MOTORCYCLE OFFICERS

OF EASTERN WASHINGTON

AND

RELEVANT CRIME STORIES

MOTORCYCLE OFFICERS

OF EASTERN WASHINGTON

AND

RELEVANT CRIME STORIES

Tony Bamonte
and
Jack Pearson

Tornado Creek Publications
Spokane, Washington 2018

Published 2018
by
Tornado Creek Publications

Printed by

Walsworth Publishing Company
803 South Missouri
Marceline, Missouri

ISBN: 978-0-9821529-7-3
Library of Congress Control Number: 2018906341

Front cover photo:
Gene McGougan, Spokane police motorcycle officer

Back cover photos:
From left: Dave Prescott, Ivan Fredrickson, Jim Finke, and Joe Pass

Illustration on end sheets:
City of Spokane motorcycle officers in the mid-1960s

Tony and Suzanne Bamonte
P.O. Box 8625
Spokane, Washington 99203
(509) 838-7114, Fax (509) 455-6798
www.tornadocreekpublications.com

DEDICATION

This book is dedicated to those hardworking police officers who consistently hold themselves to a high standard of moral responsibility in their public service.

Books written by Tony and Suzanne Bamonte:

• *Historic Wallace, Idaho, and My Unforeseen Ties*, Tony Bamonte (2017)

• *The Coeur d'Alenes Gold Rush and Its Lasting Legacy* (2017)

• *Spokane, Our Early History: Under All Is The Land* (2011)

• *Life Behind the Badge: The Spokane Police Department's Founding Years, 1881-1903* (2008)

• *Great American Wine: The Wine Rebel's Manual*, (ghost-written by the Bamontes, 2006)

• *Vintage Postcards From Old Spokane* with Duane Broyles and Howard Ness (2005)

• *Spokane's Legendary Davenport Hotel* (2001)

• *Miss Spokane: Elegant Ambassadors and Their City* (2000)

• *Spokane and the Inland Northwest: Historical Images* (1999)

• *Manito Park: A Reflection of Spokane's Past (1998)*

• *History of Newport, Washington* (1998)

• *History of Pend Oreille County* (1996)

• *Sheriffs, 1911-1989* by Tony Bamonte (1990)

• *History of Metaline Falls* by Tony Bamonte (1987)

Books written and published by the Spokane Police History Book Committee,
while Jack Pearson was a member

Another of Jack's important contributions to his community was his involvement with a small group of other professional people, the Spokane Police History Book Committee, in chronicling the history of law enforcement for the city of Spokane. Jack first became involved with researching and recording the department's history in 2003. The committee's work culminated in a series of books, titled *Life Behind the Badge*. The first volume was published in 2008, titled *Life Behind the Badge: The Spokane Police Department's Founding Years, 1881-1903*. Following that, the history book committee wrote and published *Life behind the Badge, The Spokane Police Department's Turbulent Years, 1903-1923*, in 2010. That was followed by the publication of *Life Behind the Badge: The Spokane Police Department's Transforming Years, 1923-1944*, in 2011. Next came *Photo Chronicles, The Spokane Police Department's 130th Anniversary Edition, 1881 to 2011*, in 2013. In 2014, the police book committee published *Life Behind the Badge: The Spokane Police Department's Transitional Years, 1944-1970*. In 2017, the group published their final volume titled *Life Behind the Badge: The Spokane Police Department's Progressive Years, 1970-2000*.

Table of Contents

About the Authors

Tony Bamonte wrote his first book in 1987. It was about Metaline Falls, Washington, the town in which his wife and he were raised. This ignited a new passion, and that book was followed by one on the history of the sheriff's of Pend Oreille County, based on his master's thesis.

Tony was born in Wallace, Idaho, in 1942. His mother left the family in 1948, at which time his father moved his older brother and younger sister to Metaline Falls. His father cut and peeled cedar poles in the summer and worked in the mines during the winters. In the summers and after school, Tony worked with him peeling cedar poles. During his last year in high school and for a year following, Tony worked in the Pend Oreille Mines. He then went into the army, where he served in Vietnam as a helicopter door-gunner. Also, for a while, as bodyguard for Henry Cabot Lodge, who at the time was the ambassador to South Vietnam. Following his military service, he went back to the mines for a short while, followed by a year working for Boundary Dam near the Canadian Border.

In 1966, Tony moved to Spokane, took the test to become a Spokane Police Officer, and was hired shortly after. After serving as a Spokane city police officer for over eight years, six years on motorcycles, Tony moved back to Pend Oreille County in 1974, as a political appointment for the current sheriff at the time. In 1978, he was elected Pend Oreille County sheriff and served until 1991.

Jack Pearson is a lifelong resident of Spokane and spent almost 30 years as a Spokane Police Department officer. After returning from service in the Marine Corps, he went to work for the *Spokesman-Review*, becoming a journeyman printer. He completed his AA Degree in Law Enforcement at Spokane Community College before joining the SPD in 1971.

During Jack's tenure with the Spokane Police Department, he worked patrol division and as a motorcycle officer, as well as robbery, rape, and burglary special squads. In 1981, he went to work in the combined City/County Crime Analysis/Information Support Unit, working in this position for the rest of his career. He is a history buff and collector, especially of World War II history, aircraft, and firearms. He was an original board member of Spokane Law Enforcement Museum, a member of Spokane Historical Monuments Committee, and Spokane Retired Police Officers and Spouses Association.

Tony Bamonte and Jack Pearson nearing the end of this book project in 2018. *(Courtesy Suzanne Bamonte)*

Jack was one of the key committee members in the writing and publishing of five definitive books regarding the history of the Spokane Police Department. In doing so, a group was formed called the Spokane Police Department History Book Committee. This was a 13-year project.

Preface

The inspiration for this book emerged from some reminiscing about our years as Spokane Police Department motorcycle officers. The Spokane Police Department History Book Committee, of which Jack was a key member, was completing the fifth and final volume of the *Life Behind the Badge* series, chronicling the history of the department from its inception. We both have insatiable appetites for history and agreed a lack of historical information regarding local motorcycle police left a void that needed to be filled. Upon researching this topic, we found two other books written about police motorcycle officers, but nothing by anyone who had ever served as a police motorcycle officer or anyone who had ever been in law enforcement. Consequently, in the early part of 2015, we began our odyssey that resulted in this book.

Between the two of us, both long tenured law enforcement veterans and former Spokane Police Department motor officers, we decided to put this book together based on our own and fellow motor officers' experiences. One thing we both agreed on was that working on motor was one of the most rewarding jobs we ever held during our lengthy careers in law enforcement. This book contains a number of highly interesting police responses involving both the lighthearted and darker side of our communities.

Because we both rode Harley-Davidsons during our time on motor, and because they were made in this country, we are admittedly biased toward Harleys. However, the first motorcycle to officially begin duty in our region was an Indian. On March 17, 1910, the city leaders purchased a twin-cylinder Indian for the police department. That purchase was made a year after the department purchased its first auto. Since that time, the motorcycle police officer has been an important part of the majority of police agencies. It is also one of the most coveted jobs in many police agencies for the younger officers.

We found it extremely important to stress safety to anyone who may decide to ride motor. In all police departments, officers considered for motor duty must have extensive police experience. Typically, they need at least three years as a patrol officer before they are qualified to take the test to go on motor. One of the most important assets is maturity. Motor officers need good skill sets, and be able to upright an 800-plus pound motorcycle if it gets tipped over. A motor officer has to be continuously aware of what's going on around him and the traffic flow in all directions, as there is the constant element of danger from that traffic.

There are a number of aspects that stand out in judging the skill of motorcycle riders. An experienced rider will always use both brakes to slow down or stop. This routine is important when an emergency stop is necessary and using both brakes has become automatic. One other important action is when you are stopped. If the gear shift is on the left, lean to the left with only your left foot down, keeping both the hand and foot brakes engaged. If the clutch, brake line, or cable brakes, you won't shoot out into traffic.

Assignments for motors often include more than one district, and at times, half of an entire city. The maneuverability of motors in traffic offers great advantages not provided by larger, more traditional police vehicles. The motorcycle's relatively small size allows quick access to major crimes and accident scenes. Police motorcycles are also used in police funerals, VIP motorcades, and other special events.

And last, but also important depending on the officers assigned, motorcycles can contribute significantly towards good and effective public relations. They can resolve specific problems that cannot be handled by a normal patrol vehicle, such as getting to trouble areas in a hurry.

Tony Bamonte and Jack Pearson

Acknowledgements

Doris Woodward

Duane Broyles

Sue Walker

Laura Arksey

Rae Anna Victor

Linda Habbestad

Jack and I are deeply grateful to each one of the above people who, in one way or another, contributed to or participated in this book. The contributions of those pictured above fall into two broad categories. One category includes those who contributed material (including photographs). The other includes those involved in editing and proofreading. All these friends have generously assisted us through the duration of a number of books we have been involved in writing and publishing. Each contributed time and talents for projects they recognized as a benefit to our community. It is with heartfelt sincerity that we acknowledge their help in this particular book project to help us make a record of motorcycle officers and many of their accomplishments.

Other acknowledgements

In addition, our sincere special thank you to the law enforcement officers who contributed to this project. These would include those from the Spokane Police Department, the Spokane County Sheriff's Office, and the Washington State Patrol. We are especially appreciative of Tim Downing, a former motorcycle officer with the county, and troopers Joe Pass, Lee Boling, and John Mittmann with the Washington State Patrol for taking the time to provide the necessary information to adequately cover their agencies' history and backgrounds. We also wish to thank two of Spokane's police chiefs, who were also former motorcycle officers: Interim Police Chief Rick Dobrow and current Spokane Police Chief Craig Meidl. It is also with great appreciation that we thank Washington State Patrol Chief John Batiste, who was also a former motorcycle officer with the State Patrol. However, one of the most important contributors to this major project is Suzanne Bamonte, whose expertise and time devoted to making this book accurate and grammatically correct is greatly appreciated.

And a special thank you to Don Brockett, Spokane County's longest-serving prosecutor

We were honored to have Don Brockett write the foreword to our book. In May 1961, Brockett graduated from Gonzaga Law School and soon began working as a deputy prosecutor for Spokane County. Brockett was elected prosecutor in 1969 and retired December 31, 1994. During his time in office, Brockett was president of the Washington Association of Prosecuting Attorneys, on the committee that wrote the Superior Court rules for criminal cases, and the committee that formed the Sentencing Guidelines for the state. Brockett was also engaged in many efforts regarding legislation in Washington State dealing with criminal matters. In 1996, he entered private practice. Following 52 years of practicing law, Brockett is now an honorary member of the Washington State Bar Association. In 1959, Brockett married Nerita Jean Corigliano. They have five children. One daughter, Lisa, was killed in a plane crash in Ellensburg, Washington, in 1987. Together they have 13 grandchildren and 11 great-grandchildren.

In a number of Brockett's cases, the death penalty was possible. However, because the jury could not agree unanimously, the defendants were sentenced to life without the possibility of parole or release. Two of his cases fall into this category: One was that of Lonnie Link who shot and killed SPD Officer Brian Orchard. Brockett charged Link with First Degree Murder with a possibility of the death penalty. The jury convicted Link of first degree murder, and he is serving a life sentence without the possibility of parole. Brockett also prosecuted Al Hegge, president of the Ghost Riders motorcycle club who engineered the robbery of Adolphi's weapons in Wenatchee by Lonnie Link and Donald Beach. A deal was set up later under Hegge's supervision to sell the weapons back to Adolphi, which the SPD found out about, set up a surveillance, and during an encounter with Link, Officer Orchard was killed. Brockett tried Al Hegge for his part in the crimes and was appointed a Special Assistant U.S. Attorney to assist in the prosecution of Hegge in federal court. In both cases, he was convicted.

Brockett also tried the case of the so-called "South Hill Rapist," Fred (Kevin) Coe, who was a suspect in a number of rapes and was identified after an extensive investigation by the SPD. After the trial, Coe's mother tried to hire a hit man to have the trial judge killed and Brockett beaten into a state of an "addlepated vegetable" who was to be in diapers for the rest of his life. Police learned of the plot, set up a sting operation with SPD Officer Rich Jennings posing as a "hit man," and arrested Mrs. Coe. The case became the topic of Jack Olson's book *Son* followed by a 1991 television program *Sins of the Mother*.

In 2015 Brockett wrote and published an excellent book exposing the fact that the U.S. Supreme Court has made rulings that improperly reflect court members' political leanings and have altered the balance of power in the country. He questions "How has this one branch of the federal government, meant to be the least powerful, made some of the most important decisions on how you should lead your life?" The title of the book is *The Tyrannical Rule of the U.S. Supreme Court; How the Court Has Violated the Constitution.*

Foreword

Of all the men and women dedicated to keeping us safe, the motorcycle officer has one of the most dangerous jobs. In addition to policing us as other law enforcement officers do, these officers are in a position to arrive at a crime scene in a short time due to the maneuverability of the bike. Typically motor officers are assigned to several districts, or even half of the city at one time. To become a motor officer requires a substantial amount of police experience, as they often respond to calls on their own and need to have the ability to handle those calls.

During my thirty-three years with the Spokane County Prosecuting Attorney's Office, I was privileged to meet and work with many of the motorcycle officers whose stories are presented on the following pages.

With the change to having law enforcement officers in their vehicles most of the time, we lost some of the interaction between a person in uniform and the people of the community. Officers were more insulated and drifted farther and farther away from the original idea of policing – becoming knowledgeable about the people they were tasked with directing to obey the laws. That didn't happen to the same extent with motorcycle officers because they had a more direct contact with people and were more accessible to them, especially when showing young people their bikes.

What you won't read in the following pages are the effects of the stress of the job on the individuals described or their families. These men were dedicated to making our communities safer and were very successful in doing so.

Little did I know that I would owe my life to Rich Jennings, once a motorcycle officer, because he had posed as a "hit man" to record the intentions of the mother of Fred Coe, prosecuted for several rapes. She was upset because I had prosecuted her son and wanted me to become an "addlepated vegetable" in diapers for the rest of my life. I owe Officer Rich Jennings my eternal gratitude for his professional conduct.

> Donald C. Brockett
> Spokane County Prosecuting Attorney (1969-1994)

Founding of the Spokane Police Department and Its First Use of Motorcycles

The Spokane police and other core municipal departments were established in Spokane Falls by an official act of incorporation in November 1881. Upon incorporation, the Legislative Assembly of the Territory of Washington appointed the town's first mayor, Robert W. Forrest, and the city council, which in turn offered Eugene B. Hyde the job as the town's first law enforcement officer. He accepted the position, becoming the first marshal (chief of police) of Spokane Falls. It is important to note that, during formations of early police departments, the head of the department was commonly referred to as "marshal" and the officers he hired were deputy marshals.

By the mid to late 1880s, especially as towns grew into cities, "chief of police" became the customary term for the head of a police department. Irrespective of the title, the duties were the same. An amended city charter approved on November 28, 1883, stated: "The positions of city attorney, assessor, treasurer, and *chief of police* [emphasis added] shall be elected by the qualified electors of said city ..." The election that followed on April 1, 1884, listed the office as *city marshal*. Although Hyde had an opponent by the name of F. M. Thompson, he was elected to the position by an overwhelming majority. This gave Hyde the distinction of being both the first appointed and the first elected police chief of Spokane.

Eugene B. Hyde. *(Courtesy Washington State Archives)*

Eugene Hyde moved to Spokane in the spring of 1881 at the age of 32 and, upon arrival, became involved in the real estate business. In his new profession as marshal, Hyde was described as a stalwart man who had an accurate aim and was quick with a sidearm. The following statement from the May 29, 1917 issue of the *Spokesman-Review*, three days after Hyde's death, offers a glimpse into the type of law enforcement official he was:

> Mr. Hyde served with high efficiency and courage ... By sheer weight of his strong and quiet personality he held the disorderly element under control ... and Spokane enjoyed a high reputation for law and order at a time when many other western communities allowed themselves to be terrorized by "bad" men from the plains and mountains.

Joel Warren, whose 50-year-long law enforcement career began during Hyde's tenure, provided another personal insight into his character. Warren was quoted as saying: "When I was sworn in, Eugene Hyde said to me, 'Read the ordinances, Joe, and never lose a fight. If you lose it will have a bad affect on the community and cause you lots of trouble. 'I have always tried to follow that advice.'

Hyde's Fellow Officers

Although it has been published elsewhere that Hyde's position as marshal was an unpaid one, Article 7 of the city's incorporation act addressed salaries. According to Section 1, neither the mayor nor the councilmen were to receive salaries, but Section 2 stated: "All other officers provided for in this act, or to be created, shall receive such compensation as shall be provided for by ordinance." Hyde was given one assistant when he became marshal.

On January 7, 1882, the *Spokan Times* reported: "The city marshal and his assistant receive, respectively, $75 and $40 per month. The former patrols the streets from noon till midnight, the latter, from midnight till noon." Extensive research failed to produce the name of his first assistant referenced herein, but despite the

The following statement was given by Francis Cook (the founder of the *Spokan Times*) to Herbert Gaston in June 1914: "As long as I ran my paper here I printed its name 'Spokan Times', and continued to insist on spelling Spokan without the final and positively useless 'e.'"

Spokane looking north in 1881. *(Courtesy Spokane Public Library, Northwest Room)*

scarcity of available resources from the early 1880s, a determination was made of the other officers to serve the Spokane Police Department during its formative years. Following the unnamed assistant, the officers to serve under Hyde's watch were (in the order of their employment): William Kohlhauff, appointed night watchman on June 16, 1883; Ephraim J. "Jack" Hubbard, hire date unknown, but referenced in a neW.S.P.aper article as early as March 29, 1884, in regard to a city incident involving law enforcement; and Joel F. Warren, who was sworn in on April 13, 1884. In addition, although he does not appear to be regularly employed, Frank Aiken was called in on occasion to assist with specific needs, such as guarding the jail to ensure prisoners did not escape.

Both Kohlhauff and Hubbard served primarily as night watchmen. Hubbard was tragically killed in the line of duty during James Glispin's tenure as chief. William Kohlhauff moved to Spokane Falls with his wife Johanna and their family in May 1883 to set up a mercantile business. Their home was "out in the woods" on Second between Lincoln and Monroe. Kohlhauff began as night watchman on June 16, 1883, but on July 21st, the *Spokane Falls Review* reported that he "had enough" and had resigned his position! Apparently his leaving was not permanent as there are occasional references to him as night watchman in later newspapers. He was also a city councilman for 16 years, a volunteer fireman, and a school board director. Having served under Col. Wright during the Indian Wars of the 1850s, he was influential in the naming of Fort George Wright.

An ordinance passed in the April 1884 election gave the mayor authority to appoint two policemen at the salary of $65 per month. No time was wasted in offering Joel Warren a job, but he was not satisfied with the pay. Eugene Hyde and J. M. "Mel" Grimmer, who established one of the earliest hauling and delivery services in Spokane, personally contributed to Warren's salary. According to Warren, when the offer reached $75 (another account has $72.50) per month, he accepted. That fall, Warren and Grimmer ran against each other on the same party ticket in the sheriff's election, but both lost. On November 29, 1884, the neW.S.P.aper reported that "J. F. Warren, who has made such an excellent peace officer in this

Joel Warren. *(Courtesy Northwest Museum of Arts & Culture L87-1.17327-34)*

city for months, has been laid off for the present. His discharge was not on account of inefficiency but simply because there are no funds in the city treasury to pay the salary of an extra officer." (This latter statement became an all-too-familiar refrain.) Warren was rehired a little over a year later and became chief of police in 1887.

Although not with the police department, a mention of Deputy Sheriff Lane C. Gilliam is deemed appropriate. Before the city's official incorporation, law enforcement was the county's responsibility (through the sheriff's department). Until it became evident in the late 1870s that the railroad would include Spokane Falls on its route, the tiny settlement had little need for law enforcement. In 1881, the year the Northern Pacific Railroad made its entry into the region from the west, 25-year-old Gilliam moved to Spokane from Walla Walla, where he had been was raised. He was appointed deputy by the current elected sheriff Michael Sullivan shortly after his arrival, and he was involved whenever the need for an additional officer arose. An industrious man by nature, his name was soon associated with John W. Glover, brother of the town's founder, James Glover, in the livery business, having stables located in the heart of the growing community. He later left law enforcement and became involved in the more financially lucrative professions of real estate and mining promotion.

Horse Mounted Police Patrol in Spokane

In 1881, the year the Northern Pacific Railroad came to Spokane Falls, the population was less than 500. By 1897, it had jumped to almost 40,000 and was steadily climbing. From 1881 to 1883, the city limits of the town consisted of the south riverbank, south to Sixth Avenue, with the west boundary being Cedar Street and the east boundary being Hatch Street. This was a small area and was patrolled by foot.

In 1883, the boundaries again expanded, but only a small amount to Spofford Avenue on the north and 14th Avenue on the South. By 1891, the city's boundaries had again expanded, this time significantly, to almost twelve times the size of the original boundaries that Seth Scranton and James Downey had platted.

Sometime between 1883 and 1891, because of the area that now needed to be covered, and the fact that the first automobile did not arrive in Spokane until 1900, it appears that at least four members of the police department were assigned to horse patrol.

Taking Care of Police Horses According to the Spokane Police Department Policy Manual

SECTION 1 Patrolmen during duty mounted on horses will be required to perform patrol duty on foot when their horses shall be disabled, or unfit for duty. They are to dress in the uniform of the Mounted Police Force, and each patrolman must take the entire care of, and will be held responsible for the condition and safe keeping of the equipment assigned to his use.

SEC. 2 In rural districts on long Posts distant from the Station House, the relieving point should be arranged to save unnecessary traveling in reaching the

The mounted police during President Roosevelt's first visit to Spokane in 1903. *(Courtesy Spokane Public Library, Northwest Room)*

post of duty.

SEC. 3 Mounted men in going to and from their posts will proceed in a walk, or at a moderate trotting pace, not to exceed the rate of six miles an hour. In patrolling their posts they are to proceed at a fast walking pace. They are required to teach their horses to walk at a rapid pace, and under no circumstances are they allowed to ride at a canter or running pace except in cases where the rapid movement is required in the performance of police duty.

An ordinance was passed that made it mandatory that any horse or horse-drawn conveyance be tied to a suitable hitching post or weight. On Saturdays there was not an empty telephone pole on First Avenue, one of the busiest streets in town. The next ordinance to be added was a speed limit of four miles an hour. An article in the *Chronicle* told of two citizens who were arrested for speeding down First Avenue at six miles an hour.

Spokane's mounted police during President Taft's visit in 1909. Left to right: Charles C. Manson; Frank L. Bunker; Winfield G. Boldman (also Spokane's first motorcycle officer); and Grant Bradley. *(Courtesy Spokane Public Library, Northwest Room)*

Officer Andrew Green, one of Spokane's first black officers, on the south bank of the Spokane River, circa 1893. *(Courtesy Spokane Public Library, Northwest Room)*

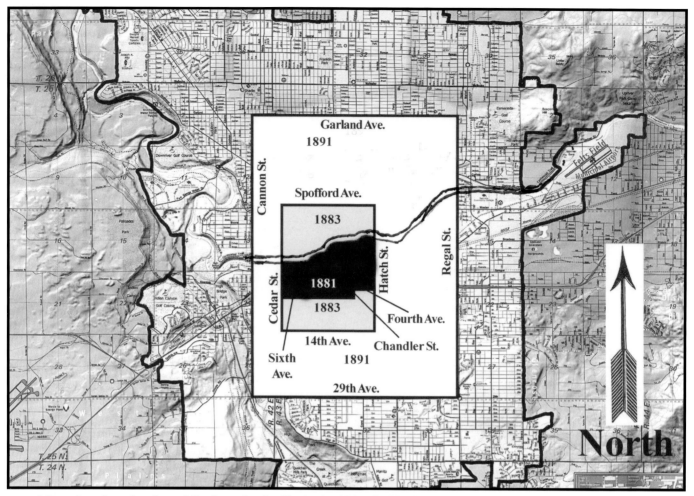

Map showing the size of Spokane's city limits in 1881 (in black)**, 1883, and 1891.** *(Bamonte generated map)*

Map of Spokane Falls in 1884. *(Courtesy Spokane Public Library, Northwest Room)*

Spokane's First Automobile and
The Ensuing Automobile Problem

Spokane's early automobile history has been clouded by conflicting information. Although businessman F. O. Berg is generally credited with owning the first car, this is not correct. On September 15, 1899, the first automobile arrived in Spokane. It came directly from the factory, consigned to the owner, Roy L. Boulter, who lived at the corner of Fifth Avenue and Haven Street.

When Boulter's auto arrived, by way of the Great Northern, he had no idea how to operate it. One of the few people in the city who did know was George Bartoo, the man who sold it to him. Bartoo soon opened the first garage and "held the first automobile agency" in Spokane. With some difficulty, Bartoo helped Boulter get it running, and they took a 50-mile drive.

Residents were excited about the prospects of seeing this car "speeding about the streets of Spokane," but it failed to meet those expectations. Two months after the car's arrival, the *Chronicle* reported: "The automobile was seen downtown once. It was being drawn along through a back alley and was tied to a good old-fashioned horse and wagon, on the way to the repair shop … After two trips to the repair shop, the automobile is now in the barn of its owner …" Accounts conflict regarding the car's ultimate fate but do agree it was a miserable failure. It did, however, stimulate plenty of discussion regarding the pros and cons of steam versus gasoline engines.

Two More Autos Arrive

On March 5, 1911, in an article summarizing the history of the car in Spokane, the *Spokesman-Review* stated that Roy Boulter's car was followed by a second one on April 9, 1900. It was owned by Fairmount Cemetery. The third, according to an article on September 11, 1900, had arrived the previous day and belonged to businessman F. O. Berg. In 1901, its first year in business, George Bartoo's agency sold a grand total of five cars. Typical of the times, these sales were transacted at Bartoo's bicycle shop. Within two years, gasoline-powered cars began to arrive in noticeable numbers and the first electric car made its appearance.

On July 26, 1903, the *Spokesman-Review* claimed: "No other town in the northwest can boast of as many automobiles as Spokane." During the early years, one of the newspapers published annual reports listing the make of every car in Spokane and the owners' names. Of course, street paving took on a higher priority, and prisoners from the city jail were kept busy sweeping the newly paved streets. By 1910, there were nine businesses that sold autos in Spokane and approximately 450 autos in Spokane County. An example: A 1910 Cadillac "30" sold for $1,600, not including shipping, from Detroit. This model included a magneto, two gas lamps, a generator, and a horn.

F. O. Berg Terrorized the Spokane
Neighborhood With His Automobile

Years later, Berg recalled the first drive in his new car and was quoted in the February 11, 1926, *The Spokane Woman* magazine as saying: "I'll never forget the night I brought it to Spokane [in September 1900]. I started from the old O.W.R.&N. depot on Cataldo Street, and before I got uptown I had succeeded in startling five runaways [horses]. They didn't have any arrest laws in those days, but I got plenty of abuse."

F. O. Berg, in his new car, the third in Spokane. *(Spokane Public Library, Northwest Room)*

The Spokane Police Department in 1901. Chief Witherspoon is in the front row, third from the left of those men sitting in chairs. He was the first police chief to clamp down on the perceived automobile "terrorist" threat in Spokane. *(Courtesy Spokane Regional Law Enforcement Museum)*

Chief William Witherspoon Initiates the First Traffic Laws in 1902

Chief William Witherspoon was on hand to help remedy the lack of motorized vehicle laws. On May 25, 1902, a "horseless carriage" moving along Riverside at a rapid clip caught the chief's attention. He jumped from the streetcar he was riding and caught up to the offender as the man reached his destination. Estimating the auto driver to be going at least 12 to 15 miles per hour, the chief issued a citation for speeding. Exceeding six miles per hour on horseback within the city was a misdemeanor punishable by a stiff fine. There were a few other traffic-related ordinances, which pertained primarily to streets and horses, including restrictions against riding a horse or bicycle on the sidewalks. But, because there were no city ordinances under the topic of automobiles, the charge was dropped.

Witherspoon wasted no time initiating an ordinance to restrict the automobile's rate of speed within the city limits. Beginning with this single law, the body of vehicle ordinances multiplied exponentially. By the time the city published its 1928 ordinance book, the double-column topical index of vehicle-related ordinances filled over four pages. Although cars dominated the streets by then, it was still a misdemeanor to willfully "frighten any horse, mule or other animal, being at the time attached to any vehicle or in charge of any person."

Chief Ren Rice begins the first major campaign against speeders. In 1907 Rice, a former assistant news editor for the *Spokesman-Review*, with no police experience, arrange to catch a large number of Spokane's elite (the people who could afford autos at that time). In July 20, 1907, the following was stated in the *Spokesman-Review*:

Ren H. Rice, Police Chief, 1907-1909. *(Courtesy Northwest Museum of Arts & Culture L83-113.172)*

ARRESTS OF AUTO OWNERS PLANNED
CITY OFFICIALS SAY SPEED LAW IS
GENERALLY VIOLATED.
HAVE TIMED FAST MACHINES

Record Kept Shows From 16 to 23 Miles an Hour Within City's Fire Limits.

Through plans quietly under way for several days by Chief of Police Ren H. Rice and his license inspector, Major R. D. Gwydir, and detectives, the biggest bunch of surprises yet to be sprung on local automobiling enthusiasts will probably be launched within the next week. These surprises are likely to come from wholesale arrests for turning the streets and avenues of the city into speedways and exceeding the speed limit.

It is known at the city hall that the officials have been quietly keeping a speed check on the different automobile owners. The record shows that one physician has been making as much as 25 miles an hour on First avenue west of Monroe street. A wealthy real estate owner has reeled off from 18 to 20 miles an hour and done it practically in the heart of the city. The lowest speed record taken on streets close in was more than 16 miles an hour.

People Narrowly Escape

It is also known that a number of people have narrowly missed being run over. Were a deaf person or a child to get in the path of one of the machines traveling upwards of 20 miles an hour, the chances of such person being killed or injured are regarded as being above the average. The accumulated information gathered against different speed offenders, it is believed, will but add to the likelihood of their conviction in police court. The contention at the city hall is that all automobile owners should know the speed laws of the city and that it is not necessary to serve notice of the limit of speed permitted. In the case of the physician named, it was pointed out yesterday that the speed of the average western express train is about 25 miles an hour and that this physician, when he was traveling through a city street at more than 23 miles an hour, must have known that he was violating all speed laws.

It was said at the police station last night that the speed law is four miles an hour in crossing street intersections, eight miles an hour between intersecting streets within the fire limits, and 12 miles an hour outside the fire limits.

On August 8, 1907, The *Spokesman-Review* wrote a follow-up article concerning the result of the Police Department's efforts:

AUTO OWNERS T0 BE ARRESTED, Anti-Speed
Crusade of Police Comes to a Climax Today.
WARRANTS FOR 30 Holders of Stigmatized Numbers Are Obtained From *Olympia Register*.
STORK RACE INVOLVED

Officers Decline to Disclose Evidence—Gwydir's Stopwatch Principal Exhibit.

"I shall ask for warrants this afternoon for the arrest of about 30 different people on the charge of having violated the speed laws by propelling automobiles too rapidly through the city streets," said Chief of Police Ren Rice yesterday. While in some instances the chauffeurs were in charge of the machines, each warrant will attempt to hold the owner of the machine responsible. One woman is on the list.

The call for these warrants for arrest was delayed until the numbers of the machines, together with the names of the owners, could be obtained from Olympia. The Olympia information came today. We are now ready to proceed.

The arrests are to be made on information furnished us by Major R. D. Gwydir, license inspector, and Detective Thomas Herndon, who timed the machines and secured the numbers. When a machine was found to exceed the speed limit the number was taken. Most of the detective work preliminary to the arrests was done during the month of July. Who – Auto Sleuths Operated.

This detective work consisted of Detective Herndon standing on one street corner, a pair of binocular field glasses glued to his eyes, and—Major Gwydir standing down the street on the next corner with a stop watch in his hand. As the machine passed Herndon, he kicked out his leg and Major Gwydir started his stop watch. The additional duty of Detective Herndon, as the automobile sped by, was to get the number with the aid of his field glasses.

As a result of the detective work, a number of citizens will probably be arrested tomorrow,. . .”

That list included many prominent owners of autos who violated the law on the specified dates: Dr. Elmer Olmstead, former mayor of Spokane, July 8; Dr. C. P. Thomas and his wife, Mrs. C. P. Thomas, July 8; Dr. C. P. Thomas, July 16; Authur D. Jones, July 17; Modern Irrigation and Land Company's machine, July 17; J. F. Canady, Coeur d'Alene, Idaho, July

Dr. Elmer Olmstead, Spokane's mayor from 1897-1898. He was instrumental in the procurement and development of Liberty Park. *(Public domain)*

17; R. C. McIntosh July 2; Fred Flint and Company, July 19; Dr. E. T. Richer, July 10; P. Welsh, July 22; Fred Flint, July 27; Dr. E. T. Richter, July 26; F. H. Epperson, Seattle, July 27; W. H. Cowles, July 27; John Markey, Wilber, Wash., July 27; license 179, July 22; license 966, July 22. Most of these people had good excuses. Former Spokane Mayor Dr. Olmstead said he was hurrying to deliver a baby.

Chief Ren Rice, before becoming the Spokane police chief, was the former assistant news editor for the *Spokesman-Review*. He was Spokane's 13th police chief, and served in that capacity from 1907 to 1909. Prior to Rice's death in 1957, he made the statement that during his tenure as Police Chief he lost half of his friends.

In 1908, Spokane experienced its first traffic fatality when a car carrying seven people plunged down the bluff overlooking the Spokane River at Ide Avenue and Walnut Street. The victim was Mary Nicholls, 28. At the time of her death she was the president of

Two autos in front of the Spokane Country Club, which, according to the *Spokane Directory* was located eight miles north on the Little Spokane River. These autos appear to be the same vintage as the ones the scofflaws were driving, and they could have easily been suspects hiding out at the clubhouse. *(Courtesy Jim McGoldrick)*

This 1909 Cadillac "30" was the first automobile officially used by the Spokane Police Department. The identified police officers in the car are: Front seat, passenger side is John W. Willis; behind Willis on left is Joseph
Daniel; behind Daniel is Thomas Herndon; and also in the rear is William D. Nelson. *(Courtesy SRLEM)*

the Spokane Woman's Christian Temperance Union.
On March 15, 1909, this article appeared in the
Spokesman-Review:

SPEED MANIACS OWN MONROE STREET
AUTO AND MOTORCYCLE DRIVERS SCORCH
BUSY THOROUGHFARES, CARELESS OF WHOM
THEY MURDER OR MAIM.

No ordinance has been passed permitting it, but by tacit
official understanding North Monroe street, since being
paved, has been surrendered to auto, motorcycle and other
developments of speed lunacy.

The only police notice of this so far is a report made by Officer
Daniels that autos shoot Monroe at the rate of 100 miles an
hour. Probably one nearly caught Daniels at the switch and his
estimate of the speed rate may be slightly exaggerated, but that
an exceedingly dangerous speed is common across the river
is a matter of apprehensive concern to everybody except city
officials charged with enforcement of safety regulations. ...

The Spokane Police Department's
First Automobile Predates the Motorcycle by
Approximately a Year

During the first decade of the 20th century, the city
was growing aggressively in population, industry,
and infrastructure. Over two-thirds of the land that
would make up today's park system was acquired
during this period. Over 80,000 trees were planted
in the city during this decade. The increased number
of parks added to the police workload. This was the
fastest-growing period – never to be repeated in the
history of the city. One of the biggest changes for
the police was the transition from horses to cars. By
1924, there were 104,000 citizens and 20,000 cars.

Prowl Car Service Begins

A 1909 Cadillac "30" was originally purchased by
the city officials for use by members of the Board
of Public Works. The September 21, 1909, edition

of the *Spokesman-Review* stated: "Auto Supplants Patrol Wagon. In order to answer emergency calls with speed, the auto belonging to the city and used by the Board of Public Works will be parked at the police station."

On September 26, 1909, the council ordered that the auto assigned to public works be used to respond to "emergency calls outside the area covered by a horse-drawn patrol wagon." This was the beginning of motorized transportation for the Spokane Police Department. It was another 18 months before the council would respond to a request from the chief and on March 23, 1911, a contract was awarded to the Metropolitan Motor Company for a 1911 Locomobile Touring Car (Type L).

As the advent of the automobile began to take effect in Spokane, many members of the police department began to embrace its arrival within the department with remarkable enthusiasm. This article from the *Spokesman-Review* on January 16, 1911, explained some of the enthusiasm that occurred when the police department received its first motorized paddy wagon:

POLICE STOP JOYRIDING
Patrol Wagon to Be Used by Department Only

Except in times of riot, street and fire emergency, none but the members of the police department will be allowed to ride in the patrol wagon after today.

This is the effect of an order issued by Police Chief W. J. Doust yesterday. The order was the result of the fondness of police station habitues to pile into the wagon at every clang of the warning bell. The last word was spoken when three prisoners and a policeman had to walk to the station because the "Black Maria" was overloaded with "joyriders."

The Popularity of Motorcycles

The following article appeared in the July 15, 1910, *Spokesman-Review*:

MOTORCYCLES WIDELY USED
Business Houses buy Machines for many Purposes.

Business firms of this city are beginning to use motorcycles extensively. James F. Stack, agent for the Harley-Davidson and the Reading-Standard, reports the following sales to Spokane business firms: Holley-Mason Hardware company, Washington

The funeral of Acting Chief John T. Sullivan on January 5, 1911. The funeral procession was traveling south on Howard Street. The Grand Hotel, on the left , was on the northwest corner of Main and Howard (1890-1914). Inset: Acting Chief John T. Sullivan 1909-1910. *(Courtesy Spokane Public Library, Northwest Room)*

Brick and Lime company, Spokane Falls Gas Light company, Idaho Lime company, Spokane Electrical Inspection company, John W. Graham, Madison Lumber company. Firms report the motorcycles a great convenience.

A July 31, 1910, the *Spokesman-Review* article stated:

MOTORCYCLES ARE GAINING IN FAVOR
Several Hundred Now Owned in
Spokane—Cheaper Than Street Cars For City Riding

The article described a motorcycle as a bicycle with a powerplant incorporated in its frame work. The cost to purchase was around $200 to $400, and the cost to run them was about one to two cents per mile. You could also purchase a sidecar that would hook onto the frame. The sidecars were a popular feature for business deliveries or campers.

The Spokane Police Department's First Motorcycle, and Why it Was Purchased

On March 17, 1910, the Board of Police Commissioners submitted a recommendation from Chief John T. Sullivan asking the Spokane City Council to appropriate $312.00 for the purchase of a motorcycle and the equipment needed to convert it for police use. This idea came about because of the number of traffic complaints being made. Also, the police commissioners had learned of other departments having success with mobility and speed of motorcycles. Consequently, the department needed an officer assigned to the duty of enforcing the newly enacted ordinances relating to all motorized vehicles.

Department Received First Motorcycle During Chief John T. Sullivan's Tenure

Acting Chief Sullivan initiated Spokane's first motorcycle traffic unit. He was Spokane's 14th chief of police since the incorporation of Spokane, when Eugene Hyde was appointed chief in 1881. The following year, Sullivan was murdered.

The Circumstances of John T. Sullivan's Murder

On January 5, 1911, at 8:45 p.m., an assassin fired a shot through the window of Sullivan's home on West Sinto Avenue. Sullivan was sitting in a chair near a window reading the . The .32 caliber bullet passed through the chair and pierced his right lung. Although Sullivan was mortally wounded, he crawled to the phone and called the police station for help. Following the attendance of numerous physicians at his home, he was taken to Sacred Heart Hospital, where he died in the morning hours of January 7th. In 1912, an arrest was made in the Sullivan murder, but he turned out to be the wrong person.

Thirteen years would pass before the case was finally solved. Victor C. Miller of Alabama had been shot by his wife, Florence, in self-defense. Prior to the shooting, he had frequently boasted to both her and one of his closest friends that he had gotten away with killing Spokane's police chief in 1911. Chief Wesley Turner and Captain Martin Burns did a thorough investigation and found the claim to be true. They also learned that Miller was responsible for a number of other murders. Whether or not a motive for the murder was ever established or publicly stated was never disclosed.

Taking Care of the Police Motorcycles According to the Spokane Police Department Policy Manual

With the purchase, use, and success of the new Indian motorcycles, those in command of the police department issued strict guidelines for their operation and maintenance. Those rules were stated as follows:

1911 Motorcycle Squad Section as worded in the Manual of the Spokane Police Department

SEC. 1: Officers detailed for duty on motorcycles will be held strictly accountable for the same and its equipment entrusted to their care. They will allow no other person to use the wheel under any circumstances without authority of the commanding officer of the station to which they are attached. All injuries to the motorcycle or equipment will be reported in writing through the regular channels. Officers will carefully inspect their wheels before going on duty, and immediately after their return. Motorcycles must be at all times kept clean and well oiled.

SEC. 2: Before new oil is put in the base of the engine all the old oil must be let out.

SEC. 3: The machine must not be run any length of time in a rack. Chain must be kept lubricated and also adjusted.

SEC. 4: Engine must be lubricated with oil every fifteen or twenty miles.

SEC. 5: All nuts and wire terminals must be kept tight.

SEC. 6: All electrical contact points to be kept clean.

SEC. 7: Coaster brakes and compensating sprockets must be oiled whenever necessary.

SEC. 8: Gasoline must be strained before putting same in tank.

SEC. 9: The following repairs must be made by members of the Motorcycle Squad, and commanding officers must not make a requisition for the same:

a.   Repairing of small punctures.
b.   Cleaning and assembling of carburetor.
c.   Adjustment of compensating spocket.
d.   Adjustment of drive chains.
e.   Cleaning of spark plug.
f.   Cleaning of all electrical contact points.

SEC. 10: Whenever a member of the Motorcycle Squad is compelled to leave his motorcycle at some place other than the Station House for any cause, whatever, he must make a report of it, stating the cause to his commanding officer, and the motorcycle must not be left for a longer period than is absolutely necessary.

SEC. 11: Members of the Motorcycle Squad to whom machines are assigned, must not allow any other member of the Force to ride the same without permission from the commanding officer, and in no case shall a person who is not a member of the Police Force be permitted to ride Police Department motorcycles.

SEC. 12: Members of the Motorcycle Squad must not leave their machines at their residence under any circumstances unless permission is granted by their commanding officer.

SEC. 13: Motorcycle men are members of the Police Force and must obey all rules and regulations prescribed for the same.

SEC. 14: The efficiency of motorcycle men will be judged not only by the number of convictions obtained, but also by the amount of repair bills of the machines.

SIGNAL BOX SYSTEM

SEC. 1: The Commanding officer must be particular to see that the following rules are observed in the operation of signal boxes, and report to the Inspector of Police, any neglect of duty or violation of any of said rules.

SEC. 2: In precincts furnished with the Police Signal boxes, Patrolmen will make the proper signals at the proper Station House from such boxes, and at such times during their respective hours of patrol duty, as may be designated by the commanding officer of the precinct or other proper authority, and whenever they make an arrest they will forthwith take their prisoner to the nearest signal box and signal for the patrol wagon.

SEC. 3: The Sergeant shall carefully instruct the members of their respective stations in the operation of the signal system, any member of the Force who is unable to comprehend such instructions or the operation of the boxes will be reported as incompetent.

SEC. 4: Each officer will be furnished with a key to the Police signal boxes, and will he held responsible therefore. Keys will be inspected at each roll call, should an officer be unable to produce his key when requested, or fail to promptly notify his station of its loss, complaint will be made against him.

SEC. 5: Should any Patrolman fail to signal from the box at the time directed, by reason of his being called away in the performance of other Police duties, he will immediately after such duties have been performed, proceed to the nearest box and duly signal therefrom, and report the cause of the delay.

SEC. 6: No Patrolman when signaling will leave the box until he has observed that his signal has been duly received at the Station House. Members of the Force detailed for duty at the telephone desk in the Station House, will promptly answer in clear and distinct manner all signals sent from the boxes, and keep a record of the same on the blotter, noting carefully from whom received and the exact time when received. The officer in charge of the apparatus at the Station House shall on receipt of any signal, answer by giving his surname to the officer giving the signal.

SEC. 7: One of the members so detailed will be on duty at the Station House at all times, and the several tours of duty will be regulated by the officer in command of the precinct.

SEC. 8: Patrolmen will be held responsible for any injury to the signal boxes during their respective tours of duty, and shall report to the Station House all accidents and breaks in the wires on their respective posts; they must not alter or disarrange the adjustment of the instrument when the bell ceases to work, but will report the same to the Sergeant on patrol.

SEC. 9: The Mounted Police will use the signal boxes when necessary, but must not attempt to open them before dismounting. In order to prevent any tampering with the instruments, the Sergeant on patrol will have supervision thereof and, will during their tours of duty visit, inspect and test as many of them as possible and notify the Station at the time of such inspection. When a signal box or instrument or line is reported out of order, the officer on desk duty will at once investigate and report the result of such investigation.

SEC. 10: Signal box keys consecutively numbered will be kept by the Inspector of Police at the Station who will issue same to respectable citizens at his discretion, taking the name and occupation of the recipient, and the number of the key delivered which will be carefully noted upon the "key record" in each Station, which "key record" will be accessible to the desk officer at all times in order that the name, occupation and residence of any person giving a false alarm or losing or abandoning his key may be ascertained instantly no matter in which district the false alarm occurred.

The earliest form of communication within the police department, the location of the signal boxes, shows where the activity and problem areas existed in 1911:

From the 1911
Manual of the Spokane Police Department

1. Howard and Riverside
2. Post Street and Riverside
3. Riverside and Monroe
4. Main and Washington
5. Stevens and Sprague
6. Post and First
7. Bernard and Trent
8. Bernard and Riverside
9. Sprague and Division
10. Division and Front
11. Pine and Second
12. Stevens and Second
13. Post and Second
14. Fifth and Howard
15. Fourth and Brown
16. Fifth and Sherman
17. Boone and Hamilton
18. Boone and Division
19. Howard and Sharp
20. Washington and Mallon
21. Broadway and Ash
22. Broadway and Cochran
23. Ash and Indiana
24. Northwest Blvd. and Ash
25. Division and Indiana
26. Washington and Mansfield
27. Illinois and Hamilton
28. Sprague and Altamont
29. Sprague and Green
30. Helena and Sprague
31. Third and Arthur
32. Fourteenth and Grand
33. Fourteenth between Wall and Stevens
34. Ninth and Ash
35. Spruce and Pacific
36. Nevada and Gordon
37. Thirteenth and Chestnut
38. Sharp and Cochran
39. A Street and Sinto
40. Maxwell and Monroe
41. Jackson and Monroe
42. Post and Garland
43. Buckeye and Howard
44. Waverly Place and East Oval
45. Boone and Napa
46. Tenth and Perry
47. Manito Boulevard and Twenty Second Ave.
48. Grand and Twenty Sixth Ave.
49. Ninth and Adams
50. Thirteenth and Madison
51. Main and Monroe
52. Oak and Second
53. Second Ave. and C. St.
54. Third and Monroe

Signal boxes also located in these locations
HOSPITALS AND HOMES in 1911
From the 1911
Manual of the Spokane Police Department

- Church Home for Children, E. 307 Empire Ave.
- City Emergency Hospital, Basement City Hall
- City Isolation Hospital, River Bank, W. End Euclid Ave.
- Deaconess Hospital and Maria Beard Deaconess Home, 715 Fourth Ave.
- Deaconess Old People's Home, E. 1905 Wellesley Ave.
- Finley, Esther C., Deaconess Rest Home, 1104 Sinto Ave.
- Florence Crittenton Mission of Spokane, E. 2335 North Crescent Ave.
- House of the Good Shepherd, Wabash Ave. corner Lidgerwood
- Sacred Heart Hospital, 8th Ave, opp. Browne, via Manito or Rockwood car lines
- St. Joseph's Orphanage, North 01016 Superior St.
- St. Luke's. Hospital, Summit Blvd. and A. Sherwood Add.
- Salvation Army Rescue and Maternity Home, S. 739 Chandler
- Spokane Children's Home, Euclid Ave. Cor. Hemlock
- Spokane General Hospital, 330 3rd. Ave.
- Washington Children's Home Society's Receiving Home, E. 1605 North River Ave.
- Washington State College Veterinary Hospital No. 2, 225 Indiana Ave.
- Woman's Club Day Nursery, 1114 Third Ave.

S P O K A N E   P O L I C E   D E P A R T M E N T

The Spokane Police Station from 1891 to 1913

The Spokane City Hall, which housed the police department, fire department, chamber of commerce, and library. This building existed from 1894 to 1913, during the time when automobiles started to become a problem and the first motorcycle officer was appointed. This photo was taken when the building was decorated for a visit from President William Taft, who came to Spokane on September 28, 1909. The city hall was demolished in 1913 to make way for the Union Pacific Railway Station. This is an especially historic photo, as it shows both an automobile and horse-drawn wagon in front of the police station. *(Courtesy Spokane Public Library, Northwest Room)*

W. G. Reggie Boldman – hired by the Spokane Police Department in 1909

This photo appeared in a March 30, 1910, *Spokesman-Review* article titled: "Officer who Keeps Check on Autos." It stated: Patrolman W. G. 'Reggie' Boldman the only [and first] Spokane policeman mounted on a wheel or motorcycle, who is making life miserable for the 'speeders' who frequent Monroe Street hill approaching Boone Avenue. Officer Boldman is mounted on a twin-cylinder [Indian] motorcycle equipped with a speedometer. He rides alongside of an auto and, watching what his speedometer records, arrests the offenders in case they are breaking the speed laws."

Spokane's First Motorcycle Officer and his "Indian" Motorcycle

Winfield G. "Reggie" Boldman had been on the department since February 1, 1909. On March 17, 1910, he was assigned as the Spokane Police Department's first motorcycle officer. Prior to being assigned to ride police motor, Boldman had already experienced an exciting career as is shown in the following article from the *Spokesman-Review*, January 2, 1910:

SPOKANE POLICE DEPARTMENT

An Indian motorcycle of the same vintage as the first police bike. This photo was taken at 11504 E. Valley Way. The caption stated the driver was Mr. Hubble. *(Courtesy Spokane Valley Museum)*

ATTEMPT TO KILL POLICE OFFICER
Friends of Man Arrested Murderously Assault Policeman Boldman
Life Probably Saved by Heavy Overcoat — Attack Follows Row at Elks Temple Dance

Following a row at the machinists' dance at the Elks Hall held on New Years Eve, Patrolman Boldman, who had arrested one of the alleged participants in the trouble, was murderously assaulted one-half block from the hall, presumably by friends of the man he arrested.

Boldman had arrested Frank Williams and Williams showed resistance while on the south side of Front Avenue between Post and Wall Streets. The officer got his man to the ground when a group of men, supposedly friends of Williams, assailed him. One of the men wielded a knife or sharp razor. The back of Boldman's $100 fur-lined overcoat was slashed in a number of places between the collar and the waistline. By drawing his revolver, the officer frightened his assailants. They took to their heels and when Boldman returned with reinforcements, none of the men could be found. Boldman's heavy overcoat, which was ruined, is given credit for having saved Boldman from serious injury as a result of the knife thrusts.

During his time on the police department, Boldman held the rank of detective before becoming the department's first motorcycle officer. Boldman had served in the Spanish-American War before coming to Spokane. In 1931, he left the department and moved from Washington State. He died at the age of 79 in Texas. When Boldman left his position on motor, he was replaced by Julius Frese.

History of Indian Motorcycles – the Choice of the Police Department in 1910

The Indian is an American brand of motorcycles produced from 1901 to 1953 in Springfield, Massachusetts. During 1910, Indian became the largest manufacturer of motorcycles in the world. The Indian Motorcycle Company was originally founded as the Hendee Manufacturing Company by George M. Hendee in 1897 to manufacture bicycles. In 1898, the name of the motorcycle "American Indian" was soon shortened to "Indian."

The first Indian motorcycles, having chain drives and streamlined styling, were sold to the public in 1902. In 1903, Indian's cofounder and chief engineer, Oscar Hedstrom set the world motorcycle speed record of 56 mph. Production of Indian motorcycles then exceeded 500 annually, rising to a peak of 32,000 in 1913. In 1905, Indian built its first V-twin factory racer, and in following years made a strong showing in racing and record breaking. In 1907, the company introduced the first street version V-twin. One of the firm's most famous riders was Erwin "Cannonball" Baker, who set many long-distance records. In 1914, he rode an Indian across America from San Diego to New York in a record 11 days, 12 hours and ten minutes. Successful competition played a big part in Indian's rapid growth in sales. From 1911 to 1915, the Indian motorcycles gained their most popularity.

An Indian motorcycle similar to the one ridden by Reggie Boldman for the Spokane Police Department in 1911. *(Courtesy Spokane Valley Museum)*

Julius "Jules" Frese – hired by the Spokane Police Department in 1910

Spokane's Second Motorcycle Officer, Julius Frese

• *Spokesman-Review*, June 21, 1911:

Three new two-cylinder seven horsepower Indian Motorcycles of the most approved type were received by the police department for the use of the motorcycle squad which will be formed to check speeding automobiles within the city limits. Previously Officer J. Frese has done this work alone, but the increase in the number of paved streets and automobile owners has made it impossible for him to cope with the situation single-handed. He will ride one of the new machines, but the riders for the other two have not yet been named, although it is expected that they will be selected from the patrolmen.

On May 16, 1911, a photo of Julius Frese as the only motorcycle officer in Spokane appeared in the *Spokesman-Review*. The article contained the following information about Spokane Motorcycle Officer Frese:

Mr. and Mrs. J. Frese make weekly trips in their seven-horsepower Indian, equipped with sidecar, to many of the lakes about Spokane on fishing trips. Often the party will

Motorcycle Officer and Wife on Machine

Spokane motorcycle officer Julius Frese and his wife, Rose Materne Frese. *(Frese family scrapbook)*

take camping utensils and fishing tackle, with bedding sufficient for two and three days away from the city, on their novel car. At times as much as 400 and 500 pounds have been piled onto the sidecar and yet the seven-horse-power engine has never balked at any of the many steep hills about Spokane and its lakes.

• *Spokesman-Review* April 2, 1911:

Julius Frese, elected road captain for April, has been forced to resign that position as his duties as a motorcycle police-man take up all his time. Mr. Frese is going to purchase a seven horsepower Indian for his own use and says that when it arrives he will issue a challenge to any and all comers for any kind of a test they want to make. By his fearless riding, he has already made himself a terror and pest to speeders and only lost one man whom he attempted to catch.

From the time motorcycles became popular in Spokane, around 1910, Julius Frese belonged to the Spokane Motorcycle Association. During that time,

he was active in motorcycle racing and won many first-place events with his wife accompanying him in a sidecar. The *Spokesman-Review* during the summer of 1910 has many articles about these events. Julius Frese died on May 2, 1958, in a Spokane hospital. He was 73 at the time.

By late June, the city had purchased three more Indian motorcycles. Officer Ben Hunt and Officer Arthur Jordan became motorcycle officers in 1912.

In January 1912, Commissioner Zora E. Hayden and Chief William Doust decided it would be more beneficial for the motorcycles to be stationed in the outlying districts of the city. At this time, a fourth motorcycle officer was added, and the motorcycles were kept at various fire stations for quick response.

From the July 31, 1910, *Spokesman-Review*: "The lower left hand picture is of Mr. and Mrs. J. Frese taking the turn in their side car." Frese, with his wife, Rose, in the side car, took first-place in the race with his seven-horse-power Indian. *(Frese family scrapbook)*

The following information was provided to the authors by Ty Brown, one of the owners of Wander-mere Golf Course, who is currently writing a book about the Little Spokane River, his family and their golf course, and Francis Cook's connections. He also provided the obituary and the following article, which appeared in a 1913 *Motorcycle Illustrated Magazine*. Julius Frese was also the father-in-law of Ty's uncle, who ran the golf course after his great-grandfather had a stroke in 1931.

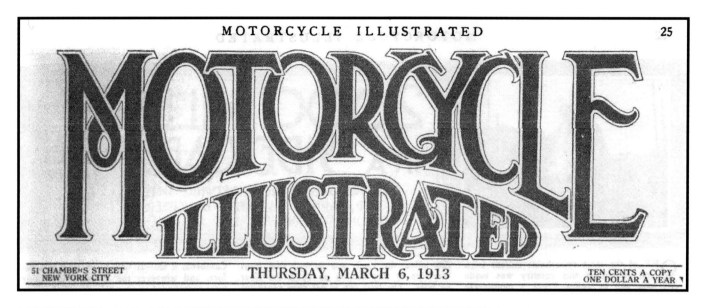

MOTORCYCLE ILLUSTRATED   25

MOTORCYCLE ILLUSTRATED

51 CHAMBERS STREET
NEW YORK CITY   THURSDAY, MARCH 6, 1913   TEN CENTS A COPY
ONE DOLLAR A YEAR

2000 MILES IN A SIDE CAR

BY CHARLES FULLER GATES

HOW JULIUS FRESE, ERSTWHILE SPEED COP, CARRIED HIS WIFE & DAUGHTER FROM SPOKANE TO LOS ANGELES

The following appeared in the March 6, 1913, *Motorcycle Illustrated Magazine*:

HOW JULIUS FRESE, ERSTWHILE SPEED COP,
CARRIED HIS WIFE & DAUGHTER
FROM SPOKANE TO LOS ANGELES

One of the most remarkable sidecar trips on record in this country was made not long ago by Julius Frese, a motorcycle repairman of Spokane, Wash., who designed his own passenger attachment and carried his wife and little daughter from Spokane to Los Angeles, a distance of more than 2,000 miles over good, bad and indifferent roads. Frese had acted as Indian agent in his district and had also served as a speed officer, so that he was well fitted to make the most of his Indian mount when he headed southward on his long jaunt.

Owing to the fact that he was obliged to carry two passengers Frese decided that a standard sidecar would not meet his requirements, and accordingly he built a roomy attachment along such lines that it afforded the regulation 56-inch tread found in automobiles and wagons. This was a bigger feature than it may appear to the uninitiated, for it is extremely difficult at times to drive a sidecar outfit with the motorcycle wheels down in a rut and the sidecar wheel bumping along in a track of its own. Frese fitted his attachment with a wide seat and with space in the rear, very much after the fashion of a boot on a stagecoach. The complete sidecar weighed 100 pounds and was large enough for two persons and some luggage.

COMPLETE ROAD EQUIPMENT.

A food box was built to fit under the seat and hold dishes, table implements, "grub" and an alcohol stove. A large telescoping luggage box was used to carry extra clothing, and for bedding there were five blankets and some lighter coverings. As the Freses were to sleep outdoors throughout the trip (and some rain was expected), a 7 by 9 tent was also carried. Mr. Frese weighs 173 pounds, his wife 125 pounds and the little girl, 90 pounds, so that with passengers and luggage in the sidecar the motorcycle was called upon to handle 886 pounds.

The start was made from Spokane on September 23, and Walla Walla. Seven miles from the Oregon border and 156 miles from the starting point, was reached the second day. On the same day the 44-mile trip to Pendleton. Ore., was made and here a stop of two days was made so that the party might attend the cowboy contests known as the "Rodeo," for Pendleton is the headquarters of the promoters of these frontier sports which are staged, so to speak in various parts of the country west of the Mississippi from time to time.

Along the route from Pendleton to The Dalles, some 250 miles of the road is good; it is the oldest road in that section of the country and runs parallel with the Columbia river. From The Dalles to Portland, about 200 miles, the roads are so bad that most travelers in that section go down the river by boat. The boat trip is not very expensive and the scenery along the river is excellent.

A THRILLING INCIDENT.

A day was devoted to sightseeing in Portland and the party figured that it had covered about one-third of the journey at this point. All had not been plain sailing, however. Soon after leaving Pendleton, for example, a six-horse freight team took fright at Frese's motorcycle and sidecar outfit and the frenzied animals got completely beyond the control of the driver. They wheeled about, broke the tongue off the wagon and did other damage, besides giving the driver a close call.

Frese went to the rescue of the driver and later paid him for all damages, to avoid the delay incident to a lawsuit. In that section of the country the motorcycle has no standing in court—certainly not with the local lawmakers —and Frese figured that it would be as well to dispose of the matter at once.

The roads are quite sandy in the eastern part of Washington, but being a motorcycle mechanic and knowing his Indian seven thoroughly, Frese managed to get through with little trouble. He carried several sets of sprockets so that he was prepared to reduce the gear ratio in unusually heavy going. Most of the time he used a 5 to 1 gear on account of the sidecar and its heavy load, but in the mountains he found 6 to 1 on the high gear none too low for the work; at times he was compelled to use even a lower gear.

ENTERING CALIFORNIA.

South from Portland it is a run of 353 miles to the California line, and 452 miles from the state boundary to San Francisco, by way of Grants Pass and Sacramento. This route is now marked all the way with signboards of the Pa-

cific Highway, the name given to a route along the Pacific which is expected by its promoters to extend in time from Alaska to South America: it is in use at present from Canada to the Mexican border. Naturally the new signboards of the Pacific Highway were a great help to Frese on his long journey, and on the whole he considered the going fairly good to Redding, which is 150 miles south of the Oregon-California border. Below Redding the roads are used more extensively. Crossroads are quite plentiful and the district begins to show signs of the population found in the central and southern sections of the state.

In this neighborhood Frese begin to notice automobiles and motorcycles and he found that the wilderness had been left behind him. Through Washington, Oregon and northern California a sidecar had never been seen before, and wherever the Freses stopped they were surrounded at once by a crowd of curious natives.

In several of the small towns it was found necessary to hide the outfit in a shed in order to avoid creating a disturbance and getting into trouble with the police. In Eugene, Ore., the outfit was left in front of a motion picture theater and in a few minutes the street in front of the amusement place was blocked.

WELCOMED IN SAN FRANCISCO.

In San Francisco, Manager Hopkins, of the Hendee branch, who has been a sidecar enthusiast for years past, extended a warm welcome to the Frese party, and Mr. Frese was introduced to many of the motorcyclists of the city before he was permitted to resume his trip southward. South of San Francisco much of the journey is along the Pacific on El Camino Real, the old mission road. In this district good roads are the rule, and often for miles at a stretch the highway is paved and as smooth and hard as asphalt. There are old missions scattered along the line and many interesting places that will repay the traveler for a visit.

All in all, El Camino Real has earned its title as "the road of a thousand wonders." All along this section of the route are the road signs of the Automobile Club of Southern California, which now has 540 members, and which spends a small fortune each year in marking highways and bringing about improvements. These signs, designed by the writer, show the topography of the road and the turns so that a traveler can follow the road at the rate of a mile a minute, if necessary, and still read the pictures and know what is ahead of him. The signs are placed about eight feet from the ground on white posts and about 200 yards ahead of the turns, crossings, etc., they refer to.

ARRIVING IN LOS ANGELES.

The Frese party arrived in Los Angeles October 17, where they were welcomed by relatives. Following a short rest after his 23 days on the road Mr. Frese disposed of his luggage, added his sister to the party and the four went sightseeing all over southern California. If that isn't a great record for a home-built sidecar and a 7 h. motorcycle we would like to have some one inform us as to just what constitutes a great performance for such an outfit.

Sidecars are so numerous in and about Los Angeles (there is a sidecar factory here) that the Frese attachment does not attract much attention in the streets, but whenever Frese can be induced to tell the story of the run from Spokane to Los Angeles he has no difficulty in finding listeners. Frese states that his running expenses were very low throughout the trip, and that owing to his intimate knowledge of the motorcycle and sidecar the upkeep has been held down practically at zero.

HELPFUL HINTS
FOR
SIDECARRISTS

by Timely Tipster

SOME funny things happen occasionally when a sidecar outfit has the brake suddenly applied. If the front wheel is turned to the left at the time the brake takes hold, a skid toward the right will occur and the faster the speed of the outfit at the instant of braking the handsomer the skid. The wheel should be kept in the line in which the rig is going or better, when possible, turned slightly to the right.

WATCH the sidecar tire to see that the chair is in proper line with the machine. The tread should be worn off evenly in the center when all adjustments are properly made but wear on either side quickly indicates misalignment. When on the left of the tread, it may mean that the chair leans in toward the machine or that the distance at the front of the wheel is greater than the distance at the rear. Wear at the right side indicates that the sidecar leans out or that the front of the wheel points inward instead of being parallel.

UNLESS you are going to tour across the Continent, carry as little luggage as possible on your trips. Every pound of dead load means extra wear and tear, and greater consumption of fuel. The springs carrying the chair are not intended to carry railroad iron or an equivalent weight as well as the passenger.

THE writer carries a jersey with him when riding at any time, and finds it particularly useful at night in summer. Another garment which is handy for long tours is a rubber poncho or cloth having a slit in the center through which the head is put when worn as a cape. This slit has a fly-flap, and the skirts can be spread over the sides of the chair when used by the passenger. When used by the rider, the skirts hang down front and back, and if the poncho is big enough the front skirt can be fastened to the handlebars so

that the arms are shielded from the rain. Eyelets are fitted to the skirts, so that strings can he used for fastening them down if desired. The skirts mentioned are the longer sides of the poncho.

FOR the owner of a sidecar outfit who smokes, wind-matches are desirable and become additionally useful when they are to he lighted. A pocket lighter using alcohol is also good, but for pipe-lighting at high speed does not compare with the wind match.

WHEN using a sidecar with a two-speed machine, don't hesitate to change gear as soon as the motor shows signs of working hard. You save the motor and its bearings by so doing, and also yourself and passenger from getting out and pushing. As the motor may run hot if kept too long on the low gear, change up to the high as soon as conditions warrant it. Change up quickly and down slowly, the latter to let the motor gather speed.

Julius Frese passed away on May 3, 1958. The following is his obituary:

Obituary
Death Takes Early-Day Resident

Early-day Spokane resident, policeman and business man who died Saturday following a brief illness will be held at Hazen & Jaeger's at 1 p.m. tomorrow.

Born in Germany, Frese immigrated to the United States with his parents in 1890 and crossed the country in a prairie schooner to settle here the following year, in 1910 Frese became a policeman and drove the department's first automobile; later he was one of the first motorcycle patrolman.

Frese was in the contracting, and road-building business for about 15 years and in 1926 went into the sand and gravel business. He was in that field for 12 years and owned pits on north Post, north Monroe and on the 3001 block on east Buckeye. In 1937 he founded the Layrite Products, company, a concrete block business that now has outlets in Spokane, Kennewick and Seattle. Frese was chairman of the board of directors of Layrite until his retirement in 1956.

Survivors include a son, Verne, Seattle; a daughter, Mrs. Mearle Ross, Pasco, Wash., two brothers, Fred and Ronald 0., Spokane; three sisters, Mrs. Emma Gemmrig, Medical Lake, Wash., Mrs. Rose Heilman, Baxter Springs, Kan., and Mrs. Pauline Schwinge of California, and three grandchildren. Burial will be at Greenwood Cemetery.

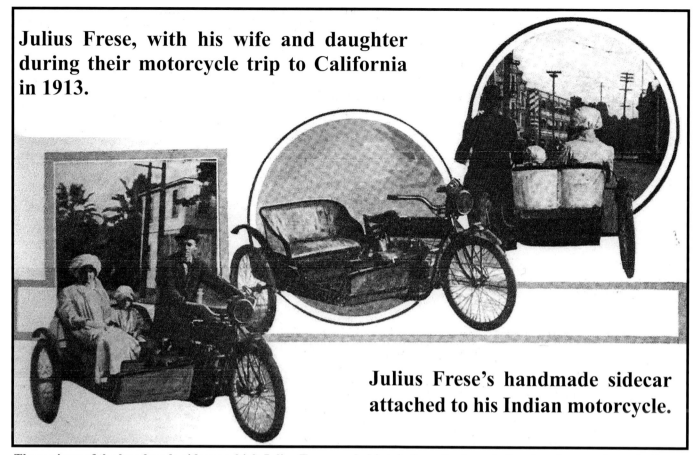

Julius Frese, with his wife and daughter during their motorcycle trip to California in 1913.

Julius Frese's handmade sidecar attached to his Indian motorcycle.

Three views of the handmade sidecar which Julius Frese made his trip from Spokane to Los Angeles are shown in the accompanying photograph. It will be noted that the sidecar attachment is unusually roomy and that the tread of the outfit is in keeping with that of standard automobiles and wagons. This feature enabled Frese to follow in the ruts of other vehicles on some of the worst stretches of his trip and obviated the necessity of trailing the sidecar wheel in a track of its own. In addition to Mrs. Frese and the child who appear in the photograph at the left, the sidecar carried considerable general luggage, including a tent outfit.

From left: Julius Frese, Rose Materne Frese (wife of Julius), Lily Materne Rogan (sister of Rose), Mearl Frese Ross (Ty's great-aunt), Robert Wesley Ross (Ty Brown's great-uncle). It is interesting that Julius married a woman named Rose and he also had a sister named Rose. *(Courtesy Ty Brown)*

Fred Frese – hired by the Spokane Police Department in 1913

In his later life, motorcycle officer Frederick Frese (Julius Frese's younger brother) wrote an autobiography of his life from the time he was born in Germany up until 1971. For a period of 20 years, Fred worked for the Spokane Police Department off and on during three separate periods from 1913 to 1942. Sixteen and a half of those years he rode police motor. The following pages are from Fred's historical and enlightening autobiography. There is a short part that addresses a situation concerning Montrose (Manito) Park. This is included because of its historical value. Fred Frese's autobiography illustrates the work of a motorcycle officer:

From the Autobiography of Fred Frese, One of Spokane's Early Motorcycle Officers:

[A baby is born at "Montrose" Manito Park on June 23, 1895]

We never traveled on Sundays. Finally we crossed the Hump and dropped down to the mining valley through Wallace, Idaho and Coeur d'Alene. After another day we arrived in Spokane, Washington from the south side. This last camp was about three miles south of the city.

It was in a fine natural park called Montrose Park, named after the many beautiful wild roses. It is now the famous Manito Park. There was a spring for water and poplars and willows for shade. Dad pitched our small tent near the spring, where mother, in a few hours on June 23, 1895, gave birth to my sister Rose, who was named after all the beautiful roses. She was the seventh child and as usual, dad was the only doctor at the child birth.

Now I must add that we were broke. I mean we had no bread, no food at all, and no oats for the horses, but there was pasture and their journey was ended, so they were no problem. There was a narrow gauge, small track electric railway that ran from the city to the park. This dinky railway was operated all day on Sundays only. It was Spokane's best resort. There was a band pavilion about one-fourth mile from our camp. The very next day after our arrival, my brother Julius, ten years old, and I, nearly eight years, were herding the old plug horses along this track when I spied something shiny between the rails. It was real silver, a great big silver half dollar! We ran the short distance to the camp and gave it to dad. He hitched the horses to the wagon, and in a couple hours he was back with a 49 pound sack of flour. That same day mother got up to bake some wonderful bread with dad's help. Rose was now one day old.

Dad must have thought it a good place to inquire where he might find some German people, as he spoke very little English. Several young ladies were there who were delighted to try out their German with dad. They were studying German in high school. This was the famous Francis Cook home. He owned and operated the Cook Excursion Electric Line to Montrose park.

Shortly following this visit, we were given everything in the line of food we needed. Dad was told that he could move into almost any vacant house, as about one-half of all the houses were vacant since owners had left the city during these hard times and their whereabouts were not known. The population of Spokane had been about 20,000, but was reduced to about 10,000 at this time. It was said that the Hypothec Bank owned about half of the city on account of defaulted mortgages. Soon we were in what I thought was a wonderful house, close to a spring where we got our water. It is now in the center of Cowley Park, several hundred feet north of the present Sacred Heart Hospital and St. John's Cathedral. Cook's mansion and most of the old houses have long since been removed. Dad sold the old team and wagon for about $20.00. Soon it was harvest time, and for sixty days dad pitched bundles in the Big Bend Country for $1.00 a day, while mother helped by doing housework. Sister Emma and brother Julius were responsible for the baby and the rest of us. In this period of about two months, the Cook girls made frequent visits to our house. We did the best we could to help them with their German, and they endeavored to teach us some English. When dad came home he had $60.00, and I'm of the opinion that mother added $10.00 to this big pot. May it be said that during the Cleveland Depression there was plenty of food, but no money.

We moved to a store building on Second Avenue, where dad opened a shoe repair shop in the front of the building [the 1896 *Spokane City Directory* lists "Fred Frese boot and shoemaker, 920 2nd Avenue"]. The first day's business was the sale of one pair of shoe strings, but business improved during the winter.

Fred takes the Civil Service test to get on the Spokane Police Department

One day my brother Julius said to me, "Fred why don't you take the Civil Service exams for police chauffeur, to drive the greyhound for the detective department?" One of the drivers, a Fred Goddard, had accidently killed himself while demonstrating the safety on his new automatic pistol for some friends in a saloon. This job paid $75 a month the first year, $85 the second, and $95 a month the third year. After two years of service, my brother Jules had quit the department for a better job as a mechanic. This looked like a mighty good opportunity for a steady chauffeur's job under Civil Service. So I took a week off from my job with the understanding that my old job would be awaiting my return.

I passed the physical easily, and filled out an application. In a few days, early in February 1913, only three applicants from the entire city showed up for this two-fold patrolman-chauffeur examination. We were Byron Graybill, 28, and a college graduate who had operated one of the city's few auto repair shops; Frank Hoffman, 34, a taxi driver; and myself, 25, a truck driver and private chauffeur. This was the first and only such Civil Service exam for this position ever held. We all were graded 100% on the physical exam. The following day, we were seated at separate tables in the City Hall for a written test. Half of the questions were on the mechanics and driving of an automobile. The others, not difficult, were pertaining to police work. On this written test, we were graded as follows: Byron Graybill, 89.06; Fred Frese, 88.50; and Frank Hoffman, 80. Seventy percent was the passing grade.

It was Police Chief Doust's privilege to choose any one of us three for the chauffeur job. The greyhound was a seven passenger car, beautifully laminated hardwood body with curtains. It was a four cylinder, four speed Locomobile. Chief Doust, who also owned the Doust Laundry, owned one of these cars and gave each of us a driving test in his car. Well, he appointed Byron Graybill, so Frank and I went back to our old jobs. We were, however, to be on the eligible list for two years just in case there was a vacancy in the five driver's positions, the three patrol drivers, and two greyhounds for the Detective Department.

My vacation gone, I reported back to work at the Union Iron Works where they told me, "Sorry, Mr. Frese, we are laying men off every day and we can't use you." Jobs were as scarce as hen's teeth. After making the rounds early every morning, especially to the fuel companies, one Monday morning a fuel yard operator told me to stick around for an hour. He had warned his man not to come one or more hours late on Monday. At 8:00, no man; no man at 9:00 which meant two hours late. He said, "Hitch up the team," so I shoveled coal and chucked wood for three weeks at $2.50 per day.

I Join the Police Department

On March 13, 1913, I received a summons from the Police Chief to report for police duty and relief driver in vacations or sickness. Thirteen is my lucky number! I showed the card to my boss who said, "Well, if you make as good a

Fred Frese replaced Fred Goddard after Goddard accidently shot and killed himself *(Courtesy Northwest Museum of Arts & Culture L93-66.164)*

policeman as you did a coal man, you will be O.K." Frank Hoffman also appeared and said, "Well, it looks like we will get a bull job out of it anyway."

In his office, Chief Doust really laid down the law to us to make sure we cared to make good. "As to you, Mr. Frese, if you are as ornery and stubborn as your brother Julius was, you will not make your six-month probation." My face must have turned colors as I stuttered "Sir, I intend to take orders from all my superiors." He said, "Well, then, I don't think you are much like him. He was the most obstinate man on the whole department." My brother had resigned when it was required that every officer had to take a rather simple Civil Service examination for old employees.

We were ordered to obtain a gun, any caliber, and buy a helmet for $1.50 at the shop across the alley, where we could also order our own broadcloth uniforms for $25.00. Then we were to report for patrol duty the next day at 8:00 p.m. For this 8:00 p.m. to 4:00 a.m. we were to wear blue suits if we had one. We were to be supplied with a five star badge wreath for our helmets, a call box key and a baton. The pay was $80 a month for the first year; $90 for the second and $100 a month thereafter.

Next night we lined up at roll call, and marched out to the corner single file with orders to fall out. Most of us took street cars to our designated beats. My first beat was about two miles north of the station, and about two miles square, with two call boxes about one mile apart. Everybody in town was looking at me. I hoped that no one would ask questions, but citizens did show respect. "Good evening, officer. Nice evening. "Officer, hi!" So I am an officer-of-the-law now, no-coaching no orders, no advice on police work outside of the chief's admonition to conduct myself always as an officer. Call it destiny or fate, it's all in the providence of God that I am still among the living.

One month on this beat, and I was assigned to the Browne's Addition beat on the South Side. This new beat of about one mile square had two call boxes. Most of the city's elite and wealthy lived here. Patsy Clark, millionaire mining man, Mr. Cowles of the Cowles Publishing Company, and many other millionaires and dignitaries. They included Zeth Richards, president of the Washington Water Power Company, and his younger brother Harry, who was married to Patsy Clark's daughter Katherine. Harry is an important character in Spokane history; and as my staunch friend, he will be an important figure in this biography.

BROWNE'S ADDITION

It is generally conceded that the most beautiful and desirable Residence Property in the city is in Browne's Addition and especially in that portion of the Addition adjoing Cœur d'Alene Park. This Property has every advantage, being near to business, with good Street Car Service, Electric Lights, Gas and City Water. There are no hills to climb, no railroad or river to cross.

Early real estate ad for Browne's Addition. *(Public domain)*

Beat assignments were for two months. I had made no arrests and had no police incidents so far. I did pick up a few shreds of advice from big Officer Ira Martin, who called in from the same box, that is, his beat adjoined my beat. After a few nights on this new beat, I made my first arrest. About 2:00 a.m. right near my call box, a giant of a logger was snoring peacefully reclined on the sidewalk with an empty bottle at his side. "My, what a bruiser," I thought. "If I wake him up, he might eat me for his breakfast." So quietly I called for the wagon. Emergency Officer Dan Phelan, over six feet tall and weighing 300 pounds, the Department's heavyweight, stepped out where I signaled. He said, "Ha, down and outer, eh? Can't wake him?" He rapped him hard on the sole of his shoe with his night stick. He certainly woke up then, staring at two policemen in full uniform. He looked so scared, I thought he would faint. I helped him into the wagon. Dan said, "Now, officer, you can get your sleep. The court bailiff will sign your complaint. Of course sometimes they plead not guilty, then their case is continued and you are notified." I thought about my job at Jimmie Durkin's, and the poor man in the patrol wagon; but for fate, and for the grace of God, there go I. ...

First Lesson in Practical Police Work

... I was about to call in at 2:00 a.m. from the Oak Street call box, when I noticed two well dressed young men standing under a tree. Unnoticed, I walked up to them and asked who they were and where they lived. As newcomers in Spokane, one handed me a card and said they had a room

Police Chief William Doust. *(Public domain)*

Police call box used during that time. *(Public domain)*

Now, Frese, tell me the details of your frisking them. So I told him I did not frisk one man. I pointed to his picture. Then he asked me where this man had his hands, and I said, "He had both hands in his coat pocket." Captain Miles just stared at me and handed me the man's picture. It read, "Wanted for first degree assault with intent to kill, very dangerous. Always carries an automatic in his coat pocket; shoots through his pocket." The captain said, "Frese, be careful in searching a suspect."

Then I rode the streetcar to my beat with a ringing in my ears. "Be careful in searching a suspect; Be careful." This was police training in 1913. "Be careful, even more careful in searching two." In the next few nights, I figured all this out. Well, these burglars who took considerable money and jewelry from my beat were not apprehended in Spokane.

Another search without seizure. I applied my police technique of "be careful." Some nights later about 2:30 a.m., as I was resting my feet in a nook of a dark alley near Hemlock Street. A man in work clothes passed

where it indicated. They had played cards downtown with a friend and seemed to have walked in the wrong direction from this place. They answered questions quite well, so I told them how to get to the address on the card; but first, I would have to frisk them for a gun. I felt the clothes of the spokesman while the other was laughing about getting lost, and commending me as a good officer. I decided not to search the other man, and said I guessed they were O.K. and let them go. After my rest period Captain Miles called me into the office and said, "Frese, you had a burglary on your beat this morning at 2:00 a.m. not far from the call box where you called in from at 2:00 a.m. Did you see anyone on the street?" "Yes, captain. I suppose I stopped these burglars, two of them and after questioning and frisking them I let them go." After telling him most of the details, he showed me two pictures from the rogue's gallery; sure enough, these were the men! Then he told me that some people at a Second Avenue address had heard a noise shortly after 2:00 am. They said that the day before, they had fed two young men who were looking for work. They identified them from many pictures of burglars.

Captain George Miles retired as a captain on the Spokane Police Department in 1929. He then was elected Spokane County Sheriff in 1930, and retired in 1936. *(Public domain)*

me without seeing me. I had covered the brass buttons and badge with the opposite lapel and turned my helmet around. I stepped lightly behind, throwing my flash light on him and said, "I'm an officer. Hold up your hands for a frisk, and don't turn around." I felt his pockets and the underarm "Do you have a gun" "No, sir. I come home from work at this time." Where are you going?" "I'm right here at my basement apartment" "O.K., Put down your hands and calm yourself, man. I'm sorry; I'm Officer Frese. What's your name?" He told me, and agreed that the front hall entrance would be used hereafter. I made a point to see him as he came home, a wonderful new friend. It was embarrassing training, but I was to use this, and similar techniques many times in the coming 29 years. A well developed wit is probably one of the best aids to a policeman's survival.

Speed Cop

In the fall of 1913, I was assigned to motorcycle duty and relief driving. This was one of the most active police assignments. Even though a man may be poorly adapted to police work in disposition and perception, and if he can ever qualify and be a public asset, he will learn much sooner on this kind of assignment. There were two other motorcycle officers, Tiny Stafford and Charlie Mason. Tiny was a Spanish American War veteran. Both of these men were valuable educators for me, police-wise. We were three of the most versatile utility officers on the department, and were called the "speed cops." There were quite a few large cars capable of sixty to seventy miles per hour, mostly phaetons, a few limousines (now called sedans) such as the Peerless, Packard, Thomas Flier, Willis Knight, Winton Six, Buick Six, Buick 37 Model and Stuts Bear-cat.

This new motive power seemed to create an urge to speed, with high pressure tires, and two wheel brakes. At speed over 35 miles, the danger was multiplied when compared to modern makes, especially on wet pavement I am convinced that the most hazardous position in existence at that time was that of speed cop.

In the first few years of this assignment, out of a half-dozen such officers, nearly all were injured, and Officer Fred Germain met death. Out of all the riders, I served the longest, sixteen and 1//2 years, and never lost time from injuries. In this, I'm sure I hold the record.

A Double Murder

When old timers gather, each one tries to excel on tall tales. It is my aim to relate briefly some of the more interesting cases up to May of 1942, especially the ones where I was involved. One afternoon in the summer of 1914, a four bell (emergency) signal sounded at the police station. "Man shot in upstairs colored club at Second and Washington." Officer Walter Lawson was driver of the Black Maria Wag-

on. I was at the station on call, and went in the wagon. Officer Mike Tinnan [Tynan] was acting emergency officer, and William Dare was the emergency steward. Upon arriving at the scene, someone on the street said that a colored man with a gun ran west on Second and turned north on Grant. Dare ran to Grant Street, then North, and at Sprague Avenue someone on the street pointed north. Just north of Sprague on Grant, there were three old houses occupied by colored people. Lawson stopped the patrol wagon about fifty feet north of Sprague, opposite the first house. Just then the greyhound stopped right back of us. It was driven by George Smith. It was carrying Sgt. Daniels and several detectives. We all jumped out of the vehicles about the same time. I was some twenty feet ahead and closer to this first house, when a colored woman ran from the front door, leaving it open and running toward the nearest house. I demanded, "Is he in there?" She said, "I don't want to get shot," and ran for the nearest house.

Officer Tinnan [Tynan] was nearest to me as I shouted, "Boys, he is in here. I'll take the back door." Officer Tinnan went straight toward the front door. The back door did not open for me as I lunged on it. One end gave and then slammed back, so I lunged a second time with the same result. I stepped back some five feet for a harder lunge when two shots rang out from the front part of the house. I stepped quickly some fifteen feet to the side of the house

Officer Michael F. Tynan.

Officer Michael Tynan. *(Public domain)*

with gun drawn, and in this position I could watch the back door and the side windows. Just then I heard Tinnan say, "Boys, I'm shot." Then there was one more shot and I saw Tinnan fall on the front porch. This shot was followed closely by five or six more shots almost simultaneously. Then the men all ran for the front door, except for Lawson, but I beat them. The colored man was lying inside near the door. Lawson and I pulled him out. Then, with a man holding each arm and leg, he was carried into the greyhound and literally tossed into the back seat. The patrol started just ahead of us with Officer Tinnan. The colored man regained consciousness in the emergency ward at the police station. With only a very superficial wound in the shoulder, he had played possum.

Washington had no capital punishment law at this time, and Jackson, a hophead, was sentenced for life. Tinnan stayed conscious and talked to his wife for more than an hour before he died, about two hours after the shooting. Officer Tinnan was in his thirties, over six feet tall and weighed 250 pounds. He was a very fine Irishman, highly respected by all who knew him. If Officer Tinnan was murdered because of inferior police work, then it is obvious that all six officers were at fault, for all of us knew that this man was a killer with a gun. To enter a house with drawn blinds from the daylight under such conditions is foolhardy, suicidal, and grossly ignorant, not bravery. The house could quite easily have been guarded until tear gas was procured. Orders are easy to take from anyone when they protect your life. Ignorance can be the cause of wrong action under stress and excitement. It was compounded

Fred Frese on motorcycle, circa 1930. *(Frese family scrapbook)*

that day. While we live, we are learners. Must we learn at the cost of a dear friend's life? Regardless of the answer, fate favored me again.

Dangers, Benefits, Fate

Up to the Spring of 1918 was a very active period of my life; many exciting events took place in my work as speed cop and trouble shooter. I had from one to six cases in court every day. My pay was now $90 per month, and would soon be $100. Later, the motorcycle officers were receiving $5.00 more than the men on the beats; sergeants received $110; a captain, $125 and the chief, $160 per month. I had traded our shack in on a new two bedroom brick house with a basement, fireplace and stove heat. We paid $1400 cash difference; $700 of it was from our bank account, and the other $700 I borrowed from Dad on a note. So now, I was in debt $700. In those days I gave little thought to the extra hazards of my job. Our motorcycles had small high pressure tires and a one wheel brake. Outside of snow and ice, the streetcar tracks were the greatest danger. We had no side cars until about 1924. I would estimate the hazards to be at least ten times that of a man on a beat, but this assignment had the greater reward potential in recovering stolen cars, for arrests and convictions of thieves, and for finding men wanted. So, I was able to pay Dad's note in one year. About $200 of this was earned from wages and $500 in rewards. This made my earnings about equal to the chief's salary. Then too, in case of serious injury, I would draw full pay for six months, and in case of retirement for any cause, my pension would be half of my salary. In case of death while performing police duty, my wife would receive one-third of my salary the rest of her life, or until she married again.

I might say that if a rider takes a spill at over fifty miles per hour and picks himself up and rides on with only a few bruises, then his guardian angel has performed his duty. If this happens several times in five years, a strong angel

Walter Lawson. *(Police and Fire Illustrated)*

has been appointed to guard him. His life is charmed. To a great extent, instincts can be developed into habit. Several times in five years, I threw my motorcycle on its side, sliding with it to avoid or dampen an otherwise dangerous collision, coming out with some burns and ruined breeches. At other times, a full throttle quickly increasing high speed has averted a really bad collision. In the preservation of life, animals usually act on instinct. Oxen will go home against the worst blizzard; birds and fish migrate to their certain places, never having been there before, and Snoopy, my son's Irish Terrier, would squat flat in the fraction of a second to let a car pass over him. Man was also created with instincts or intuition. This attribute may be more complex in him because he is the only being on earth having the power of choice, which dampens certain protective instincts. Man often does just the wrong thing in emergencies. This is one reason why professional police training should have top priority. ...

One quiet summer Sunday morning in 1916, I was as usual on call at the station. Captain Miles received a telegram. Calling me, he said, "Frese, you have been hanging around here for an hour, so go out and find this Ford car, Whitman County license number so-and-so. It was stolen from Colfax last night." "O.K. Captain," I replied, "I'll have the car and the thief here within an hour." We were accustomed to josh each other in that way. I went out and soon spotted a Ford with a Whitman County license, but not the right number. Four men were in it, somewhat intoxicated, but the driver was sober, for which I commended him. I advised the other men to call it a day. They thanked me, and one man got out of the back seat saying he wished to talk to me alone. So we stepped around the corner of the bank at Broadway and Monroe. He asked if I were looking for a stolen car from Colfax, and I said I was. "I can tell you where to find the man that stole it. His name is John Doe; you will find him at a certain hotel; he may still be in bed with his girl." We refused to bring him with us because of his youth, and the boy said to us, "O.K, I'll beat you to Spokane." I thanked him; then I searched the streets around the hotel for the car with no luck.

So I knocked on the door of the room registered to him. A man answered. I asked him if he were Mr. Doe, and he said he was. "I would like to talk to you for a minute," I said. When he opened the door and saw I was an officer, I told him he was under arrest for stealing a car from Colfax the night before. This he denied. "Well," I said, "in that case I'll have to arrest the girl too. Just show me where the car is, and give me the key and I'll forget your girl." He assented, "O.K, here's the key. I'll show you where the car is." It was only about five blocks away, so we arrived at the station just before the appointed hour was up. We had a little conversation. "Captain, this is Mr. John Doe who stole the car in Colfax last night." "Where did you make the arrest?" asked the captain. I replied, "At room so and so, in Hotel so and so."

The captain then asked, "Was the car in front of the hotel?" I replied, "No, but he showed me where he had parked it and gave me the key, so I drove it here. It's out in front." Captain Miles smiled, and just shook his head. ...

On another Sunday, Captain Miles at the police desk received a telegram. It read that a car with a California license was stolen from Los Angeles, and was probably headed north. Detective Chet Edwards was also at the desk, and he remarked as he walked to the open door, "It's just possible that this car is passing the police station this very minute." Then he yelled, "Here it is, passing the door." Sure enough, it was the California number! I ran for my motorcycle. When I got to Main Avenue, I didn't know which way to turn. I rode the streets for hours without ever seeing it again. It was not found in Spokane.

Lost Boy is Found

The winter of 1916-1917 was one of much snow. Sometimes I could ride the motorcycle only on well traveled streets. In answering calls, I often took a street car to the designated place including to and from my home. A certain desk sergeant took delight in working an officer overtime. One evening as I was going off shift at 6:00 p.m., I called off at the desk. I was about to take a street car for my home when this sergeant said, "Frese, I'll have to send you to an address north of the city limits, which was some six miles north, to look for a lost boy. He's five years old, wearing a red Sweater and has a red tassel on his cap. He had his sled and his dog with him. The dog came home, but the boy has been missing since noon." Now this could take at least four hours. We had no phone in those days, and my wife would be worried. Knowing that he could have sent the man working the beat nearest, to the address, and that others on the shift were available, I tried not to show resentment. Especially after he said, "As soon as you find him you can go home." So, to cover up my feelings, I said, "O.K., sergeant, thanks. I'll have the boy here in five minutes." At the corner of Main and Wall, I stamped my feet back and forth while waiting for a street car. Every time I turned around, some little fellow was in my way, half a dozen times in a few minutes. He was following me back and forth; I nearly fell over his sled. All at once, I noticed his red-tasseled cap. "Little boy, what's your name?" He said it was Jimmie something. "Jimmie, my Jimmie, how did you get down here?" Some boys had shown him how to hook his sled rope around the bumper of a parked car, and the car took him all the way to town before it parked so he could get the rope loose. This was about the biggest thrill in my life. I set Jimmie on my shoulder, and we were in the station just about five minutes after I left it. I set the boy and the sled on the police desk and said, "Here's your boy, sergeant. Goodbye, I have to catch my car home." "Hey, wait a minute. How do you know he's the boy?" "Ask him," I retorted. "I want to get my street car." Then, "What's your name, little boy?" "Jimmie." The sergeant just looked at me in amazement as I went out the door. ...

Trouble Shooting

In those days before we had patrol cars, two or three officers on motorcycles handled most of the neighborhood complaints and trouble calls, which ranged from vicious dogs to family quarrels, from saloon fights to home burglary. Of these calls, I think I was assigned to more than my share of neighborhood and domestic troubles. I always tried to amend things without court action. This work often taxed all of my little wisdom, but any success helped to make it intriguing. A man's bringing home a case of beer for weekends was more or less typical for those Sunday closing saloon days. Answering a call from a worried neighbor, I found a young husband, recently from Germany, who had a good job as a blacksmith. In those days there were still horses to be shod. He had sent for his beautiful wife and two very nice children, two and four years old. He had bought a nice little home, and both man and wife spoke fairly good English.

I found the wife crying and also the four year old girl. The baby was asleep in her crib. The young husband was well stewed and was sitting at the table with beer bottles on it, some full and there were empties all around. When his wife could compose herself, she told me that he was a good man, a hard worker and a good provider; but recently he had been bringing a case of beer home every Saturday evening. He would drink it all before midnight on Sunday. He had a bad temper while drinking, but the rest of the week he was a good man. Now we didn't arrest a man for drinking too much in his own home, except, of course, when there is serious disorderly conduct in our presence or evidence of immediate danger to the family. After talking quite frankly to him as to what was in store for him if he continued his weekend habit, he promised he would quit drinking.

Some weeks later I was sent out again for the same thing. Everyone was crying. The wife said he missed the next Saturday after I left, but that it was now the same thing all over again. I said, "What about the beer on the floor?" She said, "Oh, I didn't expect you, or I would have mopped it up. I mop about every hour on Sundays. You see, he don't go to the bathroom, and he just lets it go. He can't help it." "How about Monday morning? I inquired. "Oh, I just wash him up and give him clean clothes and clean overalls, and he is a good man all week." "Well, well, so he just sits there all day Sunday and stews in his own brew. "Now, my good woman, if I lock him up for thirty days, will he have his job when he gets out?" "Oh, no, officer, please don't do that. He will lose his job, and then we will lose our home." I just stood there in total silence for about five minutes, thinking that surely there must be a way for this family.

An idea began to take form in my thick head. Looking at the floor and table, I took my cue and looked straight at him. By now he was crying too with the others. I put my hand on his shoulder and said, "O.K. you'll get one more chance, and then I surprised him by saying "Herr Hein-

rich, sie haben nur eM sehr gelegheit; sie haben eine Butte frau und zwei shone kinder, und eM gutes heim und arbeit. Alles werden sie verlieren fur dies," pointing to a bottle of beer. Hearing his mother tongue in his crying jag, he ordered his wife to pour all the remaining beer down the sink which she did. He said, "Officer, I promise never to take another drink in my life." I shook his hand and said, "I will believe you, but we will see. Goodbye and good luck."

About a year later, I was talking to some officers in front of the police station when a nice looking young woman asked me, "Are you Officer Frese?" Yes, ma'am," I replied. "I'd like to talk with you alone for a minute." "Yes, I remember you, " I said, "How is everything with you?" "I just want to thank you. Heinrich has never taken another drink; our home is paid for; we have more furniture and we are happy. Heinrich wanted me to thank you for him."

I Resign the Department

In December of 1917, our daughter Shirley was born, so now we had a family. The future on the Department at $105 per month did not look too rosy when I compared it to what my brother Jules [Julius] was doing. He had paid for his four yard White dump truck and had $13,000 in the bank, all in the last year of work. Cars and trucks were getting more numerous, and better roads for them were needed everywhere. Road contractors discovered that their horse drawn wagon dumps were poor competitors for the gas truck. So I resigned to try my luck and skill in road work. It took me two years to realize fully that even with high hauling prices, one could not prosper on a shoe string start with poor equipment. In these two years I had an old 1908 Packard car fitted with a Rusksel axle and a hand hoist for the dump. Then a ton and a half new Kisselkar truck for wood and lumber; then a two and a half ton Velie for mine hauling; then a three and a half ton Federal Dump for the road work; then a five yard Packard Dump. With these I earned $33,000 in eleven months, doing my own driving from 16 to 20 hours daily except Sundays. Then the bottom dropped out of hauling prices and I quit the business with about $12,000 in assets.

Early on, Fred Frese experienced an incident that easily could have changed his future. Instead, he learned a lesson about firearm safety – and the ability of women to follow directions.

Approximately three years before Fred joined the police department, the following article appeared in the July 6, 1910, *Spokesman-Review*. This incident demonstrated both his indomitable spirit and loyalty. The lady who shot his foot, and whose name he wouldn't mention, ended up being his wife for forty years, until her death in 1952:

Motorcycle Officer Fred Frese, circa 1940. *(Frese family scrapbook)*

"SHOOT MY FOOT," HE SAYS; SHE HITS
Carpenter, 25, Is in Critical Condition Following Accident at Minnehaha.

"Shoot at my foot," jokingly said Fred Frese to a woman companion Monday afternoon as he was sauntering through the hills east of Minnehaha park. "All right, hold still," came back the joking reply of the feminine nimrod, as she leveled a loaded 22-caliber rifle and took a mock aim at Frese as he dangled his foot in the air while sitting on a rock.

"Bang," accidentally went the rifle, and the bullet tore its way through the sole and into the instep of the man's right foot. After being assisted back to his hotel room at the Kapps Hotel, 218 Bernard street, "gas bacillus infection" set in, and for 24 hours the victim has been hovering between life and death, forbidding the surgeon to amputate the foot to save his life.

The gas bacillus infection, peculiar to the feet and ankle when injured, is said by local physicians to be one of the most hopeless infections. Amputation is ordinarily the only safe process to stave off death, and even when this is done death results in more than 59 cases out of 100. Dr. A. Matthews is attending Frese. Frese's leg Is lanced from the toes to the knee in the hope that the gas will be able to escape without infecting the other parts of the body.

In City Two Weeks

Frese, who is about 25 years old, came to Spokane about two weeks ago, had registered at the Kapps Hotel. He has been doing odd carpenter jobs, and Monday afternoon started for Minnihaha park in company with a girl friend, whose name he refuses to make public since the accident. After sauntering through the park grounds Frese and his companion went into the hills back of the park to shoot at ground squirrels. They carried the 22-caliber rifle.

After shooting at a number of targets Frese and his companion sat down to rest. The girl stood beside Frese and aimed the loaded gun at various natural targets. It was at this juncture that Frese held his foot up in the air and laughingly remarked "Shoot at my foot. According to Frese little pain resulted at first, but after he reached his room the foot and leg began to swell, until about 10 o'clock Monday night the pain became so great that Dr. Matthews was called.

Before midnight, Dr. Matthews had his patient at St. Luke's hospital. At a late hour last night Frese was still alive, but with little hope for his recovery being entertained by the authorities at the hospital.

Few Recover, Says Physician

"It is an infection from which few recover," said Dr. Matthews. "Amputation is the one resort, and even this fails in 59 per cent of all cases, very few have lived through the infection and retained their foot, whole or in part. If he recovers he will be one in a hundred he recovered."

Fred and Sadie Frese. *(Frese family scrapbook)*

Joel Warren – 4th and 8th Spokane Police Chief, Chief of Seattle Police Department

Former Spokane Police Chief Joel Warren on an Indian motorcycle on the far left in this 1918 photo. During the time he was police chief for Seattle, he was favorable to the motorcycle unit, having his own departmental bike. His department included 13 motorcycle officers. *(Courtesy Seattle Metropolitan Museum)*

Joel Warren, circa 1888. *(Northwest Museum of Arts & Culture L87-1.17327-34)*

Joel Franklin Warren (1858-1934)
Spokane Police Chief
4th Chief of Police (1887-1890)
8th Chief of Police (1897-1899)

Joel "Joe" Warren was Spokane's fourth chief of police from 1887 to 1890, and the eighth police chief from 1897 to 1899. Later, from 1917 to 1920, he served as Seattle's chief of police, playing an anti-labor role during the Seattle General Strike of 1919. He also worked to enforce the Prohibition law and was a staunch proponent of the motorcycle patrol, which consisted of Indian motorcycles.

Warren was born in Sullivan County, Missouri, in 1858. As the Civil War ended, the family joined the migration west, first settling in Walla Walla and later near Spokane. Joel matured into a handsome 6' 4", 220-pound man. As a young man he worked with his father on a ranch the family owned.

In 1879, the family to a ranch west of the Spokane. Soon after Joe arrived there, at the age of 19, an Indian Chief named "Three Mountains" was murdered by an Indian, Bill Jackson. Jackson was one of four brothers whose father was a cattle thief.

After the murder, a number of men were sent out to capture Jackson, but had little success. When Warren volunteered to go after Jackson, the older element among the law abiding citizens were a bit dubious about sending him. However, Warren soon convinced them he was sincere and had the ability and courage. Consequently, it was not long before he set out on horseback to capture Jackson. Soon after, Warren came riding in with Bill Jackson walking in front of him.

Following his capture of the notorious Bill Jackson, which took place on March 26, 1884, Warren was appointed a police officer in Spokane on April 13th, thus beginning, at the age of 19, a long police career that lasted for almost 50 years.

Joel Warren, Police Chief of Seattle, 1917-1920

How he became police chief of Seattle

In 1914, voters had passed a prohibition initiative. On January 1, 1916, Washington became a "dry" state. In Seattle, liquor and vice laws were widely ignored, and the city's tenderloin district was still a place for seamen, loggers, and soldiers to go for a good time. After a serious outbreak of venereal disease at Camp Lewis, Major General H. A. Greene put city officials on notice that something must be done. After repeated warnings, on November 22, 1917, Greene put Seattle off-limits to his 36,000 troops. The navy yard at Bremerton soon followed Greene's lead. This had a major effect on Seattle's business community, as Tacoma was getting all the business. There were immediate calls for the removal of Mayor Hiram Gill and Police Chief Charles Beckingham.

Since his days in Spokane, and as a Nome, Alaska, officer and Secret Service extradition agent, Warren had gained an exceptional reputation as a fearless officer and a fine leader, who had the respect of his men. No criminal, however tough, could ever intimidate him. This reputation followed him throughout his entire career and led to his appointment as the Seattle police chief.

In 1917, before the United States entered the First World War, Warren moved to Seattle to take up a position with the Pacific Coast Steel Company, guarding their local plant. On December 17th, while working on this assignment, Warren received a phone call from Captain Foster, then in charge of the Seattle office of the United States Secret Service, and now in charge of the San Francisco office, requesting to see him and Mayor Gill at the old Post Office Building.

Following a few minutes of conversation, Warren was offered the appointment of Seattle police chief. At this time, Warren made it very plain that he must be given absolutely free rein in conducting the affairs of the department if he were to accept the appointment. Without hesitation Mayor Gill agreed to this and confirmed that Warren would become chief of the Seattle Police Department.

Warren held the position of Seattle police chief from 1917-1920. At that time, his greatest problem was the handling of the thousands of "undesirables" who flocked to Seattle to work in the shipyards.

Chief Warren had about 440 regular police and about 100 ex-servicemen, including two aviators, under his command. He also "swore in" about 3,000 responsible citizens, authorized them to carry a gun and assist in the enforcement of the laws as "special police." He also appointed his former employer, Sheriff Claude Bannick, as his inspector. As a result, Chief Warren obtained splendid results.

Chief Warren and Seattle's Motorcycle Patrol

Based on available records, and from a picture in an exhibit shown on page 35, in March of 1912, Seattle's motorcycle unit may have begun that year. The caption on that photo stated: "Seattle buys 5 Indian police motorcycles. They were used to respond to police calls, enforce auto speed limits, stop runaway horses, and the protection of the Sunday papers, which were being stolen in record numbers."

Chapter Two

Early Harley-Davidson Era

The Spokane Police Department Used Harley-Davidson Motorcycles from 1920 to 1981

Motorcycle Officer Bill Hudson told the press on December 13, 1920, that "if speeders get away from me now, they will be welcome to their freedom." He had just gotten his hands on one of the two new Harley-Davidson motorcycles purchased by the department in exchange for two older mod-els. "She is guaranteed to do 85 mph, and is one of the big 74 cubic inch displacement machines." The officer said, "I didn't open it up, but I don't believe 85 mph is any exaggeration. If they get away now, I'll think they're real drivers."

Chief Arthur Hooper's car being passed by his motorcycle officers. Adolph Windmaiser is in the lead on the left and Walter Case is in the center of the photo, circa 1930. *(Courtesy Case family)*

A brief history of Harley-Davidson motorcycles

THE AMERICAN CITY

Less than 2¢ per mile !

SPOKANE COUNTY, WASHINGTON, reports that each of the above four Harley-Davidsons has been driven 20,000 miles and that "the total operating cost has been less than two cents per mile, including depreciation."

Over 1500 cities, towns and counties use Harley-Davidsons for police service. For pursuing motorized crooks and "booze-runners," for enforcing speed and traffic laws, and for a variety of service duties, the Harley-Davidson is the most efficient, dependable and economical mount known—universally recognized as "America's Police Motorcycle."

Lightweight alloy pistons—smoother power—less vibration. Alemite lubrication—first on any motorcycle. Full-floating sidecar—49-inch semi-elliptic springs. Handsome olive green finish, maroon striped.

Your city needs motorcycle protection this coming Summer. **Now** is the time to get the facts. Write for free, special literature on Police Motorcycles. Or, see your local dealer.

Harley-Davidson Motor Co.
Dept. M.   Milwaukee, Wis.

Harley-Davidson
The Motorcycle

A full-page ad in the April 1924, *American City Magazine.*

The History of Harley-Davidson Police Motorcycles

In 1908, the Detroit Police Department received the first Harley-Davidson. In 1916, Harley-Davidson motorcycles were used in the pursuit of Pancho Villa during a military operation conducted by the United States Army against the paramilitary forces of Mexican revolutionary Francisco "Pancho" Villa from March 14, 1916, to February 7, 1917, during the Mexican Revolution of 1910–1920.

A World War I Harley-Davidson motorcycle with a machine gun mounted on it. *(Public domain)*

In 1914, sidecars were made available to Harley-Davidson buyers. Clutch and brake pedals were now available on F-head singles and twins.

About 20,000 motorcycles were used during World War I. The majority of these were equipped with sidecars and machine gun mounts.

By 1920, Harley-Davidson was named the largest motorcycle manufacturer in the world. During the early 1920s, many state police forces were being formed, and Harley-Davidson motorcycles were the motorcycle of choice. During those days, motorcycles were far faster than cars and were far more maneuverable.

In 1921, the Washington State troopers began using the Harley. The entire force consisted of six officers on Harleys. Louisiana, by contrast, had a force of just 16 Harley-Davidson motorcycles that troopers used to patrol the entire state. During the mid-1920s, due to the lack of speed enforcement, traffic fatalities on the highways were greatly increasing. As a result, Harley-Davidson motorcycles were on the forefront in an effort to enforce the speed laws and thereby curb these fatalities. By 1930, over 3,000 police and government agencies were using Harley-Davidson motorcycles.

During the Great Depression, Harley-Davidson continued marketing their product as "The Police Motorcycle" while actively supporting national traffic safety campaigns. In 1931, the three-wheeler "Servi-Car" was introduced into traffic enforcement and became popular. Also, during World War II, approximately 88,000 Harley-Davidson motorcycles were manufactured for the war effort. This included 1,000 of the XA 750 cc models, a horizontally opposed two-cylinder that was shaft-driven. It was never sold to the public.

The 1950s saw the beginning of the American iconic image of the motorcycle cop, with mirror sunglasses, hiding behind the billboard and sitting on a Harley, of course, waiting for speeders! Today, over 34,000 police agencies in the United States and police departments in over 45 different countries use Harley-Davidson motorcycles.

Spokane Police Motorcycle Officer, Walter Case on a Harley-Davidson motorcycle with a sidecar. It should be noted, this motorcycle had no front brake. In 1928, Harley-Davidson introduced a front brake and, in 1930, they came out with an option of a hand or foot clutch. Up until 1966, the Spokane Police Department used Harley-Davidson motorcycles with a foot clutch, necessary when they were still using the sidecars. In 1967, the SPD Traffic Unit discontinued sidecars and started using motorcycles with hand clutches. They also discontinued the use of motorcycles in the winter and went to cars. *(Courtesy Case family)*

Frederick Germain, first motor officer killed – hired by the Spokane Police Department in 1918

MEETS DEATH IN CHASING SPEEDER

Motor Officer Germain Is Killed in Crash.

RAN INTO TRUCK

Driver of Heavy Car Tried to Avoid Collision--Is Blameless.

"BUG" MAN ESCAPED

Victim Was Dead When Friends Reached His Side--Accident on East Trent.

Officer Frederick Alexander Germain was killed in a motorcycle accident while pursuing a speeding vehicle on July 21, 1922. The driver that he was chasing was a repeat offender. During the pursuit, a large truck swerved to avoid colliding with him. The truck went into a ditch but spun around, striking Officer Germain, killing him instantly. The radiator of the truck struck the officer squarely, and he received the full impact of the blow to his chest. The truck went about 12 or 15 feet before it stopped, and the body of the officer was carried on the front bumper. When another officer arrived on the scene a few minutes later, Germain was unconscious. By the time the patrol wagon arrived, he had died without ever regaining consciousness. As the truck did not run over Germain, the motorcycle was not badly damaged.

Officer Germain had been with the department for about two years. He first joined on May 3, 1918, but left to work as a railroad engineer. He then returned at age 32, as a motorcycle officer, about five months before his death.

The headline in the July 22, 1922, *Spokesman- Review* further stated: "Pursued Speeding Bug." Germain was lying in wait in a trap used by the speed officers when the bug flashed past going east on Trent Avenue." The accident happened on East Trent near the Carsten's Packing Plant. Captain Miles of the police department stated the driver of the truck was "blameless." *(Courtesy Spokane Law Enforcement Museum)*

Walter Benjamin Case – hired by the Spokane Police Department in 1921

THE SPOKESMAN-REVIEW, SPOKANE, WASH.

Participants in Gun Battle With Bandits

V. M. Morgan.

Walter B. Case.

Bullets whizzed past the ears of Motorcycle Officer Walter B. Case early Monday morning as he drew alongside Dick Watson, 26, and Adolph Miller, 38, bandits who held up the Lotus cafe and escaped with $80. When the policeman spotted the men near Riverside and Browne the shooting started. After the rear tire of his machine had been shot off and holes drilled through a plate-glass window across the street, Officer Case blazed away at the fleeing pair. His ammunition gone, the policeman followed the men into the dark alley between Browne and Division and Riverside and Main.

Motorcycle Officer V. M. Morgan stalked Watson in the alley behind a board fence. Refusing to surrender, Watson crouched behind the fence, gun in hand. Realizing capture was sure, he shot himself in the head as the policeman was pressing the trigger of his revolver. Believing the thug was playing possum, Officer Morgan fired into the air before he approached the body.

Miller was caught an hour later by Patrolmen Miller and Mangan, who found him hiding under an old building in the alley.

The above photo and narrative appeared in the *Spokesman-Review*, circa 1924:

Bullets whizzed past the ears of Motorcycle Officer Walter B. Case early Monday morning as he drew alongside Dick Watson, 26, and Adolph Miller, 38, bandits, who held up the Lotus Café and escaped with $80. When the policeman spotted the men near Riverside and Browne the shooting started. After the rear tire of his machine had been shot off and holes drilled through a plate glass window across the street, Officer Case blazed away at the fleeing pair. His ammunition gone, the policeman followed the men into the dark alley between Browne and Division and Riverside and Main.

Motorcycle officer V. M. Morgan stalked Watson in the alley behind a board fence. Refusing to surrender, Watson crouched behind the fence, gun in hand. Realizing capture was sure, he shot himself in the head as a policeman was pressing the trigger of his revolver. Believing the thug was playing possum, Officer Morgan fired into the air before he approached the body. Miller was caught an hour later by officers who found him hiding under an old building in the alley.

SPOKANE POLICE DEPARTMENT

The Spokane Police Department's first motorcycle detachment

The above photo, called the motorcycle "suicide squad," was comprised of Victor Hudson, Harry Davenport, Pierson Anderson, Fred Frese, Adolph Windmaiser, and Walter Case with Chief Arthur Hooper in the center. This photo was taken shortly before the winged motorcycle patch was added to the uniform. *(Courtesy Walter Case family album)*

The Spokane Police Department's first official motor squad. On May 24, 1928, three more motor officers were added, bringing the total to six. Victor Hudson and Harry Davenport were to work from 7 am to 3 pm; Adolph Windmaiser from 8 am to 4 pm; Fred Frese and Walter Case from 3 pm to 11 pm; and P.D. Anderson from 4 pm to 12 midnight. Hourly calls were made by the officers to the station so that every 20 minutes headquarters would be in touch with one of the three motorcycle officers on duty.

The above officers alongside their Harleys, 1930. *(Courtesy Walter Case family album)*

Walter Case and another motor officer responding to a call. *(Courtesy Walter Case family album)*

Spokane Police Department motorcycle "suicide squad," with Chief Arthur Hooper in the car, circa 1930.
(Courtesy Walter Case family album)

In 1929, Spokane had six men riding motor, when government statistics for the size of cities equal to Spokane indicated they should have thirty-one. The commissioner of public safety asked for an additional ten men. In January, he was given two more men. Now there was a total of eight men assigned to the traffic unit. They are identified as follows with the date they went on the department: Front row, William Gale Pitner – 1928, Walter M. Johnson – 1924, William James Hudson – 1916, and Pierson B. Anderson – 1924. Back row: Walter Benjamin Case – 1924, Clyde E. Phelps – 1929, George W. Luther – 1930, and John H. Miller – 1929. Miller died in the line of duty. *(Courtesy Walter Case family)*

Meanwhile automatic traffic signals were installed on Riverside at Washington, between Howard and Post. It seemed strange to the people back then not to see the blue-coated traffic officer in the center of the street directing traffic and admonishing, in a loud voice, the pedestrians and drivers who went against his signals.

In 1930, one of the heaviest traffic flows was at the intersection of Monroe and Broadway with 15,568 autos passing the intersection in twelve hours. The northbound traffic on Monroe was the heaviest with only 3,045 going east and west on Broadway.

On May 30, 1935, the police department motorcycles had radios installed. However, the first radios were one-way and could only receive calls. It would still be several years before two-way radios were installed on all the motors.

The following article taken from the February 7, 1932, *Spokesman-Review*, again reflects the life of a motorcycle officer with the Spokane Police Department from 1920 to 1932:

Speed Cop Wears Out Cycles
Walter Case Has Run Last Mile Out of Five Motorcycles and Has Never Been Injured— In 12 Years
He has Covered 204,000 Miles

This week's "Who's Who" on the Spokane Police Department concerns a member of the "suicide squad," a group of officers about which the public knows little. The "suicide squad" is police slang for members of the motorcycle organization of the department. The article Is about Walter B. Case.

Most persons think of motorcycle officers only in terms of getting a ticket, a tag for having only one light on an automobile, or for going through an arterial highway. There was a time when the writer himself believed all motorcycle officers were "hard-boiled" snoopers who sneaked up on one just at the moment when one was "stepping on it." But such is not the case, at least in Spokane,

JOINED 12 YEARS AGO.

Mr. Case joined the department some 12 years ago and is the dean of the motorcycle officers on the department. For the last 10 years, he has ridden these dangerous contraptions and, according to estimates, has covered 204,000 miles. He already has worn out five motorcycles which have had the best of care. But after a time, even a motorcycle slows up. When it fails to turn over 75 miles an hour, it is passed on a police department.

The estimated number of arrests made by Mr. Case in the last 10 years is 3,000. Exclusive of this number are several arrests for auto theft, burglary, robbery and many other crimes.

Now, to those who do not know Mr. Case, a word of introduction is in order. He does not smile much. Perhaps at times, he even looks sour. But at heart, he's just as likeable and good-natured as any man. His work is such that most men would have quit smiling long ago.

STICKS TO HIS FACTS.

Another thing about Mr. Case you should know; If he ever catches you speeding or driving recklessly—take his word for it if he says you were traveling at 50 miles an hour. It's dollars

Walter Case, 1932. *(Courtesy Walter Case family)*

to doughnuts you were going as fast as that, if not faster. Mr. Case has never been known to "jazz up" on a speeding ticket or in any way make the offense appear an iota more serious than it really is. So if you ever face the judge, the best bet is to plead guilty.

Before Mr. Case was made a motocycle officer he walked his beat like the rest of them. He had an amusing and somewhat dangerous experience when a new officer which might have had something to do with his wishing to quit being a patrolman. Ordered to assist the late Detective Roy Fordyce in capturing a bootlegger, Mr. Case, in plain clothes, got into the car of an Austrian from whom he was supposed to buy some liquor. Fordyce was to follow and arrest the foreigner as the deal was made. But Fordyce got lost and did not follow the bootlegger's car as arranged. Instead, a big machine with eight Austrians in it followed the first bootlegger and Mr. Case. *(Continued on following page.)*

(*Continued from page 45*)

WAS TAKEN FOR RIDE

Somewhere on High Drive the rum men became suspicions, ordered Case out of the car and demanded to know who he was. He overheard them saying now was the time to "bump him off." When he showed them his star the foreigners lunged toward him, intent on knocking him out. Case pulled out his gun and backed away, standing off his assailants. There is no doubt that Case had to fight his way out. He did not fire a shot, but escaped without a mark. What kind of marks the other fellows had, Case did not say.

To come back to the suicide squad, the reason this name was given the group is because few officers ever escape service with the organization without injury. Two or three have been killed and half a dozen had serious injury. Mr. Case has never had a serious accident or been laid up by a fall from the machine. Of course, riding a motorcycle to Case is like walking to most of us.

HIS LIFE IS COLORFUL

The motorcycle officer does not only chase speeders, as some of the readers probably believe. He does a thousand and one other tasks, assigned him by the chief, captains, sergeants, and others. So, it is no surprise to learn that Mr. Case already has saved two lives–one from drowning and the other when a small boy was hurled over an embankment when an excavation gave way. It was not his fault that nobody was in a burning house in which he dashed a year ago, either.

The last good shooting escapade Mr. Case had anything to do with was in May 1930, when two robbers who held up the Lotus Cafe cashier engaged in a pistol duel with Mr. Case and V. M. Morgan, also a motorcycle officer at that time. The rear tire of Case's machine was shot off, but he was not hurt. The battle ended in one bandit killing himself when cornered in an alley near Division and Main, and the other being captured.

MUST BE VERSATILE

Mr. Case says that a good motorcycle officer must have a sort of Dr. Jekyll and Mr. Hyde personality. One moment, he is sent out to find a lost baby. He must satisfactorily coddle it. The next moment, he must battle with a drunken driver or fight a crazy drunken man.

Walter Case. *(Courtesy Walter Case family)*

The motorcycle man must go out and look for missing persons, tell youngsters not to coast or play in the street, check up on stolen autos, hurry up and catch a burglar robbing a store, be first on the job when a prowler is breaking into a residence, find out what happens when an auto crash injures somebody, lie in wait for store holdups, drive the wagons and detective cars at times, lead parades, and escort notables around the city, and a lot more things we can not write unless this paragraph goes beyond the orthodox space limit.

Associated with Mr. Case in the suicide squad at present are officers Johnson, Anderson, Phelps, Pitner, Miller and Luther. They are all good fellows when you get to know them. Of course they have to pinch speeders. We all know how sore it makes one to get that tag.

August Bettinger and Fred Judd – Bettinger hired by the Spokane Police Department in 1922. Judd hired in 1925.

During the Depression, one of the annual highlights in Spokane was the Sportsmen's Show, held under the elevated railroad tracks on Trent Avenue. Canvas was hung from the girders supporting the tracks to form skirting around the show. Wild animals were on display, along with many stuffed animals. There were also pools of water stocked with fish. The motorcycle officers assisting here are August Bettinger (kneeling) and Fred Judd. In this photo, they are handling a baby coyote. One of the sponsors for this show was John T. Little, who owned a sporting goods store at North 111 Howard Street. *(Libby photo, courtesy Deneice Hastings, great granddaughter of John Little)*

S
P
O
K
A
N
E

P
O
L
I
C
E

D
E
P
A
R
T
M
E
N
T

Walter Melvin Johnson – hired by the Spokane Police Department in 1924

Walter Melvin Johnson. *(Courtesy Johnson family)*

mer, who was born on February 9, 1902, in Kindred, North Dakota, and a sister, Eleanor Aura, who was born on July 2, 1905, also in Kindred.

World War I
Walter Johnson is drafted

In 1917, the administration of Woodrow Wilson decided to rely primarily on conscription, also known as the draft. (The draft has been employed by the federal government in five conflicts: The Civil War, World War I, World War II, the Korean War, and Vietnam War).

During the first six weeks of World War I, only 73,000 volunteers enlisted out of the initial one million target. The Selective Service Act of 1917 authorized a selective draft of all those between 21 and 31 years of age. Later that same year, as a result of the still low numbers, the draft ages were changed to 18 through 45. Draft boards were established and issued draft calls in order of numbers drawn in a national lottery. By the end of 1918, there were 24 million men that were registered with nearly 3 million inducted into the military services.

Draft boards were localized and based their decisions on social class; the poorest were the most often drafted because they were considered the most expendable at home. Consequently, in 1917, when Walter turned 18, he was drafted to serve in World War I.

The war is ended and Walter Johnson goes to Spokane

Following World War I, Johnson ended up living in Hillyard, working as a boilermaker's helper. During that time, he met and courted another Hillyard resident, Leva Isobella McCammond. At the time of their marriage, Walter was 21 and Leva was 19. According to *Polk's Spokane Directory*, in 1924, he was a "driver" for "IPCo." When they were first married, they lived at West Fourth Avenue, then later moved to West Dalton. Walter and Leva had

Walter Melvin Johnson was born on August 11, 1899, in Kindred, North Dakota, to Milla Bertina Hanson Johnson, age 32, and Albert Julius Johnson, age 31. Walter had one brother, Alfred Os-

City's Motorized Police Out to Check Reckless Drivers

The following caption appeared in a 1931 Spokane neW.S.P.aper: With instructions to curb reckless driving, this part of Spokane's motorized police force is patrolling the city streets daily with many arrests chalked up to their credit. Left to right, the motorcycle officers are: W. G. Pitner, Walter Johnson, P. B. Anderson, John Miller, and R. J. LeBlanc. The prowl car officers pictures are: E. B. Meader, R. B. Piper, J. J. Manning, L. V. Rummer, Harry Avery, J. J. Lenhart, W. W. Herwig, and C. E. Phelps. *(Public domain)*

two children, Maxine Catherine, born on March 31, 1922, and Sydney Wilford, born on May 18, 1926. Walter Johnson's father, Albert Julius, and mother, Milla Bertina Johnson, both passed away on January 30, 1948, in Spokane, Washington. At the time his father was 80 and his mother was 81.

Walter Melvin Johnson, circa 1929. (*Courtesy Johnson family*)

Walter Johnson's police career

Walter Johnson served with the Spokane Police Department from September 29, 1924, to October 6, 1950. The first three years of his career, he worked as a prowl car officer. For 11 years of his tenure with the department, he was assigned to motor, being a member of Spokane's first motorcycle detachment, which consisted of six men.

In 1939, during Johnson's time on police motor, he received one of the city's fastest motorcycles. The following article appeared that year:

Make it tough for speeders
Policemen are supplied with motorcycles
that can do 95 miles an hour.

Escape from the Spokane mounted police is going to be difficult for law violators this year, it is declared. To that end the officers have been provided with motorcycles capable of attaining a speed of 95 miles an hour and 60 miles in a block or two after leaving the curb.

These machines are the L type, built by the Harley-Davidson Motor Company on a special order. Three of them have been delivered to the department of public safety by the Brush Cycle Company here and they are being driven by policemen Harry Davenport, Walter Johnson, and Walter Case. ...

Police in Drive on Traffic Violators

Walter Johnson working traffic, circa 1931. *(Courtesy Johnson family)*

Walter died on May 25, 1955, in Colville, Washington, at the age of 55. His widow, Leva, died in Spokane on December 21, 1988, at the age of 87. Johnson's son, Sydney, also became a member of the Spokane Police Department, serving from January 3, 1949, to December 20, 1973.

Walter Johnson's last 12 years on the department gave him much renown, largely came from his work on the Dr. Hahn murder case in 1940.

During his final tenure on the department, he worked on a large number of murders, far more than average, including that of the disreputable Dr. Rudolph Hahn.

The Dr. Hahn case has become legendary in Spokane. Many stories about the house where he and his second wife, Sylvia Fly, lived allude to its being haunted. However, few of the facts and details of the case were stated correctly.

Dr. Rudolph Hahn's first marriage

Rudolph Hahn and Annie M. Tice were married in 1885. Rudolph was 36 and Annie was 32. They were married for a total of approximately 33 years. During their marriage, Annie gave birth to nine children. However, only seven of their children lived. Sometime around 1917 to 1919 Rudolph and Annie were divorced. At that time he listed his occupation as physician.

The facts behind the
Dr. Rudolph A. Hahn murder case
Spokane's legendary abortionist
and eccentric character

According to various neW.S.P.aper accounts and court documents, Dr. Rudolph A. Hahn was one of Spokane's most widely known unsavory characters, and also a murder suspect on several occasions. He also committed a number of abortions, then illegal. There is no way to get an accurate account of how many abortions he actually performed. However, based on his record and proof that he was in that line of work, he gained a substantial reputation as being an abortionist. He was also arrested and considered a suspect in the death of his second wife in 1940, but was subsequently cleared.

Since he time of Hahns arrived in Spokane, there has been speculation about what he did, and if he really was a doctor, and reported erroneously as fact. Many stories about his life have emerged, alleging he was not really a doctor, but a barber. He, in fact, was a medical doctor. For 27 years, he was listed in the Spokane Directories as a physician. According to court testimony during an abortion trial, he stated he worked his way through medical school as a barber.

During his tenure in Spokane the *Spokane Polk Directory* lists him as follows:

• 1900 *Polk Spokane Directory*, Doctor Rudolph Hahn is listed as a portrait artist, located at South 306 Howard Street, his address is listed as the same.

• 1904 *Polk Spokane Directory*, his business is listed as Falls City Portrait Company, and his residence is listed as on Carlisle Avenue.

• 1908 *Polk Spokane Directory*, he is listed as an X-Ray specialist, with his address still on Carlisle Avenue.

• 1910, his name and information appear in the directory as "Hahn R A DR, X-Ray Specialist and Electro-Therapeutist, 401 5th Avenue, Tel Main 2340, home S. 613 Washington, Tel Main 4902."

• 1913, his name in the directory reads "Hahn, Rudolph A. phys. 207 Realty bldg. residence same." Following the 1913 city directory, Hahn is listed as a physician every year up until 1945. At that time, he was convicted for manslaughter, and was ordered to give up his medical license.

During his 48 years of residence in Spokane, Dr. Hahn often found himself in trouble with the law. On at least one occasion, he was charged with committing illegal operations (abortions). In addition, he gained much publicity for hosting numerous wild parties at his opulent residence.

Doctor Hahn and his party house

During most of his time in Spokane, Dr. Hahn and his wife, Sylvia, lived on Seventeenth Avenue, in what could be termed a mansion. It was originally built by Mrs. Sarah (Hecla) Smith, a mining baroness. The house was a 26-room, three-story Swiss chalet, surrounded by three landscaped acres containing a spacious swimming pool.

In 1929, Dr. Hahn appeared in the local newspapers after installing a huge loudspeaker for his radio outdoors so he could listen to it from any part of the grounds. Unfortunately, it disturbed the neighborhood. The doctor was hard of hearing and always turned the volume up high. His neighbors took him to court, and he received an injunction ordering him to cease his radio operations.

The former Hahn home on East Seventeenth Avenue, in 2016. *(Bamonte photo)*

Taken from the front page of the *Spokane Daily Chronicle* on May 3, 1940. In the photo on the left is the Hahn residence with an arrow pointed at Hahn's high-powered radio tower. *(Public domain)*

Dr. Hahn's marriage
and the death of his wife

Hahn divorced his second wife, Sylvia, who was 32 years younger, then remarried her 14 months later in 1934. On May 2, 1940, Sylvia was found dead in her bedroom in their home, shot through the head. Hahn immediately became a suspect and was arrested and jailed.

During the investigation, detectives found numerous bullet holes in the doors and ceilings of the room, evidence of Dr. Hahn's unstable disposition. Several days later, he was released from custody as a coroner's jury turned in a verdict that Mrs. Hahn had died from a self-inflicted bullet wound. This was based on the evidence of powder burns on his wife's hand. During their married life Hahn had filed for divorce three times, but each time the couple reconciled.

This following quote was taken from the May 3, 1940, Spokane Daily Chronicle. It describes the be-

ginning of the investigation regarding the shooting death of Sylvia Hahn:

His Attractive Wife Was Found Shot to Death.

Dr. R. A. Hahn, Spokane physician held by the police, in connection with the fatal shooting of his wife late yesterday, was spirited from the city jail this afternoon and was taken to an anteroom of the city police court for questioning.

Previously, he had been held incommunicado in the jail while police and members of the county prosecutor's staff conducted an exhaustive investigation into the death of attractive 42-year-old Mrs. Sylvia Hahn. Dr. Hahn is 74. Following a short session in the police court anteroom, Deputy Prosecutor Leslie Carroll was seen to come out and immediately was engaged in conversation with Attorney Del Cary Smith, presumed to be appearing in behalf of Dr. Hahn. Others who were in the small room with Dr. Hahn could not be determined, but it was believed the number included one or more city detectives who had been probing the mystery.

Later, Deputy Carroll vouched for the information "that the investigation has not been concluded." He added that "Dr. Hahn will be held until it is complete."

Mrs. Hahn was found dead on the bed in her own room in the Hahn home, E. 2526 Seventeenth, shot through the head. Police were summoned there by telephone by Dr. Hahn about 5 p. m.

"We're investigating every possible angle," Prosecutor Carl Quackenbush said today at the Hahn home. "I doubt if we reach any solution to the mystery of Mrs. Hahn's death today, but we will talk to Dr. Hahn some time this afternoon."

Deputy Prosecutor Leslie Carroll, in charge of the case, accompanied Quackenbush to the home.

Pistol Was Used

Mrs. Hahn was slain by a bullet fired from a Luger pistol. The gun, found on the blood-soaked bed beside her, was turned over to fingerprint experts. Mrs. Hahn, police said, had been shot shortly after 4 p.m. Dr. Hahn told the officers he heard the shot from the porch and rushed into the house and found his wife dead. He indicated she took her own life. He denied having any part in the shooting.

At least five attorneys attempted to communicate with Dr. Hahn this morning, but were barred from his jail cell by police and the prosecutor's office. No one was permitted to talk to him.

Rudolph Hahn, son of Dr. Hahn, was at the home this morning and was questioned by authorities. He could give little information. He said he was out of the city when the shooting occurred.

He had no statement to make for publication, saying he preferred to talk to his father first. He indicated he would attempt to see him this afternoon.

Police said that, prior to the shooting, a drinking session had been in progress in the Hahn home. When taken to police headquarters last night, officers said Dr. Hahn was intoxicated to the point where he attempted to do the questioning, rather than the authorities.

Coroner I. S. Collins, who ordered an autopsy last night, said today he was not ready to make an official statement. He admitted the bullet passed through Mrs. Hahn's head, and it is believed, authorities are attempting to determine from which side the shot was fired and whether there are powder burns on the body.

The room in which Mrs. Hahn met her death is on the south of the house. Near the bed is a lounge and large windows on the east and north side look out on the grounds. There is a bathroom adjoining.

Police examining the room today, found a bottle containing about halt a pint of brandy on the dressing table. It was taken for evidence.

Most startling evidence in the room, evidence confirming the idiosyncrasies of Dr. Hahn, a long time user of firearms, are numerous bullet holes, perhaps a dozen in all.

A bullet had been fired through the lock on the door. One had passed though the mahogany woodwork at the foot of the bed. Another one had struck the wall over the bed. One had passed the Venetian blinds on the east window and other bullet marks were found high and low on the walls.

Doctor Hahn Denies

The delay in developments today at police headquarters led observers to believe officers and Prosecutor Carroll may have found something new in the way of evidence which may determine whether Mrs. Hahn took her own life or was slain.

Rodney Unger, N. 1309 Adams, Postal Telegraph messenger boy, reported the following Incident to Detective Oscar Haukedahl: "I went to the Hahn home three weeks ago to collect a $13 bill. Mrs. Hahn came to the door in her negligee and said she would get me the money. Dr. Hahn was there and apparently both had been drinking.

As Mrs. Hahn went for the money I heard her and the doctor quarreling bitterly. I heard the doctor threaten to shoot Mrs. Hahn because she was spending too much of his money.

The doctor gave me a $20 bill and I had to go for change, When I returned he took all the money and said he wouldn't pay me. After considerable coaxing by Mrs. Hahn, he gave me the $13 and I left.

Friends today reported Mr. and Mrs. Hahn attended an affair at the Eagles lodge hall Wednesday evening.

Dr. Han's life in the last 20 years has been one spotted with eccentric incidents. In the early days of radio, the doctor owned a legendary set which people who had seen it said "was as long as the room." All night lasting parties were frequent, police recalled today. At one time, Dr. Hahn placed the set outside. Neighborhoods, up in arms, turned to police. Always an individualist, Dr. Hahn caused a minor sensation when he first started his practice of appearing in public wearing bedroom slippers. With his bedroom slippers, the doctor often went in for colorful clothing.

Liked racing cars

One of the most interesting phases in the career of Dr. Hahn was his passion for racing cars. Two decades ago, both the doctor and his son were widely known in the Inland Empire dirt track racing circles. Dr. Hahn was given credit as having the "fastest racing car and these parts" at that time. His winning races, however, were few.

Following his retirement from dirt track racing Dr. Hahn's penchant for speed was reflected in his choice of passenger cars, which were fast, flashy and unusually exclusive. In later years, however, autos appeared to have lost some of their fascination for the doctor.

Sued for divorce

In 1932, Mrs. Hahn filed that suit for divorce and testified in one instance that the doctor chased her from the house with a sword. But the two were still attracted to each other and in 1933 were remarried. After another year of turbulent relations, Dr. Hahn filed for divorce, but the pair became reconciled once more and the action was dismissed.

Throughout their married life, Dr. and Mrs. Hahn engaged in verbal bouts. On one occasion the doctor complained that his wife had broken two of his ribs. Within recent months, police have had at least one call to investigate trouble at the large Hahn home.

The victim, one of three triplet children, was the daughter of Mary Fly, East 1517 Eleventh, and the late Calvin Fly. The body was taken to the Smith Funeral Home.

Sylvia Fly Hahn was one of eight children. She married Rudolph Hahn for the first time in 1919, in Spokane when she was 20 and he was 53. They were divorced in 1932 and married again on June 8, 1933, also in Spokane.

Prior to his marriage, he gave his marital status as divorced and his occupation as physician. This was Sylvia's first and only marriage. She listed her occupation as office girl. Prior to this marriage she gave her residence as Billings, Montana.

Hahn's medical practice

In November 1929, Dr. Hahn was charged with performing a criminal operation upon a Mullan, Idaho, high school girl. After a trial that lasted several days, the superior court jury voted eleven to one to acquit him. During the trial, Hahn told the jury he had worked as a barber in his youth to earn money for his medical education. In June 1945, Dr. Hahn was tried in superior court on a charge of manslaughter and three charges of abortion, involv-

ing the death of a wealthy Inland Empire woman the previous December. He was found guilty on two counts, and was placed on probation by Judge E. W. Schwellenbach of Ephrata. Dr. Hahn was 79 at the time of the trial, and was in failing health. Dr. Hahn agreed, if granted probation, that he would discontinue the practice of medicine.

Dr. Rudolph Hahn is murdered

The following story was printed on August 7, 1946, in the *Spokane Daily Chronicle* immediately following the murder of Dr. Hahn:

A murderous French army bayonet firmly embedded in his heart, 81-year-old Dr. R. A. Hahn, one of Spokane's most widely known characters, was found dead late last night in his new Madison apartment – hotel rooms. The body, clad in summer slacks, was found at the foot of his bed in a small bedroom, which bore signs of a terrific struggle. Coroner C. J. Abrams said a three-carat diamond was missing from a stickpin, usually identified with the aged doctor, and that his wallet was empty, leading to a theory of robbery and murder.

Heart was penetrated

The death weapon was part of an old arms collection made by the doctor during his heyday in Spokane, and its metal sheath was found near the body. It was small, less than two feet long, sharp, pointed and made somewhat like a rapier.

The bayonet, Coroner Abrams said, entered Dr. Hahns body at the right side of his chest, penetrated the heart and stopped there.

Detective Ralph Weir said the body bore at least five stab wounds in the chest, indicating a wild struggle over the death weapon.

The murder occurred in the doctor's room, 503 at the New Madison, and the report was taken shortly after 9 p.m. by the police while the body was still warm.

Dr. Rudolph A. Hahn

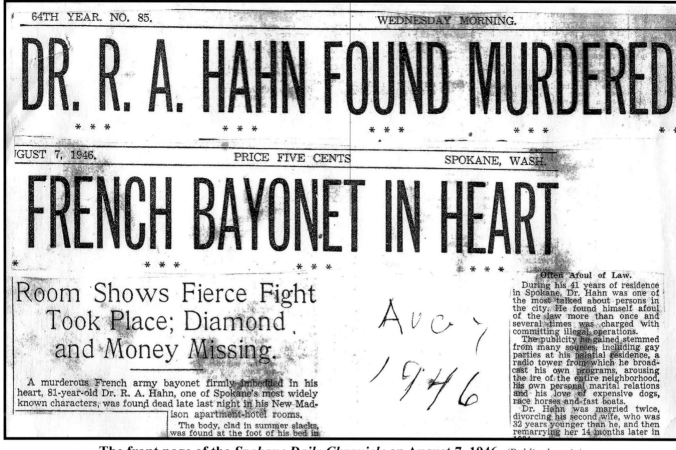

The front page of the *Spokane Daily Chronicle* on August 7, 1946. *(Public domain)*

The outcome of the Hahn murder case. *(Public domain)*

Clyde Ralstin – hired by the Spokane Police Department in 1927
Prime suspect in the murder of the marshal of Newport, Washington, during
a burglary committed at that location in 1935. Ralstin is pictured third from left

Look Out, Speeders! Cops Will Get You If You Don't Watch Out

Motorists with heavy feet are due for trouble. A light touch on the throttle is more likely to get the driver to his destination in a hurry than too much gasoline is, declare the six motorcycle officers in the picture. The police motorcycle squad now has a personnel of six men working day and night in an effort to reduce the number of automobile accidents and casualties. The officers in the picture, from left to right, are: Walter Johnson, Harry Davenport, Clyde Ralstin, V. Morgan, Walter Case and Victor Hudson.

This photo appeared in the *Spokesman-Review* on March 28, 1929. The caption read:

"Motorists with heavy feet are due for trouble. A light touch on the throttle is more likely to get the driver to his destination in a hurry than too much gasoline is, declare the six motorcycle officers in the picture. The police motorcycle squad now has a personnel of six men working day and night in an effort to reduce the number of automobile accidents and casualties. The officers in the picture, from left to right, are: Walter Johnson, Harry Davenport, Clyde Ralstin, V. Morgan, Walter Case, and Victor Hudson."

Not all motorcycle cops were good cops. Clyde Ralstin is a case in point. Ralston was the suspect in a burglary ring in the 1930s. In 1935, during the act of committing a nighttime burglary with two other men, Ralstin allegedly shot and killed the Newport, Washington, Night Marshal, George Conniff. Fifty-four years later, he was identified as the murderer, but died shortly after. This story was recounted in a best-selling book, *Breaking Blue*, by Timothy Egan, and in the television series *Unsolved Mysteries*.

How reopening the nation's oldest active murder case came about, *by Tony Bamonte:*

In 1987, during the time I was the elected sheriff of Pend Oreille County, I entered a master's program at Gonzaga University. My degree was in Organizational Leadership. When the time came to write a thesis, I approached my advisor and suggested it be on the leadership styles of each sheriff in Pend Oreille County, where I was then the eleventh sheriff. The concept was met with approval. Consequently, I began the study of each sheriff who held office and the major crimes he confronted during his tenure and how they were solved.

In 1989, my thesis was almost complete, and I was ready to defend it, which was the final phase toward getting a degree. About the same time, the Gonzaga *Signum*, a small university publication that is no longer active, ran a story about what they considered some of the more interesting theses. Mine was among them. As a result, Jim Camden, a reporter from the *Spokesman-Review* read their story and also did his own story. Following that, Timothy Egan from the *New York Times* saw the *Spokesman's* story, which was on the *Associated Press,* and wrote a piece about my thesis, which appeared on the front page of the *New York Times*.

When the first story in the *Spokesman-Review* came out, the date of the murder was not correct. That same afternoon, the son of the murdered marshal, George Conniff Jr., contacted Bill Morlin, an investigative reporter from the *Spokesman-Review*. Conniff Jr. wanted to know more about the "shooting of the marshal" story. He stated it sounded like his father, who was shot in 1935, but the dates in the *Spokesman*

Murder victim Marshal George Conniff, circa 1930. *(Courtesy Conniff family)*

On the night of September 14, 1935, Newport, Washington, Marshal George Conniff was shot and killed during a robbery of the Newport Creamery. Former police motorcycle officer Clyde Ralstin, by then a detective, and two other (non-police) associates, in a burglary ring he headed, were proved years later to have been the perpetrators. Ralstin, who pulled the trigger, had earlier shot and killed a fleeing 15-year-old boy who had just stolen a car at Rogers High School. *(Public domain)*

appeared to be incorrect. Morlin started looking up information and soon learned the dates of events in the first *Spokesman* story were wrong. He confirmed to Conniff Jr. that the story Jim Camden wrote was about his father, George Conniff, and gave him my number to call.

From that point on, Morlin became involved. During his years of working for the *Spokesman-Review*, he had developed many contacts. As a result and concerning this case, he consistently was being contacted by people who had been involved or who knew about the Conniff murder and had information to give, which he always passed along to me. Most disturbing, when Morlin contacted Chief Mangan, Mangan denied that Clyde Ralston ever worked for the SPD. This was in spite of a group photo Ralston was in, hanging in the hallway 30 feet from Mangan's office.

As a result of his help, I was able to develop what would turn out to be the nation's oldest active murder case. Had Morlin not taken an interest and developed numerous leads for me, this case would

Clyde Ralstin, circa 1927. *(Courtesy Spokane Police Department Archives)*

not have been solved. *Breaking Blue* was published about this case in 1992.

Statements from witnesses to the cover-up

A November 7, 1989, *Spokesman-Review* article by Bill Morlin details the stories of two former Spokane policemen involved in the cover-up of this murder. One of them was a former Spokane police chief:

Ex-police chief gives new version before his death, claims captain ordered partner to destroy weapon

Before his death last week, retired Spokane Police Chief Bill Parsons provided new information in what is being called the oldest active murder case in the United States.

Parsons, 79, battling emphysema and breathing from an oxygen bottle, told authorities earlier this fall that it was his partner, Spokane police officer Dan Mangan, who dropped a handgun into the Spokane River in 1935.

The handgun – believed to be the same rusty .32-caliber revolver recovered this past summer from the riverbed – allegedly was used in the fatal shooting on Sept. 14, 1935, of George Conniff, town marshal of Newport, Wash.

Conniff was gunned down when he apparently startled thieves burglarizing a Newport creamery. The marshal's murder remains unsolved.

Pend Oreille County Sheriff Tony Bamonte reactivated the case earlier this year after new information was developed from witnesses who said the shooting involved a Spokane police officer and a cover-up.

Those developments occurred following neW.S.P.aper reports about a master's thesis written by Bamonte dealing with various murders over the years in Pend Oreille County.

"From what I can see and other people say, I guess this is now the oldest ongoing murder investigation in the United States," the Pend Oreille sheriff said Monday.

The rusty handgun recovered on Aug. 22 was found close to shore on the riverbed just downstream from the Post Street Bridge. It was recovered from the spot pointed out to Bamonte by Mangan, 86.

Mangan said at the time that it was his partner, Harrison "Hacker" Cox, who had dropped the gun into the river. Cox is deceased. Mangan said the two young officers were following orders from a supervisor who knew that another police officer, Clyde Ralstin, was involved in the Conniff killing and wanted that involvement concealed.

Ralstin, now 90 and living in St. Ignatius, Mont., has denied any involvement in the murder and has not been charged in the case.

"It's all hogwash," he said last September when asked about the allegations.

Ralstin resigned from the police department on July 21, 1937, while suspended from duty, according to his resignation letter. The reason for that suspension wasn't detailed, and Ralstin's city personnel files have disappeared.

Bamonte later learned that it was Parsons, not Cox, who was Mangan's partner when the gun was tossed off the bridge in downtown Spokane in 1935.

After learning that Mangan's partner that day was Parsons, then a rookie police officer, Bamonte said he approached the former police chief, who retired in Spokane.

Parsons, in a recorded interview in September, said Mangan was ordered by a police captain to destroy the gun by dropping it into the river, said Bamonte, who released the contents of the interview last week.

Parsons offered the same version when he was filmed last month by a production crew for the TV series "Unsolved Mysteries," which is producing an episode on the case. It is scheduled to be aired Dec. 27 or Jan. 3.

The case also will be featured in a forthcoming article in the *New York Times*.

Faced with the conflicting stories, Bamonte said he arranged to have the ailing, retired police chief meet with Mangan in October and recollect the event.

Mangan's daughter, Rosemary Miller of Spokane, said her dad has suffered three strokes this year, the latest last Friday, and his memory has faded. He is in a local nursing home.

During their brief meeting at the nursing home, Mangan and Parsons discussed the shooting and disposal of the gun, Miller said Monday.

"My dad asked, 'Who the devil threw the gun over the bridge?'" Miller said. "Parsons," she said, "responded to Mangan, 'You did.' "Dad then answered, Oh, I'll be damned," Miller said.

Bill Parsons as a young officer around the time of the Conniff murder, circa 1935. *(Courtesy Spokane Police Archives)*

After discussing the event, Mangan conceded that he had dropped the gun into the river.

"When Bill (Parsons) enlightened him on things, he tended to remember," Miller said.

The gun found in the river was turned over to state crime laboratory experts for analysis.

Bamonte said they determined the handgun was a .32-caliber, like that used in the Conniff killing. "They also determined the rust on the gun is consistent with being in the water more than 50 years," he said.

The revolver, rendered inoperable by the rust, is being held as evidence in the case, the sheriff said.

The facts of the 1935 murder written and included in *Life Behind the Badge, The Spokane Police Department's Transforming Years 1923-1944, volume III* by the Spokane Police Department History Book Committee:

On Saturday night, September 14, 1935, Newport Town Marshal George Conniff was on patrol when he caught three men crouched in the alley behind the Newport Creamery. Conniff identified himself, and one of the suspects shot at him. Conniff returned fire. The suspects continued to fire, hitting Conniff four times. He died from his

A photo of Bill Parsons (left) and Dan Mangan given to Sheriff Tony Bamonte by Bill Parsons to prove they were working together, circa 1935. *(Courtesy Bill Parson)*

wounds the next day at St. Luke's Hospital in Spokane. Before becoming the Newport Town Marshal, Conniff had served as the chief of police in Sandpoint, Idaho. He left a wife and three children.

Conniff's good friend, Pend Oreille County Sheriff Elmer Black, immediately ordered roadblocks to be set up. One of the cars to pass through the roadblock on the north edge of Spokane was driven by Spokane Police Detective Clyde Ralstin. He produced his police identification at the roadblock and was allowed through. Neither he nor his passenger were ever questioned.

Detectives Charles F. Sonnebend and August H. Bettinger later found a suspect vehicle abandoned near the Northern Pacific Depot. Spokane police conducted a preliminary investigation, then handed the case back to Pend Oreille County. A crime laboratory in Seattle determined that the bullets recov-

ered from Conniff's body came from a .32 caliber revolver. A major breakthrough came with several arrests connected to creamery burglaries in Montana and elsewhere, including Detective Ralstin's friend, Acie Logan. It was believed headquarters of the theft ring was in Spokane. Stolen butter, hams, and bacon were reportedly used and fenced from a restaurant called Mother's Kitchen, located at 24 West Riverside, a favorite hangout for Spokane police officers. When Detective Sonnebend attempted to follow up on a possible connection with the Newport burglary and murder, his superior, Sergeant Daniel Mangan, ended his investigation. He also advised the detective to never divulge that Logan had ever talked about the creamery murder. Sheriff Black was also obstructed in his efforts to speak with suspect Acie Logan in the county jail.

In 1955, Pend Oreille County Sheriff William M. Giles was contacted by the prosecuting attorney of Spokane

County. He and former Sheriff Elmer Black had been re-visiting the murder of Marshal Conniff. The prosecutor advised the men that Detective Sonnebend wished to make a statement regarding the murder and the investigation. Giles was able to arrange a meeting with Sonnebend. U.S. Marshal Darrell Holmes, who had been the sheriff of Pend Oreille County from 1942 to 1953, and ex-sheriff Black also attended this meeting. The following is a condensed statement from this meeting:

In 1935, there were a lot of creamery robberies [burglaries]. Mixed up in these was a fellow who was sent to the federal penitentiary for interstate motor vehicle theft. After three weeks of questioning, Acie Logan broke and admitted his part in the creamery robberies. He also implicated Spokane Detective Clyde Ralstin, who owned a ranch a short distance from Spokane. According to Logan, there were several men connected in this ring but the stolen butter was taken to Ralstin's ranch and later disposed of through Mother's Kitchen, a restaurant in Spokane.

The night of the Conniff murder, the Spokane Police constructed a blockade at the north city limits of Spokane. It was conducted by two rookie officers. They told Sergeant

Detective C. F. Sonnebend. *(Courtesy Spokane Police Archives)*

Mangan of the Spokane Police Department that they had stopped a car that was boiling hot and appeared as though it had been driven very hard. Detective Ralstin was driving this car, and he had another person with him.

Ralstin was a very close friend of Acie Logan. Sergeant Mangan retired from the department in 1939. Mangan knows all about this murder and the affiliation of Ralstin and Logan. Ralstin is supposedly the ringleader.

At the time of his arrest, Logan was with his accomplice (Warden Spinks) and two women in a stolen car from Montana. Their car was searched as well as their hotel room. A .32 revolver and a .38 special were found in the room. These guns were kept by the department. ... This same gun [a .32 caliber revolver] was signed out of the Spokane Police Department by Ralstin just before the creamery robbery [burglary]. ... Ralstin reported it stolen. It was later reported to have been thrown into the Spokane River. ...

After Logan made his confession to Detective Sonnebend and the reports went to the chief, Ralstin resigned from the police force. Logan stated that Ralstin was in on all of the creamery burglaries. Sonnabend believed that Ralstin was the man who killed Conniff and Sergeant Mangan was in complete knowledge of this.

Sheriff Giles was unable to track down any of the people mentioned in this statement. Two years later, the dying

Dan Mangan at his home in 1989, shortly after his confession to being an accomplice to the Conniff murder. *(Photo Lynda Donoian)*

Sonnebend summoned Giles and U.S. Marshal Darrell Holmes to his hospital room and confessed that he was the officer who had signed for and taken a gun from Logan, and that he later gave it to his nephew. Sonnabend insisted again that Sergeant Mangan was aware of everything.

The suspects were never apprehended, but were identified fifty-four years later when Ex-Police Chief Bill Parsons, who was dying, confessed his knowledge of the murder to Bamonte, implicating several men in the Spokane Police Department.

Eighty-six-year-old Dan Mangan was one, forced by guilt and by his daughter, arranged for an interview with Bamonte. As detailed in Timothy Egan's book *Breaking Blue*, Mangan recalled: "I knew Ralstin fairly good. I knew he was into something. I didn't know what. I heard that he was involved in all the creamery burglaries and he was peddling. I never had much contact with Ralstin, but he hung around with some shady characters. ... He was always mixed up with some dairy business and the cafe." Mangan went on to state that Captain Ed Hinton called him and his partner into Chief of Police Ira Martin's office and gave them a package. When they came out, Harrison "Hacker" Cox said, "This was Ralstin's package. I knew about the murder... thought this might have been the murder weapon. It's been on my mind ever since."

Mangan's partner, Bill Parsons, drove the car and watched as Mangan dropped the package from the railing of the Post Street Bridge into the Spokane River. When Parsons contacted FBI agents two days later, they advised him to keep quiet about it.

The following appeared in the *Spokesman-Review* on January 10, 1990, after an interview with Pearl Keogh:

SPOKANITE WILL TELL HER STORY
1935 NEWPORT MURDER
FEATURED ON TV SHOW
By Bill Morlin, staff writer

For about 50 years, no one has really listened to what Pearl Keogh knows about the 1935 murder of the town marshal in Newport, Wash.

A year after the killing, Keogh said she and her sister gave authorities information and evidence, but were branded as "just a couple of women who should mind their own business." Tonight, the spunky 85-year-old Spokane Valley grandmother will tell her story on prime-time TV to 28 million Americans.

"I'd just like to see justice done, somehow, but I don't know how it's going to be done now, after all these years," Keogh said Monday between sips of coffee at a Spokane Valley restaurant. "I feel so bad to think that something couldn't have been done before now," she said, gazing out the window.

Keogh contacted Pend Oreille Sheriff Tony Bamonte last year after reading news accounts on the unsolved slaying of Newport Marshal George Conniff. It wasn't long before the TV cameras of "Unsolved Mysteries" showed up.

Keogh said she's convinced former Spokane police detective Clyde Ralstin was involved in the death of Conniff. He was gunned down after startling burglars stealing dairy products, then scarce, from the Newport Creamery on Sept. 14, 1935.

Ralstin, now 90 and living in Montana, has denied involvement in the killing. He has hired a lawyer, who says Ralstin is too old and ill to talk with investigators.

Keogh said her belief is based on a confession she was given in 1940 by the late Virgil Burch and butter wrappers from the Newport Creamery she found after the shooting in Burch's former home and the "Mother's Kitchen" restaurant in downtown Spokane.

Pearl Keogh, circa 1935. *(Courtesy Pearl Keogh)*

Burch, who was both a part-time plumber and restaurant co-owner, had done plumbing work at the Newport Creamery in the weeks before the shooting and may have been recognized by the town marshal, Keogh said.

She recalled hearing police officers discuss "and even joke about" the Conniff killing at the restaurant at W. 24 Riverside, where they'd stop off for free coffee and pie. She often frequented the restaurant. Her sister, the late Ruth Coffman, worked there as a cook for Burch.

"They talked about it all the time" in the restaurant, Keogh recalled. "Everybody would come in and say, 'Well, who did you kill today?'" "They were laughing and made a real laughingstock out of it," she said, "and that's what made my sister so disgusted that she finally quit."

Police complicity in the killing and subsequent cover-up were common knowledge, Keogh said. "There was no doubt in our minds," Keogh recalled. "Every place you went in Spokane, somebody knew about it and who was involved."

Mother's Kitchen bought its dairy products from Hazelwood Dairy in Spokane, but about the time of the shooting, she and her sister found Newport Creamery butter wrappers in the restaurant's garbage. Keogh also found Newport Creamery wrappers in the small North Spokane home once occupied by Burch.

In the spring of 1936, Keogh and her sister took the butter wrappers and the information they had overheard in the restaurant to Spokane County Sheriff Ralph Buckley. He promised to investigate, but never did, she said.

In 1940, after she and her husband had moved to Portland, Burch came to her home for dinner, Keogh recalled. Over dinner, Burch said that he, Ralstin and the late Acie Logan, who had been implicated in other creamery burglaries, were present when Conniff was shot outside the Newport Creamery, she said.

"I was sure of it before," but Burch didn't admit his involvement until the dinner meeting, Keogh said.

When she saw Ralstin in the restaurant and asked him about the matter, he always changed the subject, she said.

Newspaper archives and county records reveal Ralstin fatally shot a fleeing Spokane teenager in the back in 1937. A coroner's inquest ruled the shooting was justifiable.

Most police department personnel records have disappeared or can't be located, but a letter obtained by The *Spokesman-*

Review and *Spokane Chronicle* suggests Ralstin left the department while on a suspension three months later. He later became a supervisor at an atomic bomb plant and eventually became a municipal court judge.

"It's all hogwash," Ralstin said last August when questioned about his alleged role in the shooting. He has hired an attorney and refused to talk with investigators.

But still he remains a pivotal figure in what is being called the oldest, active unsolved murder case in the United States – one that is getting national media attention. It will be the lead segment at 8 tonight on the NBC show "Unsolved Mysteries."

Pearl Keogh, a witness to the confession. She and her husband were friends with Ralstin

Another important piece of evidence came to light in April 1989 from Pearl Keogh, an 85-year-old woman who knew Ralstin, Mangan, and Virgil Burch, her employer at Mother's Kitchen. She told me she had gone to the police with evidence early in the investigation, but had been told to mind her own business. Keogh corroborated facts and added information implicating Burch. At a dinner at Keogh's home in 1940, Burch talked about being with Ralstin when he shot Conniff. Burch was under a tarp in the back seat of the getaway car that was allowed to pass through the north Spokane roadblock.

Keogh also said that she had handled butter with Newport Creamery wrappers at Mother's Kitchen, and that years later, when she moved into a house once owned by Burch, she found Newport Creamery wrappers stashed away in a closet. Mrs. Keogh's husband had been a friend of Ralstin's and had sworn her to secrecy on the matter. After he died, she phoned me with the information that Ralstin had once bragged in front of her that he had shot Conniff.

On August 22, 1989, the Washington Water Power Company, which controlled the flow of the Spokane River, by means of its dams, ordered an inspection draw-down to conduct some surveying. This event gave me, and those assisting me, access to the slippery riverbed. Within fifteen minutes, I had found the corroded gun. It was about 20 feet downstream from where Dan Mangan said he had dropped it.

Prior to the draw-down, I had taken both Parsons and Mangan (individually at different times) to the Post Street Bridge site, asking them to identify the spot where the pistol was dropped from the bridge.

After resigning from the Spokane Police Department, Clyde Ralstin moved to St. Ignatius, Montana, and continued his career in law enforcement. On January 23, 1990, Ralstin died a free man, having never admitted his involvement and never being charged for the crime. His death ended a five-and-a-half decade quest for justice.

George Conniff's children 54 years after their father was murdered by former Spokane Police Motorcycle Officer Clyde Ralstin. From left to right, Mary, George Jr., and Olive. The hardest part for them was when they found out Darrell Holmes, the Pend Oreille County sheriff from 1942 to 1953, was part of this cover up. In 1953, Holmes resigned as sheriff and was appointed to the position of a United States marshal for the District of Washington, serving for eight years. He finished his law enforcement career as chief jailer of Spokane County. I took this photo at my office the day they learned their father's murder had been covered up by many law enforcement agencies who knew the facts. *(Bamonte photo)*

A television reporter and a member of the Spokane Treasure Club at the scene when the murder weapon was discovered. *(Lynda Donoian)*

The Spokane River as it looked with the water flow suspended. In this picture are members of the Spokane Treasure Club, several members of the media, and myself on the far right. The Post Street Bridge is to the right of this photo and in the direction the group is heading. *(Photo by Lynda Donoian)*

The George Conniff Murder Weapon as it was found in 1989

The murder weapon. *(Photo by Lynda Donoian)*

The murder weapon as it looked after lying in the Spokane River for over 54 years. The handle grips were completely rotted off. Also, the hammer, trigger, and trigger guard were rusted off. When I sent it to the Washington State Patrol crime lab, they stated it was the same caliber Marshal Conniff was shot with and its condition was consistent with being in the river for over 50 years. A Washington Water Power official also stated, "The location where it was found was the only area in that vicinity that had never been disturbed." Last, but also important, it was within 30 feet downstream of where Dan Mangan stated he dropped it. That location was confirmed by Bill Parsons, later a Spokane police chief, who was with Mangan when he dropped it from the Post Street Bridge railing.

This case was closely followed by the news media. About a week before the river was stopped, I contacted the Spokane Police Department and the news media to let them know the time and date I would be searching the river. I also invited the SPD, as it was a crime one of their men was a suspect in. I also invited the Spokane Treasure Club to the site, as I had no idea if the river bed would be covered with silt or debris.

However, since Chief Terry Mangan (no relation to Dan Mangan) had publicly made the statement that Clyde Ralstin had never been on the Spokane Police Department, he failed to send anyone to the scene. All of Ralston's records were missing. However, Ralston's picture was in a group police photo in the Public Safety Building's hallway, about 20 feet from Chief Mangan's office.

When that date arrived and the river was stopped, within 15 minutes I found the pistol exactly as shown in the above photo. I left it in that position for over a half hour so the press could take photos and I also had a personal photographer at the scene. After leaving it at the site of discovery for that amount of time for the news media to photograph it, I picked it up, cleaned off the mud and silt, then proceeded to my car. When I arrived at my office in Newport, I placed it in the evidence locker. Once the suspect had passed away, I donated it to the Northwest Museum of Arts and Culture in Spokane.

Clyde Ralstin, 1989. Inset: Ralstin, circa 1980. *(Courtesy Bill Morlin, Spokesman-Review)*

General motorcycle duty in 1939

This photo taken of motorcycle officers in 1939 in Spokane was the result of a prank being pulled on baseball coach Buck Bailey of Washington State College. Bailey had just gotten married. When he returned from his honeymoon with his new wife, their lawn was piled with boxes of hats. Phony return addresses said that the used, tattered hats came from General Franco, King George, Franklin Roosevelt, and boxer "Two-Ton" Tony Galento, among others. Bailey estimated that he received 27,000 hats. *(Courtesy Francis and Louise Carrol)*

Buck Bailey was famous for stomping on his hat when he disputed an umpire's call, so his fans put out a call to "send Bailey a hat."

Buck came to the university as assistant football coach and became a legend as its colorful, and winning, head baseball coach. He also had played football and baseball at Texas A & M and Bethany College in West Virginia, and was captain of the West team in the first East-West Shrine game in 1925. At WSU, Bailey's baseball teams won 11 Northern Division pennants and were second 10 times.

The 1950 team was runner-up for the NCAA title and seventh nationally in 1956. The athlete-coach of "Bailey's Angels, barnstorming basketball team" made up of WSC sports greats, toured the Northwest and entertained thousands. Buck and his wife died in October of 1964 in a car crash near Albuquerque, NM.

Buck Bailey
(Public domain)

Leonard "Jack" Lee – hired by the Spokane Police Department in 1942

Spokane Police Department Officer Jack Lee, 1944. *(Courtesy Spokane Police Archives)*

Irvin Neubauer – hired by the Spokane Police Department in 1942

Day shift patrol, late 1940s. Front Row: Sgt. George Pymm, Capt. Lloyd Ferguson, Sgt. Harry Hastings, John Robertson, Peder Bakken, Orville Gay, and Alfred Wilson. Second Row: David Lamphier, Harold Carlson, Donald Lussier, Victor Hudson, Arthur Eslick, Walter Herbert, Harry Cockburn, Harry Indahl, Perry Miles, Warren Loomis, Harrold B. Gibson, George Storasli, and Ed Stewart. Third Row: Walter Case, Edward Rooney, Roy Hamilton, Irvin Neubauer, Raymond Kenworthy, Oscar B. "Ozzie" Hoffman, Eugene Kenworthy, Fred Hunt, Roy Kelley, Raymond Byrnes, Alton Snyder, and David Watson. *(Both photos courtesy Spokane Police Archives)*

Irvin Neubauer was born on August 29, 1912 in Minnesota. He married Julia Morse on September 2, 1934, at Davenport, Washington, where his future bride resided. Irvin and Julia had two children, a son Rick Neubauer and a daughter Sherry Balocco.

Prior to joining the police department on August 19, 1942, Irvin worked in sales. His job on the police department included being a patrolman, motorcycle officer, and detective. He was on the Spokane Police Department for over 22 years. Irvin passed away in 1992.

Peder Bakken – hired by the Spokane Police Department in 1944

Spokane Police Department

Motorcycle Officer Peder Bakken, circa 1940. *(Courtesy Bakken family scrapbook)*

Peder Bakken joined the department in 1944 as a foot-beat officer. Within six months, he was riding a motorcycle.

Bakken was very innovative and instituted "Courtesy Week," working with the Spokane Chamber of Commerce. He would stop drivers and issue them "Courteous Driver of the Day" certificates.

Bakken's first accident occurred on July 2, 1946. He suffered severe head cuts and injuries to his arm, hands, and left leg.

On May 19, 1949, Bakken was involved in another motorcycle accident. He had numerous injuries. He was pronounced deceased 20 minutes after the accident. Bakken was on the way to the morgue, when he came to and was rushed to the hospital. Bakken spent over a month in the hospital, being released the end of June. He spent the next nine months recuperating at home.

Bakken returned to work as director of the Police Athletic League (PAL) in March 1950. Over the years, he taught many young Spokanites boxing, bowling, and dancing. Following his recuperation, six months later, he was back on the motorcycle.

In May 1955, Bakken attended the FBI Academy at Fort Lewis. Bakken was part of the department's dignitary detail. During his tenure with this unit, he escorted President and Mrs. Truman, Vice President Alben Barkley, Cardinal Francis Spellman, Duncan Renaldo (Cisco Kid), Governor Albert Rosellini, Bing Crosby, Bob Hope, Roy Rogers, William Boyd (Hopalong Cassidy), and Gene Autry.

In 1959, Bakken was promoted to detective and worked the vice squad, property crimes, and homicide. In 1962, he was one of two officers in the state chosen to take training in the new IDENTI-KIT system for identification. Billed as a "new system of rapid identification to aid law enforcement in the battle against crime," the system aided in assembling a likeness of a suspect for viewing by a witness. Bakken was credited with many arrests because of his work with this new tool. He retired in 1966 after 22 years of service.

Bakken's 1949 accident. *(Courtesy Bakken family scrapbook)*

George Patrick Lancaster, killed on motor – hired by the Spokane Police Department in 1942

The second motorcycle officer killed in the line of duty was Officer George Patrick Lancaster, who was struck by a car and suffered a basal skull fracture and many other injuries. *(Courtesy Spokane Police Archives)*

Officer George Lancaster joined the department in July 1942, and passed his probation to become a permanent officer on July 30, 1943. On October 21, 1943, Motorcycle Officer Lancaster was traveling northbound at Indiana and Division when his motorcycle was struck head-on by a car.

His body was thrown approximately 47-feet from his motorcycle and sustained basal skull, face, and body injuries. Lancaster was rushed to Sacred Heart Hospital. On November 18, the doctor said he expected Lancaster to make a full recovery even though he had been unconscious for the two weeks since the accident. The doctor thanked the many fellow officers who gave blood for the transfusions that were sustaining Lancaster.

Officer Lancaster did regain consciousness, but then developed pneumonia and died exactly four weeks to the day of his injuries. George Lancaster was a graduate of Gonzaga University and only 25-years old at the time of his death. He was survived by his wife and two young daughters, one who was just an infant. Pallbearers at the funeral were officers Ray Young, Ray Kenworthy, James Bricker, Glen Atkisson, Sherman Wakely, and Don Lussier. The driver of the car was booked and convicted for reckless driving.

Miscellaneous motor activity during the Harley-Davidson era, Baxter Hospital

Downtown Spokane in 1943, looking south on Division from Trent Avenue, shows a motorcycle officer escorting an ambulance convoy to Baxter Hospital. *(Courtesy Spokane Police Archives)*

On March 3, 1943, a 200-building military hospital complex with 1,500 beds opened on Spokane's north side. It grew to more than 300 buildings and 2,001 beds on a 200-acre site. It was named Baxter General Hospital in honor of a Civil War surgeon, Brigadier General Jedediah H. Baxter (1837-1890), who rose in rank and responsibility to become surgeon general in August 1890, but died four months later of a stroke.

Baxter General Hospital had 800 doctors, nurses, and military staff, and cared for soldiers from the Northwest during their final stages of recovery. The hospital emphasized a return by the wounded to civilian life and drew upon the community to help reintegrate patients back into society. Between 1943 and the fall of 1945, Baxter General Hospital treated more than 20,000 patients.

To brighten Christmas, local groups provided trees and parties, and the American Legion gave gifts to the hospitalized soldiers. Among the many distinguished visitors to the hospital was Richard F. Wood (1920-2002), son of Lord Halifax (1881-1953), the British ambassador to the United States. Wood could relate well to the patients, as he had lost both his legs in the North African campaign earlier in the war.

The last patients departed Baxter on November 8, 1945, and the hospital closed December 12, 1945. Most of the buildings were sold and removed, except for eight buildings occupied by the Naval and Marine Corps Reserve Center. In 1964, these buildings were demolished and a new center constructed.

Both Baxter, at Spokane, and McCaw General Hospital at, Walla Walla, had German prisoner-of-war camps attached. At Baxter, the prisoner camp was in the southwest portion of the hospital grounds. The prisoners took care of the grounds and worked in the laundry and other hospital areas.

Gene Kenworthy and Leslie Fleenor – hired by the Spokane Police Department in 1942 and 1943

Downtown Hillyard. Officers Leslie Fleenor and Gene Kenworthy leading a parade in the summer of 1949.

(Courtesy Spokane Police Archives)

Chapter Three

Harley-Davidson Era

The Motor Bulls of the 1946 to 1980 Era.

The above photo was taken next to Brush Cycle at South 218 Madison in 1946. It shows the new black and white motorcycle shields used for parades. Brush Cycle appeared for the first time in the city directory in 1928. At that time the address was West 1006 Second Avenue. *(Courtesy Spokane Police Department Archives)*

This photo appeared in the *Spokesman-Review* on April 8, 1946. At the time, the traffic squad had 20 officers, 16 of them motorcycle officers. Gerald S. Swartout was chief. He is shown standing on the right in coat and hat. Others in the photo are: Front Row: Ray W. Kenworthy, John Robertson, Roy Hamilton. Second Row: Jerome Potts, Irvin Neubauer, Eugene Kenworthy, Warren Alton. Third and fourth rows: Alfred Wilson, Roy Kelley, Walter Case, and Leslie Fleenor. Standing: Captain Lloyd Ferguson, Glen Atkisson, Edward Parsons, Alfred Stoeser, Warren Loomis, and Perry Miles. *(Courtesy Spokane Police Department Archives)*

Willis Glanville – hired by the Spokane Police Department in 1947

Willie Glanville, circa 1956. This photo was taken following a Lilac Parade. At this time, Willie was wearing a police motorcycle officer's dress uniform. *(Courtesy Karla Heinz, daughter)*

Willis "Willie" Glanville was born in 1917 at Proctor, Minnesota. At six years old, he moved to Everett, Washington, and in 1929, the family moved to Spokane, where he attended Arlington Grade School. When he entered his freshman year, he attended the last class of the old Hillyard High School. In 1932, to ease congestion at the small Hillyard school, John R. Rogers High School was built. It was also the last year Hillyard High School was used as a school. The 48 students who graduated in 1932 were the last to do so, thus completing the transfer of Hillyard's High School students to the new Rogers High School.

Following graduation, Willie Glanville worked for the Washington Water Power Company as a stock clerk and a timekeeper for a line construction crew. Following that, he worked for the Great Northern Railroad in Hillyard.

Willie joined the Army in 1942, serving overseas in the Pacific Theater with the 841st Aviation En-

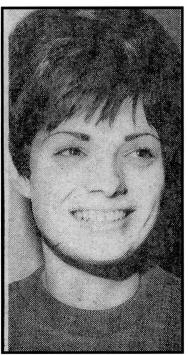

The following caption appeared under this photo:

Karla D'Ann Glanville, 18, is the second candidate to enter the Miss Spokane [twentieth] competition under the sponsorship of the Benevolent Order of Police Wives. A graduate of John Rogers High School, Ms. Glanville is majoring in physical education at Spokane Community College where she is active in Associated Woman Students activities and is a cheerleader. She is the daughter of Willis A. Glanville, who lived on north Napa. The girl chosen Miss Spokane XX will receive two modeling school scholarships worth more than $250.

Regarding the photo on the left, his daughter Karla stated: "He mostly rode the motorcycle and I always remember a sidecar (because I rode in it a lot)."

Willie Glanville and his son Lynn, with his daughter Karla shown partially visible to the right, circa 1950. *(Courtesy Karla Heinz, daughter)*

Willie Glanville's wife Lucy, daughter Karla and son W. Lynn, circa 1951. *(Courtesy Karla Heinz, daughter)*

gineers Battalion during World War II, in the South Pacific, being awarded five Battle Stars.

In May of 1947, Willie joined the Spokane Police Department, working the downtown beats, which rotated between walking a beat and working the paddy wagon. He later was assigned to prowl car duty. Following that, he was assigned to the traffic division and was a motorcycle officer for 18 years. Following a serious accident on his police motor, he retired from the department in 1968.

Willie was also an accomplished cartoonist and musician. He played drums at Rogers High School in Spokane from the time the school was founded in 1932. Both Willie and his last wife, Lucy (he was married three times), played music at the Idaho/Washington state line. Willie also played with various dance bands in Washington and Idaho. He was a drummer with the Hal Kaiser Quartet for 11 years, and also played drums at Phil's Club, which was a dinner/dance club. His wife, Lucy was also a musician and played several instruments. Willie was also a member of Eagles Lodge #2, a life member of the Veterans of Foreign Wars, Post #1474, and was the first president of the Hillyard Booster Club, which was founded in 1934.

Willie passed away on the 25th of November 2008, at the age of 91. There was a reception for his passing held at Luigi's Restaurant in Spokane.

Lynn and Karla Glanville with their dad's police motorcycle, circa 1950. *(Courtesy Karla Heinz, daughter)*

Various photos of Willie Glanville, circa 1949-50, including his 1943 Army photo. *(Courtesy Karla Heinz, daughter)*

Willie Glanville when he married Lucy Maxson, shortly after he was discharged from the Army after World War II. At the time of this photo, circa 1946, Lucy was 18 and Willie 29. *(Courtesy Karla Heinz)*

Al Wasser – hired by the Spokane Police Department in 1947

Al Wasser, circa 1949. *(Courtesy Mercedes Griffiths)*

Clifford Payne, former police chief – hired by the Spokane Police Department in 1947

The above photo was taken on Monroe Street at Maxwell, next to the Bancroft School, circa 1947. Clifford Payne is on the left. *(Courtesy Spokane Police Department Archives)*

Clifford Payne.

On January 1, 1957, Ralph E. Johnson was named the 26th Spokane Police Chief. Prior to that, he had been on the department for over 20 years. However, for unknown reasons, his tenure lasted only three months. At that time, Sergeant Clifford Payne was appointed chief.

Clifford Payne was Spokane's police chief for over nine years, from 1958 to 1967. Payne joined the department on March 3, 1947. He served for several years as a motorcycle officer until he was promoted to sergeant.

In 1962, the Washington Association of Sheriffs and Police Chiefs was formed. Spokane's Police Chief, Clifford Payne, was elected as its first president. Many of the officers who knew and worked for him recognized him as an excellent speaker and exceptionally intelligent person. *(Courtesy Spokane Police Department Archives)*

Chief Payne teaching a Spokane Auxiliary Police class about the various types of tear gas capsules and projectiles sometimes used in police work. During Chief Payne's tenure, one of the cases that confronted him was the Candy Rogers murder. That case involved a six-year old girl's abduction, rape, and murder. During the search, helicopters from nearby Fairchild Air Force Base circled above the search grid in a desperate effort to spot the girl. Tragically, one of the choppers hit a power line and crashed in the Spokane River, killing three airmen. The murderer has never been found. Inset is Chief Payne in uniform. *(Courtesy Spokane Police Department Archives)*

Floyd Jones – hired by the Spokane Police Department in 1947

Floyd Jones participating in "Police Day" at Reverend Hamp's Camp at Liberty Lake. *(Courtesy Ron Hubert)*

Although there has been little written about Floyd Jones, an article by Kim Crompton, in the *Spokesman-Review* on October 8, 1979, gives a description of one of Spokane's most well-known and well-liked police officers.

BADGE NUMBER ONE FINISHING 32 YEARS WITH POLICE.

The man wearing Spokane police badge number one retires Friday.

It was 25 winters ago that patrolman Floyd M. Jones of the Spokane Police Department first climbed aboard his Harley-Davidson three wheeled motorcycle. Ending a 32-year career with the department, he'll dismount for the final time Friday afternoon.

"Meeting the people downtown, that's probably the thing I'm going to miss the most," said the rugged, 56-year-old Jones. A mountain of a man at six-foot-five and 300 pounds, the retired police officer has worked city traffic since he started with the department on July 1, 1947.

Jones underwent open-heart surgery in 1976 when he had a four-bypass operation. He was off the job five months, then returned to his job on the motorcycle.

Being a police officer wasn't exactly what Jones had in mind when he began his job search more than three decades ago. Jones underwent four weeks of training at the old Spokane trade school at Fourth and Post, where the freeway now passes, before being assigned to a prowl car and walking beats. He didn't begin working on the marking motors, as the three wheelers are called, until June 17, 1953.

"It was retired police detective Chuck Sorini who talked me into it and we both went on the same day. They were having trouble finding guys to ride the three-wheel motorcycle back then, "Jones said." I had never ridden a motorcycle in my life until the mechanic took me up on Thorp Road in the Southwest, and said 'There it is, Go to it.'"

Since then, Jones estimates he's covered "a couple hundred thousand miles" on routine traffic routes and given out "quite a bundle" of parking tickets, along with some citations for moving violations. "I probably ticketed everybody in Spokane over some period of time," he chuckled.

Besides the traffic detail, his duties over the years have included everything from escorting funerals and parades to supervising special events, such as, and protecting players in the penalty box at hockey games from enraged fans.

Working traffic on three wheelers has meant missing out on some of the major arrest and pursuits that come naturally on the "speed motors" (the two wheeled motorcycles) and in the prowl cars. But, according to Jones, it also has enabled him to take the job more lightly. "There have always been comical things going on. Some of the guys take the job pretty seriously, but I don't," he said.

Finding clothing that would fit him was one of his first major tasks in his early career. "I was the only one who didn't have a helmet. It was a hard thing to find at that particular time. So some of the guys found a "thundermug" – the type of bowl that used to be kept under the bed for toilet purposes – and fixed it up just like the regular helmets and gave it to me to wear," he remembered, chuckling

Jones's easy-going nature is evident in his nonchalant attitude toward one of the three wheelers less enviable duties – riding the motorcycles during the winter.

Shrugging complaints aside, he said, 'I never wore "long handles' and I wore the same pair of leather gloves all the time."

Though he recalls the day when he began work in a 26° below-zero-temperature and knocked off when it was 17 degrees below, he said he was never seriously bothered by the cold temperatures.

"Seeing the pretty girls in the spring downtown made it all worthwhile," he claimed, smiling.

Despite having been in the saddle all that time, Jones holds no great love for motorcycles.

"I have no desire to ride motorcycles after I quit," he said, suggesting instead that he will use other modes of transportation to do some retirement traveling with his wife Maxine.

Meanwhile, his badge number one will be turned over to another veteran of the three wheelers, patrolmen first class Melvin T. Griffiths, who joined the police department a year after Jones.

Spokane police officers are eligible for retirement anytime after 25 years of service.

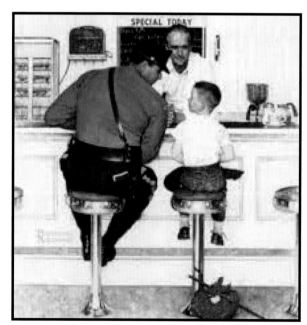

Norman Rockwell painting illustrating good public relations. *(Public domain)*

Jack Latta and six-foot five-inch Floyd Jones, circa 1966. *(Courtesy Jack Latta)*

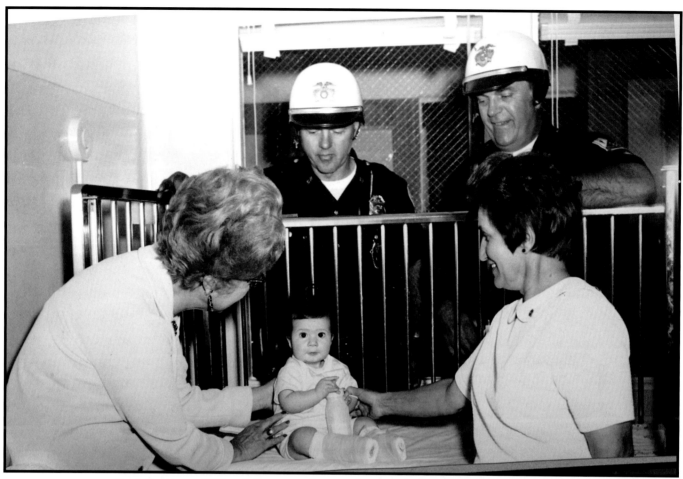

Jack Latta and Floyd Jones at the old Shriners Hospital. *(Courtesy Jack Latta)*

Jack Latta, an unidentified Shriner, and Floyd Jones at the exterior of the old Shriners Hospital. *(Courtesy Jack Latta)*

Robert "Bob" Colliton – hired by the Spokane Police Department in 1947

Robert "Bob" Colliton, circa 1949. *(Courtesy Kelly Colliton)*

Robert Colliton was born in Spokane on June 16, 1921, to John and Ellsie Colliton. The family immigrated to the United States from Ireland. Their first destination was to the East Coast. They later came by railroad to the West Coast.

In the mid-1930s Bob met his future wife, Alice M. Scott, at an informal dance or party arranged to give members of a group an opportunity to get acquainted (mixer). They were married in 1939. Together they had six children: Jeffrey, Gregory, Toberta Anne, Rodney, Courtney, and Kelly.

In 1947, Bob began his career for the Spokane Police Department. Beyond high school he did not have a formal education, but his common sense ability to see through challenges made him a success in his law enforcement profession. The biggest influence in his career on the police department was Al Wasser.

Bob's first assignment was "walking the beat" in Spokane's China Town on swing and graveyard shifts. Early in his career he applied for and passed the tests to become a motorcycle policeman, which at the time were riding Harley Davidsons. He was fascinated by the power of those cycles and probably would have spent his entire career riding them.

Bob was also elected to be the president of the "Royal Order of the Silver, Black, and White Cycles," an organization founded in April of 1951. The following swing-shift traffic officers were the charter members: Captain Lloyd Freeman, Sgt. Olan Sherar,

Tom O'Brien, Jay Wilcox, Mel Griffiths, Richard Tilton, Homer Hall, Bob Colliton, Willie Glanville, Royce Thornburg, Tom Pugh (who later changed his last name to Curtis), and Glen Atkisson who was the Cchaplain, although he didn't ride motor. The organization described itself as a semi-social and semi-business organization. The meetings were held at Sherar's home, or whoever had an "understanding wife." When they got enough money in the treasury, a party was thrown at the Garland Dental Clinic basement. This wasn't very often as the dues were only 50 cents a month. At that time, motor officers were making $300 a month. The club disintegrated due to changes in assignments after a couple of years, but the brotherhood of the motorcycle officers exits even today.

Robert Colliton, on the far right, with a "Tommy" gun, circa 1950. *(Courtesy Kelly Colliton)*

Bob soon began to climb the ladder within the ranks of the department. As he worked his way up through the police department, he passed exams for sergeant, detective, and lieutenant, taking each assignment as he rose through the ranks. He was also selected to attend the National Polygraph Academy and, upon his graduation, was assigned to the County Prosecutor's Office to assist in solving numerous crimes using polygraph procedures.

Eventually, Colliton was promoted to inspector and served in that position for several years. His last assignment within the department was deputy chief of police, which, according to him, was his most memorable experience during his time with the police department.

Bob's time on the department was filled with many accomplishments, one of which was when he allowed Sam's Pit, a black club that existed during the height of racial tensions, to remain open as an all hours club. In return Sam repaid that cooperation in many ways. All in all, Bob will be remembered by those that knew and worked with him as an honest cop who was there to back his men. Bob retired in September 1977, after 30 years of dedicated and professional service to the city of Spokane. Following his retirement he enjoyed woodworking, racing horses, and construction, such as building homes from the ground up. He even built boats and campers. Bob died on May 19, 2003, at the age of 82.

Deputy Spokane Police Chief Robert Colliton, circa 1973. *(Courtesy Kelly Colliton)*

The following article by Kenneth James appeared in "Inside Detective magazine" on October 11, 1963. It was titled "One Life Forfeited." It is an outstanding example of the interesting and excellent police work of which Bob Colliton was a part of:

It was mid-afternoon when the car pulled into the service station at Maple and Indiana Streets in the northwest part of Spokane, Wash. The driver parked at the gas pumps, turned off his radio and settled back, expecting the attendant momentarily since there were no other cars at the station, and he could see no one at the grease rack.

After a brief wait, he got out of his car and went into the office. "Anybody here!" he called out. There was no response. He walked through to the rear store room. There on the floor of the shelf-lined room lay the body of a teenage boy, blood spreading out from under him.

The customer's hurried telephone call brought Motorcycle Officer K. Baker who, after one glance at the lifeless form, radioed in for help.

It was Sunday, August 25, 1963. Most of the top police were off duty but were reached at their homes and within minutes Police Chief Clifford Payne, Inspector Robert Piper, Detective Lieutenant Robert E. Colliton and Detectives Al Wasser, Harry Simons and Harry Cockburn arrived.

Using a key that was attached to the victim's belt with a piece of leather, they opened the cash register. There were no bills in it.

The owner of the station, called from his home, shook his head sadly. "Yes ... that's the boy who worked for me," he said. "Bill Matthews. Worked weekends for about a month." He estimated that about $50 had been taken from the cash register.

The man who had discovered the body had seen no activity around the station whatsoever. He had waited in his car about two minutes before going inside and had found the dead youth at 3:40.

The officers were collecting all of the bits and ends that appeared meaningless at the time, but can sometimes make the difference between a solved case and an unsolved one. The cash register was dusted for fingerprints and the back room was searched thoroughly. On one of the can-laden shelves a detective found a piece of black metal, about three-eighths of an inch square. "Might be part of a gun,"

he suggested. "The boy probably was beaten, as well as shot" The piece of metal was carefully preserved.

By moving through the crowd that had gathered outside the station; the police found a woman who lived around the corner from the station and who had seen a man running from the station about 3:30 p.m. She described him as 5 feet 6 inches tall, brown-haired, wearing tan jeans and a white T-shirt. He looked to be in his early 20s. She heard no shooting.

Another neighbor had seen an old model black Ford moving down the street about 3:30. She thought it might have come from the service station. But the most interesting bit of information came from a young man who extricated himself from the crowd and approached a policeman with the word that he must have heard shooting. He said he and two friends had gone to the open-on-Sunday supermarket across the way, but he left them to use the washroom in the service station. It was while he was in the washroom that he heard some loud sounds. "I thought some firecrackers were being shot off," he said. "I didn't think it was anything wrong." He walked back to the supermarket after leaving the washroom, and did not notice anything amiss.

Detectives accompanied him along the route he said he took to and from the washroom, which was at the back of the station with an outside entrance door. The route would not have placed him in a position where he could have seen the rear storage room. "Didn't you see anybody leaving the station ... on foot or in a car?" he was asked. "No, sir," he insisted.

The informant was in his mid-20s, average-sized. He was recognized by some of the officers as a youth with a burglary record. His two companions were called over and questioned, but gave statements that dovetailed with the informant. The young man was taken to headquarters for further questioning.

Further questioning of bystanders turned up one woman who was employed at St. Luke's Hospital. She had walked home from work that afternoon and had seen the boy working when she passed the station. The woman's time card showed she punched off work at 3:21 p.m.. Police walked along with her at her usual pace, and found it took six minutes to get to the corner of Maple and Indiana. "That means the boy was alive at 3:27 p.m.," the chief said. "He was found dead at 3:40 p.m. That narrows the time of the crime down considerably."

"This may be more than a robbery killing," one detective suggested. "Mid-afternoon, broad daylight, heavily populated area. The killer may have been motivated by something other than robbery, but took the money as an afterthought or a cover-up."

A thorough check of the young victim's background failed to support this theory, however. The 17-year-old youth had been a junior at Lewis and Clark High School with plans to become an electrical engineer... He was an industrious youth who liked to earn his own money. He worked part time during the summer at a grocery store and had been a neW.S.P.aper junior dealer. He had taken the job at the service station a month earlier, working on weekends and liking it because he was interested in mechanics. He recently had overhauled an automobile by himself. He was a member of Westminster Congregational Church, and had played on the church basketball team in the YMCA League. "There is nothing in his background to suggest a possible motive," a detective said. "He wasn't a trouble maker, no gang fights or anything like that. He was a nice boy, clean cut, hard working, ambitious."

The questioning of the man who said he'd heard what sounded like firecrackers while in the washroom of the service station had continued and been intensified when one of his companions was found to have $70 in his pocket. "I got paid Friday," the youth said. "I got my check cashed." No weapon was found on any one of the men, but police still considered the young man worth holding for further questioning. On Monday, however, after he had submitted to and passed a lie detector test, he was released.

The Spokane County deputy coroner reported that an examination revealed the victim had been shot twice with a .22-caliber gun. One shot went in the side, passing through the lungs. The second shot went into the head. Both were fired at close range. The victim also had been struck three times on the head with a blunt instrument. There was only one small clue now on which police could rely for help – the small piece of metal found on the shelf at the service station. "We've checked it out," a technician told Lieutenant Colliton, "and we're certain this did not come from anything in the station. It probably came from whatever instrument was used to strike the boy over the head." From a gun," he was asked. "Can't tell from this small piece," was the answer. "But it's not the usual color of gun metal. It's a black onyx paint. Most guns are painted bluish." "We'll send it to the FBI laboratory in Washington," Colliton said. "If anybody can find out where it came from, they can."

The boy's tragic death had shocked and grieved all those who knew him. But the one person who tried to salvage something worthwhile from what seemed such total waste was the victim's father. In an intelligent proposal he suggested that a volunteer organization of men willing to act as confidential counselors to the boys in trouble be set up. "If they (the troubled boys) know there is a person to whom they could turn it might help. They need to he led to the realization – that they are a part of the community, and that they have a responsibility to themselves to justify their membership in it."

In a memoriam to his son, the father wrote: "His life was forfeited. Someone's son made a mistake. This can never be rectified, but another who might be tempted may be helped. He can learn from this tragedy that his temptation is a disease, which can be cured. It is for us, everyone of us, to help in every way possible."

During the rest of that week police questioned more than 200 persons, followed up all leads and stories from an aroused public, and waited word from the FBI in Washington D. C. on examination of the slugs and the bit of metal found on the shelf.

It was early in the next week that information came in from 100 miles away that stirred activity in the Spokane Detective Bureau. At Lewiston, Idaho, south of Spokane and just across the state line, authorities were attempting to pick up a 21-year-old man for a suspected parole violation when he reportedly shot and killed himself with a .22-caliber revolver. Police speculated on why he would choose such a violent and irrefutable escape from a minor infraction and the theory was suggested that he might be connected with the case in Spokane. Lewiston police and Spokane police began a combined effort to check on the man's activities and whereabouts on the day of the Matthews killing.

They still were investigating that when a report came from the FBI on the ballistics. Tests of the slugs taken from Matthews established that they could not have been fired from the gun the parole violator used on himself. This eliminated him as a suspect.

It was mid-September before police heard more from the FBI. Technicians had labored long and hard on the small bit of metal found at the scene of the crime, but they had come up with some information. The metal, the report stated, was a piece from the trigger guard of a gun. The lab tests had established that it was from a .22-caliber pistol, and the FBI technicians were even more precise. The pistol was a High Standard Sentinel Imperial Model, 9-shot pistol. The paint on the metal, as well as the design, had been of aid to the lab men. The metal had a black onyx paint because the gun carriage was made with an aluminum alloy that couldn't take the usual blue paint used on other guns. The report also showed that this model gun had been put into manufacture in 1960.

Lieutenant Colliton read over the FBI report with growing excitement. "That gun has been distributed out this way only about two years," he said. "We can get a list of the dealers who handle it." "Yes, we can trace the purchase of these guns, and check out the ballistics with the slugs we have," a detective said. "Won't even have to go that far," Colliton pointed out. "If we find a gun with a broken trigger guard, we can take it from there."

A call to the office of the manufacturer of the Imperial .22-caliber pistol brought assurance that Spokane police would be sent a list of all wholesale distributors who handled consignments of the gun. A fast alert also was sent to all suppliers to have them notify Spokane authorities if anyone had ordered a new carriage for that model gun. It was determined that anyone attempting to replace the broken trigger guard would need an entire new carriage.

Spokane police were soon informed that no order had been placed for a new gun carriage since the date of the murder. They then started down the list of wholesalers in four states: Washington, Oregon, Montana and Idaho, urging them to check their records and give any pertinent information to Spokane police.

The wholesalers in these four states supplied the gun, reportedly designed for target practice and small game shooting, to about 150 retail outlets.
.
Police first went to the stores in Spokane that had been sent orders of the .22-caliber Imperial. Records were checked, and detectives came up with the names and addresses of five men who had bought that model gun. "All we want to do is see the guns," Lieutenant Colliton said. "If a piece is missing from the trigger guard, then we can move in. The killer used that gun to pistol whip and shoot that boy." "What do we do if some purchaser says he's lost his gun?" a detective asked. "He'll be in for some stiff questioning." The five guns all had been sold within the past year and detectives started a rundown on the purchasers.

One of the purchasers' names was familiar to police. "So, Carl Leighton bought one of these guns !" a detective said. "I thought he was still in Walla Walla." They pulled the file on Leighton, and learned he had completed a robbery sentence four months earlier. He had been released without parole and was living at a Spokane address on the south side. Carl Leighton was at home when police called. He was in his 30s, with an expression that indicated anger at the intrusion. He recognized one of the detectives as one of the arresting officers on the case that sent him to prison. "Is this a social call?" he cracked. The detectives ignored it. "You bought a gun, a .22-caliber revolver," one said.

"Let's see it." "I've got a right ... I'm not on parole. ... I can ..." "No speeches, please," he was told. "We just want to look at the gun." Haven't got it," Leighton said. "I gave it to a friend. I bought the gun this summer when I went on a trip. I just wanted it around. Then, when I got back, I figured I didn't want a gun around. So I gave it away." "We have to see that gun!" he was told. Leighton gave the detectives the name and address of a man who, police soon established, also had a criminal record. He had been arrested for burglary, but was not convicted. The detective team found him home that night. He was visibly nervous when asked about the gun.

"Come on ... Carl Leighton said he gave it to you." "Oh, yes, but I never used it," he insisted. "We just want to look at it. Get that gun!" He went to another room and came back with a .22-caliber 9-shot High Standard Sentinel Imperial. It was all in one piece. The trigger guard was not damaged.

It was patently clear this was not the murder weapon. The trigger guard was so constructed that it could not be repaired without an entire new carriage, and no new carriage had been sold.

The other purchasers of that model gun in Spokane were located and all showed their guns to police. None had damaged trigger guards. "Well, we'll have to spread the inquiry," Colliton said. "We have the names of the dealers in the four-state area. We can ask the police departments in those towns to run down the gun purchasers." The calls went out, and police began making inquiries of gun dealers in Richland, Tacoma, Seattle, Bellingham, Bremerton, Wenatchee, Kennewick, Portland, Pendleton, Baker, Newport, Eugene, Albany, Salem, Boise, Twin Falls, Pocatello, Coeur d'Alene, Lewiston, Moscow, Twin Falls, Butte, Anaconda, Helena, Great Falls, Kalispell, and other cities in Washington, Oregon, Idaho and Montana.

The big four-state gun probe moved into high gear, but no broken trigger guards were found in the first wave of gun checking. Police were alerted to pay special attention to any gun purchaser who said he could not locate his gun or who might claim that he "lost" it.

During the first days, no one reported losing a gun and practically every man approached was able to produce his undamaged pistol.

Then came a report from police at Coeur d'Alene, Idaho, 30 miles east of Spokane. There were two gun purchases that police had not been able to clear. One of the guns had

Dectective Lieutenant Robert Colliton holds a murder weapon in 1963. *(Courtesy Kelly Colliton)*

been bought by a Spokane man, and Lieutenant Colliton was interested in knowing why the man bought a gun out of town. Investigation revealed that the man had purchased the gun during a trip, and given it to his brother for a present. Spokane police visited the brother's home and asked to see the gun. "It's still in the box, the man said. "I haven't used it"

He got the boxed gun. Detectives saw the trigger guard was not damaged, and that was all they needed.

Other possibilities were also eliminated that day throughout the four-state territory, but the second gun purchaser in Coeur d'Alene remained on the list, unchecked.

He was a young man named John Henault who had bought the gun two weeks before the murder and gave his address as a hotel in Coeur d'Alene. Local police had checked this and found John Henault had been registered at the hotel, but had left on August 24, owing rent, and had not come back. He had given no indication of leaving his room for good,

but it was assumed by the hotel manager that he skipped out because he could not or would not pay his bill. His clothes were held.

"We held his clothes expecting to hear from him when he got the money for his bill," police were told.

"We'd like to take a look at the clothes," an officer said. "Sorry, the clothes are gone," he was told: "Got a letter from the fellow's father. He paid the bill and asked us to send the clothes." The clothes were sent to an address in Hyannis, Mass.

"Was there a gun in the package of clothes the hotel operator was asked. The manager shook his head. He said there bad been no gun, but in cleaning out the room a gun box had been found. That box and other objects from the room were still in the hotel, and police examined them.

The box was designed to hold a High Standard Sentinel Imperial .22-caliber 9-shot pistol. The gun was no longer there, but there was a slip of paper, a receipt for a purchase at a sporting goods store in Coeur d'Alene. It was for a small amount, far smaller than the price of a gun.

"And this isn't the store from which the gun was bought," a policeman said. As other gun purchasers were checked out and eliminated, John E. Henault's name rose on the list of persons who demanded more scrutiny.

Investigation disclosed that 19-year-old John E. Henault of Hyannis, Mass., had a police record. He had been arrested several months earlier for allegedly striking a policeman. Disposition of the case had been delayed.

Lieutenant Colliton learned that Henault was short and heavy-set. He could fit the general description of the young man reported seen near the service station the afternoon of the murder.

The receipt came under further study. At the store from which it was issued in Coeur d'Alene, police were told it was for the exact price of a box of .22-caliber bullets. A salesman remembered making such a sale to a young man, who had been short and stocky.

"This Henault boy takes on more interesting dimensions all the time," Colliton told Chief Payne. "We know he bought one of the guns. And he went to a different store to buy bullets. He left his hotel the day before the murder, and kept going—all the way back to Massachusetts. His clothes were sent for. He did not leave a gun in his room, so he had it with him."

It was decided that Lieutenant Colliton should make a trip to Hyannis, Mass., to talk to Henault and to see his gun.

At 1:15 A.M., Colliton boarded a plane for Chicago. From there, he took a plane to Boston, where he changed to a third plane that took him to Hyannis, on Cape Cod. Colliton checked in with Hyannis police, examined a few records, and then conferred with an FBI agent.

"Well, it's time to talk to the Henault boy," Colliton said. "I'll soon know if I traveled across the country to arrest a murder suspect, or to clear one. All I'll have to do is to take a look at that gun to know."

A call was made to Henault's home in Hyannis, and the youth agreed to go to Collion's motel room to talk with the visiting officer.

He understood the purpose of the interrogation, and showed no emotion. He was short and stocky, with dark hair over a round face. He said he had gone west that summer and stayed for a while in Idaho Falls, working in potato fields. Then he went to Coeur d'Alene where he stayed in a hotel and just looked around for two weeks. Then he came home.

"I couldn't find a job there so I decided to come back here," he, said. "I know I left owing, rent, but I was short of money. I just had enough to get home."

"You were short of money," Colliton said. "But you bought a pistol." The youth nodded.

"I'd like to see that gun, please," Colliton said. "Haven't got it," Henault told him. "What happened to it?" he was asked. The youth shrugged. He said he had left it in his hotel room, along with his clothes, but it was not in the package sent to Hyannis from Coeur d'Alene.

"Somebody must have taken it," he said. Lieutenant Colliton studied the youth, then moved in with questions about his activities in the northwest. Coeur d'Alene, he pointed out, was near Spokane. Had Henault visited that city? The youth said he had been there.

Colliton skirted the main issue for awhile, than slowly circled back to it. The gun? Had Henault ever fired it? "No," Henault said. "I couldn't have. I never even had any bullets for it."

Colliton was surprised at this statement, but it offered the opening wedge he needed. Henault had been caught in a

lie. There was proof he had purchased bullets for the gun at a store in Coeur d'Alene.

"We found the receipt for the purchase," Colliton said.

Following additional questioning of the youth, Colliton called Chief Payne, and on Monday, October 7, Chief Payne announced in Spokane that a murder charge against John E. Henault had been filed in connection with the killing of William H. Matthews on August 25.

John E. Henault pleaded innocent in First District Court in Massachusetts on a charge of being a fugitive from justice, and his case was continued.

Later that day in Spokane, authorities said Henault had confessed to the fatal shooting. They quoted him as saying he went to Spokane, stole an automobile from a municipal parking lot, and drove to the area of the service station.

Henault reportedly beat and shot the station attendant when the latter resisted the holdup. Then, according to the confession, Henault drove off in the stolen car, had an accident, abandoned the car, and threw the gun and other items away north of Spokane.

Extradition papers were sent from Washington to Massachusetts, and police continued the investigation.

Spokane police still had a lot of work ahead of them. They were told by Colliton that Henault said the car he stole was a 1959 Chevrolet. The description of the car, and the lot from which it had been stolen, fit a stolen car report of August 25. The car was owned by a fireman and had been taken from a municipal parking lot, and later found wrecked near Ione, Washington, 80 miles north of Spokane.

Spokane police went to Ione and searched a wooded area. They reported finding a wallet containing identification papers issued to John E. Henault. They borrowed a metal detector from the City Water Department and started searching for a gun.

On Wednesday, October 9, Henault was brought before Judge Henry L. Murphy in District Court in Barnstable, and waived extradition. Judge Murphy directed that Henault be turned over to Lieutenant Robert Colliton, and the two were taken to a plane that afternoon.

The return west was delayed a day when an airline company refused to let police put Henault on a plane in Boston.

Another flight later was taken, and Colliton arrived with his prisoner in Spokane the night of October 10.

Henault was booked at the police station, then transferred to the county jail. Police meanwhile, using the metal detector near Ione, had come up with five half dollars, but no gun.

On October 11, Detective Lieutenant Colliton and several other Spokane officers drove Henault north to Ione. They returned with a .22-caliber pistol with a piece missing from the trigger guard.

"He didn't show any hesitation at all," Colliton said of Henault. "He told us where to dig, and we found the gun right where he said it would be." The gun was buried about 50 feet from the road.

Henault was quoted as saying that after the collision near Ione, he buried the gun, and made his way west to Colville, Wash. He spent a day here, then took a bus to Spokane, and then rode a bus to Seattle. Another bus took him to California, and from there he hitchhiked his way back to Massachusetts.

The Colliton family. Bottom row from left: Kelly, Alice, Bob, and Bobbie. Upper row from left: Greg, Rob, Curt, and Jeff, circa 1980. *(Courtesy Kelly Colliton)*

The Spokane Police Station, 1913 to 1960

The City Hall and Public Safety Building at 221 North Wall Street. It was in use as a police station for 47 years, from 1913 to 1962. This photo shows the new police fleet of 1954 Belvederes. From left: Assistant Chief Leighton Dugger, Chief Clyde Phelps, and Commissioner Carl Canwell. From the right of them: Officers George Storaasli, Wesley Schubbe, Edgar Lennox, John Robertson, Carl Bays, Orville Gay, Gale Morgan, James Read, Alex Karle, and Sgt. Harvey Hastings. *(Courtesy Spokane Police Archives)*

This building was a six-story brick, "Cast Stone" trimmed. It was constructed starting in 1912, and was ready for occupancy in 1913. The architectural firm of Preusse and Zittel designed it as one of the last projects of their partnership. This new building was supposedly a temporary and expediently constructed building, not monumental as the old city hall had been (a portrait of the building remained on the official seal and letterheads of the City of Spokane until the 1950s).

The new city hall was built so it could be readily converted into a warehouse. In 1990, the Olive Garden Restaurant opened on the bottom floor, occupying space that used to be a fire station. On May 23, 2015, without warning to its employees, a sign placed outside the downtown Spokane Olive Garden, announced the business was closing permanently. The restaurant's 80 employees were notified of the closure that morning.

The police station used to be in the south half of the first story, with its own entrance on Wall Street south of the main Wall Street building entrance, and a handy door to the alley across from Johnston's Coffee Shop, the unofficial annex. The police garage opened onto the alley. The jail was on the upper floors, with barred windows to the inner court, open to the sky, where sprinkler pipes sprayed an artificial rain to make the cells a bit more bearable in hot weather. In 1962, the police station moved to the Realty Building at 241 West Riverside.

Angelo Costanzo – hired by the Spokane Police Department in 1948

SPOKANE POLICE DEPARTMENT

Angelo Costanzo, circa 1952. *(Courtesy Spokane Police Archives)*

Angelo Costanzo, circa 1971. *(Courtesy Spokane Police Archives)*

Angelo Costanzo was born in Spokane on August 15, 1924. On February 4, 1943, he enlisted in the U.S. Army for the remainder of World War II. During that time he served with the Armored Division Quartermaster Corps in Europe/Germany with Mel Griffiths, who would also become a police officer.

On January 12, 1948, Angelo joined the Spokane Police Department. During the majority of his tenure, he was assigned to motor.

Approximately two years after joining the department, on September 9, 1950, Angelo married Janice Ione Brett at the Policeman's Ball. Janice was originally from Park River, in Walsh County, North Dakota.

The Spokane Police Beneficial Association, which was financed by individual dues of police officers, with the sale of tickets to the annual ball, and direct donations, sponsored its first Policeman's Benefit Ball, held at the Masonic Temple in 1912. The proceeds of this ball went to the incapacitated officers, police widows, and children of the department. In the mid-40s, the ball was held at Natatorium Park and was open to the public free of charge.

By this time, the Ball had became a large civic affair, and due to the generous contributions of individuals, Spokane businesses, and clubs, it became very successful. In 1945, this event drew nearly 5,000 people. These events were also a gala occasion for law enforcement couples to dress in their

Class A police uniforms and socialize with fellow officers and friends from the Canadian Mounted Police, who also dressed in their Class A uniforms. The public was also invited. On October 7, 1995, the event was discontinued.

On September 9, 1975, Angelo retired from the department. Following 43 years of marriage, Angelo died on February 13, 1993, at age 69. Almost 10 years later, his wife died on October 16, 2003 at the age of 75. Angelo and Janice are buried at Greenwood Memorial Terrace in Spokane.

Angelo Costanzo, circa 1973. *(Courtesy Spokane Police Department Archives)*

Angelo and Janice Costanzo during their wedding at the Policeman's Ball at Natatorium Park in 1950. *(Courtesy Spokane Police Archives)*

This photo taken at the Spokane Coliseum in 1959 included the following officers identified by retired police Lieutenant Gene McGougan. Front row from left: Isaac Gimlen, Charles Shepard, William Crumbaker, Carl Sweatt, Melvin Griffiths, Harold Tucker, William Bradley, Richard Byrnes, James Albright, Alvie Burrell, Gerald Fallgren, Leroy Cumming, Paul Warrington, J. D. Kelly, Jack Latta, Bob Browning, and Floyd Fick.

Second row from left: Floyd Jones, Robert Owens, Charles Sorini, John Bevins, Angelo Costanzo, Oscar Hoffman, John Grandinetti, (last officer in the second row to the far right is unknown).

Back row from left: Willie Glanville, with helmet standing at upper far left. To Willie's left standing is the administration and command staff left to right: Lt. David Lamphier, Asst. Chief Edward "Bill" Parsons, Capt. John Reilly, Inspector Robert Piper, and Chief Clifford Payne. *(Courtesy Spokane Police Archives)*

Mel Griffiths – hired by the Spokane Police Department in 1948

Mel Griffiths teaching traffic safety. *(Courtesy Mercedes Griffiths)*

Mel Griffiths rode motor begininng in 1948. He began with a two-wheel police "speed" motor, more than 22 years, and for the last 10 years of his career had been a familiar sight on downtown streets on a three-wheel motorcycle. A cycling enthusiast, Griffiths said he was working at Brush Cycle where police motorcycles were repaired, got to know the officers, and decided to join the force.

Griffiths was at one time a national motorcycle hill-climbing champion and motorcycle racer. He had been on the force only a few months when he was assigned to motorcycle duty. His only injury in his many years of police motorcycle riding was a minor neck injury around 1974, when his motorcycle was bumped from behind.

Mel Griffiths, Expert

Spokane, Washington

The very friendly motorcycle police man you hill climb fans have seen here fo a number of years. Mel poses a real threa here on this Lewiston hill, which in the pas has been a very good one for him.

A side-by-side 1959 neW.S.P.aper article featuring Mel Griffiths in a hill-climbing contest. *(Public domain)*

Mel Griffiths teaching a motor class, circa 1963. *(Courtesy Mercedes Griffiths)*

Police Officer Cycle Champion

A Spokane motorcycle policeman, Mel Griffiths, edged Floyd Payne, Buckley, Wash., for the Inland Empire motorcycle hill climb championship yesterday at the Devil's Arm Chair race course northeast of Spokane.

Griffiths also won the two divisions of the expert class. Twenty Pacific Northwest cyclists took part in the competition.

Event No. 1—45 novice: Jack Slone, Boise, 16.24; Tod McAllister, Spokane, 17.83.

Event No. 2—80 novice: Doug Hooper, Portland, 260 feet; Grand Bushong, 235 feet.

Event No. 3—45 expert: Mel Griffith, Spokane, 12.74; Floyd Payne, Buckley, Wash., 13.21.

Event No. 4—80 expert: Griffiths, 12.05; Jack Bloomquist, Tacoma, 13.72.

Inland Empire championship: Griffiths, 15.56; Payne, 16.09.

A 1959 news clipping about Griffiths, a national motorcycle hill-climbing champion and motorcycle racer, who was famous in the motorcycle world in the 1940s and 1950s. *(Public domain)*

During his entire career he never had to fire his service revolver in the line of duty. The closest he came was an incident in May of 1967, when he apprehended a bank robbery suspect minutes after the Old National Bank at Lincoln Heights was held up.

Griffiths was patrolling near the bank when police radio broadcast the holdup report. A bank employee pointed to a suspect walking away from the bank. Griffiths ordered the man to halt and the man pulled a gun. In turn, there was a short stand-off and then Griffiths wrestled the suspect to the ground. With the help of four passers by, they disarmed and subdued the suspect. Griffiths recovered the $25,000 stolen from the bank. Lincoln Heights merchants were so impressed they held a "Mel Griffiths Day" and a "Police Appreciation Week."

The following narrative appeared in the May 17, 1967, *Spokesman-Review*,

Police Motorcycle Officer Melvin Griffiths today was commended for his quick thinking and skill in apprehend-ing a suspect in yesterday's $25,400 holdup of the Old National Bank's Lincoln Heights Branch.

Deputy Police Chief Wayne A. Hendren said today it was "one of the finest jobs by a Spokane police officer I can recall in some time." The man arrested by Griffiths was David Donald Gibbs, 43, S. Perry. He was being held today on both federal and state charges. The holdup occurred just minutes before the 3 p.m. closing time, Mrs. Betty Jean Splichal, Spangle, told detectives Louis N. Moss Jr. and Eugene W. Kenworthy that, at that time, a man wearing a white suit and women's yellow sunglasses and with tape on the lower part of his face walked up to her teller's window and showed her a holdup note.

Mrs. Splichal told the detectives the robber showed her a gun under his coat and told her "hurry it up and no one will get hurt," She said the robber ordered her to take all the large-denomination bills from her cage, then ordered her into the bank vault where, holding the gun on her, he again told her to hurry up. She said the robber told her not to call anyone for 15 minutes, then left the bank,

Virginia M. Morton, W. 2507 Liberty, the teller in the cage next to Mrs. Splichal's said she had seen it was a

Mel Griffiths next to his police motorcycle during the cold weather season. This photo was taken during the fall of 1951. *(Courtesy Mercedes Griffiths)*

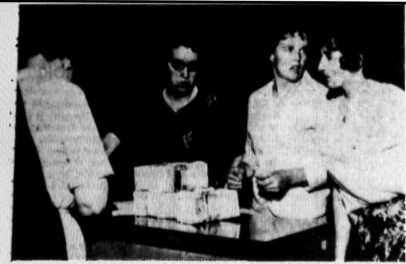

·Robbery Loot Recovered

'About $25,000 in cash lies on the table after the robbery of the Old National Bank's Lincoln Heights Branch yesterday afternoon. Gathered around it are four woman employes, including the teller who was held up and the one who pressed the alarm button that resulted in the capture of a suspect and recovery of the money. Left to right are Mrs. Milo C. Masek (back to camera), Mrs. Francis Splichal, Mrs. Perry A. Morton and Mrs. John Young. Mrs. Splichal was held up and Mrs. Morton sounded the alarm. At right, motorcycle officer Melvin T. Griffiths, who captured the suspect, holds the gun taken from the suspect. It proved to be not loaded.

* * *

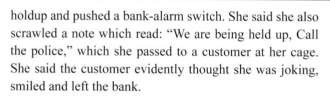

Police Officer Commended for Action in Holdup Case

Police Motorcycle Officer Mel-|bank, when he got a radio call|caliber revolver. "The gun was|

holdup and pushed a bank-alarm switch. She said she also scrawled a note which read: "We are being held up, Call the police," which she passed to a customer at her cage. She said the customer evidently thought she was joking, smiled and left the bank.

Griffiths said he was at Twenty-eighth and Southeast Blvd., about six blocks from the bank when he got a radio call about the holdup.

"As I pulled up to the bank on my motorcycle a woman pointed to a man walking down the sidewalk," Griffiths said. "I drew my gun and told him to put his hands up. He said I didn't do nothing' and I told him again to put up his hands." Griffiths said the man dropped a money bag he had in his right hand, reached inside his coat and pulled out a large revolver and pointed it at him. "As he drew the gun out, I grabbed the gun and finally managed to knock the gun out of his hand," Griffiths said. "Then he grabbed me in a bear hug. I hit him alongside the head twice with my gun and got loose. I told him again several times if he didn't put his hands up, I would shoot him. Then he tried

to grab my gun." Griffiths said, it was at this time, that four citizens came to his aid and helped subdue the suspect.

Griffiths, who had high praise for the men, identified them as Frank Stanek, Leonard Stickelmeyer, Richard Ellis, and Bill Fowler. Ellis is assistant manager of the bank. Officer Carl J. Bays arrived and helped handcuff the struggling suspect.

Griffiths, well-versed in the latest police procedures relative to arrests, advised Gibbs of his legal rights while Gibbs was still stuggling on the ground. "He told me that someone else was holding a shotgun on him and making him do what he did," Griffiths said, "but we saw no one else."

Griffiths suffered a broken left thumb in the battle, and Gibbs had two cuts on the head where Griffiths struck him with his pistol in the early part of the struggle. Detective Lt. Robert E. Colliton said that the holdup suspect had a long-barreled .44 caliber revolver. "The gun was not loaded," he said. Detective Homer C. Hall said that when

Gibbs was searched, prior to being put in to a jail cell, a holdup note was found in his pocket. The note, printed on a large white envelope, read: "Clean out vault. $100s, $50s, $20s, $10s and $5. No alarm, Will kill anyone. Hurry."

Stanek, Stickelmeyer, Fowler, and Ellis possibly risked their own lives to help subdue the bank robbery suspect. "When we read about some cities where citizens stand by and watch a policeman battle for his life. It is a good feeling to know Spokane citizens are the kind who accept their responsibility and come to the aid of an officer when he needs assistance," Hendren said.

During most of his career, Mel was the instructor for new motorcycle officers. "A motorcycle is just as safe as its rider," he said. "A smart motorcycle rider doesn't follow too closely when he's behind a car and rides a bit to the side so he has some place to go if the car dynamites its brakes." Many officers today credit Mel's defensive driving techniques with the low rate of accidents in the department. Griffiths, a 32-year police veteran, handed Badge #1 over to Officer Jack Latta when he retired in 1980.

Mel passed away suddenly November 10, 1997, but his spirit lives on in the many lives he touched along the way. He graduated from Lewis and Clark High School and served in General Patton's 3rd Armored Division during WWII. As a hobby, he coached various sports and activities in which is children were involved. He was survived by his wife of 48 years, Mercedes, who moved to Tehachapi, California; along with two daughters, Carol Anderson in Redondo Beach, California; Valarie Griffiths in Tehachapi, and son, David of Palmdale, California.

Griffiths was highly respected, well liked, and a legend in the minds of those who knew him. He always had time for everyone he came in contact with.

Mel Griffiths. *(Courtesy Mercedes Griffiths)*

Mel Griffiths in a sparsely populated portion of the Lincoln Heights area in the fall of 1952. Mel was assigned to Lincoln Heights, as he grew up in that neighborhood. *(Courtesy Mercedes Griffiths)*

Mel Griffiths, in the spring of 1953. *(Courtesy Mercedes Griffiths)*

Mel Griffiths points to a speed limit sign as part of a safety program that took place in the mid 1960s. Griffiths was the perfect person to be involved in this program as he gave motorcycle classes to new motorcycle police for over 20 years. One of Griffiths's main emphasis was safety. He consistently stressed "following too close" was the cause for the majority of accidents. During his motor classes, Mel, always instructed new motorcycle officers to remember what was printed on the top of the box the motorcycle came in: "This side up." *(Courtesy Mercedes Griffiths)*

Mel Griffiths in front of Brush Cycle at 218 South Madison. Brush Cycle was the only Harley-Davidson motorcycle dealership and repair shop in Spokane. It first appears in the *Polk Spokane City Directory* in 1928. At that time, the address was West 1006 Second Avenue. In 1933, it was still listed in the city directory, but this time their address was West 1002 Second Avenue. Also, in 1933, the Indian Motorcycle Company at West 924 First Avenue appears in the directory. In 1936, the *Spokane City Directory* listed their address as South 218 Madison, which would have been its location until Brush Cycle went out of business in the 1960s. *(Courtesy Mercedes Griffiths)*

The Royal Order of the Silver, Black, and White Cycles. The following swing shift traffic officers were charter members of the "Royal Order;" Sgt. Orlan Sherar, Tom O'Brien, Jay Wilcox, Mel Griffiths, Richard Tilton, Captain George Freeman, Homer Hall, Bob Colliton, "Willy" Glanville, Royce Thornburg, Tom Pugh, and Glen Atkisson, who was the chaplain, although he didn't ride a motorcycle. First organized as The Royal Order of the Silver, Black, and White Cycles in April 1951, all the motorcycles were actually silver. After Homer Hall had an accident, he got permission to have his motorcycle painted black and white. Eventually, all the motorcycles were black and white. *(Courtesy Spokane Police Department Archives)*

FIRST OFFENSE — and Dad doesn't even know he took the car out!

Mel Griffiths on the left. *(Courtesy Mercedes Griffiths)*

The motorcycle hill-climbers. From left: Dan Hite, Carman Hack, Spokane Motorcycle Officer Mel Griffiths, and Todd McAlister. *(Courtesy Dan Hite)*

Mel Griffiths and Willis Glanville. *(Courtesy Mercedes Griffiths)*

Mel Griffiths and his wife Mercedes, holding plaque at a retirement party held in his honor. The plaque stated: "Melvin T. Griffiths, Spokane Police Department, May 1948–September 1980, Your Fellow Officers." *(Courtesy Mercedes Griffiths)*

Homer Hall – hired by the Spokane Police Department in 1948

Homer Hall on police motor in 1949. *(Courtesy Zoe Arneson)*

Homer Hall joined the Spokane Police Department in 1948. Shortly after, he was assigned to the motorcycle squad, where he rode for about three years.

During Hall's second year as a motor officer, he had an encounter that gave him his first bad taste of law enforcement and the politics that are often involved. The incident began on April 1, 1949, when Hall put a parking ticket on a car parked illegally outside the Davenport Hotel. As he was putting it on the windshield, the owner stormed out the door of the hotel, jerked the ticket off the windshield and handed it to Hall, stating, "I'm beyond receiving them."

According to Hall's police report, he told him to take it to the station, adding the driver said, "No idiot was going to give him a ticket." Then he drove off.

Homer Hall, circa 1949. *(Courtesy Zoe Arneson)*

In the low-speed chase that followed, the errant driver, Congressman Compton I. White, Idaho's Democratic Congressman from the 1st Congressional District, "allegedly" forced Hall into the wrong lane of traffic, deliberately trying to run into him. Hall finally stopped White and arrested him for disorderly conduct. White was jailed and released on $15 bail.

Congressman White sued the City of Spokane for $200,000 and named Hall as a defendant, claiming that he was slammed against the wall and otherwise mistreated by the Spokane police. He gave his version of his arrest and imprisonment in a six-page statement dictated to a reporter. "I wouldn't treat a dog the way the police treated me," he said. He also stated that his arrest was illegal because of congressional immunity. He said, "God help America when the safeguard of congressional immunity established by the Constitution is torn down."

The case was widely publicized. Hall's young son, Michael, was very upset that they were going to lose their home and everything else. He was consoled by his mother, who told him that his dad had done the right thing, and there was no way he was going to

lose. It is understandable that a young boy would think like that.

Over time, Officer Hall was victorious. In the meantime, according to one newspaper, he was "the best-known policeman in the United States." He received fan mail from as far away as Tennessee and Massachusetts. One letter in particular, from Washington D.C., said, "I wish to convey my congratulations to that fearless officer who had the courage to arrest that misrepresentative Compton I. White." White paid $100 and court costs on conviction.

At the time, White was 71 years old and was serving his ninth term in the U.S. Congress. He said he was thinking of appealing the conviction and was preparing an article on "A Night in the Spokane Jail" for publication in the Congressional Record. White later moved to Spokane, where he died on March 31, 1956.

Who was Congressman White

White was born in Baton Rouge, Louisiana, and moved during early childhood to Rankin County, Mississippi, then to Clark Fork, Idaho, in 1890. As a young man, he delivered newspapers while attending school in the Clark Fork community. He attended Metropolitan Business College in Chicago,

U. S. Congressman Compton I. White. *(Public Domain)*

Illinois, and graduated from Gonzaga College (now University) in Spokane in 1897.

During his early years he worked on railroads as a trainman, conductor, and telegraph operator. After 1910, he worked in lumber, mining, and livestock raising.

In 1925, White received an unexpected windfall when a valuable mine of galena ore was found on his Idaho property. It was this unexpected find that gave his family a small fortune and allowed him to become a real player in Idaho politics.

Detectives Homer Hall and William Beeman shot

On August 29, 1973, detectives Homer Hall, age 60, and William Beeman, age 44, were both shot by a suspect while attempting to serve a warrant at a 31-unit apartment house, Brunot Hall, in Spokane's Browne's Addition.

The warrant ordered the commitment to a mental hospital of a Brunot Hall tenant, Jack A. Magney, 56, who had earlier that day threatened the life of the part-owner of Brunot Hall, who had objected to Magney continuing to live in the apartment house without paying rent.

Since the previous December, Magney had been asked repeatedly to move out of the building, which his father had owned but had sold to Don Gullio and other investors. Magney, who was a lieutenant colonel in the Army Reserves, had told Gullio he would leave "feet first" before paying rent.

When they arrived with the mental warrant, detectives Hall and Beeman knocked and identified themselves to Magney, who slammed the door on them. As they attempted to force the door open, Magney fired shots at them, wounding both officers. Both being shot, Hall was only able to return a single shot before the door was again slammed and secured. Sheriff's detectives Walter F. King and John Neudorfer, who were present as backup, ran to assist as Detective Hall staggered outside and fell on the lawn with bullet wounds in the chest and abdomen. An ambulance was called. Detective Beeman, shot through the arm,

was assisted by officers Bob Bailor, Larry Peterson, and others who had arrived at the scene.

The suspect then lit a trash fire in his apartment, turned on a five-gallon propane gas tank, and lit the gas. The explosion shattered windows and blasted tenant Brett Ostlind and two other persons off the front porch. The fire department and Fire Chief Al O'Connor were summoned. Soon a crew of 41 firemen arrived with aerial ladder trucks and other pieces of equipment.

The suspect, whose apartment was next to a main stairway, yelled that he would kill anyone who came near, keeping the firefighters from entering with their hoses. Additional shots were heard. Soon the fire had spread to the third floor. It was later determined that several shells had exploded as a result of the fire; the random 'shooting' had increased the risks of rescue work and fire control.

Because of the location of Magney's apartment by the main stairway, tenants were evacuated through the fire escape and windows. Officer Bob Yake lo-

SCENE OF SHOOTING, FIRE DRAMATIC

At the scene of the 1973 Brunot Hall fire. From left: Fred Fait, Sgt. Jerry Hickman, Bob Yake, and Howard Russell. *(Spokesman-Review)*

cated the wounded suspect hiding inside his apartment, bleeding from a self-inflicted gunshot wound to the head. Officers W. Reedy, Joe Machala, and firemen smashed a window and carried Magney out of the smoke-filled room. He was then placed on a gurney and carried to a waiting ambulance. He did not survive. The fire continued to burn uncontrolled for two and a half hours as attempts were made to evacuate the building.

Within a short time, the news media picked up on the shooting. Before long it was announced on KHQ television that Detective Hall had been killed. Also, believing Hall had been killed, Police Chief Wayne Hendron had Detective Charlie Sheppard sent to

Hall's residence to pick up his wife and daughter Zoe to take them to the hospital to identify the body. All along, Sheppard was believing Hall was dead and would not turn on the radio for fear the family would hear it over the news. When they got to the hospital, they learned the story the news media had put out wasn't correct. Although he had been wounded severely, Hall was not dead. Within a short time his wife was allowed to talk to him and told him that it had been broadcast on television that he had been killed, to which he stated: "Boy, I'm glad I didn't hear that, it would have scared me." Det. Hall was placed in an intensive care unit and did not return to work until 18 days after the shooting.

Top photos left to right: (1) Homer Hall and Carl Sweatt, in the 1940s. (2) Homer Hall, circa 1948. Bottom left and right: When Homer Hall passed away in 1980, a number of motor officers came to his house to pay their respects, and provide comfort to the family. *(Courtesy Zoe Arneson)*

Brunot Hall, 2209 West Pacific Avenue, built in 1892, turned to tragedy in 1973. *(Vintage Postcards From Old Spokane by Duane Broyles and Howard Ness, with Tony and Suzanne Bamonte)*

In 1891, the newly appointed Bishop of the Episcopal Diocese of Spokane, Lemuel H. Wells, was riding a train from Pullman to Spokane when he met the philanthropists Mr. and Mrs. Felix Brunot.

The Brunots, who lived in Pittsburgh, Pennsylvania, were taking a tour of the West. While on the train, Wells convinced the couple to stop in Spokane as a part of their tour. The visit went well, and, when they left, they gave the church $30,000 to build a school and an additional $22,000 for the land. The school was named Brunot Hall after its benefactor. It was a combination school, meaning that while some students lived at the school, others lived in their nearby homes with their families. Brunot Hall had room for 50 boarding pupils and reminded parents that "the school is not designated to reform bad girls, but to educate and train the well-disposed in habits of refinement and courtesy, fitting them for cultured society." Brunot Hall advertised in publications, such as *The Churchman*, in July of 1909, claiming, "Certificate admits to Smith, Wellesley, and other colleges. Advantages in Music, the very best. Fine Art Studio."

Brunot Hall had a rigorous course of study. In 1910, the subjects taught were psychology, ethics, English, German, French, mathematics, history, Greek, Latin, prose composition, science, physical culture, bookkeeping, and stenography. Brunot Hall had 11 instructors, all women. Four of the 11 instructors had obtained bachelor degrees from a university. The teachers, from across the country, came from such colleges as Vassar, Smith, Stanford, and Vanderbilt.

In 1912, Brunot Hall suffered from its first fire. It was immediately repaired at a cost $3,000. During World War I, the girls' school was suspended. Following the war, the building was used as a dance studio. In 1931, it was converted into a theatre for Spokane's "Little Theatre Group."

World War II again impacted the use of the building, when it was remodeled into apartments for workers. Brunot Hall remained apartments from 1943-1973. When the incident on the preceding pages took place, it was completely destroyed. The Pacific Terrace Apartments occupy the area now.

Thomas O'Brien – hired by the Spokane Police Department in 1950

Tom O'Brien as a motorcycle officer, circa 1953. Tom was on motor for approximately seven years. *(Courtesy Tom O'Brien)*

Tom O'Brien was born in Conrad, Montana, in 1929. His family, which included six children – Mickey, Claude, Tom, Maxine, Patsy, and Al – moved to Northport, Washington, in 1939, as his father had a job lined up working in a mine owned by a doctor. Within a year, the doctor went broke and left for California, leaving his employees without paying them.

In 1940, searching for work, Tom's father moved the family to Spokane. He worked at numerous jobs, such as road-grader operator, bartender, at Spokane Union Iron Works, and as a carpenter for Gus Bouton. Tom's father passed away at a young age in 1948. In 1954, Tom married Barbara Lemely. They have two children, twins Scott and Tammy.

Tom had many jobs, from setting pins in a bowling alley, working for the *Spokesman-Review*, Pacific Fruit & Produce unloading boxes, and working in a tire shop for 35 cents an hour. He also worked at New Method Laundry for 35 cents an hour.

While working at unloading boxcars for Pacific Fruit & Produce, he made friends with a couple of policemen, who used to stop by at times and bring him coffee. That's when he decided he wanted a steady job.

Although he took a large pay cut, to $242 a month, Tom joined the department in 1950. During his first years on the department, he became friends with another motorcycle officer, Ed Rooney. Rooney had just been discharged from the Army, having served in the Army Airborne. Tom had great respect for Rooney, who talked him into going into the Army. Two years after he had joined the department, and at Rooney's suggestion, he joined the military in 1952.

At that time, the Korean War, which had begun on June 25, 1950, was still going. It was a war between North and South Korea, in which a United Nations force, led by the United States, fought for the South. China and the Soviet Union fought for the North. The war arose from the division of Korea at the end of World War II, and from the global tensions of the Cold War that developed immediately afterwards. On July 27, 1953, an armistice was agreed to and the fighting stopped.

Tom served 33 months in the Army, and outside of his training schools, the rest of his time was spent in Airborne. One of his more memorable times in Airborne occurred when he was with a group parachuting out of a plane. During one of his jumps, he landed on top of another man's parachute, but managed to maneuver off. His best memories of being in the military were "that his chute opened during every jump" and "getting out of the military."

As his military obligation was close to being over, he applied for and received a three-month early out to attend Whitworth College (now University). Following his military obligation, he again, on November 1, 1955, went back to work for the Spokane Police Department. One of his first memorable experiences occurred when working paddy wagon duty with an older policeman named Dutch Schubbe. Schubbe was a large and muscular man. He was also an outstanding example of what a policeman should be, both in courage and competency. Schubbe was a no-nonsense type of cop, who was somebody Tom was soon to learn from.

In 1955, the paddy wagon looked like a Wonder Bread truck, the type used during the '50s to '70s. It was a marked unit, painted black and white to match the prowl cars during that time. The paddy wagon was referred to as car #80. The reason it looked like a bread truck was its size and shape. The front, where the driver and passenger sat, was partitioned with solid steel; a small, covered peephole allowed a view of the passengers in the back. It was small enough to keep from being disturbed by the prisoners. This was a two-man unit and always worked the downtown area. It was often referred to as the "drunk wagon." The back of this vehicle had two facing bench seats and another bench-type seat against the steel separating partition. All in all, the paddy wagon had a comfortable seating capacity for

Tom O'Brien, circa 1967. *(Courtesy Tom O'Brien)*

approximately 10 drunken and disorderly folks, and possibly 15 smaller people, if it were a busy night and discretion was used.

Working the paddy wagon was a unique and interesting assignment. Anyone who ever worked it for any length of time would have found it to be a most life-changing experience. It gave the opportunity to meet some of the city's most remarkable down-and-out people and also some of the worst society had to offer. Mostly, it consisted of picking up drunks. Often some of them would consider themselves as "tough guys" and resist – that's where understanding and technique came in.

In the case of Tom O'Brien and Dutch Schubbe, they were making their rounds in the paddy wagon one evening when they came upon a drunk and disorderly person in one of the many downtown skid-row taverns. Dutch told him he was under arrest and needed to follow him out to the paddy wagon. The man walked over to one of the mounted bar stools, sat down, and stated, "I'm not going anywhere with you." Dutch walked over to him, picked both him and the bar stool up and carried them out to the paddy wagon. This gave Tom a clear understanding of a no-nonsense approach when an arrest needs to be made, a lesson he learned well.

When I (Bamonte) came on the department in 1966, Tom held the position of "police inspector." I soon learned how he made it to that rank. Like Dutch Schubbe, he also was an intelligent, no-nonsense outstanding example of what a policeman should be in courage and competency. On several occasions, I was called to transport to jail people he had arrested. One of these was a fighter, a man who had been arrested for serious felony offenses on numerous occasions. This man, Jesse Lockhart, had a reputation of being an exceptionally tough man, who, at one time, had been shot by the police following a felony he had just committed. He survived being shot, was back in shape and ready for action. This wasn't good, as he was the type of person if you got a call regarding him, you could be assured you were going to be in a fight.

One afternoon a call came over the police radio involving Lockhart. He was having difficulties in

Left: Tom O'Brien and Wayne Hendren, receiving promotions from Police Chief Bill Parsons in 1967. O'Brien was promoted to inspector, and Hendren was promoted to deputy chief. Later, when Hendren made chief, the two men made major efforts to modernize policing and improve professionalism, which included a strict standard of openness and honesty to the public. *(Public domain)*

his marriage and was at his father-in-law's house, where his wife was staying. The father-in-law had made the call, as he was intimidated by Jesse and his reputation. He had armed himself with a shotgun and was about to shoot Jesse. Tom was on his way back to the station when he heard the call. The policeman assigned to that district was on another call, and I was two districts away. Tom responded to the call and, in a scuffle that ensued, he hit Jesse along the side of his head with his pistol, stunning him. When I arrived, within minutes after, he was still stunned. Fortunately, we were able to handcuff and transport him to jail.

Tom stated three cases that stood out during his career that had an impact on the city: the Candy Rogers murder case; the case in which two detectives, Bill Beeman and Homer Hall, were shot; and the South Hill rapist case (about Kevin Coe).

After serving 27 years on the department, Tom retired in 1980. To the people who worked under him, Tom was one of the best deputy chiefs the department ever had. He did his job well. Tom O'Brien passed away in 2017.

Tom O'Brien and his wife Barbara, circa 1966, at the Policeman's Ball. *(Courtesy Tom O'Brien)*

Tom and Barbara O'Brien in 2014. *(Bamonte photo)*

Lloyd A. Howard – hired by the Spokane Police Department in 1950

Lloyd Howard, circa 1955. *(Courtesy Pat Howard)*

Lloyd Howard was born in Spokane in 1925 to George and Ida Howard. His father worked various jobs, and his mother was a housewife. He graduated from Rogers High School in 1943. The first job Lloyd ever had was when he was still attending high school. During his freshman year he worked at a chicken ranch in the Spokane Valley doing cleanup work. His widow, Pat, still remembers what he made and how he spent it. He worked for the entire summer and made a total of $75. With that money he purchased a saxophone for $25, a car for $25, and a springer spaniel dog for $25.

During Lloyd's high school years he was in the school orchestra, the Rogers Glee Club, and was a member of the school student council. The Rogers School Orchestra was an essential part of the music department and was involved in many of the school's functions. The music the orchestra played was clas-

Lloyd Howard was a member of the Rogers High School Marching Band and Orchestra from 1940 to 1943. He won a competition for first place clarinet player in the Washington State high school competition for two years in a row. *(Courtesy Pat Howard)*

sical or semi-classical type. Throughout Lloyd's life music always played a major part, as he was a member of several professional musical groups. While still in high school he was awarded the best in the state for two years as a clarinet player.

When Lloyd graduated from high school in 1943, he entered the Air Force. He spent combined time in the Air Force and the Washington Air National Guard for a total of 33 years. During World War II, Lloyd spent two years in England. After the war he enrolled at Washington State College in Pullman.

Lloyd met his future wife, Pat Ashley, at her home in 1948. A friend of Lloyd's had lined up a blind date for the two of them. The date was held at Pat's house. Lloyd's date was with Pat's friend and Lloyd's friend was with Pat. Unfortunately, for Lloyd's friend, he was scheduled to ship out in two weeks for an overseas assignment. Just before he left he asked Lloyd to take care of Pat for him. Lloyd took his friend

Lloyd Howard and his father, George, circa 1929. *(Courtesy Pat Howard)*

Lloyd and Pat's wedding photo. Left to right: John Dillon; John Staley; Lloyd Howard, groom; Pat Ashley – bride; Fred Ashley, father of bride, Spokane realtor and past two-term Washington State Representative; Pat's sister Judy Ellis, widow of Captain John Ellis, Spokane Police Department; Jo Klein seated; Sadie Garberg; and John Brohhead. *(Courtesy Pat Howard)*

Left: Kathleen, Lloyd, Wayne, Pat, and George Howard. Patricia, their fourth child was born in 1957. Kathleen, who became a nurse, but was also a pilot, was killed in 1994 while attempting a take off from Lake Wenatchee State Airport, Leavenworth, Washington. Her husband Laurence, and another nurse who worked with Kathleen, also died in the wreck. This tragic day started out as a picnic with her husband and a friend. *(Courtesy Pat Howard)*

Second Lieutenant Lloyd Howard in 1954.

seriously, and less that five months later, he and Pat were married at the Westminster Congregational United Church of Christ in Spokane.

Lloyd and Pat Howard had four children, Wayne Allen, Kathleen Ann, George Robert, and Patricia Kay.

Howard was commissioned an officer in the Washington Air National Guard and went on to become a fighter pilot, rising through the ranks. On February 24, 1950, while still in the Air National Guard, Lloyd was commissioned by the Spokane Police De-

partment. He served four days short of a year and resigned the department in February during the Korean War. On October 5, 1953, following the war, Lloyd again was commissioned as an officer with the Spokane Police Department. At that time, he was assigned to the motorcycle unit, a job he held until February 28, 1957.

Lloyd Howard passed away at his home in Spokane on August 10, 2008, following a six-year-long battle with lymphoma. He was in hospice care at the time of death.

Lloyd Howard on his police motor next to his F-86 fighter intercepter at Geiger Field on October 25, 1955. Note Lloyd's name below the cockpit on the airplane. *(Courtesy Pat Howard, widow, and Fred Ashley, brother)*

The following quote appeared under this photo in the *Spokane Daily Chronicle* on October 25, 1955:

Alerted Guardsmen Praised For Speed. In 15 minutes city motorcycle officer Lloyd A. Howard shifted from chasing speeders to speeding through the skies.

The speed with which officers and airmen of the 116th fighter-interceptor squadron of the Washington Air Na-

tional guard responded to a test alert at 5:30 a. m. today brought pleased comment from commanding officers. Col. Frank W. Frost, commanding the 142d fighter-interceptor wing at Geiger field, of which the 116th is a unit., said the planes were airborne within an hour after the alert was sounded. Maj. Charles L. Nelson, commander of the 116th, also had praise for the smoothness with which the operation was carried out.

The "scramble" here was part of a nationwide practice exercise to determine the air national guard's readiness to help in defending the nation against enemy air attack.

The order for the national guard units to get into the air was flashed by air defense command headquarters in Colorado Springs at 9:28 a.m. EDT.

Handling the alert here was the Ninth air division at Geiger field. The signal for the exercise, "operation stop watch," went to 23 wings and 73 squadrons of the air guard which have been assigned an air defense responsibility.

At Camp Murray, Tacoma, officials told the Associated Press the Washington state phase of the nationwide alert was concentrated in the Spokane area. State national guard headquarters there said close to a dozen planes took to the air from Geiger field. The alert ended in about three hours.

Brig. Gen. Sam W. Agee, Ninth air division commander, said the only other fighter-interceptor squadron joining the 116th in this area for the alert was the 190th at Gowen air force base, Boise.

The 142d fighter-interceptor wing is one of the fighting units assigned under the national defense program.

Lloyd Howard. *(Courtesy Pat Howard)*

Called at Home

Fliers of the 116th were called from their homes to take to the air as speedily as possible against a theoretical enemy bomber force. Action of the squadron was restricted to the skies over the Inland Empire.

Typical of the readiness shown by the personnel was that of Capt. Lloyd A. Howard, a city police motorcycle officer, who was at the field within 15 minutes after the alert sounded and climbed into his plane in his police uniform.

Captain Lloyd Howard in a dual role as police motorcycle officer and jet fighter pilot. *(Courtesy Pat Howard)*

Lt. Colonel Lloyd Howard accepting an award for the 116th fighter interceptor squadron.

validated during the Vietnam War, with Air Guard fighter squadrons serving successfully in Vietnam. Wilson also continued efforts to integrate the National Guard, including the appointment of its first African-American general officer.

Wilson flew in Vietnam on observing and fact-finding missions and received the Vietnam Service Medal. He was appointed to a second term in 1967, and served until his 1971 retirement.

Lt. Colonel Lloyd Howard with the Winston Peabody Wilson Award his fighter group received when he was the commander. *(Courtesy Pat Howard)*

Because Howard and his unit were honored with the Winston Peabody Wilson Award, the following is a brief word about Wilson. He was a United States Air Force major general who served as chief of the National Guard Bureau. Wilson was appointed director of the Air National Guard in 1954, and promoted to brigadier general. In 1955, he was appointed deputy chief of the National Guard Bureau and promoted to major general. During his tenure as air guard director he oversaw the organization's diversification from a fighter-based force to one of fighters, bombers, observation, and transport units, as well as a modernization of its planes and facilities.

In 1963, Wilson was appointed chief of the National Guard Bureau, the first Air Force officer to be officially named to the position. Long an advocate for integrating National Guard and Reserve units into operations with active duty ones, rather than using them as a strategic reserve, Wilson's view was

This photo appeared in the *Spokane Daily Chronicle* on Wednesday, August 29, 1973, stating: "Col. Lloyd A. Howard this week was named commander of the Washington Air National Guard's 141st Fighter Group of Spokane International Airport. He succeeds Col. Donald Stack, who retired after 30 years service." At the time of this promotion, Howard was a full-bird colonel. *(Courtesy Pat Howard)*

Lloyd Howard, sixth from the left, playing the clarinet. This was called the "Potes Band." *(Courtesy Pat Howard)*

This was the "Corn Fed Five Band." All were officers in the Washington Air National Guard. From left: Lloyd Howard, Charlie Lewis, Fergie, General Lloyd Lamb, Dallas Sartz (*Miss Spokane* hydroplane driver during Coeur d'Alene races). *(Courtesy Pat Howard)*

Following his retirement from the Air National Guard in 1976, Lloyd worked for the Enstrom Helicopter Corporation as a salesman and instructor. Enstrom Helicopter Corporation designed and built light, single-engine helicopters, both piston and turbine, for personal, commercial, and government use. Their helicopters were touted as the safest and best-supported helicopters in the world. Safety has been a primary factor in all design decisions, including development of the high-inertia rotor system, rugged airframe, and robust landing gear.

All Enstrom helicopters had features that made them unique in the industry. Enstrom helicopters had a patented swashplate/control system and were the only rotorcraft with protected, internal controls. They also had an unblocked tail rotor design that gave the aircraft some of the best flight characteristics in the industry.

Lloyd's last job was driving school a bus for the Mead School District. He worked for them for eight years until he retired in 1991.

Lloyd and Pat Howard in 1978, preparing for their installation as Grand Guardian and Associate Grand Guardian of the International Order of Job's Daughters. They were the first husband and wife team in Washington State to serve in that capacity.

**S
P
O
K
A
N
E

P
O
L
I
C
E

D
E
P
A
R
T
M
E
N
T**

Harold Tucker – hired by the Spokane Police Department in 1950

Harold Tucker on motor in front of his home in 1954. *(Courtesy Tucker family)*

Harold Tucker was born in 1925 in Dahinda, Illinois, a small unincorporated community in Knox County. Harold's father was a jack-of-all-trades and his mother was a housewife. There were four boys and five girls in the family; all were raised and attended schools in Knoxville, Illinois. Harold went to both grade school and high school at Knox-ville. From the first to fourth grade, he lived on a farm, walking two and a half miles to school. Following high school, a bunch of his buddies got drafted. This was upsetting to him, and rather than wait for his draft number to come up, he went down to the recruiting station and volunteered for the United States Navy (at that time military service was mandatory).

Farragut Naval Training Center

When Harold joined the Navy he was sent for his basic training to Farragut Naval Training Center on Lake Pend Oreille in Bayview, Idaho. The history of Farragut as a Naval training center is interesting. In 1941, Eleanor Roosevelt allegedly noticed Lake Pend Oreille on a flight to Seattle. At the time, she had inside knowledge that her husband, President Roosevelt, was looking for a location to secure an inland naval training center, and she mentioned this site to him. Roosevelt quickly made a secret tour of the area. As a result, in late 1941, the U.S. government purchased over 4,000 acres. This purchase was made from private land owners, Kootenai County commissioners, and a railway company that owned much of the land. Roosevelt felt it was important to establish an inland naval base away from the western coastline, as he feared a Japanese invasion at the time.

Construction of the base began in March 1942. By September, it had a population of 55,000, making it the largest populated city in Idaho. For the next nine months, over 22,000 men were employed at the site, working 10-hour shifts for 13 of every 14 days. They built mess halls, libraries, movie theaters, living quarters, chapels, and many other buildings. A total of 776 buildings were constructed. Because of the rush and shortage of seasoned lumber, the majority of the buildings were constructed with green lumber. This was a major construction project for the entire Inland Northwest, which provided an economic stimulus for the surrounding communities. It was a good move as the area was still suffering from the Great Depression of the 1930s.

The Farragut Naval Training Center served as boot camp for Navy recruits. Basic training at Farragut typically meant recruits left home for the first time, came to Farragut, and learned basic military skills before heading off to fight in World War II.

However, as is always a condition of any military base, the recruits needed time and places to go for rest and recreation. Special trains called Liberty Trains were dedicated to the enlistees stationed at Farragut, making three trips a day to Spokane. At the time, Farragut was the second-largest training center in the world (the Great Lakes Naval Station at Chicago was the largest). This project was welcomed throughout the Inland Northwest. There was a war going on and the public appreciated the efforts of the young trainees, and the fact that once they went to war they might never come back.

During its 30 months of existence, more than 293,000 sailors received basic training at the camp. The last recruit graduated in March 1945. Farragut was also used as a prisoner-of-war camp where nearly 900 Germans worked as gardeners and maintenance men. The facility was decommissioned in June 1946.

Harold Tucker at Farragut

In 1944, Harold was going through boot camp at Farragut. On a weekly basis, recruits were allowed to obtain a pass (permission by those in charge to be away from one's military unit for a usually short period of time).

During Harold's training at Farragut, he and some of his Navy buddies, whenever they got a pass, would go to Cook's Roller Rink (now Pattison's) in north Spokane. Cook's had a reputation as a place with a wholesome environment and a good place to meet young women.

In the spring of 1944, Harold met his future wife, Shirley Campbell, at Cook's. She was 17 at the time and a senior at North Central High School. The relationship continued and grew. It eventually turned into a romance by correspondence once Harold shipped out. Harold's assignment, at age 19, was as a hospital corpsman aboard the USS *LaGrange*. His ship was anchored at Buckner Bay near Okinawa.

One night, 13 Japanese twin-engine bombers attacked. "They hit every ship around us but didn't hit us," said Harold. "We were young. We stood on the fantail and cheered the anti-aircraft fire. We hollered every time they shot down a plane."

The night before the war ended, on August 13, 1945, the *LaGrange* was attacked by two Kamikaze pilots. (The meaning of the word Kamakazi, which is "suicide," literally translates to "divine wind." Japanese World War II pilots loaded their planes with bombs and crashed them onto their target). One plane struck the ship and damaged it before crashing into the water. The other, carrying a bomb, plunged through the ship and the bomb detonated three decks below.

At the time the *LaGrange* was hit, Harold was in the ship's dental office trying to write a letter to Shirley. After a few attempts at writing, he kept coming up blank. He finally went to the mess hall to watch a movie. Within five minutes, the bomb went right through the dental office where he had just been. The next morning he found his belongings floating in the water on deck. You could honestly say Shirley saved his life that day.

The ship was a disaster area, there was fire on the deck, and many men were killed or badly burned. As a hospital corpsman, Harold did his best to care for the wounded and dying.

During Harold's tenure in the Navy, he stated the most important thing he learned was respect for everything, especially his wife. This attitude has

The USS *LaGrange*. *(Public domain)*

While anchored in Buckner Bay, on August 13, 1945, the USS *LaGrange* came under enemy air attack and suffered the last known kamikaze attacks of the war. Although heavy anti-aircraft fire responded to the attack, a kamikaze carrying a 500-pound bomb crashed into *LaGrange's* superstructure. A second suicide plane struck the top of a kingpost (post designed for handling cargo, and so are located at the forward or aft end of a ship), and splashed 20 yards from the ship. The transport suffered considerable damage in both strikes, with 21 sailors killed and 89 wounded. After hostilities ended on August 15, the *LaGrange* crew did field repairs and prepared for the cruise home. Departing Guam on September 6, she arrived at San Francisco on September 21. Because of the remaining battle damage, *LaGrange* was decommissioned there on October 27, 1945, and was returned to the War Shipping Administration and placed in the National Defense Reserve Fleet at Suisun Bay, California. In 1955, the *LaGrange* was withdrawn from the Reserve Fleet as part of a repair program, and then returned. On April 18, 1975, she was sold to Nicolai Joffe Corp. for $208,489.78, to be scrapped.

helped him immensely as he has applied it through all phases of his life.

On Nov. 11, 1945, while on a 30-day leave, Harold and Shirley were married at Pilgrim Lutheran Church in Spokane. Following his leave, Harold returned to duty, and the couple spent the first six months of married life apart.

Following his discharge in 1946, they lived for a time in Spokane and after a few months moved to Illinois. However, that didn't last long, and they moved back to Spokane, where Harold worked a number of other jobs, mostly at service stations, even owning one at 38th Avenue and Grand Boulevard. In 1950, he took

the civil service test for the Spokane Police Department and came out number 12 of 127. Tucker joined the Spokane police department on August 8, 1950.

He worked as a motorcycle officer, hit-and-run officer, safety police officer, detective, and spent 15 years playing Santa Claus at Christmas time.

Beginning duty as a patrolman, he was later assigned to the motorcycle unit. His motto during his police career was, "Do to others as you would wish to be treated."

During their first seven years of marriage, the Tuckers established their family when Shirley gave birth

Harold Tucker in front of his home in 1965. *(Courtesy Tucker family)*

Bob Browning on the far left in uniform; Jerry King, independent insurance agent; Fireman Bob Cumming; Harold Tucker in Santa outfit; Russell Fick and his dad, Floyd Fick, to the far right in uniform. *(Courtesy Tucker family)*

to three children. The first, Douglas, was born in 1947, Ronald in 1949, and Pattie in 1951. Also, to make ends meet, Shirley worked for many years at a neighborhood pharmacy.

During his tenure on the department, Harold had innumerable experiences, both good and bad. He was involved in three separate accidents while he was on police motor. His last accident occurred in 1960, when an 18-wheel truck went through a red light and collided with him.

Prior to Harold's accident, he was asked a number of times by his supervisors if he would like to go into teaching classes on "Traffic Safety." He always declined, as his preference was riding motor. Following the accident, he rode for another month and then became the traffic education instructor for the police department. Harold excelled in that capacity.

On August 30, 1953, while responding to a garage fire, with two boys suspected to be trapped inside, he was hit at an intersection, throwing him into a car.

Tucker's motorcycle came to rest against his body and caught fire. Tucker was unconscious for three days and listed in critical condition with damaged kidney, broken ribs, hip, damaged right eye, and two swollen knees. Six months later, he was back on the bike. During the 15 years he played Santa for the first and second graders in the Spokane School District, he gave out Hershey bars (the original sized ones) supplied by the Independent Insurance Agents of Spokane to every child.

After 25 years on the force, Harold retired, taking a job as an investigator for the Washington State Department of Revenue. He was also active in the Masonic Lodge, and in his 60s became a licensed minister, serving for a time as interim pastor of the United Church of Christ in North Spokane.

Harold Tucker's near-fatal motor accident. *(Courtesy Tucker family)*

Harold Tucker teaching school safety patrol to his daughter, Pattie, in September of 1961. Motorcycle Officer Mel Griffiths, who also taught traffic safety, was Harold's biggest influence in his career. *(Courtesy Tucker family)*

Harold Tucker teaching bicycle safety, circa 1959. *(Courtesy Tucker family)*

Santa (Harold Tucker) visiting and giving gifts to children in December 1961. *(Courtesy Tucker family)*

Santa was popular with everybody. Here he is with actress Jayne Mansfield in 1965. While Mansfield was in Spokane on a publicity tour she told her bodyguard that she wanted to sit on Santa's lap, which was arranged in spite of Harold's reluctance. *(Courtesy Tucker family)*

Harold Tucker and actor Ernest Borgnine at a Masonic fellowship dinner on June 20, 1989. *(Courtesy Tucker family)*

From June of 1988 to June 1, 1989, Harold was the Grand Master of the Masons in Washington State. His job was to go throughout the state and visit the different lodges during their meetings.

On his last meeting, in June 1989, which was held in Spokane, the Masons held a fellowship dinner to celebrate the achievements of Spokane's youth.

During their meeting that day, they were surprised when past grandmasters –Doug Lemons and his friend Ernest Borgnine – requested entrance. They had been in meetings in Wenatchee and heard of Spokane's Grand Lodge meeting, so they came to attend. At the meeting, Borgine was very generous with his time and visited with everyone.

The Tucker family in 1969. From left: Ronald, Shirley, Pattie, Harold, and Douglas. *(Courtesy Tucker family)*

Harold and Shirley Tucker in 1945. *(Courtesy Tucker family)*

Harold and Shirley in 2015. *(Bamonte photo)*

During Harold's time on the department, there were two incidents that stand out. The first of these occurred when he was selected to be one of the officers assigned to protect senator and presidential candidate John F. Kennedy during a 1960 campaign visit to Spokane.

The other incident involves what could have become a mass murder. Spokane has had a number of serial murders and rapists, but never a mass murder. "Mass murder" is defined by the FBI as murdering four or more persons during a single event with no "cooling-off period" between the murders. However, Spokane had what could have easily been a mass murder if it hadn't been quickly stopped.

The killing and rampage

On Thursday, November 11, 1971, at 11:30 a.m., an emotionally disturbed young man, Larry Harmon, armed himself with a .22 caliber rifle and sledge-hammer, the beginning of a rampage inside St. Aloysius Church in Spokane.

In 1960, John F. Kennedy was in a down-to-the-wire battle with Richard M. Nixon for the presidency. This photo was taken during one of his trips to Spokane that year. Spokane was a key battleground for the electoral votes of Washington. On November 8, Kennedy won by the narrowest of margins and took the oath of office as the nation's 35th President in January of 1961. Harold Tucker is to the far left in this photo. He was assigned to a group of officers tasked with protecting Kennedy as he made his way around Spokane. Behind Kennedy is Officer Leroy Cumming. *(Courtesy Tucker family)*

FORECAST TODAY

Fog

Thursday	High	Low
Airport	46	34
Downtown	45	35
(Full Report on Page 2.)

THE SPOKESMAN-REVIEW

89TH YEAR NO. 182   FRIDAY MORNING   NOVEMBER 12, 1971   PRICE TEN CENTS.   SPOKANE, WASH.

Police Kill Gunman After Wild Spree; Worker Dead, 4 Others Hit by Bullets

Gonzaga Church Interior Ruined; LSD Use Cited

By TOM BURNETT

Spokesman-Review Staff Writer

A berserk young man, armed with a .22-caliber rifle, killed a church caretaker, wounded four other persons and heavily damaged St. Aloysius Catholic Church before he was shot and killed by police at noon Thursday.

He was identified as Larry J. Harmon, 21, the son of Mr. and Mrs. E. Glenn Harmon, E12124 Twenty-first. The father, a Spokane attorney, describes the youth's experience with LSD and its effect on his life leading up to Thursday's events in a statement which appears elsewhere on this page.

The spree of death and destruction apparently began about 11:30 a.m. in the interior of St. Aloysius, a Jesuit church adjacent to Gonzaga University in Spokane. When the events ended, church caretaker Hilary M. Kunz, 69, E807 Indiana, was dead amid rubble one observer likened to the aftermath of a wartime bombing. Statues were smashed, a large portion of the Carrara marble communion railing was broken beyond recognition, an American flag was ripped from its standard, and glass was strewn about.

Those wounded were: Michael J. Clark, 18, in satisfactory condition early this morning; Robert A. Fees,

LARRY J. HARMON

This incident made the front page, plus two additional pages, in both Spokane newspapers. It had the potential to be Spokane's first mass murder. This occurred in November of 1971 ironically. In June of 2009, almost 38 years later, Douglas Harmon, the younger brother of Larry Harmon, attacked and injured a young man with a machete in Spokane at Sixth Avenue and Bernard Street. This was an unprovoked attack on a teenage couple was just sitting on the sidewalk when it happened. The victim required 100 stitches after the machete sliced his face from his ear to his jaw, shattered a bone in his left wrist, and took a chunk out of his scalp. The suspect was tasered and subdued. He later pleeaded guilty by reason of insanity and was sent to Eastern State Hospital. The officers under the headline from left to right: Jim Johnson, unknown, Carl Bays, Robert Schaber, and Richard Poole. *(Courtesy Tucker family)*

The story began when a deranged man, Larry Harmon, parked his four-wheel-drive International Scout vehicle on Astor Street, about 50 feet south of Boone Avenue. He then entered the church, killing the janitor, Hilary Kuntz, who was working on a ladder. Kuntz's body was found at the bottom of the ladder against the east wall, where he apparently had been working on a clock. This happened while Kuntz's wife was waiting for him outside.

Harmon then went to the front, or north end of the church, and began destroying everything he could find that represented religion and authority. At least six statutes were broken, the altar area was heavily damaged, the tabernacle was smashed, and an American flag located to the left of the main altar was torn down, ripped apart, and left lying over a chair.

Following this rampage, Harmon, according to witnesses, began shooting at any person he saw outside the church. Before he was killed, he had murdered one person and wounded four others.

Officer John F. Lynch was the first uniformed officer to arrive on the scene, followed by officer Carl Bays. Lynch emptied his pistol at Harmon who proceeded to chase him around his patrol car, attempting to shoot him. Officer Bays showed up as this was going

Detective Harold Tucker was the first (detective) to arrive on the scene following the murder and other attempts to murder both inside and outside St. Aloysius Catholic Church. In this photo he is on the far left interviewing a witness. The suspect's body is below his International Scout vehicle. Upon searching the vehicle, police found a large amount of ammunition in a coffee can and glove box. There was also a sledge hammer and axe in the vehicle. *(Courtesy Tucker family)*

on and immediately fired a shot at Harmon with his shotgun, and according to Lynch, this distraction probably saving his life.

Harmon immediately began shooting at them with a rifle, as he ran back behind the rectory. As he did, he dropped down behind a garbage can and fired more shots at them with his rifle. Bays told him three times to put his gun down, but Harmon continued to shoot.

At that time, Bays fired back at the gunman from a distance of about 60 feet with his 12-gauge shotgun. Bays said he could see that he had struck the gunmen in the side with a shotgun blast. He said the man, still carrying his clip-fed .22 caliber rifle, ran toward a four-wheel-drive vehicle and, as he got close to it, fired another shot which struck a bystander in the arm.

Officers Robert Schaber and Richard Poole arrived

at the scene just as the gunman got into his vehicle. They approached from both sides. As they did this, Harmon raised his rifle to shoot. At this time Officer Schaber fired his service revolver at him. Officer Poole, who said he flattened himself on the ground when he saw the man ready to fire his rifle, fired his revolver one more time. As it was obvious that Harman had been hit, Poole went up to the vehicle and took the rifle away from him. As he did this Poole said "he had to pry his gun away from him – he was still trying to shoot at me when we pulled him out of the truck."

Police Officer Angelo Costanzo, who arrived shortly after, stated "he examined Bay's prowl car and found six bullet holes in the car inflicted by the gunman."

A Letter from the Killer's Father

Note: The authors gave much consideration to printing the following letter from the "Killer's Dad." However, we felt it would be beneficial for anyone who reads this book to get an understanding of the dangers of drug use and the consequences that too often surround its effects, which often turn deadly. One of the authors (Bamonte) was there the day this incident happened. It is one of those unfortunate and preventable crimes that leaves a lifelong lasting memory.

Glen Harmon was the father of Larry Harmon, the murderer. He was also a former journalist and prominent Spokane attorney who represented the *Spokesman-Review* and *Spokane Chronicle*.

This letter and the incident left an impact on Detective Tucker and many others. The manner Larry Harmon chose to end his life had a tragic and lifetime effect on everyone involved. The final incident that caused his death was, without a doubt, drug-related and impacted many people. The day after his son's rampage and killing, Glen Harmon wrote the following article that appeared in the *Spokesman-Review*:

My son Larry is dead. Killed by police bullets, the record will say. But he was not killed by bullets, he was killed by LSD. Worse than that, the same LSD pills which did irreversible damage to his brain more than two years ago, caused him to kill another with himself. These deaths are an unbelievable tragedy, I, and my family, can only feel shock for the relatives of the man he killed with himself.

Police Had No Choice

There is little doubt in my mind that as far as the police are concerned, they had no choice than to kill Larry. Were I in their shoes, I believe I would have done likewise.

For to him, life on this earth had reached the point where he found nothing left for him to live for. He still loved his mother, his Dad, his little brother, Douglas. The rest of the world had become a place where he no longer fit, though his family fought as hard as they knew how, and with all the help medical science could offer, to undo the damage to an incredible intelligent brain, was irreversibly damaged by LSD.

It Happened at MIT

Where did this happen? Even to tell it seems unreal. It happened at MIT — Massachusetts Institute of Technology — the university which his mother and I firmly believed was the greatest university in the world for a budding nuclear scientist. For that is what Larry J. Harmon was three years ago when he enrolled at MIT. When he was graduated from University High School in the spring of 1967, he was rated by his teachers as the greatest mathematical mind they had ever known. In a nationwide pre-college test he scored a perfect score of 100 points out of a possible 100 points on the mathematics portion of the test, and, in the top one-half of one per cent in the nation in the over-all scholastic aptitude test. His teachers said they knew of no other Spokane high school graduate who had scored a perfect score in mathematics nationally.

He left for MIT, planning to study physics. He had already started college physics at Gonzaga University. Larry had great ambitions. Among other things, he toyed with joining the Students for Democratic Action, not because he approved their plans for socializing this country, but because he opposed them.

Anything Goes

He entered a dormitory at MIT. He told me later that just about anything goes in the dormitories, or the one he was in. Friends, primarily SDS friends, finally induced him to try smoking pot. He told me later he found pot "extremely enjoyable." But his friends did not stop there. They kept telling him of the marvelous "mind expanding" properties of LSD, "acid," to the initiates. On his 19th birthday, June 27, 1969, he took half of a pill, which his friends told him was LSD. He was still at MIT at that time for the summer session, because he asked his mother and me permission to stay in school for the summer so he could "finish his course faster." He got a job in the school dining room to help pay his way in summer school.

There Is a Hell

His first "trip" on LSD produced incredible hallucinations. His friends said he had a "bad trip." He told me he went to hell and back, literally, saying. "Dad, I know you don't believe me. But there is a hell. I went there. I talked to the **"devil himself."** A few days later he had convinced himself that everything that happened on his first "trip" was a hoax. He became convinced that if he just focused his will and brainpower on it, he could take LSD again and in his mind would refuse to let anything happen. That would prove to him that it was all unreal, only hallucinations. So a few days later he took a second LSD pill, this time only a quarter of a pill. He gambled with LSD against his brain. He lost. The same identical hallucinations came back to him again, this time stronger than before. He met and talked to the Devil in hell. He discovered that his friends who gave him the LSD were in fact emissaries of the devil.

Old Testament Impressed

On his second "trip," he picked up the Holy Bible. He had never been especially religious, having attended Sunday

School for a time until he didn't want to go any more. He told me later: "When I picked up the Bible and started to read, it was like revelation to me. I read the first five books of the Old Testament, and I knew then every word in them was true."

He died still believing that every word in the first five books of the Old Testament were true. Thanks to LSD, his mind perverted his beliefs into a believable and incredible mold. While he was reading the Old Testament, under the influence of LSD, he came to the words, "Honor thy Dad and thy mother." He put down the Bible and phoned his mother and me from Massachusetts. He told us he was "tripping" on LSD and wanted to come home. From talking to him we had not the slightest idea of his real condition. We talked to a doctor and officials at MIT, who deprecated the seriousness of what had happened to him and said a number of students were experimenting with LSD. We asked if he could come home alone or if we should come and get him. We were told he should be able to come home alone.

Son Is Silent, Dazed

I met him at the Spokane airport. I was a few minutes late and his flight had landed. I could not find him. After searching for some time I started to leave the airport. Then I saw Larry. He was in a daze. For a half hour he said nothing to me, despite my earnest efforts to get him to talk, to tell me what had happened. I took him home. He continued to be in an unbelievable trance-like state. We took him to the hospital. Our doctor had him under medication for about a week. It was difficult to watch. His mother stayed at the hospital overnight with him since he was afraid of the nurses and others.

The doctor told us we would have to hope and pray that the LSD had done no permanent damage to his brain. We heard, for the first time, the words "irreversible damage to a brain by LSD." We could not believe it could be true. Weren't youngsters, including those right here in Spokane, experimenting with LSD on an ever-increasing scale? Almost three and a half years later, we know it is true. Until yesterday, we continued to hope that medical science would come up with something to undo what two LSD pills had done.

LSD Becomes Poison

Amazingly enough, after those two LSD pills, he concluded that LSD was a very bad poison. He developed a dislike, to the point of hatred for LSD and "pot," which had led him to take LSD. We took him to one psychiatrist, talked to a number of others. They held out no real hope for a cure. On one subject, he was completely unchangeable. When he later read the New Testament of the Bible, he became convinced that Jesus Christ was not the real divine being or deity in the universe. Jehovah was God. Christ was an imposter in his incredibly warped mind.

Still worse that instead of an imposter, Jesus Christ was in fact the devil who came to earth to destroy the true religion of the Jewish faith. Though neither my wife nor I have Jewish blood to our knowledge, he became convinced he was a Jew, and that he had a message for the Jewish world. He wanted to tell every person everywhere that "Jesus Christ was not the true God of Creation he found in the first five books of the Old Testament.

Hard Work Prescribed

No one would listen. We, his family, moved to our summer home on Coeur d'Alene Lake last year and lived there. The doctors said that perhaps hard work would be the best therapy for him. He worked hard. He cut wood, cleared brush, bought an International Scout carryall with money he had saved from work he had done on a farm during summers before he went to MIT.

At times we thought he was being cured by time. He could talk with anyone and be wholly rational on any subject – except religion. He planned to go back to MIT after the class he started with graduated. He told me honestly that he was afraid he might attack the boys who gave him LSD if he went to MIT while they were still students there. Doctors told us there was a chance of having him committed for his mental aberrations. He could make a fool of anyone, with his great intellect, when he chose to do so. I suffered a heart attack when I tried to reason with him and became angry to the point of hysteria when his mind parried every reasonable argument I could make.

Suicide Said Objective

After that, both he and I were afraid to talk seriously about religion. He continued to believe Jesus Christ was the devil incarnate who came to earth to destroy the true religion Larry Harmon found in the first five books of the Old Testament.

I know now, with as much certainty as one can have in such a tangled matter, that he went to St. Aloysius Church yesterday to commit suicide. He could not stand it that no one would listen to the distorted "truth" he found in hallucinations from two LSD pills.

So he killed so he would be killed. I know it is true. His mother knows it is true. May God have mercy on his soul. ...

Prior to this incident, his son had previously traveled to Israel and desecrated a shrine of Jesus, for which he was jailed. It had taken the work of a congressman and the U.S. Embassy to gain his release at that time. This appeared to be a sign of future problems.

Harry McKeever – hired by the Spokane Police Department in 1950

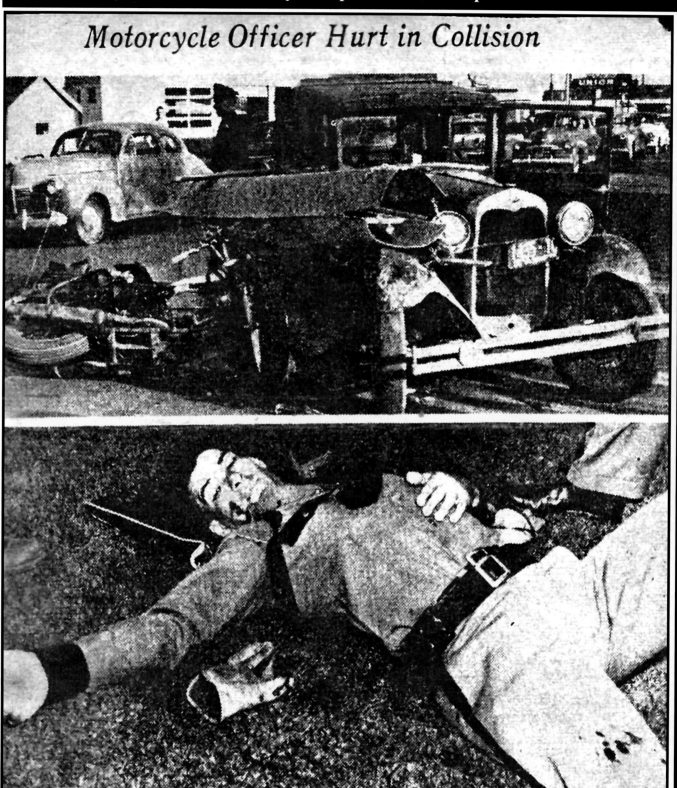

Motorcycle Officer Hurt in Collision

The caption under this late 1940s *Spokane Daily Chronicle* photo stated: "Motorcycle Policeman Harry A. McKeever lies on his back while waiting for an ambulance to take him to a hospital for emergency treatment. McKeever suffered multiple injuries when the motorcycle he was riding collided with a 1929 model pickup truck, at Nevada and Broad, early last night. The driver was charged with negligent driving." *(Public domain)*

S P O K A N E   P O L I C E   D E P A R T M E N T

A detail from Harry McKeever's Police Academy graduation class. Harry is in the top row, second from left, with arrow marking him. *(Courtesy Spokane Police Department Archives)*

Jack Latta – hired by the Spokane Police Department in 1951

Jack Latta after he finished the Aviation Cadet Program, during World War II, in 1943. *(Courtesy Jack Latta)*

A graduate of North Central, Jack Latta worked for Inland Motor Freight while still going to high school. Following high school in 1943, at age 19, he enlisted in the Army during World War II and was sent to the Aviation Cadet Program, becoming a B-24 pilot. During his military time, he flew 45 combat missions over the Philippines. He recalls bombing a Japanese oil depot in Borneo and seeing flames shoot into the sky. To avoid the flames he put his plane into a descent to gain speed. Jack's plane was dubbed "Squirrely Shirley" with the typical pinup girl painted on its side.

While overseas, Latta survived a plane crash in bad weather. That day, the pilot decided to circle the runway hoping for improved visibility, but the storm continued. As they tried to land, the wing tip and propeller struck the ground and the plane collapsed onto its belly, sliding into a gully full of rain water.

Jack had a talent for operating motorized equipment that served him well in the military and later in his vocation. Following the war, Jack worked for the Coca-Cola Bottling Company and Seven-up Bottling Company. While working for Coca-Cola, one of his jobs was to run a forklift. During that time, he developed a special skill of being able to pick up momentum from one side of the building and then stealthily slide sideways with the forklift into a perfect position to enable picking up a pallet. His boss was so impressed that one day he gathered everyone around and had Jack conduct a demonstration of how that was done.

In 1947, Jack married Patricia Courser. They had been married for 69 years when Jack died in 2016. They had two sons, three grandchildren, and four great-grandchildren.

Jack joined the Spokane Police Department in 1951. He spent his first year on routine police assignments. When the year's probation period was up in 1952, he was assigned to motorcycle patrol, where he remained until retirement.

During the 1957 Labor Day Weekend, Elvis Presley made his first visit to Spokane. He traveled for two days by train from Memphis, arriving on August 29th at 11:20 p.m. Spokane was the first stop on a four-day, five-city tour in the Pacific Northwest. He arrived at the Great Northern Depot and was taken to the Ridpath Hotel by limousine. Elvis stayed in his room all the next day. Fans, mostly young girls, stormed the lobby with hopes of getting a look at and possibly an autograph from the rock-and-roll star. Later that evening, he held a press conference in his dressing room at Memorial Stadium (now Joe Albi) at about 8:00 p.m.

Fifty off-duty uniformed officers, hired by the stadium and the releasing company, had their hands full even though the crowd was orderly. The crowd jammed the west stands of the stadium, sitting in the aisles, disregarding any assigned ticketing. Those arriving late with "elite tickets" were out of luck, as it was impossible to make the mass of humanity move. Officers made no attempt to sort it out as they formed a double cordon for the Cadillac carrying Elvis.

During his last song, Elvis jumped off the stage onto the track and sang "Hound Dog" while kneeling in the dirt. After he left the stadium, mobs rushed from the stands onto the track, grabbing dirt while screaming. The crowd was estimated at 12,000.

Spokane police officers John Bevins, Jack Lindell, and Jack Latta were hired specifically to act as se-

curity for Elvis. According to retired Officer Jack Latta: "We were all organized and planned to give Elvis and his entourage a motorcycle escort from the train to the hotel. Elvis decided he didn't want one, saying that he just wanted to be on his own. We followed the limousine to the stadium the next day for the concert and stood by the stage in case things got out of hand. I spent quite a bit of time talking with Elvis' dad. He was a very down-to-earth person and talked quite a bit about his son."

During his tenure as a motorcycle officer, Latta dealt with numerous incidents involving violence, from bank robberies to family fights to assaults. Once, in the early 1960s, Latta had just received the description of a bank robber, over his police radio. The man had just robbed the American Commercial Bank at

A B-24 bomber, the type Latta flew. The B-24 had ten .50-cal. machine guns and could carry 8,000 pounds of bombs. Its maximum speed was 303 mph and cruising speed was 175 mph. It had a range of 2,850 miles and could fly as high as 28,000 feet. Its wingspan was 110 feet and its length was 66 ft. 4 inches with a height of 17 ft. 11 inches. It weighed 56,000 pounds loaded and cost: $336,000. There were more B-24s manufactured during World War II than any other bomber. A total of 18,000 B-24s were produced. *(Courtesy Jack Latta)*

Jack Latta, front row second from right, when he graduated from the Police Academy and received his Certificate of Award in 1951. *(Courtesy Jack Latta)*

Elvis's press conference in Spokane, 1957, photographed in the building at the north end of Albi Stadium (then called Memorial Stadium). The building is now used primarily as a team dressing room. The four KNEW disc jockeys pictured with Elvis are, from left: Bob Hough, Bob Salter, Bob Adkins, and Bob Fleming. SPD Officer Leroy Cummings is in the upper right part of the photo. *(Photo courtesy Bob Hough)*

Fifth and Washington. Within minutes he spotted a man fitting that description and arrested him.

In 1961, Latta responded to an exchange-of-gunfire call. A would-be robber had just been in a shoot-out with a druggist at the West End Pharmacy at Monroe Street and Sprague Avenue. The robber and the druggist had both exchanged gunfire. The owner of the drugstore, Fred Olsen, had been shot in the face and shoulder. In return, he had shot the gunman in the head and the arm.

At the time of the call, Latta was on his motorcycle working the downtown area and quickly responded. When he arrived at the scene, he followed a trail of blood in the snow to the Herald Hotel on South Lincoln Street. He found the gunman, William Meeds, behind the bloody door of the third floor rest room still holding his gun in his hand. Latta disarmed and arrested him.

During Jack's career, he pulled a suicidal jumper off the Monroe Street Bridge and ended up in a fight with him. The man was later shot to death by a police officer in California.

Latta also survived another close call. He was hurrying to an accident scene on his motorcycle when a car pulled out in front of him. He tried to avoid the collision but hit some gravel, causing the bike to

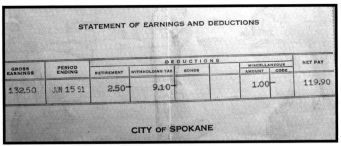

Jack's "Statement of Earnings and Deductions" for his first month on the Police Department. His gross earnings were $132.50, with $2.50 cents for retirement, $9.50 withholding tax, and $1.00 for Miscellaneous, leaving him with $119.90 take-home pay. In 1951, he was making almost .75 cents (take home) an hour for being a policeman.

drop under the car. He flew over the top but was OK. During his entire career, he was fortunate to have only been involved in two motorcycle accidents.

During the winter months, before the police motors got electric starters, officers switched to riding in cars during bad weather because the motorcycles were hard to start. During those times, Latta would hook a rope on the back of his big Chrysler, make two wraps around the center of his handlebars, and his wife would pull him to get the bike started.

In 1967, Jack received a 250,000-mile pin from the Harley-Davidson Company. He also received an engraved Harley-Davidson belt buckle.

At the time of his death in 2016, Jack Latta had the distinction of being the longest continuous motorcycle officer in department history, going back to the days the police rode motorcycles year-round. At the time of his retirement, in 1981, he had badge #1, meaning he had more seniority on the police department than anyone else.

Jack loved riding motorcycles and was a "motor bull" for 29 years. His entire career was filled with numerous incidents dealing with both the good and bad of society. When Jack retired, he left the department with a reputation for integrity. Jack was one of those guys everybody looked up to and was an asset to Spokane.

Spokane Police Training School

SPOKANE, WASHINGTON

Certificate of Award

Certifying that _John E. Latta_

Has satisfactorily completed a General Course of Instruction afforded by the

Spokane Police Training School

For a period of _One Month_ ending _October 31, 1951_ and by these presents; as a law enforcement officer, is entitled to the professional standing that accrues with this achievement.

Certificate of Award Jack Latta received when he graduated Spokane Police Academy on October 31, 1951, signed by Police Chief Clyde Phelps. *(Courtesy Jack Latta)*

These photos are of Jack Latta feature the different styles and colors of the department's uniforms. Sometime during the 1950s, the department had switched uniform colors. Another interesting fact – up until 1966, none of the police motorcycles had electric starting. To help the motorcycle during starting, the left handle-grip was designed to retard or advance the spark. This prevented the motor from backfiring during starts. Also, if you note from the photos on this and the subsequent pages, the left side of the motorcycle has a gear shift that goes up the side of the gas tank and the clutch was above the left foot board. This was necessary on the police motors, as they needed a reverse, when the side cars were attached.

Jack served as a loan officer for the Police Credit Union for 22 years and was vice president for ten of those years. It is now called the Spokane Law Enforcement Credit Union. He was also a member of the "Blue Knights" and "Goldwing Club." During that time, he participated in many rides around the country, including two large motorcycle gatherings at Sturgis, South Dakota. *(Courtesy Jack Latta)*

Jack Latta on his police motorcycle with his son peeking out of the sidecar. *(Courtesy Jack Latta)*

Jack Latta, circa 1963, with his son who was about to start Gonzaga Prep. *(Newsclipping courtesy Jack Latta)*

Jack Latta, circa 1967 at a Shriners Hospital function. *(Courtesy Jack Latta)*

From left at Shriners Hospital: Larry Williamson, Dick Edgar, Art Kathman, Mel Griffiths, and Jack Latta with an unidentified patient. *(Courtesy Jack Latta)*

From left: Bob Browning, Floyd Jones, Chuck Sorini, Mel Griffiths, Jack Latta, and Alve Burrell.
(Courtesy Jack Latta)

The Spokane Police Department Traffic Division at the old Coliseum in December 1967. This was the year that motorcycles were replaced by squad cars for use in the winter or rainy weather. Prior to this time, the motorcycle officer rode motor year around, using sidecars during the winter months. The change was a good thing, as during the winter months, motorcycles were not too functional. The radar cars are on the left. At the back of the photo are the hit-and-run detail and traffic patrol cars. In the front are the three-wheel motorcycles used downtown, plus the three scooters used by meter maids. In front at the right are Lt. Calvin Smith, day shift traffic commander, and Sgt. Leroy Cumming. First Row: Michael Kusterer, Jack Latta, June House, Genevieve Tuefert, Rose Weeden, Floyd Jones, and Angelo Costanzo. At far left with radar cars: Robert Browning and Alve Burrell. Back Row: Melvin Griffiths, John Morris, Clifford Barclay, Charles Johnson, Louis Vela, Danny Naccarato, Fred Mielke, and Mickey O'Brien. *(Courtesy Spokane Police Department Archives)*

The Latta family, from left: Kip, Jack, Patricia, and Lance. *(Courtesy Jack Latta)*

Jack and Patricia Latta. *(Courtesy Jack Latta)*

Jack and Patricia, 2015. *(Bamonte photo)*

Chuck Sorini – hired by the Spokane Police Department in 1951

Spokane Police Inspector Robert Piper in sidecar, with Chuck Sorini, circa 1963. *(Courtesy Jack Latta)*

As a motorcycle officer patrolling in the northeast section of Spokane, Chuck Sorini heard a call over his police radio that a baby had stopped breathing. The call came from the 1300 block of East Bismark. He was close by and responded quickly. The mother, with baby in her arms, said, "My baby is dead! Do something." She then handed the child to Sorini. The baby was three months old and had a blue face. Chuck took the baby, opened its mouth and with his finger felt inside and pulled out a chunk of pablum. He then breathed into the baby's mouth and gave CPR for ten minutes until the fire department ambulance arrived. The baby was rushed to Sacred Heart Hospital. Sorini was advised he had saved the child's life. Sorini worked accident investigations for over 13 years. He was later promoted and went into the detective division.

The man in the sidecar (above photo) was Robert Piper, who came on the department in 1929. When he retired in 1967, he had been on the department for over 38 years. Chief Clifford Payne had originally appointed Piper to the position of inspector in 1958, a position held until his retirement at age 67. The photo was taken during the Lilac Parade. Every year, when he was inspector, he always rode in a sidecar during the parade and always chose Chuck Sorini to be his driver.

Robert "Bob" James Grandinetti – hired by the Spokane Police Department in 1967

Bob Grandinetti with Cami, age four, one of his two daughters, July 1970. *(Courtesy Beverly Grandinetti)*

Bob Grandinetti was born in Spokane in 1937. His parents were Carmen and Carmella Grandinetti from Kellogg, Idaho, where his father worked for the Northern Pacific Railway.

When they moved to Spokane, Bob and his family lived on South Ralph Street. In Spokane, Bob attended Sheridan Grade School, Libby Junior High, and Lewis & Clark High School. Following high school, Bob joined the Air Force Reserves. He later enrolled at Eastern Washington College, which he attended for two years. During Bob's earlier years, he was quite proficient on the drums. He originally learned to play in high school. Later he played in the Air Force Band and, following his discharge from the military, he played for numerous popular bands around the area. He was one of the few drummers who could read music.

S P O K A N E   P O L I C E   D E P A R T M E N T

Bob and Beverly Grandinetti's wedding day on September 19, 1964. According to Bob, it was the best and happiest day of his life. *(Courtesy Beverly Grandinetti)*

Bob met his wife, Beverly Meyer, in 1962, while they were both attending Saint Ann's Catholic Church in Spokane, where they both belonged to the same youth group. They were putting on a play at the time. They were married in 1964 and had three children: Cami, born in 1966; Kimberly, born in 1971; and Rob, born in 1976. As of this writing, Kimberly is a pediatrician, and both Cami and Rob are civil engineers working for the Environmental Protection Agency.

Bob joined the Spokane Police Department in 1967. While in Patrol, he was assigned to various duties, enjoying them all. From there, he was assigned to the Traffic Division, where he rode motor from 1970 to 1974, later working hit-and-run cases. From 1982 to 1990, he worked Community Services and from 1990 to 1998 he worked Operational Management. During his tenure on the department, his older brother John (also on the police department) was his biggest influence.

The School Santa Safety Program

Bob worked the School Safety Santa Program for over 25 years. Before this program was formalized in the early 1900s, officers would take unclaimed items, such as bicycles, in the property room, and distribute them, in secret, to needy children on Christmas Eve after the children had gone to bed. The School Santa Safety Program sought to educate young people on child safety. Originally created by a Spokane police officer, the tradition continued through the dedication of the officers, who faithfully kept the program alive until the mid-1990s. The School Santa Safety Program took place each December when an officer dressed in a Santa suit visited Spokane elementary schools to talk to students and teachers about personal safety. Each visit concluded with gifts and holiday cards donated by local Spokane businesses. Over the decades many officers have donated much of their time to the Santa Program.

The program began in the 1940s, when Donald Lussier played the role, followed by Art Corbett in the 1950s. Ralph Weir took "the mantle" for a few years before Harold Tucker, who was one of the longest tenured Santas (for 15 years), followed by Bob Grandinetti, who served the department and the children of Spokane for many years. Duane Willmschen did a short stint before the program was permanently retired. This program has transitioned into the Shop with a Cop program.

Santa (Bob Grandinetti) visiting a school, circa 1978. *(Courtesy Beverly Grandinetti)*

Santa and the kids, circa 1978. *(Courtesy Beverly Grandinetti)*

From the *Spokesman-Review*, circa 1978, Dan Pelle photo: "THERE HE GOES! Teresa Kelly's third-graders at Spokane's Stevens Elementary School didn't get a chance to hear safety tips from the police department's Safety Santa. But that didn't stop some of them from sneaking a peek at the red-suited visitor this week as he continued his season's meandering and made his way to another school."

Bob Grandinetti with his daughter Kimberly in 1972.
(Courtesy Beverly Grandinetti)

Grandinetti family, from left: Kimberly, Cami, Santa, Beverly, and Rob, circa 1975. *(Courtesy Beverly Grandinetti)*

Grandinetti family from left: Kimberly, Cami, Santa, and Rob, circa 1979. *(Courtesy Beverly Grandinetti)*

Grandinetti family, seated left to right: Rob, Santa and Kimberly. Standing: Cami and Beverly, circa 1985. *(Courtesy Beverly Grandinetti)*

The Spokane Country and Western Music Scene
(Written by Duane Becker for *Nostalgia Magazine, permission given for this publication*)

Previous articles on Spokane's country and western music scene in *Nostalgia Magazine* have focused on the popularity of country and western bands in the 1940s and '50s. With radio playing a big part in the bands promotion, most all of the bands had their own 15 or 30 minute radio show.

There was a change brewing starting in the 1960s for local country and western music in Spokane. Radio was going another direction and no longer featured local shows. There were a few locally produced music television shows but these all were dropped by 1965. KXLY-TV's and later KHQ-TV's Starlit Stairway was the last to feature local talent. However, this did not stop Spokane's musicians. From about 1960 to the mid-1980s, nightly dinner and dancing to country and western music was a feature at almost all Spokane night clubs. The Pine Shed, The Stardust, The Slab Inn and the bars at State Line all had country music five and six nights a week. Even the small taverns and private clubs had music at least on Friday and Saturday nights.

Most bands concentrated on playing bars, as grange halls dances were few and far between. The 1960s produced a string of great local musicians playing country music in Spokane.

Robert Dennis McNutt, or Dennis Roberts as he was known to his friends and musicians, began to play music while attending high school in Ritzville, Washington. At a young age, Dennis took vocal coaching lessons to sing Opera, but his love for country music led him in a different direction. He soon moved to Spokane, starting a 40 year career as a bass guitar player and singer. By 1965, Dennis was a full time sideman playing with everyone in Spokane. In March of 1966, Dennis was involved in a near fatal late night auto accident while driving back to Spokane from a gig in Davenport, Washington. Dennis was severely injured but did recover. Dennis not only played and sang country, but he also performed pop tunes just as well. He was featured for many years at the Davenport Hotel and at the Highland House with his own band, The Dennis Roberts Trio. Sadly, Dennis passed away from cancer in 2003. He was highly regarded as one of Spokane's best singers.

"Remembering Gary 'Duck' Lewis, This popular band called The Country Squires, played the El Patio on a regular basis from 1959 through 1961. The band would continue as a group after leaving the El Patio for several years up until approximately 1966, playing various private clubs and bars throughout the Spokane area.

Mention must be made here regarding bass guitar player Paul Valsvig: Paul was one of the premier bass guitar players in the Spokane area. He was noted for his excellent musicianship not only in country but also early rock and roll, swing, and jazz. Paul started playing music at an early age. He was influenced by his mother Pauline who was a long-time piano player for social tea dances at the Sinto and Northstar senior citizen clubs in Spokane. During the mid-1960s through the early 70s, Paul played the Kon Tiki lounge at the State Line, Idaho. He later worked the The Mainsail located on the corner of Washington and Boone in Spokane and the old Heritage Inn, north of town, in what was called Heritage Village. During Expo '74, Paul played banjo in the Expo Dixie Band. The band continued on for several years after Expo playing special events and concerts. Paul still plays today. His vocal range, from low bass to high baritone was and still is extraordinary. He has been a very well-known country bass guitar player and singer for many years. Currently, you can find Paul playing casual dates in Spokane at venues including the Eagles Club on Francis.

Harry Carr, vocals and rhythm guitar; Bob Grandinetti, drums; Paul Valsvig, vocals and bass guitar; and seated is Lee Lessig, steel guitar, all members of a popular band, the Country Squires. Dennis Roberts later replaced Paul Valsvig on bass. Photo circa 1950. *(Courtesy Beverly Grandinetti)*

Thurs., Nov. 27, 1986

ST. LOUIS POST-DISPATCH

'Mr. Glad' Is Chief Of The Odd Squad

He takes the calls that no one else knows how to handle

By Karen McGrath
Of the Associated Press

SPOKANE, Wash.

OFFICIALLY, it's called the Office of Special Police Problems. Unofficially, they call it the Odd Squad.

Mainly, it's Patrolman Robert Grandinetti, a 20-year veteran of the Spokane Police Department, who has a face like Fred Flintstone and a personality that's earned him the nickname of "Mr. Glad."

Grandinetti's easygoing nature made him the perfect candidate for the Odd Squad, where he and a partner take care of all of the police calls no one else knows how to handle.

They deal with problems like the woman who had 67 dead cats stored in her freezer, piles of debris in her home, street kids who sleep in vacant buildings, the elderly who are easily exploited out of their life savings, sorry hobos who subsist on occasional meals and cheap wine, and so on

Patrolman Robert Grandinetti of Special Police Problems in Spokane, Wash.

During the time Bob Grandinetti worked for the Office of Special Police Problems, he became somewhat of a legend throughout the United States. The above news article gave a description of his duties and accomplishments. He was the perfect person for that job, as he had the kindness and patience to deal with those who needed a friend the most. The article appears below. *(Courtesy Beverly Grandinetti)*

The following article, by Karen McGrath of the Associated Press, appeared in the *Spokesman-Review* on November 27, 1986:

THE ODD SQUAD
'MR. GLAD' IS CHIEF OF THE ODD SQUAD
He takes the calls that
no one else knows how to handle

Officially, it's called the Office of Special Police Problems. Unofficially, they call it the Odd Squad. Mainly, it's patrolman Robert Grandinetti, a 20-year veteran of the Spokane Police Department, who has a face like Fred Flintstone and a personality that's earned him the nickname of "Mr. Glad."

Grandinetti's easy-going nature made him the perfect candidate for the Odd Squad, where he and a partner take care of all the police calls no one else knows how to handle.

They deal with problems like the woman who had 67 dead cats stored in her freezer, another with four-foot piles of debris in her home, street kids who sleep in vacant buildings, the elderly who are easily exploited out of their life savings, sorry hobos who subsist on occasional meals and cheap wine, and so on. "We have situations where you deal with them, or we'll be dealing with their remains," Grandinetti says. "I do what any reasonable person would do. I can't walk away from it. I've got to do something." The work started in 1974, with a grant from the state Department of Ecology intended to help clean up Spokane for its World Exposition.

Grandinetti's training included years on the force and the empathy he gained by watching his dad Carmen die a painfully slow death years before. Today, Grandinetti believes doctors would say he suffered from Alzheimer's disease. "I have real compassion because I understand," Grandinetti says. "I know it's easy to make fun of people who are suffering, but I always think, you could end up like any of them."

Grandinetti views arrest as a last resort. He says he's discovered that humor and friendliness are valuable tools when dealing with the public.

Working the department's graveyard patrol shift 15 years ago, Grandinetti and his partner received a call about a woman having a problem at her home. "We get there and she says she keeps hearing voices, coming out of her sink. So I scratch my head a while and then walk over to the sink and bend over and yell 'Shaddup', down the drain hole. "The woman tells me the voices are gone, but my partner looks at me as if I'm crazy."

His current partner is patrolman D. V. Willmschen, one of 13 officers who applied to join the Odd Squad last year when the operation fell hopelessly behind in its calls.

"He's excellent to work with" Willmschen, says, "I take the bulk of the nuisance calls. Bob was more social, especially when you deal with the elderly." Even with Willmschen's assistance, the squad, which enforces the city's public nuisance ordinance, is 200 to 300 calls behind, Grandinetti says. He and Willmschen now act on only the most important calls – those in which life may be in danger.

The Odd Squad's tiny office, which also serves as a police storage room, has an answering machine. The two officers are rarely there. Police chief Robert Panther credits Grandinetti with a superb performance.

Like the rest of city government, the Odd Squad is threatened by 1987 budget cuts. Still, it's a bright spot for a department hit hard recently by scandals ranging from a former female officer's charges of sex discrimination – a suit eventually settled out of court – to a recently fired corporal who kept evidence photos of nude, battered women in his locker.

Social workers in other agencies say eliminating the Odd Squad would leave many people out in the cold.

"Bob averts a lot of problems that could get bigger," says Bob Hansen, an official with the state Department of Social and Health Services. "He's unique in that he's got a real social conscience and compassion for people in addition to, or even greater than, his law-enforcement presence."

The pitiful situations he deals with sometimes wear on Grandinetti. He cites the case of the woman who had 12 cats. "Well, something had to be done. We told her she could keep three cats The people up at the animal shelter said she would come up every evening and hold every cat until she had decided which three she wanted to keep. They were like her children.

As Grandinetti steered his unmarked police jeep through downtown Spokane he talked about his wife and three children. His oldest daughter is a University of Washington freshman and carries a 3.6 grade point average in civil engineering. His second daughter is a high school freshman, and the son is a fifth-grader who has just started playing the drums – his Dad's instrument.

Grandinetti became a police officer in September 1967 after deciding he needed to give his family more financial security than was provided by his job playing drums in bars at Stateline, Idaho.

As the Police Department's official Santa Claus, each December he visits every Spokane grade school in his red and white suit, taking along candy, Christmas cards and safety tips.

Whether working with children or adults, Grandinetti keeps in mind the same things. "A lot of people are dealing with a police officer for the first time," he says, "each time, the situation is a big thing to them."

"I don't downplay it. To them, their situation is the most important thing in the world. So you give them your time. If you don't, you turn them off."

Bob Grandinetti's Connection With One of America's Most Violent and Murderous Serial-Killer Gangs:

The Freight Train Riders of America (FTRA)
(Information from Wikipedia)

In 1978, Officer Bob Grandinetti was assigned as a special police problems officer. As a part of his duties, he was given the assignment of monitoring the transients living along the Spokane River and the train tracks. He was responsible for conducting camp sweeps in order to relocate the transients from the downtown area.

During these sweeps, he discovered a criminal gang element living among the transient population. That element was called the Freight Train Riders of America (FTRA). This was a group of people who rode the rails committing violent crimes against other freight train riders and transients. His investigation, the first and most thorough look into this problem, lasted for over 15 years. As a result, Grandinetti uncovered one of the nation's most violent group of serial killers. Within this group there were also undertones of racism as shown by graffiti left by members.

The Freight Train Riders of America's turf covered a large area, making these cases especially hard to prove. However, it seemed that a serial killer was murdering hobos. The victims were commonly shot in the head at close range with a small caliber pistol while they slept. Ten murdered hobos were found along the rail lines between Cheney, Washington and Rathdrum, Idaho. They all had their shirts pulled over their heads and their pants twisted around their ankles.

Grandinetti stated: "Most members carry knives and axe handles they refer to as 'goonie sticks.' Officials have identified a "Goon Squad" within the gang that was responsible for many violent attacks. They're a criminal gang who will beat you for a buck and kill you for $5.00. You can't trust them and you can't turn your back on them." According to Grandinetti, over 160 members had been convicted of either rape or homicide. "To me, that's a lot."
Grandinetti took a camera along during his morning raids of transient camps, documenting the lives of the drifters passing through town. Graffiti marking the FTRA territory was found under railroad overpasses, in switch yards, on boxcars, switch boxes, and buildings in the Spokane area. The gang used swastikas, lightning bolts, and the letters FTRA, FTW (F--- the world), STP (Start the Party), and ATAPAW (Any Time, Any Place, Any Where). These messages would let other FTRA members know they were in the area and where they were headed.

Grandinetti discovered and released the information on FTRA to other law enforcement officials across the United States. As a result, he became the leading authority on that gang. Consequently, three national TV shows: America Most Wanted, 20/20, and station A&E, filmed documentaries on the FTRA. Also, local Northwest television shows provided coverage of the problem.

Following, and as a result of, Grandinetti's work, police believed the FTRA might be responsible for hundreds of deaths, beatings, and thefts along railroads that began in the 1980s. These were murders of hard-to-locate and homeless people, were exceptionally hard to investigate, and in most cases, weren't major news events. To make things worse, when Grandinetti first began his investigation, railroad officials passed these deaths off as accidental and referred to the FTRA as an urban legend that soon was shown to be factual. Before long, Grandinetti's hypothesis was proven, and he was consistently contacted by numerous law enforcement agencies throughout the nation requesting information, which he always provided, and which typically proved beneficial.

Grandinetti stated: "While little was known about the FTRA, joining appeared to be a private, violent process during which 'prospects' were beaten, women associated with the gang were raped, and loyalty was tested. These guys are basically serial killers, tying a urine-soaked FTRA bandana around a recruit's neck and securing it with the honored clasp in a rowdy, public ritual, usually fueled by alcohol and methamphetamines. Sometimes they killed each other, which was the cost of doing business within the gang. Grandinetti compiled documentation on approximately 800 known and suspected FTRA members and noted that up into the 1990s there were more than 300 unsolved murders along the rails during the decade. He suspected that many of these murders could be attributed to the FTRA.

There were a growing number of illegal immigrants and entire migrant families riding the rails. It also became a fad for college students and adventurous Yuppies to hop a freight car just for fun. This activity was considered highly insulting to most of the hobo train hoppers and especially by the FTRA. Many of these "outsiders" were robbed, beaten, or suffered worse consequences at the hands of the genuine transients.

The FTRA systematically stole high value merchandise from the trains and committed burglaries around the train yards. The Union Pacific Railroad reported taking more than 30 burglary reports per day at the Colton Yard in San Bernardino, California. Firearms and high value items were sold for large profits to the drug cartels of Mexico. The FTRA committed armed robberies near the railroad tracks and would immediately hop a freight car out of town.

A book about the Freight Train Riders of America details Grandinetti's work

The following is a quote from:

Murder on the Rails,
by William G. Palmini and Tanya Chalupa

According to retired 34-year police veteran of the Albany California, Police Department, Bill Palmini, he investigated the most notorious murderer and FTRA member,

Officer Bob Grandinetti as he is about to check on a hobo camp, circa 1979. *(Courtesy Beverly Grandinetti)*

Officer Bob Grandinetti photographs a suspected FTRA member at a transient camp near the Freya Street Bridge in 1997. *(Spokesman-Review, public domain)*

"Side Track," or Robert Silveria. His book describes how Spokane, Washington, police officer Bob Grandinetti began documenting the FTRA gang early in the 1980s. He describes how Grandinettti closely followed a series of reported bodies along the High Line between Spokane and Sandpoint, Idaho. Many of the victims had their shirts and jackets pulled up around their heads and their pants pulled down. Grandinetti suspects that many of these murders are attributed to members of the FTRA, but the cases were especially hard to prove. In a snuff magazine article by Christopher Ketcham (2/28/03) Grandinetti is quoted as saying, "The problem is the suspects and all the witnesses disappear."

In his book Palmini describes Silveria as a scarecrow-like heroin addict who had a tattoo of the word freedom on his throat. Eventually Side Track was connected to the FTRA and several of these unsolved railroad murders. He was featured on "America's Most Wanted" and dubbed the "Boxcar Killer" by the media. After his arrest, he confessed to a five-year nationwide murder spree ranging from Florida to California.

According to Palmini, "One of his victims was college student Michael Garfinkle, who was on a weekend odyssey when Side Track murdered him in a hobo jungle in the switching yard outside Emeryville, Calif. Mostly Silveria preyed on the helpless homeless, killing them for their clothing and social security cards. He confessed to 14 of the unsolved murders.

America's Most Wanted television show identified other FTRA members involved in numerous killings, including Spokane resident Hugh "Dog Man Tony" Ross, who rode with Silveria for years. The FBI and over 20 law enforcement agencies were involved in the case, evolving out of information originally supplied by Officer Grandinetti.

In 1992, Ross was convicted in Spokane County of first-degree armed robbery and sentenced to 41 months in prison. Eighteen months later, he walked away from his Airway Heights Correctional Center work crew while weeding a Liberty Lake golf course. A few days later, he was captured in Royal City, Washington.

Numerous police agencies identified specific members of the FTRA in dozens of homicide investigations throughout the country. Many turned to Officer Grandinetti to help identify, track and jail these murderers. "It took me a little while to pick up on what was going on," said Grandinetti. "I don't trust any of these guys. I guess they respect me because they know I have a gun." At his office, stacks of records, warrants, and tips overwhelmed the officer's desk. The information was constantly being shared with FBI agents, district attorneys, and detectives from around the country. Grandinetti developed over 800 criminal profiles of suspected FTRA members, including pictures, criminal records, and fingerprints. Although Grandinetti has been retired since 1998, he still has two large bins of information on the FTRA.

The following story appeared in the *Spokesman-Review* on July 30, 1997:

Killers Ride The Rails – Spokane Officer Tracks Elusive Gang of Transients Suspected of Murders Nationwide
by Robin Rivers
Reporter for the *Spokesman-Review*

A racist gang of hobos may be responsible for as many as 300 transient murders across the nation in the last decade, including at least 10 in Spokane, Kootenai, and Bonner counties, authorities say. Police are identifying specific members of the Freight Train Riders of America, thought to number 2,000, in dozens of homicide investigations.

They are turning to Spokane police officer Bob Grandinetti, a nationally recognized FTRA expert, to help identify, track and jail the elusive drifters.

Transients suspected in the killings claim the gang is a hoax intended to intimidate and scare off casual boxcar riders. To rail riders, the threat is very real. Mere men-

Robert Joseph Silveria Jr., also known as "The Boxcar Killer," is an American serial killer currently serving a double life sentence in Oregon for the murders of William Pettit Jr. and Michael Andrew Clites in December 1995. Silveria was also convicted in Kansas for the killing of Charles Randall Boyd and in Florida for the killing of Willie Clark. Silveria had confessed to murdering 28 people. *(Public domain)*

tion of the train gang evokes unmistakable fear. At a Spokane rail yard recently, Grandinetti approached a scraggly, middle-aged couple gobbling hot dogs and beer under the Freya Street bridge. "Are you FTRA?" he demanded. They yanked the necks of their shirts down to reveal skin where FTRA bandannas would hang. Stop messing with us, they screamed. "Find the guys who are killing people!" the woman raged as she rose from the filth. "Find the guys who killed Horizontal John. I'm scared, man." Under the same bridge, the body of a fellow drifter, 46-year-old Horizontal John, turned up earlier this month. Natural causes, the coroner said. Transients think the gang claimed another victim. Grandinetti thinks they're probably right.

On the average, three transients die each year along rail lines in Spokane; 70 to 90 died along tracks nationwide, according to police and the FBI. Few of the cases involving foul play are solved.

"Let's face it, most people just don't give a damn if a transient dies," said Salem, Ore., police detective Mike Quakenbush, who recently was involved in the arrest of alleged serial killer and FTRA leader Robert Silveria.

Hugh "Dog Man Tony" Ross. *(Public domain)*

An overall glimpse of freight rain riders

In the United States, freight-train hopping had become a common means of transportation following the American Civil War, as the railroads began building to the west. This was especially popular among migrant workers. This form of transportation was widely used by those unable to afford other means of transportation, especially during the Great Depression. During those times it was far more acceptable to hop the freight trains due to the poverty of the general population. Freight-train hopping is far less common today. However, most important, it is a far different and more dangerous clientele who today engage in that practice.

Freight-train riding is extremely dangerous in many ways. A large percentage of freight train riders are ex-convicts or felons, not yet caught. Consequently, violence is common among that group. Train hopping is also illegal, with increased security around railroads always a problem for freight-train riders.

Research into the lifestyle of train-hoppers, as well as the loose-organized "gangs" that exist on America's rail lines, points to more boxcar transients killed than any other group across the western states. Newer and much younger groups, such as the Wrongway Kids and the Crusty Punks, have also been implicated in criminal activity. There are also a number of separate so-called train gangs besides the random drifters that are common along the rails.

When asked who was the biggest influence in his life was, Bob referred to his brother, John, who was also on the Spokane Police Department from 1951 to 1978. During John's tenure on the department, he also went above and beyond his normal duties as a police officer in his investigation of a serial murderer in the city. (See sections on John Grandinetti and Dan Hite.)

Bob Grandinetti passed away in 2016. His was large and attended by many current and former police officers.

ABC News 20/20

December 12, 1998

Bob Grandinetti
5207 S. Dearborn
Spokane, WA. 99223

Dear Mr. Grandinetti,

I would like to express my warm appreciation for your cooperation with me and ABC News. I especially appreciated your providing us with pictures and a videotape which we are planning to use in our piece on *20/20*, and perhaps in other ABC News programs. I know that your cooperation with ABC News will enhance our coverage of the FTRA, which will be widely seen both in this country and internationally.

Once again, thank you for your cooperation and I hope that we are able to work together in the future.

Sincerely,

Jean M Alter

Jean Alter

John Anthony Grandinetti – hired by the Spokane Police Department in 1951

John Grandinetti, circa 1953. *(Courtesy Carol Johnson)*

S
P
O
K
A
N
E

P
O
L
I
C
E

D
E
P
A
R
T
M
E
N
T

John Grandinetti, front row fourth from the left, following his graduation from the Spokane Police Academy in 1951. The entire graduating class is as follows: front row: Air Force Patrolman (unidentified), SPD Officer John Doran, SPD Officer Joe Clark, SPD Officer John Grandinetti, SPD Officer Robert Ostrander, SPD Officer Jack Latta, and (unidentified) Air Force. Back Row: SPD Officer Charles Sorini, SPD Officer Alvin Halbig, unidentified FBI instructor, unknown, unknown, Chief Clyde Phelps, unknown Air Force, unknown Air Force, and SPD Asst. Chief John Lenhart. *(Courtesy Carol Johnson)*

John Grandinetti's parents, Carmen and Carmella Grandinetti, lived in Kellogg, Idaho, where his father worked as a carpenter. They later moved to Spokane where John was born on May 29, 1922. John had five siblings: Bob, Carl, Julie, Edward, and Fanny. In Spokane, John went to Sheridan Grade School, Libby Junior High, and Lewis and Clark High School. John was also the brother of Spokane police officer Bob Grandinetti (also included in this book).

When John graduated from high school in 1941, the military draft law was in effect. Not long after his graduation, he was drafted into the Army.

Following his discharge, on August 17, 1946, John married Lillian Francis Franklin. That relationship began as a result of Lillian's and John's parents' friendship. During the Grandinetti's frequent family visits with the Franklins, Grandinetti's son, John, and Franklin's daughter, Lillian, eventually began dating, which culminated in their marriage. During their marriage, Lillian gave birth to two boys and a girl. Their children, beginning with the oldest, were Christine, born in 1950, Carolyn, in 1953, and John, in 1960.

Prior to going on the police department, John worked for the Pepsi Cola Company. In 1951, he was hired by the Spokane Police Department. During that time John established a reputation of being one of the most respected and well-liked officers on the department. He was also known as an exceptionally kind man who worked hard to make a good life for his family. During his career, the majority of his time was spent in the traffic division, assigned to the traffic safety car and later as a traffic sergeant.

One of Spokane's most notorious cold cases, and one in which John played a major part, occurred on March 6, 1959, when nine-year-old Candy Rogers, a fourth grader, was abducted while she was selling mints for her Camp Fire Girls' troop.

The Spokane Police Department and Spokane County Sheriff's office immediately launched a search. Lawmen and volunteers swept the area for miles around. All known sex offenders in the area were questioned. Helicopters from nearby Fairchild Air Force Base were called in and also joined the search, circling above the search grid in a desperate effort to find her. During the height of this search another tragic fatal incident occurred when one of the helicopters crashed into the Spokane River, killing three airmen.

Sixteen days later, on March 22, 1959, hunters found a pair of girl's shoes in a remote field. Police were called and after a brief search located the remains of the missing girl. Candy lay in a clump of bushes, her body covered by pine boughs and brush. Her body had been discovered 12 miles from her home. Her legs were tied together at the ankles with parts of her own slip. "Candy had been raped and death was due to strangulation," Coroner William Jones said. Parts of her slip were found around her throat. The body, fully clothed except for her shoes and red leotard, was completely covered with underbrush except for one knee. "Death probably came on the night she disappeared," Jones said.

Almost three years after the murder, an amateur investigation took place by a Spokane motorcycle enthusiast belonging to a motorcycle club, Daniel L. Hite, who was also a mechanic at Brush Cycle Company, and Motorcycle Policeman John A. Grandinetti. They developed information that led to the arrest of a man named Hugh B. (Chris) Morse, 31.

Morse was a motorcycle enthusiast who belonged to the same motorcycle club as Hite. Hite also got to know Morse's mother, as she was the reason Morse eventually moved to Spokane. During a visit with the mother, Hite recalled that she was exceptionally excited that they were accepting her son into the motorcycle club as he had few friends.

John Grandinetti and his four-year-old daughter, Christine, standing next to the Spokane Police Department's Safety Education car in October 1957. *(Courtesy Carol Johnson)*

Hite and other club members are the ones who first became suspicious of him. In turn, Hite contacted Officer Grandinetti and passed the information the club had put together to him. This resulted in Grandinetti working the case on his own time. Soon, he became "convinced" there was a good case and enough probable cause to turn it over to the detective division. However, with requests from the detective division and his friendship with the motorcycle club members, he continued working the case with them. Hite and other members of the motorcycle club were high in their praise of the outstanding work Grandinetti accomplished from his cooperation and the information they gave to him.

At the time of the 1959 murder, DNA identification wasn't available. However, police had saved Candy's clothing as evidence. In 2002, a genetic profile was done comparing the victim's DNA. It didn't match the sample from Morse. However, circumstantial evidence against Morse was so strong that Spokane detectives weren't willing to dismiss him as a suspect even though comparatively recent DNA evidence seemed to clear him. There were too many other circumstances: Morse had a fondness for grape gum. He chewed grape gum all the time. Investigative files indicate grape gum was found at the scene of attacks in which two Spokane women were murdered and a third was severely beaten. Grape gum also was found in Morse's room when he was arrested. Most relevant to the involvement of Morse in this investigation was the fact that grape-smelling gum was smeared on Candy Rogers' sweater, coat and, possibly, her corduroy jumper. There was "quite a large quantity of this on her white Sweater," Spokane County Sheriff's Captain James Allen reported in March 1962.

Consequently, Spokane County Sheriff William Reilly still considered Morse the number one suspect. Sheriff's Capt. Allen, who interviewed Morse in the Minnesota State Prison at Stillwater, Minnesota in 1962, told a *Spokane Daily Chronicle* reporter that Morse denied killing Rogers, but was reluctant to talk about her. He said Morse told him, "If I did rape and kill Candy Rogers, I would probably be too ashamed to talk about it."

In April 2003 Morse died in a Minnesota prison while serving two life sentences for a September 1961 rape and murder in St. Paul. The Minnesota conviction ended a two-year, cross-country spree that put Morse on the FBI's Ten Most Wanted list.

Although Morse was never convicted of the Candy Rogers murder, solely based on the DNA test, there was enough other evidence to lead to the conclusion that he was a prime suspect in the murder of Candy Rogers in 1959.

John Grandinetti as a patrol sergeant, circa 1973.
(Courtesy Carol Johnson)

John and Lillian Grandinetti, circa 1985. *(Courtesy Carol Johnson)*

Dan Hite, Spokane's motorcycle mechanic, 1969-1990

CLEAN SWEEP CLIMB

Dan Hite tops both 45 and 80 inch events with Harley-Davidson in Montana State Championship Hillclimb

Report and Photos by Dave Epperson

MONTANANS caught triple "H" in their mid-June state championship Formula C hill climb at Billings. The Sunday afternoon of "H" came in the form of H-ack and H-arley—Dan Hite and Carman Hack, of Spokane, Wash., and Harley-Davidson of Milwaukee, Wis., that is.

Hite towed his pair of H-Ds over the Rockies from [Spok]ane to Billings—just to make a clean sweep of the places in the 45 cubic inch, 80 cubic inch and open hill [climb] events.

[C]armen Hack, also a Spokane H-D rider and Hite's [spar]ring partner, took home a share of the Billings payoff [with a] second place in the open and a third place in the [in]ch climb.

[T]hat's how the Montanans caught "H."

[T]imes for the 260-foot, 83 per cent grade hill were ex[celle]nt.

[I]n the open climb, Hite went over the hill in 7.05 [seco]nds. Hack's time was 7:15 seconds. Dale "Dode" Sel[leck] of Billings, former Montana hill climb champion was [fifth] with a 7.75-second ride aboard his BSA Spitfire. Troy [Geor]geson of Harlowtown, Mont., also on a Spitfire, made

the run in 7.8 seconds for fourth position. Donney Mullowney of Billings, mounting a Triumph TR-6, was fifth with a 7.9-second go at the hill.

The fact that there was less than a second time spread among the first five competitors in the open attests that the climb was a very, very good show. Fans in the Yellowstone River valley below the finish line held heavy hands on their auto horn buttons in appreciation for the riders spectacular show of skill.

In the 80 cubic inch event, Hite nipped off a cool 7 seconds flat for his first place win. Six-tenths of a second behind was Mullowney. Hack was third with 7.7 seconds Georgeson hit 8 seconds flat for fourth and Selleck was fifth with an 8.1-second grind.

Hite scored first in the 45 cubic inch climb with a 9.3 second ride. Speed Gulbranson of Great Falls, Montana astride a Triumph T-100-R, won second spot with a 9.35 second elapsed time for the uphill drag. Bob Slack, also of Great Falls and T-100-R mounted, was third with 9.8 seconds. Mac Henry of Helena, Montana, was fourth on his H-D climber with a 10.95 second ride. Ed Jellison of Billings, another T-100-R handler, took the number five slot with a time of 11.1 seconds for the course.

The Billings climb was open to either chains or tires And it was a perfect day for riders to test the traction

(Continued on Page 34)

[LEF]T: WHAT MAKES IT DO THAT?—Troy Georgeson [seem]s to be "seated" by his potent BSA Spitfire Scrambler.

[HO]W IT'S DONE—Dan Hite, of Spokane, Wash., shows [how] he made a clean sweep in three events with his [Harl]ey-Davidsons. He was declared Montana State Champ.

SURPRISED—Ed Jellison looks surprised as his Triumph T-100R turns up and over.

A September 1950 neW.S.P.aper motorcycle hill-climbing article about Dan Hite of Spokane. Hite went to work for Brush Cycle in 1957, working there for over ten years. In 1969, he went to work for the City of Spokane as the primary police motorcycle mechanic. He retired in 1990. *(Courtesy Dan Hite)*

Dan Hite at one of his racing events. *(Courtesy Dan Hite)*

Dan Hite at his home in Springdale, Washington, in March 2015. Dan was mayor of Springdale from 1994 to 2000. In this photo, Dan is holding a trophy of his 1959 National Hill Climb award. Inset is the plaque he received. *(Courtesy Dan Hite)*

The photos on the left are of Dan Hite at the city maintenance garage in a specific area used to work on police motors, which was assigned to Dan. He was the only mechanic allowed to work on all the police bikes. *(Bamonte photo)*

When Dan originally took the test to work for the city, he came out number one, going to work shortly after. When his boss at Brush Cycle found out he had taken the city test, he fired him.

Before Dan worked for the city, as the motorcycles wore out, they were traded in for new motors. Dan told the shop foreman it would be a better idea if they auctioned them off. They did this and came out ahead, getting four times the amount from the auctions than the trade-ins. Following that, they started auctioning off all of the vehicles rather that using them as trade-ins. Unfortunately for Brush Cycle, once they stopped working on the police bikes, their business declined. *(Bamonte photo)*

The top right photo is Dan standing in front of his personal motorcycle, during the time he worked for Brush Cycle. *(Courtesy Dan Hite)*

Dan Hite provides evidence in Candy Rogers murder case

An October 15, 1961, *Spokesman-Review* story showing the involvement of Dan Hite, motorcycle repairman, and Spokane police officer John Grandinetti in solving a string of rapes and murders. *(Public domain - unable to read author's name)*

Finger Points at Murder Suspect by Cycle Officer
John Grandinetti Given Credit for Sleuth Work

Amateur detective work by Spokane motorcycle enthusiasts and the persistence of a motorcycle policeman who "took it from there" paid off in spotlighting Hugh B. (Chris) Morse as a suspect in unsolved sex crimes.

Principals in the real-life private eye drama were Daniel L. Hite, a mechanic at Brush Cycle Co. here, and motorcycle Policeman John A. Grandinetti.

Morse, 31, a motorcycle enthusiast and a recent addition to the FBI list of 10 most wanted men, was arrested by FBI agents in St. Paul, Minn., Friday night,

Slayings Listed

St. Paul police said he admitted the sex slaying of a woman there a month ago and the following Spokane sex crimes:

The fatal beating of Mrs. Gloria J. Brie, 28, on Nov. 7, 1959; the murder of Mrs. Blanche E. Boggs, 69, on Sept. 27, 1960, and the near-fatal beating of Mrs. Beverly Myers, 23, on Oct. 25, 1960.

Spokane police also are questioning Morse in St. Paul about the sex slaying of Candy Rogers, 9, on March 6, 1959.

Morse was a member of the Spokane Motorcycle Club when he lived here at intervals. Hite and other club members are the ones who first became suspicious of him.

It was on the night of the beating of Mrs. Myers that we first got suspicious," Hite told the *Spokesman-Review* Saturday. Mrs. Myers was beaten savagely in the early hours of the following morning. She recovered but could not remember anything that happened.

We were at a friend's house that night. Chris and several club members were there.

It was about 10 p.m. and Chris said he was going to a drive-in movie. We asked him if he had a girl out in the car and he said no, he was going alone.

It was an odd hour to go to a drive-in, especially alone. We asked him where he worked and he said at the Matador Room. As it turned out later, that's where Mrs. Myers worked. And we found out later, too, that Chris didn't work there. He was a bus boy at another place. We first began wondering about him that night.

Became Suspicious

Then the next day, when we heard about the beating and noticed that Mrs. Myers worked at the Matador, we really got suspicious. Besides, Chris left town the next day, the day after the beating, and that didn't look good.

So then we got to putting things together. Most of the club members helped. Each one would put in something he knew.

We got out a city map and we placed the location of each one of the unsolved crimes. Then we put our heads together and figured where Chris lived at the time each one of these happened.

We discovered then that he lived within five blocks of each of the victims at the time she was attacked. (This includes Candy Rogers, Mrs. Brie, Mrs. Boggs and Mrs. Myers.)

Then we compared notes and found that Chris had left town a day or a few days after each one.

Turned Up Later

Every time after something happened, he'd just disappear. Nobody knew where he'd go. Then he'd turn up again after a while.

We remembered, too," said Todd McAllister, another club member, "that when we were in the shop (at Brush) talking in a group and a policeman would walk up, Chris would back off. He didn't seem to take to' policemen.

Brush Cycle Co. maintains police motorcycles and policemen are in and out of the shop daily.

And we got to looking at some of our old club movies," Hite said. We noticed that every time Chris was in a shot—and that was seldom—he'd fidget around and turn his head. He sure was camera shy. You won't find many pictures of him around.

Participated in Hunt

Then, we remembered that a month before Candy Rogers was killed, Chris was along with the club when we made a turkey run (a form of competitive motorcycle riding) in the area where her body was found. Chris went right down to the road where her body was found. Morse even participated briefly in the hunt for Candy's body.

But he wasn't much help. McAllister said. We hunted south of town and Chris was along for only half a day, and he spent most of his time just sitting on the road, while we hunted.

Then, the next day – the day the body was found – he disappeared from town again.

Hite collared Grandinetti and passed him all the information the club had put together. Grandinetti, working more than 100 hours on his own time, began talking to people who knew or lived with Morse. He became "convinced," he said. When Grandinetti assembled what he considered was a good case, he turned it over to the detective division. But he went on working the case with detectives.

Mixed with Public

What kind of a man was Morse? "He was a clean, likable, fellow," Hite said, "the type you'd never suspect of such things. "He mixed with the public real well. He could go right up into a group and make friends. But, at the same time, no one ever got to know him real well – men, that is. "He didn't get too Pally with men. When we had a party, he'd always seem to be off with the women most of the time. He considered himself a ladies' man, I guess. He was real good looking.

Always Had Money

"He always seem to have money, although he didn't have good paying jobs. He didn't have large amounts of money, but he always had some."

Hite said he and club members can't recall that Morse ever joined in their discussions about the unsolved sex crimes before they began to suspect him.

"He always disappeared after these things happened," Hite said," "and there was no chance for him to talk with us about them."

Hite and other club members were high in their praise of Grandinetti.

Spokesman-Review story by John Meidl in March 9, 2009,

The 1959 rape and murder of 9-year-old Candy Rogers, arguably Spokane's most infamous unsolved crime, has haunted Dan Hite.

Now 74, the former Spokane Motorcycle Club secretary remembers the day 49 years ago when he drove past the isolated spot where Rogers' body would be found less than a month later.

Hite believes the man riding in the sidecar of his Harley 74 – a likable, "clean-cut guy" who turned out to be a serial killer – made a mental note of an abandoned rock quarry and returned with Rogers less than a week later.

"You'd never know it, to talk, that he was off his rocker," Hite said of his companion, Hugh Bion Morse, whom he knew as Chris.

Hite and Morse had been marking the course for a "hare-and-hound" motorcycle event. Spokane Motorcycle Club members had to track the bags of red lime that Morse tossed out of the sidecar.

Rogers disappeared the evening of March 6, 1959, while selling Camp Fire Girl mints near her home. The Holmes Elementary School student's body was found about 3 1/2 miles northwest of Spokane Falls Community College – five miles due north of Spokane International Airport – that March 22. The body was under a pile of pine needles and boughs about 200 yards south of the quarry and 130 feet off Old Trails Road.

Police later discovered that Morse lived within a couple of blocks of Rogers' home.

Similarly, Morse lived within a few blocks of two Spokane women he later admitted beating to death and a third whom he nearly killed. And Morse vanished after each crime, popping up later at a different address.

Hite said he thought nothing of it at the time, but Morse's first disappearance was on the day Rogers' body was found.

Morse was helping the Spokane Motorcycle Club search for the missing girl when two marmot hunters found her shoes. Rogers' body was found the next morning, and Morse was gone when Hite went to Morse's home to tell him the search had been called off, Hite said.

That and other circumstantial evidence against Morse is so strong that Spokane Police Detective Brian Hamond isn't willing to dismiss him as a suspect even though comparatively recent DNA evidence seems to clear him.

Hamond is the latest in several generations of detectives to work the Rogers case. He's the only person assigned to a case that originally was investigated by dozens of police and sheriff's officers.

DNA identification wasn't possible when Rogers was murdered, but Rogers' clothing yielded her rapist's genetic profile in 2001 and it didn't match a 2002 sample from Morse.

Morse died in a Minnesota prison in April 2003 while serving two life sentences for a September 1961 rape and murder in St. Paul. The Minnesota conviction ended a two-year, cross-country spree that put Morse on the FBI's Ten Most Wanted list.

Right on the Money

Eight women or girls were beaten, sexually molested or killed before Morse was caught.

Hite is "right on the money" in suspecting Morse, Hamond said last month. Coincidentally, the detective had just received a big box of prison medical and psychological records on Morse.

"I can't wait to read it," Hamond said. "That's what I'm going to do this weekend."

Hamond said his interest in Morse "blossomed all over again" about two months ago when someone called to tell him about Morse's connection to the now-defunct Spokane Motorcycle Club. Detectives who investigated the Candy Rogers crime scene photographed what appears to be a motorcycle tire track in the vicinity.

Hamond's tipster mentioned Hite as a motorcycle club member who might remember Morse. Hite now lives in Springdale, Wash., where he has operated a septic-pumping business and served as mayor.

Independently, Hite called the *Spokesman-Review* to pass along his information about Morse. "I've been trying to find somebody to tell it to," Hite said. "I don't want to go to my grave knowing nobody knew about it."

He bows only grudgingly to DNA evidence that someone else killed Candy Rogers. "I know, I just KNOW, that it was Chris," Hite said. "But," his voice trailing off, "I don't know."

Hamond knows the feeling

He knows something else about Morse: "He had a penchant for grape gum. He chewed grape gum all the time." Investigative files indicate grape gum was found at the scene of attacks in which two Spokane women were murdered and a third was severely beaten. Grape gum also was found in Morse's room when he was arrested.

And grape-smelling gum was smeared on Candy Rogers' Sweater, coat and, possibly, her corduroy jumper. There was "quite a large quantity of this on her white Sweater," sheriff's Capt. James Allen reported in March 1962. Hamond said he plans to submit the gum for DNA testing.

Confessed to all but one

News accounts said Morse confessed to all the crimes in which he had been suspected – except the murder of Candy Rogers.

Authorities in Spokane said Morse passed two lie-detector tests about the Rogers murder, and a detective magazine report that he admitted raping Candy Rogers without killing her proved false. Morse consistently told investigators he had nothing to do with Rogers.

Spokane Police Chief Clifford Payne said in 1967 that he was attempting to contact the magazine writer who said Morse admitted raping Rogers. But Payne no longer believed Morse was "much of a suspect."

With Morse already serving two life sentences and having confessed to so many other murders, Payne could see little reason for him to lie about Rogers.

However, Spokane County Sheriff William Reilly still considered Morse "a prime suspect."

And Morse was still "the No. 1 suspect" for sheriff's Capt. Allen, who interviewed Morse in the Minnesota State Prison at Stillwater, Minn., in 1962.

Allen told the *Spokane Daily Chronicle* that Morse denied killing Rogers, but was reluctant to talk about her.

He said Morse told him, "If I did rape and kill Candy Rogers, I would probably be too ashamed to talk about it."

The Spokane Motorcycle Club, circa 1960. *(Courtesy Dan Hite)*

A 1952 Harley-Davidson ad promoting the Spokane Police Department motors

Twenty-six Harley-Davidson motorcycles give Spokane one of the most efficient traffic squads in the Pacific Northwest. Directing this force, are (L. to R.) Sgt. George Pymm; Assistant Chief of Police John Lenhart; Chief of Police Clyde Phelps; Traffic Captain George Freeman."

GOOD CITIZEN. "Thank you, officer —
let's hope it teaches me a lesson"

OUTRAGED INNOCENCE

Floyd Morton Fick – hired by the Spokane Police Department in 1954

Floyd Fick circa 1965. *(Courtesy Floyd Fick)*

Floyd Fick was born in 1931 in Iowa at the peak of the Great Depression. In 1942, his family relocated to Spokane as part of a national "great migration" to the coasts and larger cities to find work in defense jobs triggered by World War II. At the time, Floyd and most of his male high school classmates joined a military reserve (Navy) program.

In 1948, he was accepted for active duty at a newly established training base and was assigned to serve on both a destroyer and an aircraft carrier. Following the Korean War, he worked as a pipe fitter for Kaiser Aluminum and in late 1954, he joined the Spokane Police Department.

S P O K A N E   P O L I C E   D E P A R T M E N T

Floyd and Jacqueline Fick in 1955. *(Courtesy Floyd Fick)*

In 1955, Floyd married Jacqueline Garner and has, to this date (2018), been married over 60 years. In 1961, their son Russ Fick was born. Russ later became a deputy sheriff for Los Angeles County.

During the 1960s, Floyd returned to school on a part-time basis and graduated with a bachelor's followed by a master's degree in education.

In 1980, he retired from the police department. However, since his wife was still working (she was a tenured professor for Whitworth College), he decided to try other careers, starting with real estate sales. In 1985, they relocated to Seattle, where his wife had accepted a new job, and in 1987, he was hired by a Los Angeles property management firm as an area manager and relocated to California. His area included properties from Simi Valley to San Dimas.

In 1992, during the Los Angeles race riots, he was assistant director of security for the Beverly Center,

a 13-story fashion mall in Los Angeles. During the riots, the Los Angeles Police Department called to them the rioters were coming to burn down the center and they would not be able to direct force to help them. For some reason, the rioters stopped a half block short of the center. At that time, he told his wife and son, an L.A. deputy sheriff, "I think it is time for us to go home." In 1994, the family moved to the Seattle area for a real retirement.

Tour of Duty on the Spokane Police Department

Floyd's first job on the department was to roll large boulders around to form a foundation for the house that would be the Police Academy and firing range. The house was a gift from Washington Water Power to the department. His next assignment was walking a beat. His first beat was to walk from Washington Street east to Division Street, on Trent, Main, and Riverside avenues on swing shift. The call box was

Russ Fick and his dad Floyd. Russ was on the Los Angeles Sheriff's Department during the race riots in the spring of 1992. *(Courtesy Floyd Fick)*

The first house and part of the firing range at the Spokane Police Academy, circa 1954. This was the new academy building Floyd Fick helped relocate. *(Courtesy Floyd Fick)*

at Riverside and Division, which was close to Ma Penna's Tavern where he would stop to get warm before continuing his beat. Floyd recalls, "After a couple of warm-up stops the bartender told me not to come back because it was bad for his business. At the end of the shift, Fred Fait and Mick McCabe, who drove the downtown wagon, picked me up and took me to the station. They asked me how the night went and I told them about the bartender." Nothing more was said, and they dropped him off and went back to work. Later he learned the two had gone back to the tavern and made several arrests, including the bartender, and closed the place down. It never reopened.

The next assignment Floyd had was to attend the Police Academy, where he would learn the duties of a policeman and how to carry them out. At the time, the Police Academy was one room in the trade school on Fourth Avenue across from Deaconess Hospital. Both police and sheriff's officers trained together. At the academy, Floyd met classmates who would become future partners and great friends. He asked two of them, Robert Browning and Jim Albright, to serve as ushers at his wedding in July of 1955. Corky (Ed) Braun, one of the sheriff's deputies, overheard the conversation and said he would volunteer to sing at the wedding. Floyd told him this was to be a big church wedding and Corky said fine with him, so Floyd agreed. When the day came, Corky surprised everybody at the wedding by giving a very professional performance. After that, Corky became a lifelong friend of the Ficks.

Corky Braun, circa 1954. *(Courtesy Glen Whitely)*

After a few months on graveyard shift, Floyd and Robert Browning got the chance to become motor officers in the traffic division. One Friday a mechanic from Brush Cycle, the company that maintained the police motors, dropped off a motor at Floyd's house, a 1955 Harley with a sidecar. Floyd explained he had never ridden a motorcycle before so the mechanic showed him how to start it. He then advised him to

Bill Bradley, circa 1954. *(Courtesy Floyd Fick)*

Partial membership from the first motor bull party. From left: Jerry McGougan, Danny Naccarato, Floyd Fick, Bob Browning, and Ray Gimlin. *(Courtesy Floyd Fick)*

ride it around the neighborhood for a couple of days and he would be ready to go by Monday.

When Monday arrived, Floyd made it to work. At work, his police supervisors told him his partner would be Bill Bradley, but he had been in an accident and was off sick. They told him to just go out and ride around – Bill would be back in a week or so. Bill returned and he started showing him the ropes. They went to Natatorium Park to check the parking lot where they made a slow turn on gravel. During the turn Floyd fell over and jumped off the bike as it went down still running. A couple of young men who were in the park shut the motor off and stood the bike up for him with a "here you are, Officer." Bill laughed all night.

One night at muster the traffic lieutenant announced he was starting a new shift, 7 p.m. to 3 a.m. He asked for volunteers. Floyd was standing next to Robert Todd (R. T.) Browning. Floyd grabbed Browning's arm and raised it with his and said they would take it. That was the start of a great friendship and the best of times for Floyd on the police department. They would come to work at 7 p.m., check in with the lieutenant. Then after 12 p.m. they were on their own. After a short time, the inspector had them doing specialty work instead of traffic.

One night they were sitting on their motors in a parking lot across from the Top Hat Drive-in. Without warning and for no known reason, the kickstand broke on Floyd's bike, causing it to fall over on top of him, pinning him to the ground. Browning was unable to get it off, so he went to the Top Hat and recruited some "hot rodders" to help with the rescue.

Radar was very new at this time, and everyone was interested in adapting it to police work. The traffic lieutenant borrowed a radar unit from the Washington State Patrol to try it out. It was just a box on a tripod with a long line, allowing the user to be out of sight. The lieutenant, who was a rather excitable fellow, would man the radar and line up the bikes awaiting his instructions. When he yelled out the speed, the first bike in line would take off and stop and issue a citation to the driver. When it came

Fick's turn, he could not get his bike started. Soon, the lieutenant's yells turned into screams. As he finally roared away from the curb, the last thing he heard was the lieutenant's scream, "You are fired!" The next day he heard the chief and the inspector were walking down the hall when the chief reported "the lieutenant had fired Fick last night." The inspector was heard to say, "Oh, not again!"

On another radar event the lieutenant had a new strategy. He sat in the car using a walkie-talkie with an antenna, which he would wave wildly as he leaned out the window and called out the speed to Fick and Browning. Fick was just returning from his run when he saw Browning running back and forth alongside the car trying to keep up with the

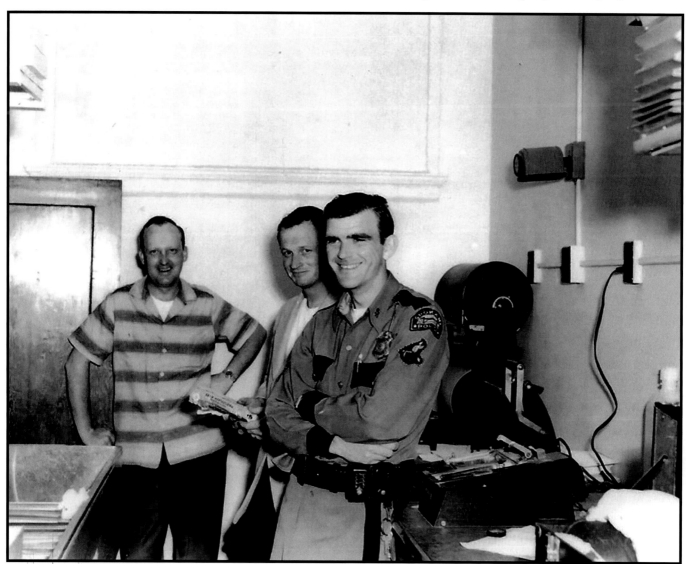

From left to right: Bill Bradley, unknown, and Floyd Fick at the photo lab in the City Hall, which at the time was located on Wall Street. *(Courtesy Floyd Fick)*

antenna which the lieutenant had somehow managed to hook into Browning's nose. Browning was hanging on to the antenna with both hands as the lieutenant was waving the radio. The lieutenant was hollering and Browning was swearing until the antenna came loose.

At that time, motor officers rode year around. In the winter, they attached sidecars. Winters were always hard on motor officers, as there were few places to get out of the weather. Browning came up with the idea of buying electric socks with small batteries. Fick figured out a quick disconnect so thcy wired them to the bike battery. Fick found a place in England where he ordered sheep-wool-lined boots.

When he left traffic everyone wanted his boots. Fick went into Safety Education as Harold Tucker's partner. Here he started making training films and presentations. They went to Eastern Washington University to get state certified to teach driver education.

Later Tucker went into the detective bureau, and Fick went to planning and research where he could apply some of the training skills they had developed. While there, he also wrote federal grants for funding to get a hold-up reduction program started.

From that assignment, he was transferred to a new department, crime prevention, where he remained until he retired in 1981.

From left: City Police Officer Floyd Fick; County Deputy Chuck Anderson, and Washington State Patrol Trooper John Mittmann, circa 1968. *(Courtesy Floyd Fick)*

Robert Todd Browning – hired by the Spokane Police Department in 1954

Bob Browning, circa 1956. *(Courtesy Rob Browning)*

S P O K A N E   P O L I C E   D E P A R T M E N T

Robert Todd "Bob" Browning attended Hill Military Academy in Portland, Oregon. This distinguished school, founded by Joseph Wood Hill, was modeled after similar institutions in the United States. It was in operation from 1901 until 1959. The cadets wore uniforms, received military training, and took academic college-preparatory classes. The academy accommodated both boarding and day students. Its graduates served in wars from World War I through the Korean War, some rising to high ranks.

Following this education, at the age of 17, in 1945, Bob joined the U.S. Marine Corps. He served in World War ll in the Marine Detachment BB-41 on board the battleship USS *Mississippi*.

During his tenure on the department, Bob was a mo-torcycle patrolman and later a detective in the intelligence unit. Bob was always considered an outstanding officer and well liked by the public and his peers alike. In 1981, Bob retired from the Spokane Police department at the age of 53.

However, 26 years with the job had taken its toll. During an interview when he retired, he stated he had enough, "Regardless of what area of police work you're talking about, you are working with problems. All these negative things are thrust at [policemen] every day, if a policeman is working narcotics, what kind of people is he going to run into? … Working narcotics you often deal with dopers, pimps and hookers. It's depressing because they are going nowhere but down. And I just don't want to see that anymore."

The battleship USS *Mississippi*, circa 1940. *(Public Domain)*

Bob Browning next to his police motor and inset, circa 1967. *(Courtesy Rob Browning)*

HARLEY-DAVIDSON 100,000 MILE CLUB MEMBERSHIP

It is a pleasure to state that

Robert T. Browning   Spokane   Washington.
Name   City   State

has ridden more than 100,000 miles on one or more Harley-Davidson motorcycles, and is a bona fide member of the Harley-Davidson Mileage Club.

Wm H Davidson
President, Harley-Davidson Motor Co.

F.A27

Bob's two sons, Rob and Dee, on his motor. Riding on his motor was always a highlight for them. As they lived next to a church parking lot, he would often give them rides.

A Harley-Davidson 100,000 Mile Club membership, signed by the president of the Harley-Davidson Company, W. H. Davidson. Bob also attained a 250,000 Mile Club membership. *(Courtesy Rob Browning)*

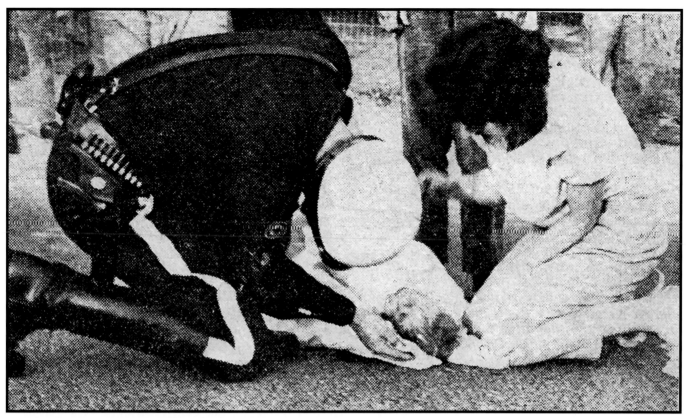

In this photo motorcycle officer Robert Browning and an unidentified woman comfort a two-year-old boy after he was struck by a car while playing in the street at 5200 North A Street. The boy was admitted to Sacred Heart hospital for treatment of his fractured left shoulder, skull fracture, and cuts. *(Public domain)*

Mark Robert "Rob" Browning, son of Bob Browning, circa 1968. *(Public domain)*

Rob Browning, the son of motorcycle officer Bob Browning, was exceptionally proud of his father. He devoted much time working with the authors and furnishing the information and photos in his father's section of this book. Rob was polite, respectful, and an all-around good person and will be missed by many. The following was copied from his obituary:

Musician, friend and father, Robert Browning passed away at home October 10, 2017 in his hometown of Spokane. He was born June 26, 1951 to Robert Todd and "Patricia" Browning in Spokane, WA. His wide variety of interests led him to career opportunities with the Spokane Police Department, in the Insurance field, and later Property Management. What he's best known for, however, is his love of music. He was a master guitar player, mostly self-taught, and played in bands his whole life beginning with "The Henchmen" while at Lewis and Clark High School, and most recently with the regarded Spokane rhythm and blues band "Cool Stack." Rob was a known expert of Northwest music history, and had a passion for police history and the culture of the Old West. This modern day cowboy loved Western films, always had a joke to tell, and collected law enforcement memorabilia, antiques, music, etc. He is survived by his daughters Paige and Claire, his brothers Dee, Todd and best-buddy/brother Guy, and many friends including Judy Ray. We love you. In lieu of flowers please send donations to the Inland Empire Blues Society/Foundation. He will be honored in a quiet gathering.

The Beginnings of the Annual Motor-Bull Reunion

The following was written by Bob Browning's first motor partner, Floyd Fick, shortly after Bob died

Robert Todd Browning was more affectionately known by friends as just R. T. The first time I came in contact with him was when we were testing for the position of police officer of Spokane, at the YMCA for a physical test and then again for the written test. We both came out near the top of the list. I can't remember if he was third and I was fourth or the other way around, it doesn't matter. We were both close to each other, and we were put out on the street about the same time. We were on swing shift walking a beat in the downtown area for awhile. Then we were sent to the police academy, which was one room in the Trade School. We became even better friends as we worked together on some small projects. So when I was going to be married the next July, I asked him if he would be one of the ushers at the wedding and that was over 52 years ago!

While working graveyard shift we did some off-duty work to make extra money just to get by, even though both of our wives were also working. Economic times were not the best. So, when the opportunity came along for both of us to transfer to the traffic division and ride motorcycles, at 16 dollars a month more, we became known as motors 14 and 17.

One day at muster the lieutenant asked for volunteers to work a two-man shift from 7 p.m. to 3 a.m. R.T. and I were standing together. I grabbed his arm and raised it with mine and said, "We will take it." We spent several great years working that shift together. Those years were some of the best of my career. Just a few months ago when R.T. and I were together, we again agreed those were the times! This is not the place to talk about the many great memories we had, since a lot of them were about giving the lieutenant heartburn – but you could write a book about that – as we were just two friends working together and enjoying it to the utmost. I hope R. T. took those memories with him, because I know I will.

Over the years I tried to get R. T. to go duck hunting, fishing and water skiing. I don't know if he really liked any of these sports, but let me tell you I remember many days seeing a wet swim suit on the handlebars of motor 17 on his way home with the sun coming up. I will never hear the sound of a Harley without thinking about my partner, R. T., and all of those great times.

R.T. went into the detective division, and I wound up in one of the other offices. We still saw each other as our work would come together from time to time. One day R.T. said, "It is time to retire; why don't we join a few others and throw a party?" So it was a retirement party at the Police Guild, and his police career was over.

But as in all great friendships, that was not the end and even though I moved away, we still kept in touch. I was living in California when one day I got a call from R. T. How about coming up to another party. It was just to be a one-time motorcycle get-together and it turned out to be an annual reunion for R. T. and me to reminisce about the good old days. I have been told some of those stories are still floating around.

R. T. and I talked a lot the last few months of his life, about the past, health, and the unknown future. I do not know where R. T. is now but it has to be a good place because he was a good person and a great friend. For me this is not a farewell because he will always be in my memories of all the good old times.

Bob Browning and wife, Pat, at a lake. *(Courtesy Rob Browning)*

Senator Barry Goldwater during his run for the presidency. The photo was taken at the Spokane International Airport. Bob Browning is on the lower right in plainclothes with hat. *(Courtesy Rob Browning)*

This photo was taken circa 1960, during a coffee break, at a drive-in restaurant on Spokane's north side. Browning's motor partner, Floyd Fick, had a new camera and took this photo of Browning. While looking for photos for this book, Floyd came across it. *(Courtesy Floyd Fick)*

Bob Browning and wife, Pat, circa 1976. *(Courtesy Rob Browning)*

Left: Jerry and Patty McGougan. Right: Bob and Pat Browning, circa 1973. The other couples were not identified. *(Courtesy Rob Browning)*

Carl Sweatt – hired by the Spokane Police Department in 1955

Carl Sweatt, circa 1958. In 1973, Sweatt was a sergeant in charge of Spokane's first SWAT team. *(Courtesy Randy Albright)*

Carl Sweatt was team leader for the first Spokane Police Department SWAT team, formed in conjunction with the Sheriff's Department to provide security for Expo '74. The SWAT (Special Weapons and Tactics) team is described in detail in the later section on Ron Scholz, who was also a member.

One of the duties of members was to serve as potential snipers, which did require special weapons. At the time, the only sniper weapon they had was a 30.06 rifle with a scope, which had been donated. The SWAT team would have preferred a .223 as it hits hard, but gives only a slight kick. The 30.06, which the SPD had, kicked about three times as hard. Consequently, as the trigger was pulled, knowing it was going to kick hard, the shooter would often flinch, throwing him off target. Also, with Spokane's first SWAT team, every person was trained in every other person's position on the team.

Fully-trained SWAT member

The cartoons on this page were posted in one of the FBI's training rooms. Bamonte took photos of them while he was attending SWAT training at the FBI Academy.

They were used as levity to bring humor to the intense training sessions.

The SWAT training camaraderie was an important component of the SWAT training.

Squat thrust champ

Pull up Champ

Push up champ

SWAT Hall of Fame Gymnasium Heros

Spokane Police Department (vertical left margin)

James Albright – hired by the Spokane Police Department in 1955

Jim Albright at Manito Park, August 1959. *(Courtesy Randy Albright)*

Jim Albright leading the Lilac Parade, circa 1959. *(Courtesy Randy Albright)*

S P O K A N E   P O L I C E   D E P A R T M E N T

Jim Albright assisting a motorist, circa 1959. *(Courtesy Randy Albright)*

Floyd Jones, Mel Griffiths, and Mickey O'Brien – went on the department consecutively in 1947, 1948, and 1963.

In front of the old Shriners Hospital. From left: Floyd Jones, Mel Griffiths, and Mickey O'Brien, 1968. Following his retirement from the SPD, Mickey moved to Montana, where he was elected sheriff of Mineral County for two successive four-year terms. *(Courtesy Mercedes Griffiths)*

Paul Warrington – hired by the Spokane Police Department in 1956

Spokane Police Department

Paul Warrington, circa 1970. *(Courtesy Frank Warrington)*

Paul Warrington was born in 1932 at Libby, Montana, to Marshal and Blanche Warrington. He had a sister, Berry, who was eight years older and a brother Marshal, three years older.

Paul Joined the Spokane Police Department on July 31, 1956, and retired the same month and day in 1981, serving exactly 25 years to the day.

During his police career, he was a patrolman, motorcycle officer, and detective. One of his many accomplishments was forming, organizing, and serving on the first Spokane Police Bomb Squad. He was a member of the bomb squad for four years.

Paul's cousin, Frank Warrington, has an interesting story about Paul:

> During the time Paul was riding motor, they rode bikes year around and had side cars during the winter. As these bikes did not have electric start, some times when it was cold we would get someone to give us a pull. (We all carried a tow rope with us.) Paul said one morning he had his wife Ann give him a tow with their car, and as he was being towed Ann made a right turn onto a side street and when she did, his motorcycle tipped with the side car up and he was being dragged down the street on his crash bars. He said he was dragged for about a block before he was able to get Ann's attention and get her to stop." [This story made quite an impact on Paul as both the authors of this book also remember Paul telling us that same story in late 1970, when he returned from Vietnam.]

Paul also served in both the Korean and Vietnam wars, serving with the 1st Cavalry Division. He retired from the Army Reserve as a command sergeant major at the age of 60 with a total of 44 years active and reserve service.

His reserve service included the Naval Reserve, Coast Guard Reserve, 12th Special Forces (Green Berets), and 104th Division. During his service, Paul was awarded the combat infantry badge, a bronze star, an air medal, an army commendation medal, a good conduct medal, and parachute jump "wings."

Paul passed away on April 8, 2011, and is survived by his wife, Ann, of 55 years; sons Brad and Jon; daughters-in-law Carmenla and Debby; and grandchildren Keenan, Jordyn and Wyatt; his brother Marshal; sister-in-law Pat; nephews Kenneth, Robby, David and Steve; nieces Mary Henderson and Kathy Henderson; sister Betty; as well as several other nephews and nieces. He was also instrumental in the nurturing and mentoring of several young people throughout his life and therefore adopted them in spirit. One such person he was especially close to was Sgt. 1st Class Carl Pucker, United States Army.

Paul's funeral was held on April 15, 2011. It was followed by a full military service and presentation of the flag at the Washington State Veterans Cemetery, Medical Lake, Washington.

Karman Baker (left) and Paul Warrington, circa 2009. *(Courtesy Frank Warrington)*

Paul Warrington (left) and Fred Mielke, circa 2006. For a number of years, Mel Griffiths and Paul Warrington were prime movers in promoting the Annual Motor-bull Party. *(Courtesy Frank Warrington)*

The Paul Warrington family, from the left: Brad holding Keenan, Ann, Paul, Carmenla, and John, circa 2001.
(Courtesy Frank Warrington)

Ronald Curtis Scholz – hired by the Spokane Police Department in 1958

S P O K A N E   P O L I C E   D E P A R T M E N T

Ron Scholz, circa 1961 during the fall. This was during the time when those assigned to motor rode year round and sidecars were necessary during the freezing season. *(Courtesy Scholz family)*

Ron Scholz was born in Portland, Oregon. When he turned 14, the family moved to Spokane, where he graduated from West Valley High School. Ron served in the Navy during the Korean War, spending time at sea on a naval destroyer. He liked being on the water and enjoyed the action that was involved. During that time, the draft was in effect and it required that every able bodied man had a military obligation. Ron did not like military life, but had no choice due to the draft, and was pleased when he got out.

Ron's first job was playing piano in a bar. Although he was underage at the time, he looked older and

there were no questions asked; the bar owner needed a piano player. His worst job was running parts for Babcock Motors in Spokane. His favorite job was with the Spokane Police Department, which he joined on February 1, 1958. During that time, one of his favorite assignments was the Special Weapons and Tactics (SWAT) team.

The Spokane Police Department SWAT team

During the 1960s, Los Angeles was plagued with race riots and violent crimes that required stronger tactics and heavier weaponry than the capabilities of the average police officer. Chief Darrel Gates, the

Los Angeles police chief at the time, tasked his staff to develop a unit that could handle violent situations and SWAT was the result. SWAT was designed to utilize heavier weapons, to always act as a team, and to take suspects into custody. The perfect SWAT call was when no one got hurt. The concept for a SWAT team had the appearance of something that would work well. Consequently, the FBI decided to adopt it, and build a SWAT school at the Marine Training Base at Quantico, Virginia.

The Spokane Police SWAT team was scheduled to attend training at Quantico, ahead of the newly formed sheriff's team. This was in preparation for the Spokane EXPO '74. At the same time, Spokane Police Chief Wayne Hendren also had a national police chiefs' meeting scheduled at Washington D.C.

To my knowledge, no one in our group had ever been to our nation's capital before, which the police chief recognized. As a considerate gesture for that fact, the chief arranged for us to leave on a Friday afternoon. He also went with us. His plan was to give us all a weekend to see and tour Washington, D.C. He was our tour guide, as he had been to our nations capital numerous times before, and knew the city well. This was a great experience for Spokane's first SWAT team, as it gave us all a unique opportunity. Everything we saw was memorable

From left: **Carl Sweatt, Gary Lacewell, Dennis Hooper, Ron Scholz, and Spokane Police Chief Wayne Hendren in front of theUnited States Capital Building during the spring of 1974. Of the original SWAT team only Dennis Hooper and Tony Bamonte are still living. Chief Wayne Hendren passed away in 2017.** *(Bamonte photo)*

and left lasting impressions on our group. Interestingly, this trip was Ron's first time he had ever ridden on an airplane.

Fortunately, during the same time Spokane's first SWAT team was formed, I (Bamonte) was completing my requirements for a degree at Whitworth College. One of the fill classes I was taking for credit was a photography class, which required each student to produce a slide presentation on a selected topic. Both the assignment and trip to Quantico came at the same time. As a result, I made a slide presentation on SWAT training at the FBI Academy. I ended up with over 200 slides taken during various training sessions. Some of the photos in Ron's section of this book are from that trip and the various training we all were involved in over 45 years ago. Being on Spokane's first SWAT team was an honor for all of us. Later, when President Nixon came to Spokane to open EXPO '74, Ron became a part of that.

Ron met his wife, Betty, when their families lived across the street from each other. Ron became a friend of Betty's brother, Frank Warrington, who was also on the Spokane Police Department and is in this book. Ron and Betty were married in 1952.

Ron Scholz, circa 1961 during the spring. *(Courtesy Scholz family)*

Some of the SWAT "Spiderman" training we received at the FBI Academy at Quantico. This particular photo shows Tony Bamonte on the side of a building. Gary Lacewell, Bamonte's motor partner at the time, took this photo. *(Bamonte photo)*

Carl Sweatt, Ron Scholz, and Dennis Hooper at the Columbus Doors to the U.S. Capitol Building. These doors, also known as the Rogers Doors, are a pair of massive bronze doors modeled by sculptor Randolph Rogers for the east front of the United States Capitol. They open into the Rotunda, and depict events from the life of Christopher Columbus.

Rogers, an expatriate American artist trained and living in Italy, was a Neoclassical sculptor noted for his carved works in marble. He visited the United States in 1855, and was awarded the commission for the doors. He had never done anything on this scale, and was not known for working in bronze. The theme consisted of scenes from the life of Columbus. Each door has four panels, regarding significant events illustrating Columbus's landing in the New World. Including transom, the doors are 16 ft. 8 in tall, and 9 ft. 9 in wide. They weigh approximately 20,000 pounds (10 tons) Narrative from *Wikipedia.* *(Bamonte photo)*

Spokane Police Department's first SWAT team. From left: Ron Scholz, Tony Bamonte, Gary Lacewell, Dennis Hooper, and Carl Sweatt. *(Courtesy Wayne Hendron)*

One of the more humorous calls that Ron handled during his time on the SPD was there was about a cougar in a ladies bathroom. When he arrived and went to the bathroom door, he quickly found the cougar was actually a hamster.

According to Ron, his happiest memories were with the Spokane Police Department. He retired on March 15, 1989, after over 30 years with the department. His final assignment was as a patrol sergeant in charge of the 911 call service until it went under civilian operation. His retirement consisted of wood carving, bowling, golfing, and furniture making. However, his most cherished activity after his retirement was his social life with people he had worked for and with, and respected for over 30 years. He started going to the Jackpot Service Station and having coffee at 6:00 every morning with his buddy, Frank Warrington. Soon Gene McGoughan stopped by and before long a coffee group was started. Many retired people came, both civilian and patrol. They kept up on "what was happening" on the department and, in

Ron and Betty Scholz's children. From left: Pam, Ken, Teresa, and Debbie. *(Courtesy Scholz family)*

the world. Ron was there daily until he died on November 5, 2009. Frank, Gene, and all the others still meet to discuss local and regional events. To all who knew him, Ron was a well-respected, excellent policeman who was fair in all he did.

Ron and Betty Scholz wedding photo, Jan 20, 1952. *(Courtesy Scholz family)*

Ron and Betty Scholz, still a happy couple after 52 years of marriage. *(Courtesy Scholz family)*

Karman F. Baker – hired by the Spokane Police Department in 1958

Karman Baker, circa 1964. *(Courtesy Karman Baker)*

Karman Baker was born in Coeur d'Alene, Idaho, to Robert and Era Baker. He attended grade school in Coeur d'Alene and high school in Spokane. His father was a baker by vocation. There were seven children in his family. He enlisted in the Navy, where he spent four years on active sea duty aboard the USS *Rochester*.

Karman attended both Washington State University and Eastern Washington University. Karman's first wife was Connie Paterson, with whom he had several children, both boys and girls. His second wife is Betty Bray Baker.

Karman joined the Spokane Police Department on February 1, 1958, and quit on May 5, 1965. The majority of his time with the department he spent on motor.

In early 1962, his four-year-old daughter, Linda Baker, had one dream. She wanted to go to Disneyland. The only difference between her and a million other children was that she had been diagnosed with acute leukemia.

At that time, the salary of a police officer and the mounting medical bills made it impractical, if not impossible, for that dream to come true. Fellow officers decided they would make Linda's dream come true. They contacted local businesses and the Police Benevolent Fund and made personal contributions. Soon they had collected enough funds for three first-class airline tickets, food, and general expenses.

When the Los Angeles Police Department heard of the situation, they offered a car and driver for the duration of the Bakers' stay in California. The Los Angeles Police Protective League agreed to make arrangements for lodging and to pick up the entire bill. When the Bakers arrived at the Los Angeles Airport, they were met by a delegation from the department. When the final itinerary was complete, it included not only Disneyland, but also a visit to Marineland of the Pacific, and many other attractions. There were so many included that the Bakers had to stay a week to see them all. Linda passed away on November 1, 1963, in Spokane.

The majority of Karman's time in the military was spent on the USS *Rochester*, the most heavily armed cruiser in the U.S. Navy when commissioned. On the morning of July 3, 1950, the first U.N. air raids against North Korean forces were launched. On July 18 and 19, the *Rochester* supported landings on Pohang Dong by the Army's 1st Cavalry Division. She continued to serve with Task Force 77 until August 25, 1950. Just before daylight, at 0550, on September 17, a North Korean Yak-9 and an Il-2 made an attack run on the cruiser *Rochester*, anchored off Wolmi-do. Initially the aircraft were thought to be friendly until they dropped four bombs over the American ship. All but one missed and the one that did hit smashed the *Rochester's* crane but failed to detonate. *(Public domain)*

Gene Donald McGougan – hired by the Spokane Police Department in 1959

Gene McGougan, circa 1965. *(Courtesy Gene McGougan family)*

Gene McGougan was one of Spokane's most active police officers during his entire 30-year tenure on the department. Over five of these years, he was assigned to motors. Gene was one of those people you would like to see arriving at the scene if you needed backup or advice. He had a reputation for always being at the right place at the right time and doing the right thing.

During this same time, Gene's brother Jerry was also on the department, spending about five years as a motor officer. Both were well known and respected by the public and within the department. If Gene said he was going to do something, or was given an assignment, you could count on it getting done. (See front cover of this book for a confirmation of the depth of respect for him.)

John Welton and Gene McGougan, circa 1967. *(Courtesy Gene McGougan family)*

Gail and Gene McGougan at the Rogers High School 1982 50th reunion to celebrate when the students first started attending the new Rogers High School

In 1932, to ease congestion at the small Hillyard High School, John R. Rogers High School was built. This was also the last year the Hillyard school was in use.

The last graduating class of Hillyard High School was in 1932. The 48 students in that class were the last to do so, thus completing the transfer of Hillyard's high school students to the new Rogers High School. The first graduating class from Rogers was in 1932. This was a celebration of that landmark event.

Gene graduated in 1953 from Rogers High school.

One of the many arrests Gene was involved in. The photo and caption appeared in the *Spokesman-Review* in 1966: "The End of Chase. Damon M. Turner Jr., South 213 Bernard, is put into a police prowl car last evening by motorcycle officers William H. Crumbaker, center, and Gene McGougan following Turner's arrest near Second and Stevens after chase on foot from Boge Furriers, N. 8 Post. Mrs. Shirley Hoffman, a clerk at the store, led the chase after she told police Turner took a $1,000 mink stole from a mannequin in the display window and walked out of the store. She was aided by several male passersby, including Harry L. Carl, Tacoma, a state parole officer." *(Courtesy Gene McGougan family)*

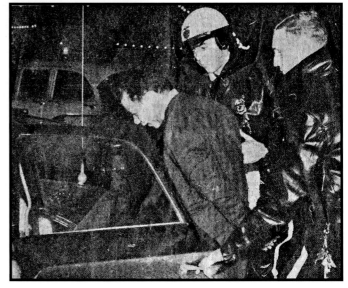

This photograph from the *Spokesman-Review* was published on August 18, 1966. It centered around a story about the Century Auto Club in Spokane, which consisted of 65 teenage boys. Regarding this photo, the caption stated: "They are placing safety bumper stickers on vehicles. Watching them is motorcycle policeman Gene McGougan. Over 20 cities in the Inland Empire have joined Spokane in this second annual observance, designed to tell the story of the important role the policeman plays in a community." *(Courtesy Gene McGougan family)*

Gene McGougan, then a lieutenant assigned to the detective division with the Spokane Police Department, was put in charge of the famed "South Hill Rapist" investigation in 1980.

The investigations ultimately led to the arrest of Kevin Coe. Following his convictions his mother was also arrested for attempting to hire a hit-man to kill the judge and the prosecutor who, she felt, were responsible for the conviction of her son.

The following pages cover the case in some detail.

Kevin Coe and his mother, Ruth Coe, circa 1981. This photo was taken during the time of his many court appearances. *(Public domain)*

Kevin Coe, after many years of prison incarceration. *(Public domain)*

One of Spokane's More Infamous Rape Cases, "The Kevin Coe Case"

Beginning in August of 1978, Spokane began experiencing a series of rapes that subsequently accelerated at a rapid rate. Between August 1978 and March 11, 1981, approximately 40 incidents of rape, attempted rape, and indecent public acts were reported. They were all believed to have been committed by the same male. The suspect terrorized Spokane's South Hill for over four years and took on a special significance as the rapes continued to progress.

Lt. Gene McGougan is put in charge of the South Hill Rapist case

In June of 1980, two years after the first rape, Detective Lt. Gene McGougan took over the investigation. When that happened, the first thing McGougan did was read every sex crime report that went through the department, beginning in 1978. He concluded that one particular individual was probably involved.

On February 25, 1981, McGougan ordered full-time surveillance of Kevin Coe. He also had the officers disperse to the entire surrounding area. By March 4, hundreds of man-hours had been spent on the Coe surveillance and investigation. The suspect's father was the managing editor of the *Spokane Daily Chronicle*, one of two daily newspapers in Spokane.

In 2010, *HistoryLink.org,* an online encyclopedia of Washington State History, hired Jim Kershner to write about that story. Kershner, a veteran writer for the *Spokesman-Review*, and an accomplished historian, wrote the following:

Spokane's South Hill Rapist: the Kevin Coe Case
HistoryLink.org Essay 9484 by Jim Kershner

From 1978 to 1981, a rapist who committed as many as 37 brutal assaults kept the city of Spokane terrified. Police scoured the city for the "South Hill rapist" so-named because many of the rapes took place in the city's upscale South Hill neighborhood. In 1981, Frederick Harlan "Kevin" Coe (b. 1947) was arrested in connection with several of those rapes. The arrest was particularly sensational since Coe was from a prominent family, the son of the managing editor of the *Spokane Daily Chronicle*.

In a dramatic 1981 trial, Kevin Coe was convicted on four of six rape counts. In a sensational twist, his mother, Ruth Coe, was arrested months later for trying to arrange a "hit" on the judge and prosecutor. She was caught on tape asking an undercover officer to turn the prosecutor into "an addle-pated vegetable."

In 1982, she was tried and convicted of solicitation to commit first-degree murder, but received a surprisingly light sentence. Kevin Coe's four convictions were overturned by the Washington Supreme Court in 1984 because some of the victims had been hypnotized by police in hopes they would remember more details. In a second trial in 1985, Kevin Coe was found guilty of three of the four counts of first-degree rape. Two of those convictions were overturned in 1988, again because of the hypnosis issue. Yet the third conviction was upheld and Coe went on to serve all 25 years of his sentence at the Walla Walla State Penitentiary. Before he could walk free, however, a civil jury declared Coe to be a sexually violent predator in 2008, and he was sent to a Special Commitment Center at McNeil Island. He remained there as of 2010.

The Terror Begins

In 1978, a 19-year-old Spokane woman was walking home late at night when a man wearing jogging clothes popped out from behind a parked car, grabbed her, dragged her into the nearby bushes and raped her. He repeatedly jammed his fist into her mouth to prevent her from screaming. Police could locate no suspects.

Over the next two years, Spokane police noticed a baffling increase in the number of brutal rapes in the city. In 1978 there had been 49; in 1980 there were 127. Many of these rapes had a few traits in common. The women reported that the rapist jammed a fist – often covered with a glove or an oven mitt – into their mouths. He also talked to them during the rape, asking them questions about themselves. He also said that if they told anybody, especially the police, he would find them and kill them. He said he knew where they lived.

Police Suspect a Serial Rapist

Many of the victims had just gotten off a bus or had been out jogging. The rapist himself was usually described as wearing a tracksuit or jogging Sweatts (Spokane was already becoming famous as a jogging city since the advent of the massive Bloomsday race in 1977). The Spokane police began to suspect that they had a serial rapist at work. They formed a task force in 1980, but quietly. They didn't want the city to go into a panic. Yet panic was already beginning to take hold, especially on Spokane's upper-middle-class South Hill, where many of the rapes had taken place. People were beginning to talk about a rampage by the mysterious "South Hill rapist."

Chris Peck, a metro columnist for the *Spokesman-Review*, one of the city's two dailies, wrote a column about one traumatized victim in March 1980. The number of rapes kept escalating, and on September 7, 1980, he wrote a column that "hit the prosaic old town like a bomb," in the words of author Jack Olsen, from his definitive account of the case, *Son: A Psychopath and His Victims* (Olsen, p. 138). Peck wrote:

"A horrible specter is back on the South Hill. In jogging clothes, threatening with a knife, it has begun again to strike at women in one of Spokane's classiest neighborhoods. ... Women on the South Hill, be furious together. Look for clues, find the courage to open your eyes, press charges if you can. Otherwise, creeps will prevail" (Peck, "Specter").

Then in January 1981, the *Spokesman-Review* published a map showing the rape locations and their correlation with the bus routes, along with a story titled "How the South Hill Rapists Work." Police theorized at the time that there might have been three or four different rapists committing as many as 37 different rapes.

By then, the city was in a full-blown state of alarm. The only voice of calm seemed to come from the city's other daily, the *Spokane Daily Chronicle*, whose managing editor wrote an editorial that said, "It is hoped that every man out jogging is not hounded off the streets because some rape reports have said the attacker wore jogging clothes" (Olsen). That managing editor's name was Gordon Coe (1916-1999).

A Suspect and an Arrest

Yet rapes were being committed more frequently than ever, including two in February 1981. One of those – the rape of a 51-year-old woman jogging at Hart Field, near Sacajawea Junior High School -- would prove to be crucial to breaking the case. An employee at the school reported seeing a silver Chevy Citation parked there that morning with unusual license plates. The plates were yellow, like the state's personalized plates at the time, but without personalized numbers or letters. The car was registered to Gordon Coe, yet it was being used by his 34-year-old son, Frederick Harlan Coe, who liked to call himself "Kevin" for reasons known only to himself (in 1982 he would officially change his name to Kevin).

On February 25, 1981, police begin watching Kevin Coe, who was working, with a conspicuous lack of success, as a real-estate agent. They discovered that his car had yellow cellophane over regular license plates. Police then showed a picture of Coe to the Hart Field victim, who immediately said, "That's him!" It was the break Spokane police were waiting for. Yet they didn't feel they had enough solid evidence to make an arrest. Police and prosecutors decided to try to nab him in the act, so they put him under surveillance. They discovered he often cruised High Drive on the South Hill – where several rapes had occurred – and he often followed bus routes.

Coe eluded his watchers numerous times and in one case exposed himself to a woman, so police eventually decided it was unsafe to wait any longer. On March 10, 1981, police went to Kevin Coe's real-estate office and arrested him for the Hart Field rape. Later that evening, a steady stream of rape victims were brought down to the police headquarters to view police lineups. Several of them picked Coe out of the group. ...

The First Trial and Sentencing

The evidence against Coe was voluminous, if mostly circumstantial. Police and prosecutors believed he was responsible for as many as 20 or 30 other rapes. Coe's defense, orchestrated by Kevin himself, was one of flat denial. He insisted that it was all just a massive case of mistaken identity. He chose to accept a public defender as his lawyer, probably because he felt that he would be able to direct his own defense more easily. When his lawyers suggested that he plea-bargain for hospitalization instead of prison, he rejected the notion by saying, "I'm not a sexual psychopath and I'm not guilty"

The trial was delayed several times, but finally began on July 20, 1981. Impartial jurors were tough to find in Spokane – the populace was immersed in every detail of the biggest scandal in the city's history – so a jury was impaneled in Seattle and brought to Spokane for the trial before Judge George Shields (1928-2006).

Both of Coe's parents took the stand in his behalf. Ruth provided her son with an alibi for every rape; she said he was often at home with them. Ruth, 60, was a well-dressed, flamboyant woman who wore a jet-black wig. She testified that she and "Son," as she called him, had actually attempted a kind of citizen's arrest of the South Hill rapist. The two of them, she said, had actually gone out several times on their own surveillance excursions. "Son would jog, and I would follow in the car at a very slow pace," she testified. "[We were] very unsuccessful, so we did give up" That would explain, she said, why he and his car had been seen so often near the bus routes and near the scenes of the crimes. His former girlfriend, however, took the stand for the prosecution and told about his suspicious behavior, the mysterious cuts he would receive and the fact that she once found him washing an oven mitt at 7 a.m.

Coe took the stand on his own behalf. In between telling virtually his entire life story – large segments of which were absurdly exaggerated – he adamantly denied ever owning gloves, ever owning oven mitts, ever owning a stocking cap and, of course, ever raping anyone. "His mother, seated in the back of the tiny courtroom, smiled and nodded as he made his points and occasionally emitted a loud sigh or muffled comment when the prosecutor [Donald Brockett] registered objections," wrote Olsen (Olsen, p. 354). The jury bought little of it. On July 29, 1981, Kevin Coe was convicted of four counts of first-degree rape.

Yet the story was far from over. Coe's mother was angry and defiant. Ruth told *Spokesman-Review* columnist Chris Peck that she believed that Judge Shields had not played fair. She said that, in hindsight, she would "never try to play fair again, because the law doesn't play fair" (Peck, "Ruth").

Sentencing

At this point, Kevin and his parents were terrified that he would be sent to the Walla Walla State Penitentiary, where they were convinced the other inmates would declare open season on the famous "rapo" (they were eventually proven right, when in 1994 Coe was slashed across the throat with a homemade knife at Walla Walla). Prosecutor Brockett had raised an even more alarming sentencing option; he pointed out that state law still allowed convicted rapists to be castrated. So the Coes grasped at one final straw – that Judge Shields would sentence him as a sexual psychopath, meaning he would be sent to a state mental hospital, not a prison.

For the sentencing phase, the Coes hired Carl Maxey (1924-1997), a well-known Spokane civil rights lawyer. Maxey, a family acquaintance, had heard the judge raise the possibility of sexual psychopathy at one of the early sentencing hearings, and believed he could nudge the judge toward a sexual psychopath ruling. The strategy was risky. The judge had earlier said that he couldn't recommend the sexual psychopath option because Coe's flat-out denials indicated that he would not be amenable to treatment.

So Maxey arranged for Dr. Robert A. Wetzler, a well-known psychiatrist in the field of sexual psychopathy, to interview Coe one more time. This time Coe told Wetzler that he had committed one of the rapes and would be willing to accept treatment for his sexual problems. Even then, Coe was coy about his admission. He told the psychiatrist he was "jealous of the South Hill rapist" and had committed a "copycat rape." Still, when Maxey put Wetzler on the stand during the sentencing hearing, Wetzler dropped the bombshell: Coe had confessed and was begging for treatment.

It didn't work. On August 17, 1981, in a proceeding broadcast on live TV, Judge Shields announced his sentence: a prison term of 20 years, a second term of 25 years, a third term of 30 years and a fourth term of life, all to be served consecutively. Within two months, Coe was sent to the Corrections Center at Shelton and then on to Walla Walla. Coe later reasserted his innocence and said his confession had been a ruse. "As a strictly legal ploy, it makes good sense, but it didn't work," Coe told the *Seattle Times*. "The judge, in fact, tricked us" (Olsen, p. 380). Ruth Coe reserved all of her scorn for Brockett and Shields.

Ruth Coe's Druthers

In a discussion with a stranger a few months later, Ruth Coe said these words: "I want the prosecutor out and I want the judge out" ("The Coe Tapes"). This conversation was captured on tape because the stranger was actually an undercover police officer. He was posing as a hit man after police had received a tip that Ruth Coe wanted to take out a contract on Brockett and Shields. The conversation continued:

Undercover officer: "We are talking about the same thing; you want those people ..."

Ruth Coe: "Gone."

Officer: "Dead?"

Ruth Coe: "Dead. Right. If I had my druthers, I'd have that prosecutor just made a complete vegetable so that he could never, ever be anything but a vegetable, so that they had to care for him forever, and he lived on and on that way. And the judge ..."

Officer: "Just tell me what you want."

Ruth Coe: "Well, uh, and that judge, I'd like him gone – dead – and I'd like both of 'em dead, really, except that with Brockett, I felt that – he's a man about 46 or 47 and he has been so filthy, and my feeling for him is that I would love to see him just an addlepated vegetable that had to be cared for – that his family had to take care of the rest of his life. I mean diapers and all the rest of it. He wanted 42 years of my son's life gone. I'd like to see him sit 42 years in ... umm, as a baby. But, um, to have him gone would be great, too. I mean, you can never be sure, I suppose, how you clobber them, that could be the way it'd come out. So dead is great. But I do think he should suffer ..." ("The Coe Tapes").

Ruth Coe was arrested the next day, on November 20, when she handed the officer a $500 down payment. When the officers approached her in the parking lot and arrested her on charges of soliciting first-degree murder, she muttered disgustedly, "I thought so. I thought so. That's right, I really did think so" (Olsen, p. 399).

"A Greek Tragedy"

Ruth's arrest made national and international news; the London Daily Mirror ran a headline that read "Sex Shame of Town's Top Family." the *Spokane Chronicle* ran the story on the front page as well, with the headline, "Coe's mother faces death plot counts."

The non-jury trial, in front of Judge Robert Bibb, began on May 17, 1982. "It was just like watching a play," said reporter Rick Bonino, who covered the trial for the *Spokesman-Review*. "It wasn't like any other trial – it was just like entertainment. There were all these unexpected twists and turns" (Kershner, p. 215). For one thing, Maxey's defense was based on portraying Ruth as crazy (or at least "diminished"), which didn't prove difficult in the least. One psychiatrist testified that Ruth saw "horns grow-ing out of the head" of Judge Shields when he pronounced sentence. Her husband took the stand and testified that she had for years abused a variety of prescription drugs – "an absolutely appalling jumble of chemicals" – and that after Kevin's verdict, suicide had seemed to loom on the hori-zon" (Olsen, p. 412). Meanwhile, the prosecution's case was straightforward enough: Forget about all of that psy-chiatric mumbo-jumbo – Ruth was motivated strictly by old-fashioned revenge and hate.

At one point, the trial had to be delayed when the hysteri-cal Ruth Coe was put on suicide watch at a local hospital. Yet the trial soon resumed, and within days Judge Bibb announced that he had reached a verdict. He said the en-tire case reminded him of a "Greek tragedy by Euripides or Sophocles – a symbiotic family relationship, catastro-phe caused by man or the gods, avengement and the judg-ing of the avenger again by the gods or fate or by men" (Olsen, p. 424).

He pronounced Ruth Coe guilty as charged. Yet the judge was moved to pity. His sentence was virtually the lightest possible one: 20 years in prison, suspended; one year in the county jail of her choosing; and 10 years of probation. The whole thing amounted to one year of easy time, with the possibility of work release.

"In essence, the judge bought the diminished capacity de-fense," a satisfied Maxey later told the *American Lawyer* magazine (Bruck). Brockett later called it "a sentence of the heart and not the head" (Bruck).

Meanwhile, in the prison at Walla Walla, Kevin Coe told the *Seattle Post-Intelligencer* that he couldn't understand why the defense hadn't utilized every weapon at its dispos-al, namely, himself. He bragged that he would have made an excellent witness.

Reversal and Second Trial for "Son"

Yet the Coe story was still far from over. In 1984, the Washington State Supreme Court overturned all four of Kevin Coe's convictions, on the grounds that a number of witnesses and victims had undergone hypnosis to "assist" them in recovering memories. A new trial was ordered, this time in Seattle. The victims were brought back to the stand to relive their horror again. On February 12, 1985, Kevin Coe was re-convicted on three of the rape counts and sen-tenced to life plus 55 years.

However, the hypnosis issue still tainted the case, and on January 29, 1988, the Washington State Supreme Court re-versed two of the convictions again. The third conviction was upheld; it carried a 25-year sentence. Theoretically, Coe could have been released in four years. But it didn't turn out that way, at least in part because Coe refused to attend any of his parole hearings.

Coe's Indefinite Incarceration

By 2006, Coe had served his full 25-year term. He had spent nearly his entire sentence researching the case in what he called an attempt to find the real rapist. "That's all I do," he told a reporter during a prison interview in 2006. "I'm probably the world's leading expert on this case." Coe's release was blocked when the state attorney general filed a petition to have him civilly committed under the state's Sexually Violent Predator Act.

The civil trial was delayed until 2008. During the month-long trial, new evidence emerged, including DNA evi-dence linking him to one of the rapes. A jury declared Coe to be a sexually violent predator, a designation that gives the government the power to hold him indefinitely at the Special Commitment Center on McNeil Island. As of July 2010, Coe remained at McNeil Island, where he continued to churn out letters and legal challenges from his cell. Olsen's best-selling book chronicled the case in 1984 and spawned a made-for-TV movie in 1991, "The Sins of the Mother," starring Elizabeth Montgomery as Ruth Coe and Dale Midkiff as Kevin Coe.

And Spokane's wave of brutal rapes? From virtually the moment that Coe was arrested, it subsided, never to return.

Sources used for this story

Jack Olsen, Son: A Psychopath and His Victims (New York: Atheneum, 1984); Connie Bruck, "Will a Prosecu-tor's Missteps Free the South Hill Rapist?" The American Lawyer, December 1982; Jim Kershner, Carl Maxey: A Fighting Life (Seattle and London: University of Wash-ington Press, 2008); "The Coe Tapes," (transcription of the undercover Ruth Coe tapes), Spokesman-Review, May 19, 1982, p. 11; Chris Peck, "Trying to Forget a Face That Won't Go Away," Spokesman-Review, March 16, 1980, p. B-1; "Rapes Spotlight Police," Spokane Daily Chronicle, January 14, 1981, p. 4; Chris Peck, "A Horrible Specter Rises Again on the South Hill," Spokesman-Review, Sep-tember 7, 1980, p. A-16; Chris Peck, "Ruth Coe: Profile of a Mournful Mother," Spokesman-Review, November 24, 1981, p. 6; Shaun Higgins and Rita Hibbard, "How the South Hill Rapists Work," Spokesman-Review, Janu-ary 11, 1981, p. A-1; Dave Reagan, "Sex Assaults Alert Police," Spokesman-Review, January 6, 1980. p. B-1; John Harris and Rita Hibbard, "Spokane Man, 34, Held in Rape on South Side," Spokesman-Review, March 11, 1981, p. A-1; Tim Hanson and John Webster, "Bond Rais-es to $100,000 for Rape Suspect," Spokane Daily Chron-icle, March 11, 1981, p. 1; Rita Hibbard, "One Man, One Charge and Many Questions," Spokesman-Review, March 15, 1981, p. A-1. Tom Clouse, "The Case Has Consumed Me," Spokesman-Review, May 21, 2006, p. A-1.

A Suspect and an Arrest

. . . the rape of a 51-year-old woman jogging at Hart Field, near Sacajawea Junior High School -- **would prove to be crucial to breaking the case.** An employee at the school reported seeing a silver Chevy Citation parked there that morning with unusual license plates. The plates were yellow, like the state's personalized plates at the time, but without personalized numbers or letters. The car was registered to Gordon Coe, yet it was being used by his 34-year-old son, Frederick Harlan Coe, who liked to call himself "Kevin" for reasons known only to himself (in 1982 he would officially change his name to Kevin).

Charles and Earnestine Williams. (*Courtesy the Williams family*)

The preceding story by Jim Kershner, former journalist for the *Spokesman-Review,* was posted on HistoryLink.org Essay on July 20, 2010. It summarized one of Spokane's most active serial rape investigations. The South Hill rape investigations continued from 1978 to 1981.

It is with great respect and appreciation, almost 40 years later after the rape case, that the authors of this book would like to acknowledge Charles Williams, an employee of Sacajawea Junior High School, who was responsible for providing crucial suspect vehicle information that ultimately led to Kevin Coe being identified as the prime suspect in the South Hill rape investigations.

The following quote, from the preceding story by Kershner, illustrates the importance of Mr. Williams in the solving of this crime and others:

An Addendum to the South Hill Rapist Investigation

The night of the sexual assault at KJRB radio station on 57th Avenue, police radio advised this author (Jack Pearson) and my partner, Gale Meenach, that the sheriff's department was taking a rape report at the radio station.

We responded to the location and contacted the on-scene deputy, Fred Ruetsch, who advised the suspect was last seen northbound, on foot, through the field behind KJRB. We proceeded to 49th Avenue, which was the first street north of the field at that time. We were headed eastbound when we observed a dirt bike, whose rider was wearing a full-face helmet, coming from this general direction. As we approached him, he immediately fled at a high rate of speed. This led us on an approximate two-minute chase before he left the roadway and escaped into a wooded area.

Until Coe was named as a prime suspect we had wondered if we had allowed a rapist to escape. I talked to Coe's girlfriend a couple years later and when asked if Coe had ever ridden a motorcycle, she advised no.

It would be interesting to have coffee with that motorcycle rider nearly 40 years later and reminisce about "old times."

The Police Station from 1962 to 1971 (former Realty Building)

In 1962, the police station moved to the former Realty Building at 242 West Riverside. Inset is Jim Manson, circa 1967, working the front desk, located on the first floor and just to the left of the building's entrance.

An article in the *Spokesman-Review* of September 25, 1910, stated: "The Realty Building was started early last spring and is now being completed. Albert Held is the architect and H. J. Farney is the contractor." It was an eight-story steel frame building. The upper floors of the building had been operated as the Realty Hotel until the 1920s, when the building began to have more office rentals. As it was well outside the central business district, its office space, although of high quality construction, never could command high rent and was never filled. The ground floor was also a poor location for any type of business. In the 1950s, KSPO radio station had its office and studio on the second floor.

A north-south alley was located exactly next to and on the west side of the building, which was originally platted in Havermale's Addition, and extended from Trent to Sprague. During the time of its use as a police station, that alley was used for a drive-up window for people to pay their parking tickets. The elevated ramp still exists as of this writing.

Note above that almost half of the block in front of the station was reserved for parking police vehicles. The front of the building was kept open for the paddy wagon, which made two runs a day, almost filling the wagon with drunks each time. The paddy wagon looked like one of the old bread trucks. It had a partition separating the drunks from the police. Two policemen always manned the paddy wagon. The area in front of the building and to the east (where the two motorcycles are parked) was reserved specifically for police motorcycles.

During its use as a police station, the men's jail was located on the second floor, the women's jail on the third, the drill hall, where roll call was held, on the seventh floor, and the chief's office on the sixth. There was an elevator that traveled to all floors. During those years, there was no prisoner classifi-

Police radio room at 242 West Riverside. From left: Mickey O'Brien, motorcycle officer, Joe Kaley (standing), Jack Teigen (sitting closest) and Dick Olberding (sitting at the back). *(Courtesy Spokane Police Archives)*

cation. Almost all prisoners, upon being booked, would be placed in the "drunk tank," which was approximately 30 x 40 ft. Most often, the bookings would go well until the prisoner was taken to that room. The drunk tank had the semblance of a smelly garbage dump, where the majority of prisoners typically smelled offensive as many would drink to the point of being unable to control their bowel movements. A prisoner's biggest résistance was typically during the initial arrest and then the final placement in the drunk tank. During the entire time this building was occupied by the police department, the two most commonly used statutes were drunkenness and state vagrancy.

The police front desk was located on the ground floor at the south side of the building with plate glass windows facing Riverside Avenue. It was usually manned by at least two or three policemen.

That was where the general public went to file a complaint or request services. The city courts were also located on the ground floor, but at the north end of the building.

The Old National Bank "Parking Branch" was located directly across the west alley from the elevated drive up "ticket paying" window. One day there was an armed robbery at that bank, which had an alarm directly to the police station. The desk sergeant walked over to the bank and arrested the holdup man, who asked the question, "How did you get here so fast?"

When the city offices moved in 1971, the interior of the building was thoroughly altered to transform it into "The Delaney," subsidized apartments that opened in 1972.

Roll call on the seventh floor of the police station when it was located at 242 West Riverside, circa 1967. The motor officers are on the far left. There are two rows of men, but only one showing. The civilian in the white shirt is Dave Morris, a longtime radio operator. Bamonte is on the far right. *(Bamonte collection)*

Jerry McGougan – hired by the Spokane Police Department in 1960

Jerry McGougan, circa 1964. *(Courtesy McGougan family)*

Jerry McGougan joined the Spokane Police Department in 1960. He was born in 1937, at Anaconda, Montana, and his family moved to Spokane when he was a young boy.

In 1955, Jerry graduated from Rogers High School and soon after, joined the Coast Guard Reserves. In 1956, Jerry married his high school sweetheart, Patty Massuto. Prior to going on the police department in 1960, Jerry worked for Saad's Shoe Repair.

Both Jerry and his brother Gene were part of numerous major crime investigations in Spokane. In 1968, Jerry was put in charge in the first vice, intelligence, and narcotics units (ADVIN) in the department's history. Jerry was fearless and had a knack for solving seemingly impossible cases – mostly by good police work.

Jerry was nicknamed "Zip" by his colleagues, who joked about his hyperactive and sometimes impetuous personality. Jerry was known as a hard-working cop who became personally involved in many cases, often as an administrator.

During most of Jerry's time on motorcycle, his partner was Jerry Oien. Anyone who worked for, or with, Jerry McGougan respected him. He also had many contacts in all segments of the community. Jerry retired in 1980, and started his own private investigating business, McGougan Investigations.

From left: Patty and Jerry McGougan, Gene McGougan's wife, Val, and Glenda and Jerry Oien at the 1965 Policeman's Ball. *(Courtesy McGougan Family)*

This newspaper photo shows the start-off leading the Lilac Parade in 1965. At the head of the parade were Jerry McGougan and Jerry Oien. At that time, the signal that the parade was starting began with a drive through the entire parade route by police officers on motorcycles. These included city, county, and the state patrol. The officer taking this photograph was **Al Burrell**. *(Courtesy McGougan Family)*

From Left: Gene McGougan, Danny Naccarato, and Jerry McGougan. *(Courtesy McGougan Family)*

Police Drama involving Jerry McGougan

Final Fireside Edition

Spokane Daily Chronicle

The Weather
Occasional snow or rain through tomorrow, rising temperatures and southwesterly winds from 10 to 20 miles an hour. Low expected tonight, near 30; high tomorrow, about 40. High yesterday, 24 at 4:45 p.m.; overnight low, 23 at 12:30 a.m.; 28 at 10:30 a.m.; 27 at 1:30 p.m.

87TH YEAR. NO. 95.   32 PAGES   2 SECTIONS   SPOKANE, WASH., FRIDAY, JAN. 12, 1973.   10 CENTS   MA 4-1121   WANT ADS TE 8-4664

Police Star in Drama on City Streets

The following article appeared on the front page of the January 12, 1973, *Spokesman-Review*. This interesting article involved four motorcycle officers:

It was the old cops-and-robbers intrigue with – well, you'd have to say a storybook ending. The hour-long suspenseful episode in Spokane yesterday afternoon saw, in this order:

- An armed robbery in a downtown beauty salon.

- A hair-raising foot chase on crowded and snowy downtown streets, capped by the crackle of gunfire.

- A police officer confronted face-to-face by a gun-wielding man.

- Squads of shotgun-armed policemen ringing and searching buildings at Sprague and Monroe.

- A city transit bus commandeered at gun-point, with the driver forced to take the empty rig to the Garden Springs area in west Spokane.

- Police helicopter pressed into use for the second criminal activity need in the past two months.

Suspect Seized

The "storybook ending" came at about 3:15 when a suspect was arrested inside a house at S. 1208 F in the Garden Springs area. Police zeroed-in on the area after the bus driver, Fred Wise, whose coach was commandeered, showed officers where the gunman got out.

"We went to one house, that one over there, and the lady said she was O.K. and hadn't seen anybody," said Police Officer A. J. "Tony" Bamonte, one of the uniformed policemen on the scene when the arrest was made.

"We went to check out this second house and the man who answered the door wouldn't let us come inside. He said he had a vicious dog inside, so we became a little suspicious."

Bamonte and officer Gary A. Lacewell guarded the residence while detectives Jerry N. McGougan and Det. Lt. James F. Haynes entered the dwelling after the man who answered the door was told to hold his "vicious dog."

Within minutes, police detectives, led by Deputy Chief Robert E. Colliton, emerged from the flat with a handcuffed suspect. The suspect was found hiding under a bed and was pulled out by Lt. Haynes, who said the man offered no resistance.

Revolver Found

A revolver was found inside a box spring, directly above where the suspect was found under the bed, Haynes said.

A black, Labrador-type pup and a second dog, a red puppy, also came bounding out the door into the freshly fallen snow, both wagging their tails and romping amidst the squad of policemen who converged for the arrest. "Good police work if I say so myself," said Colliton as smiling officers led the young and slender, slightly bearded suspect up a snow-covered hillside to a police van parked on Sunset Boulevard.

The suspect taken into custody was identified as Carl G. Smith, 23, who was booked at the County-City jail on two charges of armed robbery, one of first-degree assault and one of kidnaping.

Detective Capt. Calvin D. Smith said that the robbery charges involve yesterday's Ridpath Hotel Beauty Shop holdup and a Tuesday night holdup at Third Avenue Drugs, W. 327 Third. The assault and kidnaping charges grew out of events following the holdup, Capt. Smith said.

Holdup Described

He said that a man walked into the Ridpath Beauty Shop on the corner of First and Stevens, pulled out a revolver and announced the holdup. The robber scooped about $80 out of a cash register and ran out the door.

Capt. Smith said that Carlos T. Vazquez, a beauty shop employee, chased after the holdup man.

"Outside the hotel," Smith said, "Vazquez caught up with the robber and hit him on the head with a can of hair spray." The captain said the robber ran west on Sprague from the hotel, pursued by Vazquez, who was running down the middle of Sprague, shouting at the fleeing robber.

"It was at Sprague and Post that the robber stopped for a moment and fired a shot at Vazquez," Capt. Smith said.

A witness told police that the robber had the hammer cocked on his revolver when he was confronted by Officer Melvin T. Griffiths.

Officer ducks

Griffiths, who was wearing a raincoat and heavy jacket, said he jumped off his three-wheel motorcycle and ducked behind a car trying to get at his service revolver and it was then that the suspect disappeared.

Haynes said the suspect then ran into the Metro Mall building, S. 13 Monroe, then fled east on Sprague to Lincoln and commandeered the bus driven by Wise.

Haynes said witnesses told police that a charter bus had been used in the getaway and officers felt it might have been one of the downtown shuttle buses or one of the buses that carry Eastern Washington State College students back and forth to Cheney. For that reason, Haynes said, the search shifted to the Coliseum area. But the suspect, holding a gun on the bus driver, forced him to drive

to the Garden Springs area, where the gunman got off the bus, Haynes said. Wise, the bus driver, telephoned police and told them what had happened, then showed police where the suspect had alighted from the bus.

Haynes said officers followed footprints in the snow to the house where Smith was found under a bed.

Haynes said the second time he was asked, the owner of the house gave police permission to go in and search the frame dwelling.

Capt. Smith credited the "inquisitiveness and intuition" of Officers Bamonte, Lacewell and Philip J. Ostendorf with being key factors in the apprehension.

"A chase from downtown to West Spokane involving dozens of police ended yesterday afternoon with the arrest of a robbery suspect." The *Chronicle's* Chris Brown photographed Carl G. Smith, 23, as he was escorted from 1208 South F. Street by Deputy Chief Robert E. Colliton (left) and Detective William A. Beeman. *(Public domain)*

Frank Marvin Warrington – hired by the Spokane Police Department in 1960

Proud Pops List Tots

Motorcycle Policemen Gene McGougan, left, and Frank Warrington register their babies in the Chronicle Baby Contest with contest secretary Carlene King. The two officers stopped off at the Chronicle office yesterday afternoon before going on duty. Hundreds of babies, all under 2 years old, have been entered in the 1962 contest.

From left: Proud fathers, Gene McGougan and Frank Warrington, registering their babies for the Chronicle Baby Contest. *(Courtesy Frank Warrington)*

Frank Warrington was born in Kalispel, Montana, in 1934 to Marvin and Lillian Warrington. For the first five years of his life, the family lived in Kalispel, prior to moving to Spokane.

In Spokane, Frank attended Browne Elementary School and North Central High School. Following graduation, he worked for a short time as a box boy for Albertson's supermarket. He later joined the United States Coast Guard, where he served four years active duty and nine years active reserve, attaining the rank of E-7. Following his active duty time, he attended Spokane Community College for two years and Spokane Falls College for a year and a half, majoring in general law enforcement. Frank met his future wife, Nancy Schoenwald, on a blind date. They were married in 1958.

On April 1, 1960, when Frank went on the Spokane Police Department, he worked out of the Wall Street police station under Lieutenant Roy Ginnold. In 1962 the police department moved to 242 West Riverside. During that time he worked for Lieutenant Wayne Hendren (who later became Spokane police chief) and Sergeant Calvin Smith. In 1970, he moved to the new station at West 1100 Mallon. This gave him a working knowledge of all three facilities and their advantages and disadvantages as they relate to police work.

He was assigned to the traffic division during the summer of 1961 and rode motor until September 1967.

During his time, his primary motor partners were Gene McGougan, Mike Kusterer, and Fred Mielke. During the entire time Frank was assigned to motor they rode year around, which meant they put sidecars on their motors during the icy winter months. This was also during a time when the motors were maintained and repaired by Brush Cycle.

One of Frank's most memorable events was a natural gas explosion at the Safeway store at Monroe and Montgomery, which occurred in the spring of 1962.

Frank was later assigned to the police academy for three years, which he describes as was one of his best jobs. As Frank rose through the ranks, he later became the swing shift traffic sergeant working with Lieutenant Carl Sweatt. Frank was later promoted to lieutenant.

Frank's family, from left: Heidi, Ed, Kate, Hans, Sue, Megan, and Benny. *(Courtesy Frank Warrington)*

Nancy and Frank Warrington, with Pepe, in 2014. *(Courtesy Frank Warrington)*

Bob Allen – hired by the Spokane Police Department in 1961

Bob Allen working the Lilac Parade in mid 1960s. *(Courtesy Bob and Fran Allen)*

Bob Allen was born on July 6, 1939, and raised in Sault Ste Marie, Michigan, on the northeastern end of Michigan's Upper Peninsula, near the Canadian border. The city is 346 miles from Detroit. In the 2010 census, the population was 14,144, making it the second largest city in the Upper Peninsula of Michigan.

While still living in Michigan, Bob's family made a trip to California, which left a favorable impression. Later, wanting to go back to California, he joined the Marine Corps, entering a special two-year program. Consequently, right out of high school, he was sent to San Diego for training.

While in the Marines, one of the things Bob felt he learned, which benefitted him throughout his life, was discipline. During his two years in the military, Bob was promoted to lance corporal. When he got out of the Marines, he moved to Spokane, where his parents had already moved. Bob's mother was a homemaker and his father was a purchasing agent for a hardware company.

Bob's first job in Spokane was working as a rough carpenter while he was going to Eastern Washington College. He graduated from Eastern Washington with a bachelor of arts in political science.

Bob was hired by the Spokane Police Department on January 1, 1961. Early in his law enforcement career he happened to be investigating an accident at the top of the Post Street Hill with Cliff Barclay, an older officer and an ex-marine. At the time, Cliff's daughter, Fran, was also at the scene watching her dad. That encounter soon sparked a relationship that led to their marriage. They became the parents of two girls and later a boy. Bob and Fran now have grand and great grandchildren. During Bob's lifetime, there are two significant political events that left an impression on him: the assassination of President Kennedy and, later, the Bush administration's actions that precipitated the United States involvement in the Iraq War, which many Americans felt was a bad move.

During Bob's tenure on the department, he advanced through the ranks, becoming a captain. Some of his assignments included: assistant director of the police academy from 1973 to 1977, working on the Coe retrial task force, and the War Room (a designated and secure room for addressing ongoing incidents). One of his favorite assignments was riding police motor

for five years. Of Bob's many accomplishments, the one that was most significant to him was when he graduated from Gonzaga Law School and passed the bar. Bob retired from the police department on January 30, 1988. During his time on the department, Bob Allen established a reputation for being a fair and honest cop.

In his retirement, he writes and studies computer issues relating to privacy and technology. Bob practices law on a limited basis.

Bob Allen, circa mid 1960s, on a police motor with a sidecar, during a time when the police rode motors year around. *(Courtesy Bob Allen)*

Spokane Police Academy, which Bob Allen attended in February 1961: Bob is fourth from the right in the front row. Front Row: SPD Officer Ray Bolstad, SPD Officer Richard Luders, SPD Officer James Whitman, SPD Officer Jerry Phillips, SPD Officer Bill McCrosky, SPD Officer Gary Fallgren, SPD Officer Frank Warrington, SPD Officer Bob Allen, SPD Officer Fred Uttke, SPD Officer John Morris, and SPD Officer Jack Tenney. Back Row: SPD Supervisor Perry Miles, SPD Officer Chuck Ailie, SPD Officer Dan Naccarato, SPD Officer Neal Peoples, SPD Officer Ken White, SCSO Deputy Jerry Baldwin, SCSO Deputy Bob Sennett, SCSO Deputy Don Manning, SCSO Deputy George Schee, SPD Officer Jim Scott, SPD Officer Jerry McGougan, SPD Officer Harold Osborne, and SPD Officer Al Hales. *(Courtesy Bob Allen)*

Man Wanted in California

From left: Marriott, Johnson, Coffey.

One of three armed robbery suspects scooped up by Spokane police shortly after a North Side grocery store was held up late Tuesday will be returned today to San Luis Obispo, Calif., to face charges of first degree murder.

Harold E. Johnson, 47, who

3 Arrested for Robbery

Three men were arrested by police late Tuesday 16 minutes after the armed robbery of a North Side grocery store. They later were charged with the holdup.

Booked into the city jail were James Ray Delong, 41; Calvin Clay Coffey, 38, and Earl Freemont Moore. Police said they were checking to determine if the names were aliases. The suspects did not reveal where they were from but officers said the auto they were driving had California license plates.

Mrs. Lurene B. Stone, owner of the Bantam Food Shop, E2904 Francis, told police detective John F. Leahy she was alone in the store about 10:20 when two men walked in. One said he wanted to buy some beer and the other then obtained a description of the auto and its direction of travel.

The description was broadcast to all police units converging on the area and at 10:33 motorcycle officer Robert J. Allen spotted an auto matching the description at Division and Bridgeport. It contained three men.

Aid Asked

Allen radioed for assistance and at 10:35 the auto was halted at Post and Cleveland and the three

A news clipping of three men from California who Bob arrested. The man in the center, Harold E. Johnson, had an outstanding warrant for first degree murder from that state. *(Courtesy Bob Allen)*

Bob Allen, mid 1960s, by his police motor with training wheels installed by fellow motor officers. *(Courtesy Bob Allen)*

Bob Allen and his wife, Fran. Inset, Bob during Christmas season in earlier years. *(Courtesy Bob Allen)*

Bob and Fran Allen, circa 2013. Bob retired as a captain. *(Courtesy Bob Allen)*

Jerold Edward Oien – hired by the Spokane Police Department in 1961

Jerry Oien, circa 1964. *(Courtesy Jerry Oien)*

Jerry Oien was born at Potlatch, Idaho, on January 12, 1938. He has three brothers, two younger and one older. He was raised in Spokane, attending Holmes Grade School, Havermale Junior High, and North Central High School. Following graduation from high school, he went into the military, joining the Navy, where he spent four years, some of that time in Japan. Prior to his military discharge, he had attained the rank of E-5. He later attended Eastern Washington University.

Jerry met his future wife, Glenda, when they were teenagers ice skating at the old Elm Street arena. Glenda was a figure skater, Jerry was a hockey player. They were married in 1961. Together they have one daughter and two sons.

During his time on the department, his favorite job was riding police motor. During that time he met great people, both on and off the job. Jerry's biggest influence in his life and one of his best friends was his motorcycle partner, Jerry McGougan. Jerry's other motor partners were Howard Russell and Jerry Hick-man. Jerry's happiest memory was when he swore his son in as a Spokane police officer. The accomplishment he is most proud of was his assignment to the Spokane Police Academy as the lieutenant in charge. Also, he values the time he spent in the major crimes unit.

Jerry Oien and Chuck Johnson, circa 1964. *(Courtesy Jerry Oien)*

Persistent 'Bulldog' Oien Gets His Man After All

If they start calling Patrolman Jerold E. Oien "Bulldog" it will probably be because he doesn't give up until he gets his man.

Oien arrested a burglary suspect last week who allegedly stole about $2,000 in tape recording equipment from an apartment of a friend of Oien's—an apartment that Oien was keeping an eye on while the tenant was on vacation.

The motorcycle officer explained that in July, an acquaintance of his, David Yost,

even though he couldn't have prevented the burglary which occurred while he was off duty, kept an eye out for the stolen items. Thursday night, while making a routine check of a downtown tavern, he saw a recorder matching the description of the one reported stolen, being offered for sale.

He said he checked serial numbers with the theft report. They matched.

Loren Eugene Griffith, 21, W2826 Dean, was arrested in connection with the burglary Friday and booked into the city

The headline on a 1965 *Spokesman-Review* read: Persistent "Bulldog" Oien Gets His Man After All:

If they started calling Patrolman Jerold E. Oien "Bulldog" it will probably be because he doesn't give up until he gets his man.

Oien arrested a burglary suspect last week when he allegedly stole about $2,000 in tape recording equipment from an apartment of a friend of Oien's – an apartment that Oien was keeping an eye on while the tenant was on vacation.

The motorcycle officer explained that in July, acquaintance of his, David Yost, left on vacation, but first asked Oien to periodically check his apartment at S. 930 Lincoln. But while Yost was gone, someone broke into the apartment and stole two stereo tape recorders and about 80 stereo tapes.

Oien, who felt responsible, even though he couldn't have prevented the burglary which occurred while he was off duty, kept an eye out for the stolen items. Thursday night, while making a routine check of a downtown tavern, he saw a recorder matching the description of the one stolen, being offered for sale.

He said he checked the serial numbers with the theft report. They matched. Loren Eugene Griffith, 21, W. 2800 Dean, was arrested in connection with the burglary Friday and booked into the city jail on a charge of second degree burglary. Bond was set at $1,500.

Oien, after winding up the paperwork, left the station Friday night to inform his friend that all the items stolen from his apartment had been recovered.

Left: Shane Oien and his father, Jerry Oien, at Shane's swearing in as an officer for the Spokane Police Department on March 1, 1996. *(Courtesy Jerry Oien)*

Jerry and Glenda Oien sailing on Priest Lake, Idaho. *(Courtesy Jerry Oien)*

Jerry and Glenda on a cruise. Glenda died in an auto accident on Friday, June 7, 1996. Glenda and Jerry were married for over 35 years. She worked as a secretary at Deer Park Junior High School for 20 years. This photo was taken six months before her tragic death. *(Courtesy Jerry Oien)*

In 1964, a suicide attempt at the Red Shield Hotel, 200 West Main, occurred. The SPD was housed at the old Realty Building at 242 W. Riverside. The hotel was located directly across the alleyway from the police station. Oien's partner, Jerry McGougan, and he were in the station finishing up some paperwork when they received a call of a man claiming he was going to jump off the fire escape at the rear of the Red Shield Hotel. It took only minutes for officers Oien and McGougan to reach the hotel. Oien went to the third floor hallway that led to the fire escape. McGougan went to the roof, one floor above. Several hotel residents were out on the fire escape trying to talk to the man, but he wasn't listening. Suddenly he made a move to jump. Oien had been able to move onto the fire escape, and when he attempted to jump Oien was assisted by two bystanders to restrain the man. Officer McGougan can be seen climbing down the ladder from the roof. The man was taken to a hospital for mental evaluation. *(Courtesy Jerry Oien)*

John Morris went on the Spokane Police Department on December 16, 1960, and retired on March 31, 1994. *(Courtesy Jerry Oien)*

John passed away in 2003. He was assigned to Patrol Division. He went on motor in the early 1960s, and promoted to detective, working the auto squad.

John remarked that, when he started arresting the third generation in one family, he felt he had been on the SPD long enough. He always dealt with people well and referred to those he arrested as his "clients." He always had his pile of little folded-up papers in his shirt pockets, which held more information than the file cabinets in the office.

Frederick Robert Mielke – hired by the Spokane Police Department in 1961

Fred Mielke (far left, under arrow), Ron Scholz, and an unidentified motor officer sitting on his motor to the far right, with some of the children at St. Joseph's Children's Home. St. Joseph's was originally an orphanage, which opened in 1890. The Sisters of St. Francis of Philadelphia saw a growing need to care for orphaned children in the Spokane community. In order to help meet the needs of these children, they arranged to build St. Joseph's Children's Orphanage. The sisters took in children whose parents could no longer care for them, as well as those who were orphaned. The Spokane community raised the funds for the building and supplies needed to support the children. The sisters never turned anyone away. The original facility served as an orphanage until 1973, and then as a group home for children, before becoming a personal growth center. In 1987, St. Joseph's Children's Home evolved into a counseling and retreat center. *(Courtesy Terry Mielke)*

Fred Mielke was born on February 25, 1939, to Robert and Kathryn (Teen) Mielke. He was the oldest of three children. He grew up in northwest Spokane and graduated from North Central High School. He married his wife, Karlynn, on July 30, 1959, and also entered the U.S. Coast Guard.

Fred's first job with the city was for the Spokane Maintenance Garage. Shortly thereafter, he was hired as a Spokane police officer, where he served for 26 years. For 18 years, Fred rode police motorcycle. He was also a hostage negotiator, taught at the police and state patrol academies, and was one of the initial officers assigned as a community relations officer. During Expo '74, he oversaw police operations at Peoples' Park.

The following article appeared in the *Spokane Daily Chronicle* on Monday, August 6, 1984, 10 years after Expo '74:

People's Park: The hippie hotel
Officers in (grubbies) kept the peace at Hangman Creek during Expo '74
by Jim Spoerhase

Not all visitors to Expo '74 stayed in hotels and relatives homes. People's Park, a dusty 35-acre campsite at the confluence of Hangman Creek and the Spokane River was "home" for thousands attracted here by the world's fair, including a number of self-described hippies and "yippies."

Fred Mielke, then a Spokane police officer assigned to the park, which included the city's unofficial nude beach, said the transient population of the park peaked at about 6,000.

Mielke and eight other officers in plain clothes, actually in "grubbies," were assigned to patrol the park. "We didn't hide the fact we were cops, but we didn't flash it around,"

Fred Mielke circa 1970. *(Courtesy Terry Mielke)*

Mielke recalled recently, "It was scary to walk through the camp after 11 p.m. You never knew what might happen."

Mielke recalled a fight between two young men, who apparently had been friends. "One of them had a big snake around his neck, which I thought was rubber or plastic," Mielke said. "They got into a fight over who was going to 'wear' the snake. One started slashing with a knife and the fella with the snake got cut on the ear and lip, then was stabbed in the side."

"After we broke it up," Mielke said, "I bent over to look closely at the cut the young fella had on his side. It was then that the snake moved. It was real! There I was, looking that snake eyeball to eyeball. I aged a lot that night."

Some of the problems were generated by those not staying at the park, Mielke said. "We had lots of local kids who wanted to come in, drink beer, and act tough. There were the pimps who wanted to get close to the young girls in the park, some of whom were runaways and a target for the pimps. There was also the problem of hard core drug dealers," Mielke said. "Marijuana was smoked in the park, we knew it and they knew we knew it, but most of them didn't make a show of it in front of us," he said.

Mielke said several groups of transients using the campsite had their own forms of government and police helped organize a "tribal council" of group leaders. The park residents helped police keep order. "We had knifings and the like, but never a homicide that whole summer," Mielke said. However, one of the transient residents drowned on May 22, 1974.

He said the only problem, nude swimming, involved curious city residents who tried to drive in close for a look. It became necessary to install a gate and dig a trench to stop vehicles from entering the beach area.

On July 5, the yippies scheduled a "smoke out" at nearby High Bridge Park. About 200 showed up and there was talk of storming the gates at Expo. Mielke said many in the group marched toward the fairgrounds. But by the time it got to Main and Monroe they were met by police who told them they would have to stay on the sidewalks – the number had dropped to 50. Eventually 16 of them got to the Expo grounds and made a disturbance. All were arrested.

The People's Park campsite was officially closed in September 1974.

Another article appeared in the Tuesday, June 6, 1995, *Spokesman-Review*. This came about as the result of Spokane's notorious, but often easily embarrassed reporter, Doug Clark, who was assigned to investigate and report his findings at People's Park, 21 years following the closure of Expo '74. Doug did not enjoy this assignment, but he had a job to do.

People's Park Nudists Unglued About Being Labeled Lewd

Cindy Lambert isn't the least bit ashamed to be interviewed while she sprawls in warm sand as "nekkid" as a peeled onion.

The woman invited me to Spokane's famed haven of ungirded loins the other day to chat about something that really embarrasses her: Being considered lewd for her nudist ways.

Lambert, 38, is one of a handful of sun lovers who got their bare buns ticketed during a recent police sweep of People's Park, along the banks of the Spokane River just west of the city. They were cited for "lewd conduct," which Lambert finds highly offensive because the misdemeanor can be applied to far sleazier things than mere nudity.

According to the city code, sickos who masturbate, urinate, defecate, or engage in intercourse in public can also be popped for lewd conduct. A conviction carries up to a $1,000 fine and 90 days in jail.

In the minds of Lambert and her free-spirited friends, there is nothing remotely lewd about being nude. "I was asleep on the beach. The cop had to wake me up to give me the ticket," says Bob Grothe, 45. "How can you be asleep and be lewd?" The nudists have contacted a lawyer. They vow to fight this in court and I hope they win.

Getting an all-over tan is normal behavior at People's Park. Grothe has been part of the People's Park fleshscape since 1975. Lambert began doffing her duds there in 1984.

"I won't say that there's a grandfather clause," she adds, "but police have allowed us to be nude down here for at least 20 years. "So why do they suddenly come out of the bushes like a bunch of vultures and pluck out a few of us?"

In the early 1980s, four People's Park nudists fought their lewd conduct citations. Helped by the ACLU, the sun lovers won when the ordinance was ruled unconstitutional. The city drafted another lewd law, but it apparently hasn't been tested. Until now. Just what Spokane needs, another asinine court battle.

People's Park is just a few minutes west of downtown Spokane, but you have to be a determined voyeur to see any skin. It takes a quarter-mile hike down a dusty trail to reach this secluded spot where Hangman Creek meets the Spokane River.

During Expo '74, this lovely place was jammed with camping hippies, many of whom frolicked naked in the river. A national nudist hot line still lists People's Park among America's nude beaches. Workers at the Peaceful Valley Community Center will gladly give the curious step-by-step directions.

On hot summer weekends you may find 100 people, lounging near the rushing water in various stages of undress. I encountered about 25 naked strangers during my visit to see Lambert. Walking clothed among the unclothed is a weird sensation, let me tell you. Paul, a man with nothing to hide except his real name, said entire naked families gather on Sundays to relax and barbecue burgers. I'll bet when you're a nudist you learn real fast not to dangle too close to the ol' hibachi.

Lambert and Grothe are worried their citations are the beginning of a new People's Park purge.

Spokane Police Lt. Jim Nicks says not to worry. No new nudist-hassling policy has been issued. Nicks was vague about what happened to Lambert and the others on May 22. He didn't say why, but a brother officer apparently decided to use "officer discretion" and nail a few unclad sunbathers. It's a bum rap. Apparently there weren't any crack dealers, gang bangers or burglars to arrest. Ticketing nudists "is not high on our priority list," Nicks agrees, chuckling. "It must have been a slow day."

More Fred Adventures

Fred Mielke held numerous side jobs throughout his life, including driving commercial trucks, owning both a pilot car service, an excavation business, and a funeral escort business.

He grew up vacationing at Priest Lake, Idaho and made it his primary home after retiring.

Fred had many passions in life including his family, friends, kids, dogs, classic cars, and speed. Throughout his life, he raced motorcycles, cars, and eventu-

ally settled on racing boats, achieving the top points in his class for the nation.

Fred was one of the author's (Bamonte's) motor partners for several years. I remember him as always having a great sense of humor. One incident that stands out was the time he became involved with boats. He had a friend who was trying to sell him a sleek-looking large racing boat. The only thing that Fred didn't like about the boat was its color, which was pink. Upon seeing his friend's boat for the first time, Fred immediately objected to its color. His friend quickly corrected him about the color stating it wasn't actually pink, but was champagne colored, and that most people he knew just loved that color. Fred bought the boat. However, the next time Fred saw his friend that sold him the boat, he was greeted with, "Hi Fred, how's your pink boat?"

From left: Mike Kusterer, Ron Scholz, unknown, and Fred Mielke entertaining a group of kids, circa 1960.
(Courtesy Terry Mielke)

One other thing I should mention, Fred was exceptionally good on a motorcycle. He also had a number of his own motors and could do a commendable wheel stand for a long distance.

He also had a great appreciation for classic cars, starting when he was a teenager. He owned many throughout his life and was a member of the Dukes Car Club. Fred loved kids and was an especially proud grandfather. Early in his career, he volunteered with Morning Star Boys Ranch and helped Rev. Clifton Hamp arrange an annual summer camp at Liberty Lake for disadvantaged youth.

Following lengthy complications from a previous stroke, Fred passed away on April 4, 2015.

Fred Mielke and his father, Bob, holding a motorcycle trophy Fred must have "accidentally" won. *(Courtesy Terry Mielke)*

John Lynch, foreground facing camera; Jim Spoerhase, back to wall with glasses; Fred Mielke, guarding the door; and Tony Bamonte behind Fred – mostly hidden by Fred's "slouchy posture," and at the far right, Angie Costanzo. *(Courtesy Terry Mielke)*

Louis Vela – hired by the Spokane Police Department in 1961

S
P
O
K
A
N
E

P
O
L
I
C
E

D
E
P
A
R
T
M
E
N
T

Louis Vela, circa 1965. *(Courtesy Louis Vela)*

Lou Vela was born at Ozona, Texas, in 1937, where he and his younger sister attended both grade and high school. During his time in Ozona, Lou learned ranch work from his father, Francisco "Pancho Vela," who was a ranch foreman. Lou was six years old when his mother passed away. His dad raised both Lou and his four sisters, Juanita, Francisca, Josepha, and Rosa. A fifth sister, Rosario, was still a baby and adopted by an aunt and uncle. Lou's dad never remarried. Only Rosa is alive today. She lives in Midland, Texas.

Following his graduation from Ozona high school in 1956, Lou enlisted in the Air Force. His final tour of duty was at Geiger Field in Spokane County. Part of Geiger Field was later turned into a work release facility.

In 1960, Lou married Florine Heine. The following year he joined the Spokane Police Department. In 1972, Lou attended Spokane Falls Community College on the GI Bill, studying law enforcement. In 1987, following 26 years on the department, he retired.

During his time on motorcycle with the Spokane Police Department (1963 to 1970), his greatest source of pride was that he and Flo raised four children who all became accomplished swimmers, representing the Spokane Swim Team. They all attended Shadle Park High School in Spokane.

His oldest son, Steve, placed in multiple events at the Junior Olympics and several national meets. He missed qualifying for the 1980 Olympic trials by tenths of seconds. He went on to swim collegiately at the University of Oregon and University of Washington, where he became an All-American. He recently retired as aquatics director at Queen Anne Pool in Seattle.

A 1959 photo of Lou Vela standing on his 1953 Ford Fairlane. *(Courtesy Lou Vela)*

l Join Force

ere are Spokane's 10 newest police patrolmen and new policewoman—there are three policewomen the department—shortly after they were sworn recently by City Clerk Alex A. Brown. The patrolmen this week started a six-week course on all hases of police work at the Spokane Police Acad-emy. Left to right, front row, are Michael C. Kuterer, Robert L. Kriek, Sharon J. Price, Louis Vela and Charles R. Johnson; back row, left to right are Jerold E. Oien, Frederick R. Mielke, Michael D. Connors, Roy S. Allen, John D. Skow and Michael R. Fitzpatrick.

Photo taken in 1961 shows 10 of the newest police patrolmen and a new police woman. It was taken shortly after they were sworn in. They are from left to right starting with the front row: Michael Kusterer, Robert Krick, Sharon J. Price, Louis Vela, and Charles Johnson. Back row: Jerold E. Oien, Frederick R. Mielke, Michael D. Conners, Roy Allen, John D. Skow, and Michael R. Fitzpatrick. *(Courtesy Lou Vela)*

Lou's son Stan also swam at the University of Washington, later transferring to Central Washington State College, (now university in Ellensberg). He was voted for two consecutive years as the National Association of Intercollegiate Athletics (NAIA) swimmer of the year. He was featured in *Sports Illustrated*, and was inducted into the Swimming Hall of Fame at the Ellensburg school. During this time, he was still active in master class swimming, setting a world record for his age group in the United Kingdom. His daughters Starla and Stacy also swam in what was a family project.

After Lou retired in 1987, he participated in local rodeos and team roping with former policeman, and best friend, Stan McGee. In 2014, he quit roping when his horse Sammy passed away. Horses have always been a passion with Lou.

One of the most important lessons Lou stated he learned in life, and especially while on the police department, was to always be kind and considerate to other people and in turn they will be the same to you. This lesson was practiced well throughout his life. It especially came through during his years on the police department as he was respected and well liked by all who knew him.

An advertisement promoting minority hiring for the Spokane Police Department. The name of the girl standing next to Lou is Penny (unknown last name), who worked in records. This photo was taken in 1986. *(Courtesy Lou Vela)*

Lou Vela on horse patrol for the Spokane Police Department. The horse is "Lil Big Enuff," formerly owned by John McFall, the sheriff's posse secretary. Lieutenant Isaac "Ike" Gimlin is in the background. This photo was taken at Riverfront Park, circa 1974. *(Courtesy Lou Vela)*

Upper photo: Lou's daughter, Stacy, is the first girl in the upper left.

Lower photo: The girl second from the left is Lisa Brodie. She is the niece of John Brodie, a quarterback for the 49ers. Stacy Vela is on the far right.

Other members of the Spokane swim team, at the time, were nieces of Lt. Ken White of the Spokane Police Department, Tonya and Tersa Angelo, and nephew Joe Angelo.

Other law-enforcement related members on the swim team were the sons of state patrolman Joe Kimball, Deputy Sheriff Richard Lovejoy, and FBI agent Les Dieckman. Also, Officer H. Clark had two sons on the swim team at the same time Vela's boys swam. *(Courtesy Lou Vela)*

Swimming: Togetherness for Vela Family

The Vela family gathers around the trophy case to examine some of the more-than-200 trophies they have won in swim events. Family members are (left to right) Steve, age 17, father Lou, Stan, 16, Starla, 12, Stacy, 14, and mother Florence.

Lou and Florence look in on their family at a recent practice session at Shadle Park High School pool. During the summer the swimmers have twice-daily practices.

Sisters Follow Brothers Into Competition

By SUE VAUGHAN

"Swimming has kept our family together, giving us a special closeness. It has taught the kids self discipline and kept them out of trouble. We are grateful to God for the wonderful ability He has given our children."

These are the heartfelt sentiments of Lou Vela, father of one of Spokane's most successful swimming families.

Between the boys—Steve, age 17, and Stan, age 16 — the Vela family has been represented at 11 national swim meets. And there are two more Velas coming up—Stacy, age 14 and Starla, age 12.

But, to Lou, the children, and his wife, Florence, their participation in competitive swimming is what ties the family into a close-knit group, providing the encouragement often essential for success in athletics.

"We have seldom prodded or pushed the kids to go swimming. Their accomplishments have been on their own, with long yardage and hard work," Lou explained.

Indeed, instead of rivalry between the children as to who brings home the most trophies—there are more than 200 trophies in the Velas' trophy case—it is admiration between the swimmers.

"It has really drawn us closer together. I understand that Steve has put in the necessary work to get what he has and that I will have to put in that much work," Stan said. "Really, our family is the only one who understands exactly what we have accomplished with the hard work. Our friends at school don't know about swimming. Like I went to the regional meet and took fifth place, which was really an accomplishment for me.

"I came home and told the kids at school and they said, 'gee, you didn't do very well, you didn't win'."

Steve was the one who got the family started in the water sport.

When he was eight he was swimming and boating and we told him he would have to chose between the two," Florence related. "We kind of pushed him toward swimming because we thought it would be less expensive.

"Stan started swimming shortly thereafter because he kept following Steve over to the pool." And, in turn, the girls wanted to do what their brothers were doing and they jumped into the pool, too. All, now are members of the Spokane Swim Team.

"We are really thrilled and thankful that Stacy can swim at all," Florence said. "She had open heart surgery when she was five, she only weighed 32 pounds. We are thrilled to death she can swim with the other children."

But, Florence was wrong about the financial end of the sport. "This costs more than I ever imagined," she said.

"Each boy must finance his own trips. The only help they get from Spokane Swim Team is when they go to national competition."

But, Lou was quick to add, "We have been blessed with help." Lou is a detective on the Spokane police force and said they have been so good about working his hours around traveling with his children.

"And the guys all chipped in to help the boys go to nationals. We really want to thank the police guild and the Footprinters, another police agency, for helping us."

Lou and Florence both try to attend all of the children's meets.

"Sometimes he is at one and I am at another, and it used to be quite a time trying to get them all to practice," their mother, who works selling greetings cards, said. "Especially in the summer when they swim at 6:30 a.m. and 4:30 p.m. and at different pools."

And, Florence added that one of the most difficult things about having the whole family involved is finding time to have a family dinner. "It was so hard to ever have everyone there, but it is getting better now. We have adjusted our dinner around the swimming."

The Vela swimmers do not suffer one malady often facing dedicated athletes—the monotony of daily workouts with little public recognition or appreciation of what they are working for, something that has tempted more than one swimmer to quit.

Both boys have their sights set on the 1980 Olympic Games and the girls want to follow right along behind their older brothers.

"The workouts are so hard sometimes," Starla agreed. "Your muscles get sore but you have to suffer sometimes to get what you want."

Steve recently returned from the National AAU Indoor Meet in Austin, Texas where he placed 21st in the 200 intermediate. He was seeded 45th going into the meet so he was pleased with his showing.

Stan attended the National AAU Junior Meet in Huntsville, Ala., the week before where he placed 35th in the 200 backstroke. "I was seeded about 24th so I didn't do that good. I think I was nervous."

Starla, has her sights and goals set on something within a shorter reach than her brothers. She attended the junior nationals at Eugene, Ore., when she was 10. Now she says, "When I grow up, I want to go to the senior nationals."

It looks like the Vela family will have several more records to enter in the books before it is finished in swimming.

And, Lou could very well have been describing his own family when he commented—

"*The Spokane Swim Team is a super organization with well-mannered, good kids and caring parents.*"

With goggles atop his head, Stan takes a breather during workouts.

Photo by Clint Watkins

Labor of Love

The swimmers' grandmother made each one of these quilts out of their swim patches.

Starla (left) says every swimmer gets tired once in awhile but hard work got her to a national age group meet, one Stacy wants to attend.

Stan (left) and Steve often race against each other in practice. Stan said when they were young, he almost beat Steve once.

A full page of the May 12, 1978, *Spokane Daily Chronicle* was devoted to the Vela family. In the upper left photo they were gathered around some of more than 200 trophies the children had won in various swim events. *(Courtesy Lou Vela)*

Lou Vela at Spokane Community College in 1976 as a member of a running group. To this day, Lou continues to work out on a daily basis. *(Courtesy Lou Vela)*

Upper left photo: Lou Vela's dad, Francisco "Pancho" Vela, holding his first son Steve. When Steve was born, Pancho's father took a bus from West Texas to Spokane to meet his grandson. Lou's dad's nickname was "Pancho." In Spanish Latin America and in the Philippines, people with the name Francisco are nick-named "Pancho." As a teenager, Lou's dad was a horse wrangler for Pancho Villa in the early 1900s. The relationship and thoughts about his dad were expressed in Lou's statement: "My daddy was the kindest and most affectionate dad a child could have, just the best dad in the world and my lifetime hero."Lower left photo: Lou and his dad in 1970, during a visit to a cousin's ranch in Texas. *(Photos courtesy Lou Vela)*

Pancho Villa, born in 1878, was a fearless Mexican revolutionary hero. The son of a field laborer, he was orphaned at an early age. In revenge for an assault on his sister, he killed one of the owners of the estate on which he worked and was afterward forced to flee to the mountains, where he spent his adolescence as a fugitive. During the rebellion, Villa, who lacked a formal education, learned to read and write, displaying his talents as soldier and organizer. Those gifts enabled him to be a key figure in the Mexican Revolution. In the lower photo, he is pictured with a 1914 Indian motorcycle. Villa's exploits were regularly filmed by Hollywood movie companies. *(Public domain)*

Mounted drill team from left: Gary Lacewell, Joe Machala, Tom Scott, Mark Grumbly, Joe Bokor, Lou Vela, and Monte Johnston. *(Courtesy Lou Vela)*

Lou was happiest when he was sitting astride his horse. This photo was taken at Long Beach, Washington. *(Courtesy Lou Vela)*

Spokane Police Academy, July 1961 - Front Row: SPD Officer Mike Kusterer, SPD Officer Bob Krick, SPD Officer Ron Wayerski, SPD Officer Richard Apperson, SPD Officer Sharon Price, SPD Officer Lou Vela, SPD Officer Fred Mielke, SPD Officer John Skow, SPD Officer Charles Johnson, and Lt. George Berg. Back Row: SPD Officer Jack Tenney, SPD Officer Jerry Oien, SPD Officer Mike Fitzpatrick, SPD Officer Ron Cahalan, SPD Officer Lynn Howerton, SPD Officer Roy Allen, SPD Officer Chuck Staudinger, SPD Officer Al Teeples, SPD Officer Joe Kaley, and SPD Officer Jack Carter.

Lou in the Air Force. He served from 1956 to 1960. During that time, his MOS was as communication operator. In 1960, he received an honorable discharge and settled in Spokane.

Lou and Florine Vela when they were married in 1960 in Spokane. Florine's maiden name was Heine. They divorced in 1987, the same year Lou retired. They still have remain good friends, and neither of them has remarried. Their kids are a bond that keeps them connected. *(Photos courtesy Lou Vela)*

James Frederick Moore – hired by the Spokane Police Department in 1961

Jim Moore, circa 1968. *(Courtesy the Moore family)*

Jim Moore was born on May 11, 1939, and raised in Spokane. He went to Willard and Bemis elementry schools and graduated from Rogers High School in 1957. Jim and his wife had five children: Cassandrea, Dorothy, Timothy (deceased), Elaine, and Gregory. Jim joined the Spokane Police Department in 1961.

He was assigned to Traffic in 1965 and rode motor until he made detective in 1968 or 69. During Jim's riding days they rode motor year around, attaching a side car during the winter months, which typically began in October. Sometime in the spring, usually in March, they would remove the sidecars.

During all of Jim's riding years, they used Harley-Davidsons. This was during the time there was no electric starting on the bikes. During the winter, starting the bikes was always a problem because the oil would be so thick.

As a detective, Jim worked with five police officers in a Special Squad for about six months. Their assignment was to reduce burglaries, identify patterns showing specific areas of town, and known burglars. In that assignment, officers averaged two misdemeanor or traffic and one felony arrest per day. As part of that assignment, they interviewed all suspects, which then would lead to more arrests, and then executed search warrants. They consulted with the prosecutors on a regular basis and the overall results were great. Burglaries dropped from 10-15 daily to one to two daily. Jim was very proud of the work done by this group of officers. I recall those with him on that assignment were: Sgt. Lou Moss, Steve Christian, Larry Williamson, Jim Peterson, and Bob Yake.

Jim retired from the police department in March of 1988. He was a well-liked officer and could always be counted on. He took great pride in serving his community and was proud to be a Spokane police officer.

Jim Moore, circa 1968. *(Courtesy the Moore family)*

Monte Emmitt Gaunt – hired by the Spokane Police Department in 1962

Monte Gaunt, circa 1965. *(Courtesy Rhea Gaunt)*

Monte Gaunt was born in Spokane on September 10, 1934, and was a lifelong resident. He graduated from Lewis and Clark High School and worked as a bricklayer prior to going on the Spokane Police Department in 1962. When Monte went on the department his first duties as a patrol officer were walking a beat in the downtown skid row area, the downtown paddy wagon and the jail, which at the time was located at 242 West Riverside. Several years later, Monte began five years on motor. This assignment was temporarily interrupted by a debilitating accident involving his motor and an automobile. Upon his recovery, he went back to riding motor, this time with Lou Vela as his partner.

During 1967, while Monte was still on motor, he would often work the district around Playfair Racetrack, an area of occasional crime. There was a tack shop on the racetrack grounds, which was operated during the racing season by Rhea Richards Shipley, who was the granddaughter of early Spokane mining magnate Patrick "Patsy" Clark. One day Monte asked her what she did with the money she took in every day from her business. She replied that she

took it home. This would have left a woman nearing her 50s in a vulnerable position for a strong-arm robbery. Monte realized that, so whenever he was working that area and had time he would check in on her, seeing that she made it to her car safely. As time passed they became friends and Rhea grew to respect Monte.

As a friendship grew between Monte and Rhea, she learned Monte also had a passion for horses. Rhea had a daughter, also named Rhea. Both mother and daughter were well known in the Spokane area for teaching horseback riding lessons in the Spokane Valley. When Rhea learned Monte was looking to buy a horse, she told her daughter about the good looking policeman who used to look out for her at the racetrack. The daughter, Rhea, had a horse to sell. Within three years, in 1970, the 25-year-old Rhea married Monte. When asked, Rhea said she was married to Monte 28 years – up until he died. When I asked how they met, she said, "Monte bought a horse from me."

Following his tenure on motor, Monte went into the the detective division. He served in the Spokane Police Department for 30 years from 1962 to 1992 and retired as a detective. Monte passed away at the age of 62 on October 29, 1996, and is buried at Pines Cemetery in the Spokane Valley. He was survived by his wife, Rhea Gaunt; his six children, Barbara, Jody, and James Gaunt, all of Spokane, Tammy Gaunt of Vancouver, Washington, Rick and Terri Williams, both of Seattle; a brother, Bill Gaunt of Springfield, Oregon; two sisters, Penny Prentice of Cheney, and Sally Fields and Connie Saxon, both of Spokane; six grandchildren and three great-grandchildren.

The George Grammer Task Force

George Grammer was described by Judge William Grant as "a Beast of Prey who stalked and raped women as if it were a full time job." This description was given by Judge Grant in 1989, when he sentenced Grammer to 95 years in prison.

The George Grammer Task Force was made up of Monte Gaunt, Earl Ennis, Marilyn Simon, Shirley Rice, Judi Carl, Lloyd Schaffer, Jim Peterson, Joe

THE SPOKESMAN-REVIEW

25 CENTS/50 CENTS OUTSIDE SPOKANE AND KOOTENAI COUNTIES   SPOKANE, WASHINGTON 106TH YEAR, NO

Rapist gets 95-year term

Extraordinary sentence lin to Grammer's vicious atta

By Jim DeFede
Staff writer

Describing George Grammer as "a beast of prey" who stalked and raped women as if it were a full-time job, Judge William Grant sentenced him Thursday to 95 years in prison.

With time off for good behavior the 26-year-old, seventh-grade dropout will be eligible for parole in 62 years — the year 2051. He would be 88 years old.

"The sheer enormity of the crimes is something that has impacted this community tremendously," the Spokane County Superior Court judge said before ordering the sentence, believed to be the most severe since the Legislature passed the Sentencing Reform Act in 1984.

"The picture here is that of a true serial rapist," Grant said.

Grammer has admitted to raping eight women between 1985 and his arrest in October 1987. On Jan. 17, he pleaded guilty to four rapes, including an attack on a 5-year-old girl.

Prosecutors had asked for a sentence of 75 years and corrections officials recommended no more than 90. But Grant's anger toward Grammer and his crimes was evi-

dent in the judge's v talked about the effect had on his victims as entire city.

"An exceptional sen be imposed," Grant said standard sentence for was 17 to 23 years.

Arguing for the exce tence, Deputy Prosecut ble said Grammer's a particularly vicious in ning and execution. Hi tion was intense, Skibbi

"Mr. Grammer's f was stalking women, came very good at it," "At any one time he four or five houses u lance."

He said that as nev tacks spread, everyon became a victim.

Grammer's attorn Bechtolt, said "severe is warranted" and th tional sentence in the child was warranted, judge should make it Grammer to someday ciety.

The temptation warehouse George in
(See Sentence on

Serial rapist George Grammer is led from the courtroom where a judge sentenced him to 95 years in prison. *Staff photo by DAN PELLE*

George Grammer, escorted from court by Deputy Jerry Brady, was a serial rapist who operated in the Shadle area from 1985 to 1987. He could easily be considered one of Spokane's most dangerous criminals, rivaling the horrendous *modus operandi* of serial rapist Kevin Coe – both in brutality and savageness. When Judge William Grant sentenced Grammer to 95 years in prison, he considered the enormity of the crimes and how they impacted the Spokane community. The judge said he believed the sentence to be the most severe since the Legislature passed the Washington State Sentencing Reform Act in 1984. *(Public domain)*

Peterson, Minde Connelly, Jimmy Johnson, Jerry Hendren, Mark Bennett, Chief Terry Mangan, and Larry Lindskog.

Because of the seriousness of the crimes, many officers worked hard to bring this case to a successful end. They also felt it was important, for the benefit of the community, to be aware that such dangerous criminals existed. Due to Grammer's viciousness and predatory attacks on women, a decision was made to place it in Monte Gaunt's section, both as a tribute to him and to all who worked it.

George Grammer's crimes

Grammer admitted to violently raping eight women between 1985 and his arrest in October 1987. On January 17, he pleaded guilty to four rapes, including

an attack and rape of a five-year-old girl. Grammer showed no remorse toward any of his victims. In a psychiatrist's report, Grammer is quoted: "If I cared about these women, I wouldn't have raped them."

Psychiatrist David Grubb who examined Grammer after his arrest, described him as "a sociopath who is not capable of empathy, remorse, or caring for other people."

Six corrections officers testified how Grammer continued to make threatening statements while in jail, telling several female officers he would love to rape them some day.

In the courtroom, as the judge began describing each of Grammer's attacks, a broad grin spread over Grammer's face. However, as the hearing continued,

Grammer became annoyed that the process was taking so long and at one point gestured with his hands for the judge to speak faster – tapping the chains that shackled him against his chair.

As the judge pronounced the sentence, Grammer told his attorney he regretted pleading guilty and that he should have taken the case to trial. Grammer told his attorney he was afraid of what would happen to him in prison, as inmates typically don't look favorably upon child rapists. He threatened to kill a deputy or correction officer before leaving Spokane in the hopes it would make him a hero to other convicts at the state penitentiary.

On his way back to the jail, Grammer said; "Death to society." A few minutes later he got into a scuffle with sheriff's deputies and spit in the face of one of the officers.

The following, by Jim DeFede, was written in the *Spokesman-Review* on November 13, 1987, following a combined interview by columnists from both the *Spokesman* and *Chronicle*:

"I'm sorry they had to be raped" Grammer confesses he's Shadle rapist; Had plans to kill.

George Grammer says he is the Shadle Park rapist, He says he has terrorized Northwest Spokane since 1985, prowling the streets at night and raping a least eight people – from a 5-year-old girl to a 60-year-old woman.

"I hate women," Grammer said. "I hate women so bad that a lot of times I'll think about how I hate so bad, that I can actually make myself start puking up blood."

In five hours of Jail interviews with the *Spokesman-Review* and *Spokane Chronicle*, the 25-year-old Grammer said that if he had not been locked away Oct. 8 for exposing himself to a woman, he would have continued raping and then would have turned to murder.

Grammer said he already would have assaulted District Court Judge Christine Cary – who he said he had been spying on for nearly two months. From there, he planned to kill Superior Court Judge John Schultheis and several police officers.

Every rape, Grammer said, was a cry for help from a man who bad been sexually abused as a child, who was continually at odds with the law and who spent half his childhood in foster homes and detention centers.

"The only way I thought I could get help was to do the rapes," he said.

Grammer was identified Thursday by Police Chief Terry Mangan as the key suspect in the Shadle Park rapes. Mangan expects rape charges to be filed against Grammer within two weeks.

Grammer, who has lived in the Shadle area for 15 years, said he plans to plead guilty.

He is in Spokane County Jail now on $250,000 bond for attempted kidnapping.

Last summer, a special police task force was established to capture the rapist stalking the quiet residential neighborhoods east of Joe Albi Stadium, as well as a second serial rapist who has preyed on children in the Mission Park area.

"I enjoyed it" when they formed the task force, Grammer said, "mainly because now at the same time I was hunting down victims, I had people hunting me.

"It brought excitement to what went down.

In chilling detail Grammer – dressed in a white T-shirt and blue pants – explained from the sixth floor of the jail how simple the attacks were to accomplish.

"It's about like doing a burglary," he said. "There is nothing to it. All you have to do is go down a street, see a house, see a light on and go up to the house and look in."

Grammer said he would watch several houses in an area for a period of days or even weeks, keeping track of the comings and goings of the occupants, waiting for a time when he was sure the victim would be home alone at night.

When he was ready to strike, he said, he would approach the house by bicycle, cut the telephone lines, force open a window and climb inside.

In one rape, he recalled, "I got into the lady's house and went to her back bedroom. She was still asleep. I opened the door and she stood up, she didn't scream, she didn't say nothing. I told her, 'come with me.' As I walked down the hall I told her I was going to (rape) her." Grammer said he led the woman to the back of the house, assaulted her and left.

Most of the victims, he said, he would lead outside, to their back yard or a nearby alley, before raping them. He said one of his victims talked throughout the incident, and another tried to grab a kitchen knife as they walked out of the house. She "fought like the dickens," said Grammer who is 6 feet 4 1/2 inches tall, But she quickly gave up, he said.

"The rest of the rapes were basically the same. They only fought for maybe five minutes, then I basically got what I wanted and left." The rapes had little to do with sex Grammer said, "It did not matter," he said, "if the victim was young or old, skinny or fat, pretty or plain."

"I'm sorry they had to be raped, he said. "I'm sorry for the emotions that they are going to have to live through, of being afraid at night."

He said that raping the 5-year-old was the most psychologically enjoyable at the time. It was part of a fantasy he was having about a virgin.

"It was not so much that I wanted to do it," he said. "It was a plea for help. It was getting to the point where I didn't know what to do with myself. I didn't know what to do with my life."

Grammer said he went into the child's bedroom while she was asleep, scooped her into his arms and carried her away on his bicycle. He stopped in a vacant lot near the girl's home and raped her.

"She wasn't scared at all," he said. "She wasn't crying, she wasn't screaming... .

"She took it, as I took it when I was first – you could say raped when I was 10 years old," Grammer said, his upper chest and arms trembling, "What could she do?"

Initially, Grammer said, he left the girl in a vacant lot. "It's like the bad side of me said leave her there to die, and I rode down the alley," he said. Then "the good side came out of me and I basically went back and made sure she stopped bleeding," After he checked on the girl, Grammer said he placed her near a parked car so she would be found easily.

Police say that in most of the cases, the rapist usually helped the victim to her feet, led her back to her house and made sure she got inside and locked the door before he would leave.

One of the victims suffered a broken Jaw, police said, but no one was beaten and no weapon was used.

Before leaving the rape scene, Grammer said, he would try to find the victim's purse or wallet and take it with him.

Because he believed the police always were watching his house, he never would go home immediately, he said. Instead, he would wander the streets for hours, sometimes watching patrol cars scream through the neighborhood on their way to the victim's house.

He then would find someplace quiet and sit. "I would sit there for a half-hour, 45 minutes, staring at the victim's driver's license and her face, I would basically start crying, telling myself, "Why the hell did I do this? I know I'm sick, I know I need help," Then the other side would come out and say, "Well, you did it because you wanted to do it. You're a criminal,'"

Asked why he raped, Grammer replied in two words: "My life."

Born Aug. 1, 1962, in Portland, George Nicholas Grammer was the second of four children. He was raised and baptized a Catholic by his parents - Eileen and George Grammer.

For nine years, he said, life seemed relatively normal. Dad worked for the park service in Portland. Mom raised the kids.

Then one day, Grammer said, he walked into his Dad's bedroom and found him dead.

"That freaked me out. I went off the deep end from there."

Grammer said he began getting into trouble with Oregon police almost immediately. When he was 10, he and his family moved to Spokane. But instead of using the move as a fresh start, Grammer said, he began getting into trouble with police for such things as shoplifting and vagrancy.

Gammer became a ward of the court. Depending on the type of trouble he got himself into, he was shuffled as a teenager among juvenile detention centers, foster homes and work ranches.

Growing agitated as he spoke, Grammer pointed to scars he said he accumulated during his childhood as a part of "the system." "In all of these places I was abused quite a bit, both sexually and physically.'

Grammer's juvenile records are not available. Police Chief Mangan said the police are working on confirming details about Grammer's life, and have been told he was raised in foster homes and spent time in detention centers.

Grammer, who said he attended school through the seventh grade, said even as a juvenile, he was asking for help from the judicial system. "I never did get any," he said.

"I'm very intelligent," be said later. "I probably have an IQ higher than you or anybody in this jail, But my IQ is for the wrong stuff, you know, crime and drugs."

At 18 Grammer said he met and fell in love with a woman, his first and only girlfriend. He has lived with her for the last seven years, and three months ago she gave birth to their first child – Georgie Jr.

"The way it's going now," Grammer said, "we are going to have to change his name."

In the last seven years, he has been employed for six weeks – two weeks as a dishwasher and a month as a laborer. The rest of the time he said, his girlfriend supported him.

Grammer's history of crime has been a gradual progression, starting with shoplifting and burglary, moving into sex-oriented crimes such as indecent exposure and peeping.

"When you've done as many years in institutions and have such a resentment toward society, and you have a brain like mine, crime is easy to do.

"Because I understand exactly how the cops work, what their next move is going to be. I begin to think as a criminal. I can think as a cop. And I can think as a victim."

Next on Grammer's list of victims was District Court Judge Cary. Grammer appeared before her in 1988 for possession of marijuana. She fined him $150 and gave him a 90-day suspended sentence.

Grammer said he had watched her house for nearly two months, but couldn't plan an attack because her husband kept different hours every day.

Then, Grammer said, he planned to kill Superior Court Judge Schultheis. He said he appeared before the judge several times for traffic tickets while Schultheis was a District Court judge.

"I was going to move up from rape to murder," Grammer said, "because I have so much hatred in my body."

In Grammer's head is locked the memory of a day when he said Schultheis scolded him before a courtroom filled with people. Grammer lowered his voice and mimicked the judge's deep tone: "By God, George, if you come into my court again, I'm going to send you to prison until you are 21."

Then, he planned to move on to police officers. Grammer said he began spying on an officer's wife earlier this year, at one point cutting the phone line to the house. He did it only to scare the officer.

I wanted them [police officers] to know that I am watching them." Law enforcement officers believe Grammer intended to do that to. Luckily, they said the night the phone was cut, the officer tried to call his wife. When he realized the phone was dead, he raced home. His wife was safe but one of the windows to the house looked as if someone had tried to pry it open. Grammer denies tampering with a window.

Grammer said he "probably would beat" the rape charges but plead guilty, "I feel sorry for my victims and don't want to see them go through a long trial.

He said he is hoping to be placed in a sex-offender treatment program, but believes he probably will get a lengthy prison term instead.

Several times during the interviews, Grammer offered to have himself castrated if his victims requested it.

"If all of the victims got together and said (castration) would make them happy and make them feel like they were getting something. ..., then I would do it."

He is just as emphatic about his need for counseling while in jail. He predicts that he will be sentenced to 40 years in prison for the rapes, an estimate some officers say probably is close to the sentencing range. With time off for good behavior he thinks he will be out in 18 years.

"I'll be 43 years old, and they'll turn me loose on the streets, Grammer said. "What am I supposed to do? Every time I go on the streets, I don't know what to do with myself."

Rhea and Monte Gaunt in 1978 at the Policeman's Ball. Prior to her marriage to Monte, Rhea showed horses and taught horseback riding, a skill and vocation she learned from her mother, Rhea Richard Shipley, who was one of a total of seven children born to Parick "Patsy" and Mary Clark. The patriarch of the family, Patsy Clark, was one of early Spokane's most successful mining magnates, well known for his friendship and kindness. The Patsy Clark Mansion still exists in Browne's Addition. *(Courtesy Rhea Gaunt)*

William Gene Ferguson – hired by the Spokane Police Department in 1963

Bill Ferguson, circa 1966. *(Courtesy Bill Ferguson)*

Bill Ferguson was born at Versallis, Missouri, and raised in Denison, Iowa. He attended Arlington Grade School in Iowa, Rogers High School in Spokane, and Metaline Falls High School in north Pend Oreille County, Washington. Bill had three brothers and a sister.

Following high school, he attended Spokane Community College and Eastern Washington University, where he obtained a BA in psychology. He spent two years active duty and six years with the Marine Corps reserve. Bill's first job was as a farm hand. His worst job was as a bouncer at a tavern. However, he stated the best job he ever had was being a husband to his great wife, Glenna. They met at the Crescent Department Store and were married in 1956. Glenna died on July 29, 2010. Bill and Glenna had three sons and a daughter: Bill Jr., Keith, Kelley, and Karen.

During Bill's 31-year tenure on the department, two of those years he was assigned to motor. Jim Moore, now deceased, was his motor partner.

One of Bill's most difficult experiences was a call he responded to that involved a mother who shot and wounded her son who was only two-and-a-half-year, and then committed suicide. The child was listed in fair condition at Holy Family Hospital. He suffered from three bullets, two in the chest and one in the leg.

Officers Bill Ferguson and Donald Jolley said the husband called police at midnight when he returned from work and found his wife and child.

Bill's happiest memory while on the department was of all the people he worked with. Bill always did the best he could on any assignment he was ever given. It could easily be said that Bill Ferguson lived by the Golden Rule throughout his life.

The following caption was taken from the 1965 *Spokane Chronicle*: "Five Spokane policeman today received the new badges they will wear when promotions they have received take effect Saturday. The badges were presented by Chief Clifford N. Payne (right). Receiving the promotions are (left to right) Officer Bill G. Ferguson, promoted to motorcycle officer), Officer John H. Leahy, promoted to detective; Sgt. Leroy G. Cummings Junior, promoted to detective, Officer Charles H. Crabtree to Sgt., and Sgt. Richard Olberding, to Lieutenant." *(Courtesy Bill Ferguson)*

The source and date are unknown but the caption was as follows: Girl Scouts drive – Sock dolls, made by members of Girl Scout Troop 424, have been added to the *Chronicle* Christmas drive for Lakeland Village. The troop is sponsored by Lidgerwood Elementary PTA. From the left are Mrs. Bill G. Ferguson, troop leader, Michelle Holcumb, Kathy Yates, Shelley Clemens, Cathy Gheri, and Karen Ferguson. Many other groups were also donating gifts for Lakeland. *(Courtesy Bill Ferguson)*

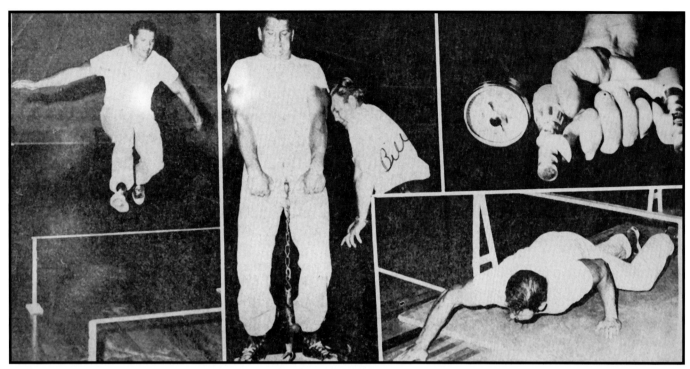

From the *Spokane Daily Chronicle*, circa 1972. Bill Ferguson is the third from the left. At the time of this photo, he was a lieutenant. This photo was at a civil service exam test. Ferguson, who was always a physical fitness buff, helped administer this test to new recruits for both the police and fire departments. The other person in this photo is fire fighter David J. Willman. *(Courtesy Bill Ferguson)*

From left: Motor officers Jim Moore, unknown, Bill Ferguson, and Bob Krick in report room. *(Courtesy Bill Ferguson)*

Flowers, You Say?

During Bill Ferguson's entire law-enforcement career, he established a pattern of consistently showing consideration for others. In this photo, he received a gift of flowers from a man who called himself "a satisfied citizen." The plant contained a card that said "keep up the good work."

Baby Arrives in Stalled Car

The following was a portion of an undated article that appeared in the *Chronicle:* "While her husband was urgently telephoning the police, his 18-year-old wife early today gave birth to a baby boy in a car parked in front of East 1100 29th Avenue. Police Officer Bill Ferguson reported the child was born shortly after 5 a.m. today and both the new son and mother were doing well at Deaconess Hospital. Ferguson reported he received a call to go to East 1100 29th. When he arrived he said in a report, the child already had been born. The dad was in the house at the time, still on the telephone. Strahl told officer Ferguson he started for the hospital and that his car ran out of gas in front of East 1107 29th. Mrs. Strahl and her son continued the trip to the hospital in a private ambulance."

Veteran officer to lead reserves

By ROBERT ALLEN
Spokesman-Review staff writer

New assignments are not unusual for Spokane's newly appointed police reserve unit chief Lt. Bill G. Ferguson.

During his 13 years on the police force, Ferguson, 38, has been a patrolman, a detective, a special investigator, a patrol and traffic sergeant and he has worked each of the day, swing and graveyard shifts.

Currently a lieutenant for the police patrol division, Ferguson's new assignment requires him to work one day a week with reservists.

He replaces James F. Haynes at the helm of the reserve unit. Last month Haynes was promoted to deputy police chief.

Working under the direction of Police Chief Wayne A. Hendren, Ferguson will train, schedule and coordinate the activities of the city's more than 40 reserve police men

LT. BILL FERGUSON
Heads Police Reserve

A partial quotation from an undated *Spokesman-Review* article. One of Bill Ferguson's last assignments was heading the Spokane Police Reserve. During his career he was well liked by both department members and the public, receiving numerous letters of commendation for police work well done.

Donald Jolley – hired by the Spokane Police Department in 1964

S P O K A N E   P O L I C E   D E P A R T M E N T

Don Jolley rode police motor for approximately eight years. Following that, he was assigned to Hit and Run, and ended his career investigating fatal accidents. *(Courtesy Don Jolley)*

Don Jolley was born in Orofino, Idaho, to Clyde and Mabel Jolley. He had two older brothers. Don and his brothers attended Forest and Winchester schools in Idaho. When he attended Forest School, a one-room school serving grades one through eight, he was the only one in his class. At that time, the town of Forest consisted of 28 people. Today it is a ghost town, with the remains of only one building still in existence. The town of Forest is a short distance north of Winchester. While attending Winchester, there were seven in his class. Winchester is a town within the Nez Perce Indian Reservation in Lewis County, on the Camas Prairie in the north central part of the state. The population was 340 in the 2010 census. The city was named in 1900 during a meeting to establish a school district. While considering the possibilities, an individual looked at the stack of Winchester rifles at the door and suggested the name, which was approved.

During the time the Jolley family was living at Winchester, Don's father worked for the main sawmill in town. The sawmill closed in May 1965 after the mature timber in the area had been cut. The mill was operated by Boise Cascade for its final five years. Its closure followed a fire, which destroyed much of downtown Winchester. When Don's father was working for the sawmill, he basically had two jobs: he was the main dry kiln operator and also pulled lumber from the "green chain." Anyone familiar

An early sawmill in Winchester, Idaho, circa 1910. Winchester was a small logging and sawmill town from its early beginnings in the 1900s. Don's father worked in the sawmills. *(Public domain)*

The entrance to the town of Winchester, where Don Jolley grew up. *(Public domain)*

with sawmill operations will be aware of the physical condition that job demands. Both of Don's older brothers also worked on the green chain.

In 1957, Don volunteered for the Army draft. During that time, he spent 16 months of his tour in Korea and spent the remainder of his time at Fort Lewis in Washington State. Following his discharge, Don went back to Winchester, but soon after moved to Spokane, where his future wife was living. Don met his wife, Wanda Hartwig, in grade school. She moved to Spokane, where she attended Kinman Business University. He moved to Spokane to marry her in 1962. Don's happiest time were the birth of his two children.

Don and Wanda divorced after 27 years of marriage. The have two children, Ken and Crystal. Wanda retired from the Spokane County Sheriff's Office as an administrative assistant after serving for many years. Their daughter, Crystal, is an officer for the Spokane Police Department.

Prior to going to work for the Police Department in 1964, Don worked for the Northern Pacific Railroad. During his time on the department, he served as a motorcycle officer, specialist, corporal assigned to motorcycles, hit-and-run and fatal accident investigation in the traffic division. Don rode motor from 1966 to 1974. During that time, his motor partner was Mickey O'Brien.

One of the significant events in Don's life was his participation in a new law that took effect July 1, 1980, which authorized tougher penalties against hit-and-run drivers who flee from accidents involving injuries or fatalities. That new law elevated the crime of hit-and-run from a gross misdemeanor to a Class C felony. Under the new law, a driver convicted of a felony could be sentenced to five years in prison and fined $5,000. Prior to that, the offender could only be charged with a misdemeanor and faced a possible year in jail and a $1,000 fine. The case that brought this to a head was the death of Donald R. Christianson of Spokane, an accident investigated by Don Jolley. In 1978, Christianson was struck and killed by a hit-and-run driver as he was crossing Sprague at Altamont. His body lay in the street until another vehicle ran over it and stopped when the driver saw it was a person.

That case culminated in September when an extensive investigation resulted in mailing a citation to a suspect who had moved to Texas. The suspect was charged with failure to leave information at the scene of a fatal accident, which is a gross misdemeanor. The suspect, who had moved back to Spokane at the time, agreed to meet with police but failed to keep his appointment. Jolley later learned he had left the state. Prior to that time, prosecuting attorneys rejected possible charges of negligent homicide, a felony, as there were no witnesses to the accident and most of the evidence was collected from paint samples at the accident scene and from the suspect's car. Frustration over the case led to Spokane Police Chief Wayne Hendren and Deputy Chief Robert Panther becoming involved. This was one of the significant cases, in which Don played a part.

Just as important, though, was the freedom the new statute afforded law enforcement officers against suspect drivers who had left the state. In the past, it was almost impossible to issue arrest warrants for hit-and-run drivers who fled to another state because the crime was not a felony

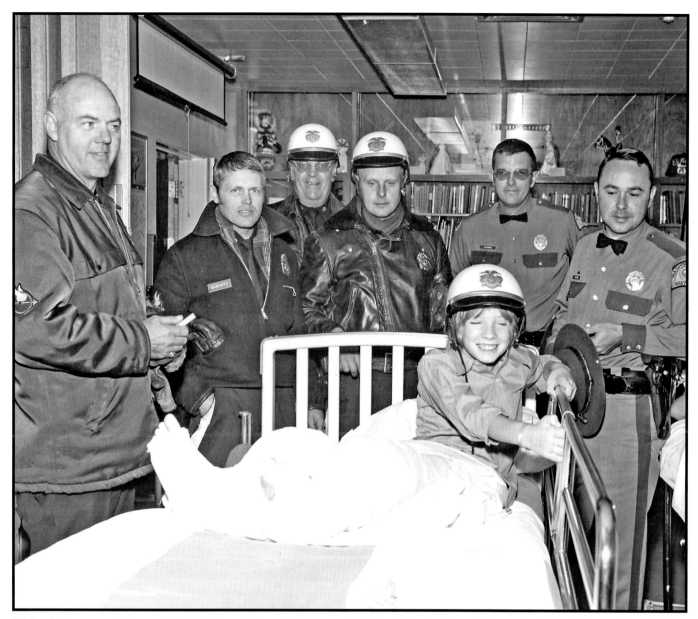

This picture was taken at the Shriners Hospital. From left: Jack Latta, Tony Bamonte, Floyd Jones, Don Jolley, John Ahrens, and Dale Olsen. The name of the little girl in the bed is unknown. Visits to the hospital were an annual event for motor officers. Visits were always appreciated and welcomed by the young patients, and were an enriching experience for the motor officers.

The Shriners Hospital for Crippled Children opened as a unit at St. Luke's Hospital on Summit Boulevard on Spokane's north side on November 15, 1924. Then, as now, children up to age 18 with orthopedic conditions, burns, spinal cord injuries, and cleft lips and palates were eligible for care. There was no charge, regardless of financial need, for any of the children who were sent there.

On November 3, 1930, after years of intense fund-raising, the Shriners broke ground for a new hospital on the campus of St. Luke's Hospital. It was a big community event. According to the *Chronicle,* the Shriners' "imperial potentate" for North America "stuck a spade in the ground" where the new $50,000 Shriners Hospital for Crippled Children would rise.

In 1988, the Shriners designed its new hospital across the street from Deaconess Medical Center, at 911 West 5th Avenue. The $20 million hospital, which opened in 1991, is now a place where physicians perform 650 surgeries each year. *(Courtesy Don Jolley)*

The Spokane Police Credit Union

During Don's tenure with the police department, the accomplishment he was most proud of was his management of the Spokane Police Credit Union. It was first organized on November 23, 1966, when eight police officers signed 20 Articles and Bylaws to incorporate. The officers were Richard Tilton, Lee Elliott, Royce Thornburg, Robert "Bob" Owen, Paul Hook, Mark Bauer, Frank Davis, and Harold Tucker. On December 5, 1966, these articles were filed and accepted by the State of Washington. The same day, the first deposit was accepted in account #01-00, opened by Robert Owen.

The first board of directors meeting was held on December 26, 1966. The directors were Herschel Libey, Clifford Harding, Gary Johnson, Robert Owen, Donald Jolley, Mickey O'Brien, and Jack Thornton. The Supervisory Committee present at this first meeting consisted of Charles Shepherd, Charles Sorini, Louis Moss, and Bob Owen as the first treasurer/manager. In another action at the first meeting, the board was authorizing the signature loan limit at $200 and the secured loan limit at $500. Local 1461 of the Spokane Police Labor Union donated $100 to purchase supplies to get the credit union started.

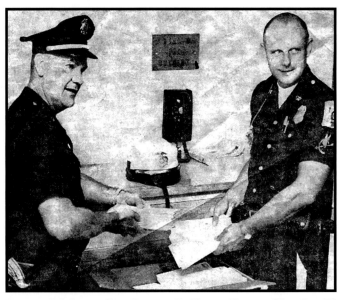

Dance Tickets Go Out – Police officers Charles V. Dotson and Donald Jolley prepare for mailing some of the 2500 invitations to the annual Policeman's Ball September 14, at the Coliseum. The dances are sponsored, free of charge, for Spokane residents by members of the Police Department. Chairmen of the event were detectives Robert E. Colliton and Sgt. James F. Haynes. *(Spokane Daily Chronicle, public domain)*

Bob Owen served as treasurer/manager from 1966 to 1969. He died in 1969 while serving on active duty during summer camp in the Washington Army National Guard with the 1st Battalion, 161st Infantry Mechanized at the Yakima Firing Center in Yakima, Washington. Following Owen's death, Don Jolley took over from 1969 to 1978, and Jerry Hickman from 1978 to 1986. Don will always be remembered as an exceptionally honest person and one of the good guys. He retired from the department in 1990.

SPCU Board of Directors, 1986. Front row: Larry Lindskog, Sue Walker (first female elected to the board and wife of former Spokane Police Officer Robert Walker), and Gary Johnson. Back row: Don Jolley, Dick Jorgenson, Bill Bradley, and Jack Latta.

(Spokane Police Credit Union Photo)

Bob Owen joined the SPD in 1948. He passed away in 1969.

Bob had credit union account #1. His framed history hangs in the entrance to the Spokane Law Enforcement Credit Union on West Sinto.

At the Spokane Police Guild, circa 1973. From right at the table: Don Jolley, Wanda Jolley, Fred Fait, and Gerri Fait. *(Spokane Daily Chronicle, public domain)*

Don Jolley's motorcycle training class from the *Spokane Daily Chronicle* on July 27, 1966. The caption below the article stated: Cycle Officers Training. A week's rigorous training for potential motorcycle officers ended last week for these young law-enforcement men. Instructors at left are Sgt. William Crumbaker, left, and motorcycle officer Melvin Griffiths. On the lineup of cycles are [from right] city police officers Gary Lacewell, Howard Russell, Monty Johnston, Bruce Nelson, sheriff's deputy Mike Bosch, Tony Bamonte and Donald Jolley. Much of the instruction was carried out in the Coliseum's spacious parking lot. *(Courtesy Ron Hubert)*

James V. Johnson – hired by the Spokane Police Department in 1964

Jim Johnson at his residence, circa 1970. *(Courtesy Jim Johnson)*

Jim Johnson was born in 1937 and raised in Spokane. His parents, Vearl and Sunny, owned a small business, the Blue Mountain Steak House, in Pomeroy, Washington. Jim and his sister Sharon went to West Valley High School, and upon graduation, he attended Eastern Washington State College. His first job was working on a farm, and later, he went to work for 7-Up Bottling Company. Jim married Evie Richardson in 1964. He started out dating her sister, but ended up marrying Evie. Jim and Evie have two children. He went on the Spokane Police Department In 1964.

Jim rode police motor from 1968 to 1971. During those years, his various motor partners were Gene McGougan, Don Jolley, and Gary Johnson.

Jim's most memorable experience was the Gonzaga shooting on Thursday, November 11, 1971. Larry Harmon, a young man high on drugs, desecrated the interior of St. Aloysius Church at Gonzaga University. He armed himself with a sledgehammer and a .22 caliber rifle. Inside the church he began destroying everything that represented religion and authority. Before it was over, he had killed the janitor, wounded four other people, and exchanged gunfire with numerous police who had responded to the scene. This incident is recounted in further detail in the sections on Harold Tucker and John Lynch.

Jim retired from the department on March 31, 1992. Since retiring he has been a collector of old railroad artifacts and memorabilia.

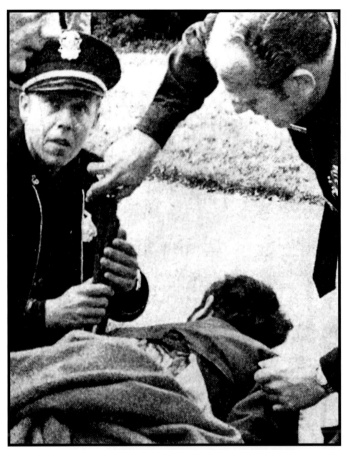

Left: Officer Jim Johnson tends to Michael Clark of Tonasket, Washington, who was wounded by Larry Harmon. Clark was placed on a stretcher at the intersection of Boone Avenue and Astor Street while waiting to be taken by ambulance to the hospital. Following Harmon's rampage inside the church, he moved out onto the street and began shooting at any at anyone who moved. During this time, he tried to shoot a number of police officers. One incident stands out during the encounter. As Officer John Lynch was exchanging shots with Harmon, he was using a parked car as a shield. Crouched next to Lynch was one of Gonzaga's most popular priests. As this was taking place, and they were both being shot at, the priest kept yelling to Lynch, "shoot him, shoot him." This is one of the stories of my (Bamonte) days on the Spokane Police Department that is clearly etched in my memories.

Lower: Crowds gathered outside St. Aloysius Church and rectory just after the shooting. The church is at the right. Across Boone Avenue are Robinson Dormitory and the Cataldo Dining Hall where Robert Schroeder, an ROTC cadet, was standing when he was struck by one of Harmon's bullets. (Boone Avenue runs east and west. In the photo Boone is diagonal to the scene.)

outside St. Aloysius Church and rectory just Thursday. The church is at right. Across Boone Avenue are Robinson dormitory and Cataldo Dining Hall where Robert Schroeder, ROTC cadet, was standing when struck.

Jim Johnson and his two daughters, Julie (the older) and Jeania. *(Courtesy Jim Johnson)*

Ronald Ray Hubert – hired by the Spokane Police Department in 1964

Ron Hubert, circa 1973. *(Courtesy Ron Hubert)*

Ron Hubert was born in Chewelah, Washington, on September 22, 1937. He had two siblings, a brother and sister. At the time, his father worked for the Northwest Magnesite Company located just south of Chewelah. The company was started in 1916 to help supply the American steel industry for World War I production, then later for World War II.

During war times, the Northwest Magnesite Company, employed as many as 800 men. For those interested, magnesite is a mineral related to marble, dolomite, and limestone. It was needed for the lining of open-hearth steel furnaces and extremely important for the steel-manufacturing technology used at the time. Prior to World War I, the United States imported it from Austria-Hungary and Greece. As the war began, these sources were no longer available. Consequently, the federal government circulated an appeal to geologists throughout the nation to search for magnesite. The mineral was soon discovered in the Huckleberry Mountains in Stevens County, just west of Chewelah.

As a result, the Northwest Magnesite Company built a large plant and began shipping magnesite to the steel manufacturers of the East and Midwest. industry. It continued operations until 1968, when new steel-manufacturing technologies eliminated the need for the type of magnesite produced in Stevens County.

From 1916 to 1968, the magnesite industry provided considerable employment for people in the Colville Valley, as well as a product essential to the steel industry. Now all that remains of the Northwest Magnesite Company plant are partially dismantled hulks of the former buildings along Highway 395 just south of Chewelah.

At the age of five, Ron and his family left Chewelah and moved to Spokane, where Ron attended Logan

Elementary School and North Central High School. Shortly after graduation, Ron joined the Navy Reserves. Following his military obligation, he worked in the grocery and construction businesses, two years for Kaiser at the Mead plant, and two years for the Pepsi Company.

In 1964, Ron was hired by the Spokane Police Department, where he rode motor for over 17 years. On July 17, 1969, Ron married Marlene Frances Gepford, his next door neighbor. They were married for almost 44 years. Marlene passed away June 27, 2013.

A partial photo of a train stopped on the tracks, near the Northwest Magnesite Company, for the purpose of displaying captured World War I trophies, circa 1919. This was a special destination for this train as the company had played a major role in the war. Visible on the train are a number of cannons and a German tank.
(Courtesy Chewelah Historical Society)

Ron Hubert starting his "kick start" police motor, circa 1967. *(Courtesy Ron Hubert)*

From left to right: Ron Hubert, Mel Griffiths, Floyd Jones, and Jack Latta. As these motor officers aged, they were assigned to three-wheel motors. "This was done as a safety precaution to keep them from tipping over." *(Courtesy Ron Hubert)*

Police Day at Rev. Clifton Hamp's Camp, located on the east side of Liberty Lake in 1979. Hamp started Police Day, when members of the police department would show up at the camp and give the kids rides on their police motorcycles and cars in the ballpark area of the camp. Ron said giving these kids rides was one of the most rewarding experiences of his life and the kids loved it. *(Courtesy Ron Hubert)*

Ron and Marlene Hubert. Married for almost 44 years before Marlene passed away. *(Courtesy Ron Hubert)*

Jack Thornton – hired by the Spokane Police Department in 1965

Jack Thornton on motor with Lt. Lee Elliott adjusting a new radar mount. Jack rode motor from 1967 to 1974. He later rode a three-wheeler from 1983 to 1984. His various motor partners were John Welton, Jim Johnson, and Jerry Hickman. *(Courtesy Jack Thornton)*

Jack Edward Neumiller – hired by the Spokane Police Department in 1965

Jack Neumiller, circa 1973. *(Courtesy his wife, Judy Neumiller)*

Jack Neumiller was born on August 22, 1940, at Wolf Point, Montana, to Edward and Margaret Neumiller. He has an older sister, Arlene, and two younger brothers, Vern and Doug. He was raised in Spokane where his father worked for the Washington Water Power Company and his mother worked for a bakery. He attended Franklin Elementary and Lewis and Clark High School. He also attended Spokane Community College, Eastern Washington State College, and Whitworth, taking both core and business classes. During his early life, he was also a member of the United States Marine Corps Reserve.

Jack was hired by the Spokane Police Department on October 1, 1965. He began his career as a police officer, PFC and detective, assigned to patrol three years, motorcycle officer five years, detective in a burglary task force, and special investigations unit

(SIU) for over 19 years. In 1985, he was assigned as the case manager for the burglary task force. The unit consisted of detectives Sheldon Reeve, Joan Schmick, Andrew (Skip) Pavlischak, Ken Krogh, officers Dick Poole, Larry Lindskog, Larry Williamson, Joe Peterson, and Sgt. Mark Sterk. Their goal was to identify perpetrators of high profile burglaries, arrest, determine where stolen property was fenced, and shut down fencing operations.

Neumiller attended seminars and sting schools in Portland, Oregon, and Las Vegas, Nevada. "Pillowcase burglaries" were occurring all over the county, with thieves taking a pillowcase from a bed and filling it with sterling silver and jewelry. They made numerous arrests and shut down fences. They also did effective sting operations with cooperation from businesses, who supplied them with large quantities of merchandise to be used as stolen property for sting operations, thus stopping major fencing operations. One year they arrested 135 persons. All pleaded guilty or were convicted. They also aided other communities and executed search warrants, recovering property in Sandpoint, Coeur d'Alene, and Colfax.

Jack met his wife, Judy, in early 1978, while he was a detective investigating a burglary at her place of work. They were married three years later on April 25, 1981. At the time, they both had long term, full-time careers and frequently worked different shifts, which made their days off together very important. They spent warm weather weekends in their backyard swimming pool or on camping trips in north-

Jack Neumiller at the scene of a suspect's home, following an armed robbery of a north side grocery store. Two suspects were traced to this residence. One of the robbers was found hiding under this house and the third was found hiding in a house across the street. This photo appeared in the *Spokane Daily Chronicle* on May 12, 1973. *(Courtesy Judy Nuemiller)*

eastern Washington. For their 10th anniversary they booked a tour of the New England states. That was the start of a great love of travel and later cruising. They set a goal to visit every state, national park, and national monument, but didn't quite make it. Along with camping and travel, they always enjoyed the Policeman's Ball and the Marine Corps' Birthday Balls. They spent a lot of free time remodeling their house, until they ran out of room inside and out.

They later bought 11 acres of land and designed a new home, doing much of the finish work themselves once the house was built, along with all of the landscaping and planting.

Jack and Judy have two sons, Michael and Brian, and daughter, Michele, six grandchildren and five great grandchildren. Jack retired from the SPD on March 1, 1993, and passed away on March 30, 2017.

Jack and Judy Neumiller, circa 2016. *(Courtesy Judy Nuemiller)*

Gerald Olcott Hickman – hired by the Spokane Police Department in 1965

Jerry Hickman photographed in February 1967. *(Courtesy Jerry Hickman)*

When Jerry Hickman went to work for the Spokane Police Department, he began his probationary duty as a rookie officer. From that position he advanced to private first class, specialist, detective, sergeant, and lieutenant, assigned to patrol, traffic, police academy, internal affairs, vice and narcotics, and intelligence.

During his tenure as a detective, the unit had two armed robbers staked out for three weeks. They had hit many jewelry stores in the western states and were now casing stores in Spokane. An informant gave the police information, and they bugged the suspect's vehicle. They chose Chuck Howard Jewelry on Post between Riverside and Main to stake. One team was following the suspects, and one team with snipers watched the store 24 hours a day. The following quote is from Jerry Hickman:

The stake-out took so long that even some of the employees knew we were there. One Sunday, one of them brought his girlfriend down to point out our hiding places. We thought our cover was blown. But on April 14, 1975, at about 10 a.m. we watched as two well-dressed men walked into the store. We could hear with a hidden microphone as they locked down the store and tied up the employees. It took them less than five minutes to clean out the store. We blocked off the one-way street at Main, and the pedestrian overpass quickly filled with curious people. The robbers hid guns in briefcases as they exited into our waiting arms. No one was injured and not a shot was fired. We got a standing ovation from the crowds on the overpass and at each corner of the street.

Gary Lacewell – hired by the Spokane Police Department in 1965

S P O K A N E · P O L I C E · D E P A R T M E N T

Gary Lacewell, circa 1969. *(Courtesy Lacewell family)*

Gary Lacewell was born in 1937 and raised in Oakesdale, Washington. Gary was raised by his grandmother after his father passed away. Gary's first job out of high school was working for an independent mail carrier.

In 1962, Gary married Connie Lisenbee from Farmington, Washington, a small community twelve miles from Oakesdale. In 1965, Gary went on the Spokane Police Department. Several years later, he was assigned to motor. Gary was a member of Spokane's first SWAT team and also a motor partner of Tony Bamonte. During their early years on the department, Lacewell and Bamonte started a Spokane County baseball team for grade school children. Their sponsor was Everett Hite, the owner of Hite Crane and Rigging. They named their team the "Hite Hitters," who went on to win first place in the playoffs.

On January 11, 1973, Gary was part of a chase where a suspect accused of robbery had hijacked a city bus and fled to the Garden Springs area of West Spokane. This incident followed a frantic chase through downtown Spokane during which the suspect committed a first-degree assault, kidnapping, and the armed robbery of a drug store at 327 West Second Avenue.

During the robbery, a salon employee struck the robber over the head with a hair spray bottle and then chased him east on First, north on Stevens, west on Sprague, south on Howard, west on First, north on Wall, and west on Sprague until the suspect fired a shot at him and he gave up the chase.

At the time of the hijacking, the bus was empty. The bus driver stated the suspect ran in front of his bus and ordered him to halt on Lincoln between Sprague and Riverside. When the man attempted to board the bus, the driver told him it was headed for the bus yards, but the gunman told him "No, you're going my way" and directed him to the Holiday Inn. On the way there, the suspect changed his mind, ordering the bus driver to take him to the Garden Springs area, where he got off.

During the time of this incident, a slight dusting of snow had just fallen. Consequently, officers were able to track the suspect to a house at 1200 South F street, where he was arrested. At the time of his arrest, the suspect was hiding under a bed.

During his career, Gary was involved in numerous police-related arrests. Gary died in 1993 from lung cancer.

Gary Lacewell, on right, was also a member of the Spokane Police Department's mounted patrol. *(Courtesy Lacewell family)*

Gary Lacewell was one of five members of the first SWAT team.

AFTER SWAT
TRAINING... HONED
TO A KEEN EDGE...
A FINELY TUNED
DESTRUCTIVE FORCE

Spokane
Police
Department

Gary Lacewell was also a member of the Spokane Police Department's first Special Weapons and Tactical Squad (SWAT) team. This photo was taken in the fall of 1973 and is a partial view of the FBI campus at Quantico, Virginia. The campus was quite large, with other training grounds and rifle ranges within driving distance. Spokane's first SWAT team was made up of five members: Carl Sweatt, Gary Lacewell, Dennis Hooper, Ron Scholz, and Tony Bamonte. Four of the five SWAT members were motor officers, or had been at an earlier time.

At the time this photo was taken, Bamonte was finishing a degree at Whitworth College. In the process of obtaining the proper amount of credits to graduate, he took a photography class. One of the assignments was to prepare a slide presentation. Consequently, Bamonte made a slide presentation of the SWAT team training. Chief Hendren, who had a meeting in Washington, D. C., during the SWAT school, accompanied us as far as Washington, D.C. At that location, he arranged for our SWAT team group to go a day earlier so we could tour the capital. *(Bamonte photos)*

The Lacewell family, from left: Brian, Gary, Brenda, and Connie. *(Courtesy Lacewell family)*

Dave Anderson – hired by the Spokane Police Department in 1965

Dave Anderson parked across the street from his residence, circa 1973. *(Courtesy Dave Anderson)*

During Dave Anderson's tenure as a police officer, he attained the following ranks and positions: Patrolman, PFC, specialist (Cpl.), detective, sergeant, lieutenant, captain, patrol, traffic, radio, investigative, records, property, academy, administrative and, during Expo '74, Dave was a shift supervisor.

His education included a BA and MBA from Gonzaga University. He also was a graduate of the following police schools: The National Crime Prevention Institute, Spokane Police Department Officer Profiles Institute, University of Louisville, FBI Academy, and Northwest Law Enforcement Command College.

A couple of the best officers Dave said he worked with were Fred Uttke and Cliff Harding. Dave was easy to get along with and had a good way with peo-

Spokane Police Department

ple, including his fellow employees. Dave rode motor for about two and a half years, minus the time he worked for Expo '74.

One of his more interesting calls was when a car careened through a corner going north from Main Street onto the Monroe Street Bridge. The driver lost control and went across the oncoming lane of traffic, going through the bridge railing, and plummeting to the rocks below. Both people, a man and woman, were instantly killed. People standing near the bridge looking down stated: "It appeared the driver was going too fast as they approached the bridge."

In researching this incident, Dave learned that there was nothing in any regulations that says the bridge railing is required to keep cars from going through. However, city officials later installed barriers by the bridge to prevent such an accident from occurring again.

Dave Anderson (left) and Mel Griffiths in the cab of the Union Pacific engine, number 8444, that was at the Expo '74 site. It was raining at the time, and both motor officers were in rain gear. Photo taken in 1974. *(Courtesy Dave Anderson)*

Dave Anderson riding the perimeter during the Junior Lilac Parade in 1973. *(Courtesy Dave Anderson)*

Bruce G. Nelson – hired by the Spokane Police Department in 1965

"Motor 10," Bruce Nelson, circa 1973. *(Courtesy Dick Lovejoy)*

Bruce Nelson was born on December 27, 1941. He was raised in Spokane and graduated from North Central High School. In 1965, Bruce went to work for the Spokane Police Department where he remained for over 27 years. He retired in 1991.

Bruce started his career with the department as a patrolman, eventually going to the traffic department where he rode motor. He later advanced to detective. His detective career included narcotic and major crimes investigations, focusing on homicides.

Bruce was also a senior bomb technician on the bomb squad. He was also instrumental in forming the international drug task force between Spokane and Canada.

Bruce's Extracurricular Activity

Beginning in 1952, Bruce had a 53-year hobby of making model and radio controlled airplanes. He got started at the age of ten through the youth program at a nearby church. In 1970, he joined the Barons Model Club in Spokane, of which he was president many times over the years. He was also active in the River City Modelers. Through both organizations, he was involved in the following activities and achievements:

• His club hosted the first "U.S. Scale Masters" in the Pacific Northwest in 1981, and he was the contest director. The next two years, he was the contest manager and then the contest director again.

• As a representative, he flew at the 1982 U.S. Scale Masters and placed second after having only flown the plane three times.

• Helped find a location for the AMA Nationals when they came to the Pacific Northwest and worked in the public relations office for the Nationals.

• Was club president of the Barons Model Club several times.

• Was manager and charter member of the Barons Flying Circus air show team, the first air show team west of the Mississippi River.

• Was a member of the air show team advisory committee for more than 20 years and chaired the committee five times.

• Served as an associate vice president for the AMA's District XI for 21 years and became vice president in 2000.

• Helped local clubs become AMA-sanctioned clubs.

• Helped teach model group leaders.

• In 1999, he received the AMA Distinguished Service Award.

Following his retirement from the Spokane Police Department in 1991, Bruce started a business called Professional Investigation Consultants.

Bruce passed away at Hospice House in Spokane on September 27, 2016 at the age of 74. He was predeceased by his wife of 26 years, Marcie A. Nelson. He is survived by his four children: Richard Nelson, David Nelson, Denise Chandler, Wendy Nelson-Lloyd, and their families, as well as his sister, Susan Henley.

Ron Hubert (left) and Bruce Nelson, circa 1975. *(Courtesy Dick Lovejoy)*

John Bardette Lynch Jr. – hired by the Spokane Police Department in 1966

John Lynch. *(Courtesy Laura Duda, daughter)*

John Lynch was born at St. Paul, Minnesota, on August 1, 1938, to John and Gertrude Lynch. Lynch and his four brothers were raised and attended school in St. Paul.

During Lynch's early life, his first job was delivering the morning, evening, and Sunday papers, as did all of his brothers. Shortly out of high school, he joined the Air Force, spending a total of nine years in that branch of the service. He entered the Air Force in 1955 from the Minnesota National Guard, then transferred to the regular Air Force in 1956. He was stationed at Park Air Force Base in San Francisco for boot camp. From there, he was assigned to Chanute Air Force Base in Illinois for training as a parachute rigger. He was eventually stationed at Geiger Field near

A Sniper at St. Aloysius Church
The First Responder

One of Lynch's interesting encounters, in fact one in which he could easily have been killed, occurred when he was the first responder to a call involving a sniper at St. Aloysius Church, next to Gonzaga University. Although the story of this incident has been told earlier in this publication from officer Lynch's perspective.

On Thursday, November 11, 1971, around 11:30 a.m. the call came out. A man had just been shot and killed inside St. Aloysius Church by a man with a rifle. That man was also in the process of shooting at anyone within his sight.

Lynch, who was assigned as the city traffic investigator, an assignment that was typically a one-man operation, was near the scene. Consequently, by himself at the time, he immediately responded, which made him the first and only policeman at the scene for a period of at least two minutes.

John and Elaine Lynch ready for the Policeman's Ball, circa 1973. *(Courtesy Laura Duda, daughter)*

Spokane. In 1958, he married his first wife. They had a daughter, Laura Lynch Duda. In 2000, he married his wife, Bobbi.

In 1964, Lynch was discharged from the air force as a corporal. On January 23, 1966, he was hired by the Spokane Police Department. He started his police career as a patrolman, then in 1969, he was promoted to motor. However, that assignment only lasted for nine months as he was promoted to corporal. During his time on motor he had two partners: Bruce Nelson and Tony Bamonte.

During Lynch's time on the department, he also worked in the jail, was an identification officer, traffic accident investigator, and worked in the licensing department.

Laura Duda, daughter of John Lynch, circa 2015.
(Courtesy Laura Duda)

As he arrived at the location of the shooting, he began driving slowly east of Gonzaga, looking up toward the church steeples, thinking the sniper may be in one of the two steeples attached to the church. Suddenly he heard a loud knock on the window of his prowl car. The knock had come from an excited priest who was fervently committed to getting the officer's attention, which he did. Lynch stopped, got out of his car, and followed the priest to the east side of the rectory. Almost immediately, both Lynch and the priest came upon Larry Harmon, a young man high on LSD (lysergic acid diethylamide), who was armed with a .22 caliber rifle, sledge-hammer, and a five gallon can of gas.

Harmon had just murdered the janitor and vandalized the interior of the cathedral, then headed back to his car to get the can of gas. Once he had the gas, he headed back to the church, undoubtably to set fire to the interior of the building. As soon as Lynch observed Harmon, he yelled at him to freeze. Harmon dropped the gas can and immediately began firing at Lynch, who ducked behind a parked car. As this was happening, the priest who was with Lynch became excited. Lynch directed him to run to the rectory, which he did.

Following the priest's hasty exit, gunfire between Lynch and Harmon immediately broke out. Harmon began running toward Lynch, at the same time, shooting at him. In an act of self preservation, Lynch also began shooting back. Consequently, Lynch, with his Smith & Wesson six-shot revolver, was now up against a man charging and shooting at him with a rifle. However, in the heat of the gunfight, both were missing their intended targets. Lamentably, Lynch quickly ran out of bullets, but not before he inadvertently shot the side of St. Aloysius Church, which was directly behind Harmon, a number of times.

Unfortunately, a ruling had just come out within the Spokane Police Department that all shotguns, formerly mounted in plain site next to the driver, were to be kept in the trunk of the vehicle. This wasn't good, as in emergency circumstances such as this, there was no time to get a shotgun out of the trunk.

As Harmon continued to advance and Lynch was attempting to reload, Harmon reached the opposite side

Carl Bays, credited by Lynch for saving his life, circa 1971. *(Courtesy Spokane Police Department Law Enforcement Museum)*

of the parked car Lynch was using as a shield. Lynch had ducked down on the opposite side of the vehicle during his reloading effort. Harmon continued shooting at him by leaning across the top of the parked car shielding Lynch, firing down at the officer. Now, more than ever, Lynch needed a priest.

More officers soon arrived, including Carl Bays. As Bays approached to within about 90 feet from where Harmon was shooting at Lynch, he exited his prowl car, grabbing his shotgun from the trunk. Once this was done, and seeing Harmon about to shoot Lynch, Bays yelled several times to Harmon in an attempt to divert his attention from Lynch. That worked, as Harmon then turned his attention toward Bays and began shooting at him.

Bays fired back at the gunman from a distance of about 60 feet with his 12-gauge shotgun. Bays said he could see that he had struck the gunman in the

Dave Prescott in the traffic office, circa 1972. *(Courtesy Coleen Prescott)*

time a police officer had been killed in the line of duty, in the Spokane area, in over 54 years.

After shooting Officer Orchard, Link sped away from the scene under a hail of gunfire from five detectives positioned to assist with the bust. The suspect's Lincoln careened around a corner and, within two blocks, crashed into a street light pole. Link jumped from the car and fled on foot. Beach was caught a short distance from the shooting scene, while tying to escape on foot.

During the investigation, it was suspected, and then confirmed, that Link went to Portland, Oregon, as it was one of the few places where he knew people and would feel safe. Following a massive manhunt, three days later, on July 21 at 8:45 p.m., Lonnie Link was arrested in Portland as he walked to a convenience store. By the time he was arrested, he had already dyed his hair blond in an attempt to disguise himself, but the police already knew too much about

him for that to work. When he was arrested, he was easily identified, was not armed, and didn't resist.

Both Link's and Beach's girlfriends were located by police. These women would soon play a part in the overall scheme of the stolen guns and extortion plot in Spokane from the burglary that took place in Wenatchee. During the separate murder trials for each man in the later part of 1984, they were both allowed to marry their girlfriends while in jail, prior to going to court.

Lonnie Link and Donald Beach both were married in the Spokane County/City Jail while awaiting trial for the murder of Detective Brian Orchard

Following the arrests of Lonnie Link and Donald Beach, detectives quickly learned they both had girlfriends they were deeply in love with. These relationships were at such a level of allegiance that Link and Beach would do anything to spend even a small amount of time with them. Also, Link's girlfriend was pregnant and had their baby while he was in jail. In an affidavit filed with the court, Link stated, "I would like to be allowed to marry before my trial starts on September 17, 1984, so that I can put it behind me and concentrate on the most serious business of my life, my trial for aggravated first-degree murder." While Link was in jail, Don Manning, the commander of the county-city jail, allowed him to get married under certain conditions. The conditions required the wedding to take place with the glass in the jail visiting room separating the couple.

Unknown to Link, his co-defendant, Donald Beach, was already married. That event had taken place in June 1984, also in the county-city jail under similar conditions.

There was a major problem for both Link and Beach with their marriages. Neither, although they were now legally married, were allowed to have any type of contact with their brides.

The main players were Alvin Hegge, president of the Ghost Riders Motorcycle Club, and Billy McEwen Without their involvement Brian Orchard would have not been murdered

There was one more element to Brian Orchard's murder – an important one. The key players in Orchard's murder were Alvin Hegge and Billy McEwen. Alvin Hegge, the president of the Ghost Riders Motorcycle Club, had a background in numerous criminal activities, trials, and convictions, including unlawful interstate transportation and receipt of firearms. They had orchestrated the entire scenario that led to Orchard's murder, using Link and Beach as minions in this and some of their many other organized criminal activities.

Hegge's name immediately surfaced during the investigation of Detective Orchard's death. The two individuals arrested on the murder charges, Lonnie Link and Donald Beach, were reported to have been in a car that was, or had been, registered to Mr. Hegge. Hegge was immediately charged in connection with Detective Orchard's death, but, in 1989, both he and McEwen were charged with second-degree murder in aiding and abetting the murder of Detective Orchard. This conviction came about when the prosecutor built his case on proving, though not present at the time of the shooting, they were guilty of murder due to the fact that they directed the robbery of the Wenatchee antique gun collector. Also, their subsequent extortion attempts had led to Detective Orchard's death. They were able to prove this when both Link and Beach testified against Hegge under a witness protection program. Their testimonies proved invaluable.

Spokane Police Detective David Prescott works out an exchange with Link and Beach

Sometime during the early part of the incarceration of Link and Beach in the Spokane County-City Jail, Tony Bamonte was contacted by Detective Prescott. Bamonte had resigned from the Spokane Police Department in 1974 and taken a political appointment with the sheriff of Pend Oreille County, where he had grown up. When the sheriff who hired him lost his election, Bamonte ran for sheriff the following term. He was elected in 1978, and in that capacity was in charge of the county jail.

During the time he was on the Spokane Police Department, Bamonte had been Prescott's motor partner for about four years. Bamonte had great respect for the department, Police Chief Wayne Hendren, and his old motor partner, Prescott. He also knew and was a friend of Brian Orchard, as he was one of Orchard's training officers just before Orchard went on motor in 1968. Bamonte felt Orchard was an excellent officer and a tragic loss for the department. Bamonte knew if Prescott wanted help, it would be for a good cause, no matter how unorthodox the favor proved to be.

Prescott had been working on the Link/Beach case and knew the connection. However, Link and Beach were terrified of Hegge and McEwen. They had both been threatened to be killed if they disclosed any part Hegge or McEwen had played in the murder.

Dave Prescott and Tony Bamonte outside the Spokane Police Guild Building, circa 1971. *(Jim Spohaese)*

The exchange

As Bamonte recalls from conversation with Prescott prior to being asked for his help, the circumstances were as follows: Al Hegge and Billy McEwen were the key players in the death of Brian Orchard., but he needed Link and Beach to testify against them. Link and Beach refused to do that unless they received a favor in return. They were each asking for a conjugal visit with their girlfriends (they weren't yet married). Also, at the same time, Prescott gave Bamonte a short rundown on the background of Lonnie Link, the triggerman in the Orchard murder. He stated, based on information from Link's mother, Maxine Depner, many of the problems in her son's life were attributed to his adoptive father,

Jim Link, who committed suicide in 1983. Maxine had married Jim Link in 1964, and Link adopted four-year-old Lonnie, the youngest of Depner's five children. She related that, when Lonnie was eight or nine, his dog had puppies. She remembers coming home one night to find her son crying in front of their house in Black Eagle, Montana. Mrs. Link found out her husband had taken the puppies and Lonnie to a nearby field and made the boy shoot them one at a time.

This was only one many incidences that Prescott related to Bamonte concerning the influence Link had on his adopted son. There were others—all examples of Link's disregard for others taught to him by his stepfather. Although he had shot and killed a police officer, he was also a human being with his own story. He was going to spend the rest of his life in prison for his crime.

For reasons that need to remain confidential, the visits between Link, Beach, and their girlfriends were not allowed to take place in the Spokane jail. Consequently, if Link and Beach weren't allowed to have this visit, Hegge and McEwen may never have been charged in the murder of Detective Orchard.

In 1984, with permission from the author (former Pend Oreille County Sheriff Bamonte), conjugal visits from Link and Beach's girlfriends took place at the Pend Oreille County Jail in Newport, Washington.

As close as Bamonte can recall, each couple was granted four hours. Two cells were provided, with army blankets covering the inside cell windows. Spokane police officials paid to have a Newport doctor examine each female prior to entering the jail. This was done as a precaution for contraband. This conjugal visit was a small favor for the results it brought, as shortly after this, Link and Beach each testified against Hegge and McEwen. As a result, Link and Beach were both placed in the witness protection program while in prison.

Lonnie Link was found guilty of aggravated murder and sentenced to life, without parole. Donald Beach pleaded guilty to second degree murder and received a life (20-year sentence) with a 12-year minimum. Alvin Hegge was found guilty of second degree murder. Billy McEwen was acquitted of the murder of Orchard.

Following is a excerpt from a March 11, 2010, *Spokesman Review* article by Jim Camden:

> The state Clemency and Pardons Board heard what members agreed was an extraordinary plea to commute Link's sentence of life without parole and make him eligible for release. The prosecutor who convicted him, former Spokane County Prosecutor Don Brockett and one of the detectives involved in the case joined Link's former defense attorney Mark Vovos in arguing for clemency for Link. "I believe the verdict was unjust," Brockett said. "I'm here today because I think it's the right thing to do."

But the current prosecutor, Steve Tucker, joined Orchard's family and the state's law enforcement community in arguing against clemency. While it's true Link later helped convict many members of the Ghost Riders by testifying in later trials in the late 1980s, that's no reason to commute his sentence, Tucker said: "His reward was to be put under the federal witness protection program."

Link was a 24-year-old convicted burglar in 1983 and an associate of the Ghost Riders when the gang's president, Al Hegge, told him and another man, Donald Beach, to steal guns from a Wenatchee couple. They later arranged to sell the guns back in an extortion plot, and were supposed to collect the money at a downtown Spokane hotel. Link told detectives later that he had planned to double-cross Hegge, take the money and flee, cutting all ties with the gang.

But police were tipped to the extortion scheme, and were waiting for Link and Beach that night near the hotel. Link was waiting in a car while Beach went to the hotel room; Orchard and another plainclothes officer approached the car. Police and witnesses said the officers identified themselves and told Link to put his hands on the dashboard. Link said he thought Orchard, who had a shaggy beard, was either Hegge or another gang member, saw a flash and feared for his life. He shot and fatally wounded Orchard and escaped, but was later captured in Oregon.

Dave Prescott passed away on October 2, 2007. Prior to his passing he was a integral part of the Spokane Police Department History Book Committee.

Dave Prescott about the time he was working the Brian Orchard murder. *(Courtesy Coleen Prescott)*

Dave Prescott and his wife, Coleen, circa 2001. *(Courtesy Coleen Prescott)*

Tony Bamonte – hired by the Spokane Police Department in 1966

Tony Bamonte and his son, Louie, in the summer of 1972. *(Bamonte photo)*

I was born in Wallace, Idaho, in 1942 and was raised in Metaline Falls, Washington, in north Pend Oreille County. I married Suzanne Schaeffer in July of 1994 and have one son, Louis Bamonte, from a previous marriage. Suzanne and I presently reside in Spokane. I have a bachelor's degree from Whitworth College and master's degree from Gonzaga University. I spent 26 years in law enforcement, starting with my experience as a military policeman, then as a Spokane police officer (1966-1974), and finally, as a three-term elected sheriff of Pend Oreille County (1978-1990).

My other occupations were hard-rock miner, logger (mostly cedar-pole peeler and sawyer), construction worker on Boundary Dam, licensed Washington State general contractor, sawmill builder, owner and president of an all-electric, three-phase sawmill (Tornado Creek Lumber Company Inc.), and licensed Washington State realtor. In 1995, my wife and I founded Tornado Creek Publications. We specialize in writing and publishing Inland Northwest history.

During the over eight years I spent with the SPD, six were as a motorcycle officer. I especially liked riding motor, as it enabled me to quickly respond to serious calls. Because of that, I was able to arrest the first man to ever plead guilty to first-degree murder in Washington State (see Bon Marché murder, following). In 1974, I resigned from the police department and took a political appointment in Pend Oreille County.

In 1978, I ran for sheriff. During my tenure as sheriff, as a master's thesis in organizational leadership at Gonzaga University, I researched and wrote a history of the sheriffs of Pend Oreille County. It was subsequently published as a book titled *Sheriffs, 1911-1989: A History of Murders in the Wilderness of Washington's Last County*. In the process of writing this book, I solved the nation's oldest active murder case, the 1935 murder of a Newport, Washington, marshal by a former Spokane motorcycle policeman (see Clyde Ralstin story in this book). A national best seller, *Breaking Blue*, by Timothy Egan, was written about that case.

A cold-blooded killer shoots and kills a cashier at the Bon Marché while committing an armed robbery

The Incident As I Remember It
by Tony Bamonte

On October 16, 1971, at approximately 5:00 p.m., I was working an extra assignment to help cover the heavy traffic immediately following the Washington State University/California football game at Joe Albi Stadium. At the time, I was assigned to the traffic division and rode a Harley-Davidson police motorcycle. While directing traffic at the south end of the Monroe Street Bridge, a call came over my police radio that there was an armed robbery in progress at the Bon Marché (later Macy's) and someone had just been shot. I immediately abandoned my assignment and rode to that location. Because I was on a police motorcycle and riding against traffic on a one-way street, I was able to arrive within two minutes of the time of the actual murder. I parked my motorcycle on the sidewalk in front of the southwest entrance to the building (the main entrance).

Knowing that someone had been shot, I immediately unholstered my pistol, holding it down next to my right thigh to keep it inconspicuous, in an attempt to keep from frightening store customers.

I entered the building at the main entry door on the southwest side of the building and immediately began running up the descending escalator. As I reached the second floor, I observed a man coming down the stairs at a quick pace. At that point, I did not have a description of the suspect and stopped this man at gunpoint. Thinking I was going to shoot him he stated, "It's not me. Follow me, I'm security – I'll point him out." (I later learned that my "first suspect" was the store's unarmed security guard, Mike Yates, who later joined the Spokane Police Department, serving over 27 years.)

Believing Yates, and realizing time was of the essence, within four or five seconds, I followed him as we quickly descended the same down escalator I had just run up. He led me to the west entry of the Bon Marché, where there was a secondary entry

door (which later was removed). When we reached that location, as I recall, there were two or three policemen blocking the doorway and also a number of people in the immediate vicinity, especially behind me. There was also a black man standing about five to 10 feet east of Motorcycle Officer Ron Graves.

Within seconds of our arrival at that doorway, my 'then" suspect (the security guard Yates) pointed to the killer, Jerry Lewis, saying, "That's him." Lewis was standing near Motorcycle Officer

Ron Graves, holding an office-sized wastebasket. Due to his casual attire, he had the appearance of a janitor. He was just standing by, detained by Officer Graves and one or two other policemen assigned with securing the entryway. Lewis, along with others in the lobby were prevented from leaving the store. For a minute or so without causing any problems, and being mistaken for a janitor, Lewis hadn't aroused any suspicions. Consequently, the other officers were not paying much attention to him.

Within a second or two from the time the suspect was identified by Yates, and now realizing that, he drew a pistol from his black trench coat pocket and aimed it directly at me. As I was cognizant of the inherent danger, due to the number of people in the store, I had no other recourse than to shoot him before he shot me. I still had my pistol inconspicuously down at my side and, without hesitation, I raised it to hip level and fired a single shot. Had I hesitated and given him the chance to shoot first, he would either have shot me or, because that section of the store was filled with people, there was a high probability of his wounding or killing one or more store customers. The identification of the suspect by the security guard and the shooting process lasted all of about two seconds.

I immediately shot the suspect to halt him in his tracks. I doubt he even saw my pistol. Lewis was wearing sunglasses, which my bullet struck directly on the bridge, breaking them in two. Because he was aiming his pistol at me, his head was turned sideways. After entering the middle of his forehead, the bullet exited the left side of his head. He instantly fell forward and onto his pistol. Having his head turned to the side saved his life.

When Lewis fell, the wastebasket he was holding spilled out some of the $8,323 it contained. Immediately after this happened, one of the officers standing right next to him, still thinking he was the janitor, made the statement: "Bamonte just shot the janitor." Although the killer, Jerry Lewis, lived, he spent the rest of his life in a wheelchair as a result of losing about a third of the frontal lobe of his brain from the gunshot.

According to Chief Wayne Hendren and Spokane County Prosecutor Donald Brockett, Lewis was

---

FORECAST TODAY
Mostly Fair
Saturday High Low
Airport 50 29
(Full Report on Page 2)

THE SPOKESMAN-REVIEW

89TH YEAR. NO. 156.   SUNDAY MORNING.   OCTOBER 17, 1971.   PRICE 25 CENTS.   SPOKANE, WASH.

Valley Woman Killed During Robbery

Murder Charged in Robbery Death

By JIM SPOERHASE

A 35-year-old Spokane man, alleged to have killed the Bon Marche Department Store credit manager Saturday afternoon during an armed robbery, today was charged with first-degree murder.

Pros. Atty. Donald C. Brockett said the murder charge was filed against Jerry Lewis, who police said lives at 23320 Congress.

Detective Capt. Calvin D. Smith said that Mrs. Walter J.

Jerry Lewis

(Peggy Jean) Palmer, 45, E8316 Valley Way, was shot and died almost instantly when an armed man held up the fifth floor business office at the department store.

Lewis, shot in the head by Motorcycle Officer Anthony G. Bamonte as he was fleeing from the store, was reported in critical condition, but showing improvement, today at Deaconess Hospital where he is under police guard.

Held in the County-City Jail under $10,000 bond each as material witnesses were Joe Gibson, 50, who gave an address of E605 Bismark, and James E. Boyd, 27, who said he lived at N2418 Hamilton.

Incident Described

Describing what happened at the store, Smith said:

"Shortly before 5 p.m. on Saturday three men were observed acting in what Bon Marche employes thought was a suspicious manner on the fifth floor, near the credit office.

"An employe notified a store security officer, who was in the act of telephoning police when the incident happened.

"Our investigation indicates that one man confronted Mrs. Palmer with a gun and told her to open the door to the credit office. She said she couldn't open it, that it had to be opened from the inside. Witnesses tell us that the gunman and Mrs. Palmer wrestled a bit—then she was shot."

Capt. Smith said that the robber then jumped over a counter and brandishing the gun—a .22 caliber revolver—ordered three cashiers to help him put money into a pink wastebasket which he picked up in the store.

The employes ordered to hand over the money were identified by homicide Detective Homer C. Hall as Hilda T. Roberts, 56, E1224 Central; Maxine L. Stephens, 52, S6722 Plymouth Road,

and Sandra L. Brncick, 22, W1805 Ninth.

"After the robber stuffed the money into the waste basket he went out the office door and down the escalator," Smith said.

By this time, he said, several police officers who had been in the downtown area on traffic duty because of the Washington State-California football game descended on the Bon Marche in response to a call of an armed robbery in progress.

Smith said the armed man got to the first floor of the store and was nearly outside the entrance at Main and Wall when he was confronted by Officer Bamonte.

Gun Is Spotted

Bamonte, who had his gun out and in his hand at his side when he entered the store, said he saw the man grab into the waste basket and come up with a gun.

Bamonte reported the man had the gun at eye level, aimed at Bamonte when the officer fired. The bullet struck the man in the head and he fell. A pistol was found underneath the wounded man, Smith said.

When the suspect was shot by Bamonte he dropped the money-filled wastebasket which spilled out onto the store floor.

Homicide Detective C. R. Johnson said the cash in the wastebasket amounted to $8,323.

Smith said that soon after Lewis was shot by Officer Bamonte the two material witnesses were taken into custody by other officers in other parts of the department store.

Detective Johnson said an autopsy performed yesterday on Mrs. Palmer's body disclosed that she was shot in the right arm and that the bullet went into her body, killing her almost instantly.

Lewis underwent surgery Saturday night, police said. Lewis had been scheduled to go to trial next month on a sec-

Mrs. Walter J. Palmer

party was allegedly in progress.

No one was hurt in the incident in which several bullets were fired into the house, the Superior Court was told at the time Glover was sentenced.

Philip W. Alexander, managing director of the Bon Marche, said Mrs. Palmer was "a very popular employe and a good friend of everyone in the Bon Marche organization.

"Mrs. Palmer had an outgoing, friendly personality and all personnel of the store feel a tremendous loss and the circumstances of her death have clouded the spirits of her friends," said Alexander.

In addition to her husband, Mrs. Palmer is survived by five children, Judith 24; Mrs. Vickie Louise Taylor, 22; Joseph, 19; Jerry, 16, and Susan, 9; her parents, Mr. and Mrs. Arthur J. Franklin, N1402 Mamer; a sister, Catherine Franklin, Spokane Valley, and brother, Floyd A. Franklin, Sunnyside, Calif.

A Bon Marche employe since 1958, Mrs. Palmer was promoted to credit manager little more than a month ago.

Assailant Shot by Patrolman

(Also see picture, page 6.)

By TOM BURNETT
Spokane-Review Staff Writer

A cashier's assistant was shot and killed moments before her assailant was shot and critically wounded by a police officer during an $8,000 armed holdup Saturday evening at the fifth floor credit offices of the Bon Marche, Main and Wall.

The victim was identified as Mrs. Peggy J. Palmer, 47, E8616 Valley Way, mother of five children.

The two shootings occurred at about 5 p.m., a prime shopping time for the busy downtown department store, and hundreds of customers were inside the store.

Witnesses said three men entered the store, walked to the elevator and rode to the fifth floor. The elevator is located near the rear of the large department store, leading police to believe that the men were inside for some time before using the elevator.

Two Go to Office Area

At the fifth floor, one man remained at the elevator while the other two men walked into the "cash office" area. The cash offices — five teller windows and a credit office — are located about 100 yards from the elevator, through the store's toy section.

Police said one of the men in the cash office area sat on a bench in the area and was not involved in the actual holdup.

The second of the two men — the man who eventually was shot — proceeded into the cashier credit office. The office is staffed by three persons. However, only one — the victim — was on duty at the time of the robbery, police said.

The man reportedly grabbed Mrs. Palmer and forced her into a small area behind her desk. The shooting apparently occurred in that area, police said. One shot was fired at Mrs. Palmer, who fell to the floor mortally wounded.

After the shooting, the gunman walked from the credit area to the cash offices and approached one of the five windows. The man leaped over the counter, grabbed a small plastic waste basket and stuffed it half full with paper money, police said.

Others Unaware of Incident

Store employes in the immediate area were totally unaware of the incident until the fatal shot was fired.

After the gunman took the $8,000, he jumped over the counter and out into the customer area. The man who had been seated on the bench and the gunman then walked swiftly away.

They were joined by the third man, and the trio then dodged store customers as they ran down the four flights of escalator stairs to the first floor.

The Bon Marche store detective, who arrived at the scene of the shooting moments after it happened, followed the three men to the first floor.

At the time of the incident, police officials were assigning patrolmen who had handled the heavy traffic after the Washington State-California football game to downtown areas for the remainder of the evening.

At least 50 policemen were in the general downtown area when the shooting of Mrs. Palmer occurred, and about 40 officers went immediately to the store after the initial alarm went out over the police radio network.

As the trio neared the first floor, Police Sgt. Gene McGougan, who arrived within one minute after hearing the alarm, was riding the escalator to the second floor.

Men Told to Stay in Store

As the three men neared the Wall Street entrance, Patrolman Ronald B. Graves was coming into the store. He ordered the men to "remain in the store" and not try to leave.

Graves said the men turned around and walked a few feet to a point where they were about 10 feet from him.

Patrolman Anthony Bamonte, who had entered the store through the main entrance, arrived at the scene.

As the men turned, they confronted Bamonte.

The man carrying the plastic wastebasket reached into the receptacle, produced a revolver and pointed it at Bamonte, the officer said. Bamonte pulled out his service revolver and fired once at the man, with the bullet striking the man in the head.

The man was reported in critical condition at Deaconess Hospital.

As the man fell, the wastebasket landed on the floor and the money spilled onto the stairs. Sunglasses the man had been wearing later were found shattered a short distance away.

Pair Held by Authorities

The two other men were arrested and held as material witnesses Saturday night.

When the shooting occurred, the two patrolmen and the three men were by themselves at the store entrance except for a young girl who was making a telephone call nearby.

No customers or employes were in any immediate danger, police said.

A large crowd of sightseers gathered at both store entrances after the incidents. Police set up a barricade to seal off the store. Police then searched the en-

normal Saturday night closing time. All employes were escorted out of the building through a rear door, except for those who work in the areas where the incidents had occurred. They remained to answer detectives' questions.

Deputy Chief of Patrol Thomas J. O'Brien took charge of the investigation, assisted by Capt. Calvin Smith. County Pros. Atty. Donald C. Brockett and Asst. Pros. Atty. James Krum were called to the scene as was County Coroner Dr. William E. Jones.

The above headline and article were from the October 17, 1971, *Spokesman-Review*. The motorcycle officer shown with one of the handcuffed suspects was Gary Lacewell, who had just identified and arrested the second suspect.

There were three people involved in this robbery. Two of them were arrested at the scene. The third, Jerry Lewis, had shot and killed the cashier (Peggy Palmer) approximately three minutes before he attempted to shoot Officer Bamonte, who shot him first.

The partial article on the left appeared in the October 18, 1971, *Spokesman-Review*. It contains a photo of the murderer, Jerry Lewis, and Peggy Palmer, the victim.

Man Apprehended After Robbery
Police were holding two men as material witnesses Saturday night.

the first person in the history of Washington State to ever plead guilty to a first-degree murder charge. However, that was a technicality, as he was then confined to Eastern State Hospital due to his debilitated condition. Once he had recovered sufficiently, it was far cheaper to imprison him at the Washington State Penitentiary, a Washington State Department of Corrections men's prison, located in Walla Walla, than to keep him at Eastern State Hospital.

This incident happened during a time of a lot of racial tension. Because the murderer was black, the shooting created a bit of controversy. As a result, Spokane Police Chief Wayne Hendren immediately contacted the news media and provided them with the circumstances surrounding the shooting.

The information that the murderer had gunned down the mother of five children, then attempted to shoot a policeman, was all the black community needed to reach the conclusion that the shooting was not racially motivated. Also, firing only a single shot clearly indicated I only did what was necessary.

Following that incident, I went back to work feeling fortunate there were no other victims. It was a terrible tragedy for the victim's family and an incident that left grim memories for many people for years to come.

Almost 40 years after Peggy Palmer, the cashier at the Bon Marché, was shot and killed by Jerry Lewis, I had the occasion to meet her oldest daughter, Judy Palmer Bendewald. Judy had many questions for me, which had remained unanswered since her mother's tragic death. One of them was whether her mother had done anything to provoke this man into shooting her. My answer was, "No, she did everything she was asked to do, including giving him over $8,000." There was absolutely no reason for him to have shot her.

As an aside, at the time her mother was shot, Judy was the president of the International Elvis Presley Fan Club. Shortly after her mother's death, Elvis and his wife, Priscilla, sent her a sympathy card. It is among her most cherished possessions.

The Bon Marché Shooting
by Michael Yates
(The security guard at the Bon Marché, who later became an SPD police officer)

Author's note: The following is a description of the events and circumstances surrounding the armed robbery and fatal shooting at the Bon Marché of a cashier in the credit department. At the time, Michael Yates was employed by the store as an unarmed security guard and kept the suspect under surveillance from the time he shot and killed Peggy Palmer, up until he was shot while attempting to shoot a motorcycle police officer.

Immediately following this shooting, he followed the murderer from the scene at the cashier's office on the 5th floor to the main floor. It was Mr. Yates's efforts that led to the arrest of the first person in the history of the state of Washington to ever plead guilty to first-degree murder. The following is Michael Yates's firsthand account:

This is my story of the October 16, 1971, homicide of Peggy Palmer. Peggy was a Spokane Bon Marché credit office manager when she was murdered by Spokane transient Jerry Lewis in a failed robbery attempt.

I was a store loss prevention (security) officer and had worked for the Bon Marché in Seattle, Everett, Columbia Center (Kennewick), and Spokane.

On the afternoon of Saturday, October 16, 1971, I was notified by the store telephone operator that she had been advised by Peggy Palmer that three black males on the 5th floor were acting suspiciously. The operator mentioned one of them was in the record section and the other two went to the "cash office" (Credit Office).

I was wearing plain clothes (undercover) and carrying a Bon Marché merchandise bag to disguise myself. It was customary for the store operator to page me to check out potential shoplifting suspects reported by store clerks and other employees. When they did, I would surveil the suspects and their activities.

When I arrived on the 5th floor, I immediately saw one of the suspects in the record section thumbing through albums. I continued to the credit office, posing as a customer, and observed the other two suspects. One of the suspects was slumped on a bench wearing a tan trench coat and holding a brown lunch sack with the neck of a bottle protruding out the top. He appeared to be an intoxicated transient. Another suspect, later identified as Jerry Lewis, was standing at the credit office counter filling out a credit card application.

I saw Peggy standing behind the counter watching Lewis as he continued filling out the form and asking questions. I noticed that she nodded toward the other suspect on the bench. I acknowledged that I saw both suspects and left the credit office to go to a register area to call the operator. I advised the operator what I saw and told her I would remain on the 5th floor to keep the suspects under surveillance, but as of yet, there wasn't any apparent criminal activity.

I positioned myself across from the record section where I could observe one suspect as well as the credit office. I told the record section clerk that, if I gave her a signal, she was to call the store operator and tell her to call the police. Then I called the operator and advised her of the plan if anything were to happen.

One of the credit office tellers came out to give me an update on what was going on in the credit office, and she told me that Peggy was getting nervous about how long it was taking for Lewis to complete the application. I asked her to have Peggy come out and meet me.

After a few minutes, Peggy did come out and said that she didn't think Lewis would be able to finish the application and was uncomfortable because of his behavior. She told me that he was mumbling, and asking incoherent questions. I advised Peggy that we had a plan if anything happened and that the store operator was aware of the plan. At that point, Peggy said she should get back to the credit office. A little while after Peggy went back to the credit office I noticed some activity near the credit office. Customers in the area were looking that way

as if something unusual was happening (apparently customers nearby heard the gunshot). Then I saw Lewis rush from the credit office and climb over the teller's windows.

I signaled the records clerk to call Ruby and get the police. I then started walking toward the teller's window and, as I approached, Lewis climbed back over the counter with a wastepaper basket and began walking in my direction. He had a silver pistol in his hand and the wastepaper basket in the other hand. As we approached each other, it occurred to me that Lewis' companions were possibly accomplices.

As we approached each other, Lewis put his gun hand in his pocket. As we passed, I looked down and saw the wastebasket was about half full of loose cash. I stopped to see where his accomplices were and didn't see them. At that point, I heard Mr. Alexander, the store president, standing in front of the teller windows, yelling for someone to call an ambulance.

I turned and saw Lewis heading for the escalator. He went down and at each floor, I would follow him at a discreet distance. Near the interior doors, I pointed out the suspect to Officer Tony Bamonte. Then there was a gunshot, and I saw Lewis disappear between the double doors of the foyer.

I jumped to the wall expecting something else to happen, but after a couple of seconds I looked and saw Bamonte still aiming at the open door. I then saw Lewis lying face down on the floor of the foyer surrounded by money and the wastebasket next to him. I couldn't see the gun and was concerned that Lewis might not be unconscious and was lying on it. An officer came into the foyer and I told him Lewis had a gun. He rolled Lewis over, and the gun was found under him. There was a lot of confusion after that but the other two suspects were apprehended by responding officers.

I was still near the west doors when Sgt. McGougan told me that Peggy Palmer had been shot and killed in the credit office on the 5th floor. Then I understood why Mr. Alexander was calling for an ambulance.

Over the years I have second guessed myself many times on what I might have done differently that may have saved Peggy's life and I have often thought about the family she left behind. I have replayed the scene many times and tried to reconcile the events that happened with a better ending. The memory of this tragedy remained with me throughout my career as a Spokane Police Officer. I know that during my 36 years in law enforcement, I was especially, specifically committed to the protection of life. It was in honor of Peggy Palmer.

Michael Yates, the security guard at the Bon Marché, later became a Spokane police officer. The photo above shows him (front row, right) during the time he was on the SPD graveyard SWAT Team in 1975. Top row: John Henry was on the police department from 1973 to 1987; Neal Peoples was on the department from 1961 to 1984; Roger Bragdon was on the department from 1973 to 2006. Bragdon became Spokane's chief of police in 1999. Bottom row: Skip Pavlischak, a U.S. Marine Corps Vietnam veteran, was on the department from 1972 to 1999. Pavlischak had 26 years experience as an SPD SWAT team member, team leader, and commander. Michael Yates was on the department from 1973 to 2005. As a sergeant, he was assigned to Patrol Division and later to Planning & Research, SIU (Special Investigations Unit), and Crime Analysis. *(Courtesy Spokane Police Archives)*

In 2009, Judy Palmer Bendewald, the oldest daughter of Peggy Palmer, authored a book about Elvis (left photo), which included her many encounters with him. From 1966 to 1972, Judy was the president of the "Kissin' Cousins" Elvis Presley fan club in Spokane. Her book is titled *My Treasured Memories of Elvis*, published by Memphis Explorations, Memphis, Tennessee.

Judy's book is a great read and offers a short lesson in Spokane history. Judy was inspired to write her book following a chance encounter with Carla Savalli, at the time assistant managing editor for the *Spokesman-Review* – also an Elvis fan. Above photo, from left: Sandy Schmidt, Elvis Presley, and Judy Palmer. *(Courtesy Judy Bendewald)*

Judy Palmer Bendewald's book titled *My Treasured Memories of Elvis. (Courtesy Judy Bendewald)*

The preceding story by Michael Yates gives a good representation of the Bon Marché shooting. Though unarmed at the time, Yates had the courage to follow a killer from the fifth floor down to the ground floor. Because of his alertness in identifying Lewis, and following him as he was escaping down the escalator, the three murder suspects were caught almost immediately after the murder of Peggy Palmer.

The following two pages are to honor Yates for his role in solving this horrific crime.

As an interesting aside, 47 years after this incident occurred, Mr. Yates expressed his gratitude and appreciation to me for not mistaking him for the killer of Mrs. Palmer and shooting him instead of Lewis.

Michael Yates, the security guard who was working at the Bon Marché on the date of the Palmer murder. Immediately after the murder, Yates followed the suspect to the first floor and pointed him out. Two years later, in 1973, Yates joined the Spokane Police Department. This photo shows Michael and his wife Brenda Jo, who was also a Spokane police officer, with their two horses and their dog, Lucy. Mike tells a story of an incident that occurred before he married his wife. In 1989, he arrested two suspects in a drug deal he observed in a doorway. One escaped while he was handcuffing the other. He called for backup and Officer Brenda Dahlstrom responded and chased the suspect in her car and ran on foot through the train station parking lot. Yates had one prisoner in the back seat of his unmarked sergeant's car following her. Brenda caught up to the suspect, and he pulled away and ran into a parking meter or signpost. She eventually reached and pounced on him as Officer Jay Jones arrived on his three-wheeler in front of them. Jones leaned over from his bike to help Brenda, and his helmet fell off, hitting Brenda in the head while she was cuffing the suspect. Mike watched from his car in awe as this was happening. Mike retired in 2005 and Brenda retired three years later.

(Bamonte photo)

Ever-resourceful Sgt. Mike Yates
"I told you to get outta town!!"

Downtown police "David-Sector" Sgt. Mike Yates, upper left, standing in the open hatch of the first tank in 1989, escorting the Washington Army National Guard tanks to the form-up area for the annual Armed Forces Lilac Parade. In route, Mike had the tanks swing down through the 1100 west First area, where officers usually had more problems than in other areas of the downtown. Symbolism being what it is, there was obviously no problem too big to handle. *(Photo courtesy Sgt. Jim Culp)*

My Reasons For Becoming a Policeman
by Tony Bamonte

During my career in law enforcement I learned there were two types of policemen: Those who wanted to be in a position to help other people who are being victimized, and unfortunately, those with self-serving motives, who wanted the power of the position.

As a small boy, my family life was filled with habitual violence. Often the police would respond to calls at our house. During those incidents, they did their job, but it was with kindness, compassion, and understanding shown toward my sister, brother, and me. I grew up respecting police and someday wanted to be one. Fortunately, I have found there are far more good people in law enforcement than bad. A bad cop hurts his entire department. Those who are unprofessional in their actions or demeanor should be recognized, disciplined, or removed by their commanding staff.

Louis Bamonte, 1927, as a marine. He was also a great role model. *(Bamonte)*

ARGUMENT OVER WIFE MEANS JAIL, HOSPITAL

One man was jailed on an assault charge and a second was taken to Sacred Heart hospital yesterday after the first reported he met the second coming from visiting his ex-wife and beat him up.

Louis Bamonte, 43, E517 Heroy, was in jail on the assault charge after, detectives said, he beat Henry Malina, N603 Oak. First he used a piece of a shovel handle, then a sharp piece of ice, it was said.

The detectives recalled that Malina had been beaten up several months ago, supposedly by Bamonte's father and brother.

The above article appeared in the December 26, 1948, *Spokesman-Review*. This happened on Christmas morning, when both our mother and dad went to jail. We went to live with our maternal grandparents. The statement, "Beaten up several months ago by Bamonte's dad and brother is inaccurate." He actually was beaten up by my mother's dad and her brother. Two months later my grandmother and grandfather got in a heated argument in the middle of which my grandfather died from a stroke. The police also responded to that. In a court battle that followed, my father was given custody of all three children.

On a regular basis, police officers encounter people when they're at their worst – drug addicts, alcoholics, gang members, thieves, spousal abusers, etc. A good policeman should sincerely want to make a difference, set a good example, and remember he or she is a public servant, with the sole purpose of protecting the community.

As policemen, we may be the only good influence some of these criminals will ever see, typically because of their circumstances and the atmosphere they grew up in.

Tony Bamonte, 1947, with black eyes from abuse from my mother after I told my dad about the nice man my mother was seeing. She waited until he had left before this happened. My dad took this photo for evidence. *(Bamonte, evidence photo)*

The Biggest Influence in My Life
My Father

My dad, Louis Bamonte, was born in New York City in 1906 to Grazia "Grace" and Domenico Bamonte. They came from Roccadaspide, Italy, a town in the province of Salerno in the Campania region of southwestern Italy. His father passed away in 1910, and three years later his mother passed away, leaving their six children orphans. At that time, my dad's older brother and sister, Ralph and Edith, took over raising the family.

In 1926, at the age of 19, my dad hitchhiked across the United States to San Francisco and joined the Marine Corps. Most of his tenure in the marines was served aboard the USS *Maryland* and in Nicaragua. The United States Marines occupied Nicaragua from 1912 to 1933, except for a nine-month period beginning in 1925 with the evacuation of U.S. Marines. Another violent conflict between liberals and conservatives took place in 1926, which resulted in the return of U.S. Marines. It was during this time that my dad was stationed in Nicaragua. From 1927 until 1933, there was a sustained guerrilla war against the Conservative regime and subsequently against the U.S. Marines. My dad was in Nicaragua from 1926 to 1928.

In 1930, following his discharge, my dad had become friends with another marine from Kellogg, Idaho, George Harvey. As the United States was just in the beginning stages of the Great Depression, employment was scarce. However, there was lots of work in the Idaho mines, which was my dad's next move. From the age of 23, he worked for over 18 years in the various mines, and logging, in the Coeur d'Alenes – mostly the mines. Today, as I think back, I wished I had asked him more questions about his early life. I know of three mines where he worked: the Bunker Hill, Sunshine, and Polaris.

The hazards of the mines

In the history of the mining world, and specifically the Coeur d'Alenes, mining has always been a dan-

My father, Louis Bamonte, in 1928, shortly before he finished his term in the Marine Corps. *(Bamonte photo)*

My brother Dale, my dad Louis, me, and my mother Lucile in Wallace, Idaho. *(Bamonte photo)*

gerous and unhealthy way to make a living. During my lifetime, I have spent a little over two years working in the Pend Oreille Mines. Before I quit I was working as an apprentice miner. Prior to that I was beating boulders through a grizzly, mucking belts, and driving diesel trucks underground. The most important thing I learned was that mining was not a career my father wanted me to follow. In 1966, at the age of 61, he died of "Miners Consumption." This was a disease common to anyone who worked in the mines. It's caused by the inhalation of particles of industrial substances, particularly inorganic dusts and silica. Symptoms include shortness of breath, chronic cough, and expectoration of mucus containing the offending particles.

In his well-researched book *From Hell to Heaven: Death Related Mining Accidents in North Idaho*, Gene Hyde documented, with names and incidents, 3,238 mining deaths in the Coeur d'Alene Mining District from 1887 to 2001. These are only the mining accidents. The graveyards in the Coeur d'Alenes are full of men, like my father, whose lives were shortened by breathing the dust and oil fumes of the mines.

The move to the Metalines area

By 1946, mining had left my father in poor health and susceptible to frequent bouts of pneumonia, and as my mother didn't want to live so far away from a large city, he moved his family to Spokane. At the time, my brother was six, my sister wasn't born yet,

The "Old Red Rooster," where my family lived for over seven years. The horse we are on was named King. He was a kind and gentle workhorse that was mistakenly shot by a poacher. His death was a heartbreaking event for our family. The cabin on the right is where my family lived. The partial log house on the left is part of what was, at one time, called a crib (a small duplex brothel). *(Bamonte photo)*

My sister, Star, and my aunts. *(Bamonte photo)*

My brother Dale, my dad, and sister. *(Bamonte photo)*

From left: Star, Dale, and Tony. *(Bamonte photo)*

My sister, Star (Bamonte) Bieber, holding her first born, Lani Jo. Star was 15 1/2 at the time, and had run away from our home, as our dad was strict. Her daughter, Lani, turned out to be beautiful – both inside and out, and a blessing to the family. *(Bamonte photo)*

and I was four. In the winter of 1949, while my dad was working in the mines and woods of the Metaline region of Pend Oreille County and my mother and we children were living in Spokane, my mother began having an affair. On Christmas morning of 1948 my dad confronted her and her lover. By the time the police arrived, he had beaten the man unconscious and was still in the process of beating him, with the intent of beating him to death. My dad was jailed on assault charges as a result of this incident, which made the neW.S.P.aper the next day. Needless to say, this was a sad Christmas for us.

Shortly after, my mother left her family and moved to Hawaii. For two months, my brother, sister, and I lived with my maternal grandparents in Spokane on Euclid Street. At the end of the two months, and shortly after midnight, my grandparents got into an argument. My grandmother wanted to tell a lie in court to help my mother during her trial for child abuse, and my grandfather was adamant about telling the truth. In the middle of the argument my grandfather suffered a stroke and died in their home.

Living next door to a former brothel

My father's next move was to relocate his kids to an old dance hall building, ten miles north of Metaline Falls and two miles south of the Canadian Border. Living at that location allowed him to work in the

The "Old Red Rooster" again. Directly behind our horse was the original dance hall where we first lived. The two log cribs were on the left. When we first moved there, another couple lived in the house to the right. Occasionally, my dad would have his wife baby-sat my sister when he was working. Her husband owned a shingle mill about a half mile away. One evening my dad came home and found the husband had molested my little sister. Immediately behind the cabin was a water trough. I heard some noise and went to investigate. My father had the man begging for his life, swearing he hadn't touched my sister. Two days later, the man's shingle mill burned to the ground and they left the area. I'm almost sure he burned it himself as an excuse to leave the area out of fear of my dad. Several weeks later, we moved into the abandoned cabin on the right as it was a much better place to live. *(Bamonte photo)*

woods in the summer making cedar post, and later in the cedar pole business and logging.

The house we moved into was formerly known as the "Old Red Rooster," an early 1920s dance hall. Several other buildings surrounded it – a small log "crib" duplex and a 15' x 15' frame cabin. There was no indoor water or plumbing in any of the buildings, one light bulb, no telephone, and we used wood for heat. We lived there six years. During the summers, my dad worked in the woods as a cedar post maker. To keep from being left alone during the summers, we went to work with him. During that time, I became proficient at splitting, peeling, and trimming fence posts. In the meantime, my dad made arrangements for my sister to live with a family in Metaline Falls, with the exception of weekends. Since we had no indoor plumbing he felt that was the best for a four-year-old girl.

When my parents divorced, it was an easy decision for me to be with my dad. He was the most important person in the world to me. He was totally devoted to raising his children. He never remarried, drank or smoked, always worked hard, and was exceptionally honest. The only entertainment he ever indulged in was reading. On Saturday evenings, he would take us kids to the movies in Metaline Falls.

His life consisted mainly of working by himself in the woods, year after year, with the only exception being when I was with him, which was as often as I could. I worried constantly, especially since I knew he had health problems – the result of working in the mines for so many years. I often think about how lonely and hard his life was.

Among the best times in his life, and when I saw him the happiest, was in 1954 when his three sisters traveled from New York City to spend over a month with us. My dad and us kids picked them up in Spokane. From there we drove to our home near the Canadian border. My aunts slept in the old dance hall behind our cabin. That was the first time any of us had ever heard our father speak Italian. It was also one of the best times of my life.

This photo is of my dad's 1940 Chevrolet truck with a load of fence posts. From left: Dad's middle sister Rose, my dad, his youngest sister Ann, his oldest sister Edith, my brother Dale, my sister Star, and myself. My aunts worked in garment factories in New York City. *(Bamonte collection)*

The worst, then best, day of my life

The worst day in my life involved my dad, in the fall of 1951, when I was nine. My brother and I had just returned home from school, a 10-mile school bus trip from Metaline Falls, and were awaiting our dad's arrival. Typically, when my dad was working in the woods, he would get home sometime between 6:00 and 7:00. By 9:00 p.m. he still hadn't come home, and it was completely dark out. We had no phone and lived two miles from the Canadian Border, which shut down at 6 p.m., meaning there was no traffic on the road. Consequently, there was no one to ask for help. I needed to find him. In my mind, I was sure he was injured or maybe even dead. I tried to get my brother to come with me, but he felt he needed to stay at the house if anyone did, by chance, come by. I knew the immediate area where my dad had been working, as we worked with him on weekends. It was about five miles from our house.

That night was exceptionally dark; the moon was about at a quarter of its glow. I had a flashlight to use for going to the outhouse after dark, but the batteries were almost dead. As I started out, I used the flashlight as little as possible, only enough to get a quick glimpse of where I was walking. I felt it was important to save the light for when I found my dad. All the time I was walking my mind was focused on my dad and why he hadn't come home. This had never happened before; he was always there for us. He had an old 1940s truck he always drove. I watched him drive and felt confident I would be able to drive it if I went slow. I had studied what he did when he drove. I knew I would only have to use one gear to make it back home.

As I continued my walk, I sang what songs I knew. This was my attempt to scare off any predatory animals, as we had recently seen both a cougar and a wolf. My biggest fear was finding my dad dead. I walked in almost complete darkness for about three miles, as my mind raced to the various scenarios I might encounter. Suddenly I heard the noise of a truck moving toward me from about a half mile away. It was my dad. His truck had been stuck in a cedar swamp near where he was working. This was the worst/best day of my life.

The move back to Osburn, Idaho

In 1955, my dad got a timbering job at the Polaris Mine in the Coeur d'Alenes. It was to last about a year. During the years he had worked in the Shoshone County mines he had acquired a reputation of being a good worker and dependable. We packed all our belongings on the bed of my dad's '40 Chevrolet truck and moved to Osburn, where, for a year, we rented a two-bedroom unit at a place called the Royal Autel, which has since been torn down.

My most memorable experience at Osburn was when my dad made me take accordion lessons. He found out there was a man in Wallace giving lessons, bought an accordion, and enrolled me for lessons. I remember three things about this experience: 1.) My accordion teacher's name was Mr. Arnold. 2.) Mr. Arnold formed an accordion band. There were ten kids in it. He would have ten chairs placed all in a single row facing an audience of about 20 people and we would all play accordion songs, and 3.) I wasn't good at playing the accordion.

The Bamonte family getting in wood. The house on the far right was the former dance hall. The washing machine sitting on the porch had a gas motor to run it. However, it didn't work. My dad had a Kodak camera that had a built-in timer to allow for the entire family to be in the photo. The chainsaw he was using was an IEL, made in Canada, which was his first gas-powered saw. *(Bamonte photos)*

By 1956, my dad's contract at the Polaris had been completed. In the meantime, he got an offer to go back to Pend Oreille County and construct a small concentrator mill at the Oriole Mine, which was the first mine in the county to ever produce and ship ore. We then moved to the town of Metaline Falls, in the same 1940 Chevrolet truck my dad had owned for years.

Prior to Dad's beginning construction of the concentrator mill, the people who owned the mine wanted him to recruit other men to begin developing the mine. One of those he recruited was Bill McCoy from Kellogg. Bill and his family moved to a small cabin next to ours on the mine site. Bill's family consisted of his wife, Sally, and their three children, Terry, Ronnie, and Dawn Marie.

They were at the mine site for almost ten months. I became friends with their second son, Ronnie, who was my age. His ambition in life was to become a jet fighter pilot. When they moved, I lost track of the family for about ten years. I later learned he made it to the Air Force Military Academy and was training to fly fighter jets. He died in a mid-air flight accident with another jet fighter pilot trainee when they collided. Both pilots died instantly. Unfortunately he Oriole Mine venture turned out to be a flop.

Our family lived at the mine site until fall when we moved into a small house in Metaline Falls. My dad then again went into the cedar pole and logging business. From 1957 to 1961, until I graduated from high school, I worked for him peeling cedar poles at $5 a day. The cedar-pole-peeling business begins in the spring, when the bark starts slipping and ends in the mid-summer when the bark starts to stick.

Things that stand out in my mind are: Poles should always be peeled on the same day the trees are sawed down or the bark will begin sticking. The average length of the poles we peeled was from 25' to 65'. We peeled a lot of 45 to 50 foot poles. When you peel a pole, you peel up one side and then down the other. After the first bark strip is taken off both sides, it becomes easier to peel. I was able to peel from six to twelve poles a day depending on the diameter and length of the pole. Also, if I recall correctly, B.J. Carney and Company paid approximately $20 for a 35' cedar pole and $40 for a 65' pole, with the payment increments adjusted accordingly for the sizes of the others.

My dad, Louis Bamonte, in the spring of 1956, building a concentrator mill at the Oriole Mine (a silver and lead mine) west of Metaline, Washington. The Oriole was the first producing mine in Pend Oreille County. My dad was in partnership with four other men. When my dad passed away, his last wish was to have his remains scattered at the mine site. I scattered them 60-feet northwest from where he is standing in this photo. *(Bamonte photo)*

I spent many hours after school, on weekends and during summer vacation working with my dad. He passed away in 1966 at the age of 61, from silicosis, the result of his years in the mines. Not a day goes by that I don't think about him and his influence on my life – mostly about the tough life he lived.

The cabin on the left was our home from 1956 until my dad died in 1963. My beloved dog, Butch, is in the center of the photo. The vehicle on the right was a 1942 Studebaker Champion, which my dad made into a pickup. *(Bamonte photo)*

My father, Louis Bamonte on far left at one of the many mining leases he was involved in during the time he spent in the Coeur d'Alenes. This photo of him and three partners was taken at the portal of the mine. This mine, including many of the smaller mines, had no water or air to run any types of drills. Consequently, the blasting holes were all drilled with hand steel. This is the same type of mining August Paulsen was doing when he discovered the **Mighty Hercules Vein.** *(Bamonte photo)*

This is the site of the Oriole Mine located at the base of Mt. Linton in Pend Oreille County. It was my dad's last mining venture.

The Oriole was a lead, silver and zinc mine. The arrow indicates the portal to the mine. Pictured is the ore bin to the far right, the compressor shed in the middle, the black-smith shop to the left, a partial of a small cabin to the far left, and to the lower right is a horse garage. *(Bamonte photo collection)*

During the time I was the elected sheriff of Pend Oreille County, as a sideline and for exercise, I used to build log houses. I built a total of 11, almost one a year. Photo circa 1985. *(Bamonte photo)*

My son, Louie. *(Bamonte photo)*

My brother, Dale, circa 2015. He's is a seasoned and skilled union electrician. *(Bamonte photo)*

Tony and Suzanne Schaeffer Bamonte, in 2005. Both grew up in Pend Oreille County, Washington.

Military Experience

Implementation of the Draft (conscription) and why I joined the Army (Civil War soldiers would have experienced the same frustration, which was one of my reasons for describing it)

The draft, going back to the Civil War, was one of the most significant crises that hung over the heads of every young man throughout the Vietnam War. Every male in the United States was required to register for the draft within 30 days of his eighteenth birthday. Because of the draft, if a young man attempted to find work in any type of job that held a future, one of the first questions he was asked was if he had completed his military obligation. It seemed the companies offering good jobs didn't want to hire young men and then lose them to the military. This was the reason many young men voluntarily joined the military.

The small town I grew up in was a logging and mining community. It was easy to get a job in that line of work, but it was not stable and had no benefits. Consequently, after working at the Pend Oreille Mine for over a year, I enlisted in the Army on the 20th of November 1961. My choice of the Army was because it was an obligation of three years versus four years for all other branches of the military. The obligation was only two years if you were drafted. The Army was the only branch of the service that was drafting men. I felt it was worth that extra year to be able to get my military obligation out of the way. Although I had little understanding about the Vietnam War at that time, I had a strong sense of doing my duty for our country.

Consequences of avoiding the draft

The penalties for failing to register for the draft were great. You would be considered a "draft dodger." Draft dodgers faced many direct consequences, which were enforced by the federal government. Draftees who did not report as required were arrested and sent to a federal prison for a maximum of five years. They lost their voting privileges while in prison and were also subject to a $10,000 fine.

In addition to this, there were many indirect consequences, such as loss of respect from fellow Americans; draft evaders were often characterized as cowards and unpatriotic. They often left the United States and became illegal immigrants in the countries where they were hiding. Jobs were difficult to find. Families were separated due to the draft dodger's self-imposed exile; they were unable to see their children or other family members.

How men dodged the draft

There were three ways most commonly used to avoid the draft during the Vietnam War. 1.) Flee the country to Canada or Mexico. 2.) Enroll in college because students didn't have to register for the draft. This exemption favored those who could afford and were academically qualified to go to college. 3.) Get a doctor's note stating a reason you were unable to be in the military.

The end of the draft

The draft changed the lives of many men in the United States. From 1940 to 1973, during both peacetime and periods of conflict, young men were drafted to fill vacancies in the United States Armed Forces that could not be filled through voluntary means. In 1973, the draft, which was highly unpopular, finally ended when it was repealed by an Act of Congress, changing to an all-volunteer military force.

My military service, 1961 to 1964

After enlisting in the Army in 1961, I attended basic training at Fort Ord, California. From Fort Ord, I was sent to military police school at Fort Gordon, Georgia. Toward the end of my training at Fort Gordon, I applied for Airborne. However, I was sent to Lackland Air Force Base to attend K-9 school. While there, I was given the most beautiful German Shepherd dog, who would be with me for almost a year and a half. Upon completion of that school, my dog and I were assigned to Monroe, Michigan, to an underground Nike-Hercules missile base.

I was at Monroe for approximately eight months, including the time of the Cuban Missile Crisis in October of 1962. Following the missile crisis, I was transferred to another Nike/Hercules site, located on Belle Isle Park in Detroit. In my opinion, Belle Isle Park is Detroit's nicest park, being located in the most serene, peaceful, and scenic parts of the island, with trails along the river and the Blue Heron Lagoon. During my time in the Army, Belle Isle was the best location where I was ever stationed and the best duty, being with my dog.

I had been at Belle Isle about six months when I was promoted to corporal. Within weeks of that promotion, I received orders for duty in Vietnam. The directions on these orders were for men with the rank of corporal. I was forced to give up my dog. None of the training and bonding was taken into consideration. Fifty-four years later, a feeling of sadness washes over me when I think of the bond I had with him. I was told he would be assigned to another handler, but I miss him greatly to this day.

Vietnam

My arrival in South Vietnam was in 1962. I was assigned to the 560th military police company at Tan Son Nhut Air Base. Within weeks I was transferred to downtown Saigon, where I was assigned to MAC-V (Military Assistance Command Vietnam). MAC-V was the main headquarters for the brass responsible for the military actions being taken in South Vietnam. During my time working at MAC-V and living in Saigon, my residence was in a six-story hotel in the downtown area.

The MAC-V compound consisted of two buildings, one of which was used by the majority of the officers involved in the conflict and the other housed the offices of Ambassador Henry Cabot Lodge; Robert McNamara, Secretary of Defense from 1961 to 1968; and the Commander of Forces in Vietnam, General Paul Harkins. Harkins was later replaced by General William Westmoreland, who had been his deputy.

My assignment at that location was at the entrance to both buildings. My job was to greet each officer with a salute and greeting. A number of things stuck out at that time: 1) The higher ranking officers, from colonels to generals, were far more polite and gracious than those of lower rank. 2) Henry Cabot Lodge, the ambassador to South Vietnam, always rode in a solid black 1961 "Checker" automobile driven by his chauffeur. 3) Whenever the president of South Vietnam went anywhere, he traveled in a motorcade made up of at least ten American-made, high-end, vehicles. During my time in Saigon, I observed his motorcade on at least five different occasions. 4) The presidential palace for President Diem was far more opulent than that of the presidents of the United States. 5) Much of the lifestyle enjoyed by the presidential family during the Vietnam War came from the American taxpayers' military aid to South Vietnam. President Diem and his family members were highly inefficient and corrupt. Corruption abounded in all forms, especially with the large amounts of money the United States poured into the country in the form of military aid. President Diem's family was the biggest practitioner of nepotism. His close relatives filled the top ambassadorial, cabinet, and civil service posts.

By 1963, the number of U.S. military advisors had grown to over 16,000. Also, by that time, President Diem was perceived by the United States as an impediment to the accomplishment of its goals in Southeast Asia. Henry Cabot Lodge, the ambassador to South Vietnam, would play a part in his downfall.

Events leading to the military coup to remove President Diem

Diem's increasingly dictatorial rule succeeded in alienating the majority of the South Vietnamese people. Also, in the summer of 1963, Diem's brother, Ngo Dinh Nhu, had raided the Buddhist pagodas of South Vietnam, claiming that they had harbored Communists that were creating the political instability. The result was massive protests on the streets of Saigon, causing a number of Buddhist monks to commit suicide in public by pouring gas on themselves and lighting it. Numerous pictures of monks engulfed in flames made world headlines. During the time I was in Saigon, on one occasion, I was a witness to one of these self-immolations by a monk. Seeing that gave me a sad and helpless feeling.

The coup and the killing of President Diem

During the summer of 1963, American officials decided the time had come for the Diem regime to be overthrown. Ambassador Lodge was to play an important role. When the time came, and with Washington's approval, the coup took place. Diem and his brother were captured and killed. Coincidentally, three weeks later, our own President Kennedy was assassinated on the streets of Dallas.

At first, the United States publicly disclaimed any knowledge of or participation in the planning of the coup that overthrew Diem. It was later learned that American officials had met with the South Vietnamese generals who organized the plot and had given them encouragement to go through with their plans.

The very small part I played in the military coup of President Diem

I received an unexpected assignment in early October 1963, 21 days prior to the overthrow of President Diem on November 2, 1963. Along with five other men, all military police, we were moved to a house that was five doors away from the residence of Henry Cabot Lodge. Our assignment was to become familiar with that house, and, when or if the time came, we were to protect and evacuate him if necessary.

During his time in Saigon, Lodge and his wife lived in one of the nicer areas of the city. It was a quiet residential section where they had a two-story house with a balcony. The commanding officer of our group of six had made arrangements for our meals to be furnished in the home, walking distance away, with an elite Vietnamese family. This proved to be a good experience. At the time, we didn't know what we were going to protect Lodge from. However, our job was to enable him and his wife to be evacuated from the roof of his home. Our group of six men was there to provide cover for him. A helicopter would quickly swoop down and pick up him and his wife, delivering them to an undisclosed safe area. This was all pre-planned, in case the coup went the wrong way and his life would have been in danger. Everything went as planned, and although ready, we were never needed.

Within days of the military coup and the killing of Diem and his brother, my detail came to an end, and I went back to my hotel in Saigon. At this point in my Vietnam tour, I volunteered for duty as a helicopter door gunner.

My next assignment: Helicopter door gunner duty

I was assigned to the Utility Tactical Transport Helicopter Company (UTT) at Tan Son Nhut Air Base, which was an Air Force facility. The UTT, the first armed helicopter company of any army in the world of combat, was originally organized in Okinawa and sent to Vietnam in September of 1962. However, the company's designation changed three times and was given a different name each time.

I served as a door gunner for most of February until sometime in March 1964, when it was my time to return to the United States. My training as a helicopter door gunner, which was only three days long, consisted mostly of first aid and how to administer morphine. During the first few weeks as a door gunner, I flew with various pilots and copilots. I was soon assigned as the door gunner for Major Patrick Delavan, who was the commanding officer of the UTT. I quickly learned that Delavan, by all accounts, was a legend as far as helicopter pilots go. He was fearless, to the point of seeming like he had a death wish. I later learned that none of the other door gunners

Tony Bamonte standing next to his assigned helicopter, Sabre 6, in early April of 1964. *(Bamonte photo)*

wanted to fly with him because of that reputation. His helicopter was named Sabre 6, a number that was proudly passed on to other commanders.

An article about Delavan that appeared in the *New York Times* on June 12, 1964, stated: "Major in South Vietnam Gets 7th Purple Heart." It went on to say: "... His eyelids were wounded when a rocket on his helicopter exploded after being hit..."

I was Delavan's door gunner when that incident took place. As I recall the incident, the rocket not did explode. A bullet hit the fuel propellant igniting the fuel, which in turn flared up. This caused severe burns to the crew chief and minor injuries to Major Delavan, who was directly in front of the crew chief. It also caused minor injuries to others in the aircraft. Had the rocket itself exploded, as stated in the *New York Times* article, it would be highly unlikely that anyone would have survived.

In 1964, the United States was still in the role of military advisors. As such, we were required to have a South Vietnamese soldier accompany us on our missions. Also, whenever the media wanted to fly with us they would go with the flight commander. That particular day our helicopter had six people aboard. Major Patrick Delavan was in the left front pilot's seat, to his right the copilot, behind him from left to right was the crew chief, a TV cameraman from one of the national news networks, a Vietnamese observer (referred to as an ARVIN), and then myself.

When the fuel propellant exploded, it flared up, discoloring the left side and left front plexiglass windows of the helicopter. The person most seriously injured was the crew chief, as the explosion was just to his left and about three feet from him. The crew chief almost died as result of this, and to the best of my recollection, he was in the hospital for several months.

Whenever we flew, both the left and right sliding back doors would be open. The other people to suffer injuries were, as stated, Major Delavan, whose window was open at the time, and the news reporter, who was sitting next to the crew chief, was burned on the neck. The ARVIN was burned slightly on his left arm and hand. The copilot and I suffered slight injuries as we were the farthest away from the explosion.

What stands out most about that incident was when we were finally able to land, everybody exited the aircraft and we removed our flight helmets. When the TV cameraman took his off, he looked quite different than he did prior to this incident. In 1964, the Beatles' haircut style was in vogue. That was the type of haircut the news reporter was wearing. As he removed his helmet, it was immediately obvious his hair had been trimmed up a bit by the fiery blast. That was the one bit of humor attached to that incident.

General Joseph Stilwell Jr. and the UTT Helicopter Company

General Stilwell served as commander of U.S. Army Support Group, Vietnam (renamed US Army Support Command, Vietnam on March 1, 1964) from August 26, 1962, until June 30, 1964. During my time as a door gunner, I came to know General Stilwell. Prior to my departure to the States, he asked if I would be his driver. If I had taken that assignment, it would have been an immediate promotion to sergeant. However, I would have had to reenlist to extend my stay in Vietnam for another year. General Stilwell was lost at sea on 25 July 1966, while flying a C-47 to Hawaii with a longtime friend and pilot. The C-47 had been scheduled to continue on to Thailand.

Based on a database from the Pentagon, an estimated 40,000 helicopter pilots served in the Vietnam War. Total helicopter pilots killed in the Vietnam War was 2202. Total non-pilot crew members was 2704. I was one of the fortunate survivors.

General Joseph W. Stilwell at Tan Son Nhut Air Force Base in 1963. *(Bamonte photo)*

Joe Machala – hired by the Spokane Police Department 1966

Joe Machala escorting an armed robbery suspect across a downtown skywalk to an awaiting prowl car. *(Courtesy Joe Machala)*

During Joe Machala's career as a police officer, he served as a motorcycle officer and was later assigned to work hit and run, radio supervisor, tactical team, and mounted patrol. His most memorable event was the shooting of detectives Bill Beeman and Homer Hall while serving a warrant at Brunot Hall, 2209 West Pacific Avenue in Browne's Addition. When Hall and Beeman knocked on the suspect's door and identified themselves, he immediately slammed the door on them. As they attempted to

SPOKANE POLICE DEPARTMENT

force the door open, the suspect fired shots, wounding both officers.

The suspect then started a trash fire in his apartment, turned on a five-gallon propane gas tank, and lit the gas. The explosion that followed shattered windows and blasted two people off the front porch.

Machala was the first officer on the scene and helped clear residents from the burning building. At one point, as he was going through the hallways of the building evacuating people from their residences, the fire and smoke had exhausted the oxygen to the point that he couldn't breath and was able to just make it out of the smoke before he was overcome.

The fire department quickly responded with a crew of 41 firemen who arrived with aerial ladder trucks and other pieces of equipment. However, there was a major problem. The suspect, whose apartment was next to a main stairway, threatened to kill anyone who came near, keeping the firefighters from extinguishing the fire. Soon the fire had spread to the third floor, additional shots were heard. It was later determined that several shells had exploded as a result of the fire.

Joe Machala, circa 1975. *(Courtesy Joe Machala)*

In a short time, one of the firemen located the wounded suspect hiding inside his apartment, bleeding from a self-inflicted gunshot wound to the head. Officers W. Reedy, Joe Machala, and Fireman D. Albin smashed a window and carried the suspect out of the smoke-filled room. He was then placed on a gurney and carried to a waiting ambulance. He did not survive. The fire continued to burn uncontrolled for two and a half hours as attempts were made to evacuate the building. In the end the building was completely destroyed. (see pages 117-119) regarding Brunot Hall)

Other incidents that Machala vividly remembers included the shooting death of Detective Brian Orchard, who was a close friend, and the motorcycle accident of Officer Joe Bokor that almost cost him his life.

Joe Machala, circa 1975. *(Courtesy Joe Machala)*

Joe Bokor – hired by the Spokane Police Department in 1966

Joe Bokor, circa 1970. *(Courtesy Joe Bokor)*

Joe Bokor was born on November 17, 1942, in New Jersey. He graduated from Garfield High School in Garfield, New Jersey in 1960.

After graduation he joined the Air Force and was discharged four years later. He was stationed at Fairchild Air Force Base, where he met and married Sharon Trainer. They had two children, Jodi and Tammy. On October 2, 1966, he was hired by the Spokane Police Department as a patrolman and in February of 1970, began his career as a motorcycle police officer. This lasted for only six months, when on September 18, 1970, he was involved in an accident that nearly cost him his life. Around 10:30 p.m., Bokor and fellow motorcycle officer, Patrick Henry, were en route to the police station following the end of their shift. Both were southbound on Nevada, riding side-by-side in the four-lane roadway. Suddenly a pickup truck went through a stop sign on Liberty and entered the intersection less than 15 feet in front of the motorcycles. Both men applied their brakes, but not in time. Bokor's motor slammed into the rear quarter of the truck, knocking it from Henry's path of travel.

Bokor sustained a broken upper right arm and wrist, a compound fracture of the right femur, and second-degree burns on the right thigh. As Bokor was crawling away from the scene, the driver attempted to leave, but couldn't because of the damage. A female on the sidewalk took her coat off and extinguished the flames on Bokor's feet and legs. Bokor was rushed to the hospital where he technically died three times. After three weeks in the hospital, he was taken home in an ambulance at his insistence. He went back to work in the Hit-and-Run Unit just under six months after the accident and was back riding motors in June 1971. Bokor had seven surgeries, which included the complete reconstruction of the right knee. He also suffered retrograde amnesia. His last operation was two years after the accident, to remove two plates in his right arm and the plate and rod in his right leg.

Joe Bokor's motor after his wreck in 1970. *(Courtesy Spokane Police Depatment Archives)*

Charles Edward Helmuth – hired by the Spokane Police Department in 1966

Chuck Helmuth, photo taken at Liberty Park, circa 1969. *(Courtesy Chuck Helmuth)*

Chuck Helmuth was born August 20, 1942, at Burlington, Iowa. His father, Bud, was a laborer and his mother, Leona, a housewife. Chuck has four sisters and one brother, who were all raised and attended schools in Burlington, Iowa.

Shortly out of high school, Chuck joined the Air Force. Upon completion of his four-year tour of duty, he was stationed at Fairchild Air Force Base in Spokane, which was the location of his discharge.

Chuck joined the Spokane Police Department on May 1, 1966. Prior to that, he was working other jobs that included a gas station and laying sod for landscaping. During his times in the Air Force he worked in the finance office. He attended Spokane Community and Whitworth colleges, studying law enforcement and sociology. In 1974, he earned an associate of arts degree in law enforcement. In 1977, he earned a bachelor's degree in sociology.

Chuck rode motor from 1968 to 1976. The highest rank he attained on the police department was detective. The biggest influences in his career were Lieutenant Al Halbig, Bill Ferguson, Lou Moss, Jack Tiegen, and Ray Collela. During his time on motor he had several partners, He rode with Bob Grandinetti for three years. During the time Chuck was on motor, there were from 12 to 14 officers per shift riding motor for two shifts – day and swing shift.

One of Chuck's most interesting cases took place in the early 1980s when he was working as a detective on the burglary detail. It was still daylight when he and detectives Jim Johnson and Brian Breen were attempting to serve a felony warrant on a female who lived in an upper floor apartment on Monroe Street between Bridge and College avenues on the east side of Monroe.

Apparently the woman, who was armed, jumped out of the window onto the roof of the building and was running to the south—on the roof. At the time, Chuck was close by and pulled into a large parking lot off of Post Street, behind a series of adjoining buildings.

One of the buildings to the south, near Bridge Avenue, had an outside fire escape ladder from the ground floors to the roof. Chuck climbed the ladder to the roof and went to the north edge of the building. From that point he was able to see the next building's roof, which was a couple of stories down. However, the next building to the north was only one level lower than where he currently was. He noticed a large rectangular skylight running west to east about six to eight feet high on this roof.

From that point, everything went into slow motion. He saw a female with a long-gun moving slowly in a semi-crouch on the south side of the skylight heading east towards the southeast corner. He also saw Brian Breen out in the middle roof moving from north to south towards the same corner with his firearm drawn. To this point, they hadn't seen each other.

Chuck had a clear view of the woman. He drew his firearm, a Smith & Wesson .38, and loudly

Chuck and Vicki Helmuth visiting Mt. Rushmore. *(Courtesy Chuck Helmuth)*

identified himself to the suspect in order to alert Breen and Johnson. He also yelled at her to drop her weapon. At that time, she turned and looked at him, with her long-gun being held across her chest. At the same time, the other officers on the roof took cover. They could see Chuck but did not have a view of the suspect.

Chuck spent the next few minutes trying to convince her to give up and that she would not be hurt. It seemed like hours to him. The other officers who were closer to her were also telling her to give up. Following a short amount of time, she finally gave up. She was cuffed and taken off the roof via a fire department ladder truck.

Chuck's most rewarding accomplishment in life was the furthering of his education. He was able to get two college degrees while working swing shift and going to school during the day. As the authors remember Chuck, he was honest, hard-working, and eager to learn. Chuck retired on May 5, 1992.

In 2008, Chuck married Vicki. At the time, they both worked for the Mead School District. Chuck's children include one son and two daughters. He has five grandchildren, four girls and one boy.

The lesson he's learned in life is that hard work and honesty pays off in many ways.

Chuck Helmuth's motorcycle

An accident at Division and Main on October 1, 1974. The car Chuck was chasing stopped, but Chuck wasn't able before impact. The inset on the lower right is what Chuck and his motorcycle looked like, both in an upright position, before he re-configured it. *(Courtesy Chuck Helmuth)*

Ron Graves – hired by the Spokane Police Department in 1967

SPOKANE POLICE DEPARTMENT

Ron Graves leading a group of cirus elephants in 1972. During his career, Ron experienced interesting incidents. One of these occurred at Sam's Pit, a Spokane roadhouse that was often the scene of trouble, when shots were fired and one of the bullets just missed him. Another occurred when he was investigating the kidnapping of a baby. He searched the alleys and found the baby, alive, in one of the garbage cans. Ron also worked in the Major Crimes Unit. *(Courtesy Ron Graves)*

Family Ties

The more things change, the more they stay the Same.

Ron Graves- 1972 and his son Jeff Graves – 2001 were assigned the same work detail three decades apart.

A poster of Ron Graves depicting family ties in 1972. His son, Jeff, is in the lower photo in 2001. *(Courtesy Ron Graves)*

Skylstad said. "Certainly, it's very sad behavior associated with that drinking. That would be my observation." Asked about Kosnoff's theory that Welsh and O'Donnell kept each other's secrets, Skylstad said, "I don't have any information about who knew what. Clearly, there was a drinking problem. I just don't have any information."

Vicar General Steven Dublinski, who said he first saw the 1986 police report Wednesday when police officials showed it to him, also commented on Welsh's behavior. "It's not the behavior we would expect by any leader of the church," Dublinski said. "It's not behavior we would expect of people in society. It's very tragic. It's part of a sickness that he had."

Dublinksi also said: "The problem of sexual abuse of minors by clergy is much bigger than Bishop Welsh."

Spokane Assistant Police Chief Jim Nicks said from his reading of the 1986 report, Bishop Welsh received no special treatment. "We did the follow-up as requested. We contacted the church leadership. There was nothing here to indicate there was any crime in our jurisdiction," he said. Nix also said the report met today's standards of good police work. "I don't see where we would have done much different in this matter," he said. "I hope we looked at other cases we had locally to see if the bishop had been involved. I hope we would have done that back then too."

Motor Officer Ron Graves, circa 1978. *(Courtesy Ron Graves)*

This photo was taken when motor officer Ron Graves responded to a house fire west of Felts Field in 1976. Graves received a sincere and heartfelt response when he showed interest in this group of children. In response to asking the youngest of these kids, "How old are you?" the boy's answer in sign-language was "four."

This is an excellent example of the positive effect that public-relations-oriented police officers can have on kids of all ages. Kids always seem interested in motorcycles. The fact that he is not encased in a vehicle makes the motorcycle officer more approachable. *(Courtesy Ron Graves)*

Phillip Ostendorf – hired by the Spokane Police Department in 1967

Phillip Ostendorf. *(Courtesy Spokane Police Department)*

Phillip was born in Cincinnati, Ohio, in 1941. Following his high school years at North Central High School in Spokane, he joined the United States Navy. In 1964, while in the Navy and stationed at Whidbey Island, he married Janet Roberta Willard, who was a bookkeeper at the time.

Phillip was on the Spokane Police Department from June 11, 1967, to July 11, 1993. He began his career as rookie police officer, PFC, motorcycle officer, and later was assigned to patrol, traffic hit and run.

Brian Frederick Orchard – hired by the Spokane Police Department in 1968

Brian Orchard was murdered in the line of duty on July 18, 1983. *(Courtesy Spokane Police Department)*

Brian Orchard joined the Spokane Police Department on April 28, 1968. He grew up in Spokane, graduating from Lewis and Clark High School in 1963, and serving in the U.S. Army until 1968. Fifteen years later, he was killed while attempting to make an arrest, when he was shot in the head on, July 18, 1983. He died at Scared Heart Hospital, 33 hours after receiving the wound.

On that day, Orchard was one of the detectives called in to assist two Chelan County Sheriff's detectives in a stakeout at Spokane's Holiday Inn on Fourth Avenue. The stakeout was the result of a June 1st robbery in Wenatchee, Washington, of gun collector Robert Adolphi, who was held at gunpoint in his home, beaten, and locked in his large vault. The two assailants made off with coins, jewelry, and rare firearms valued at over $100,000. A few weeks later, the robbers contacted Adolphi and demanded $20,000 for the return of his guns. Adol-

phi was to drive to the Spokane Holiday Inn on July 18th and leave his vehicle with the money under the driver's seat. Adolphi complied, after notifying the Chelan County Sheriff s Office.

Brian Orchard and the other officers kept watch on Adolphi's vehicle. At approximately 10:30 p.m., 24-year-old Lonnie J. Link and 34-year-old Donald E. Beach parked a black Lincoln Continental about half a block away from the motel, with the stolen firearms in the trunk. The passenger, Donald Beach, got out of the Lincoln and walked to the motel parking lot to locate Adolphi's car. After Beach got out of the car, Detectives Orchard and Bruce Nelson pulled their unmarked Ford Mustang in behind the Lincoln. The two had been working undercover and both had full beards and were wearing T-shirts, blue jeans, and sneakers. As the detectives approached the Lincoln, with their guns drawn, they identified themselves and ordered Lonnie Link to exit the vehicle. Link did not comply.

Orchard was approaching the rear of the car on the driver's side when Link raised a pistol and shot through the car window, critically wounding Orchard on the right side of his head. Link then attempted to shoot Detective Nelson, who returned fire. As Lonnie Link sped away, six officers emptied their weapons into the fleeing automobile, flattening its tires. Barely two blocks away, Link crashed the car into a light pole but was able to escape on foot.

Donald Beach was arrested near the Holiday Inn after a sheriff's K-9 located him hiding in some bushes. Lonnie Link was found in Portland, Oregon, where he was arrested on July 21st and returned to Spokane. Both suspects were paroled ex-convicts. They were charged with aggravated first-degree murder for killing Detective Orchard. The two men were members of the Ghost Riders Motorcycle Club, an outlaw gang, and the Lincoln Continental they drove belonged to Alvin L. "Burr Head" Hegge, the gang's leader. The Ghost Riders had between 75 and 150 members with chapters in Washington, Montana, Indiana, Wisconsin, British Columbia, and Alberta, Canada.

Brian Orchard, circa 1969.

During his trial, Lonnie Link claimed he had shot Detective Orchard in self-defense, because the officers had not identified themselves and looked as if they were criminals coming to kill him. This defense allowed Link to escape the death penalty by creating some doubt as to whether or not the police actually had identified themselves. However, he was convicted of first-degree murder and sentenced to life in prison without the possibility of parole.

Donald Beach pled guilty to felony second-degree murder in a plea bargain, sparing him from the death penalty. He was sentenced to life in prison, subject to parole after a minimum term of 12 to 16 years.

In August 1987, 47-year-old Alvin L. Hegge and his accomplice, Billy C. McEwen, were formally charged with second-degree murder in the death of Detective Brian Orchard. Lonnie Link and Donald Beach initially refused to implicate motorcycle gang leader Hegge and McEwen as the two masterminds of the Adolphi robbery/extortion for fear of being murdered in prison.

Following Link's and Beach's conviction, they agreed to testify against Hegge under the conditions they both be allowed a conjugal visit with their girlfriends. This visit took place in the Pend Oreille County jail. (See Dave Prescott section of this book)

At the time of the formal charge against Hegge, he was serving a prison sentence in Wisconsin for his part in a 1983 murder in that state. Billy McEwen was on probation for a federal firearms violation and living in Espanola, Washington, near Medical Lake. Al Hegge and Billy McEwen were each tried separately for their roles in the murder of Detective Orchard.

On April 21, 1989, after deliberating for ten hours, the jury found McEwen innocent. Hegge was found guilty of second-degree murder and, on May 4, 1989, was sentenced to life in prison. This new prison sentence was to begin upon the completion of the one he was serving in Wisconsin.

As a last act of giving back to the community Detective Orchard had served, his family donated Brian's kidneys and corneas. Over 1,300 people attended his funeral. In an unparalleled display of unity for law enforcement, at least half of those in attendance were law enforcement officers from throughout the Pacific Northwest and Canada. Brian Orchard left behind his ex-wife, two daughters, and one son.

The final tribute for Brian Orchard in 1983. *(Both photos on this page courtesy Spokane Police Department Archives)*

James Garry – hired by the Spokane Police Department in 1968

James Garry, circa 1975. *(Courtesy James Garry)*

James Garry was born and educated in Ireland. Prior to graduating from high school, and with parental consent, he enlisted in the Irish Army Reserve. He served for over three years in the reserve before emigrating to New York City in 1961. Based on the fact that he was a citizen of a friendly country, that same year, Gary enlisted in the United States Air Force. In 1965, he was discharged while stationed at Fairchild Air Force Base.

In 1967, Gary became a United States citizen and, in 1968, he was hired by the Spokane Police De-

partment. He rode motor from 1973 to 1981. During that time, his motor partners were Charlie Helmuth, Joe Machala, and Jim Bunch. In 1995, he retired from the Spokane Police Department.

In 1972, while on the police department, he enlisted in the Coast Guard Reserve and served for three years. In 1975, he transferred to the Washington Air National Guard and retired from there in 1998, with more than 30 years in the Reserve.

President Ronald Reagan flanked by police officers Scott Johnson (left), and James Garry in 1986. This photo was taken in a stairwell at the Sheraton (now Doubletree) Hotel, where Garry and Johnson were stationed. The president and his secret service detail agreed to a photo with the SPD officers. It was a nice public-relations moment and a good souvenir for the officers. *(Courtesy James Garry)*

On October 31, 1986, President Ronald Reagan delivered a hotly debated statement about the controversial Hanford Nuclear Reservation, while campaigning in Spokane for Senator Slade Gorton, who was locked in a tight re-election race against former U.S. Secretary of Transportation Brock Adams. The next morning, the *Spokesman-Review* ran a story headlined, "Did President Reagan Address Hanford Issue or Not?," which pointed out that one federal law forbade test drilling at Hanford, while another law mandated a nuclear-waste repository in the West. Ambiguous statements about Hanford were clearly not what voters wanted to hear. Gorton's pollsters showed that Gorton was "eight points ahead when Reagan arrived and six points behind the day after he left." On November 4, 1986, Brock Adams beat Gorton by a narrow margin, knocking Gorton out after one term.

James Garry in dress uniform for the 1975 Lilac Parade. This was the type of uniform worn for special occasions such as parades, VIP escorts, funerals, etc. *(Courtesy James Garry)*

Guy Hawks – hired by the Spokane Police Department in 1968

(Story by Guy Hawks)

I started riding motorcycles in 1960 when I was 16 years old. I rode a Harley Hummer that summer to save money on gas, which was around 25 cents a gallon. I was making $5 a day for board and room on a local farm so had to save money for school clothes.

I never got on a motorcycle again until 1973 when I went to motor school with Mel Griffiths as my instructor. The first day I almost got into a head-on collision at Boone and Adams heading to the Coliseum for practice. From that day on it was all up hill and easy. Mel was a great teacher. The things I learned from him carried over for the next 40 years that I rode motorcycles. I started riding police motor the summer of 1974 and rode for nine years. I took Tony Bamonte's place and my Motor Number was 408. My first partner was Brian Orchard and my last partner was Larry Williamson, with several in between. Those nine years were some of the best years of my police career. Why wouldn't it be? I got to ride a Harley Davidson Motorcycle. Those nine years were filled with writing lots of tickets, lots of accidents, lots of traffic control, and lots of fun. During my riding career I worked Riverside Ave., and the tooling traffic. I worked hit and run and went to the traffic school at the W.S.P. Academy, and Jay Jones and I took over Mel's spot and taught motor school until the traffic units were disbanded in the 1980s. At that point I was done riding for the department.

Since then, I have owned several Harleys and have continued riding until I was 70 years old. Special memories were riding in the Lilac Parade, where the public always appreciated the work we did. Probably the best thing is the camaraderie and friendships that were developed from being a motor bull that extended for my whole career and on. That camaraderie is shared every year with our annual motor bull party.

Guy Hawks on police motor, circa 1978. *(Courtesy Guy Hawks)*

Guy Hawks became the new police motor school instructor, replacing Mel Griffiths, when Mel retired in 1980. This photo depicts one of his classes, circa 1982. From left: Deputies Marv Patrick, Ron Seitz, Tim Downing, and Phil Shatzer. *(Courtesy Guy Hawks)*

In front of the Public Safety Building, circa 1978. From left: Guy Hawks, Larry Peterson, and Connie Caler. This was a public relations photo for the police department. *(Courtesy Guy Hawks)*

Guy Hawks visiting kids at St. Joseph's Children's home in 1976. *(Courtesy Guy Hawks)*

Guy Hawks, second from left on motor, in front of St. Joseph's Children's home in 1976. *(Courtesy Guy Hawks)*

Robert "Bob" Yake – hired by the Spokane Police Department in 1969

S
P
O
K
A
N
E

P
O
L
I
C
E

D
E
P
A
R
T
M
E
N
T

Motor Officer Robert Yake and his daughter Jennifer, circa 1976. *(Courtesy Joy Yake)*

Robert "Bob" Yake was born in Spokane on October 28, 1943, to Harley and Virginia Yake. He graduated from Lewis and Clark High School in 1962. Following graduation, he enlisted in the U.S. Marine Corps, serving a tour in Vietnam. After his service in Vietnam, he was stationed in Bremerton, Washington. It was there he met his future wife, Joy. They were married in 1966, and returned to Spokane that same year, both completing their degrees at Eastern Washington University. On February 2, 1969, Yake joined the Spokane Police Department. He began his 12-year career with the department in patrol, rode motor for several years, and ended up as a homicide detective.

The most dramatic incident during Yake's police tenure occurred on January 10, 1972, in north Spokane. Officers Robert Yake and his partner, Robert "Bob"

Walker, were responding to a 10:30 p.m. suspected-prowler call, on a snowy evening, at the 4900 block of North Atlantic.

For approximately half an hour, Yake and Walker followed footprints in the snow on West Joseph, going in and out of yards and around houses. While tracking the prints, they observed a male suspect walking south, down Normandie Street. As they attempted to approach him, the suspect took off running. Yake pursued him on foot as he ran between houses and across an alley. At the same time, Walker, who was close to his prowl car, ran to the car and sped in the direction the suspect had headed in an attempt to intercept him from the direction Yake had chased him.

Although the suspect eluded the officers for a short time, he quickly realized that trying to outrun two policemen coming at him from different directions was not a good thing. Consequently, once out of sight of the officers, he hid behind a nearby bush.

As Yake continued his chase, he observed one of the suspect's legs jutting out from behind a bush. Yake ordered the man to get up. As the suspect arose, he began shooting at Yake. The first three rounds from the suspect's .357 magnum misfired. However, the fourth round struck the spiral wire on a notebook in Yake's shirt's breast pocket that deflected it before it entered his body, resulting in only a flesh wound. However, the force of the bullet caused a major impact and bruising on Yake's chest. Yake doubled over, returning fire as he grabbed for the suspect's coat. The suspect broke free, leaped over a fence, and fled.

Officer Walker was just entering the alley in the patrol car when he heard the shots. The suspect bolted directly in front of the prowl car, pushing away from its hood with both hands. Walker exited his vehicle and continued chasing the suspect on foot. As the suspect ran east, he scaled a wooden six-foot fence a short distance from him. As Walker continued his chase, he did not notice the suspect had fallen and collapsed at the bottom of the opposite side of the fence. As Walker jumped the fence, he almost landed on the suspect. At this time, the suspect appeared to be completely out of action as a result of the bullet wounds he had received following his attempt to kill Yake. Consequently, Walker quickly began an

Bob Walker on the left and Bob Yake on the right. Inset Douglas Pagnossin. *(Courtesy Joy Yake)*

examination of the suspect and found he had been shot in the groin area and twice in the left arm. He immediately summoned an ambulance, and the suspect was taken to Holy Family Hospital.

Walker was then informed that his partner had been shot and was also en route to Holy Family Hospital in a prowl car driven by Officer Jim Culp, who had arrived in the area just as the shooting occurred. After the scene was secured, Officer Walker left for the hospital. There he learned the suspect had died 15 minutes after the arrrest. Police records later revealed the suspect, Douglas Pagnossin, was a repeat offender who was on unsupervised parole from western Washington.

Yake retired from the Spokane Police Department on August 7, 1981. Following that, he and his wife acquired the Joy Bell Christian School House, which they owned and operated for over 40years. Bob passed away on March 22, 2015, at Spokane's Hospice House, following a year-long battle with cancer.

Wounded Officer Quits Hospital

Police Officer Robert D. Yake, wounded in a shootout in which a prowler suspect was killed Monday night, was released from Holy Family Hospital today.

Officer Yake suffered a gunshot wound in the chest.

"I think I'll carry a notebook in each pocket," Yake said today, referring to the fact that a notebook in his shirt pocket and a zipper in his jacket took up most of the force from a bullet which struck him.

Killed when shot four times by Yake

Douglas R. Pagnossin, 23, Bellingham. The shooting incident happened in the yard at N4904 Normandie after Yake and Officer Robert D. Walker had followed footprints in the snow many blocks while trailing a prowler suspect.

Yake said today he and Pagnossin were about four feet apart when Pagnossin fired at him.

"I didn't even know he had a gun until he started firing," Yake said. "I fired three or four times at him at close range, then shot some more as he ran."

Pagnossin's wife, Bonnie, and the small child, who were living in a van type camper truck, parked in the 2 block on East Pacific.

Detective Harry M. McKeever s Mrs. Pagnossin, who didn't know of husband's death, fainted when gi the bad news.

The camper van was impounded police. Mrs. Pagnossin now is sta with relatives in Spokane, police s

Pagnossin, at the time he was ki was on unsupervised parole after 1966 burglary convictions at Bel

Bob Yake.

As he was dying, Douglas Pagnossin told the police where his wife, Bonnie Pagnossin, could be found. Pagnossin had converted an old ton-and-a-half van into living quarters for him, his wife, and their child. The van and his wife were located at the East 200 block of Pacific Avenue. When found and questioned, she told detectives she and her child were downtown during the shooting and had no knowledge of what had happened. Upon learning of her husband's situation, she immediately fainted. She remained in Spokane and was reportedly staying with friends. Inside the van police discovered a large quantity of jewelry including watches, necklaces, rings, and assorted stones. Police also found a small quantity of what they believed was marijuana. Police also reported Pagnossin had an extensive criminal record.

Connie A. Caler – hired by the Spokane Police Department in 1969

S
P
O
K
A
N
E

P
O
L
I
C
E

D
E
P
A
R
T
M
E
N
T

Connie Caler, circa 1972. Connie joined the Spokane Police Department on February 2, 1969, and retired on September 25, 1992. *(Courtesy Spokane Police Department archives)*

Robert C. Van Leuven – hired by the Spokane Police Department in 1969

Robert Van Leuven, circa 1973. *(Courtesy Barbara "Van Leuven" Stumph)*

Robert Van Leuven joined the Spokane Police Department on October 26, 1969. While on the police department, he rode motor for a period of time before being promoted to detective, sergeant, and later to lieutenant. He retired in April 1998 and is now deceased.

Among the more notable and sadder cases he worked, along with numerous other police officers, was the abduction, murder, and dismemberment of 13-year-old Nanette Marie Martin in 1976.

Nanette was abducted early on April 3, 1976, while delivering the *Spokesman-Review* newspaper. At the time, her route consisted of 100 newspapers, which she had just begun delivering on her early morning route on the city's North Side. Her parents called the police about 8 a.m. after she failed to return home. Assessing the information the parents provided, the police immediately felt she was not a runaway.

Nanette had left her home on West Spofford about 3:30 a.m. She picked up a bundle of newspapers at Sinto and Lincoln and began delivering her route.

Prior to her disappearance, Nanette had delivered almost a half dozen newspapers to two apartment houses and a single-family residence before disappearing with the remainder of her papers.

As a result of their investigation, Spokane police detectives noted: "The missing girl had no reported family problems and had never been a runaway." They expressed concern that "she may have been abducted." They said the girl sometimes was joined on the route by a girlfriend, but this morning had gone alone. "Nothing has been found – not the missing papers, not the paper bag, not her," police said at the Public Safety Building, where they filled out a missing person report. Detective Robert C. Van Leuven of the department's Young People's Bureau was interviewing the parents.

Nanette, who had delivered newspapers since the previous September, was believed to be wearing a blue ski jacket, two-tone blue jeans, and tennis shoes. She was described as being 5-foot-8, about 115 pounds, with brown, shoulder-length hair, and greenish eyes. She was wearing tear-drop shaped, silver-frame glasses.

Discovery of the body

Within a short time numerous uniformed police officers canvassed the immediate neighborhood, surrounding neighborhoods, and locations of her paper route. Spokane Police Detective Robert Bailor, also a former motorcycle officer, found Martin's dismembered body two days later when he followed up a hunch that she was the victim of a copycat crime.

Lt. Fred W. Fait, who headed the investigation, said a four-man homicide detective team was assigned to the case.

Thomas Edward Mahrt, 28, 5104 East Union was

Nanette Marie Martin. *(Public domain)*

ing the Nanette Martin Reward Fund to Mahrt's landlord. The reward fund was established through a Spokane bank by the *Spokesman-Review*, after the dismembered body of one of its neW.S.P.aper carriers had been found.

According to Detective Robert C. Van Leuven of the Young People's Bureau, at the time, Thomas Edward Mahrt committed the murder. He had a son, Thomas Junior, who was four years old. His son was turned over to juvenile court authorities and was placed in a foster home. Van Leuven said the child had been in Mahrt's custody during a divorce action.

Thomas Mahrt pleaded guilty in June 1976 to kidnapping and murdering Martin. He is serving two consecutive life terms at the Airway Heights Corrections Center.

charged with first-degree murder and first-degree kidnapping in the case. Mahrt's arrest followed 16 days of intensive investigation after her body was found in plastic bags about five miles west of the city.

According to Lt. Fait, police detectives, working with a search warrant, searched Mahrt's basement. As a result, they found clothing, glasses, a neW.S.P.aper bag, and papers that were believed to be Nanette Martin's.

The arrest came after Mahrt's landlord discovered some allegedly incriminating pictures at Mahrt's apartment and notified police. The landlord had gone to Mahrt's apartment to fix a broken window and discovered photos of Nanette Mahrt he had taken while in the process of dissecting her body. Police Chief Wayne Hendren recommended award-

Bob Van Leuven and his wife, Barbara, on Easter 1980. *(Courtesy Barbara Van Leuven Stumph)*

Bill Gasperino – hired by the Spokane Police Department in 1969

Bill Gasperino, circa 1976. *(Courtesy Bill Gasperino)*

Bill Gasperino was born in Butte, Montana, on January 8, 1946. He went to school in Billings, and then the family moved to Spokane where he attended Saint Francis Elementary and Gonzaga High School. Immediately out of high school, he joined the Marine Corps Reserve for eight years, where he attained the rank of sergeant. Upon completion of his service, he worked a number of jobs from railroad work to construction work. For a short time, he had a job selling shoes, which he felt was the worst job he ever had. Bill joined the Spokane Police Department in 1969.

Bill and Kathy were married in 1971. He has two brothers, one younger and one older, and a younger sister.

Bill worked swing shift traffic motor from 1975 to the early 1980s, up until the time the police department did away with the traffic division. During that time his motor partner was Ron Beekman.

When the traffic department was activated again in 1989, Gasperino went back to riding motor on the day shift. At that time, his partner was Larry Lindskog. Gasperino rode motor for approximately 15 years, retiring in 1999, after 30 years with the Spokane Police Department. Gasperino loved the old Harleys, but he felt that during later years they lost out to the newer bikes, which were far more dependable.

During his lengthy service with the Spokane Police Department, Gasperino handled numerous and varied types of situations, from the mundane to potentially life-threatening. However, one incident he was involved in stands out among the rest.

In either 1976 or 1977, while he was working swing motor on a warm summer night, he responded to an armed robbery call at Jack's Mission Village. It was about 11:30 p.m., and as he was approaching Trent and Napa, a car blew a red light. It was a robbery suspect car, fleeing from the scene. Gasperino hit his lights, and the chase was on. The suspect then shut his lights off and took off onto the dirt streets in the warehouse area near where the chase ended up. The suspect's car was making so much dust it was unable to be seen. At about the same time, and in the spirit of the chase, which was now a blind chase at high speeds, the suspect dropped down about four feet onto a section of railroad tracks which Gasperino failed to see.

Consequently, Gasperinos's bike bumped over the tracks, hit the bank on the opposite side, throwing him over his windshield. At the same time, his bike went into a cartwheel, resting a distance away and in pieces. Gasperino suffered a few small scratches and a broken lens on his wristwatch, but was not finished with the chase.

As this was happening, a nearby citizen in a company truck, who had just witnessed the incident, stopped to see if he was okay. Still in the anxiety mode of catching the armed robber, Gasperino, without saying anything to the driver, jumped into his truck and took off after the suspect. He chased the car for several blocks where the suspect came to a dead end, and at that time Gasperino arrested him. Although this was a bit unorthodox and may be frowned upon by some people, Gasperino went above and beyond the line of duty to catch his man. Of most importance, the suspect had just held up a business at gunpoint and was fleeing.

Bloomsday

After the 1974 World's Fair (Expo '74), a fun run took advantage of the newly renovated downtown and Riverfront Park area took place. It was the first Lilac Bloomsday Run which took place in 1976. A local runner, Don Kardong, who had competed in a number of national races, had moved to Spokane in 1974. Kardong suggested to a local reporter that Spokane should have a downtown run of its own. The suggestion made its way into the newspapers headlines, and the race became a reality in 1976.

Following that success, Spokane Mayor David Rodgers encouraged Kardong to pursue the idea, and the local Jaycees adopted it as a project. On May 1, 1977, over a thousand runners participated in the inaugural Bloomsday Run, which was billed "Run With the Stars" in posters announcing the event. Olympic gold and silver medalist Frank Shorter crossed the line first, followed by Herm Atkins of Seattle, and founder Kardong.

Bloomsday, like all other major attractions in the city, requires a strong police presence, especially from the traffic unit.

The success of the first year's race led to an even greater turnout in 1978, which was over 5,000 runners. By its second year, Bloomsday was already enormous by any standard, and a victory by Boston's Bill Rodgers helped spread the event's national reputation.

In the years that followed, Bloomsday continued to grow, reaching 57,300 in 1988. In 1991, Bloomsday took another jump to 60,104, and in 1996 the event reached its all-time high of 61,298. During its history, the Lilac Bloomsday Run added prize money for top runners (1982) and wheelchair racers, and the event consistently attracts the world's top competitors.

Bloomsday has been held on the first Sunday of May since 1976. The course is 7.46 miles long and starts in downtown Spokane. It heads northwest along the far west end of town, passes by Mukogowa Ft. Wright Institute and Spokane Falls Community College before heading up "Doomsday Hill," back downtown to the Spokane County Courthouse, and crossing the Monroe Street Bridge.

Bill Gasperino, Kim Thomas, and John Clarke were the motors that led off the Bloomsday Run, circa 1997. *(Courtesy Bill Gasperino)*

Larry Lindskog and Bill Gasperino crossing a bridge at Riverfront Park. *(Courtesy Bill Gasperino)*

Robert "Bob" Walker – hired by the Spokane Police Department in 1969

Bob Walker, circa 1976. *(Courtesy Bob Walker)*

Bob Walker was born at the Providence Hospital in Wallace, Idaho, on May 15, 1941. The family later moved to Spokane where he attended Hamilton Grade School and John Rogers High School, graduating in 1959. Bob got his first job at the age of 16 while still in high school, working in the auto repair business.

In 1964, Bob married Susan S. McConnell, the daughter of Dr. Graham S. McConnell, former Spokane County coroner (1986-1994), and Laura May McConnell. Bob and Sue have two sons, Mark and Chris.

Military obligation

From 1940 until 1973, during both peacetime and periods of conflict, men were drafted to fill vacancies in the armed forces, which could not be filled through voluntary means. During the years of the draft it was hard to get a good job if you hadn't performed your military obligation. Employers didn't want to hire and train people and then lose them to the draft. In regard to fulfilling his military obligation, in 1958, Bob joined the Army National Guard. During his military time, he went on exercises, once to Japan and twice to Korea. Bob felt his military experience was a great benefit to him in his leadership skills. He enjoyed his military time and as a result learned there were many good people in the world. He retired in 2001 from the Army Reserve with the rank of Lt. Colonel after 43 years of duty.

In 1969, Bob was hired by the Spokane Police Department. He started out as a patrol officer, where he worked for four years. He passed a test as a police officer first class and was assigned to motor, where he worked for eight and a half years. His most memorable experience occurred when his motor partner, Bob Yake, was shot in 1972.

In 1973, Bob was assigned to the Special Weapons and Tactics (SWAT) Team, replacing Tony Bamonte, who had quit to take a political appointment for the sheriff of Pend Oreille County. Bob remained on the SWAT Team for 15 years. During his tenure, he was also assigned many important details, such as honor guard, pistol team, explorer scout advisor, EVOC (Emergency Vehicle Operation Course) instructor, where he worked for 20 years, traffic law instructor, challenge course manager and builder. He also developed the Lead Academy, bike patrol in Riverfront Park, and the national level programs for the Boy Scouts.

Of all the people Bob worked with, his favorite was Chief Terence Mangan. He stated Mangan would always go along with whatever programs he suggested. With ten years in Volunteer Services, Chief Mangan allowed him to develop a unique program consisting of Police Reserves, Senior Volunteers, Explorer Scouts, and Co-op education students. Following Bob's retirement from the department in 1998, he worked for the United States Marshal's service for nine years.

Bob and Sue Walker

Sue and Bob Walker met in 1960 through mutual friends. They dated off and on throughout Sue's high school years, and became engaged in February of her senior year. They married on July 18, 1964.

Sue attended business school until their first son, Mark, was born. Bob's job with the Washington National Guard took them to Pullman, Washington, where they lived for almost two years.

They moved back to Spokane in 1967, and Bob began working for the Spokane Police Department. They moved to Mead, Washington, in October 1969, where they still reside today. They were blessed with the birth of their second son, Christopher Walker.

During their early years of marriage, Sue worked many jobs to help make ends meet. Of her more interesting jobs, in the mid 1970s, she worked as a playground supervisor at Farwell Elementary, substituted for the school secretary, and was also a health room aid. For many years, Sue has volunteered in many capacities including Cub Scouts, athletics, school activities and sports, and church. Sue became the first woman on the board of directors for the Spokane Police Credit Union and served as their secretary for 15 years.

On the police department Bob was asked by the chief to start a Volunteer Services Unit for the department. He worked in that capacity until he retired in 1998 with nearly 29 years of service. Sue worked part-time with Bob until she retired to stay home to care for their first grandchild.

Throughout the rest of Bob's law enforcement career, Sue was by his side, volunteering wherever needed. Their home was a revolving door as young people stayed for a night, a week, or several months. Over the years, several hundred people have occupied the couple's home and continue to do so.

Bob was an officer in the Washington Army National Guard, and Sue was an active member of the State Auxiliary, the local Militia Auxiliary, and Family Support Group. The friendships they made have continued throughout their lives. Bob is a retired Lt. colonel with the Washington State National Guard having given 43 years of service to the nation, and a life member of the National Guard Association. He was inducted into the OCD Military Hall of Fame at Fort Benning, Georgia.

Bob and Sue volunteer for the Inland Northwest Honor Flight project for military vets, a project that sends the veternans back to Washington, D.C., to visit military memorials. They have acted as guardians on trips.

When Bob retired, he and Sue became a driving force to preserve local law enforcement history with the Spokane Law Enforcement Museum and the Hallways of History. In June of 2003, Sue helped start a project putting a committee together (SPD History Book Committee) to write the history of the City of Spokane through the eyes of the Spokane Police Department from 1881. The committee met on a weekly basis for 14 years and, in 2017, completed the final book *Life Behind the Badge, Volume V*, which covers 1998 to 2000. They also completed a 550-page *Photo Chronicles* book of a more personal nature for officers and their families for the 130th anniversary of the department.

Sue and Bob are involved in many local activities, which include the Spokane Law Enforcement Officer's Memorial Project that honors all law enforcement officers who have been killed or died in the line of duty in the State of Washington. They have also forged a partnership with Fairmount Memorial Park Association to dedicate historical monuments in their cemeteries to honor those who supported law enforcement, as well as others who left their mark on the City of Spokane who were not significantly recognized for their place in our local history. As of 2014, 24 monuments have been dedicated.

Bob volunteered to run the Happy Feet Program on a medical mission in Equador where he assisted in fund raising and helped deliver over 800 pairs of shoes and socks. He washed the feet of the recipients and put the shoes on for them. He also became

Bob and Sue Walker's wedding photo July 18, 1964.
(Courtesy Bob Walker)

Sue and Bob Walker, 50 years later, on May 2, 2014.
(Courtesy Bob Walker)

the Challenge Course Manager for the YMCA Camp Reed course at Fan Lake from 1998 to 2008. He provided challenge course activities during the spring, summer, and fall for groups from area schools and programs. He trained facilitators and built and maintained the course. He has volunteered for Bee Kind Gardens in the Spokane Valley for underprivileged children, 6-12, and was also able to help build the new Challenge course on the campus of Eastern Washington University in Cheney, Washington.

Bob has earned many accolades, including the United Way Volunteer of the Year and NSDAR Community Service Award.

Bob and Sue are both outdoor enthusiasts and love to travel. He is the former director for Winter Knights Snowmobile Search & Rescue Unit and was responsible for any and all snowmobile search & rescues in Spokane County. He also sits on the board of SAR (Search and Rescue Council), and assists in teaching youth snowmobiling courses annually. They have spent a number of years traveling together on his

Harley Davidson motorcycle, which they replaced with a 1931 Model A pickup. Bob restored it, and they enjoy their affiliation with the Inland Empire Model A Club and going on a variety of tours. Sue was a member of Footprinters Chapter 34 in Spokane, The Westerners Spokane Corral, and the Jonas Babcock Chapter NSDAR. Both Bob and Sue donated well over a 1,000 hours of service to their community yearly for over several decades.

In July 2014, Bob and Sue celebrated their fiftieth wedding anniversary by throwing a party for family and over 200 close friends, who told many stories of the difference Bob and Sue have made in their lives. The "wedding cake" was served with napkins from the original wedding that Sue had dug out of a box of memories.

In August 2004, Bob and Sue stood up for the wedding of two of their best friends – Diane Erickson and Denny Hooper. Diane's husband had died several years earlier from cancer and Denny's wife had also passed away from cancer. Denny had served

Bob Walker and Roger Gehrig, circa 1978. *(Courtesy the Walker family)*

with Bob on the original SWAT Team of the police department and retired with 24 years of service.

An interesting side note

In 1912, Bob's grandfather, John Walker, was killed in a mining accident in the Hercules Mine at Burke, Idaho. The Hercules Mine was one of the richest discoveries made in the Coeur d'Alene Mining District. The wealth from the Hercules Mine made millionaires of a number of people who later settled and invested in Spokane. Some of these mine owners were May Arkwright and Levi Hutton and Myrtle and August Paulsen. In the book *From Hell to Heaven, Death-related Mining Accident's in North Idaho,* author Gene Hyde describes Walker's death:

WALKER, JOHN, trammer, age 46, [killed] 17 November 1912, Hercules Mining Company, Partnership; Hercules Mine, Burke, Idaho; Shoshone County. Walker made several trips hand-tramming ore from a chute to an ore pass on the 400 ft. level. A shift boss came by and noticed the car was off the track and no one around. The shift boss thought Walker went to the upper level to check the amount of ore left to pull. After an hour went by, and Walker was not seen, the boss lowered another miner down the ore chute and he found Walker had slipped into the ore pass and had fallen 110 feet to his death. Reverend Willis Luce of the Methodist Church officiated at services held at 10 a.m. in Wallace on 20 November. Improved Order of the Red Men and members of the Miners Union carried out the burial services. Walker was a resident of Burke for nearly 12 years, worked all this time at the Hercules, and was well-thought-of by the company and fellow miners.

Bob Walker in front of St. Joseph's Children's Home, circa 1976. *(Courtesy Bob Walker)*

Larry Herman – hired by the Spokane Police Department in 1970

Larry went on the Spokane Police Departmant on March 1, 1970. He was assigned to motor during the spring of 1979, and rode swing shift with Jay Jones. His motor number was 424 and Jay's was 415. He rode until the traffic unit was disbanded. His children are Lisa, age 4, and Brett, age 1.

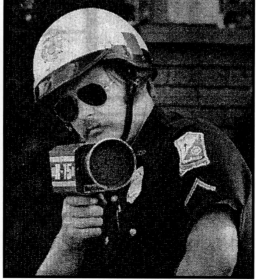

Lower left: Larry's wrecked motor after a crash and burn at Main and Division at 2:00 a.m.

Lower right: Larry working radar.

Spokane Police Department

Michael Eugene Hobbs – hired by the Spokane Police Department in 1970

Michael Hobbs, circa 1974. Michael was on the Spokane Police Department from April 26, 1970, to September 11, 1984. Mike worked primarily with Mel Burchfiel. *(Courtesy Michael Hobbs)*

SPOKANE POLICE DEPARTMENT

Lyle Boeck – hired by the Spokane Police Department in 1974

Lyle Boeck, circa 1976.

Lyle was hired January 6th 1974. He rode swing shift motor for the last two and a half years that the Harleys were used before the traffic unit was disbanded. Greg Sprague was his motor partner and they went to swing shift patrol when the traffic unit was terminated. The picture of Lyle's daughter Nicole, sitting on the bike with him, was taken in 1980 when she was six years old.

"How'd it go, Lefty?"

This cartoon was used to demonstrate the day in the 1960s when the police station was located at 242 West Riverside Avenue and there was a bank about 200 feet to the west of the station. One day that bank was held up by an armed robber, who was quickly caught and made the statement that he "should have checked out the area better." The names drawn on the cartoon are Bill Beaman, Al Halbig, Roscoe "Rock" Walker, and John Ellis.

James Keith Bunch – hired by the Spokane Police Department in 1970

James Bunch

Jim Bunch went on the Spokane Police Department on February 2, 1970, where he served until 1997, when he retired.

The photo on the bottom of this page are of Jim Bunch during a 1971 Spokane Police Academy judo class. Jim is the fifth from the left in the third row from the bottom. Front Row: Unknown, Bob Gibbs, Bob Major, Gale Meenach, Orie Hurst, and Jim (unknown last name) Second Row: Stan McGee, Jim Powell, Dave Weidmer, Mike Hobbs, Mark Grumbly, and Steve Braun. Third Row: Mel Burchfield, Jim Culp, Unknown, Linda Donley, Jim Bunch, Larry Herman. Back Row: Paul Nolan, Mike Albright, Duane Sivanish, Unknown, Unknown, Roger Gehrig, Don McCabe.

S P O K A N E   P O L I C E   D E P A R T M E N T

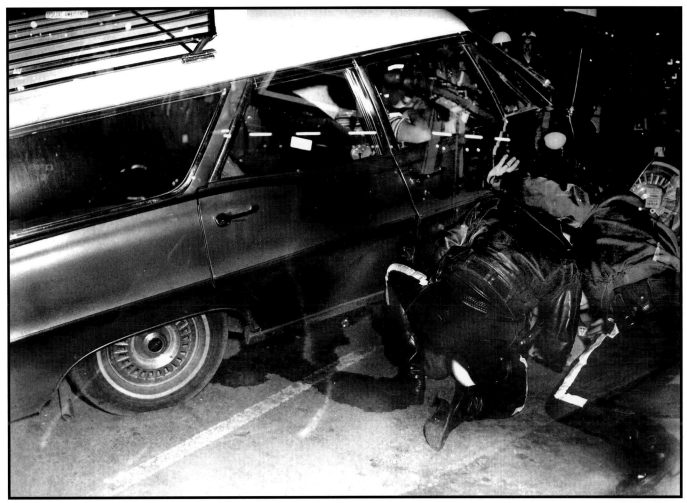

Kneeling are officers Gale Meenach and Steve Braun trying to get Officer Bunch out from under the vehicle.
(SPD archives)

On June 24, 1977, Officer Jim Bunch was returning to the basement of the Public Safety Building to park his motorcycle. As he turned into the station, an intoxicated driver in a station wagon heading northbound hit him. The force pulled his motorcycle under the car, trapping Bunch between the underside of the car and his motorcycle, as the driver continued to drive through the parking lot, dragging Bunch over 40 feet. Sparks were flying and he became soaked in gasoline. As the driver approached the median, Bunch thought he had breathed his last, when the car stalled. As the driver attempted to restart the car, officers came running to give assistance, and Bunch forced himself from between the car and the motorcycle. Bunch spent thirteen days in the hospital. Doctors had to wait four days until they could perform surgery. He then spent two years on crutches. Bunch returned to work three months after the accident but was on light duty until he was able to walk on his own.

Bunch's mangled motorcycle after it was removed from under the above vehicle.

Larry P. Lyle – hired by the Spokane Police Department in 1971

Larry Lyle circa 1977. *(Courtesy Jeff Graves)*

Larry P. Lyle, was born March 5, 1945, to Mary and Jessie Lyle in Dallas, Texas. He was the youngest of four children. He was in the United States Marine Corps from 1964-1968. On February 2, 1967, he married Linda Lee Clark in Reno, Nevada. They lived in Hawthorne, Nevada for four years where their daughter Paula was born. During that time, he worked as a deputy sheriff for the Mineral County Sheriff's Department. His son Larry G. was born two years later in Fallon, Nevada.

In 1971, Larry moved to Spokane with his family and went to work for the Spokane Police Department. In 1974, his son Dallas was born.

Larry graduated from Whitworth University in Spokane in 1986. Following 37 years of police work, Larry retired from the Spokane Police Department.

During Larry's lifetime, he often exhibited a wonderful sense of humor. His character and goals in life were defined by integrity and a determination to support his children and grandchildren. Larry often worked as a volunteer guide at the Spokane Law Enforcement Museum.

He enjoyed police work because of the positive influence it can have on others in the community. He always felt, "With just a little bit of time and consideration, as an officer, you can influence somebody's life." Also, following his retirement from the department, he helped provide primary care for three of his grandsons: Chad, Paul, and William.

Larry passed away at the North Spokane Hospice House on September 20, 2016, at the age of 71. He was preceded in death by his parents and sister, Elta Lee. He is survived by a brother, J.A. Lyle, sister JoAnn Hines of Texas, and three children: Paula Oliver in Puyallup, Washington, Larry G. Lyle in Spokane, and Dallas Lyle in Spokane, formerly from San Diego. He is also survived by five grandchildren; Chad, Paul, Will, Joe, Taylor, and his loving dogs, Maxwell, Smokey, Bratwurst, and Scooter.

In 2005, Spokane police officers, for use in a police *Photo Chronicles* book, were requested to answer a questionnaire. The following was Larry's response:

"One of my memorable experiences was a week on jury duty with Sue Walker. When I came on the department with Frank Cramer and Cheryl Stuart Graves, we walked to City Hall to be sworn in. We were excited, but that faded when a man came to the counter, had us raise our right hands, and make a pledge. We then walked back to the police station where we were given our police equipment – including weapons and ammunition.

Jack Douglas Pearson – hired by the Spokane Police Department in 1971

Jack Pearson, circa 1990. *(Courtesy Jack Pearson)*

Jack Pearson was born in Spokane and attended Hutton Grade School and Lewis and Clark High School. In 1960, following his graduation from high school, he joined the United States Marine Corps Reserve. In 1962, he went to work for the *Spokesman-Review* as a printing apprentice. Upon completion of his apprenticeship, he became a journeyman printer.

In 1969, he enrolled in the law enforcement program at Spokane Community College, receiving an Associate of Arts Degree in criminal justice. He then took the police test and went to work for the Spokane Police Department, where he served for 30 years. During Jack's time on the police department, he worked patrol, motor, numerous robbery, rape, and burglary squads, and spent over 20 years working in the Crime Analysis Unit.

One of Jack's more interesting cases was the Kevin Coe case, which was being worked as a serial rape case before they knew the suspect was Kevin Coe. The police department received a tremendous break in this case when the custodian for Sacajawea Middle School spotted Coe's car parked in a no-parking area and notified the police. Jack was one of the officers assigned to track him. Because Coe was considered an extremely dangerous person, he needed to be tracked continuously.

This proved to be a problem as Coe would get up every morning between 4:00 and 5:00 a.m. to check out the common jogging areas on the South Hill. As he did this, it became even more of a problem trying to track him. In high anticipation of a possible victim, Coe would frantically race between locations, typically driving 50 miles an hour or more. With little traffic on the road that early in the morning, it was easy for a tracking car to be spotted. Consequently, the police would often use multiple cars – using police radio contact, one would pick up where the other left off. Jack was also involved in monitoring body wires on female decoys with Jim Culp.

As this was going on, there was another problem. Gordon Coe, the managing editor for the *Spokane Daily Chronicle*, was consistently criticizing the police department for not being able to catch the South Hill rapist. Unfortunately for Gordon, he was also the father of Kevin Coe, the South Hill rapist.

Shooting incident

On July 10, 1973, Jack was involved in a shooting that, although a heavyhearted part of police work, was, on occasion, a necessary part of the job. The incident is best described in the following article by Jim Spoerhase and Jim Dullenty for the *Spokane Daily Chronicle* on July 12, 1973:

Chase Ends In Airman's Death
Captive injured Following Chase

An abduction and chase ended in the captor's death in a near downtown intersection in Spokane early today.

S P O K A N E   P O L I C E   D E P A R T M E N T

Shot and killed by Spokane police at Second and Cedar was an airman assigned to the 92nd Operational Maintenance Squadron, Fairchild Air Force Base.

Shot in the arm during the gunfire that killed the suspect, was T. Sgt. Lee R Martin, 37, 105 Armstrong, Geiger Heights, a flight chief air policeman who had been taken hostage by the suspect.

Martin underwent emergency surgery at Deaconess Hospital for his arm wound and was reported in good condition," Sheriff's Chief Criminal Deputy Dean A. Lydig said. Sheriff's officers are conducting the investigation because city officers were involved in a shooting. It is a policy that an outside agency investigate any shooting involving law enforcement officers," Lydig said.

"The suspect was shot several times," he said. "He died at the scene." Lydig also said an autopsy would disclose how many times the suspect was struck by police bullets.

– About midnight, occupants of a barracks at Fairchild noticed a man using a key to enter the room of a airman, who was currently off the base on temporary duty.

– The barracks residents called the air police, and Martin and another air policeman investigated.

– Martin found the door to the room locked, and his partner went outside to watch the window to prevent any escape.

– Martin obtained a key to the barracks room, entered, and was confronted by a man with a gun.

– Martin was disarmed and forced at gunpoint to a nearby parking lot where they got into a car (later identified as being owned by the suspect) and fled from the base.

– Martin's partner ran to a nearby telephone and alerted the base police, who flashed an alert to area law-enforcement officers.

Car Spotted

Sheriff's Deputy Douglas E. Tucker said he was just about at Airway Heights when he spotted the wanted car.

Lydig said that the suspect had forced Sgt. Martin to do the driving.

Police Day at Rev. Clifton Hamp's camp on Liberty Lake, in 1979. Hamp was totally dedicated to his community and started this camp for kids. He also started Police Day, when members of the police department would show up and give the kids rides on their police motorcycles and cars in the ballpark area. The above SPD officers are Larry Adams, Joe Boker, and Jack Pearson (on the far right). *(Courtesy Jack Pearson)*

Deputy Tucker and two Washington State Patrol units chased the car and attempted to stop it near the city limits. Tucker said the pursuit continued off the freeway and on to the Lincoln Street exit where he rammed the fleeing car. The chase continued until Tucker again was able to ram the car and stop it at Second and Cedar.

Chief Lydig said that four W.S.P. units, and five city police cars were on the scene as the fleeing car was finally halted.

"The suspect kept his gun pointed at Martin as they got out of the suspect's car, Lydig said. He added Martin was forced at gunpoint to walk to a state patrol car and ordered to get in behind the steering wheel in an apparent attempt by the suspect to steal the state patrol car and to escape with Martin still as a hostage.

Surrender Urged

Lydig said that police, sheriffs, and W.S.P. officers, their weapons drawn, ringed the area, and several officers told the suspect "to put down his gun and give up" but he didn't.

Then officers at the scene heard what they thought was a shot, and the suspect turned and pointed his gun at some of the officers. Three of the city officers, two with revolvers, one with a shotgun, opened fire and hit the suspect, Lydig said.

Lydig identified the city policemen involved in the shooting as Connie A. Caler, Jack D. Pearson, and Ronald A. Reavill.

The hostage, Martin, was wounded in the arm. Lydig said examination of a .22 caliber pistol that the suspect had held in his hand showed it had been fired twice.

Fairchild Air Force Base officials said the suspect had been on temporary duty in Guam and had returned to the base last month.

Because of the continuing shift in personnel, the base spokesman said it is not difficult to understand that the suspect would have been turned in as a stranger. Barracks personnel are trained to turn in any suspect person.

Although he would not normally have been involved in the security police response, Martin went along with one of his patrols "because he is new on base and wanted to see the patrols at work," a Fairchild spokesman said. ...

Biased and cavalier reporting
by the *Spokesman-Review* (1993)

Following a police involved shooting on August 3, 1993, at Buckeye and Division, which could have easily proved to be a major public disaster, *Spokesman-Review* representatives wrote and published a scathing article regarding the policeman involved. Their biased report was quickly rebutted with letters to the editor by Officers Jack Pearson, Tom Sahlberg, and a citizen. Those letters of rebuttal were printed in the *Spokesman-Review* on August 15, 1993, are as follows:

Officer demonstrated skill, prevented
runaway tragedy

On Aug. 5, an armed suspect was shot and killed by a Spokane Police officer at Buckeye and Division before that suspect had the opportunity to shoot anyone.

Almost weekly, local news media carry accounts of similar incidents around the nation in which armed suspects enter an office building, fast food restaurant, post office, or stand on a public roadway and randomly shoot innocent people at leisure. This situation had all the ingredients for one of these tragic multiple-victim occurrences.

The first officer on the scene (Officer Jeff Harvey), exercised a decisive, effective response to the situation, stopping the suspect before he could commit further acts that would have caused untold suffering and earned Spokane a slot on the national news.

Officer Harvey epitomizes the individual officer hired by the Spokane Police Department, officers selected on the basis of numerous criteria. Those include the ability to think and act effectively, alone when necessary, to ensure the highest level of police service to the community.

Officer Harvey positioned himself, increasing his risk of being killed, so as to minimize the chance of innocent bystanders being injured. After the suspect was down, the officer, indicative of professional control, maintained his position in case there were multiple suspects. He stayed in his position until back-up arrived.

If any innocent bystanders had been shot by the suspect, I have no doubt the Spokane Police Department would have been dragged over the coals in the local newspaper for not having responded in such a way that carnage would be prevented.

Despite the way the *Spokesman-Review* reports most stories about the Spokane Police Department, Spokane's citizens are fortunate to have such a dedicated and highly trained organization to confront the negative social element that will always be in our midst.

Jack Pearson, Crime Analysis Officer SPD

Newspapers reporting effort
was irresponsible "a travesty"

This newspaper's handling of the officer-involved shooting last week was a travesty. To solicit a report with inaccurate and incredible accounts, without researching, was irresponsible. Including the officer's personnel record was completely irrelevant to the incident he was thrown into. By all fair standards, Officer Harvey's response was appropriate and stopped a deadly threat to himself and hundreds of citizens in the immediate area. Now, not only does he have to deal with the post-critical-incident trauma that all human beings experience, he has been subjected to personal attacks from the *Spokesman-Review*.

We support and applaud the actions of all the officers at the scene of what could have been a violent tragedy for many more innocent citizens. The overwhelmingly positive response for Officer Harvey's actions shows the real heart of Spokane. Too bad its only newspaper cannot raise itself to the standards of the community that it serves.

Tom Sahlberg, Spokane Police Chaplain Advisory Board

Police, deserving of support, instead get bad rap in print

It seems as though each time I pick up your newspaper after a police incident, your paper immediately zeroes in as though it's the policeman's or policewoman's fault.

These dedicated people go out on their jobs each day knowing that whomever they stop, they are going to be hated no matter what the reason is. They put their lives on the line each time they put that uniform on and even the paper stamps them as guilty before the facts are known.

We owe these people our respect and thanks. With the recent shooting of the man at the army surplus store, instead of commending the officer, your paper makes the announcement that he had been disciplined previously for other matters. What did that have to do with the incident? We all need to come to terms with the fact Spokane has a growing problem with violence. Police should be able to do their job without continued scrutiny from some citizens and the only newspaper in town.

Officers do not have the right to provoke, escalate or promote a violent situation. However, they should be allowed to do what is necessary to protect and serve Spokane in a manner that they're trained and paid for.

Despite the desperate need we have for an increased force, our officers are doing a great job. We need to offer our continued support, not constant criticism.

Private citizen, Spokane

Authors' opinions

The previous letters to the editor, which reference the police-involved shooting at Buckeye and Division, were reprinted in this book by the authors to illustrate the occasional bias expressed against the Spokane Police Department, to one degree or another, over the past 30-plus years by some *Spokesman-Review* employees.

In the authors' opinions, the Spokane Police Department, with few exceptions, is one of the finer organizations in the country when it comes to professionalism, integrity, and high-quality police work. While we recognize the necessary role of a free press to provide the checks and balances for police organizations, the investigative reporting needs to be fair, impartial, and objective. Questionable integrity and anti-police bias, of some media organizations, appears to have been a nationwide problem for many years and in the present time.

Officer Jack Pearson issuing a citation on a Saturday night, downtown on Riverside Avenue. *(Courtesy Jack Pearson)*

Spokane unit focuses on 'career criminal concept'

By TIM HANSON
Of the Chronicle

Police Intelligence Officer Jack D. Pearson pointed to one of several mug shots tacked to the wall of his tiny, cramped crime analysis office at the Public Safety Building.

The photograph showed a man in his mid-20s with a sparse beard and a shock of shoulder-length, semicurly hair.

For the past seven years, said Pearson, that man either has been convicted of or been a suspect in crimes ranging from theft and burglary to rape and armed robbery.

"We are continually working with a high number of repeat offenders," said Pearson. ". . . If (the system) could take the three-time losers and put them in jail and keep (them) away from society for two years with no work release or other means of getting release, then I'd bet you that the crime rate would drop significantly."

Jorgenson agrees and said that the crime analysis team's explanation for the November, 1981, burglary rate drop was probably right.

"I think their hypothesis was valid," Jorgenson said. "That is the basis of the career-criminal emphasis.

"You ought to see the rap sheets on some of these guys."

Officer Pearson

"One person might be responsible for (multiple) burglaries before he gets arrested. If they get 56 of them in jail, then statistically it would show a decrease in crime."

After three years of operation, Jorgenson said the crime analysis unit has "worked out well," but said he hopes the division could be expanded.

"We need to do more pure analysis," the chief said. "We need to know as much as possible when and where the crimes will occur.

"We've got to continue to try and pick out (crime) trends."

The above article was published in the November 17, 1987, issue of the *Spokane Daily Chronicle*.

During the above interview with the *Chronicle* reporter, Police Intelligence Officer Jack Pearson pointed to several mug shots tacked to the wall of his office at the police station. He explained to the reporter that all of these people on his wall are career criminals, with exceptionally long rap sheets, ranging from theft to burglary, rape, and armed robbery. Most of these people will have rap sheets of serious crimes they have committed in excess of five or more pages. These are the repeat offenders who have committed felony crimes against the communities they live in. When these felons are arrested and appear in court, their crimes will typically be plea-bargained down to lesser crimes. These same people are able almost immediately to get back on the street to commit more crimes. When they get caught again, the same scenario is repeated. The lesson most of these career criminals learn is that crime does pay, especially if you have the right attorney.

Jack Pearson's job in police intelligence was to make a record of these career criminals, making sure all concerned, police and especially the judges, were aware of them. He felt if there was less plea-bargaining for these hardened and repeat offenders, there would be far less crime. Jack has a hypothesis: If you filled up three city buses with the worst of Spokane's career criminals and kept them in jail for a significant amount of time (20 to 30 years, or until they became too old to do violent felony-type things) based on the actual crimes they committed, Spokane would be almost crime-free and a much safer city.

Swing shift traffic unit in 1979, left to right: Deputy Chief Bob Panther, Captain Bob Allen, Officers: Jim Powell, Jay Jones, Gale Meenach, Jim Garry, Paul Meissner, Don Jolley (standing), Jack Pearson, Larry Lindskog, Mel Burchfiel, Mike Hobbs, Larry Lyle, Bill Gasperino, Ron Beekman, Lt. Carl Sweatt, and Sgt. Jim Moore.

(Courtesy Spokane Police Department Archives)

Top photo: Jack Pearson in the mid 1970s, when assigned to swing shift patrol division and just prior to being assigned to police motor. *(Courtesy Jack Pearson)*

Bottom photo: A 1970s Harley-Davidson Motor Company advertisement.

You may notice the majority of the photos in this book and on the cover are of Harley-Davidson police motorcycles. Many include sidecars, during a time when motor officers rode their bikes year round. *(Courtesy Jack Pearson)*

Rare original vintage Harley-Davidson advertising poster, circa 1950s-60s when foreign motorcycles were being considered by some United States police departments. *(Public domain)*

Left to right, Spokane Police Department officers Gale Meenach and Jack Pearson; Spokane County Detective Mike Myhre; and SPD Detective Jim Culp in summer of 1980-81. They formed a squad to track residential burglars. They wound up working this for approximately a year and a half. Pearson and Culp were also involved in the South Hill serial rapist investigation that culminated in the arrest of Kevin Coe. *(Courtesy Jack Pearson)*

Mike Albright – hired by the Spokane Police Department in 1970
George Raul Benavidez – hired by the Spokane Police Department in 1974

Mike Albright (right) and George Benavidez in Riverfront Park, circa 1992. Both Albright and Benavidez were on the department during the Harley-Davidson years, but later were assigned to ride foreign bikes. *(Couresy George Benavidez)*

Mike Albright went on the department on June 7, 1970. He rode motor from 1979 to 1981. His first motor partner was Art Kathman. He again went on motor from 1992 to 1995. During that time, he was motor partners with George Benavidez and Rich Jennings. Mike retired from the department in January 1999. At the time of his retirement, he was working at the regional drug task force.

George Benavidez had already been assigned to SPD motor when it was started up again in 1989 by Sgt. Mark Sterk. He originally went to the motor

school put on by Mark Sterk and Larry Lindskog in September but remained in patrol until January 1990, when he was assigned to the new unit.

His first partner was Dennis Barley for 1990 and 1991. Barley went back to patrol and Mike Albright, who went on the SPD in 1970, became his partner. In September of 1992, George made detective but remained assigned to traffic until November or December. During his law enforcement career of 29 years, riding motors was the best job he had. George felt it was hard to believe he was being paid to ride a motorcycle and work day shift after 16 years of the graveyard shift (mostly by choice). He considered turning down the promotion so that he could continue to ride, but the pay raise and the future retire-ment pay prevailed. Sterk still allowed him to work Bloomsday, parades, and special events for the following four years. He applied the skills learned riding those few years riding his own motorcycle.

George Benavidez, circa 1992. *(Couresy Georgw Benavidez)*

Conley 'Mel' Burchfiel – hired by the Spokane Police Department in 1972

Conley 'Mel' Burchfiel (right) and Mike Hobbs.

Conley "Mel" Burchfiel was born in Tacoma, Washington, in 1944. He graduated from Lincoln High school, at Tacoma, in 1962. In 1966, he graduated from Olympic Junior College and, in 1972, he graduated from Washington State University. Mel married Lorraine Pfaff.

He was hired by the Spokane Police Department in 1972 and retired in 1994. During that time, he rode motor for five years, until the traffic unit disbanded in the early 1980s. Following that, he rode a 3-wheel motor, downtown, till discontinued. Mel's riding partners were Mike Hobbs, Gale Meenach, and Paul Meissner.

Friday and Saturday nights were spent downtown patrolling the "cuisers" on Riverside Avenue. It seemed that every kid who had a car or access to one was downtown "tooling the gut." They were there to see and be seen. Especially important was "burning rubber," speeding, drinking beer and hanging out the windows, and riding on the outside of the car. Summer was especially oppressive with hot asphalt and cars packed together going about five mph, creating even more heat.

Watching for speeders and then taking out after them was always problematic. One notable incident involved Mel pursuing a motorcycle north on Nevada from Wellesley at over 60 mph, then West on Francis, north on Standard, east on Lyons, then South on Nevada. This action received lots of attention from fellow officers. Officer John Henry joined the pursuit. At that point, he was more concerned with his distance than with any thought of catching the violator. The end for the violator came when his partner, Mike Hobbs, cut him off at Wellesley and Nevada by kicking the rider off his bike at the gas station on the northwest corner of the intersection.

Mel said, regarding his time on motor, "I never went down or (crashed), I probably should have died or been severely injured many times over, as adrenaline overcame good sense."

Mel Burchfiel was a gold medalist in the 2002 Can-Am games. The Can-Am Police-Fire Games started as the Northwest Police-Fire Games in 1977 when officials from two state police and fire games (Washington and Oregon) and a police-fire sports group from western Canada formed an organization that conducted a multi-sport event, for police officers and fire fighters, on an annual basis. This continued until 1996.

Through aggressive marketing and tremendous interest from the law enforcement and fire fighting industry, the event grew so large that cities large enough to host the event were limited to the northwestern U. S. and western Canada. The group reorganized, renaming itself the Can-Am Police-Fire Games, to better represent the athletes demographically.

Richard Hillis Jennings – hired by the Spokane Police Department in 1974

Richard Jennings, circa 1980. *(Public domain)*

Front-page story about Richard Jennings's undercover assignment. *(Public domain)*

Richard Jennings was hired by the SPD in March of 1974 for Expo '74, and laid off in December 1974. He was rehired in March of 1975, but only worked uniform for a week. He then started working drugs with Jerry McGougan and Tom Morris. The three of them framed houses together for years. Richard also worked on building the police guild with Tom Morris. It was also around the time Tom's son, Bill, was murdered.

Richard rode motor #15 for about three years, taking over the bike from George Benevidez when he made detective. He rode with Mike Albright for quite a while until Mike went to the Task Force.

In 1981, Richard was given an undercover assignment that made history in the Inland Northwest. The following story, written in the *Newport Miner* by Don Gronning, appeared on November 29, 2017, regarding the Kevin Coe serial rapist case:

Jennings undercover for most of career
Ruth Coe solicited him to kill prosecutor, judge

NEWPORT — People in court may see bailiff Rich Jennings passing papers forward to the judge, reminding people to remove hats and on at least one occasion jumping on an unruly defendant to help subdue him.

What they might not know is that Jennings had a career as an undercover narcotics officer for the Spokane Police Department. He worked cases large and small for nearly 24 years, but his most high profile case happened in November 1981.

He was posing as hit a man named "Terry" when Ruth Coe, the mother of convicted South Hill rapist Kevin Coe, paid him $500 as a deposit to arrange a hit on prosecutor Don Brockett and Superior Court Judge George Shields, who were involved with her son's conviction. Coe offered $4,000 to kill both the prosecutor and judge. "Brockett was irritated," Jennings laughs. Brockett thought it should cost more to kill a prosecutor.

Jennings contacted Coe after being tipped off by an informant: He got her phone number and called her, claiming he was from Peoria, Ill., and was in trouble in Seattle and needed some money. They arranged to meet at a K-Mart parking lot. "I was wired," Jennings said. The car was also wired with a recorder in the dome light and another in a pair of gloves placed on the dash.

Part of the conversation between Jennings and Coe was documented in the book "Carl Maxey: A fighting life." Here's how the conversation went.

Jennings: We are talking about the same thing. You want those people ... Coe: Gone. Coe: Dead. Right. If I had my druthers, I'd have that prosecutor just made a complete vegetable, so that they had to care for him forever, and lived on and on that way. And the judge ...

Jennings: Just tell me what you want. Coe: Well, uh, and the judge, I'd like him gone — dead — and I'd like both of 'em dead, really, except that with Brockett, I felt that — he's a man about 46 or 47 and he has been so filthy, and my feeling for him is that I would love to see him just an addle-pated vegetable that had to be cared for — that his family had to take care of the rest of his life. I mean diapers and all the rest of it. He wanted 42 years of my son's life gone. I'd like to see him sit 42 years in ... ummm, as a baby. But to have him gone would be great, too. I mean, you can never be sure, I suppose, how you clobber them, that could be the way it's come out. So dead is great. But I do think he should suffer...

Coe was arrested the next day. She was eventually convicted of solicitation to commit first degree murder and sentenced to a year in jail. [She served some of her time at the Pend Oreille County jail. Coe served only two weeks of her time in the Pend Oreille County Jail as she proved to be high too high maintenance and was sent back to Spokane by Sheriff Bamonte.]

The Coe case brought Jennings undercover work to an end "My cover was blown," he said. He went back to work as a patrol officer.

Jennings came to undercover police work in a roundabout way.

He was raised in Illinois, where he worked on the family's small farm. He always had an interest in vehicles. "I was given my first vehicle at age 10," he says. He still has that 1947 Willys Jeep.

After he got out of high school, he enlisted in the Air Force, where he worked fixing damaged aircraft. He ended up stationed at Fairchild.

He got out of the service as a sergeant. He used the GI Bill to go to school at Spokane Cornmunity College, where he got into the law enforcement program.

"Then along came Expo '74," he says. The Spokane Police Department was hiring 50 police officers. About 500 applied and took the test, including Jennings. He finished 13th and was offered a job.

But he didn't work Expo. "I worked the drunk wagon," he said. After Expo '74 was over, the Spokane PD laid off 43 officers, including Jennings. He was off the force three months before he was hired back. "I came back and worked a week as a patrol officer."

One day at shift change his boss came down and said the chief wanted to talk to him. Jennings wondered what he did now.

"They sat me down and asked me how I would I like to work undercover drugs," Jennings remembers. "I said I didn't know anything about drugs and they said they'd train me."

He agreed and they said to come to work in his grubbiest clothes and start growing his hair out. "They said I would work six months," he says. Then in March 1975, they said six years.

His undercover work led to his own pseudo arrest from time to time. "I got thrown in jail two or three times," he says. "SWAT liked that and would kick the (stuffing) out of me. Me biggest fear was they would forget to come let me out." His undercover work consisted of going around, knocking on doors and meeting with dopers.

"The philosophy of druggies, is that they only want the money," Jennings said. He was flashing money around, so he had access.

"I bought everything from weed to guns," he says. His biggest bust involved 113 pounds of marijuana.

He doesn't remember the dollar value, but in those days he remembers marijuana was sold in $10 "lids" (about an ounce), so it likely wasn't too much.

Jennings was involved in the arrest of John Lee Forester, a man still in the penitentiary. Forrester was 17 when he killed an elderly couple and demanded $10,000 or he would kill again.

As for Jennings' most high profile criminal, Kevin Coe, Jennings said he never met Coe when he was working that case, although he followed him a lot.

The city created a rape task force to catch the man responsible for a series of rapes in the Spokane area.

Jennings installed the tracking device on Coe's car.

Jennings and his partner would get up about 3 a.m. and follow Coe, who drove around a lot in the early morning hours.

"He liked to follow bus routes," Jennings remembers.

One of the special squad activity files notes the activity that occurred March 2, 1981.

"0555 Coe left 29th address & tracked by Keane and Jennings using the tracking device," reads the file. The pair followed Coe to a half dozen different locations before handing off to another crew who followed him at night.

Coe eventually was convicted of three rapes, and sentenced to life plus 55 years. All but one of the cases was overturned on appeal and Coe served 25 years and was committed to McNeil Island after the sentence to be confined indefinitely.

Jennings went back to work as a patrol officer after Coe's trial. His career with the Spokane PD included a stint teaching pursuit driving, being a hostage negotiator and working as a motorcycle officer.

Jennings, 68, retired from the SPD after nearly 24 years. He moved to Pend Oreille County, where he had long owned property, and started work for Pend Oreille County in 2000.

Looking back, he says he enjoyed the undercover work. "I loved every minute of the job," he says.

(See forward by former Prosecutor Don Brockett in the front of this book.)

Mark Karl Sterk – hired by the Spokane Police Department in 1974

Mark Sterk joined the Spokane Police Department in 1974 and retired in 1998. In 1999, he ran for sheriff of Spokane County and was elected. During his career with the Spokane Police Department, he supervised the motor unit when it was reinstituted in the late 1980s.
(Courtesy Spokane Police Department History Book Committee)

Mark Sterk started his career in law enforcement in May of 1974, with the Spokane Police Department's Patrol Division. He was later promoted to sergeant, and served as the administrative assistant to patrol in 1984. He then served as the assistant director of training at the Spokane Law Enforcement Regional Training Center.

During the time he was a Spokane police officer, he responded to an animal related call north of Hillyard. When he arrived at the suspect's residence, he ran a computer check on the registered owner of a vehicle out front, and found there were warrants for the owner. Prior to that, Sterk had observed a man sleeping in the front room of the house. When he made contact, he advised the man that his dog would be taken by animal control for testing, and that he

was under arrest for outstanding warrants. The suspect began to run toward the back of the house. Sterk chased and caught up with him and, while attempting to apply a control hold, the suspect was able to flip Sterk over his back. As he landed, Sterk caught a fish aquarium with both heels, suffering severe damage to his achilles tendon on his right leg, requiring long-erm recuperation. He felt the pain but continued to struggle with the suspect and was finally able to restrain and handcuff him by the time backup arrived.

In January of 1999, Mark Sterk was elected sheriff of Spokane County. Prior to being elected, he had been a Spokane police officer from May 5, 1974 to December 29, 1974, then again from May 2, 1976 to December 31, 1998. Some of that time was spent on motor.

In 2006, Mark Sterk resigned as sheriff of Spokane County to become a minister in the Church of the Nazarene and the director of Pinelow, the church's camp and conference center at Deer Lake in Stevens County. He made this career change after more than 30 years of public service, which included 24 years in the Spokane Police Department, four years as a Republican representative in the Washington State Legislature, and six years as sheriff of Spokane County.

In 2014, Sterk became the director of safety, security, and transportation for Spokane Public Schools. In summing up his accomplishments in public service, Mark Sterk stated he wanted to be remembered as one who "cared about the people of this community and worked very hard to provide the services they deserve."

Sterk said in an interview, that stories in the *Spokesman-Review*, were a contributing factor to his resignation. Stating they were unfairly reported that his office delayed the release of documents regarding Deputy David Hahn, who killed himself in 1981. "It was just one of the things that helped persuade me that I wanted to do something else," he said.

Mark Knight – hired by the Spokane Police Department in 1974

Mark was born in Kellogg, Idaho. His family moved to Mead, Washington after his father's death in 1959.

Mark graduated from Mead High School in 1968. He worked at Mead Market with his mom and later worked in the logging industry with his Uncle Kelly and cousins.

Mark received a Criminal Justice AA degree at Spokane Community College He also worked for the Washington State Patrol for just under two years. In January 1974, Mark transferred to the Spokane Police Department, where he worked until April 2000. During his time with the SPD, Mark served on patrol, SWAT, dignitary protection and motor traffic units.

Mark was also a master police motorcycle instructor and held the course speed record. During the time he was on motor, his partners were Mike Reynolds and Craig Meidl, who is now the chief of police. Mark also taught Traffic Law at Spokane Community College.

Mark Knight. Mark was hired by the SPD in 1974 and served until 2000. He passed away on May 8, 2018.

Following his retirement, Mark worked for Columbia Paint, State Liquor Control Board, and at the "Grand Lady" Davenport Hotel. He volunteered for Safe Kids on the Spokane Regional and Kootenai Medical Health Teams, teaching families to properly install child safety restraints.

Mark loved all animals and enjoyed stained glass, art, boating, water skiing, RV camping, target shooting, gardening, watching Seattle Mariners and Seahawks, and attending the Gonzaga Lady Zags basketball games. He helped out the Spirit of Spokane Sweet Adeline Chorus Shows, making props, transporting risers, and so much more. Mark is survived by his loving wife, Cindi; sister Kathy (David) Salerno, Priest River; brother Mike (Candy) Knight, Sun City, AZ; son Chris Knight, Omaha, NB; and stepdaughter Heidi (Ken) Farr, Spokane; grandchildren: Alan, Jackson and Courtnay Knight, Omaha, Nebraska, and Jocelyn Farr, Spokane. Preceded in death by parents Delbert and Lora Knight and his son Tom Knight.

SPOKANE POLICE DEPARTMENT

Chapter Four

1980 to 2015

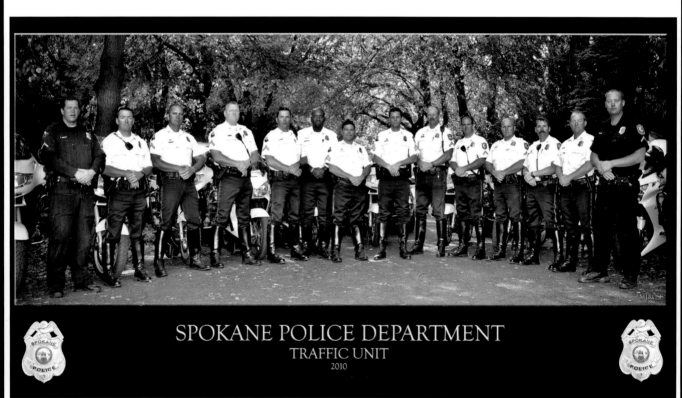

SPOKANE POLICE DEPARTMENT
TRAFFIC UNIT
2010

2010 Motocycle Unit: John Griffin, John Gately, Nate Spiering, Ryan Snider, Bill Workman, Ken Applewhaite, Sgt. Jason Reynolds (Chachi), Sgt. Eric Olsen, Dave Kennedy, Tyler Cordis, Derek Bishop, Ron Tilley, Chris Lewis, and Brad Moon. *(Courtesy Matt Rose)*

The Spokane Police Department had used Harley-Davidson motorcycles since 1920. Prior to that, they were using the Indian brand. They continued to use the Harleys up to 1981.

In 1981, due to budget cuts, the entire motorcycle squad was discontinued, which at the time consisted of 24 men who each shared a motor with another officer. At the time, there were two shifts for motors–day shift and swing shift.

The elimination of the motors came as the result of what was called the McManus Report, following a request from Chief Bob Panther for an additional 17 officers. The response by the mayor and council was a recommendation to the city to save money by eliminating the motorcycles rather than adding personnel to the department. Chief Panther did not agree with that recommendation.

In 1987, and almost immediately after he took office as police chief, Terence Mangan reintroduced motors to the department. In his autobiography, Mangan wrote the following: "The motorcycle/traffic squad which had been eliminated in prior budget cuts was reinstituted. This was done with support of the General Contractors' Association and other service clubs who donated the money to buy two used motorcycles from the sheriff's department. These motorcycles had originally been part of the old Spokane Police Department motorcycle squad. Eventually, the new unit grew with the help of a supportive city council to a total of one sergeant and 16 officers with all new motorcycles and equipment."

New motor officers, from left: Brad Moon, John Gately, Ryan Snyder on their BMW motorcycles. *(Courtesy Spokane Police Department Archives)*

Jeffrey Bruce Graves – hired by the Spokane Police Department in 1990

S
P
O
K
A
N
E

P
O
L
I
C
E

D
E
P
A
R
T
M
E
N
T

Jeff Graves, 2000. *(Courtesy Jeff Graves)*

Jeff Graves was born in Spokane in 1967 to Ronald and Kaye Graves. He has a younger sister. His father was also on the Spokane Police Department, spending most of his patrol years on motors but ending his career years as a major crimes detective. His mother, Kaye, graduated from Eastern Washington University with a bachelor's degree. Ronald Graves retired in 1992, after serving for 25 years.

Jeff and his sister were raised on Spokane's South Hill and attended Jefferson, Adams, Sacajawea schools and Ferris High School. While still in high school, Jeff got his first job, selling shoes at the JC Penney store at University City. Following graduation from high school, Jeff enrolled at Spokane Community College, where he graduated from the law enforcement program with an AA degree. In 1989, he married Joani DeWalt, the sister of a good high school friend. He and Joani have three children, two boys and a girl, who are now grown and working in various careers.

Jeff was hired by the Spokane Police Department on December 16, 1990. He felt this was the best and most interesting job he has ever had. He attended motor school in 1999 and served in that capacity through 2003. Jeff's motor partner was Dave Kennedy. They were partners in patrol and on motor for over 20 years. They still keep in contact. The author (Bamonte) clearly remembers Jeff when he responded to a burglary call next to Bamonte's residence. Jeff was a good cop. He did everything right, quickly catching the criminals and leaving a good impression with his professional, yet down-to-earth manner.

In an interview with Jeff, for the purpose of this book, he stated his law enforcement career has created value in his life by teaching him that, as individuals, we have a responsibility and duty to be productive, help others who need a hand, hold people accountable, and be accountable yourself, with a duty to achieve self-reliance.

Jeff said the people who were the biggest influence on his career were those he worked with day-in and day-out. The people who showed up for work in spite of not feeling well, people who took the routine calls, the undesirable calls, and the calls outside their own district, those who were selfless, caring, and compassionate. These were the type of people he looked up to and strived to be like.

Jeff Graves and the Gypsy Curse

One of the more interesting police cases Jeff was involved in, during his 23-year career on the Spokane Police Department, involved a contact with the well-known Gypsy family, the Marks family.

In 1997, Jeff was dispatched to a burglary in progress occurring near Twelfth and Thor. As he arrived, the housebreakers were speeding away. He immediately pursued them as they drove through several neighborhood yards, furiously attempting to avoid capture. In doing so, they ended up going north on the Ray/Thor hill. Unfortunately, at this same time, the funeral procession for Spokane's Gypsy King, Grover Marks, was pulling up to the deceased's home at Fifth and Thor. As they approached Fifth Avenue, the burglars attempted a high-speed turn, west bound,

onto Fifth from Thor, losing control of their vehicle. In the process, they crashed into one of the just-parked funeral procession's cars. This all went down as the family members had just exited their vehicle and were going into the deceased's house.

As this happened, the burglar's car became wedged against one of the cars from the funeral procession, jamming the door closed and trapping the suspects inside their getaway car. As one of the suspects was attempting to escape, out the passenger side window of his disabled vehicle, he was arrested by Graves.

This was not a good thing to happen, especially in light of earlier events that had occurred between the police and the Gypsies. The Spokane Police Department and the Marks families were not on good terms. The Marks's resentment and problems with the Spokane Police Department began on June 18, 1986, at 9:36 a.m., when members of the Spokane Police Department entered two homes belonging to he Marks families. The case grew out

Dave Kennedy and Jeff Graves, circa 2001. *(Courtesy Jeff Graves)*

of a joint city and county investigation of a string of residential break-ins in 1986. The police suspected the gypsies were a fence for stolen goods. The police used a 17-year-old boy, who was connected to the residential burglaries, as an informer. He was wired with an audiotape and made several visits to the two homes, offering to sell the Gypsies silverware and stolen jewelry. According to court records, at least one family member made remarks on tape that indicated he knew he was buying stolen property.

What Brought on the Gypsy Curse
and
What It Was About

When the police raided the two Marks family homes on June 18, 1986, they also took $1.6 million in cash, some of which was sewn into family and religious quilts. The search warrant, which was later ruled illegal because it was issued after the raid, did not specify that cash could be taken. But once the police found the money, they assumed it had to have come from criminal activity.

Consequently, a $40 million lawsuit followed. The family said, from the start, that the police did not have a warrant. Later, in a court hearing on the admissibility of the evidence, a police videotape showed that detectives began searching the houses two hours before a legal warrant had been signed. Two years after the search, Judge John Schultheis of Spokane County Superior Court ruled it illegal.

According to the indictment, members of the Marks family, while also claiming to be fortune tellers, clairvoyants, and spiritual advisors, "falsely represented to their victims that they could remove purported evil spirits or curses from their lives or that of their loved ones."

The case received national media attention. According to the Associated Press, the Marks family claimed to confer with gods and spirits to cure diseases and break curses, asking for and accepting jewelry, gold coins, and luxury cars in return. The family's defense attorneys said they believe their Gypsy religion gave them the ability to heal psychically and that their business was legitimate

The lawsuit also made national news in 1994, when CBS News' *Eye to Eye With Connie Chung* did a story on the dispute. Mr. Marks and his family also became the subject of a 2000 PBS documentary, *American Gypsy*, which detailed the legal fight.

Following the death of his father Grover Marks. In 1997, Jimmy Marks became the leader of Spokane's Roma Gypsy community. The family then began a civil rights lawsuit against the city. The city settled out of court for $1.4 million. It was also ordered that the seized cash and jewelry be returned.

As a result of the described events that took place between the police department and the Marks, Grover Marks placed a curse on the city. After Grove's death in 1997, his son Jimmy Marks continued publicly epitomizing the curse with every episode of bad luck that would befall the city of Spokane. Jimmy died on June 27, 2007.

An Unfortunate Shooting

One of the more significant things that happened to Jeff Graves occurred on February 24, 1998. He was partnered with the police chaplain, Ron Alter, when they were dispatched to an address on Fifteenth, east of Lincoln. The parents of a disturbed young adult called to report that he was out of control and had barricaded himself in a basement crawl space.

Upon arrival, Jeff spoke with the parents of the young man and then entered the residence to assess the situation while waiting for backup. Inside, he encountered a basement doorway that had been barricaded with an upright box-spring mattress and shower curtain. Thinking the suspect was in a crawl space, he moved the shower curtain and peeked into the room. To his surprise the suspect was standing there armed with a long-handled, axe-type weapon, which he immediately swung at Jeff. The axe blade narrowly missed his face and got stuck on the box spring and curtain. That gave Jeff enough time to back up and pepper spray the suspect.

However, the pepper spray enraged him, and he began tearing down the barricade. At that point, Sergeant Mullenix and Officer Turman arrived to help. The suspect came out of the room armed with a large knife in each hand. He refused all verbal commands and pursued all of the police on the scene through the basement and up the stairs to the home's main floor. At this time, with no other place to go, the officers held their ground at the top of the stairs as the suspect advanced up. As the assaulter got within four feet, Jeff shot him through the right shoulder, causing him to collapse and fall to the bottom of the stairs. He was taken into custody and did survive his injuries. He was later convicted of several felonies, including second degree assault against Jeff. His parents expressed their gratitude at the way the officers handled the situation. Ten years later, the suspect obtained a handgun and committed suicide.

Jeff Graves and Cpl. Tom Sahlberg with George H. W. Bush, during the 2000 presidential campaign. *(Courtesy Jeff Graves)*

Another interesting event involving Jeff Graves occurred in April of 1992.

The body in the basement

After he purchased a house on West Chelan from the estate of Graciano "Rocky" Ortiz. Ortiz was a 48-year-old real estate broker who had committed suicide in a friend's garage on November 30, 1991. The following is Jeff's account:

After living in the house several months I noticed there seemed to be a lot of small fruit fly type bugs infesting the place. I had an exterminator check it out, and he concluded that the bugs were likely originating from a source in the basement crawl space. There was a main door in the basement, which opened to a dirt crawl space underneath the living room.

In September 1992, I began excavating the crawl space in hopes of determining the source of the bugs and also creating an additional room.

During excavation an object tumbled out of the dirt where I'd been digging. I picked the object up thinking it looked like an old leather shoe. I took it outside and sprayed it off with the hose, after which I thought it looked more like a human foot than a leather shoe.

My dad, Ron Graves, had recently retired as a major crimes detective so I called him to come over for his opinion. He also concluded that the object was a human foot, not a shoe.

The SPD major crimes unit converged on my house and sealed off the basement.

My wife Joani, was nine months pregnant with our son Michael when this was occurring. Our doctor decided to admit her into the hospital instead of subjecting her to the stress of home.

I found myself running back and forth between home and the hospital.

On September 11, 1992, my son Michael was born. I videotaped the birth and panned the camera up to the television in the room. The TV news was showing officers removing a body out of my basement.

The body was determined to be an 83-year-old man named Leslie Monohon, who had been reported missing in June 1991. Monohon was known to loan friends and acquaintances money.

Ortiz and Monohon did know one another. It is thought that Monohon "loaned Ortiz" several thousand dollars and when Monohon came to collect from Ortiz, Ortiz murdered him by strangulation and buried him in the basement crawl space.

We lived in the Chelan house until April 1998. I never finished digging out the crawl space and never had another bug infestation.

This photo was taken in downtown Spokane. This young girl, whom he did not know, came up to Jeff and asked if she could get a photo with him for her yearbook. *(Courtesy Jeff Graves)*

This was a spring motorcycle training course in 2001, which took place at Mead, in the fire department's back lot. *(Courtesy Jeff Graves)*

Jeff Graves is second to the right. The three officers to the right of him are Bill Workman, Kim Thomas, John Clarke. Jason Reynolds is to the far right in the photo. Photo was taken next to Spokane County Courthouse, at Law Enforcement Memorial, in 2003. *(Courtesy Jeff Graves)*

Jeff's wife, Joani, 2003. Joani works at Sacred Heart Medical Center Childrens Hospital. She is an electrophysiology technician who works with children and adults with heart defects. *(Courtesy Jeff Graves)*

William D. Workman – hired by the Spokane Police Department in 1991

Innocent William Workman stands for a photo, while unbeknownst to him, he is about to be menaced by a "suspected" predator (Ken Applewaite) who was lurking in the background. *(Bamonte/Pearson photo)*

William Workman was born in Sandpoint, Idaho, in 1967 to Gerald and Carol Workman. His father worked for the railroad and his mother was a nurse. Workman has three siblings: twin brothers, Jeff and Mike, born in 1963, and a sister, Gina Stebbin, born in 1965.

Workman grew up in Spokane and attended North Central High School. Following graduation in 1985, he attended Spokane Community College, receiving an Associate of Arts Degree in Criminal Justice.

Workman and his fiancée Michelle DeSpain, have twin girls, Raychel and Ciarra, both born in 1994. He also has four stepchildren: Grant, Hailee, Lily, and Christian.

Prior to going to work for the Spokane Police Department, Workman worked loss prevention for a private company. He joined the Spokane Police Department in 1991. Prior to that he served two years in the Spokane Police Reserves. He was assigned to motor unit in 2002, and has ridden motor for over 14 years. During that time he has had two motor partners, Paul Taylor and Ken Applewhaite.

One of the highlights in his career was escorting President George Bush when he came to Spokane.

He enjoys spending his spare time at Priest Lake.

St. Patrick's Day Parade in 2002. William Workman is the first motor on the right. *(Spokane Police Department archives)*

At the the Spokane Law Enforcement Memorial adjacent to the Public Safety Building. Left: Ken Applewhaite, William Workman, Deputy Mike Brooks, and John Gately. *(Spokane Police Department archives)*

At Riverfront Park when the police department resurrected the traffic unit, circa 1980. From left: Tom Sahlberg, Mike Albright, Mark Knight, Mike Reynolds, John Clarke, Bill Gasperino, Sergeant Mark Sterk, Larry Lindskog, Kim Thomas, Rich Jennings, and Harry Kennedy. *(Spokane Police Department archives)*

The police motor division in 2016, left to right: Dean Draper, Trevor Nollmeyer, Shaidon Storch, Ken Applewhaite, Bill Workman, Chris Lewis, and Jim Christensen. *(Bamonte/Pearson photo)*

Patrick Michael "Rick" Dobrow – hired by the Spokane Police Department in 1994

Patrick "Rick" Dobrow, Interim Chief of Police, just prior to his retirement. *(Courtesy Rick Dobrow)*

Rick Dobrow is a 33-year-plus veteran of law enforcement, who started his career in a mid-sized California police department. He joined the Spokane Police Department in 1994.

His experience is diverse and has included patrol, street crimes, Special Weapons and Tactics Team (SWAT), dignitary protection, traffic/motors, drug recognition, general investigations, vice, criminal intelligence, major crimes, patrol supervisor, traffic unit supervisor, training supervisor, patrol watch commander, training director, dignitary protection team commander, commander of the office of professional oversight, assistant police chief, and interim chief, up to his retirement.

As training director for the Spokane Police Department, Rick was responsible for the recruitment, selection, and hiring of police personnel. He was also responsible for managing the on going training of the police department's 305 commissioned personnel and the development of the department's training plan.

As commander of the Office of Professional Oversight and Training, Rick was responsible for both Internal Affairs and Training. As assistant chief, he was responsible for all Uniform Field Operations. When he became interim chief, he was responsible for leading the police division of the second largest city in the State of Washington.

Spring 2003 on Mount Spokane on a long ride to put break-in miles on a new BMW motorcycle. *(Courtesy Rick Dobrow)*

Rick was born in San Fernando, California, in 1960. Both of his parents were public health educators. Rick has two sisters, one older and one younger.

Rick's family relocated to California's Central Valley when he was very young. He grew up in a rural area outside of Stockton, California, attending school in and around the Stockton area.

Rick always wanted to be a police officer. He heard stories from his grandmother about her father, who was a policeman in St. Louis, Missouri, around the turn of the century. Rick's great-grandfather unfortunately died at 28 years of age from a cerebral hemorrhage, leaving a widow and two small children. Following his death, she moved to Richmond, California, where she met and married a Contra Costa County reserve deputy sheriff.

Rick had two other relatives in law enforcement, one a police officer in Walnut Creek, California, the other, a chief of police in Martinez, California.

When Rick was 14 years old, he became a Stockton police junior cadet. He remained in that program until he was 18. He then joined the Stockton Police Senior Cadet Program, becoming "captain" of the program after two years of active participation.

While attending community college, Rick worked various jobs at St. Joseph's Medical Center in Stockton, where, in 1980, he met his wife DeAnn. They were married in March 1982.

Rick attended the first class of the C. A. POST Police Academy held at San Joaquin Delta College in Stockton. He was a police trainee from October 1, 1981, until graduating in May 1982. He then went to work for the Fairfield Police Department in Califonia.

While in Fairfield, Rick worked patrol and as an investigator. He joined the SWAT Team in 1984, filling a vacancy created when his best friend "Art" was killed in the line of duty.

Former President H. W. Bush on the stump, in Spokane, for his son in the fall of 2001, shaking hands with Rick Dobrow. The state trooper to the right is Bruce Clark. *(Courtesy Rick Dobrow)*

While living in the Fairfield/Vacaville area in California, Rick and his wife started their family, having Jeffrey in 1984 and Gregory in 1986.

Rick left the Fairfield Police Department when he was hired as Stockton's first "lateral entry" police officer in February 1987.

During his time with Stockton's police department, Rick worked in patrol, on the Street Crimes Team, as an investigator in the Vice/Criminal Intelligence Unit, and as a patrol sergeant.

Rick is a graduate of the Southern Police Institute's 126th Administrative Officer's Course, where he was recognized for achieving the highest academic average (the Director's Award for Academic Excellence). He attended the FBI's 36th Command Institute for Law Enforcement Executives. He holds executive level certification from the Washington State Criminal Justice Training Commission.

Rick was awarded the Medal of Valor in 2002, Chief's Citation in 2002, the employee of the quarter in 2006, and the Spokane Police Department's Purple Heart for injuries, while on duty in 2007.

In 1994, Rick and his family relocated to Spokane in an effort to improve their quality of life. At the time, the Spokane Police Department did not hire

Rick's sons, posing by his motorcycle at their home on North Monroe Street in the spring of 1999. Greg is on the left with Jeff on the right. *(Courtesy Rick Dobrow)*

out-of-state lateral entry officers. Consequently, Rick had to attend a Washington State Basic Law Enforcement Academy.

Following his completion of the police academy and the field training program, Rick worked as a patrol officer. He became a field training officer in 1996, then was transferred to the traffic unit as a motor officer in June 1997. Rick was a motor officer from 1997 until March 2002. While on motor, Rick became a motor instructor and was active in regional motorcycle training. In addition to motorcycle training, Rick was certified as a breath-test instructor, a firearms instructor, and taught traffic law for the basic academy.

In 1999, Rick became a "drug recognition expert," the first for the Spokane Police Department.

Rick was promoted to sergeant in 2002 and returned to graveyard patrol as a supervisor. He returned to the traffic unit, as a supervisor, in January 2003.

Rick continued to be involved in motorcycle training, obtaining "Master Motor Instructor" certification. Rick had the good fortune to lead a presidential motorcade, when President George W. Bush visited Spokane. All members of the Spokane Police Motor Unit, Spokane County Sheriff's Motors, and Washington State Patrol were needed for the motorcade.

On September 26, 2006, after spending all day working on the motorcycle training course, Rick was critically injured on his trip home. He was attempting to catch a reckless driver when a minivan pulled out in front of him. As a result, Rick had extensive injuries to his face, neck, back, and shoulder, requiring emergency surgery to save his life. He was in intensive care for seven days, then remained hospitalized for additional time.

Rick returned to light-duty in late January 2007, and got back on his motorcycle in May 2007. He remained in the traffic unit until January 2008, when he returned to patrol as a day-shift supervisor.

Rick was transferred to the police academy in 2010, as the assistant director of training. He remained in that position until May 1, 2011, when he was promoted to lieutenant. Rick returned as a patrol shift commander and the traffic unit lieutenant.

In August 2011, Rick had the opportunity to attend the Southern Police Institute, an intensive three-

month law enforcement command college, at the University of Louisville, Kentucky.

In October 2012, Rick returned to the Spokane Police Academy as the director of training. He remained in that position until September 2013, when he was promoted to captain. He was then assigned as the captain in charge of professional accountability and training. He remained in that position until appointed to assistant police chief in February 2014. As assistant chief, Rick was responsible for uniform operations (patrol division).

Rick was appointed as interim chief of police on September 22, 2015, by Mayor David Condon, following the departure of former Chief Frank Straub. Rick retired from the SPD on March 1, 2016.

Spring 2003. Rick Dobrow (left) and Paul Taylor leading the Barnum and Bailey Circus to the Spokane Arena. They were traveling west on Mallon Avenue, west of the Flour Mill. *(Courtesy Rick Dobrow)*

Rick Dobrow (left, looking at the camera) and Ken Applewhaite working speed enforcement on Rockwood Boulevard in 2005. The photo is from a *Spokesman-Review* article. *(Courtesy Rick Dobrow)*

With Spokane as a backdrop, motor officers pose on Gordon Avenue, west of Monroe Street, in the fall of 2001. From left: Brad Hallock, Dave Kennedy, Jeff Graves, Mike Reynolds, Rick Dobrow, Kim Thomas, John Clark, Paul Taylor, Joe Walker, and Tom Sahlberg. *(Courtesy Rick Dobrow)*

John "JD" Anderson – hired by the Spokane Police Department in 2000

Sgt. Jon Anderson and Kenneth Applewhaite in front of the Budweiser wagon, 2014. *(Courtesy J D Anderson)*

Jon "JD" Anderson was born in 1968 to Spokane Police Captain Dave Anderson. In 1987, he graduated from University High School in the Spokane Valley. In 1991, he graduated from Gonzaga University with a Bachelor Degree in Business Administration with an emphasis in accounting. His original intent was to work for the FBI or another federal law enforcement agency. However, he was told he needed experience to go with his education.

Anderson's law enforcement career began in Pierce County, Washington, in 1991 due to a hiring freeze in Spokane. Spokane offered him a job in 1992, so he moved back to Spokane.

After being a police office for a few years, he decided against joining the FBI, so contrary to his original plan, he began working as a patrol officer, on mostly graveyard, for several years. He spent most of his active patrol time in traffic enforcement. Following that, he was a neighborhood resource officer for a couple of years and then was promoted to corporal. As a corporal, he was trained to work in the Technical Collision Investigation Unit. While there, he was also trained in collision reconstruction for auto versus pedestrian, bike, and motorcycle. He investigated numerous serious injury and fatal collisions during the time he was a corporal and a detective.

He was promoted to sergeant and, after a few years, was assigned as the special events coordinator. During that time, he shared an office with the traffic unit sergeant, Tony Meyer. They worked together on several events that utilized the Motor Unit.

SPOKANE POLICE DEPARTMENT

Jon "JD" Anderson escorting the Budweiser wagon in 2014. *(Courtesy JD Anderson)*

In 2014, Anderson was authorized to go through the motor school as a sergeant. The school was 80 hours over two weeks, and the hardest training he had ever done. He was assigned as the special event sergeant and May was the height of special event season. During that time, he worked 80 hours of overtime due to scheduled events. He passed the motor school class and was allowed to ride that summer, when time allowed, even though he was the special events sergeant. When Tony Meyer decided to retire early to take over his family farm, Anderson was selected because of pressure on the administration by all the motor officers, to replace him. In July, before Tony actually left, Anderson was promoted to lieutenant.

Anderson thought his riding days were over before they really even began. He even debated about turning down the promotion. However, the chief's office then informed him he would be the administrative lieutenant and the traffic unit would still be assigned to him, so he could ride as a lieutenant. Consequently, Anderson became the first regular riding lieutenant since he had been on the job. Being a riding supervisor gave him a clearer understanding of the needs for his unit to have plenty of training time and reliable equipment.

Anderson remembered the first day he rode without a training officer. The entire traffic unit was working a special event on North Division. A former motor officer, James Erickson, put out a code 99 (emergency call) near Division and Cozza. Erickson was out on a call with a subject that had a knife and was refusing to drop it. Anderson was the farthest motor to the south on Division. At the time, he kept thinking to himself, "It is always the last guy through an intersection that gets hit." Fortunately, he carefully cleared each intersection and safely arrived at the call.

After motor school, his left shoulder bothered him. For four months, he took anti-inflammatory drugs while Labor and Industries was slow to respond. During that time, he passed out twice for no apparent reason. As a result, he went to the hospital in Newport, where the doctor determined he was bleeding internally from the anti-inflammatories he had been taking. He was given blood transfusions and flown by a Life Flight helicopter to the hospital in Spokane. Once he became stable, L & I immediately authorized surgery to find out what was wrong with his shoulder. It turned out he had a labral tear in his left shoulder that did not show up on a previous MRI. Once it healed, he continued to ride motor. In 2015, he was moved to patrol as a watch commander but kept the traffic unit and continued to ride.

His most stressful moment came during the spring of 2016, when Sgt. Griffin (the current guild president and traffic sergeant) and Anderson were in a labor management meeting. The meeting was interrupted by a call stating a motor officer was down at Crestline and Rowan and they were performing CPR. Both Anderson and Griffin rushed to the scene expecting the worst, knowing the only motor riding that day was Officer Shaidon Storch. While en route, they were advised the CPR information was false. He was alert, talking, and was in an ambulance en route to the hospital. They both diverted to meet him there, where they learned he was banged up and had

a concussion but would be okay. Later, they learned he was going after two vehicles racing northbound on Crestline, and an elderly driver was westbound on Rowan. The elderly driver pulled out in front of him and they collided, sending him over the top of the car.

At the time of that accident, Anderson had the infamous upside down wings. (The upside down motor wings are assigned to the last person within the unit to drop a motor outside the training environment.) An elderly female had pulled out in front of him, in the fall of 2015, and he managed was able to avoid crashing into her driver's door, but laid the bike down.

It would have been insensitive to give Storch the wings while he was still recovering from his injuries. He had totaled what was supposed to be his new motorcycle, so he could make his 2007 Honda a spare bike when he got his 2015 Honda, as they had just purchased four brand new bikes. Officer Storch was saved the humiliation by Officer Ken Applewhaite, one of the master instructors, who no doubt felt sorry for him. Ken had made a traffic stop on a hill when he heard a scraping sound and loud bang. He looked back to find his bike on its side. Applewhaite's bike had shifted on the hill and tipped over. He was by himself, so he could just pick it up and nobody would know – except the fall had broken a mirror and one bag. Consequently, Applewhaite had to confess, thus saving Shaidon Storch from the wings of shame.

Some of Anderson's best memories from riding motors were the escort assignments. He escorted the Budweiser Clydesdales, Dignified Remains of U.S. Servicemen, Sgt. Greg Moore (LODD from Coeur d'Alene PD), disabled children in Grant County Chief For a Day, and floats in the Lilac Parade. In all, he was able to ride for three years before he was transferred out of the unit at the end of 2016.

A list of Anderson's family members that rode motors with the Spokane Police Department are as follows: Retired Captain Dave Anderson's father; retired Sergeant Jim Moore (mothers's cousin); retired detective Bob Yake (uncle); and Officer Ryan Snider (brother-in-law).

In 2016, Anderson planned the city servility plan for the political campaigns. Donald Trump asked to take a picture with him because he planned everything. *(Courtesy JD Anderson)*

Craig Meidl – hired by the Spokane Police Department in 1994

Spokane Police Chief Craig Meidl, circa 2016. *(Courtesy Craig Meidl)*

SPOKANE POLICE DEPARTMENT

Craig Meidl was born in Carmichael, California, in 1971. His parents were Carl Meidl, a career Air Force enlistee, and Donna Meidl, an office manager. Both parents were from Wisconsin. Meidl has two siblings: Scott Meidl, born in 1967, and Kim Meidl, born in 1969. Meidl was raised in California, Michigan, Illinois, and Washington state. He attended elementary school in Illinois, and middle and high school in Seattle. He has a Bachelor of Arts Degree in Law and Justice from Central Washington University and a Master's Degree in Organizational Leadership from Gonzaga University. He obtained his master's degree because he felt it would help him in the supervisory position he held at the time.

Meidl's first job was delivering newspapers in Illinois at the age of 10. Following that, he was hired at Wendy's Burgers as soon as he turned 16. At 17, he transitioned to a job at Pizza Hut.

Spokane Police Chief Craig Meidl with his wife, Tracie, circa 2016. Tracie, also a commissioned officer with the Spokane Police Department, joined the department in 1993. *(Courtesy Craig Meidl)*

While he was still 17, he joined the United States Marine Corps, and remained in the active reserves until after he was hired by the Spokane Police Department. He also worked for Central Washington University, moving furniture, while attending college.

During the time Meidl was in the Marine Corps Reserves, his unit was activated for Desert Shield and Desert Storm. Consequently, he served in both Saudi Arabia and Kuwait. In his early career, he started out driving M-60 battle tanks, but, due to being color blind, was soon moved to a supply unit. Meidl served in the United States Marine Corps Reserves for six years, from 1989 to 1995. At the time of his discharge, he held the rank of corporal.

In January of 1994, Meidl joined the Spokane Police Department. He was assigned to the motor unit in 1998, where he worked for two years. During that time, his primary motor partner was Mark Knight, though he did frequently work with Paul Taylor, Rick Dobrow, and Kim Thomas. When he first started riding motor, there was a total of eight men assigned to that unit, which was increased to 16 by the time he was reassigned to other duties. Meidl was also a member of the SWAT team.

During Meidl's time on motor he learned a lesson that he felt should be passed on to anyone who is new with motorcycles. The first week he was assigned to motor he was on a Kawasaki 900 cc. He was working a school zone, watching a speeding car go by. It appeared the driver was attempting to get away from him when he saw Meidl start out after him. As he leaned his bike into a turn, he didn't pay attention to the large school zone letters painted in the middle of the street. Slick painted letters are like ice for a motorcycle if the motorcycle is leaning in a turn. Consequently, his bike slid out from under him, costing several thousand dollars to repair. Besides feeling the embarrassment, Meidl felt this was information that should be passed on.

Meidl met his wife, Tracie Mayer, at work. They both worked for the Spokane Police Department and were assigned to the same patrol team. They married in 1997 and have two children, a son born in 2000, and a daughter, born in 2002. According to Meidl, his wife has been the biggest influence in his career. She is extremely stable and consistent and has great compassion for others.

The highest rank Meidl has held on the police department is that of chief of police. Asked about what he has learned during his career, he stated it has created value in his life by helping him appreciate what he has. His job has demonstrated the importance of making good choices, in everything he does, which he is instilling in his children. As he has gained more years of experience, the knowledge from what he has learned in police work has helped him leverage the opportunities he has been afforded. Being a police officer, and interacting with people at their lowest points in life, created in him a desire to always be compassionate toward people who truly need compassion and understanding.

The Intermodal shooting

One of Meidl's memorable experiences happened in 2003. It involved a shooting incident at the Spokane Intermodal Center. A number of officers, including Chris Lewis, who is now a motor officer, were also involved.

On January 7, 2003, at 1:20 a.m., Lewis made a traffic stop at Sprague and Bernard. As he made the stop, the two occupants in the vehicle immediately began shooting at him and then sped off. A short time later, they crashed their vehicle at the Intermodal Center.

Following the crash, two men got out, and one, carrying a semi-automatic assault rifle, climbed onto some elevated railroad tracks and ran into the depot. The train and buses had just arrived, making it an extremely dangerous situation, due to the number of people in the area. Police chased the man outside the Spokane Intermodal Center terminal to avoid hitting civilians, at which time the suspect with the assault rifle began firing at the officers. Before it was over, he had fired two dozen rounds at the officers. In return, the officers fired three shots at the gunman, one of which hit him in the leg. After he was shot, he put

down the rifle and was wrestled to the ground and arrested. The second man, who was injured in the car crash, had surrendered earlier.

At the time of the shooting, there were an estimated 250 passengers aboard the train and 100 were aboard three buses. In addition, there were numerous people in the terminal. It was later learned that rounds from the suspect's assault rifle hit an Amtrak train, a bus, and a police car. Although the train was in the process of loading and unloading, none of the shots hit any passengers or officers who responded to the scene.

On June 14, 2003, Spokane County Superior Court jurors found the suspect guilty of attempting to kill police officers during a gun battle at a crowded downtown train and bus station. He was convicted of two counts of attempted first-degree murder, four counts of first-degree assault, and one count each of second-degree assault with a deadly weapon, possession of stolen property, taking a motor vehicle without permission, and unlawful possession of a firearm.

Among Meidl's happiest memories are going out with the SWAT Team after a hard day of training and enjoying the camaraderie.

Meidl says he gets much of his personal identity from his job. He feels that learning life's lessons from the perspective of a police officer has made him a better person overall, in both his career and life in general. The main lessons he has learned in life is to do unto others as he would like them to do unto him, a central premise that he strives to achieve every day. "This doesn't mean we always can give people what they want, but it does mean we treat them how we would hope to be treated if we were in the same position as they are."

Although Meidl doesn't claim to have a specific role model, he sincerely tries to emulate the expectations presented to him from reading the Bible. Although his father died when Meidl was 13, he left a tremendously good and lasting impression on his son, which continues to shape his life.

The Macabre History of the Intermodal Center

RNING SEPTEMBER 7

MANY ARE DEAD

An Awful Disaster in
This City.

THIRTY-FIVE VICTIMS.

Eighteen Dead Bodies Taken
Out.

TWENTY-SEVEN STILL MISSING

Terrible Scenes of Death—A Pre-

The Intermodal Center, located at 221 West 1st Avenue, was originally built, in 1891, for the Northern Pacific Railway. It now serves as a railway station, and a re-fueling and service stop for the Amtrak Empire Builder, as well as the Greyhound and Trailways bus station for Spokane.

The location of this building is especially historic to Spokane. In terms of lives lost in one location, a tragedy occurred related to the Northern Pacific Railroad that is unparalleled in the history of the city.

On September 6, 1890, the Northern Pacific Railroad had a large labor crew working on a rock-cut at the intersection of Sprague and Division. They were in the process of numerous construction projects for the railroad, one of which included the above train station. Just minutes before the shift was to end at 6:00 p.m., over 200 pounds of dynamite prematurely exploded, instantly killing and wounding scores of workers and horses. A concentration of workers had been in the immediate area. Most had no chance to run and were buried under as much as 15 feet of falling rocks, some weighing several hundred pounds. An eyewitness reported seeing the two men who were setting the blast – foreman James McPherson and powderman Joseph Rhea – blown into the air in a dense column of smoke. The scene was one of horrifying terror and confusion, and the air was pierced by the agonizing cries of the injured survivors. One observer likened the aftermath to a "battlefield with dead men lying around, broken carts and mangled horses."

An alarm was sounded, and the police were enlisted to hold back the well-intentioned crowd that quickly gathered. Several hundred volunteers, including almost every physician in town, worked feverishly to save lives and rescue those who were trapped. Many family members lined the rock-cut and crowded outside the morgue in total despair. Sadly, the blast claimed about 26 lives (24 were positively accounted for).

At the time, little concern was placed on workers' safety or well being. In life, these laborers, mostly immigrants, were little more than numbers to their employer. Each wore a brass tag etched with his identifying number. When the foreman wished to summon a man, he called him by number. Now in death, a majority of the laborers were buried in unmarked graves in a humble section of Greenwood Memorial Terrace, and the families who depended on them were left with no means of support. In 1996, Fairmount Memorial Association placed a monument at the site to acknowledge the uncelebrated contributions of Spokane's early laborers, who, as these men did, often risked their lives during the building of the city.

Christopher Lewis – hired by the Spokane Police Department in 1995

Christopher Lewis, May 4, 2016. *(Jack Pearson photo)*

Christopher Lewis was born in Spokane on December 4, 1968. Christopher's father, Michael, was a small business owner and his mother, Doreen, was a homemaker. Christopher had two siblings, Mike, born in 1960, and Pat, born in 1961. Chris and his siblings all graduated from Central Valley High School.

Shortly after graduating from high school, Chris enrolled at Washington State University, where he received a Bachelor of Arts Degree in Criminal Justice. In 1985, Chris met Sonja Giampietri. They were married in 1998 and now have two children, Jacob 16 years, and Abby 12 years.

Chris joined the Spokane Police Department on April 10, 1995. Prior to tha,t he worked for Northwest Culvert Company, as a yard laborer, and the Washington State Patrol. He was assigned to motor in 2004 and has been on motor ever since.

S P O K A N E   P O L I C E   D E P A R T M E N T

James Christensen – hired by the Spokane Police Department in 2000

James Christensen, 2016. *(Jack Pearson photo)*

Jim was born in Spokane on March 11, 1969. His parents were Harry Christensen, who was the production manager for Columbia Lighting, and Gerry Christensen, who was the manager for Early Dawn Ice Cream. James has five siblings: Judy Reiter, born 1955, Mike Christensen born 1957; John Christensen 1959; Carol Madhtare 1961; and Kim Coan 1963. They were all raised in Spokane.

Jim attended Cooper School and graduated from John R. Rogers High School. Following his grad-

Jim's mother Gerry on his Honda ST 1300 motorcycle. *(Courtesy Jim Christensen)*

uation, he attended Spokane Community College and graduated with an Associate of Arts Degree in Administrative Justice.

Jim met his wife, Theresa Smith, while going to school. They were married in 1990, and have two children. Jim joined the Spokane Police Department on August 3, 2000. Prior to that, he worked for the Spokane County Jail from October 1, 1990 to 8August, 2, 2000. Jim's core philosophy is to work hard and do the right things in life.

Bank robber gets away but is later caught with record speed

Spokane police officers responded to the report of a bank robbery on February 11, 2015, just after 4:00 p.m., at the Inland Northwest Bank in the 2100 block of North Ruby. The suspect was not located at the time, but officers in the area found discarded clothing along with a bag that contained some of the money from the robbery. That clothing was submitted to the Washington State Patrol Crime Lab for testing. The crime lab later advised Major Crimes detectives that DNA found on the clothing matched a suspect's DNA. That suspect was later arrested by Jim Christensen.

Arrest of a suspected armed robber eight minutes after he committed the crime

In March 2017, at approximately 3:30 p.m., Spokane police received a report of a holdup alarm at the Washington Trust Bank on Indiana between North Division and North Ruby streets. Spokane Police Neighborhood Conditions Officer James (Jim) Christensen, on his way home from work, located and arrested the suspect eight minutes after the initial emergency call.

The original police report indicated a male had entered the bank and demanded cash, but did not display a weapon. Washington Trust Bank employees said a man, dressed in a dirty grey sweatshirt and pants and a Spider Man mask, entered the bank at 27 East Indiana around 3:30 p.m. He put a black canvas bag on the counter and demanded cash before fleeing. As the suspect was fleeing, Spokane Police Officer Jim Christensen spotted a man he believed fit the description of the suspect riding a bike at Nora and Division. Christensen tried to stop the man, identified as "Doug" Burns, but the suspect rode his bike south on Ruby as Christensen gave chase in his patrol car, according to court records.

The chase headed down alleys and through yards, and Burns dropped the backpack he was carrying behind a home near Augusta and Division. As other officers converged, Christensen cut the suspect off, forcing him to ride into the side of the police car. The suspect then tried to get away but was tackled and handcuffed.

Later, as a result of the arrest, Spokane Police Major Crimes detectives charged David C. Burns (45) with an additional count of first-degree robbery after his DNA was discovered on clothing discarded after the robbery on February 11, 2015.

Assault with baseball bat

A man was arrested after charging at two Spokane police officers with a baseball bat early Saturday morning. Michael A. Bernal, 29, was arrested after Officers James Erickson and Jim Christensen responded to the 200 block of East Crown Avenue at 1:57 a.m., following a 9-1-1 hang-up call. A dispatcher had called back, and a woman told the dispatcher she could not speak freely.

When officers knocked on the door, Bernal allegedly "whipped the door open, armed himself with a baseball bat and then swung it at the officers, almost hitting them both," police said in a news release.

Police said Bernal refused to drop the bat. As he charged at officers with the bat, the woman, whom police did not identify, grabbed him around the waist. Police said he then threw the bat at the officers, broke free, and yelled, "Bring it on!"

All three ended up on the ground when they tried to arrest him. During the struggle, Bernal grabbed one of the officer's flashlights in "another apparent attempt to assault the officers," police said.

Officers arrested Bernal on two counts of second-degree assault. They determined there was no crime committed between Bernal and the woman.

City, county and state motorcycle officers line up, and then perform for the start of the 80th Lilac Festival/ Armed Forces Torchlight parade in 2018. *(Photos courtesy Linda Habbestad)*

Dean Draper – hired by the Spokane Police Department in 2000

Dean Draper, 2016. *(Pearson photo)*

Dean Draper was born at Fort Presidio in San Francisco, in 1973. His father was in the Army at the time. He was raised at Martinez, California, and attended Achambra and Martinez schools there. Dean later moved to Spokane, where he attended Whitworth College (now university). He met his future wife at Whitworth, and they were married in 1997. Together they have three teenage children, two girls, and a boy.

Prior to joining the Spokane Police Department, Dean was on the Pittsburgh (California) Police Department from 1998 to 2000. In August of 2000, he went on the Spokane Police Department. In August of 2011, he was assigned to motor.

Dean is very active in sports and coaches youth basketball, baseball, and softball. During his off-duty time, he is active in many outdoor activities.

Trevor Nollmeyer – hired by the Spokane Police Department in 2003

Trevor Nollmeyer, 2016. *(Pearson photo)*

Trevor Nollmeyer was born in Tacoma, Washington, in 1978, to Meidl and Patty Nollmeyer, both from Tacoma. His father was a police officer with the Tacoma Police Department, and his mother was a nurse. Trevor has one sibling, a sister Emily, born in 1980. Trevor was raised in Tacoma and attended Harvard and Franklin Pierce schools. Following graduation, he attended the University of Washington, where he received a Bachelor of Arts Degree in business.

In 2004, Trevor married his wife Shawna. Together they have two boys, a two year old and a six-months old.

In July of 2003, Trevor moved to Spokane when he learned he had scored high on the Spokane Police Civil Service test and had passed all the other requirements, making him eligible to be hired. In 2013, he was assigned to ride police motor.

Shaidon Storch – hired by the Spokane Police Department in 2006

Shaidon Storch was born in Reno, Nevada, in 1983. He was raised by his mother, Lauri Burns, who was from California. He has no siblings.

Shaidon was raised at Nine Mile Falls, north of Spokane. He went to Nine Mile Elementary, and Lakeside Junior High, and Lakeside High School. Following his graduation from high school, he attended Spokane Community College, receiving an Associate of Arts Degree in Law Enforcement.

Shaidon joined the Spokane Police Department in February 2006. Prior to becoming a police officer, he worked corrections and miscellaneous odd jobs. He rode motor one year prior to being assigned to motor duty, and in 2011 he was assigned to motor permanently. Although he was in a motorcycle accident in 2017 (See page 419) some of his most memorable times, during his tenure on the police department, occurred while working motor duty.

Shaidon met his wife, who also works for the Spokane Police Department, and they were married in 2011.

During his off-duty time Shaidon enjoys all outdoor activities.

Shaidon Storch, 2016. *(Pearson photo)*

Chapter Five

Sheriff Motorcycle Officers

The Spokane County Sheriff's Department Began using Motorcycles in 1919

The following information regarding the Spokane County Sheriff's Department was researched and provided to the authors by retired Spokane County Sheriff Motorcycle Officer Tim Downing. Downing began his research with the Spokane County records pertaining to the sheriff's office. He bracketed his research around the time motorcycles came into use by law enforcement agencies around the United States. He also used numerous original source newspapers and personal contacts. As such, he provided the following:

• On May 14, 1914, the Spokane County Sheriff's Department consisted of seven deputies. $8,400 was budgeted for the year, and there was also a six-month allowance for temporary deputies at $2,160.

• In September 1916, the department consisted of three sheriff deputies, one criminal deputy, and eight regular deputies, with a total budget of $9,600.

• In September 1917, the department budget was $14,180. It consisted of the sheriff, a chief deputy, a chief clerk, six deputies, and no motorcycle officers.

• In September 1918, the total budget was $23,048. The department consisted of the sheriff, chief clerk, and six deputies.

• In September 1919, the budget was $30,000. This was the first time the classification of motorcycle officer appeared. On Saturday, September 6, 1919, during the county commission's board meeting, Sheriff George Reid, who was the sheriff of Spokane County from 1917-21, requested a classification of two motorcycle officers. According to Sheriff Reid, it was a classification C, meaning motorcyclist, which is a higher pay grade status. A class-A status was the highest pay grade in Spokane County. The grading goes from A to E. Pay is adjusted according to skill, experience, risk, etc. A regular deputy (patrolman) is classified as D.

• On October 10, 1919, on page 360 of the commissioners meeting records, the 1920 budget was authorized. Two motorcycle officers were listed for 1920. The total cost to the county was $2,640. The department at that time had a total of six deputies.

• On Monday, October 4, 1920, the commissioners called for a meeting to approve the 1921 budget presented at the September 7 meeting. The minutes were approved, and it indicated that class C motorcyclists for Spokane County, totaling three deputies, would be paid $5,940 and three outside deputies would receive $5,400.

• On Friday, January 14, 1921, at the beginning of a new year, all departments submitting their declarations of their prospective departments had listed their total personnel. Also, a new sheriff had been elected, Clarence Long, who served from 1921 to 1923. Sheriff Long submitted the names of two motorcycle officers. Those officers were M. Hamilton and J. S. McCormick.

• From 1920-28, the county commissioners provided funds for the sheriff's department to employ from two to three deputies as motorcycle officers. Today, deputy sheriffs are required to take an exam and are hired from civil service lists. The only exception is the law allows each sheriff of a county to have a certain number of political appointments depending on the size of the county.

History of the English Sheriff
(Paraphrased from Wikipedia)

The Office of Sheriff is distinguished from other law enforcement agencies in its historical roots. The sheriff came into existence in England in the ninth century, which makes the office of sheriff the oldest continuous, non-military, law enforcement entity in history. In early England, land was divided into geographic areas among a few individual kings – these areas were called "shires." Within each shire, there was an individual called a reeve, which meant guardian. The reeve was originally selected by the serfs to be their informal social and governmental leader.

As the kings observed how influential this individual was within the serf community, they soon incorporated that position into the governmental structure. The reeve soon became the king's appointed representative. His job was to protect the king's interest and act as mediator with people of his particular shire. Through time and usage, the words shire and reeve came together to be shire-reeve, guardian of the shire, and eventually to the word "sheriff."

Because taxes on the poor were oppressive and even poaching was a hanging offense, the sheriff became increasingly hated by the common people. The most notorious in English folklore is Robin Hood's nemesis, the Sheriff of Nottingham.

As time passed, the responsibilities grew, and soon the duties of the sheriff included keeping the peace, collecting taxes, maintaining jails, arresting fugitives, maintaining a list of wanted criminals, and serving orders and writs for the King's Court. Most of those duties still remain as the sheriff's responsibilities in the United States. In England, the sheriff eventually began to lose responsibility and power, and by the early 1800s, his role was largely ceremonial.

The first sheriff in America is believed to be Captain William Stone, appointed in 1634 for the Shire of Northampton in the Colony of Virginia. The first elected sheriff was William Waters, in 1652, in the same shire. ("shire" was used in many of the colonies, before the word "county" replaced it).

A brief history of the sheriffs in the United States

The early sheriff's office in America was much less social, and had less judicial influence. However, it was much more responsive to individuals than the English sheriff. The duties of the early American sheriff were similar in many ways to its English forerunner, centering on court-related duties, such as security and warrants, protection of citizens, maintaining the jail, and collecting taxes. As the nation expanded westward, the office of sheriff continued to be a significant part of law enforcement. Today, the elected sheriff is a major part of the USA's judicial system.

In 1776, Pennsylvania and New Jersey adopted the Office of Sheriff in their Constitution. The Ohio Constitution called for the election of the county sheriff in 1802, and then state-by-state, the democratic election of sheriff became not only a tradition, but in most states also a constitutional requirement. In the United States today, of the 3,083 sheriffs, approximately 98 percent are elected by the citizens of their counties or parishes.

The early American sheriff was important to the security of the people and was granted much power. The early frontier sheriffs administered punish-

A circa 1915 photo of an early motorcycle. Being a motor officer has always been one of the most coveted positions in many police agencies. *(Public domain)*

ment, not only conventional as we know it now, but also by flogging, banishment, or execution by hanging. The American books on sheriff's duties included many of these, even a diagram for building and erecting a gallows.

Although some of the earliest sheriffs were appointed, one of the main characteristics that distinguish the present office of sheriff from other law enforcement agencies is its direct accountability to citizens through the election process. The office of sheriff is not a department of county government, it is the independent office through which the sheriff exercises the powers of the public trust. No individual or small group hires or fires the sheriff, or has the authority to interfere with the operations of the office. Elected sheriffs are accountable directly to the constitution of their state, the United States Constitution, statutes, and the citizens of their county.

The sheriff is the only head of a law enforcement agency in this nation that is accountable directly to the people of his/her jurisdiction. In Washington, each sheriff of the 39 counties is an elected official serving a four-year term, which has no term limits. In essence, the sheriff is the chief law-enforcement officer of a county and is empowered to enforce the state criminal laws of the State of Washington and the county their office represents, as well as to serve or execute civil processes; to maintain county jails; to provide courthouse security; and to provide general law enforcement in unincorporated areas. In many cities, police services are contracted to the sheriff's department in lieu of a city police department. Such is the case with the City of Spokane Valley, which contracts with the sheriff to provide all its law enforcement. Another example was early Spokane Falls. When the city incorporated in 1881, it could have chosen to hire the sheriff to perform their duties. Rather than do that, the city officials chose to form a police department to provide services, along with the other necessary branches of government, including the courts and a jail.

During the early 1900s, transportation was rapidly evolving to motorized vehicles. Law enforcement agencies began purchasing automobiles, but soon recognized the advantages of using motorcycles in police work. Within a year or two, motorcycles would follow.

The first American police motorcycle patrol unit was recorded to have been started by the Detroit Police Department in 1908. This same year, the Evanston (Illinois) Police Department also purchased a motorcycle for patrol purposes. Soon, the nickname of "motor" was the term of choice used to refer to motorcycle patrol officers.

One of the first dedicated motorcycle patrol units created was in California, in 1911, by Chief August Vollmer of the Berkeley Police Department. The Berkeley Police Department also developed some of the first motorcycle patrol training, policies, and procedures, as well as modified their Harley-Davidson and Indian motorcycles specifically for police patrol with saddlebags for extra storage.

The speed and maneuverability of a motorcycle offered advantages not provided by larger, more traditional police vehicles. The motorcycle's relatively small size allows it to get to accident scenes more quickly. Police officers typically use motorcycles for

Spokane County Sheriff George L. Reid, served as Spokane County sheriff from 1917 to 1921. Reid was the sheriff who, in 1919, originated the first motorcycle patrol for the sheriff's department. *(Courtesy Spokane Police Department Archives)*

the enforcement of traffic laws. However, motorcycle officers handle many tasks, as they are quick to arrival at the scene of an emergency or crime.

History of the Spokane County Sheriff's Office

The history of Spokane County is somewhat complicated, but the present-day county was officially formed on October 30, 1879. At that time, Washington Territorial Governor Elisha P. Ferry appointed Spokane County's first three commissioners: W. C. Gray, John H. Wells, and Andrew Lefevre. Those commissioners appointed Noah M. Tappan as the first sheriff of Spokane County. Tappen held office until the first election, which occurred in 1880, when Michael Sullivan was elected sheriff.

In 1929, motorcycles were no longer listed in the sheriff's budget. It is important to note that in 1928 Motorcycle Deputy Valentine McDavis was killed on his motorcycle while on duty. Following this accident and his death, the motorcycle unit was dis-

banded. The decision was made by Sheriff Floyd Brower, who was sheriff from 1925 to 1930.

The following article appeared in a 1940 Spokane newspaper (specific source and date unknown). Although it was written 10 years after Brower disbanded the sheriff's motorcycle unit, it was still applicable in some circumstances, and echoed many of Brower's arguments:

"MAN KILLERS" VALUE IN DOUBT
Motorcycles for Police Patrol
Work Not Practical--
Danger Is Great.

The recent tragic accident in which State Patrolman Lang W. Sheldon lost his right leg brings up the question, "Does it pay to use motorcycles for police patrol duty?"

In the opinion of the writer, who has had close contact with police activities for years and has ridden motorcycles in the largest cities in both Europe and America, the an-

Motorcycle Deputy Valentine McDavis, the first Spokane County Sheriff's Department officer to be killed on his motorcycle while on duty. *(Courtesy Spokane Police Department Archives)*

Sheriff Floyd J. Brower was the sheriff of Spokane County from 1928 to 1932. Following the death of Valentine McDavis, he disbanded the sheriff's motorcycle unit for safety reasons. (*Courtesy Spokane Police Archives*)

swer is no. It is his belief that the motorcycle, with few exceptions, is obsolete as a means of police transportation or for the prevention or detection of crime.

Before going into details the following incomplete list of motorcycle casualties in local law enforcement in recent years is recalled:

Dead

• Officer F. A. Germain, police officer, killed July, 1922, when his motorcycle collided with a truck.
• Deputy Sheriff V. J. McDavis, killed near courthouse June, 1928, when his motorcycle collided with a truck.

Injured

• Officer Ralph Harper, fractured skull.
• Officer Walt Johnson, fractured shoulder in collision.
• Deputy Sheriff J. R. Cashatt, shot off motorcycle by bandit.

• Officer Gail Pitner, fractured leg, alighting from sidecar.
• Officer Vic Hudson, fractured jaw in fall.
• Officer John Miller, fractured arm in fall.
• Officer P. B. Anderson, fractured leg in collision.
• Officer Harry Davenport, fractured leg in collision.
• Sergeant A. Windmaiser, fractured leg in collision.
• Officer A. J. Karle, fractured ribs in collision.
• Officer M. M. Ettenborough, ruptured blood vessel.
• Deputy Sheriff Emil Vecchio, serious injuries-accident.
• State Patrolman Gilbert Hyde, fractured skull in fall.
• State Patrolman Lang Shelton, loss of leg in collision.

Others Hurt Also

The foregoing is only a partial list. More have been laid up with injuries of a minor nature after collisions and falls in the last 14 years. The writer believes that motorcycles, known to officers who ride them as "man-killers," are obsolete for the following reasons:

1. Nearly every modern automobile can now travel as fast, if not faster, than a motorcycle, unless the latter is especially geared and "doctored" for high speeds.

2. An officer alone often faces two, three, or more persons when an arrest is to be made, and he can not transport these persons without first calling for additional transportation.

Lone witness at Disadvantage

3. The officer alone is the only witness when an arrest takes place his word often is disputed in court by two, three or more persons in the automobile involved.

4. In the event of an accident he can not transport the injured to a hospital.

5. If he himself is injured or wounded, being alone, he is helpless until another person arrives to help him.

6. In at least four months of the year riding a motorcycle is uncertain because of weather conditions, icy streets, etc.

7. The lone motorcycle officer is not as good as a patrol officer is, with two men in a car. Two heads are better than one, and in any event, the officer not at the wheel at the time can watch what is going on, all the time. In dangerous situations one man should never be exposed to unnecessary risk.

The police cars of today are equipped with veritable arsenals that can not be carried on a motorcycle. The latter are now loaded down with radio sets.

Another reason uniformed motorcycle officers are handicapped in patrol duty is that guilty motorists can both see and hear them coming for miles.

Police Chief Ira Martin believes the motorcycle on the whole is not practical. Inspector Frank Keenan says it is a necessary evil but not as satisfactory as two-man cars in patrol duty.

The Spokane County Sheriff's Department's first motorcycle probably was an Indian

In 1901, bicycle racing champion promoter and champion, George Hendee, hired Oscar Hedstrom to build gasoline engine-powered bicycles to pace bicycle races. In February, Hedstrom began work on the motorized pacing bicycle in a shop in Middletown, Connecticut. He completed the first motorized bike in May and shipped it the 38 miles to Hendee in Springfield, Massachusetts. The machine, and the other two bikes Hedstrom built in 1901, proved to be powerful and reliable, establishing the company's reputation for outstanding performance.

By 1909, the Hedstrom's factory introduced the first Indian Scout, a mid-sized model with a 606 cc

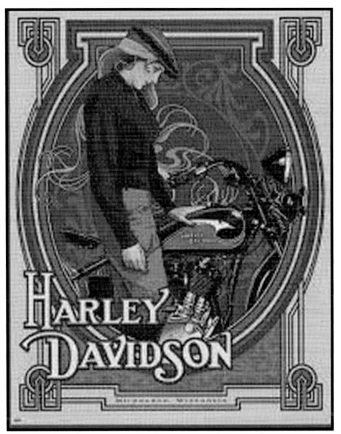

A vintage Harley-Davidson ad. The subject in this ad almost appears reluctant to try out this new bike. (*Public domain*)

side-valve V-twin engine. It was reliable, fast, and highly maneuverable, and it enticed many people to start riding.

In 1917, the United States entered World War I. The company provided the U.S. military with nearly 50,000 Indian motorcycles from 1917-1919, most of them based on the Indian Powerplus model. This durable, dependable, and powerful model served the troops well, and when the war was ended, had been noticed and admired by many World War I veterans who were now in law enforcement and able to make buying decisions. Also, those men purchasing motorcycles for the various law enforcement agencies may have admired the beauty and form of the Indian ads more than they did the Harley-Davidson ads.

A vintage ad for Indian motorcycles, which may have in some small way, played an integral part in the purchase of Indian motorcycles for law enforcement agencies. (*Public domain*)

Both the City of Spokane in 1910, and the Washington State Patrol in 1921 chose Indian motorcycles as their first bike. Spokane used Indians from 1910 to 1920. It was only natural the Spokane sheriff should also choose to use them.

Jesse Richard (Dick) Cashatt – hired by the Sheriffs Department in 1922

Jesse Richard "Dick" Cashatt, 1923. This photo appeared in the *Spokane Chronicle* on April 17, 1923, following an incident where he was shot from his police motor, while chasing a murder suspect. *(Public domain)*

Jesse Cashatt was born June 10, 1900, to John and Elizabeth Cashatt, who lived at West 600 Maxwell Avenue. His first job was as a meter reader for the city of Spokane. In 1922, he joined the Spokane County Sheriff's Department where he worked until 1926. In 1926, he then joined the Washington State Patrol. Jesse lived with his parents until he was married in 1927.

In 1927, Jesse married Estella Gladys Lynn, who lived in Opportunity, Washington. He was 28 years old, and she was 26. This was a first marriage for both, at which time he and his new wife moved

to 4400 North Nevada Street in Spokane. According to records, Jesse's mother passed away on July 9, 1942, in Seattle, and his father, shortly after, on October 18, 1943, in Spokane.

In 1926, Jesse was hired by the Washington State Patrol and served that agency until his retirement. Jesse passed away in Spokane on the 27th of August in 1956. His wife passed away on April 30, 1998. They are both buried at Pines Cemetery at 1402 South Pines in the Spokane Valley.

Dick Cashatt, while on police motor, was shot through the lungs while chasing an escaped murderer from San Quentin

While working for the Spokane County Sheriff's Department assigned to police motor, Cashatt was shot while chasing a man who was in the process of abducting a Spokane waitress.

On May 11, 1923, Gladys Homer, an 18-year-old waitress, while at work at a Spokane restaurant, had agreed to go for a ride with George Burt after she finished her shift. She had ridden with him, unbeknownst to her, in a stolen car on one or two other occasions and knew him only through the restaurant. Burt, who was 24 at the time, became infatuated with her and had devious criminal plans, which included Gladys becoming his victim.

Shortly after Burt picked up Gladys from the restaurant, he headed south, away from Spokane. As they sped southbound, his talk and manner became frightening to Gladys. Once they had driven several miles south of Spokane, she asked him to stop the car and let her out. He refused and kept speeding toward the direction of Spangle. Now, clearly sensing the terrifying demeanor of Burt, her fear reached the point that she felt she immediately needed to escape from both the car and him. Several miles from Spokane, when the car was going at a high rate of speed, she opened the car door and leaped out, violently tumbling and severely injuring herself. Her most serious injury was a skull fracture, which for a while the doctors felt was going to be fatal.

As this happened, another vehicle was behind them. The driver stopped, gathered her up, and immediately transported her to the hospital in Spokane, where they called law enforcement and reported what happened.

Sheriff Motorcycle Officer Dick Cashatt was assigned to the call and quickly headed that way in an attempt to overtake the driver. Just before entering the small town of Spangle, he caught up to the car, a newer model "Star," stopped it, and placed Burt under arrest. A search by Cashatt produced a loaded revolver, which he confiscated and placed in his pocket. He then ordered Burt to drive ahead toward Spokane. As Burt started off and drove only a short

DEPUTY SHERIFF WOUNDED BY MAN SEEKS TO ARREST

SPOKANE OFFICER SERIOUSLY HURT; ASSAILANT ACCUSED BY A WOMAN.

The above news clipping from the *Spokane Daily Chronicle* **appeared on April 17, 1923.** (*Public domain*)

This is a 1923 Star automobile. The Star was assembled by the Durant Motors Company between 1922 and 1928. Also known as the Star Car, it was envisioned as a competitor against the Ford Model T. It was built from parts supplied by various outside companies. Originally, Stars were powered by a four-cylinder engine. In 1926 the line introduced a six-cylinder engine. (*Public domain*)

distance, he suddenly turned toward Cashatt and, with a revolver he had concealed in the stolen car, began shooting at him as he was being pursued. One of the bullets hit him in the chest, with the impact knocking him from his motor. However, he soon recovered enough strength to get back on the motor and ride to a farmhouse to call his office for help. In the meantime, Burt sped away from the scene.

The abductor and his convict pal were both escaped murderers from San Quentin Prison

Records from San Quentin, following Burt's conviction for murder in San Luis Obispo County, document him arriving at the prison in 1919.

At the time of his escape on June 24, 1923, Burt was with a fellow convicted murderer, Thomas Walton, who also had an official record for a murder he committed in California in 1915. He was sentenced to life imprisonment in San Quentin for that murder. Consequently, both Burt and Walton were life termers in San Quentin.

In a confession to police following their capture, after Burt's shooting of Cashatt, he made the following statement concerning their jailbreak:

> We were working on the outside of the prison with a large gang, and, without any plans, jumped into a "flivver" parked near the gates. As we passed each of the guards we waved and they waved back at us. They did not recognize us. Four of the guards, stationed with machine guns, kidded us as we sped outside. We drove north along the coast and stole two other cars.

After their escape from San Quention, both Burt and Walton were on the run for over four months. As part of their plans, they moved to the Inland Northwest and set up a home base near Rosalia, Washington. They now began committing numerous auto thefts and burglaries throughout the Spokane area. It also appeared they were operating a chop-shop near the Rosalia area where they were now living.

How they were identified and caught

The discovery that the two men were escaped convicts, both doing time for murder, came as the result of Sheriff Clarence Long's (1921-1923) networking with other law enforcement agencies in the northwestern United States. As such, and as part of the procedure, Long provided a description and *modus operandi* of the suspects committing burglaries and auto thefts in the Spokane area to a special detail committed to auto theft, who was attending a law enforcement convention being held at San Francisco. Fortunately, that group had been compiling information on auto-theft suspects and had numerous data already recorded. As a result, Sheriff Long was advised to look up the photo of Burt, alias Edward Langson, and Walton. To the sheriff's advantage, the Spokane Police Department had photos of both suspects, which they had earlier received from Long's networking.

The photos were soon shown to Deputy Cashatt and Gladys Homer, who both positively identified Burt. Approximately three weeks later, both George Burt and Thomas Walton were arrested by the chief of police at Des Moines, Iowa, following a sensational auto chase. At the time of their capture and arrest, they were going by the names of Fred Fletcher and Jack Haines. However, once they were taken into custody, they were quickly identified by their fingerprints, as Burt and Walton. Their capture also cleared up many of the burglaries and auto thefts going on in Spokane County. Following their arrest, Burt confessed to the shooting of Cashatt and the abduction of Miss Homer.

The strangest of events the murder of two convicts

George Burt and Thomas Walton were sent back to prison for life, this time at the Walla Walla State Prison. While serving his time there, Walton took a disliking to his former pal, Burt, and Burt's friend, George McDonald. Consequently, while all three of them were in the prison chapel at noon during the

BURT ADMITS SHOOTING OF DICK CASHATT

Complete Confessions Secured From Escaped Lifers Held in Iowa.

George P. Burt, arrested yesterday at Des Moines, Iowa, with Thomas Walton, has confessed to the shooting of Deputy Sheriff Jesse R. (Dick) Cashatt last month near Rosalia and has admitted his escape, together with Walton, from the San Quentin penitentiary in California.

The confession was made to the Iowa officers today, according to Associated Press dispatches.

Sheriff Long also received a telegram from Des Moines today confirming the confession of Burt.

He announced that Deputy Sheriff Bradley of Spoane and Sheriff Cole of Whitman county will leave for Des Moines as soon as extradition papers can be prepared at Olympia.

"Wo wired to Olympia today asking for the papers, and hope that the

May 17, 1923, *Spokane Daily Chronicle.* (Public domain)

Sheriff Clarence Long, circa 1923. *(Courtesy Spokane Police archives)*

Sunday service, Walton attacked both Burt and McDonald with a knife he had crafted while in his cell. Following a violent struggle in the prison church, Walton fatally stabbed both Burt and McDonald. Later in court, he stated he killed Burt "to put an end to too much talking." He killed McDonald because he was Burt's friend and simply didn't like him.

Thomas Walton is hanged
Goes to the gallows with dignity

The following article appeared on page 7 of the *Ellensburg Daily Record* on December 11, 1924:

Tom Walton pays for killing prisoner
Penitentiary inmate murdered three men;
Had no fear of death

Walla Walla, December 12. Thomas Walton, convicted of the murder of S. P. Burt, a follow Convict, in the state

SLAYER SAYS "NOT GUILTY"

Walton, Spokane Convict Who Killed Former Pal in Prison, to Face Trial.

WALLA WALLA, Wash., Oct. 9.—His head swathed in bandages bloody from his encounter of Sunday noon when he killed two fellow convicts, S. P. Burt and George McDonald, Tom Walton stood before Superior Judge E. C. Mills this morning and coolly pleaded "not guilty."

The charge was first degree murder, filed in behalf of Burt, a former pal of Walton's, made notorious in Spokane through the shooting of Deputy Sheriff Richard Cashatt last spring when the pair attempted to get away with an automobile on the Inland Empire highway. Until Walton is tried for Burt's murder the charge of killing McDonald can not be filed

Lawyers Appointed.

Asked if he cared to be represented by counsel, Walton readily assented and T. M. McKinney and J. C. Hurspool were appointed. Expressing a wish to "get this thing over with," the attorneys conferred for a few moments with their client and the plea then was entered.

Walton sauntered from the court room, without sign of emotion, puffing at a cigarette.

Can't Plead Guilty.

Under the laws of Washington a plea of guilty is not permissible when the death penalty is involved.

Walton is charged with having attacked Burt and McDonald in the chapel line Sunday noon, stabbing both with a knife he had made and

Taken from the October 9, 1923, *Spokane Daily Chronicle*. *(Public domain)*

penitentiary here on October 7, 1923, was hanged at the penitentiary this morning. The trap was sprung at 5:06 a.m., and the prison physician pronounced him dead 10 minutes later.

Walking to his death with the same fearlessness that he has displayed since the beginning of his prison career, he refused to make any final statement, and even refused to talk with Rev. A. R. Liverett, prison chaplain, or Father Buckley, Catholic priest, in his cell prior to the execution.

Prison officials had expected Walton to either break down or show fight and were prepared for both emergencies, but he went to his death as coolly and calmly as any man who ever mounted a scaffold here.

His body will be shipped to his relatives in Montague, California. Although Walton paid the penalty for killing Burt, he has an official record of having killed two other men. The first was in 1915 in California for which he was sentenced to life imprisonment in San Quentin prison. The other was George McDonnell, cell mate of Burt, whom he stabbed following his attack on Burt.

Walton and Burt were life termers in San Quentin and made their escape together in a prison automobile in January, 1923.

South of Spokane they established a camp where they assembled automobiles and other stolen loot. Burt became infatuated with a waitress in Spokane and on one occasion took her for a ride in a stolen car. The girl became frightened and jumped from the car while it was traveling at a high speed, suffering a skull fracture. Motorcycle officer Richard Cashatt was detailed to the case.

Arrested in Des Moines

Cashatt found Burt enroute to Rosalia, disarmed him and ordered him to drive to Rosalia. Burt shot Cashatt through the lung with another gun the officer did not see in the car.

Walton joined Burt south of Rosalia and they were apprehended several weeks later in Des Moines, Iowa.

Valentine "Val" McDavis – hired by the Spokane County Sheriff in 1926

SPORTS EDITION

Spokane Daily Chronicle

42D YEAR. NO. 230.   26 PAGES   SPOKANE, WASH., THURSDAY, JUNE 14, 1928.   PHONE MAIN 1121.   PRICE:

DEPUTY SHERIFF KILLED BY AUTOMOBILE CRASH

PLACE HOOVER FIRST TONIGHT

VICE PRESIDENT SELECTION WILL NOT BE HURRIED

UMPIRE DODGES FLYING BOTTLES

BOSTON, June 14, (AP)—Umpire Pfirman was the target of a barrage of pop bottles thrown by Boston fans today when the crowd resented his driving Manager Rogers Hornsby from the ninth in the fourth inning of the St. Louis-Braves game at Braves field. The Rajah had protested a third strike called on him.

In Third Olympics

McDavis Dies in Hospital Two Hours After Motorcycle and Auto Hit --- Deputy Prosecutor Is Hurt.

Deputy Sheriff V. McDavis died at 3:10 this afternoon from injuries received about 1 p. m. when a motorcycle on which he was riding collided with an automobile driven by Newton Vinther, W1024 Jackson avenue, at Mallon and Adams.

Deputy Prosecutor Del Cary Smith Jr., who was riding on the motorcycle with the officer, was pain-fully injured and at 4 p. m. had not sufficiently re-

BOY DROWNS

Ralph Heyer, 3, son of Mr. and Mrs. Julius C. Heyer, E1023 Sinto avenue, was drowned in the Spokane river this afternoon when he fell from the Dora avenue bridge.

REPUBLICANS KILL EQUALIZATION FEE

Platform Formally Adopted at War Session --- Ignore Plea of McNary Haugen Boosters.

Spokane Daily Chronicle **headline of fatality.** *(Public domain)*

Valentine McDavis and Del Cary Smith: The Fatality

The death of a county motorcycle officer under conditions that today would spark controversy

On June 14 1928, at the intersection of Adams and Mallon, Valentine McDavis, a motorcycle officer for Spokane County, was traveling east on Mallon Avenue, when a vehicle driven by Newton Vinther, going north on Adams Street, failed to yield the right-of-way and struck his motorcycle. McDavis was transported to Sacred Heart Hospital, where he was pronounced dead.

Worthy of note, Officer McDavis was driving the motorcycle while straddling the gas tank. Sitting on the motorcycle seat behind him was Del Cary Smith, who at the time was a Spokane County deputy prosecutor and a man from a Spokane family of some historical prominence. McDavis and Smith were returning to the courthouse after an investigation at the county garage, where they just completed inspecting a vehicle in an attempt to learn information regarding a criminal case they were working.

In 1928, operating a motorcycle in this manner, was dangerous but not illegal. As early as 1921, Washington State had a driver's license requirement, but it wasn't until 1937 that the state instigated a driver's license examination. In addition, as time passed, stricter laws were added to the books. Today in many third world countries, entire families with three or four people on a motorcycle or motor scooter often can be seen.

The Spokane Police Department initiates an investigation

In 1928, Floyd Brower was the sheriff of Spokane County. At the time, he was combatting bootlegging on a countywide basis trying to enforce Prohibition laws. Two days after the accident, on June 16, a story about Sheriff Brower appeared in the *Spokesman-Review* about conducting liquor raids

Valentine "Val" McDavis. *(Courtesy Sue Shipton)*

The investigation

According to Spokane Police Motorcycle Officer Walter Case, who with the assistance of Deputy Prosecutors Frank Funkhouser and Ralph Foley, stated: "Vinther had been driving north on Adams Street and didn't see the motorcycle going east on Mallon Avenue as he had turned to wave to his fiancée, whose home was located at Dean and Adams." Motorcycle Officer Case further stated "the Ford vehicle Vinther was driving skidded 66 feet before it struck the motorcycle." The first word of the accident came when a citizen ran into the courthouse with McDavis's revolver. One witness said she saw the youth (Vinther) looking back just before the crash.

Motorcycles during that time, and the ones typically used by police departments, were either Indians or Harley Davidsons. An interesting comment regarding this accident was the fact that neither Indian nor Harley-Davidson motorcycles were equipped with front brakes until 1928. This is significant as it related to this accident. There is no record of either the make or year of McDavis's county-owned motorcycle. However, since this accident happened in 1928, there is a good chance it was an older bike and did not have a front brake.

It is common knowledge among experienced motorcycle riders that the use of a front brake is very important in stopping the motorcycle. It is generally accepted that approximately 70% of a motorcycle's total stopping power comes from the front brake and 30% from the rear. The main reason is that when the front brake is applied, most of the bike's weight, thus stopping power, is focused on the front tire. If the motorcycle McDavis was operating was not a 1928 model, it wouldn't have had a front brake, greatly eliminating his chances of stopping in time to save his life.

Also, during the investigation, Del Cary Smith, Valentine's passenger, said that at the last minute McDavis turned the motorcycle in such a way that prevented the impact of an oncoming car from striking him. He felt McDavis was trying to protect him and saved his life.

in Spokane. As the chief law enforcement officer of a county, a sheriff also has jurisdiction in all cities and towns in the county of his election, and if he feels it is necessary, he can supersede the city's jurisdiction, which is what he was doing. That article was specifically criticizing the city police department for not cleaning their own house. Brower made sure the addresses of those raided were listed in the paper, especially the ones in the city. Consequently, there was a bit of bad blood between some in the sheriff's office and the city police department. However, it did not affect this investigation, as it was properly conducted.

Walter Case, 1926, was the city motor officer who investigated the McDavis fatality. *(Public domain)*

County prosecutor files manslaughter charges against Newton Vinther

As a result of the fatality investigation, which resulted in the death of Motorcycle Officer McDavis, manslaughter charges were filed against Newton Vinther alleging he was directly responsible for the death of the deputy. "The right-of-way unquestionably belong to the motorcycle," Prosecutor Greenough said. "Vinther had a clear view of the street upon which the motorcycle was approaching for half a block. He had plenty of time to stop if he had been watching for crosswise traffic. We found that he later stopped his car at his girlfriend's home, and had been talking to her, to whom he is engaged." Newton Vinther died in 2006, age 97.

A short history of victim Motorcycle Officer Valentine John Henry Mc'Naught'Davis

Valentine McDavis was born in Farndon, Newark, England, in 1891. He came from a large family con-sisting of 16 children: nine boys and seven girls. In 1909, while still in England, he became quite a proficient boxer. All nine boys in his family served in World War I. Two of his brothers died in the war. The family name was originally Mc'Naught'Davis. When Valentine entered the Army in England, he shortened his name to McDavis. He served with the Royal Horse Artillery British Expeditionary Force.

Following the war he met his future wife, Lillian Brown. Upon their marriage, the McDavises immigrated to Grand Forks, Bitish Columbia, Canada. During the early 1920s, they moved to Spokane. The McDavises bought a home at 2700 East Hoffman in Hillyard, where the family lived. His family attended the neighborhood Holy Trinity Catholic Church.

His first job in Spokane was working for the Great Northern Railroad as a fireman. While working for the railroad, he came close to being killed in a derailment in 1925 near the Deer Park area. He was pinned underneath the railroad engine. From that job, he joined the Spokane County Sheriff's Department and had been on that job for about two years before he was killed.

The McDavises had three boys: Eric, Reginald, and Donald. Eric, the oldest, was attending Hillyard High School at the time of his father's death. Eric also played football and was active in boxing, like his father.

The original Hillyard High School building was built in 1907 and had an initial enrollment of 14 students and one teacher. It closed down 25 years later, in 1932. The 48 students who graduated that year were the last. From that point on, students who would have attended Hillyard High School were transferred to the new Rogers High School. It was on the day of his father's death, while at Hillyard High School, that Eric learned about it from one of his classmates who made the statement: "Your dad is dead and his brains are all over the sidewalk." Valentine's two youngest sons, Reginald and Donald, were attending Arlington Elementary School at the time of their father's death.

Valentine and Lillian McDavis with two of their three boys. *(Courtesy Sue Shipton)*

Photos of two motorcycles similar to the year of Valentine's. Note the absence of a front brake on both bikes. *(Public domain)*

Valentine McDavis's funeral took place on June 16, 1927, at the Holy Trinity Church in Hillyard. His widow, Lillian, was now left with the task of providing for and raising three boys. Although she never remarried, she realized she must work to support her family. Thankfully, two other people were a great help. Her oldest son, Eric, became very protective of his mother and younger brothers. Also, George Elmer Brown, a lawyer, whose office was located at North 5012 Market Street in Hillyard, became a close and caring friend to the family.

George Elmer Brown of Hillyard, The family's champion

George Elmer Brown took on the role of helping the family and mentoring the three boys. Through Brown's influence with county government, Lillian was given a job as a court bailiff for Spokane County. This made her the first woman in Spokane to hold that job. George Brown was also active in the Hillyard Booster Club and continued to help and guide the McDavis boys.

Lillian passed away in 1954. Both Lillian and Val are buried in Spokane at Riverside Memorial Cemetery. Eric went to college at Gonzaga and Whitman. During World War II, he was a Navy officer stationed in the Pacific. He maintains the original family name – Mc'Naught'Davis. He went to work as a social worker for the state of Washington. Eric married Tad Glazebrook and continued his civilian life in LaJolla, California. Eric and Tad raised two girls, Janet Lee Mc'Naught'Davis/Nelson, and Valerie Jean Mc'Naught'Davis/Parker. Reginald stayed in Spokane and became an agent for Standard Insurance. He and his wife raised two children, Marylyn and Stan. Donald also served in WWll. He served in the Army and was stationed in Alaska. Donald eventually became a principal for School District 81 in Spokane. He and his wife raised two children, Susan /McDavis/Shipton and Bruce McDavis.

The patriarch of the Smith family in Spokane an interesting piece of early Spokane history

Del Cary Smith, the man on the motorcycle with Val, was the second of three generations of lawyers bearing that name. The first was born in New York in

The old Hillyard High School building at 5313 North Regal. On November 8, 2010, a groundbreaking was held by the Spokane Housing Authority when it was remodeled for the Agnes Kehoe Apartments. The building was turned into a 51-unit, low-income apartment complex. Agnes Kehoe (1874-1959) served four terms in the Washington State Legislature, beginning in 1938. She never actively campaigned, but had no trouble getting re-elected on the basis of promising never to get drunk and never to sell her vote. *(Public domain)*

1869, spending his early years as a neW.S.P.aper reporter before becoming a lawyer. In 1927, he moved to Spokane from Port Townsend, Washington. In Spokane he practiced law until his death in 1939. His most notable case occurred when he defended George Webster, the last person in Spokane County to be officially hanged by the sheriff. During that time, Del Cary Smith went out of his way to help Webster. This support continued up to the last moments of Webster's life on the gallows.

George Webster terrorizes a family

In 1897, the Aspland family consisted of five members: Andrew, age 57; his wife, Lize, age 44; twins John H. and Ella May, age 13; and daughter Jennie C., age 11.

George Webster, an itinerant laborer, age 25, had been working various jobs around Spokane County for about four years. Webster had a reputation in Spokane County for being a hard worker and skilled handyman. However, he was allegedly an alcoholic.

On May 5, 1897, Webster was in Cheney and had been drinking in several saloons. At approximately

7:00 p.m., while Webster was still able to function, the Cheney constable ordered him to leave town. Webster was heading up the road toward Medical Lake. As it became dark, he stopped by the Aspland family farmhouse and asked to be put up for the night. Webster visited with the Asplands, offering to share his bottle of whiskey. Unfortunately, they agreed to let him stay — a fatal mistake. During his drunken condition, Webster attempted to force himself on Mrs. Aspland and her 13-year-old daughter. In the process he shot the mother in the stomach, and she died shortly after. Before his conviction for murder, his main defense was that he felt he should not be hanged for this crime because, due to his drunken condition, he did not remember committing it.

Preparations for the Hanging of George Webster and the Stay of Execution in 1899

Ten days prior to the hanging, Sheriff Robert Speck ordered the scaffold be taken out of storage and erected in the enclosed yard between the courthouse and the jail. It had originally been constructed in 1897 and stood 15-feet high and 10-feet square. There were 13 steps leading to the platform, which had a three-foot-square trap in the middle. The trapdoor had a 50-pound iron weight attached underneath and was sprung by pulling a single lever. The area where the scaffold stood was in the enclosed yard between the courthouse and the jail. It had been covered with a large awning, concealing it from public view. The newly elected Spokane County Sheriff, Charles A. Cole, was determined to make the hanging as private as possible with admission by engraved invitation only, as this was part of his prescribed duties. Attendance was limited to 200 people, principally composed of police chiefs and officials from other counties, physicians, and members of the press. The first execution date of 1899 was postponed until 1900 due to a stay of execution.

Spokane's Last Official Execution at the County Courthouse, March 30, 1900 – "Farewell, George"

On Friday morning of the execution, March 30, 1900, Webster arose at 7:00 a.m., had a simple break-fast of eggs, toast, and coffee, and then met with his spiritual advisors. Shortly after 9:00 a.m., Sheriff Cole entered his cell and read him the lengthy death sentence. Afterward, Webster visited with a number of acquaintances. His last visitor was his attorney, Del Cary Smith, who bade Webster farewell as he left the cell.

At 11:00 a.m., flanked by sheriff deputies Francis K. Pugh and Henry Desgranges, Sheriff Cole led the prisoner from the jail and across the courtyard to the gallows. Reverend Perine and Captain McClelland followed behind. The group climbed the stairs to the platform. Sheriff Cole then asked Webster if he had any last words. He had nothing to say except "Goodbye." As Reverend Perine prayed aloud, Webster was positioned upon the trap and the deputies fastened leather belts around his torso, holding his arms and wrists close to his body, and around his legs and ankles. A black hood was pulled over his head, followed by the hangman's noose. Deputy Felix Pugh carefully adjusted the large knot just in front of Webster's left ear where it would instantly break his neck when he fell. Sheriff Cole pulled the lever, releasing the trapdoor and dropping George to his death. George was buried in an unmarked grave at Greenwood Cemetery in Spokane.

Del Cary Smith II, the Motorcycle Passenger

Del Cary Smith II, of Spokane fame, was born in 1902, graduated from Gonzaga Law School, and was admitted to the bar in 1924. He practiced law at Colville for two years. Smith then moved to Spokane and, from 1926 to 1930, served as deputy prosecutor under Charles W. Greenough. It was during that the fatal motorcycle accident occurred. In 1942, Mr. Smith became president of the Spokane Bar Association, and, in 1951 he served as president of the Washington State Bar. In 1953, his son, Del Cary Smith III, joined his practice and, in 1961, his younger son, Lawrence Smith, was added to his practice to make the law firm of Smith, Smith, and Smith.

The first invitation to the execution of George Webster, dated July 28, 1899. Due to an appeal by Del Cary Smith, the actual hanging didn't take place until Friday morning on March 30, 1900. At that time there was a second invitation was issued with the new date. *(Public domain)*

The following information was neatly printed on the back of George's execution invitation giving everyone due credit for their involvement:

• Presiding Judge: Hon. Leander H. Prather.

• Prosecuting attorneys: Hon. John A. Pierce & Hon. James Z. Moore.

• Defendant's Attorneys: Hon. James E. Fenton and Hon. Del Cary Smith.

• Trial Jury: William Gill, J. F. Roadnight, John Valentine, U.H. Morgan, I. Libschuetz, John Q. Van Ness, C. Thomas, W. P. Gould, N. C. Hair, Thomas

James, H. W. Doane, R. J. Frazier.

• Sheriff: R. D. Speck.

• Sheriff's Force: H.W. Desgranges, F. K. Pugh, Karl Brauns, E. C. Thompson, Charles Cole, J. W. Charlton, George Von Eschen, E. G. Sherman.

Also of interest in 1899, when Webster was executed, there was an elected county sheriff with eight full-time deputies.

William C. "Bill" Seitz – hired by the Spokane County Sheriff in 1957

William Seitz, circa 1960. *(Courtesy Ron Seitz)*

William C. Seitz was born July 3, 1919, in South Dakota. He was orphaned at age 10 and raised in the Hutton Settlement, a distinguished home for children in the Spokane area.

William's mother, Catherine, was born in 1881, and passed away at Yakima, Washington, in 1929. His father, Jacob, was born in 1879, in Russia. He died April 13, 1930, also at Yakima, Washington. Both are buried at the Tahoma Cemetery in Yakima County.

William had one son, Ron, and four stepdaughters. He was in the Army and served in World War II. He was a prisoner of war for 3 one-half years, working in Japanese coal mines. He was also a survivor of the Bataan Death March.

William joined the Spokane County Sheriff's office in 1956. He rode motor for five years and later became a sergeant for the patrol division. His son, Ron, remembers his dad riding motors with the side car in the winter months. He also remembers riding in front of him on the motors as a child going to a flag dedication at the Liberty Lake Golf Course when it first opened.

Staff from the Fairmount Memorial Association: Orville Clouse, Duane Broyles and granddaughter Sierra Broyles, Steve Pratt, Dave Clark, Tom Stokes, Kevin Smith, Carl Ellis, Dave Peters, Alex Crosen and Diane Perry surround the first double monument created in honor of Levi and May Arkwright Hutton who were partners in philanthropy. Their legacy lives on in the Hutton Settlement, dedicated to helping children for nearly a century. The memorial was dedicated on April 3, 2008. *(Bamonte photo)*

S P O K A N E   C O U N T Y   S H E R I F F

Chance Meeting in Spokane Reunites Bataan Death March Buddie

Patrolman Walter Mathers (left) and Deputy William Seitz.

The following is from a news article describing William Sietz's experience when he was captured by the Japanese and went through the Bataan Death March.

(Courtesy Ron Seitz)

Chance Meeting in Spokane Reunites Bataan Death March Buddies

Two Spokane law enforcement officers met last month in the courthouse parking lot. Each recognized the other from somewhere.

After comparing notes they decided they must have known each other in Wenatchee some years ago. Comparing notes again in Sheriff Roy A. Betlach's office yesterday, however, they remembered where it was they had met: They had known each other during the front-line fighting in the Philippines early in 1942 and had made the Bataan death march together. State patrol officer Walter Mathers, district license examiner for six northeast Washington counties, and Deputy Sheriff William Seitz found they had several more things in common.

They enlisted the same day, February 14, 1941, Seitz from Spokane and Mathers from Ellensburg.

They were sent to the Philippines on the same ship and took basic training at the same time in Manila, although they were assigned to different units.

Each was in his barracks when bombs started falling in Manila December 8, 1941.

They were sent to northern Luzon to meet the Japanese invasion from Lingayan gulf, and fought together on the retreat to Bataan. In February, 1942, Mathers was attached to Seitz's company, and the two men met for the first time. The men were captured, with nothing but Manila bay behind them, on April 9.

Then the week-long, 140-mile death march began.

"I" company's 85 remaining troops had dwindled to 35 men by the end of the march. After five months of night-and-day fighting and shrinking food rations, many were in no condition to withstand the rigors of the march.

Mathers and Seitz had become separated before the death march began and although they were interned in two of the same prison camps at the same time, they apparently did not meet again until last month.

The death march ended at Camp O'Donnell. Seitz stayed there three months and Mathers seven. Both were shipped from there to another camp in cattle cars, packed shoulder to shoulder with prisoners.

"When a man passed out on the trip, he stayed standing up." Seitz recalled. "He didn't have room to fall."

Seitz then was shipped to Cebu and other islands in the area on Japanese work details.

Mathers was in a prison in Manila September 21, 1944, when the first American bombs began to fall.

Seitz, who had been sent to Japan, recalled that when American bombers first were sighted there, the prisoners waved to them. They were told that anyone caught waving again would be shot. The waving came to a stop.

Mathers was sent to Formosa, where he worked in a logging camp carrying logs out of the woods on his shoulders.

"We could always tell when there had been an American victory by the increase in brutality from the guards," Seitz said. "One time, just after we came in from swing shift, we were ordered to fall out. After we lined up, a guard came down the line and hit each of us in the face with his fist."

Travel in Ships' Holds

Each had left the Philippines in the hold of a ship. That in which Mathers rode was 40 feet square, had a one-foot layer of coal on the bottom and held 730 men. Each man was allowed a pint of water every 48 hours, and they remained in the hold from October 1, 1944, until November 24. "It got so that men were knifing each other over water," Seitz said. Food in the camps consisted largely of rice once per day. Seitz, who weighed 178 when he enlisted, was down to 98 pounds at the end of the death march and 118 when he was released.

Mathers weighed 184 when he enlisted and 94 when he was released. This year, 10 years after his release, he finally was able to bring his weight above 170. He now weighs 175. Realization that the war was over came slowly, Seitz said. Sixteen days after the surrender, a Japanese lieutenant announced that the prisoners should "be proud to be from one of the greatest nations on earth and that Japan had surrendered.

History of the Hutton Settlement
by Laura Arksey for Historylink

In late November, 1919, the first orphans arrive at the Hutton Settlement, Spokane's new children's home built and endowed by mining millionaire Levi W. Hutton (1860-1928). The opening of the home is the fulfillment of a dream of a man who himself was an orphan, raised by uncaring relatives. Hutton designed and will manage his orphanage along the most enlightened principles of the time, with a goal of providing a happy, healthy environment in which orphaned and needy children can grow up. Although not the first orphanage in Spokane, it quickly becomes the most prominent institution of its type in the region.

Levi Hutton was a locomotive engineer in the "Silver Valley" of the Idaho panhandle. In his off-duty hours, he, August Paulsen, and other shareholders toiled at a claim they had named the Hercules Mine. His wife, May Arkwright Hutton (1860-1915), kept the miners well fed during their backbreaking labor.

In 1901 they struck a large vein of silver and lead, and soon the newly rich Huttons moved to Spokane. Hutton expanded his business operations into Spokane real estate, May became a major force in the woman suffrage movement, and both gave time and money to philanthropy.

After May's death in 1915, Levi Hutton began working toward the realization of his dream. He purchased 111 acres, enough land to function as a working farm, in the valley just east of Spokane. He then sent Spokane architect Harold C. Whitehouse (1884-1974) on a nationwide tour to research orphanage facilities. Hutton did not want his children's home to have a grim institutional character, and together he and his architect decided on the cottage plan as the best of existing options. The facility Whitehouse designed consisted of an administration building and four "cottages" -- each in reality a gracious and functional Tudor-style home able to accommodate 20 children under care of a matron or house parents.

Hutton not only oversaw the planning of the physical facility, but also outlined the total administration of his orphanage and laid down the principles that would guide it over decades. The Deed of Trust and other founding documents specified that the home be non-sectarian; that siblings be admitted together; that the children be educated in the local public schools until graduation; that special consideration be given to orphans from the Coeur d'Alene mining district; and that the children do reasonable farm and house chores.

To carry out his wishes, Hutton named an all-woman board, many of whom were carry-overs from the Ladies' Benevolent Society and its then still-existing Spokane Children's Home. Most of these women were society matrons, the wives of Spokane leaders, yet they were a working board, furnishing the cottages, sewing for the children, and seeing to their educational, health, social, and recreational needs. Over the years, the board relinquished some of these tasks to paid staff as it assumed a more professional supervisory role in terms of personnel, admissions and business decisions.

Until his death in 1928, Hutton himself did much of the administration of his orphanage. The children loved and mourned "Daddy Hutton," the closest to a father most had ever known. Hutton bequeathed to the Settlement his mining shares as well as his downtown Spokane commercial properties, including the beautiful Hutton Building. His handpicked assistant, young Charles S. Gonser, took over management of these assets as well as the administration of the Hutton Settlement, serving until his retirement in 1970. He was succeeded by Robert K. Revel, who retired in 1995, then by Michael Butler, the current administrator.

The Hutton Settlement has survived various challenges over the years -- threatened development and road encroachments on Settlement land, fluctuating revenues, complicated relations with the social work establishment and state regulations, difficulties in finding and keeping good residential staff, and the changing nature and needs of the children served. Because there are few full orphans today, the Hutton Settlement serves a different clientele -- children who for a variety of reasons cannot be raised by their own parents. Its beautiful buildings are now on the National Register of Historic Places. Through it all, the board and administrators have kept the Hutton Settlement true to the vision of its founder, and it continues to provide an important service to children of the region.

Deputy William Seitz with his three-year-old son, Ron, in 1957. *(Courtesy Ron Seitz)*

One of the many buildings at the Hutton Settlement. This photo was taken in 1922 and pictures Levi Hutton standing in the middle of the doorway, surrounded by children. *(Courtesy Hutton Settlement)*

Opinions Differ
Candidate for Sheriff Charges He Was Fired

In 1962, William C. "Bill" Seitz ran, as a Republican against Sheriff William Reilly. At that time his brochure listed the following:

- Seitz has the experience for the job
- Reared an orphan at the Hutton Settlement in the Valley.
- Attended Millwood grade school and West Valley High School.
- Veteran of World War II. Received the purple heart. Wounded in action. Bataan death march. Prisoner of war for 3 1/2 years.
- Father of four stepdaughters and one 8-year-old son.
- Merchant policeman in Seattle.
- Guard for atomic works at Richland, Wash.
- Sergeant of sheriff's patrol division for 6 years, patrol man for 2 1/2 years.

Immediately after he announced his candidacy, Sheriff Reilly fired him. The following is an article from the *Spokesman-Review* about that incident:

Opinions Differ
Candidate for Sheriff Charges He Was Fired

William C. Seitz, patrol sergeant in the sheriff's office, said today he will be a candidate for the Republican nomination for sheriff in the September primary.

He also charged that he was fired as a deputy Friday when he told Sheriff William J. Reilly, that he was going to run for the office.

"I did not resign as was reported – I was fired," Seitz said, "and I intend to take this matter before the County Civil Service Commission. I had not planned to quit or take leave of absence and make a public announcement before the end of the month."

Firing Denied

Reilly said he did not discharge the patrol sergeant but accepted his resignation in compliance with Civil Service regulations prohibiting deputies from taking part in political activities.

"I told him that under Civil Service, if he was to be a candidate for public office he couldn't work here any longer," Reilly said. "The question of a leave of absence was not discussed or considered. It was Seitz who brought up the matter of his running for sheriff, not I."

Seitz, in the sheriff's office for more than eight years, served as patrol sergeant under both Roy A. Betlach and Reilly. He was first employed there under Sheriff Ralph M. Smith.

An orphan, Seitz was reared at Hutton Settlement and attended schools at Millwood and West Valley. He entered the army in 1941 and was on the Bataan death march. He was a prisoner of the Japanese in Luzon for 3½ years. He had the rank of sergeant.

Before joining the sheriff's office he was a security guard at Hanford Atomic Works and served as a merchant policeman in Seattle. He also followed the welding trade and was a truck driver.

Seitz said he is running for sheriff because he believes there is room for much improvement in the area of employee relations, work assignments, training personnel, and protective measures for rural and suburban areas. He said that with the fast growth of suburban residential areas more mobile equipment and manpower and the reassignment of existing forces are necessary.

Ronald Laws – hired by the Spokane County Sheriff in 1962

Ron Laws on East Sprague. *(Courtesy Tim Downing)*

SPOKANE COUNTY SHERIFF

Richard "Dick" Lovejoy – hired by the Spokane County Sheriff in 1964

Dick Lovejoy in 1968 on a 1968 Harley. *(Courtesy Dick Lovejoy)*

Dick Lovejoy was born in Spokane on March 16, 1938. His father was Louis C. Lovejoy from Iowa. His mother was Margaret (Ennis) Lovejoy from Fort Steele, British Columbia. His father was a metal worker, his mother a housewife. Dick has one brother, Kenneth, born in 1930.

Dick attended Finch Grade School. Following that, he attended and graduated from North Central High School in 1956.

In 1956, Dick joined the United States Marine Corps, spending four years serving his country. He fulfilled his obligation and was honorably discharged as a lance corporal in 1960.

On October 29, 1964, Dick went to work as a deputy for the Spokane County Sheriff's Office. Prior to that, he worked for Carnation Dairy in Spokane.

In 1968, Dick was assigned to the traffic division, where he rode motor for over three years. His motor partners were Bob Bean and Chuck Anderson, who are both deceased. When Dick originally went on motor, there were four people assigned to motor, which combined both day shift and swing shift. Unlike the Spokane Police Department, each deputy was assigned his own motor. In addition to motor officer, he was a motor training officer up to his promotion as sergeant in 1971.

One of Dick's most important accomplishments was being assigned as the sergeant for Spokane County's newly formed and first SWAT Team, and attending SWAT school at the FBI Academy at Quantico, Virginia. This occurred in 1973, just prior to and in anticipation of Expo '74.

One of the most important and helpful things Dick learned during his time with the department was tolerance and understanding. During that entire time, it should be noted that he had tremendous respect for Captain John McGregor, who was his role model of what a police officer should be. Dick retired in 1995 with the rank of lieutenant. During his time with the sheriff's department, Dick was well liked and respected by other members of the department.

Dick Lovejoy in 1972 with his son Steve. *(Courtesy Dick Lovejoy)*

Left to right: Motor officers Dick Lovejoy, Chuck Anderson, and Bob Bean, in 1969, on the west side of the Spokane County Courthouse. *(Courtesy Dick Lovejoy)*

Dick Lovejoy in 1969 during a police visit at the Shriners Hospital. *(Courtesy Dick Lovejoy)*

Sergeant Jack Teagan and motor officer Dick Lovejoy in front of the Shriners Hospital in 1969. At the time, the hospital was located at 820 North Summit Boulevard. These visits were regularly scheduled by the Spokane Police Department, the County Sheriff's Office, and the Washington State Patrol. The visits meant a great deal to all the children at the hospital, and the officers also looked forward to them. *(Courtesy Dick Lovejoy)*

Infant Born in Motel
Stork Outruns Deputy's Vehicle

Deputy Sheriff Richard S. Lovejoy delivered a baby boy about 6 this morning—with the aid of an interpreter.

Answering a radio call to the Locust Grove Motel, E.4824 Sprague, Lovejoy said he found that Mrs. Yam Kwong Lee was starting to give birth.

Richard S. Lovejoy

"Well, the baby was being born," Lovejoy said, "so I just hoped I remembered my first aid training and I did my best and delivered the baby."

The mother and her husband speak no English, so Harry Huey, a relative of the new parents, translated from Chinese for Lovejoy as he handled his obstetrical duties.

"The mother got a big grin on her face after the baby was born and Mr. Huey translated my remarks that it was a fine baby boy."

Just minutes after the baby had been delivered, an ambulance arrived and the new parents and infant were taken to Sacred Heart Hospital.

But Huey and the family doctor went to St. Luke's. Sacred Heart was notified and the parents and baby went to St. Luke's.

Hospital attendants reported both mother and son doing fine. As for Officer Lovejoy, himself the father of two small children, he admitted "I'm a bit shook."

It was the second maternity case in a month for Lovejoy, who last month stopped a car on the Spokane Valley freeway only to find an expectant mother en route to the hospital had already had her baby, right in the car.

Fellow officers today were calling Deputy Lovejoy such nicknames as "Doc" and "The Stork."

And what was Deputy Lovejoy's reaction after the whole affair was over. Said he with a grin:

"I'd rather catch burglars—it isn't so nerve-wracking."

The new arrival is the second child for the Lees, who came to Spokane from Hong Kong last December. The father is employed in the kitchen at the Far East restaurant. The Lees have another child, a son 2 years old, who was born in Hong Kong.

Cops once made special deliveries

Shawn Jacobson/The Spokesman-Review
Robert Lee and Lt. Dick Lovejoy at the motel where Robert was born.

Helping with births was part of the job

By Kelly McBride
Staff writer

Veteran cops like to reminisce. Mention a crime, an officer with more than 15 years experience can one-up the story with a tale from his early days on the beat.

Drunks? Patrolmen used to be on a first-name basis with rabble-rousers and skid-row bums. A good cop didn't arrest them. He'd convince them to check into the drunk tank and dry out.

Drug houses? Well, in the days of the Ghost Riders and other motorcycle gangs, dozens of notorious hideouts plagued Eastern Washington and North Idaho.

As a cop reporter, I've heard the stories. As a pregnant cop reporter, I've heard a lot about babies — namely their unpredictable arrivals.

There are a handful of older cops in Spokane and Kootenai counties who can brag that they brought more than crime fighting to the streets they patrolled.

Some actually brought life — new babies.

They describe themselves as young and eager to help in the late 1960s when they were on patrol. Most were rookies working graveyard shifts.

It's been more than 20 years since a cop delivered a baby in Spokane or Kootenai counties. The emergence of paramedics, regional ambulances and medical helicopters has pushed police out of the baby buggy's path.

They are now supervisors or detec-

Please see **BABIES** A12

Top: In 1964, Deputy Sheriff Dick Lovejoy was called on to deliver a baby at the Locust Grove Motel at 4824 East Sprague Avenue. Bottom: Thirty years later the opportunity was made for him to meet the young man he had delivered. *(Courtesy Dick Lovejoy)*

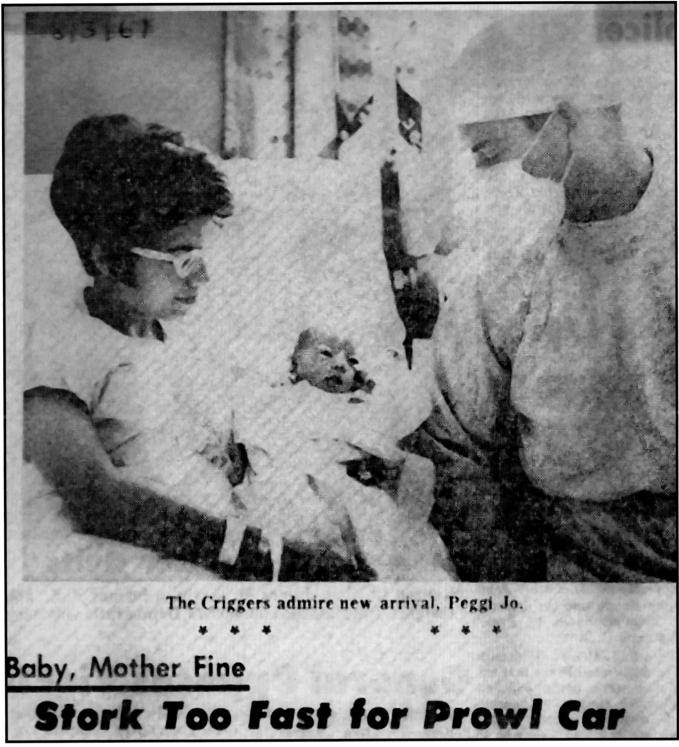

The Criggers admire new arrival, Peggi Jo.

★ ★ ★   ★ ★ ★

Baby, Mother Fine

Stork Too Fast for Prowl Car

Deputy Lovejoy had another occasion to help deliver a baby in 1967. Deputy, Kenneth Crigger was writing a report when his wife called to tell him the arrival of their second child was imminent. Crigger immediately rushed home, where he was met by fellow deputies Richard Lovejoy and Ron Dashiell. They immediately started toward the city on the freeway. Before they could get to the hospital, Mrs. Crigger had delivered a five-pound ten-ounce girl with the assistance of her husband and instructions from Deputy Lovejoy.

This was the first time for delivering a baby for the father, although he had received training at the Police Academy. However, since Lovejoy, who was sometimes called "Doc" by his fellow officers, had already been through this type of situation before. As a result, all involved felt everything was under control. *(Courtesy Dick Lovejoy)*

This photo is from the book *Son, a Psychopath and His Victims* by Jack Olsen. From left: Dick Lovejoy, Atty. Julie Twyford, Fred (Kevin) Coe, Atty. Roger Gigler, and Sgt. Norm Nickerson. *(Courtesy Dick Lovejoy)*

The Kevin Coe case is covered in other chapters of this book. The following description was taken from the dust jacket of Jack Olsen's book *Son*:

This is one of the most remarkable true crime books you will ever read. It is many things at once. For months, the story of a mother, a son and a city enmeshed in tragedy made headlines across the nation. This is the story behind the headlines. It is also an extraordinary examination of the mind of a psychopath and of the women – and men – who were his victims. And it is a chilling investigation of the consequences of a crime that does not kill – but which destroys as surely as any knife or gun. For more than two years, a rapist prowled the night streets of the homey, 'All-American' city of Spokane, Washington, terrorizing women, sparking a run on gun stores, and finally causing one neW.S.P.aper to offer a reward, the calls taken by the distinguished managing editor himself, Gordon Coe.

In March 1981, luck and inspired police work at last produced an arrest, and Spokane shuddered. The man was clean-cut, teetotal, conservative – and Gordon Coe's son. The family rallied behind Fred Coe. They had an explanation for everything.

Fred's mother, Ruth, gave detailed alibis for the rapes. But the evidence was overwhelming. As Fred was led away. Ruth Coe was heard to say, "Down, but not out. It was no mere gesture of defiance. Ruth Coe was bent on revenge, and soon the judge and the prosecuting attorney would feel the full force of her murderous wrath....

For eighteen months, Jack Olsen researched the cases of Fred and Ruth Coe to try to learn not only what happened within that family, but how and why. He interviewed more than 150 people, and slowly, bit by bit, built up a portrait not only of that extraordinary family, but of the mind of a psychopath. Talking with the rape victims, he probed the devastating effect the violations had had on their lives two weeks afterward, two months afterward, two years afterward. And searching the memories of the women in Fred Coe's life, he unearthed a most horrifying question: What is it like to love and live with a man for years – and then discover he is a psychopathic criminal? The answer to that question, to all the questions Olsen asked, and the bizarre conclusion to an evermore-bizarre series of crimes, make "Son" the most riveting account of villainy and dark obsession since *In Cold Blood*.

Bob Bean – hired by the Spokane County Sheriff in 1962

Deputy Bob Bean, circa 1969. *(Courtesy Dick Lovejoy)*

Bob Bean was born in Spokane on September 24, 1938, to Eugene Carter Bean and June Herbert Bean.Bob graduated from North Central High School in June 1956. He entered the U.S. Navy on September 10, 1956 and served until September 16, 1959.

On May 23, 1962, Bob joined the Spokane County Sheriff's Office. While there, he became one of the first motorcycle patrolmen when that unit was reactivated in the 1970s. Chuck Anderson and Dick Lovejoy were also part of that detail. Bob also served the sheriff's department as a rescue diver.

In the later 1970s, the office switched from Harley-Davidson to Kawasaki 1000 police motorcycles, and the sheriff's office continued with a much-reduced Traffic Unit until Sheriff Mark Sterk was elected to the office. One of his first projects was to expand the Traffic Unit with new deputies, new Harley "Hogs," new unmarked cars, and new uniforms. It was now common to see sheriff's motorcycles and traffic cars patrolling county roads and enforcing the county traffic code. As a result, accidents decreased by 30 percent. Sterk went to a leased fleet of vehicles and motorcycles, which reduced the cost and increased the number of units available.

Motor riders came and went, but Bob stayed with the motorcycle unit until a number of injury accidents forced him into retirement on June 30, 1994, after 32 years of service.

Following his retirement he joined the Blue Knights Motorcycle Club, traveling throughout the United States and Canada.

Bob died doing something he loved doing. As a result of injuries he suffered in a motorcycle accident he passed away on September 18, 2011.

April 1967

Sheriff's Traffic Force

Sheriff William J. Reilly talks over the duties of his new three-man motorcycle patrol today with Deputy Sheriff Ronald A. Laws, the department's senior cycle officer. The other motorcycle officers are Robert E. Bean (center) and Michael J. Bosch. Reilly said the motorcycle officers will concentrate on traffic enforcement and will be detailed mostly on residential and suburban streets outside the city.

A 1967 news clipping concerning Sheriff William Reilly's formation of a new three-man motorcycle patrol. From left: Ron Laws, Sheriff William Reilly, Bob Bean, and Michael Bosch. *(Courtesy Tim Downing)*

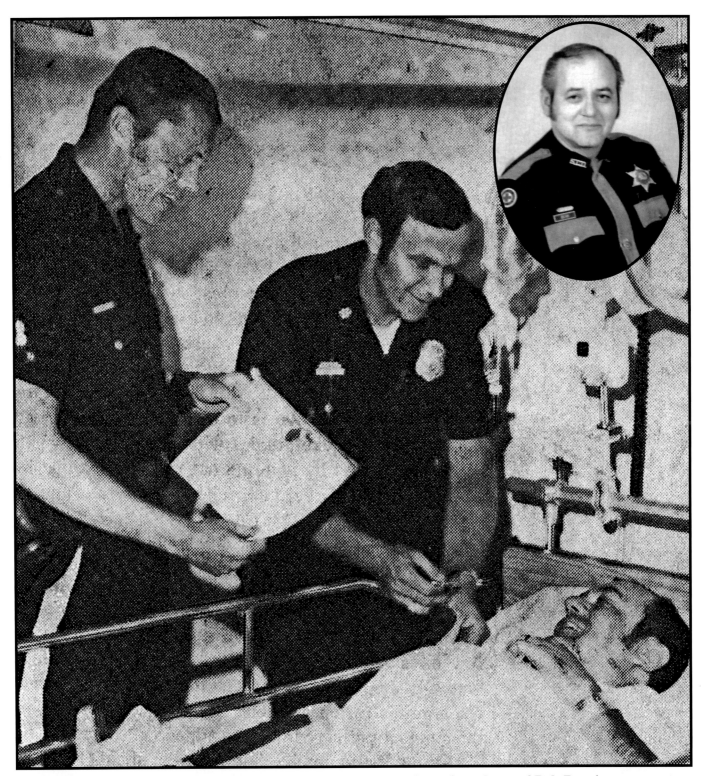

In 1972, motorcycle officers Tony Bamonte and David Prescott investigated one of Bob Bean's many motorcycle accidents, which seemed to occur with regularity. It seemed like he was one of those officers who often was at the wrong place at the wrong time when unfortunate circumstances came his way. The caption under the photo states: "In Line of Duty – City police officers A. G. Bamonte (left) and David S. Prescott present a purple heart of sorts – and a bit of kidding – to Sheriff's Motorcycle Officer Robert E. Bean, who was injured yesterday when his motorcycle slid 80 feet after hitting an oil slick at Illinois and Green. The officers, who investigated the accident, said Bean, on routine patrol at the time was observing the speed limit when his machine made its spectacular slide." Inset is the late Bob Bean in an upright position, circa 1990. Photo taken at Sacred Heart Hospital. *(Courtesy Dick Lovejoy)*

The Spokane Police Department's "Dry Squad;" circa 1925. Bob Bean's grandfather was a member of the Spokane Police Department for 25 years. During Prohibition, as a detective in Spokane, he was assigned to the "Dry Squad." *(Courtesy June Bean)*

Prior to the death of Bob's mother (June Bean), Bob told me (Bamonte) I should contact her as she had some family photos involving the police department. She actually didn't have many police-related photos, but provided the above photo, along with an interesting story:

According to June, he Dry Squad was specifically designed to enforce the prohibition of alcohol while Prohibition was in effect nationally (1920 – 1933). During that time, June's father, Walter Hubert (pictured third from the left) joined the force in 1922 and retired in 1947. As a member of the Dry Squad, Hubert was often required to work with a partner. He later confided to his daughter he hadn't enjoyed working with his partner because "He was a heavy drinker and to cover the alcoholic aroma, he'd eat garlic before coming to work and smoke cigars in the car. Somehow the combination produced a lot of gas, which didn't make for pleasant working conditions."

About halfway through Prohibition's hold on the nation, based on official figures, there were already 140 casualties as a result of enforcing it, 49 of which were prohibition officers and 92 were violators. Most of these deaths came about as the result of gun battles that broke out between federal dry agents, bootleggers, moonshiners, and rum-runners. The most interesting thing about Prohibition is that the government, at one time, allowed officers to shoot people for the sale of alcohol, now the government collects millions of dollars in tax revenue on its sale.

Frustrated that people continued to consume so much alcohol after it was banned, federal officials ordered the poisoning of industrial alcohols manufactured in the United States. This included alcohol regularly stolen by bootleggers and resold as drinkable spirits. The idea was to scare people into giving up illicit drinking. By the time Prohibition ended in 1933, the federal poisoning program, by some estimates, had killed at least 10,000 people.

Jerry Brady – hired by the Spokane County Sheriff in 1967

Jerry Brady went to work for the sheriff's office August 16, 1967. He rode motor from 1970 to 1975. During several of those years, he rode motor three days a week and worked the boat patrol for two. His various motor partners were Bob Gibbs, Mike Mc-Clanahan, Bob Bean, Jim Alma, and Dick Lovejoy. He worked for the sheriff's department for over 41 years and retired as a captain. During his career, Sheriff Mark Sterk was his biggest influence.

The upper photo shows the presidential motorcycle escort provided for President Nixon when he came to Spokane to officially open the World's Fair (Expo '74) From left: Wayne Wilson (city motor), Philip Ostendorf (city motor), Jerry Brady (county motor), Tony Bamonte (city motor), and Bob Bean (county motor). Inset – Jerry Brady. The lower right photo is of Police Chief Wayne Hendren greeting President Nixon and Mrs. Nixon upon their arrival in Spokane. The chief was the first person to greet him when he departed the plane. Chief Hendren had these photos taken and gave copies to all the motorcycle officers shown. *(Courtesy Wayne Hendren)*

S P O K A N E   C O U N T Y   S H E R I F F

James "Jim" Donald Alma – hired by the Spokane County Sheriff in 1967

Jim Alma, circa 1973. *(Courtesy Jim Alma)*

Jim Alma was born on September 13, 1942, at Memorial Hospital, Logansport, Indiana, to John William Alma and Vivian Maxine (Maddock) Alma. Because it was during World War II, and his father was in Charleston, North Carolina, waiting to be shipped overseas, his mother was staying with her parents. Just before his father left for China, Jim's Grandfather Maddock called him with the news he had a son. His father didn't return home until October 1945, when Jim was three years old. After his father arrived home, he worked in a factory, farmed with his grandfather, and was parts manager for a Ford tractor dealership.

Jim has one sister, Janice Marlene (Alma) Hoover, born March 29, 1948; and two brothers, Richard Lee Alma, born October 22, 1950, and Timothy Joe Alma, born March 20,1953. His brother Timothy died on June 5, 1953.

From 1942 to 1960, Jim's family resided in Burnettsville and Idaville, both in Indiana. He attended first and second grade in Idaville. After the family moved to Burnettsville, he attended the third through eight grades at the Burnettsville country school from 1950-1956. He attended high school, from 1957 to 1960, also in Burnettsville.

In 1960, Jim traveled to Spokane to visit his aunt and uncle, and subsequently chose to attend Eastern Washington College of Education, Cheney, Washington, from 1960-1961. In 1962, he attended Moler Barber College in Spokane. Following that, from 1962 to 1963, he worked at Scotty's Barber Shop, which was located at the Washington State University Campus at Pullman.

In 1963, Jim enlisted in the Washington Air National Guard, 242 Mobile Communications Squadron. In 1964, he received his basic training at Lackland Air Force Base, San Antonio, Texas. In 1965, he was sent to Communications Tech School at Keesler Air Force Base in Biloxi, Mississippi. Jim completed his duty with the Air Force in 1969.

In 1966, Jim married Susan Rae Loucks in Spokane. They had one daughter, Diana Sue (Alma)

Kautzman, who was born on January 27, 1967. On September 12, 1971, they had a son, Brian James Alma, who died almost four months later, on December 23, 1971. Another son, Jeffrey John Alma, was born on January 17, 1973. Jeffrey died less than a month after he was born, on February 2.

In 1967, Jim joined the Spokane County Sheriff's Department, and in 1968 he attended the Spokane Police Academy's 400-hour school in Spokane. In 1970, he took the motorcycle officer 40-hour-training school in Spokane and began riding motor. In 1978, Jim attended the Washington State Criminal Justice 80-hour Crime Prevention School. From 1978 to 1995, he was assigned to the sheriff's department's Crime Prevention Task Force as a specialist.

On April 14, 1984, Jim, being single again, married Karen Patricia (Lynch) Templeton in Spokane.

Jim Alma working the Lilac Parade. *(Courtesy Jim Alma)*

Jim Alma, circa 1974. *(Courtesy Jim Alma)*

In 1995, after 28 years with the Spokane County Sheriffs Department, Jim retired and went to work for Silver Car Auction and Bartlett's Collector Car Appraisal Service. He stayed with that job until 1998, when he went to work for the Federal Court Security, U.S. Marshal's Service, in Spokane. He retired from that job in 2006, and moved to Columbia Falls, Montana, near Glacier National Park, where he currently resides. Following his retirement, Jim pursued his interests in woodcarving and American western history.

Jim Alma's personal memories

In 1974, Spokane hosted a world's fair. It was my last season as motor officer, and I had a new partner, Bob Gibbs. Bob's dry sense of humor fit both our personalities. We had good times working together and making memories that summer.

The Maple Street Toll Bridge

Working swing shift, we were suppose to get off at 11 p.m. but often it was later. Bob would have me stop by his house on the way home for pie and coffee. I'm sure his neighbors appreciated the rumble of motors in the neighborhood late at night. Sometimes his wife would already be in bed, but often she would get up, turn on the coffee pot, and cut us a piece of pie. I would ask him, "How does she put up with you for as long as she has?"

I remember once when we were about ready to get off shift, we received a call of a woman at Fairchild Arms Apartments in Airway Heights. She had taken an overdose, but that soon changed to a family disturbance and assault. Bob and I were the only units available, and it was going to be a long haul as we responded from near Francis and Division. Since Bob had an electronic siren on his motor, and I still had the old windup type, I hollered for him to lead the way and I would be right behind him. Ash Street was one-way traffic southbound until we reached the north end of the toll bridge, where it merged with Maple Street. Each sheriff's vehicle had a pad of vouchers and stopped at the toll gate each time you crossed the bridge. However, in emergencies the toll collector lifted the gate and allowed us through without having to stop.

At night when the traffic was light, the man in the toll booth would be half asleep or be reading the neW.S.P.aper, as in this case. Bob had cut his siren several blocks before we got to the bridge, so the toll booth operator did not know we were coming. Then out of the darkness and to his surprise he heard our motors go through the gate, outside of the arms, at a high rate of speed. No doubt, this caused him to throw his neW.S.P.aper in the air, probably leaving him to say to himself "What the hell." Bob and I both had to chuckle at the idea he never knew who it was but probably thought it was a couple of city motors.

Going Fishing

This story is unbelievable, but it really happened. Two of my closest friends from the Sheriff's Department, Bob Gibbs and Denny York, decided to go fishing with a few of their buddies. For weeks they planned this wonderful out-of-town fishing trip. They knew the river they were going to fish and where they were going to be staying.

Since Bob needed some fishing gear, his wife decided to surprise him by going out and buying him everything he would need for the trip. He arrived home from work one evening to find a mountain of fishing gear stacked high in the middle of the living room floor.

The next day, traveling to their destination to meet the others, Bob asked Denny if maybe they could find the nearest Emergency Room. It seems he wanted to get a head start on fishing by attaching the hook to the line, and in doing so, he had run the fishing hook through his right thumb. After considerable work by the hospital staff to remove the hook and carefully bandaging his throbbing thumb, they were back on the road with high expectations of a great weekend of fishing.

It was a beautiful warm morning as Bob and his buddies lined the side of the river, each of them eager to catch their share of the fish. Spotting a rock further out in the water, Bob decided he would have more success by climbing upon the rock and fishing from there. It was a prime location, but the rock was slippery and without warning, he slid off the back of the rock, scraping both shins on the way down. He not only was soaking wet, but now has two badly skinned shins to go with his throbbing right thumb.

That evening at the motel, everyone was preparing for the short drive into town for dinner. Hurting from his previous mishaps, Bob limped toward the shower with a bandage on his right thumb and bandages on both of his shins. The warm water should sooth the pain and he knew he would feel much better after he had something to eat and a good night's rest. Suddenly, Denny heard a loud thump and a yell that could be heard over the noise of the TV. Hurrying to the bathroom to see what happened, he found Bob had fallen in the tub and possibly broken or cracked his ribs.

Arriving home, Bob was greeted at the door by his wife, who could hardly wait to hear about his fishing trip. Just grateful to be home, with his thumb still throbbing, barely able to walk, and holding his painful ribs, he tells her: "Take all that damn fishing gear back to the store, and don't ever buy me any more. "I'm never going fishing again."

Motor Down

On July 23, 1974, Deputy Chuck Anderson, who was working the radar car, and I decided to team up and work a section of Sprague Avenue. We set up radar with me being chase motor on the north side of the street, on either North McCabe or North Blake Road, which is a couple blocks east of McDonald Road.

I was sitting on my motor next to the driver's door of the radar car when the alarm went off indicating a speeder had entered the range of the radar unit. Chuck yelled out the speed of a red pickup truck traveling westbound at 50 mph in the posted 35 mph zone. Catching the slowing vehicle at the traffic signal at McDonald Road, the pickup turned north around the corner and stopped on McDonald, about 100 feet from the intersection. I positioned the motor a few feet behind the driver's side rear corner of the vehicle. After calling radio to indicate I would be out with the Idaho plate, I cautiously approached a slender male driver in his early 20s. The vehicle engine was still running, so I asked him if he would turn it off. He responded that if he did, he wouldn't be able to get it started.

At the time it seemed like just another write-and-release routine traffic stop. I had asked for and received his driver's license, but when I asked for the registration, he began to look around like he didn't know where it was. He finally reached over and opened the glove compartment, where I caught a glimpse of the handle of a gun just before he quickly closed it. I told him to stay put and upright as I returned to my motor to use the radio. Standing on the right side of the motor, which placed me near the center of the pickup, I called for the radar car to come for backup, and then called radio to run a records check on a Mark Crowder.

Others must have recognized the name, as I recalled there was some chatter on the radio, just as the pickup truck instantly accelerated in reverse, smoking both tires. I started to back up and side step toward the curb but was knocked off balance. My motor crashed to the right side, landing beside my left leg. As I fell backwards, I grabbed what I believe was the tailgate.

The vehicle traveled about the length of itself before coming to a stop with the left rear wheel on top of the front of my motor and the right rear wheel up on the curb. The driver then put the vehicle in a forward gear and accelerated away again, smoking both tires. With this action, I let go of what I believe was the bumper, leaving me uninjured. This occurred as Deputy Anderson came around the corner, which started a hot pursuit. Blowing the stop sign at Broadway, the vehicles reached a speed of 70 mph, before Crowder's vehicle was broad-sided at the next major intersection of Mission Avenue. There Crowder exited the pickup, apparently without the gun, leaving the scene on foot.

Interesting notes are that I still had Mark Crowder's drivers license. The 1967 or 1968 Chevrolet pickup was stolen out of Idaho, as well as the gun in the glove compartment. Deputy Tony White working District #1 was involved in a T-bone accident at the intersection of Sprague Avenue and Park Road, while responding to my location. Detective Lucky Lang fired a shot at Crowder near Mission Avenue to try to get him to stop, and Deputy Bruce Mathews with his partner, chased down the fleeing suspect after responding from Highway 27 near Freeman.

A Dirt Bike Problem

Over a number of weeks, a dirt bike had been eluding the sheriff's patrol cars in the area of East 53rd Avenue, between South Regal and South Perry Street on Spokane's south side. Deputies reported the Sheriff's Department had received several complaints from local citizens about a teenage rider believed not yet old enough for a driver's license, running his red-colored dirt bike up and down 53rd. They indicated the unlicensed bike was loud, appeared to be speeding, and not always making room for the automobiles. It usually occurred in the late afternoon or early evening, so our swing shift spent a number of days patrolling the area. When the rider spotted a patrol car, he would leave the road using a dirt bike trail and go into an open field to elude them. He would then stop some distance away and taunt the officers.

One evening I thought I would see if I might be able to catch him. I was hoping if he saw my motor he might not head for the field. I was wrong....but I did not attempt to follow him that time. A few nights later I thought I would give chase using the same bike trail that he used to leave the roadway. There was some brush, a few trees, and a couple of big rocks, but the problem was the rut was cut so deep I was rubbing the foot boards on my motor. Again, he got away, then stopped some distance away and taunted me.

It had somehow become personal! The next evening I was back there and caught him traveling on the roadway coming my direction. I was hoping to cut him off at the bike trail, but no such luck, as he was closer to the exit and again eluded me. Sitting on the roadway pondering my next move, a pickup truck came down the road. The vehicle pulled up, stopped beside me, and this gentleman asked, "Would you like to know where he lives?"

What a break! I pulled off 53rd onto South Perry, and stopped at the second house on the left. A man answered and asked if he could help me. I inquired

if he had a son, how old the son was, and did his son have a red dirt bike. Bingo!

The dad was very cooperative and told me that his son had permission to ride the bike in the field, but that he was instructed to push the bike the short distance to and from their house. He asked if I would like to talk to his boy. When I answered "Yes," he responded that his boy would probably not come home if he saw the police motor parked in the street. He invited me to put my motor inside the garage with the garage door down. Seated on my motor, we waited as I sat visiting with mom and dad. Before long we heard a noise outside. The suspect knew his mom and dad were there, so he had walked the bike home and was now pushing the button on the outside garage door opener. This allowed the garage door to open where he had an unexpected surprise when he came face to face with a Spokane County Sheriff's Department motor officer. It was one of those moments when a picture would have been worth a thousand words.

Jim Alma, Spokane Valley, after being run down by a fleeing felon. *(Courtesy Jim Alma)*

Mike Ebel – hired by the Spokane County Sheriff in 1971

Mike Ebel, 1976, in the Spokane Valley, Ponderosa neighborhood. *(Courtesy Tim Downing)*

Marv Patrick – hired by the Spokane County Sheriff in 1974

Marv Patrick at Greenacres, 1982. *(Courtesy Tim Downing)*

SPOKANE COUNTY SHERIFF

Marv Patrick, 1980s. *(Courtesy Tim Downing)*

1978 Motor School. From left: Spokane County Sheriff's Officers: Marv Patrick, Ron "Oscar" Seitz, Tim Downing, and Phil Shatzer. Spokane Police Officers: Paul Meissner, Kenneth Krogh, Terry Morehouse, Mike Prim, Jay Jones, and Earl Ennis (with full face helmet). *(Courtesy Tim Downing)*

Marv Patrick 1980s. *(Courtesy Tim Downing)*

Deputy Mike McClanahan, Deputy Marv Patrick, Deputy Ivan Frederickson, Lt. Carl Sweatt, Sgt. Ray Bolstad shaking hands with President Jimmy Carter, and W.S.P. trooper Ron Snyder. This photo was taken around 1980 when Jimmy Carter was again running for president. The motor bulls in the photo were assigned to escort the president from the airport to the downtown area. At this time, the city was still using Harley-Davidsons. However, the county motor bulls had just changed from the Harley-Davidson to Kawasaki 1000s. *(Courtesy Tim Downing)*

Ivan Dale Fredrickson – hired by the Spokane County Sheriff in 1974

S
P
O
K
A
N
E

C
O
U
N
T
Y

S
H
E
R
I
F
F

Ivan Fredrickson, circa 1981. *(Courtesy Tim Downing)*

Jim Finke, Ivan Fredrickson, and Marvin Patrick. *(Courtesy Tim Downing)*

Ivan Fredrickson was born in Compton, California to Olai and Violet Fredrickson. His father was a cement contractor, and his mother a homemaker. He has two surviving brothers, Norm and Lewis. Norm is two years older and Lewis is two years younger.

Ivan was raised in Compton, Turlock, and Long Beach, California. He attended grade school and high school in Milliken and Long Beach. He attended two colleges, Cerritos in California and Eastern Washington University. He earned a degree in criminal law from Eastern Washington.

As a young man, prior to going into the Marine Corps, he was a dishwasher. He later worked as a crop picker in Turlock and a bobtail truck driver and a railroad guard for Union Pacific.

In the Marine Corps, he was stationed in South Vietnam from '68 to '69 as a sniper. At the end of his obligation in the Marines, he was honorably discharged as a corporal.

Ivan came to Spokane in 1974 during Expo '74. Following his move to Spokane, he joined the Spokane County Sheriff's Office, where he met his current wife, Shauna, at Nature's Kitchen in the Spokane Valley. They were married in 2002. He has one son, Nathan.

During Ivan's tenure with the sheriffs department he rode motor for a total of eight years. During his time on motor, there was a total of four deputies. Two worked day shift and the other two swing shift.

All in all, his time as a deputy sheriff made him feel as if he were making a difference in serving the public. Ivan's biggest influence in his career was Lt. Dick Lovejoy, who he worked for when he was assigned to patrol and the SWAT Team. He also has great respect for his motor training officer, Mike McClanahan, and John Simmons, patrol training officer. His motor partners were Mike McClanahan, Marv Patrick, and Oscar Sietz. Among his most memorable experiences during his entire time with the sheriff's department was being assigned to motor, especially on warm sunny days, as well as the escorting the Lilac Parade and presidential motorcades. His happiest memories on the department were when he was assigned to motor and when he joined the SWAT Team. Ivan will be remembered by his peers as a person who can always be trusted – he could be counted on to always have his partner's back. Since his retirement, Ivan's main pastimes are riding his Harley, boating, and especially hiking with his wife. The main things he has learned in life are trying to look at the bright things and put his faith in the Lord.

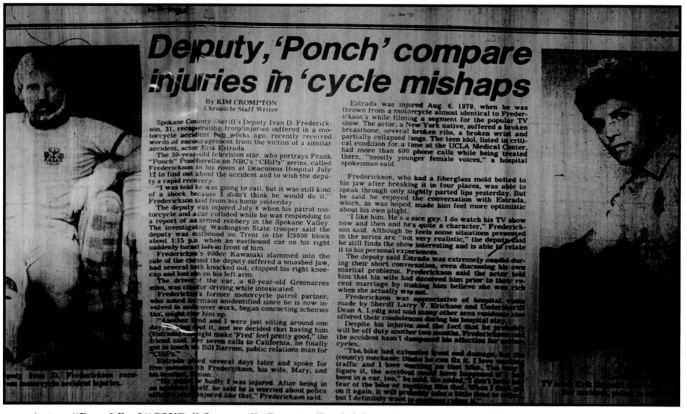

Actor, "Ponch" of "CHiPs" fame calls Deputy Fredrickson to compare accidents. *(Courtesy Tim Downing)*

The following is a quote taken from the *Spokesman Review* on July 9, 1979:

**Deputy, 'Ponch' compare injuries
in cycle mishaps**

Spokane County Sheriff's deputy Ivan Fredrickson, 31, recuperating, from injuries suffered in a motorcycle accident two weeks ago, recently received words of encouragement from the victim of a similar accident, actor Erik Estrada.

The 30-year-old television star, who portrays Frank Ponch Poncherello on NBC's "CHiPS" series, called Fredrickson in his room at Deaconess hospital July 12 to find out about the accident and to wish the deputy a rapid recovery.

"I was told he was going to call, but it was still kind of a shock because I didn't think he would do it," Fredrickson said from his home yesterday. The deputy was injured July 8 when his patrol motorcycle and a car collided while he was responding to a report of an armed robbery in the Spokane Valley. The investigating Washington state trooper said the deputy was eastbound on Trent in the East 9800 block about 1:15 PM when eastbound car on his right suddenly turned left in front of him.

Fredrickson's 900cc Kawasaki slammed into the side of the car and the deputy suffered a smashed jaw, had several teeth knocked out, chipped his right kneecap and lost skin on his left arm. The driver of the car, a 60-year-old Greenacres man, was cited for driving while intoxicated.

Fredrickson's former motorcycle patrol partner, Marv Patrick, began concocting schemes that might cheer him up.

"Another friend and I were just sitting around one day, talking about it, and we decided that having him (Estrada) call might make Fred feel pretty good," the friend said. After several calls to California, he finally got in touch with Bill Barroom, public relations manager for "CHiPs."

Estrada phoned several days later and spoke for five minutes with Fredrickson, his wife, Mary, and his brother, Norman. "He asked how badly I was injured. After being in an accident himself, he said he is worried about police officers who get injured like that," Fredrickson said.

Estrada was injured August 6, 1979, when he was thrown from a motorcycle almost identical to Fredrickson's while filming a segment for the popular TV show. The actor, a New York native, suffered a broken breastbone, several broken ribs, a broken wrist, and partially collapsed lungs. The teen idol listed in critical condition for a time at the UCLA medical center, had more than 600 phone calls while being treated there. "Mostly younger female voices," a hospital spokesman said.

Fredrickson, who had a fiberglass mold bolted to his jaw after breaking it in four places, was able to speak through only slightly parted lips yesterday. But he said he enjoyed the conversation with Estrada, which, as was hoped, made him feel more optimistic about his own plight.

"I like him. He's a nice guy, I do watch his TV show now and then, and he's quite a character," Fredrickson said. Although he feels some situations presented in this series are not very realistic, the deputy said he still finds the show interesting and is able to relate it to his personal experiences.

The deputy said Estrada was extremely candid during the short conversation, even discussing his own marital problems. Fredrickson said the actor told him that his wife had deceived him prior to their recent marriage by making him believe she was rich when she actually was not.

Fredrickson was appreciative of hospital visits made by Sheriff Larry D. Erickson and Undersheriff Dean Lydig and said many other area residents also offered their condolences during his hospital stay. Despite his injuries and the fact that he probably will be off-duty another two months, Fredrickson said the accident hasn't dampened his affection for motorcycles.

"The bike had extensive front end damage, but the (county) mechanic thinks he can fix it. I love working traffic and I love working on that bike. The way I figure it, the accident could have happened if I had been in the car, too," he said. He added, "I don't have any fear of the bike or anything like that. When I first get on it again it will probably take a little time to adjust, but I definitely want to continue riding it."

The cast of CHiPs, from left: Erik Estrada as "Ponch", Robert Pine as Getraer, and Larry Wilcox as Jon. *(Photo from Wikipedia)*

Information on CHiPs from Wikipedia

Larry Wilcox (Jon) and Erik Estrada did a great deal of their own motorcycle riding, and performed many smaller stunts themselves. Although Wilcox emerged relatively injury-free, Estrada suffered various injuries several times throughout the run of the series. In several early first season episodes, a huge bruise or scar can be seen on his arm after he was flung from one of the motorcycles and skidded along the ground. But his worst accident came when he was seriously injured in a motorcycle accident while filming a season three episode in August 1979, fracturing several ribs and breaking both wrists. The accident and Estrada's subsequent hospitalization was incorporated into the series' storyline.

Prior to being cast in CHiPs Estrada had no experience with motorcycles, so he underwent an intensive eight-week course, learning how to ride. In 2007, it was revealed that he did not hold a motorcycle license at the time CHiPs was in production, and only qualified for a license after three attempts, while preparing for an appearance on the reality television show Back to the Grind.

Jim Finke – hired by the Spokane County Sheriff in 1974

Jim Finke, circa 1980, new 1000 cc Kawasaki. *(Courtesy Tim Downing)*

Jim Finke went to work with the Spokane County Sheriff's Department on February 1974. In May of 1977, he was assigned to motor, where he rode for six years. He was trained on motor by Jerry Brady. Some of the other partners he rode with were Marv Patrick, Ivan Fredrickson, Jim Graves, Bruce Minor, and a little with Ron Seitz. During that time he rode many Lilac Parades, escorted Jimmy Carter and his wife, Bob Dole, Dick Cheney, George H. Bush Sr., Al Gore, and several other presidential candidates and dignitaries who came to town. Jim was one of the only riders who did not crash and get hurt.

Jim was on the SWAT Team for six years, being assigned as sniper at the end. Following his motor career, he was promoted to detective in 1984, where he worked auto theft, checks, and fraud cases. He was also on the hostage negotiations team. In 1990, he was promoted to sergeant. He was in patrol for six years on all three shifts. In 1996, he was promoted to lieutenant. He stayed in patrol for a couple of years. In 1998, Jim went to the FBI National Academy in Washington, D.C., where he met Director Louis Freeh, Henry Kissinger, and Frank Abernathy, the character depicted in the movie *Catch Me If You Can*. During his time in Washington, also in 1998, he had great educational experiences, including touring the White House, the Capitol, and the Mall. It was a busy year!

Finke was the day shift patrol manager and traffic manager for six years. He then went into Community Services and managed the SCOPE people and stations, Critical Incident Management commander, worked with the Dispatch Center and Explosives Disposal Unit, and did special projects until he retired January 10, 2010. He had 36 years of a very enjoyable career. He liked going to work and doing the things he was called on to do. He looks back fondly on all of those years, and all of the people he had the opportunity to work and serve with, including the civilian staff.

Larry Olson – hired by the Spokane County Sheriff in 1974

Larry Olson, circa 1979. *(Courtesy Larry Olson)*

Larry Olson was born on July 12, 1948, in Spokane at the old St. Lukes Hospital, which was located on West Boone, near the old Natatorium Park site. Larry's father, Lon R. Olson, was born in Minnesota and was the son of German/Norwegian immigrants who later settled in Spokane. When they married, Larry's mother was 15 and his father was 18. Following their marriage, his father joined the U.S. Army, 82nd Airborne Division. He served in Germany as part of the Occupational Forces in 1945.

Following his discharge, his father joined the Iron Workers Union. However, in that work there were frequent periods of unemployment. To supplement his income, he became a major neW.S.P.aper car-

rier (a motor route) in the Airway Heights/Fairchild Air Force Base area. After paper deliveries, which generally ended at 7 a.m., his father found further income by starting his own salvage business. In that business he dismantled buildings at the base. The materials from this salvage were used for resale as building materials.

For two years, Larry and his brother Rex, who was three years younger, would help their father with both of his sideline jobs, which included Sunday paper deliveries (the largest paper of the week) by wrapping them in rubber bands or, when it was raining, wrapping them in wax paper and rubber banding. Their days started at two in the morning. Larry had that job from the age of from nine to twelve. Consequently, beginning in 1957, when he was nine and his brother was six, they both began developing their strong work ethic. Although there were child labor laws designed to prevent this, they both had to work at early ages.

When Larry reached the age of 17, he became the boss—overseeing their last salvage job, which was the dismantling of the Boise Cascade Lumber mill in Winchester, Idaho. That mill had been closed since 1964. The Winchester salvage project lasted for a year and a half, during which time his family lived in Winchester.

At Winchester, he attended Highland High School as a junior (a class of 35 students). While there, Larry lettered in football, was on the honor roll, and supervised the salvage crew at the lumber mill – assigning jobs, overseeing their work, making deliveries and payroll. Also, at this same time, his father was employed as an iron worker at Little Goose and Dworshak dams.

During the course of his salvage work, one of the deliveries Larry made could have easily ended in his death. He had 3,000 bricks loaded on pallets on a 1952 Ford 2-ton flatbed truck headed for Lewiston. While going down the new Winchester grade, he attempted to slow the truck by down-shifting the two-speed rear end to a lower gear, at which time the motor died, leaving him free wheeling. Even pressing the brake and pulling the emergency brake lever (which was on the driveline) as hard as he could, he was unable to stop the truck. He contemplated jumping at 35 mph because he was gaining speed. However, he felt it would be too dangerous to abandon the truck, especially if any other vehicles happened to be coming toward it. He finally brought the truck to a stop with all brakes glowing and smoking. After the Boise Cascade mill salvage job was finished, his family moved back to their home in the Spokane Valley.

Larry's mother was a typical mother of English descent. She maintained the household, overseeing a family of five children, two boys and three girls. Larry was the oldest. Larry's siblings are Diana

Crane, born in 1949; Rex Olson, born in 1951; Candice Halvorson, born in 1952; and Francine Lamb born in 1965.

Larry started school at Opportunity Elementary in the Spokane Valley; University Elementary (2nd through 5th grade), Spokane Valley; Greenacres Elementary (6th grade), Spokane Valley; Sunset Elementary (7th and part of 8th grade), Airway Heights; North Pines Junior High (second half 8th and 9th grade),Spokane Valley; University High (10th and 12th grades), Spokane Valley; and Highland High (11th grade), Meidlmont, Idaho.

Beyond working for his father, Larry worked for Perfection Tire, mounting/balancing tires while a senior in high school. After graduation in 1967, he worked for a paving company, based in Moses Lake, that had contracts all over Washington and Idaho. His uncle Fred got him that job. It paid union scale of $3.25/hr when minimum wage was $1.60/hr.

As a result, Larry managed to save over $4,000 for his freshman year at WSU. He didn't have a bank account at the time, so he sent his money to his mother to open an account and deposit it. However, when Larry came home, he learned his alcoholic parents had spent all but $400.

During his early years, Larry's mother managed to feed her family with minimal income. To help the family, Larry shoveled snow in the winter and eventually worked for Perfection Tire. He later got a job at Brown Building Supply, doing salvage and yard work. His father introduced him to Richard (Dick) Brown, owner of Brown Building Materials. He worked for Dick for two years while attending school at SFCC. He attended Spokane Community College at the Falls from 1967 to 1969, graduating with an AA. During his first two years at Spokane Community College, he was a liberal arts student with goals of becoming a teacher.

Larry enlisted in the U.S. Marine Corps in September 1970 and went to basic training in San Diego. His training was cut short by a sudden onset of hyper-thyroidism, which sent his metabolism and blood pressure to an over-acceptable high rate. As a result, he was given a medical discharge and sent home to deal with the problem with his personal physician. He asked the Marine doctor what was wrong and was told the Marine Corps didn't have time to help him find the problem and to continue his boot camp training. Larry was discharged 45 days into boot camp.

He then enrolled at Eastern Washington State College (prior to the name change to Eastern Washington University), graduating in 1971 with a BA. At EWU, he pursued his goal of being a math/science teacher. However, due to being self-supporting (working 40 hours a week on swing shift at a cut-shop, making little boards out of big boards), his dedication to studying suffered and his grade point average was under 3.0. During his junior year at EWU, he looked at the teaching job prospects, which were dismal considering his competition with the full-time students with higher GPAs.

Larry met his wife, Marcia Erickson, during the 1967/68 school year. Marcia, a Mead High School graduate of 1967, was also attending SFCC. At the time, she was studying for her associate of arts degree, with an emphasis on secretarial skills. They dated for the next two years and married August 23, 1969, at the Opportunity Presbyterian Church.

Marcia got a secretarial job for Weyerhaeuser at a cut shop at Spokane Industrial Park, which led to Larry getting a job there with higher pay and medical benefits. He worked there for two years on swing shift while attending and paying his way at EWU. He worked his way up to swing shift foreman. He took a cut in pay to hire on with the Spokane County Sheriff.

Larry got a job for a returning Vietnam veteran friend and U-High classmate, Mike Chapman. One day he asked him if he was interested in taking the test for the Spokane County Sheriff's Department, which Chapman stated he was planning to take. Larry signed up and took the test, which was the first civil service test he had ever taken. He finished 40 out of 250 – not high enough to be hired.

Following this setback, he took the test for the Spokane Police Department. Prior to taking this test,

he reviewed some study material, which helped him greatly. As a result, he placed 11th on the Spokane Police Department test. The following year, he placed first on the testing for the Spokane County Sheriff's Department. On February 8, 1974, Larry was hired by the Spokane County Sheriff, William J. Reilly, as part of a surge in anticipation of policing needs created by Expo '74 in Spokane.

After finishing motor school in 1976, Larry was assigned "dirt bike patrol." In that capacity, he patrolled and responded to complaints in suburban areas for dirt bikes on the roadway or trespassing on private property. They rode Yamaha 250 enduros (set up as police bikes). They always rode in pairs. Larry's career as a motor officer covered both day and swing shift and dirt bike patrol and traffic patrol.

He eventually had several partners, including Jim Finke and Larry Miller. However, his longest tenured partner was Marv Patrick, whom he sees periodically at retired deputies meetings and social functions.

In 1977, he was reassigned to traffic motor and rode a Kawasaki KZ900. His partners were Marv Patrick and Larry Miller. In that position he worked some swing shift and day shift. He was reassigned to patrol after the 1978 riding season. In 1986, he was promoted to detective/corporal. During the time Larry rode motor, there were four motors on both day shift and swing shift. Larry also rode motor at the opening ceremony of the Lilac Parade.

During Larry's career in law enforcement, he has been surrounded by friends of good character, mostly other law enforcement people. As a law enforcement officer, his goal was to set a good example for everyone he came in contact with, both in his job and during his lifetime. During his son's formative years, he got involved in Cub Scouts/Boy Scouts. He was Cub Master for two years and Scoutmaster for six years. His wife and daughter went on many of the outings as well. His troop had seven boys who eventually achieved the rank of Eagle Scout, his son being one of them. He had a great support group of parents.

During his career, his biggest influence was his training officer, Jim Hill. Hill had served with the Washington, D.C., police and was very passionate about providing the best service possible to the public.

Some of the more interesting events that have occurred during Larry's law enforcement career are paraphrased from his written experiences as follows:

In traffic patrol, they almost always worked in pairs. One hot summer day, Larry and his motor partner Marv set up on Crestline about two blocks north of Francis in the shade of a tree. They both heard a car accelerating hard coming their way. Marv grabbed his radar gun and held it up for Larry to see and said, "Start your motor." A late '60s Mopar hit the radar at 75 in a 35 zone. Larry gave chase on the KZ900, which took about two blocks to catch up to the Mopar. After the stop, he performed all the usual for issuance of a speeding ticket, but kept looking for Marv to join him.

Finally, after Larry issued the ticket, Marv showed up. Larry then asked him, "What took so long?" Marv explained that, in the excitement, he threw his motor over to the right to pull up the kickstand harder than usual and ended up tipping his motor over in the grassy swale next to him. Unfortunately, it had flooded the engine and took awhile to start. This would have made a great YouTube video, on what not to do, if you tube had existed at the time.

Then there was the case of the world's most expensive hamburger. This happened when Larry was in an unmarked car while his motor was in the shop for service/repair. He was eastbound on Trails Road, near Spotted Road, with the moving radar. Westbound was a late '60s early '70s Chevelle. He picked his speed up at 93 in a 55 zone. Larry had to come to a stop and turn around and accelerate hard to catch up with the Chevelle, which he wasn't able to do until Hayford Road and Highway 2, where he saw him pull into the Longhorn Burger stop. He ordered a hamburger, but the fine for 38 miles over the limit increased the cost of the hamburger to over $100.

Another adventure in traffic enforcement was a pursuit he was involved in with an unlicensed dirt bike with a passenger on the county road near Thorpe and Assembly. Having ridden dirt bikes from the time he was 16, he knew the awkwardness and instability of having a passenger. The dirt bike failed to stop and turned on an abandoned trolley track/roadbed east of Assembly. It was smooth and practically flat. His pursuit lasted about a mile on this trolley roadbed when a dip in the dirt roadbed caused him to lose control and dump his bike on its side. He broke the windshield, headlight and tore his britches but was unhurt. He could see the dirt bike and rider were both on the ground about 50 feet ahead of him and his passenger was gone.

At this time, Larry ran up to the dirt bike operator, who was attempting to restart his motorcycle, and took him into custody. Directly in front of the downed dirt bike were two concrete retaining walls of a missing bridge about 20 feet apart and a ravine about 20 feet deep. Had the dirt bike not gone down, it very well could have resulted in a death. The dirt bike driver had to pay for all the damage to Larry's motor as well as a pair of new britches.

Larry's partner, Marv Patrick, was frequently coming up with quotes and actions that were humorous. One frosty morning, Larry had on his leather jacket. Marv had only his short-sleeved shirt. While they were on Sprague eastbound from I-90, Larry noticed Marv was covered in goose bumps and was shivering. Larry asked him if he was cold. He took a deep breath and relaxed, allowing the goose bumps to fade and said, "No, my badge keeps me warm."

As a detective, many of Larry's cases came and went, but two cases come to mind. Both were burglary investigations. The first was the burglary of the Fairfield Pharmacy. Larry had developed information on suspects who buried the drugs they stole in a field behind their house. However, the suspects had moved from the house. With permission of the property owner, Larry went to the house with two members of the Spokane Metal Detectors club. They located the buried stash and were able to charge and arrest the suspects.

Also, during the time Larry was a detective, he initiated the licensing and reporting requirements of pawn shops and secondhand dealers. In that position, he worked with TIEPIN (The Inland Empire Police Information Network) to established a means of creating a database. He supervised volunteers to enter the data. While reviewing some pawnshop reports, he saw property that appeared to be related to an extensive burglary of a Spokane secondhand dealer.

When AIDS was a little known disease, he arrested a man who knew he was infected as a result of heroin addiction/needle sharing. That man was very active sexually with many women and infected his wife, who bore a daughter who was born with AIDS. His investigation resulted in the suspect's arrest and sentencing to prison. Unfortunately, his daughter passed away at around age six or seven.

Larry loves old cars and hot rods and has restored five custom cars/hot rods in his lifetime. He still owns three: a 1933 Plymouth coupe, a 1957 Ford Fairlane 500 2dr hardtop, and a 1969 Ford Mustang Mach 1. Two others he restored and sold were a 1957 Ford Fairlane 500 sport coupe and a 1957 Fairlane 500 Sunliner (convertible).

While on the sheriff's department, Larry felt his role model was Bob Bean, who sometimes came across as cantankerous but had a heart of gold. Bob rode motor for quite a few years for the sheriff's office, and later became the president of the Washington Blue Knights chapter, of which Larry is also a member. Bob rode until he was 73, when he suffered a stroke while riding his motorcycle and received life-threatening injuries to which he later succumbed.

Larry also likes to carve wood and has won several ribbons at the Spokane County Fair. By all of Larry's co-workers, he was known and will be remembered as an exceptionally hard worker with integrity, who stands up for his beliefs.

A late '60s Mopar, similar to the one Larry gave chase to, which took about two blocks to catch up to. *(Public domain)*

Larry Miller – hired by the Spokane County Sheriff in 1973

Larry Miller, Spokane Valley, 1979. *(Courtesy Larry Miller)*

Larry Miller joined the Spokane County Sheriff's Department on August 1, 1973, as a cadet. On September 1, 1974, he became a communication officer for the department and, on February 20, 1975, he became a deputy.

His law enforcement motor experience began in 1977, when he attended motor school and was assigned that same year to dirt bike patrol with Larry Olson as his motor partner. In 1979, he was assigned to street patrol with Gary Grose as his motor partner. At that time, he was assigned a 900 cc 1976 Kawasaki.

In 1981, Larry was promoted to detective and, in 1996, he took over the job for the department as the polygraph examiner. Following 32 years with the Spokane Sheriff's Department, Larry retired in 2005.

In looking back at his life, Larry said his law enforcement career was inspired by one of his old neighbors, retired Washington State Patrolman Sergeant Dwight Nye, who was a trooper during the 1950s.

Interestingly, other members of Larry's family have also been, and are, members of the law enforcement community. His wife, Lieutenant Laurie Miller, retired from the Spokane County Sheriff's Department in June of 2017. Laurie's daughter, Sarah, works in the Spokane County Jail as a secretary and Sarah's husband is Deputy Chad Ruff. Larry's brother, David Miller, is a retired Washington State Trooper (1975 to 2005). His last assignment was working patrol in North Spokane. Also, Larry's brother-in-law, Roy Meye, is also a retired Washington State trooper.

Larry and Laurie Miller, circa 2016. *(Courtesy Larry Miller)*

Ronald W. Seitz – hired by the Spokane County Sheriff in 1974

Ron Seitz, circa 1982. *(Courtesy Ron Seitz)*

Ronald Seitz was born in Spokane, to William and Thelma Seitz. Ron and his four sisters were all raised at Liberty Lake. He went to Greenacres Grade School and Central Valley High School. He received an AA Degree in Law Enforcement from Spokane Community College.

On May 1, 1974, Ron joined the Spokane County Sheriff's Office. In 1982, he was assigned to the traffic unit, where he rode motor for a year. Shortly after, the unit was disbanded over politics with the sheriff and county commissioners.

Ron met his wife, Sabrina, while guarding a prisoner at Sacred Heart Hospital. They have three children – one daughter and two sons.

Ron feels the most important thing he has learned from his career was patience. He always felt it was important to teach his three kids honesty, respect, and love for each other – something he also felt was important to show the public during his career.

The biggest influence and role model in Ron's life was his father William, who also was a deputy with the Spokane County Sheriff's Department beginning in 1956. In honor of him, Ron wore his father's SCSO collar insignia for the duration of his tenure on the department. William Seitz's biography is also in this book, as provided by Ron.

During the time Ron rode motor, his partners were Ivan Fredrikson, Jim Finke, and Marv Patrick. He is still in touch with all of them. During Ron's time on motor, there were only four people with that assignment, two on day shift, and two on swing shift.

One of Ron's most memorable and saddest experiences was finding and saving a five-year-old girl who fell in the river while she was feeding ducks. Unfortunately, she died three months later.

Another meaningful event in Ron's career was being involved in the capture of the FBI's 15th most-wanted person on a SWAT callout. This occurred in August in 1984. The arrest was made in Elk, Washington, with the following members of the SWAT Team involved: Knetchtell, Fredrickson, Seitz, Downing, Howard, Mulvey, Wakefield, Ellingson, Shatzer, and Aubrey. Ron was on the Spokane County SWAT Team for 13 years. During that time he attended many SWAT team schools, consistently receiving a #1 rating from them.

Among Ron's happiest memories was being hired by the Spokane County Sheriff's Department on May 1, 1974, and watching his oldest son being sworn in for the Spokane City Police Department in January of 2016.

The accomplishments he's most proud of is set-

Ron Seitz and Ivan Fredrickson at Geiger Field for motorcycle qualification in 1982. *(Courtesy Ron Seitz)*

ting his goals to become a member of the SWAT team, and riding motor for the department. Among Ron's best qualities was being able to inspire team members and achieve many competitive goals. He also took pride in the fact the he could be counted on as a reliable and dependable team member. The main thing he feels he has learned in life is to be respectful of others, and not to pre-judge anyone. During Ron's spare time he enjoys taking care of his five-acre farm and an additional 20-acre piece of property.

Ron Seitz and his father, William Seitz, in 1959. *(Courtesy Ron Siitz)*

Retired sheriff deputies, left to right: Mark Henderson, retired detective Spokane County Sheriff's office; Jim Graves, retired detective and motor officer, Spokane County Sheriff's Office; Tucker Seitz, third-generation law enforcement in Seitz family, Spokane Police Department; Ken Downing (Don't know his department), Bellevue Washington, Ron Seitz, retired motor officer, Spokane County Sheriff's Office and second-generation law-enforcement; Bart Carlson, retired Los Angeles Police Department motor officer; Ivan Fredrikson, retired motor officer Spokane County Sheriff's Office. *(Courtesy Ron Seitz)*

Among Ron's saddest memories from his law enforcement career, was the death of Kaila Ann Snyder. She was the five-year-old girl who fell into the river while feeding ducks. Ron located her and pulled her from the water. Sadly, she died, as a result of her accident, three months later.

Ron wanted this photo of her to be printed in this book to honor her memory. *(Courtesy Ron Seitz)*

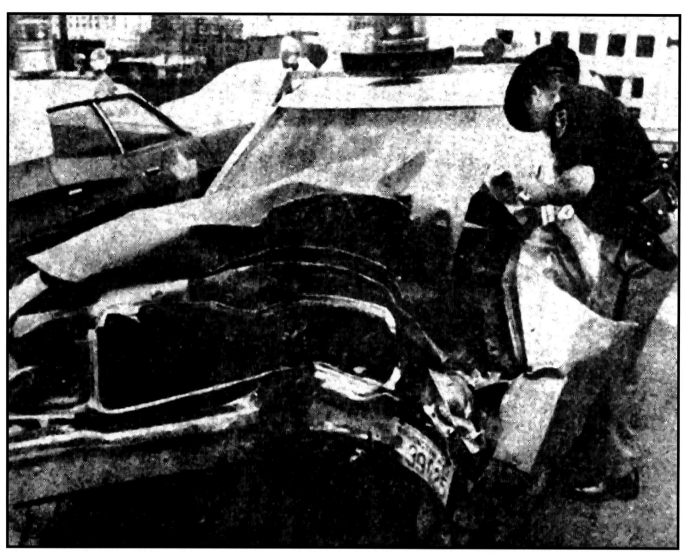

Damage to Sheriff's Department prowl car in which deputy Ronald W. Seitz suffered multiple lacerations in a high-speed chase is inspected by Sheriff's Lt. John H. McGregor. In another accident, John McGregor lost his leg while he was directing traffic on East Sprague, but he continued in service with a prosthetic leg. *(Courtesy Ron Seitz)*

The following narrative was written about the above news photo, which appeared in the *Spokesman-Review* on Saturday, July 9, 1977:

Deputy Hurt During Wild Valley Chase

A Spokane County Sheriff's officer narrowly escaped serious injury or possible death early today when his prowl car plowed into a tree during a high speed chase.

Deputy Ronald W. Seitz suffered multiple lacerations in the accident near Fourth and Dishman-Mica Highway. He was treated at Valley General Hospital and released shortly after the 5 a.m. accident.

The 16-year-old driver of the fleeing auto, which was reported stolen last night by Spokane Valley residents, was booked into the County-City Jail on charges of reckless driving, sheriff's officers reported. He was expected to be turned over to juvenile authorities later on a charge of taking a motor vehicle without the owner's permission.

Seitz, whose vehicle looked like an accordion from the impact, said he had chased the stolen car earlier at an estimated 90 miles an hour south on Bowdish before losing sight of it. A half-hour later, he reported. he again spotted the car and he and other officers gave chase, again at speeds of 90 miles per hour. Heading north on the Dishman-Mica highway, Seitz apparently attempted to "bump" the fleeing car to halt the driver, officers reported. However, the prowl car veered off the roadway and struck one of the few trees in the area.

Other deputies continued the chase north on Argonne until the youth abandoned the car at Knox and Argonne and officers apprehended him on foot.

Richard Timothy Downing – hired by the Spokane County Sheriff in 1974

Motorcycle Officer Tim Downing, circa 1999. *(Courtesy Tim Downing)*

Tim Downing was born in Spokane in 1954 to Richard and Margaret Downing. At the time, the family lived in Hillyard, where his father worked for the Great Northern Railroad. Tim has one sibling, a brother. They were both raised in Hillyard. Tim's family came from a long line of railroaders.

Tim attended Linwood Grade School, Salk Junior High, and North Central High School. Following graduation from North Central, Tim attended Spokane Community College and Whitworth, where he studied criminal justice, public administration, and education. In 2012, he received a degree in criminal justice.

In 1974, Tim married Susan Johnson, whom he had met in the eighth grade. They were married for 37 years. During their marriage, they had five children, one girl and four boys. Tim's wife passed away in 2013, following a lengthy bout with cancer.

In 1974, Tim joined the Spokane County Sheriff's Department. Shortly after, while working the front desk with Mike Hirst, they decided to join the Air National Guard, where he served as a reservist for 20 years. Part of his time as a reservist was spent in Bosnia, where he was involved with a United Nations effort refueling fighter planes.

From left: Motorcycle Officers Eric Epperson, Phil Shatzer, Randy Strezlecki, Tim Downing, Tom Warner, and Don Manning, circa 1999. *(Courtesy Tim Downing)*

From left: Motorcycle Officers Tom Warner, Tim Downing shaking hands with Dick Cheney, Dave Vanwormer, Don Manning, Eric Epperson, and Dave Thornburg (far right), circa 2000. *(Courtesy Tim Downing)*

During Tim's time with the sheriff's department he rode motor from 1985 to 1987, then again from 1999 to 2002. One of his most rewarding and memorable experiences occurred when he saved the life of a suicide victim. In 1989, at approximately 11:00 p.m., he came upon a vehicle parked on the side of Rutter Parkway. He was traveling about 35 mph and caught a glimpse of what appeared to be a plastic hose fitted to the exhaust of a parked vehicle going into the driver's window. He immediately backed up and saw the car was running with a female passed out in the driver's side, with several photos of her family on the dashboard. The doors to the vehicle were locked, so he broke out a window, removed the victim, and immediately began giving C.P.R. However, when she was revived, she became immediately upset that he had saved her. Shortly after, he had her transported to the Sacred Heart psychiatric ward in an attempt to get her the help she needed. He later learned that she was successful in another suicide attempt.

During Tim's career, he learned that creativity works in all situations, which he always applied. Often when he was working traffic on motor, he had a rubber iguana lizard in his saddlebag, which he would bring out when he saw the person was upset. This typically always was met with a smile by the offender and a sudden mood change.

Robert Lee Yates, Jr., serial killer
Spokane, Washington
Murdered 14 women and one man

The following story was taken from *Murderpedia*, which is a free online encyclopedic dictionary of murderers and the largest database about serial killers and mass murderers around the world. The authors are familiar with this case and can vouch for the authenticity of this study.

Robert Lee Yates, Jr. (born May 27, 1952) is an American serial killer from Spokane, Washington. From 1996 to 1998, Yates is known to have murdered at least 13 women, all of whom were prostitutes working on Spokane's "Skid Row" on E. Sprague Avenue. Yates also confessed to two murders committed in Walla Walla in 1975 and a 1988 murder committed in Skagit County. In 2002, Yates was convicted of killing two women in Pierce County. He currently is on death row at the Washington State Penitentiary.

Yates growing up

Yates grew up in Oak Harbor, Washington, in a middle-class family that attended a local Seventh-day Adventist church. He graduated from Oak Harbor High School in 1970, and in 1975, he was hired by the Washington State Department of Corrections to work as a prison guard at the Washington State Penitentiary in Walla Walla. In October 1977, Yates enlisted in the United States Army, in which he became certified to fly transport airplanes and helicopters. Yates was stationed in various countries outside the continental United States, including Germany and later Somalia and Haiti during the United Nations peace-keeping missions of the 1990s. He earned several military awards and medals during his 18½ year military career, including three Army Achievement Medals, three Army Commendation Medals, two Armed Forces Expeditionary Medals, and three Meritorious Service Medals. Yates left the Army in April 1996.

Murders

The murders Yates committed between 1996 and 1998 in Spokane all involved prostitutes in Spokane's "Skid Row," area on E. Sprague Avenue. The victims were initially solicited for prostitution by Yates, who would have sex with them (often in his 1979 Ford van), sometimes do drugs with them, then kill them and dump their bodies in rural locations. All of his victims died of gunshot wounds to the head; eight of the murders were committed with a Raven .25-caliber handgun, and one attempted murder was linked to the same model of handgun. Autopsies of two of the victims indicated that the killer was a marksman aiming for the heart. One particularly bizarre detail of Yates' murders involved the case of Melody Murfin, whose body was buried just outside the bedroom window of Yates' family home.

On August 1, 1998, Yates picked up prostitute Christine Smith, who managed to escape after being shot, assaulted, and robbed. On September 19, 1998, Yates was asked to give a DNA sample to Spokane police after being stopped; he refused, stating that it was too extreme of a request for a "family man."

Convictions and appeals

Yates was arrested on April 18, 2000, for the murder of Jennifer Joseph. After his arrest a search warrant was executed on a 1977 white Corvette that he had previously owned. A white Corvette had been identified as the vehicle that one of the victims had last been seen in. Coincidentally, Yates had been pulled over in this vehicle while the

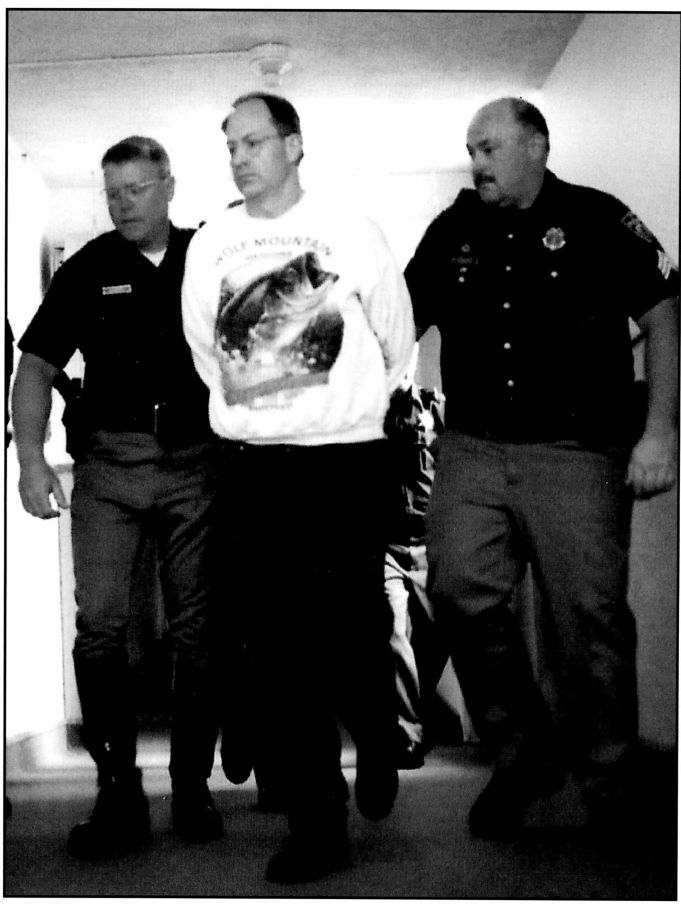

Robert Yates, serial murderer, being escorted to his first Spokane Superior Court appearance by Motorcycle Officer Tim Downing (left) and jailer Jay Hughes. *(Courtesy Tim Downing)*

Task Force was searching for it, but the field interview report was misread as saying "Camaro" not "Corvette," thus the incident was not realized until after Yates had been arrested. After searching the Corvette police discovered blood that they linked to Jennifer Joseph and DNA from Yates that they then tied to 12 other victims. In 2000, he was charged with 13 counts of first-degree murder and one count of attempted first-degree murder in Spokane County Superior Court. As part of a plea bargain in which Yates confessed to the murders to avoid the death penalty, he was sentenced to 408 years in prison.

In 2001, Yates was charged in Pierce County with the murders of two additional women. The prosecution sought the death penalty for the deaths of Melinda L. Mercer in 1997 and Connie Ellis in 1998, which were thought to be linked to the killings in Spokane County. In October 2002, Yates was convicted of those murders and sentenced to death by lethal injection.

The 2002 death sentence was appealed on grounds that Yates believed his 2000 plea bargain to be "all-encompassing," and that a life sentence for 13 murders and a death sentence for two constituted "disproportionate, freakish, wanton and random" application of the death penalty. The arguments were rejected in 2007 by the Washington Supreme Court. A September 19, 2008 execution date was stayed by Chief Justice Gerry L. Alexander pending additional appeals.

In 2013 Yates's attorneys filed a habeas corpus petition in federal district court, stating that Yates is mentally ill and, "through no fault of his own ... suffers from a severe paraphilic disorder" that predisposed him to commit murder. The still-pending motion is regarded as a "long shot" by most observers. "I don't think Mr. Yates helps his cause by relying on the fact that he's a necrophiliac," said Pierce County Prosecutor Mark Lindquist.

Yates remains on death row at the Washington State Penitentiary. His case has been further complicated by Washington Governor Jay Inslee's 2013 declaration that he would not sign death warrants for anyone on death row while he is in office. Inslee cited the high cost of the appeals process, the randomness with which death sentences are sought, and a lack of evidence that the penalty serves as a deterrent to other criminals. In July 2015, the Washington Supreme Court once again rejected an effort by Yates to overturn his conviction and death sentence.

Left to right: Phil Shatzer, Randy Strezelecki, Tim Downing, Tom Warner, Eric Epperson, and Don Manning. *(Courtesy Tim Downing)*

Robert Yates during his trial, circa 2000, and, right, a prison photo. *(Public domain)*

Taken from the *The Associated Press*, July 23, 2001:

Serial killer's wife suspected Yates was having affairs

The wife of confessed serial killer Robert L. Yates Jr. knew something was wrong when he started going through the family's bills. For years, the bills had been Linda Yates' job. But in late 1999, she found her husband tossing credit card statements into the fireplace of their Spokane home. That's when she noticed the charges for Al's Spa Tub Motel, a place she had never been and where customers can pay by the hour. "Did you have someone else there?" Linda Yates asked her husband, according to Tuesday's editions of the *Spokesman-Review*.

Linda Yates' comments were published in the 24th installment of a 31-part series the Spokane neW.S.P.aper is publishing on the hunt for the serial killer.

Yates, father of five, denied to his wife that he had taken women to the motel. He contended he used the motel's hot tub to soothe his aching muscles after 12-hour shifts at a nearby Kaiser Aluminum plant. But the credit card bills confirmed for Linda Yates an old suspicion that her husband was having affairs. The bills showed he'd been going to the motel for at least a year.

"I was raised with old-fashioned values," Linda Yates recalled. "When you marry, you marry. Apparently he didn't take it seriously like I did."

The Yates family settled in Spokane in 1996 after two decades of traveling around the world for Robert's job as an Army helicopter pilot. Shortly after, women began disappearing from the streets of Spokane.

Linda Yates had hoped the return to their home state would help the troubled marriage, but it didn't. Daughter Sonja Yates found her father's address book one day and called the numbers of some women whose names she did not recognize. "Do you know Robert Lee Yates Jr.?" she would ask the women. Each denied knowing him. Robert Yates explained that the women were selling him car parts for his many vehicles.

Around that time, Linda Yates noticed the family was running out of money. She complained to her husband about his frequent withdrawals from ATMs. For the first time in their 26-year marriage, Robert Yates began badgering his wife to get a job.

Robert Yates also began having trouble with impotence and talked about using Viagra. "It's OK," she told him. "You're probably tired and I'm tired."

Linda Yates found magazines featuring orgies and lists of people interested in group sex. Robert asked if she had ever fantasized about making out with another woman. "I don't believe in that stuff," Linda Yates replied.

Linda Yates also noticed that her husband's military colleagues always seem surprised that he had a wife when they went to parties together. At the parties, Yates would drink heavily, moon other women, and tell them his name was James Bond, 007.

Much earlier in their marriage, she left her husband for a month when she discovered he had drilled a hole in an attic wall so he could watch a couple having sex in an adjoining apartment.

Linda left her husband again in the mid-1980s, moving the children back to her hometown of Walla Walla while Yates remained on duty in Alabama. She loved the separation, but the couple reunited in June 1988 after being separated for a year and a half. "The girls were pleading to be with their dad," Linda said. "They didn't want to be poor and not have anything anymore." Linda said the romance was gone, but she felt guilty about splitting up the family. "They loved their dad and I just kind of suffered through it," Linda Yates said. "I didn't love him like a wife should. He killed that."

Yates, 49, was arrested as he drove to work in April 2000. Under a deal to avoid the death penalty, he pleaded guilty in October to 13 murders and one attempted murder. Ten of the victims were women in the Spokane area, killed from 1996-98. In each of those cases, the victims were involved with drugs or prostitution or both.

Yates also confessed to killing a man and a woman in the Walla Walla area in 1975, and to the 1988 murder of a woman whose body was found in Skagit County. He was sentenced to 408 years in prison.

Now he faces murder charges in the deaths of two women in Pierce County and could face the death penalty at a trial scheduled to begin next April 29.

Mike Reynolds SPD officer, and Tim Downing on top of Steptoe Butte, last day of ride for motor class in 2002.
(Courtesy Tim Downing)

Top row from left: Mike Reynolds, Jason "Chachi" Reynolds, Tom Hendren, Ryan Snyder, Dave Kennedy, Bill Workman, Brian Bunker, and Kurt Henson. Bottom row: Paul Taylor, instructor Mike Brooks, Jeremy Jeske, and instructor Tim Downing, at the Spokane Arena, 2002. *(Courtesy Mike Brooks)*

Front row from left: Joe Bonin, Greg Lance, Craig Chamberlin, and Tim Downing. Back row: Glen Bartlett, Brad Moon, Mike Carr, David Kennedy, Jerry Hensley, Paul Taylor, Jordan Ferguson, John Clark, and Mike Reynolds, April 2002 motor school, Spokane Arena. *(Courtesy Tim Downing)*

Greg Lance (left) and Joe Bonin at Paul Taylor's and Tim Downing's motor school at the Spokane Arena, circa 2002. *(Courtesy Tim Downing)*

This photo was taken at the starting of the Lilac Festival Torch-light Parade in 2001. The two motor officers in the center are Tim Downing and Tom Warner. *(Courtesy Tim Downing)*

This photo was taken in 2001 at the Spokane County Courthouse. It was a memorial for former slain law enforcement officers slain in the line of duty. *(Courtesy Tim Downing)*

Tom Warner and Tim Downing in front of the Spokane Club at an insurance company Appreciation Lunch for law enforcement, circa 2001. *(Courtesy Tim Downing)*

Safety Tips For New Motorcycle Riders
by Tim Downing

I will never forget the advice that Undersheriff Larry Lindskog gave me when I became a motor officer. He said, "If you make it to five years as a motor officer and do not sustain any serious injuries, you will have done well." I took those words of advice and incorporated that caution into the lesson plans when teaching new motor officers. The following facts are important to remember.

According to the National Highway Traffic Safety Administration, motorcycle riders are 27 times more likely to be killed in an accident than someone in a car.

The numbers are even scarier for older riders, who are increasingly taking up or returning to motorcycling after many years. Because of slower reflexes, weaker eyesight, more brittle bones, and other disadvantages, riders over 60 years old are three times more likely to be hospitalized after a crash than younger ones.

Riders without a helmet are 40 percent more likely to suffer a fatal head injury in a crash and are three times more likely to suffer brain injuries than those with helmets, according to government studies.

Before each ride, do a quick walk-around to make sure your lights, horn, and directional signals are working properly. Check the belt, or shaft and the brakes. Inspect the tires for wear. And then preform a checklist.

Pre-ride checklist

1. Check the tire pressure and tread depth.

2. Check the hand and foot brakes.

3. Operate your headlights to ensure they are clear.

4. Check your emergency lights for operation.

5. Compare your fluid levels to previous rides and top them up when necessary.

6. Check under the motorcycle for signs of oil or gas leaks.

I would stress to the officers that the motoring public visualizes oncoming traffic in a horizontal perception. A car sits horizontally on the road, it's wide and has two headlights. A motorcycle appears vertical or in a straight line with a top and a bottom. These two distinctions are why most motorists do not perceive motorcycles as a vehicle and explains why motorists often pull out in front of a motorcycle.

When I was a teenager going through driver's education our instructor emphasized to make eye contact with other drivers when approaching intersections, or when a driver is entering the roadway from a driveway. This is not good advice. Our officers are taught to watch the front wheel of the vehicle that is waiting to enter the intersection or roadway. The wheel will be the first visual indicator that the vehicle is moving.

The Downing family in 2011. Left to right, front row: Anne Margaret Gilbert; David Michael Downing; Jacob Matthew Downing. Second row, from left to right: Richard "Tim" Timothy Downing; Margaret Mercedes Hoiland; Molly Margaret Downing; Richard Fuqua Downing; Benjamin Earl Downing; Janine Louis Lindberg. Third row, from left to right: Sue Ellen Johnson; Joseph Richard Downing,; Beth Elaine Hammerstrom; Todd Randall Massie; Andrew David Downing; Sara Beth Johnson; and Tammy Lynne Hiler.
(Courtesy Tim Downing)

The crew of a Boeing KC-135 Stratotanker refueling plane: Left upper seat, Maylon Dirks; right upper, Mike Boyington (Mike Boyington is also a deputy sheriff for Spokane County); lower left, Tim Downing; and right, Dave Stockdill. When this photo was taken, Tim Downing was in the Air National Guard. He was with the Washington 141st Air Refueling Wing, but was assigned to the 116th Air Refueling Squadron at Fairchild Air Force Base, circa 1998.

All of these photos were taken by a Thunderbird photographer over the Grand Canyon. The Thunderbirds had just completed an aerial demonstration and were on their way back to their home base in Las Vegas, Nevada. *(Courtesy Tim Downing)*

The Thunderbirds returning from an aerial demonstration in their F-16 C Fighting Falcons.

Tim Downing was the boom operator for the Boeing KC-135 Stratotanker that was assigned to refuel the Thunderbird planes to facilitate a non-stop flight.

Tim Downing operating the boom during the refueling of an F-16 C Falcon plane en route to Las Vegas, Nevada. It was typical for a photographer to accompany these flights to take promotional photos for the Air Force. Jack Pearson, co-author of this book, stated he attended one of these flights. The observation he made regarding taking photos was that photographers were not allowed to use a flash. This rule came about when someone used a flash, causing the pilot to immediately break away from the refueling plane, mistaking the flash for an explosion an explosion. *(Courtesy Thunderbirds photographer given to Tim Downing)*

Michael D. Brooks – hired by the Spokane County Sheriff in 1991

Mike Brooks, 2005. *(Courtesy Mike Brooks)*

Michael D. Brooks was born in Moscow, Idaho in 1967. He has a brother, James Brooks, born in 1969, a half-brother, Kevin Palmer, a step-brother, Todd Standish, and two step-sisters, Tina Fowler and Tracy Just, all living in the Spokane area.

Brooks was raised in Idaho, two miles east of Palouse on a small farm surrounded by wheat fields, which he often used for motorcycle riding after work.

Brooks attended elementary and high school in Potlatch, Idaho. His grandfather and mother also attended school in Potlatch. Brooks was in the last class (6th grade) to be held in the same small school building as his grandfather and mother, as it was torn down that year.

He graduated in 1985. Following graduation he attended North Idaho College, receiving an Associate in Science Degree in Business.

In 1988, he met his wife, Vickie Gately, while working a summer job as a roofer at Washington State University. At the time, he was working with her cousin's husband, who set him up on a blind date.

In 1996, he moved to Spokane and began looking for work. He continued to date Vickie, while she attended dental hygiene school. They have two girls, Jordyn born in 1997, and Erika in 1999. Jordyn is in college at Indiana Tech, playing Lacrosse and getting a degree in mechanical engineering. At the time of this writing, Erika is attending Mt. Spokane High School.

Mike Brooks, his wife Vickie (front center), and daughters Jordyn (top) and Erika (right), circa 2014. *(Courtesy Mike Brooks)*

Other members of the Brook's family have also been in law enforcement. Mike's great-grandfather, James Baker, was a law enforcement officer in Gandview, Washington, in the 1950s. His brother and sister-in-law, John and Kelley Gately, both work for the Spokane Police Department.

When he was 14, Mike started doing summer farm work. While attending college, he worked at Washington State University as a roofer, eventually becoming a journeyman. Prior to that, he had worked at a lumber mill for one year before moving to Spokane and finding a job at a pawn shop in the Hillyard area.

In 1991, he was hired by Spokane County Sheriff Larry Erickson. He worked as a corrections officer

in the jail for six and a half years. In 1997, he became a Spokane County deputy sheriff .

In 2002, Mike joined the Spokane County motor unit and passed the motor school in April of that year. He rode motor for ten years. During his riding career, he became a motor instructor in 2005 and attained the level of master instructor in 2012.

When he first began riding motor, the unit was staffed at 15. The county didn't have enough Kawasaki 1000s for everyone to ride, so several of the men had to share a motor. During Mike's time riding motor, he had several partners but rode most with Jeremy Jeske. They became friends and still share family vacations.

Brooks remembers applying for the Spokane Police Department while working at the jail. At that time, officer Mark Sterk was on his oral boards and asked where he wanted to be in five years, which was the standard question asked by the oral board. Brooks told him, not knowing he was a motor officer for the city, that he wanted to be a motor officer and eventually a motor instructor. Sterk seemed to like the answer. After Sterk had been elected sheriff, he put effort into returning motors back to Spokane County.

Brooks started his motor career on Kawasaki 1000s, receiving training through Tim Downing's motor school. He remembers Downing making everyone do a front wheel lock. Often while doing the max front braking, the front wheel would slide out and the rider would end up bouncing down the pavement. Brooks can still see the tire marks at Joe Albi Stadium from Downing's practice sessions. Thanks to Downing, Brooks used that same skill when he taught motor school to demonstrate a front wheel lock and how to recover from it. Brooks believes he was good at max front braking. However, he thinks he may have been asked to demonstrate the skill because he was the only one foolish enough to teach it.

Brooks takes pride in being an instructor and always passed the qualification course on all police motors from the KZ 1000 to the Harley Road Kings, BMW, Honda, and Yamaha ST. However, the motor he enjoyed most was the Kawasaki Concourse. His drive to become a good rider came from his instructor, Paul Taylor. Taylor and Brooks had ridden dirt bikes together prior to Taylor becoming his instructor. His dirt bike skills led him to winning a week's worth of lunches from Taylor on a bet. Although Brooks was better as a dirt bike rider, he now had to try to reach Taylor's skill level on a police motor. Taylor constantly pushed him to improve his skills and technique. Brooks found he often used many of his dirt bike skills to teach others. Nonetheless, Taylor was the person who made it possible for him to reach the level of master instructor. As a result, Brooks was able to instruct motor schools all over the Northwest. As the motor school in the Spokane area began to grow and get reviews as one of the best schools in the state, the departments from Oregon, Montana, and Idaho began sending officers to be certified as a police motor riders.

After SPD Motor Officer Rick Debrow was involved in a serious on-duty motor crash, a void for someone to put on motor escort training occurred. Debrow, who had been teaching this course for Eastern Washington, requested Brooks to take his spot. With the help of the city of Spokane, he put on several of these courses. He was consistently nervous about putting on a motor escort class, as the danger of this exercise for the riders involved was huge. However, the payoff was worth it. Also, the camaraderie with other motor units was invaluable. He has always enjoyed reuniting with those from Grant County and their hospitality, along with the great motors from Yakima, Ritzville, Wenatchee, and a few from the Washington State Patrol.

Though he's no longer in the motor unit, he still gets asked to remain qualified and ride during the summer and special events. For that opportunity, he is truly grateful to the department for keeping him involved. Rick Johnson is now the lead instructor for the sheriff's office. Johnson was one of Brooks's students.

Motors was the most fun and hard work but he also had other duties as a deputy. Brooks is currently on the SWAT Team and has been for over 14 years. As a member of the team, he specializes in the less lethal riot and chemical munitions. He is currently a EVOC/driving instructor and has been for 16 years. In 2014, Brooks became a firearms instructor, and he continues to work on his teaching skills. He has taught traffic school for eight years and has done the traffic reports on KXLY radio. In 2015 he applied for the school resource deputy (SRD) at Riverside High School and has been enjoying the challenge of building the trust of the students and faculty.

Brooks feels gaining the respect from other department motors as a rider and instructor has been his greatest accomplishment. He hopes to add to that accomplishment in SWAT, Firearms, and as an SRD.

In their spare time, his family likes to vacation camping or traveling. He recently purchased an adventure motorcycle and hopes to ride on trips to mountain lakes and off-road destinations.

His main lesson in life is that there is always someone who is better than you and that you can learn from them.

Riding Tips from Mike Brooks
Motor Instructor for the Northwest

1. You need to ride a bike that doesn't make you nervous to ride. I've seen more crashes due to the rider not being used to the bike or nervous riding it.

Mike Brooks. *(Courtesy Mike Brooks)*

Mike Brooks demonstrating a lean while he was teaching motor school. *(Courtesy Mike Brooks)*

2. Never show off.

3. Cover your clutch and brake at intersections, especially when there is a left turn lane in front of you.

4. Look way down the road for hazards.

5. Stay out of other vehicles' blind spots.

6. Never ride behind a vehicle hauling or towing anything. I have used this rule and have witnessed sheetrock or wood fall off the vehicle in front of me. I was lucky I had moved to the other lane.

7. Check the air pressure in the tires.

8. Pay extra for a good, comfortable helmet.

9. Keep your feet up and stop duck walking.

10. Practice, practice, practice braking. Find a place to practice your maximum and your threshold and braking. And don't forget to practice braking and evading.

The Beginning of Brooks's Sheriff Motor School at Seven-Mile.

Motor school practice in the sand hills at the Seven-Mile area. *(Courtesy Mike Brooks)*

The Ending of Brooks's Sheriff Motor School in 2007

High-speed training class with Mike Brooks as the instructor, 2007. *(Courtesy Mike Brooks)*

Mike Brooks at the Fairchild Air Force Base air show. *(Courtesy Mike Brooks)*

Deputy Jeremy Jeske and Mike Brooks at air show at Fairchild. *(Courtesy Mike Brooks)*

Bret Gores at the Hanford high-speed training class with Mike Brooks as the instructor, 2007. *(Courtesy Mike Brooks)*

Bret Gores and Kevin Nave at the Spokane Valley Sheriff Precinct in 2002. *(Courtesy Tim Downing)*

Craig Chamberlin – hired by the Spokane County Sheriff in 1999

Deputy Craig Chamberlin. *(Courtesy Tim Downing)*

The following interview with Craig Chamberlin was taken by Tim Downing to fulfill a public relations and communication assignment at the criminal justice department at Spokane Community College on April 8th, 2016:

I had the privilege of interviewing Craig Chamberlin of the Spokane Sheriff's Office. Deputy Chamberlin is very close to celebrating his twentieth year for the sheriff's office. The interview took place at Spokane Community College.

Craig is a Spokane native who graduated from University High School and graduated from the University of Puget Sound with an undergrad degree in economics in 1992.

After graduating from college, Craig went to work with the Okanogan Sheriff's Office as a road deputy and left that department to come to the Spokane Sheriff's Office in 1999. Once in Spokane, Craig has served as a motor officer, road deputy, S.W.A.T member, and public information officer.

I found Craig to be a high energy individual with a can do attitude. It doesn't take long to see Craig's confidence in himself and the passion for his chosen career field. Craig is a father of three girls.

INTERVIEW

The following questions were discussed with Craig. The answers are a combined response from a Law Enforcement officer's perspective and as a Public Information Officer, P.I.O.

1. What is your organization's primary mission?

To protect, serve and educate the citizens of Spokane County and the City of Spokane Valley.

2. How does public relations contribute to the mission?

It is the most important aspect of our job. The community trusts that law enforcement in general will not abuse or overstep its color of authority, especially with recent events involving law enforcement across the nation. The tone of the interaction between an officer, deputy, trooper, etc. sets the tone for that citizen's image of law enforcement from that point.

3. What is the relative position of PR as a management priority?

One of the most important positions in the agency. That person is the "face" of the organization, and the public's perception of that agency is largely influenced by that individual's ability to communicate with the public.

4. Who are the organization's primary audiences?

The entire community that the organization serves. Businesses, schools, citizens, private and public organizations, etc...

5. What methods of PR are used to communicate with those audiences?

SPOKANE COUNTY SHERIFF

Taking your job serious is not a joke – see next page. *(Public domain)*

Craig Chamberlin plays no favorites, as he unashamedly gives his daughter Courtney a ticket in 2002. Based on her smile, she knows her mom will FIX her ticket. *(Courtesy Tim Downing)*

Social media is very beneficial because an organization can reach out to a far greater number of people instantaneously as well as traditional television and print. However, being accessible to the public in person is by far the most powerful tool, so people can interact with that person and get a genuine feel for the image of the department.

6. What are your core messages?

For citizens to trust their law enforcement agency, to be approachable and accessible, and to encourage citizens to be involved in their community.

7. What challenges exist in conveying your messages?

Officer's making bad choices. With the explosion of social media, these choices are highlighted almost instantaneously, rightfully so. This can jeopardize the trust of the community even if it was in a different state.

8. How is the public relations function staffed (number of people, their duties)?

Usually there is one individual assigned as the PIO. However, if not available, ranking officers should be trained to provide media with basic information when requested.

9. Do you have formal education in PR or communications? If yes, where? If no, how did you acquire the necessary training?

There are seminars you can attend to assist with your presenting ability. However, in my experience people are either comfortable or confident with speaking to the media, large groups, etc... Or not. Law enforcement is unique because information you release could either jeopardize or assist in an investigation, so you have to be seasoned in the profession so as to not jeopardize an investigation.

10. Does your current position extend beyond PR and include other areas of responsibility? If yes, what other areas?

Yes. I am one of our department's collision reconstructionist as well as a patrol deputy in Spokane Valley.

11. Can you share any "war stories" – actual events, good or bad, that have happened to you in the course of your PR career? What went well? What didn't? What did you learn? What would you change?

At a homicide scene I was going to give the media a heads up on what our game plan was so they could plan accordingly for their evening news. However, it was information that could not be reported until I told them it was time. One reporter, in front of many, said she could not make any promises so nobody got the information. The other outlets were not happy.

12. What do you do to stay current in the PR industry?
Stay on top of national and current news dealing with our industry.

13. If there is such a thing as a typical week, how do you spend most of your time?

My time is spent responding to calls for service in Spokane Valley. It is never typical because there is absolutely no way to plan your day. You have to have the ability to "switch gears" in a split second depending on the situation you are dealing with.

14. How have technology and social media changed public relations?

It is the most powerful tool we have to communicate with an enormous number of people, worldwide.

15. How does your organization use social media?

By utilizing our own Facebook and web page, as well as other social media outlets.

16. In comparing traditional media to social media, do you consider one more effective than the other – or are they of equal value, just different?

I still think traditional media, television, is by far the most powerful. It puts a face to the organization as well as a personality. You can't do this with a Facebook post.

17. Beyond the growth of social media, are there other significant changes you have seen in the PR industry over the course of your career? Explain.

No. Social media has basically taken over. As an officer, you should fully expect to be recorded on every incident and to see it on a social media outlet.

18. What do you consider the essential skills and competencies of a public relations professional today? Where do you place writing skills on the list of competencies?

Writing skills is number one. If you can't write, the community will see that and their perception of the agency you represent will be a direct reflection of the inability to communicate in an intelligent manner. Speaking ability is just as Important. If you are not comfortable speaking to media or large groups, citizens will pick up on it and base their opinion of the agency on their perception.

19. How do you measure PR effectiveness? How much of your PR work is driven by data (Facebook Insights, Google Analytics, etc.)?

PR is the bread and butter of an agency. If you don't represent your agency in a fair, competent, professional manner, you will have an extremely difficult time earning their trust and respect.

Miscellaneous Spokane County Sheriff deputies

New Harley-Davidson motorcycles, 2004. *(Courtesy Tim Downing)*

From left: Phil Shatzer, Randy Strezlecki, Tom Warner, Kevin Nave, Don Manning, and Eric Epperson.
(Courtesy Tim Downing)

SPOKANE COUNTY SHERIFF

Dave Kennedy (left) teaching a motor school at Fire Station 9, in 2007. *(Courtesy Tim Downing)*

Combined city/county motor school, April 1 to April 12, 2002. From Left: John Clark, Craig Chamberlin, Greg Lance, Paul Taylor, Brad Moon, Jordan Ferguson, Tim Downing, Joe Bonin, Mike Reynolds, Mike Carr, Jerry Hensley, and Dave Kennedy. *(Courtesy Tim Downing)*

Fallen Officers Memorial in front of the Public Safety Building. From left: Phil Shatzer, Randy Strezlecki, Mike Brooks, Joe Bonin, Greg Lance, Jesse DePriest, Eric Epperson, and Craig Chamberlin. *(Courtesy Tim Downing)*

Deputies Tom Warner and Eric Epperson in front of the Spokane Valley Police Station. *(Courtesy Tim Downing)*

Spokane County Sheriff's Office
Spokane, Washington

From left: Dave Vanwormer, Darren Shaum, Eric Epperson, Randy Strezelecki, Don Manning, Jeremy Jeske, Tom Warner, Brad Gilbert, Craig Chamberlin, Mike Brooks, Joe Bonin, Jesse DePriest, and Tom Thompson. Photo taken at Mirabeau Park, Spokane Valley, in 2006. *(Courtesy Tim Downing)*

A combined city and county funeral escort. *(Courtesy Tim Downing)*

Brett M. Hubbell – hired by the Spokane County Sheriff in 2000

Brett Hubbell, circa 2016. *(Courtesy Tim Downing)*

S P O K A N E   C O U N T Y   S H E R I F F

Brett M. Hubbell was born in Spokane on July 7, 1975, to Michael and Laurie Hubbell. He has a sister who was born on August 12, 1971. His grandfather grew up in Spokane, and the family has remained here since. His father was an ironworker and business owner, and his mother was a loan officer.

Brett went to Lake Spokane Elementary, Nine Mile Falls Middle School, and Lakeside High School. Following that, he went to Spokane Community College and obtained an Associate of Arts Degree in Mechanical Engineering.

Brett has been married since June 2005 to Tracie L. Kromm, who worked at Juvenile Detention. They have two children, Brennan Rosendahl (stepson) and a daughter, Baylie Hubbell.

In November 1996, Brett joined the Stevens County Sheriff's Office, and in January 2000 he made a lateral entry to the Spokane County Sheriff's Department. Prior to joining the sheriff's department, Brett was an ironworker.

Brett has been assigned to motor from 2014 up to the present time. There are six members who are assigned to motor, all on one shift. His current rank is corporal. He believes his job has given him a sense of pride in doing a good job and making a positive difference in people's lives. His mother encouraged him to be a police officer, as she always thought he would do a great job in public service. His motor partner is Corporal Jeff Welton. They still work and ride together.

Brett's most memorable experiences on the sheriff's department involve riding motor. He has also been a member of the SWAT Team for 13 years. During that time, he worked his way from team member to team supervisor. In that position, he was able to secure a lot of training and equipment for the team.

Brett's happiest memories have been with his family and also his time in law enforcement. Brett's ambition is to always be dependable and trustworthy.

Among his favorite off-duty activities are camping, riding ATVs, and basically being outdoors.

His role models on the sheriff's office are Jack Rosenthal for his knowledge and drive in SWAT, and Richard Johnson for his drive and "never give up attitude" while riding motors.

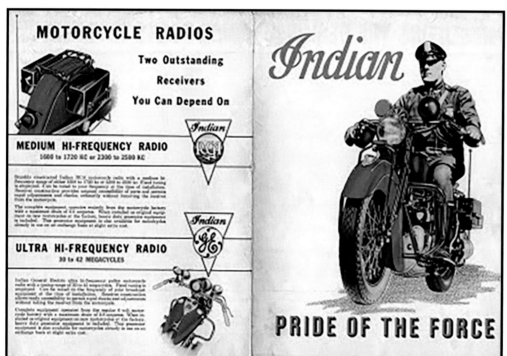

An ad for an Indian Police motorcycle equipped with a General Electric radio.

Indian motorcycles and communications have come a long ways since the 1940s. The Spokane Police Department started using two-way radios sometime in the 1940s-1950s. *(Pubic domain)*

Rick Johnson – hired by the Spokane County Sheriff in 2000

Deputy Rick Johnson, circa 2013. *(Courtesy Tim Downing)*

Rick Johnson was born in 1974, in Rapid City, South Dakota, to Robert and Paula Johnson. His father worked for Northwestern Bell for 43 years. His mother was a legal secretary. Rick has a sister, Heather Gordon, born in 1972. They were both raised in South Dakota and received all their schooling in Rapid City. Rick received an Associate in Arts Degree from North Idaho College in Law Enforcement.

Rick met his future wife, Erin Legreid, in college. Meeting and marrying her has brought him deep happiness in his life. They have two children, a son, Gunnar and a daughter, Kyra.

Rick enlisted in the Coast Guard, where he served for four years. When he was discharged, he had at-tained the rank of petty officer. Prior to going on the sheriff's department, Rick was a boat rigger for Gull Boats. He joined the Spokane County Sheriff's Department in May 2000, and has been riding motor since 2010. The best job he ever had is, hands down, riding motor. Mike Wall is his motor partner. Rick's best role model is Mike Brooks, who pushed him to become a better rider.

Rick's father was the biggest influence in his life. From him, he learned to be a hard worker and a person with a good attitude. He also feels being a deputy is important to all citizens, if you can set a good example as a law enforcement officer.

A new generation of motor bulls. *(Courtesy Tim Downing)*

Newer, faster motor bulls up close. *(Courtesy Tim Downing)*

Jeffrey L. Welton – hired by the Spokane County Sheriff in 2001

Deputy Jeffrey Welton, 2013. *(Courtesy Tim Downing)*

Jeffrey L. Welton was born in Omak, Washington, on December 16, 1964, to Joseph and Karen Welton. His father is retired, and his mother works for the Chelan County Public Utility District. Jeff has a sister, Michelle Welton, who is two years younger.

Jeff was raised by his mother in Wenatchee, from age 4 to 15, then by his father in Omak from ages 15 to 17. He returned to live with his mother in East Wenatchee from age 17 to 18.

Jeff went to a number of schools during his time at Wenatchee: Lincoln Elementary School, Lee Elementary School, Sterling Middle School, and 6th-7th grades at Eastmont Junior High. He then went to Omak High School, then back to East Wenatchee to complete his senior year.

Jeff joined the Washington State Army National Guard and served from 1992 to 2000. His military occupational specialty (MOS) was infantry. He later transferred to mechanized infantry, where he was assigned as an operator on a Bradley Fighting Vehicle.

Jeff served a total of six years active guard and two years inactive guard. He was an E-4 Specialist when his obligation ended. He was then awarded an honorable discharge.

Following his guard service, Mike attended Eastern Washington University at Cheney from 1993-1996, where he completed his junior year studying criminal justice for a future career in law enforcement. In 1996, out of college after his junior year, he worked as a reserve deputy for Okanogan County Sheriff. To make ends meet, during the day he worked at a lumber yard, and during the evenings he drove a tow truck.

At the age of 22, he received his first permanent position in law enforcement when he was hired as a police officer for the Okanogan County Sheriff in October 1997. He attended the Washington State Tactical Officers Association in Burien, and graduated in January 1998. He worked as a deputy for the Okanogan County Sheriff's Department until April of 2001. In 2001, he moved to Spokane as a lateral hire from that department. He also returned to Eastern Washington University and enrolled in the Criminal Justice Program. He graduated in 2004 with a Bachelor of Arts in Criminal Justice.

In 2003, Jeff met his future wife, Jill N. Cusick, while at Eastern Washington University. They were married March 18, 2005. They have one daughter, Gabriella Sophia. She was born April 23, 2009. Jeff also has a son from a previous marriage, who was born March 31, 1999.

Jeff became a detective/corporal and is a motor officer in the traffic unit, which he joined in March 2012. He graduated motor school in May 2013.

In regards to Jeff's attitude towards his job in law enforcement, he feels a sense of purpose about keeping his community safe. Jeff finds it hard to name just one person who has influenced him or his career. On a daily basis he is surrounded by numerous influen-

tial individuals whom he respects. To name a few, he mentioned Sergeant Jack Rosenthal (previous traffic corporal partner and SWAT supervisor), Corporal Brett Hubbell (current traffic corporal partner and previous SWAT Team leader/supervisor). These people have been influential in his success both in Traffic and SWAT. Most important, his wife, Jill, is very supportive of his career and understands the responsibilities Traffic and SWAT require.

Jeff clearly understands and reflects the importance of a good work ethic, being honest, having integrity, and being kind and selfless in all his actions. The accomplishments Jeff is most proud of are being a part of the SWAT team, motors, traffic unit, dive team, and detectives.

During Jeff's time off he enjoys boating, spending time with family, and his daughter's gymnastics.

A Bradley Fighting Vehicle similar to what Jeff Welton was assigned to. Consequently, he switched from a track vehicle to a two wheeler. *(Public domain)*

Michael R. Wall – hired by the Spokane County Sheriff in 2002

Michael R. Wall, circa 2016. *(Courtesy Mike Brooks)*

Michael R. Wall was born on November 3, 1973 at McKinley General Hospital, Gallup, New Mexico. His father is Michael R. Wall Sr. of Gallup. His mother is Marcia Wall, a retired teacher. He has one sister, Jolie M. Medrios, who was born in 1971.

Mike has been employed since he was 14 years old. He has worked as a paperboy, cook, prep cook, maintenance man, valet, and also in a lumber yard.

Mike was raised in Wallace, Idaho, where he attended Wallace High School.

Mike started in law enforcement at the Osburn, Idaho Police Department on June 18, 1994, as a Patrol Officer. He transferred to the Post Falls Police Department on May 17, 1997, where he served as a patrol officer, SWAT member, DUI car, and patrol sergeant. Later he attended the Idaho Peace Officer Standards and Training's (POST) basic academy, and the Washington Law Enforcement Basic Equivalency Academy. He has earned Idaho's basic law enforcement and Washington's law enforcement certifications.

Mike has three children, Austin, Aubrianna, and Abigail. He brought his family to the Spokane area to work in law enforcement. He transferred to the Spokane County Sheriff's Department on January 14, 2002, and is currently assigned to the Spokane Valley Police Department as a motor officer.

Mike grew up riding motorcycles. He started as a kid, racing motocross. He purchased a road bike in 2000 and was assigned as a motor officer in 2012. He is currently a deputy. He enjoys working in law enforcement and believes his job has value in reducing collisions through enforcement and education. When he first started as a motor officer, there were eight motors in the unit (six full time motors, two part-time motors within the unit. They rode when they could, but also had other duties). Currently in the unit there are three full-time motors due to downsizing and two part time motors.

The biggest influences in law enforcement have been Sgt. Diane Hogan (retired) from the Osburn Police Department and Sgt. Marc Anderson, formerly of the Post Falls Police Department. He feels they were greatly instrumental in molding him to the person he is today. Mike is currently partners with Rick Johnson, with whom he is in touch daily.

Mike has several memories from his two decade in law enforcement. One that sticks out is a bond he made with a seven-year old boy on a double homicide call.

Mike's happiest memory is when he became a motor officer. He is extremely proud of the unit he works in. He feels they have a great work ethic and push each other to become better at their duties and rid-

ing skills. His peers will remember him as a level-headed person with a good sense of humor, someone who was detailed in his work and produced quality outcomes.

Off duty, Mike likes to do as much as possible with his children. His youngest has a disability so they play quite hard and have a strong bond. His oldest daughter plays ice hockey, and he helps coach her. His son plays baseball, and he has coached him most of his career. His son also plays ice hockey and he also coaches him in that sport. Off duty Mike enjoys playing ice hockey, camping, fishing, and spending time with his friends.

The main lesson Mike has learned in life is that you cannot always count on other people. If you want something done the way you envision it should be done, then you need to do it by yourself. He has learned that, as a police officer, people watch what you do, and it is important to provide a good example to kids and others.

Mike's father is his role model. There have been people who have been a huge influence on him as a motor officer, such as his current partner, Rick Johnson, and former motor officer, Mike Brooks.

The Northern Pacific Depot in Mike's hometown of Wallace. This photo was taken during the move in 1986. The Northern Pacific Railroad Depot was moved 200 feet across the south fork of the Coeur d'Alene River to make room for two massive highway columns, which were to be used during the Freeway construction. This building now houses the Northern Pacific Railroad Museum and Gift shop. *(Courtesy Butch Jacobson)*

Jason C. Karnitz – hired by the Spokane County Sheriff in 2005

Jason Karnitz was born in Spokane in 1978 to Paul and Darlene Karnitz. He has five brothers, all raised in Spokane.

Jason went to the Gethsemane Lutheran Grade School in the Spokane Valley and University High School. Following his graduation, he attended Washington State University, where he received a Bachelor of Arts in English. His goal was to become an English teacher.

Prior to going on the sheriff's department, Jason worked in roofing and siding. Later he worked in general services at a law firm.

Jason met his wife, formerly Miss McConnell, on a blind date. They were married in 2009. Since that time they have two children, both girls.

Jason went to work for the Spokane County Sheriff's Department as a deputy sheriff in 2005. He feels that one of his best accomplishments with the sheriff's office is being a Field Training Officer (FTO), which is an experienced or senior member responsible for the training and evaluation of a junior or probationary level member. That role is used extensively in law enforcement, fire departments, and emergency medical services. In addition, he feels being assigned to motor with the sheriff's department was an honor. During the time Jason rode motor, his partners were Michael Wall and Richard Johnson.

Jason feels his uncle was the biggest influence in his career. As far as the job of being a deputy sheriff, Jason knows it is a job that many people can't or won't do, for good reasons. However, he knows that always being honest and hardworking typically overcomes most of the negative aspects of law enforcement. During his off-duty time Jason likes to do things that involve being in the country.

Jason Karnitz. *(Courtesy Tim Downing)*

A Spokane County sheriff poster advertising for new hires. *(Courtesy Tim Downing)*

Chapter Six

Washington State Patrol

The Washington State Patrol Began as the Highway Patrol in June 1921, and Commenced Service With Six Indian Motorcycles.

George Olin Potter, one of six highway patrolmen appointed September 1, 1921, by the Washington State Legislature. At the time of their appointment, that agency was called the "Highway Patrol." The first motorcycles used were Indians. *(Courtesy John Mittmann)*

By 1923, the Washington "Highway Patrol" had added two more troopers to the original six. Up until 1928, they rode Indian motorcycles. In 1933, the Highway Patrol officially became the Washington State Patrol. This photo was taken in 1923 in Olympia. Left to right: Harry Harkins, Gil Hyde, ? Cottle, ? O'Brien, ? Leidy, ? Newell, William Clark, and Harold Lakeberg. *(Courtesy John Mittmann)*

The Washington State Patrol's History Began with Motorcycles
(The source of the following is the Washington State Patrol Archives)

On June 8, 1921, the Washington State Legislature authorized the appointment of six motorcycle highway police with the power of peace officers. The governor of Washington State, at that time, was Louis Folwell Hart, a Republican, who served from February 13, 1919, to January 12, 1925.

The first patrolmen were Harold Lakeburg, Harry Harkins, Henry Shuk, William Clark, Eugene Russel, and George Potter. They were commissioned September 1, 1921, and were each issued a badge, a sidearm, and an Indian motorcycle. That was the beginning of the Washington State Patrol. However, at that time, they were simply called the Highway Patrol. The initial appropriation for maintenance of the motorcycle patrol was $70,000. The first two Highway Patrol directors were called supervisors.

The first arrest for speeding occurred in August 1921. The speed limit at the time was 35 mph. The first siren was used on a Highway Patrol motorcycle in 1922. It was a crude device that was activated when the officer pushed down on a foot lever that put pressure on a type of roller attached to the rear wheel of the motorcycle. The faster the wheel turned the louder the siren.

The Highway Patrol adopts a uniform

The patrol made arrangements with a local clothing store to provide the same uniform for every man. Attired in motorcycle caps, grey Norfolk jackets, riding breeches, brown leather puttees and boots, the Divi-

Helen Shaw was the first chief of Washington Highway Patrol, albeit for just a short period of time. In this 1927 photo, she was riding with Motorcycle Officer Gil Hyde. *(Courtesy Claude Shea Collection)*

The Washington State Patrol paddy wagon, in 1936 at Grand Coulee Dam. *(Courtesy John Mittmann)*

sion began to realize the value of good public relations. In 1928, Chief William Cole changed the color of the uniform from grey to forest green, and added black trim, Sam Brown belt, and "cap" style hat.

By 1937, as the uniform was designed and redesigned, one apparel feature, unique in law enforcement, was introduced that remains to this day – the bow tie. Originally red, the bow tie was changed to black after a couple of years. It has remained a standard part of the W.S.P. uniform, which evolved to its present crisp blue shirt with dark blue pocket flaps, French blue pants striped with dark blue, and royal blue campaign hat. In 2007, the agency was recognized as the "best dressed state law enforcement agency" by the National Association of Uniform Manufacturers and Distributors (NAUMD).

Appointing the agency's chief

Prior to the official appointment by the governor of the first chief of the Highway Patrol, Helen Shaw (Christensen) assumed the duties of chief for a short time, possibly just weeks. Consequently, based on the W.S.P. history, the first chief of the state patrol

A Washington Highway Patrol trooper on an Indian motorcycle, circa 1932. *(Courtesy John Mittmann)*

Washington Highway Patrol Officer Claude G. Shea, 1927. *(Courtesy Claude Shea Collection)*

was a woman. The first chief to be officially appointed by the Washington State governor was William Cole, in 1925. Although it was not mandated by the legislature for the governor to appoint the chief until 1933, Governor Roland H. Hartley made the appointment because there was a need and he was in a positioned to do so. Hartley, a Republican, served as governor from January 12, 1925 to January 9, 1933.

Transportation

By 1925, there were 28 officers. Just one year later, the patrol had grown to 42. By that time, Harley-Davidson was the motorcycle of choice. It would also become the standard for law enforcement agencies for years to come. The Highway Patrol switched from Indian motorcycles to Harley-Davidsons in 1927.

By 1933, automobiles were beginning to replace the patrol's motorcycles. By the late 1950s, it began to phase in its current patrol car door design, diagonal royal blue spear and black and white badge insignia. By 1968, all patrol vehicles were white.

The patrol had acquired its "paddy wagon" by 1927. It was a Ford panel delivery truck, which was as-signed to the major mountain highway crossing Snoqualmie Pass. The paddy wagons were eventually phased out, around 1949, in favor of four-door sedans, with improved police equipment and special engines, transmissions, and high-speed gears.

From Highway Patrol to Washington State Patrol

In 1933, the Legislature acknowledged the need for a police organization that was mobile and could be concentrated immediately, at any place in the state, where public safety was endangered. The Highway Patrol Division officially became known as the Washington State Patrol, which had been given full police powers. However, the police powers were not to be used unless ordered by the governor or requested by other law enforcement agencies. The Washington State Patrol, at that time, was placed directly under the governor, who had just been officially authorized to appoint the chief. The headquarters were in Olympia, the state capital.

Communications

From 1931 to 1940, communications were haphazard. Troopers received some of their orders by mail, some from county sheriffs, and some from their supervisors by telephone. They worked out of sheriffs' offices, city police stations, and often from their own homes. Most of them did quite a bit of work for the sheriff in their particular area, helping police the numerous country dance halls and investigating robberies or an occasional murder. The sheriffs usually paid by reimbursing them for gas and swearing them in as temporary deputy sheriffs.

The first radio was installed on a motorcycle in the Vancouver area in 1933, by Patrolman Harry Williams. Operating on a City of Portland (Oregon) police frequency, the unit gave accident and traffic information. The agency installed its first radio station (communications center) in 1942. Naturally, it was located in Olympia. The following year, the patrol set up its own communications network, completing the installation of two-way sets in all vehicles.

Establishing districts and divisions

In 1936, the patrol divided the state into four patrol districts, with a captain in charge of each district: District 1, with headquarters in Tacoma, consisted of 14 counties, including all of southwest Washington and the Olympic Peninsula; District 2, with headquarters in Seattle (moved to Bellevue in 1971), consisted of six northwest counties; District 3, with headquarters in Yakima, consisted of eight southeastern counties;

and District 4, with headquarters in Spokane, consisted of 11 counties in the Big Bend and Palouse areas and the northeastern part of the state.

In 1939, District 5 was established, with headquarters in Vancouver, and included some of the counties formerly in District 1. District 6 was established in 1948, with headquarters in Wenatchee, from some of the counties formerly in District 4.

The Criminal Investigation Bureau was formed in 1937. In 1940, the patrol was known to have one of the largest fingerprint files west of the Mississippi. Imagine the impact when new technology result in an Automated Fingerprint Identification System (AFIS), which was adopted by the W.S.P. in 1987.

Safety Education, which started in 1929, was formalized in 1942 with the formation of a Public Relations Division staffed by seven officers. The Safety Education Program was discontinued in 1980, due to lack of funds, but was reinstated in 1987.

In 1943, the Motor Vehicle Inspection Division and Weight Division were created, and were responsible for checking trucks for size, weight, and license violations. Both divisions previously were under the Department of Highways. In 1955, the patrol began to hire civilian weigh masters to work stationary and portable scales. Most of the troopers working weight

Washington State Patrol officers at an airport in 1958. *(Courtesy John Mittmann)*

Twenty-three Washington State Patrol motorcycle troopers turned out in force for the 1927 Spokane Air Show at Parkwater, which later was renamed Felts Field. In 1927, motorcycles did not have front brakes. This was also the first year that the Highway Patrol switched to Harley-Davidson motorcycles. *(Courtesy John Mittmann)*

A scene from the 1927 Air Show at Parkwater, later renamed Felts Field. *(Jim McGoldrick collection)*

control in the field were later transferred to traffic duty. The Weight Control Division became known as the Commercial Vehicle Division. In the spring of 1996, Commercial Vehicle Enforcement Officers (CVEOs) began special training, which included firearms. CVEOs were being armed for the first time in more than 20 years, when the last of the troopers assigned to weight control returned to traffic duty.

In 1972, the Vehicle Identification Section began with eight employees assigned to wrecker yard inspections.

Governor Dan Evans served as a Republican governor for the State of Washington from 1965 until 1977. Evans was the only governor in Washington State history to serve three four-year consecutive terms and the second to be elected to three terms following Arthur B. Langlie. A 1981 University of Michigan study named him one of the ten outstanding American governors of the 20th century. He declined to run for a fourth term. As an interesting aside, serial-killer Ted Bundy served as a campaign aide for Evans. During the 1972 campaign, Bundy followed Evans's Democratic opponent around the state, tape recording his speeches, then reported back to Evans personally. A minor scandal later followed when the Democrats found out about Bundy, who had been posing as a college student. *(Public domain, information from Wikipedia)*

Operations were expanded in 1973 to the inspection of all vehicles first licensed in Washington, except new vehicles sold by a Washington dealer. This section became known as the Auto Theft Section.

In 1946, the Washington State Patrol had the distinction of being number one out of eleven western states regarding traffic safety. In 1951, it implemented the use of radar with a stationary type unit. In 1954, the W.S.P was awarded the National Safety Council's Grand Award, recognizing it as one of the finest law enforcement organizations in the nation.

Training

The State Patrol initiated its first cadet class in 1937. Ten years later, in 1947, it gained its own training center in the former Navy bachelor officers' quarters near the Shelton Airport. In 1968, a new W.S.P. Training Academy was built on 23 acres near the existing facility. The patrol's drive course was constructed on 165 acres adjacent to the academy and is considered one of the finest in the country. Construction of a new multipurpose building was completed in 1987.

An aviation program of its own

In 1959, the patrol's started its own aviation program, with its primary responsibilities being search-and-rescue operations, aircraft accident investigation, and enforcement of aeronautics laws. It leased its first aircraft, a Cessna 172, in 1960. A year later, realizing the value of aircraft, the patrol purchased its own Cessna Skylane and subsequently used it for traffic surveillance and enforcement, search operations, emergency relays, and transportation duties. In 1967, the Aviation Division was given statewide responsibility for aircraft registration. The following year, the division was moved from Boeing Field to their new quarters at the Olympia Airport.

In 1962, Seattle hosted the World's Fair "Century 21," and the patrol received the Governor's Distinguished Award for Outstanding Service. In 1965, under the governorship of Daniel Evans, the patrol became responsible for the safety and protection of the governor.

A chronological account of further advancements and changes within the Washington State Patrol from the agency's archives

In 1970, the Drug Control Assistance Unit was established by state law due to increasing drug trafficking and abuse.

The Investigative Assistance Division (IAD) was established in 1973, and included the Narcotics Section, Organized Crime Intelligence Unit, and a Clandestine Laboratory Response Team. The IAD is also the law enforcement contact with Interpol for the state of Washington. In 1974, the Identification and Criminal History Section was established, and two full-service crime laboratories were set up in 1975, in Seattle and Spokane.

In 1975, the State Patrol hired its first female troopers and, in 1977, its first department psychologist. The first woman trooper to be promoted to sergeant was in 1987.

In 1979, the Walla Walla State Penitentiary was set on fire by rioters. The patrol was involved with security, and troopers walked the prison walls for weeks.

In 1980, Chief Robert Landon attempted to talk Mr. Harry Truman, Mt. Saint Helens Lodge caretaker, into leaving the Spirit Lake Lodge at Mt. Saint Helens, and 12 hours later the volcano erupted and buried Harry.

In 1980, the Legislature created the patrol's crime laboratory system.

In 1981, four more crime laboratories were added in Tacoma, Marysville, Kelso, and Kennewick.

In 1982, the W.S.P. Historical Advisory Board was established.

In 1983, an entirely new Washington Crime Information Center data base was brought online, and provided faster response time, as well as access to the Federal Bureau of Investigation's National Crime Information Center computer (NCIC) system and direct entry of missing adults and runaway children.

Washington State Patrol Chief Annette Sandberg. She served as a commissioned officer in the State Patrol for 18 years. Her appointment to chief was by governors Gary Locke and Mike Lowry. She served in that position from 1995 to 2001. *(Public domain)*

Also, in 1983, the Washington State Patrol Memorial Foundation was created as a non-profit charitable organization, which provides financial assistance to employees in time of need, including their children.

In 1987, the Computer Aided Dispatch (CAD) system was installed as a pilot program in Olympia (which was used statewide in 1989), and an Automated Fingerprint Identification System (AFIS) was implemented.

In 1989, the Legislature passed a bill to incorporate a DNA typing laboratory into the existing Seattle Crime Lab, staffed by specially trained personnel. This also helped in the creation of a DNA data bank to aid future investigations. The patrol purchased five "Total Stations" in 1989, which are used as survey devices to determine the reconstruction of traffic collisions and aid in the investigations.

In 1991, the National Governor's Conference deployed over 200 State Patrol personnel for security.

In April 1995, at the age of 33, Annette Sandberg was appointed chief by Governor Mike Lowry.

In July 1995, the State Fire Marshal's Office joined the agency when the Legislature transferred Fire Protection Services to the Patrol. The office provides for mobilization of resources to wildfires, firefighter and hazardous materials training, fire and life safety inspections, and other services.

In 1996, the Special Weapons and Tactics Team (SWAT) combined with the Methamphetamine Lab Response Team, to create a Statewide Incident Response Team (SIRT). The Problem Oriented Public Safety (POPS) philosophy was initiated by the agency in 1997, following the award of a Community Oriented Policing grant from the federal government. The award added 72 trained POPS officers to the patrol over the ensuing three years. POPS signaled the beginning of a new problem-solving philosophy that fosters the development of partnerships among the W.S.P., citizens, and other stakeholders, who together help solve public safety problems in communities throughout the state. The department made a commitment to bring POPS and Governor Gary Locke's Quality Improvement Initiative together and to train all employees in this new philosophy of public service.

In 1997, the W.S.P. Canine Unit began with the deployment of two explosive detection teams.

In 1997, the Computer Crimes Unit was established as a full-service computer evidence retrieval and analysis unit. The Criminal Records Division launched a new Web site in January of 1998 called WATCH (Washington Access To Criminal History), where the public can obtain criminal history information online. The patrol started its Aggressive Driving Apprehension Team (ADAT) program, utilizing unmarked patrol cars to proactively locate and arrest those who drive aggressively on Washington roadways.

In May of 1998, the patrol published a five-year strategic plan after a year-long effort. As part of this, all organizational units of the department are required to develop operational plans and performance measures that support the goals of the strategic plan.

In 1999, the patrol began a Strategic Advancement Forum (SAF) process, ensuring increased accountability among districts and divisions. Strategic planning was integrated with POPS and a quality philosophy to help the agency meet future demands. By integrating long-range planning with quality business practices, and by developing partnerships, the patrol ensures that the service needs of Washington's citizens are met.

In 2002, SIRT was changed back to SWAT after tactical responses began to arise as a result of the Terrorism Attacks on the World Trade Center in New York on September 11, 2001.

In 2003, the "Tom Neff Industrial Park" was completed in Tumwater and houses the W.S.P. Fleet, Supply, and Property Management Sections. Mr. Neff was instrumental in a large land swap with the patrol's Martin Way property, in order to gain the new property. On February 20, 2003, the El Protector program began. This program was implemented to address the increasing concern of Hispanic/Latino-surnamed drivers being over represented in fatal and felony collision in the Mid-Columbia Valley. The program provides educational materials to people with limited English-speaking abilities. In 2003, the W.S.P. implemented the Tissue Donation Program, which, works to ensure that potential donors, via next-of-kin, are given the opportunity to donate usable tissue/organs to save and/or improve the quality of life of fellow citizens. Also, in 2003, the Drug Control Assistance Unit (DCAU) was established.

In 2004, the patrol provided approximately 500 personnel for security and other responsibilities during the National Governor's Association (NGA) Conference in Seattle. At the NGA Conference, the AMBER Alert Web Portal was launched as a national model for recovering missing children. The patrol played an integral part in this public/private partnership.

In 2005, the patrol developed a Vessel and Terminal Security Division which provides security for the Washington State Ferry System. On June 28, 2005, they opened a new Crime Lab at Eastern Washington University. In 2005, the SWAT Team participated in the largest fugitive operation in American history. Operation FALCON, sponsored by the U.S. Marshal Service, arrested a total of 10,340 fugitives and cleared more than 13,800 felony warrants.

In 2006, the patrol began issuing tasers to troopers throughout the state in an effort to reduce injuries to officers and non-compliant individuals.

In 2007, the International Association of Chiefs of Police (IACP) named the W.S.P. as the best state police agency of its size. The agency was also recognized as the "best dressed state law enforcement agency" by the National Association of Uniform Manufacturers and Distributors (NAUMD). Judges for both awards reviewed many aspects of the agency to include professional appearance and operations.

In 2008, W.S.P. launched an innovative, first in the nation DUI Aerial Response Team (DART). This effort combines fixed-wing aircraft using forward-looking infrared cameras and ground troopers to respond to citizen complaints of DUI as well as initiate stops of intoxicated and reckless drivers. The patrol also became the first state police/highway patrol agency to host the International Problem Oriented Public Safety (POPS) conference.

In 2009, the transition to new side-arms was begun. The Smith & Wesson M & P (Military & Police) .40 caliber semiautomatic was selected as the standard issue weapon for all officers throughout the agency.

In 2010, the patrol underwent re-accreditation from the Commission on Accreditation for Law Enforcement Agencies (CALEA). Being accredited by CALEA requires police agencies to prove their compliance with 459 standards that detail every major aspect of law enforcement, including traffic operations, crime analysis, performance evaluation, recruitment, evidence collection, strategic planning, public information, and communications. These standards are designed to make an agency more efficient, more accountable, and more responsive to the needs of citizens.

Mike Wayno – hired by the Washington State Patrol in 1926

Washington Highway Patrol Trooper Mike Wayno, 1926-51. *(Courtesy Rod Mittmann)*

The following narrative was written by Harriet Fish, historian for the Washington Association of Sheriffs and Police Chiefs. Michael Wayno was born on July 22, 1891, and lived in Tacoma, Washington. He passed away in February 1979, at age 87:

Many times, when doing in-depth research, tremendous admiration wells inside me for someone I never have or will know, someone whose life is filled with the details of greatness, which so often just "laces" another's lifetime. Such a person was Mike Wayno, No. 17 to join the State Highway Patrol in 1926.

Mike Wayno was a patrolman from 1926 to 1951, before the term "Trooper", when the organization still was called the Highway Patrol, when uniforms were "in the making," when transportation moved from motorcycles to panel trucks and four-door sedans, and when operations were flying into gear, as growth developed statewide.

Born in Carbonado, Washington in 1891 to Austrian-Czech parents, Wayno learned to speak six languages and grew up working in coal mines, blacksmith shops, meat packing plants and a shipyard during World War I.

After applying for a state position, he was guided toward the newly-organized Highway Patrol and, in his words, "It was pull and who you knew, not what you knew" that got you into the Patrol then.

He didn't know how to ride a motorcycle, but spent three days falling off. Then he could ride one. The roads were mostly gravel, and after one spill he spent nine days in a hospital.

Henry Huseby, behind the wheel of a new 1928 Model A Ford, was stopped by officer Mike Wayno in January of 1928. Mr. Huseby was not receiving an order to appear in court; the car he was driving was so attractive that Washington State Highway Patrol Officer Mike Wayno stopped it so he could place an order for one for himself. Henry Huseby was a veteran salesman for the V. R. Dudley Motor Company in Tacoma.

In 1928, Ford stopped production on its 20-year-old Model T in favor of the more streamlined and powerful Model A. The vehicle could produce 40 horsepower, and its starting price was around $460. The V. R. Dudley Motor Co. was an authorized Ford dealership. *(Courtesy John Mittmann, from the Tacoma Sunday Ledger, 1/29/1928)*

Mike Wayno. *(Courtesy W.S.P. archives)*

Given a badge, motorcycle, ticket books, a garrison cap, and assignment to the 292-mile "Mountain Highway" beat to Mount Rainier, Wayno often showed his understanding nature and dislike for giving tickets.

Once, because of a violator's interfering and nagging wife, he tore up a speeding ticket, saying, "A man who has a wife like that has all he can handle." And usually he gave a stick of gum with his tickets.

Ultimately his motorcycle had a siren mounted on the fender to help him patrol before he was given a panel patrol vehicle in 1947. He was involved in escorting celebrities and in handling traffic at the Western Washington Fair in Puyallup.

He also manned a 24-hour roadblock at the time of the George Weyerhaeuser 1935 kidnapping in Tacoma. It wasn't until he requested relief that he found out the roadblock had been called off. Weyerhaeuser had been found alive.

Caring about his life as a patrolman, Mike kept a scrapbook in that much history is preserved. It contains accounts of such events as the annual convention; speech topics which each patrolman had to prepare to present at the convention; complete contents of talks prepared for school patrol training; and correspondence, some pro and some con, of his work as a patrolman.

There are letters that implore Chief William Cole not to change Mike's work area because the National Park people found his services "very essential and helpful."

When he was 44, Mike won a Packard sedan in a contest in which friends participated. Each of the 500 friends received a handwritten thank you letter from him.

Mike became an appointed sergeant in 1949. After leaving the Patrol on July 31, 1951, with a retirement of $64 a month and a letter of commendation from Gov. Arthur Langlie, Wayno became a member of the Civil Service Office of the Pierce County Sheriff's Office. He served until he was 70 years old in 1961.

By 1976, Mike and his wife, Bertha, had been married for 60 years and raised three sons and a daughter, and had six grandchildren and six great-grandchildren.

Early Washington State Patrol motorcycle troopers

Washington Highway Patrol troopers, in the late 1920s. *(Courtesy W.S.P. archives)*

WASHINGTON STATE PATROL

Hank Hyatt in 1935. *(Courtesy W.S.P. archives)*

Highway Patrol motorcycle officers with sidecars on their motors in 1927. *(Courtesy W.S.P. archives)*

1936 uniform and 1929 Harley-Davidson motorcycle, at W.S.P. Academy. *(Courtesy W.S.P. archives)*

Washington State Patrol Trooper Grover Cannon, 1936, on a Harley-Davidson. *(Courtesy W.S.P. archives)*

Presently the Washington State Patrol has 42 motorcycle troopers assigned primarily to the urban I-5 corridor. Motorcycle detachments are located in Seattle, Tacoma, Marysville, and Vancouver. Additional motorcycles are assigned to Kennewick, Bremerton, and Spokane.

Motorcycles are highly effective in apprehending speeders and other aggressive drivers, particularly in heavy traffic. They are often the only emergency vehicle able to reach collision scenes and other incidents on crowded freeways with narrow shoulders.

Furthermore, with the Northwest as a favorite destination for national leaders and visiting heads of state,

W.S.P. motor officers are frequently involved with dignitary escorts.

W.S.P. Motorcycle Trooper

The Washington State Patrol is recognized as a leader in police motorcycle training. Motorcycle training is conducted annually at the W.S.P. Academy in Shelton. In addition to classroom and dormitory facilities, the academy features a 2.7 mile drive course with an off-road environment, a low-speed skill course, and high-speed pursuit exercises.

A Washington State Patrol officer at the State Capitol at Olympia, circa 1950. *(Courtesy Spokane Valley Heritage Museum)*

West side motorcycle officers. *(Courtesy John Mittmann)*

Washington Highway Patrol Officer Doc Austin, 1928. *(Courtesy Claude Shea Collection)*

Stacy G. Mattson – hired by the Washington State Patrol in 1939

Washington State Patrol Sergeant Stacy Mattson, circa 1950. *(Courtesy Scott Mattson)*

Stacy Mattson was the son of John G. and Nelly Mattson. He was born in 1913, at Swedish Hospital in Seattle. He had one sister, born in 1910. He was raised at Coal Creek, New Castle, and Olympia, where he attended both grade and high school. He also attended Saint Martin's College in Lacey, Washington. Saint Martin's was founded in 1895 as an all-boy boarding school by monks of the Benedictine Order. It became a degree-granting institution in 1940. The college became coeducational in 1965. In 2005, it changed its name from Saint Martin's College to Saint Martin's University.

Mattson met his wife, Arlene Waters, at Saint Peters Hospital in Olympia, where she was a nurse. They were married in 1939. Their first child, Jeffery, was born in 1940, followed by Scott in 1943.

Prior to joining the Washington State Patrol, Mattson worked at a plywood plant in Olympia and later as a bartender, also in Olympia.

Mattson's sons, Scott (left) and Jeffrey, circa 1948. *(Courtesy Scott Mattson)*

In 1939, Mattson joined the Washington State Patrol. His training for the patrol took place at Fort Lewis. At the time, the Patrol Academy was also located at the Army base. While he was going through the Patrol Academy, a *Seattle PI* photographer, who had been following the class progress, asked Stacy if he would be a model for the firearms training, to which he agreed.

In 1931, at the age of 18, Stacy had purchased a Tacoma Police Department surplus Harley-Davidson motorcycle, which started him on his love for motorcycles. During his career he rose through the ranks and was promoted to major in 1971. Among his many career highlights his assisting the FBI in apprehending a Russian spy. For that he received a commendation

Stacy Mattson with his first son Jeffrey, circa 1942. *(Courtesy Scott Mattson)*

Stacy Mattson, at age 18, with his first motor. This was a surplus bike he had just purchased from the Tacoma Police Department in 1931. *(Courtesy Scott Mattson)*

letter from J. Edgar Hoover, the director of the FBI at the time.

Stacy was a respected lawman by all who knew him. He was considered by those who worked under him as a good and fair boss, and one with many exciting and interesting stories to tell.

Stacy loved the State Patrol, but was forced to retire in 1973 because of his age (60 was retirement age then). Following his retirement, Stacy and his wife went into the antique business, operating it out of their home eight miles south of Spokane. The name of their business was "Hanging Tree Antiques." It was located at 1208 East Excelsior, off Highway 195. They both enjoyed this business and made many out-of-town buying trips.

Stacy passed away in 2004 at the age of 91. His wife passed away four years later.

The caption on this neW.S.P.aper photo stated: "Tommy" Guns and Pistols fit into the Patrol's Training course. A target 200 yards away has the eye of a student (above) sighting a "Tommy" gun. *(Courtesy Scott Mattson)*

Stacy Mattson taken just before World War II. *(Courtesy Scott Mattson)*

Stacy Mattson, circa 1947. *(Courtesy Scott Mattson)*

Stacy Mattson in Lakefair Parade at Olympia, circa 1958. *(Courtesy Scott Mattson)*

Stacy and Arlene Mattson, on October 15, 1938, on their wedding day. There was no expensive wedding dress as Arlene wore what they could afford. *(Courtesy Scott Mattson)*

Stacy Mattson congratulating his son Scott the day he became a new trooper in December 1973. *(Courtesy Scott Mattson)*

Stacy Mattson as captain and district commander in Spokane. *(Courtesy Scott Mattson)*

Stacy Mattson's son Scott with his first patrol car. Following a four-year enlistment in the Navy, from 1964 to 1968, Scott joined the Washington State Patrol. In his early career, he worked the W.S.P. radio in North Bend. Later, upon graduation from the Patrol Academy, he was a line trooper in Kittitas County until he retired in 2001. *(Courtesy Scott Mattson)*

Stacy Mattson with actress Joyce Taylor and actor David Janssen during the filming of a movie titled *Ring of Fire*, is a 1961 drama film directed by Andrew L. Stone. It stars David Janssen, Joyce Taylor, and Frank Gorshin. The film was shot in Vernonia, Oregon, and Wynoochee River, Washington, featuring footage from two real forest fires. The title song was written and performed by Duane Eddy. As a deputy sheriff, Steve Walsh (Janssen) encounters a trio of young people in Washington between Shelton and Aberdeen, in a rural Mason County forest, and is taken hostage when the girl, Bobbie, produces a gun. Bobbie later tries to seduce Walsh, who is twice her age and resists. Her companion, Roy, tries to push Walsh off a cliff but plummets to his own death instead. When a search party comes to Walsh's rescue, one of his captors, Frank, accuses the lawman of having improper relations with Bobbie, who is a minor. Before the matter can be resolved, a cigarette carelessly tossed earlier by Frank sets the forest ablaze. This was one of the W.S.P.'s duties. *(Courtesy Scott Mattson)*

David Janssen was born in 1931. He was a film and television actor best known for his starring role as Dr. Richard Kimble in the television series *The Fugitive*, which aired from 1963 to 1967. Janssen also had the title roles in three other series: *Richard Diamond, Private Detective; Harry O*; and *O'Hara, U.S. Treasury*. In 1996, *TV Guide* ranked him number 36 on its "50 Greatest TV Stars of All Time" list.

He attended Fairfax High School in Los Angeles, where he excelled on the basketball court setting a school scoring record that lasted over 20 years. His first film role was at the age of 13, and by the age of twenty-five he had appeared in 20 films and served two years as an enlisted man in the United States Army. During his Army days, Janssen became friends with fellow enlistees Martin Milner and Clint Eastwood while stationed at Fort Ord, California.

His films include *To Hell and Back*, the biography of Audie Murphy, who was the most decorated American soldier of World War II. At one time he co-starred with Angie Dickinson. *(Both photos public domain and information from Wikipedia)*

Born in Taylorville, Illinois, Joyce Taylor sang in amateur shows at age ten and turned professional at the age of 15, signing on with Mercury Records. For seven years, in the 1950s, she was under contract to Howard Hughes' RKO. However, the eccentric multimillionaire only allowed her to act in one picture, a small part in *Beyond a Reasonable Doubt*, which was filmed in 1956. After the end of seven frustrating years bound by a contract to Hughes, she became a regular on the TV sci-fi/adventure series *Men Into Space* which began airing in 1959. She also acted in many other TV shows and a handful of other features.

The films she was in included: *Beyond a Reasonable Doubt; The FBI Story; Atlantis, the Lost Continent; Ring of Fire; Beauty and the Beast; Twice-Told Tales; The Windsplitter.*

The television programs she acted in included: *77 Sunset Strip; Sea Hunt; Lawman; Lock-Up; The Adventures of Ozzie and Harriet; Men Into Space; Bat Masterson; The Untouchables; Tales of Wells Fargo; Bonanza; The Man from U.N.C.L.E.; The Littlest Hobo.*

Two movie posters advertising *Ring of Fire*, one in French, the other in English. *(Courtesy Scott Mattson)*

Joyce Taylor sitting on the back of Stacy Mattson's motor. This is an example of one of the duties the W.S.P. is sometimes called upon to perform. *(Courtesy Scott Mattson)*

THE WASHINGTON Trooper

1928 Harley Davidson Restoration Update

By Trooper Mark Soper

1928 Harley-Davidson at 99 percent completion.

The 1928 Harley Davidson motorcycle, which has been undergoing major restoration, is 99 percent complete. There are just a few minor parts left to be installed. There has been some additional good news about this project; a sidecar has been found which will also be restored and attached to the motorcycle. This will make the motorcycle and sidecar a very unique addition to the WSP's historical fleet.

The restoration is being done by Vintage Motorcycles Northwest of Spanaway. The owner, John Burgin, along with his staff, Steve White and John Condon, have put countless hours into the restoration. They have tracked down the original parts for this era of bike and when the

bike and sidecar are finished, it will be classed as excellent condition. A very large thank you is due to the staff at Vintage Motorcycles Northwest for all their hard work, attention to detail, and dedication to this project. The WSP Historical Advisory Board (WSPHAB) has been spearheading the project, which has been funded by donations from current and past WSP employees and friends of the Patrol. Retired Lieutenant George Engledow and retired CVEO Phill Bellgardt have been the main organizers of this project. Both serve as members of the WSP Historical Advisory Board. Both have assisted in locating parts and keeping a picture diary of the progress of the project.

The motorcycle has been restored to running condi-

Vintage Motorcycle Northwest staff, (left to right) Steve White, John Burgin and John Condon.

tion, but has had the engine packed with grease. The WSPHAB recommended to the Chief that it would be best if the motorcycle could not run. The reason for this is that this motorcycle will be a very unique piece of history for the department and it is best to lessen any chance of having it damaged. Pushing power would be the safest. An old motorcycle trailer is being modified by the Fleet Section to have an enclosed storage and transport trailer. Like the other two historical vehicles, the motorcycle will be available for display at fairs and community events.

Very rough sidecar at the beginning of the restoration

This is a copy of information published in the *Washington Trooper* magazine, which was with Stacy Mattson's memorabilia. It is the same year as his first motorcycle. *(Courtesy Scott Mattson)*

Staff photo by Bart Rayniak

Arlene and Stacy Mattson have collected antiques for 45 years.

Hanging Tree Antiques does business at home

By Jim Spoerhase
Staff correspondent

Business

Stacy and Arlene Mattson are surrounded by antiques at their large home eight miles south of the city.

It is only natural because the Mattsons own Hanging Tree Antiques at E1208 Excelsior, off Highway 195.

The couple started collecting antiques 45 years ago, and it developed into their business in its present form about 14 years ago. They built their own home, with one wing for the antique shop, by working seven days a week "and living in sawdust for three years," as they put it.

Hanging Tree specializes in country artifacts and accessories, with some items dating back to the 1700s.

Furniture of pine, lighting fixtures and wall-hangings are featured items.

Their stock includes large chairs, tables, chests, cupboards and fireplace accessories. Their country furniture is definitely not formal, some is even homemade.

The Mattsons buy most of their antiques in the Midwest or on the East Coast. They have even made two trips to England to make purchases. In all, about 75 percent of their items are American.

It is not uncommon for them to have antique items dating to the 1700s.

Hanging Tree is open from 10 a.m. to 4:30 p.m. Thursday through Sunday. Other times are available by appointment. The business can be reached by calling 448-1803.

An article from the *Spokesman-Review* and *Spokane Chronicle*, March 1, 1990. *(Courtesy Scott Mattson)*

John Mittmann – hired by the Washington State Patrol in 1950

John Mittmann, circa 1956. *(Courtesy John Mittmann)*

John Mittmann was born on April 23, 1927, in Illinois. He joined the Washington State Patrol in Seattle in 1950, and was transferred to Spokane in 1957. John rode motor for the patrol for a total of 25 years, starting on the west side in 1956. During his time on motor, he typically rode Harley-Davidson motorcycles.

John met Anna Marie Nilson in Seattle, while she was attending the Seattle Art Institute. They were married on December 24, 1950. In 1957, John was transferred to Spokane. Together they raised four boys, Randy, Rodney, Paul, and John, which became a full time job for Anna. Anna passed away in 2017. John and Anna were married for over 67 years.

Trooper John Mittmann providing escort for Governor Albert Rosellini. *(Courtesy John Mittmann)*

John Mittmann, Gayle Stokes, Captain Horn, and a Game Department pilot with his airplane in a 1970 Traffic Enforcement Program. *(Courtesy John Mittmann)*

Motorcycle units escorting John F. Kennedy's motorcade as his presidential campaign swept through Spokane in 1960. W.S.P. Trooper John Mittmann (far right) participated in this historic event with his partner, Trooper George Engledow. *(Courtesy John Mittmann)*

Troopers George Engledow (left) and John Mittmann prepare to take their motors on patrol, 1958. *(Courtesy John Mittmann)*

Thirty-five years later, John's son Rod Mittmann and Joe Pass, in front of the same building at Appleway Avenue and Park Road. *(Courtesy John Mittmann)*

Retired Washington State Patrolman John Mittmann and his wife, Anna, 2016. *(Bamonte/Pearson photo)*

The following article, a testimony to John Mittmann's commitment to helping people, appeared in the *Spokesman-Review* on Feburary 6, 1996:

Road Rangers Senior Volunteers Cruise Highways Offering Help, by Gita Sitaramiah

Linda Stonehocker's motor blew up, leaving her stranded on Interstate 90 near the Sullivan interchange east of Spokane.

"The motor went bang," the 47-year-old Spokane woman said last week during Friday's bitter cold spell.

With her bare hands, she gathered up parts of her motor strewn on the freeway and stashed them in her pickup. Then Stonehocker trudged up the Sullivan on-ramp to a nearby gas station.

Suddenly, help arrived. Two Washington State Patrol senior volunteers, John Mittmann and Dick Novotney, drove up and offered her a ride to a gas station to call a relative. The telephone didn't work, so they did even better. They offered her a ride home. "This is really nice," she said. "Thank you fellows a lot."

In the new program put on by W.S.P. and the state Department of Transportation, senior volunteers drive a van around Spokane County's state highways and I-90 helping drivers whose cars have broken down. They're equipped with tools to help change or inflate tires, or put gas in a car that's run dry. Soon, they'll have a cellular telephone to call for a tow or a ride for those stranded on the roads. In one case, Mittmann arrived at the scene of a van rollover and handed two startled young girls teddy bears.

"That settled them down," he said.

Then Mittmann took the family to W.S.P. headquarters while the van was righted.

Lt. Bruce Clark said the volunteers ease the workload of troopers who need to be available for higher priority calls.

"It's extremely important that we serve the people. That's why they hired us," Clark said. "We don't just give tickets all the time."

The only trouble now is that W.S.P. could use more volunteers. They have only four volunteers to hit the road, so the van will only be out when volunteers have the time and inclination.

In the three hours Mittmann and Novotney spent on the road Friday morning, they stopped to help four drivers, including two men whose truck had a flat tire.

They spotted other cars stopped along I-90 heading west to the county line, such as a GMC truck with California plates and its emergency lights flashing.

Novotney got out of the van, circled the truck and peered inside. "Somebody must have picked him up because there's no tracks in the snow," Novotney told Mittmann.

They spotted a few other abandoned cars and at each one, the same scenario followed.

The volunteers do no police work and leave impounding cars to troopers.

Mittmann, a retired trooper, enjoys getting back on the road, helping people. Novotney is a retired State Department of Transportation maintenance supervisor.

"Some people play golf. John and I drive the roads," Novotney said. "It gets us out of the house and our wives' hair."

Dale Olsen – hired by the Washington State Patrol in 1966

Dale Olsen, circa 1978. *(Courtesy Dale Olsen)*

Dale Olson was born in Walla Walla, Washington, in 1943, and was raised in Sandpoint, Idaho, where he attended both elementary and junior high. He graduated from Pasco High School and later received an AA degree from Spokane Community College in Spokane.

Dale served four years in the Air Force. During his term in Vietnam, he was assigned to the 555th Fighter Squadron (the Triple Nickel), which provided combat air power to U.S. and NATO as well as the National Command Authority. In January 1964, the 555th re-emerged at MacDill Air Force Base, in Florida as the 555th Tactical Fighter Squadron (555 TFS), operating the McDonnell Douglas F-4C Phantom II.

Dale was hired by the Washington State Patrol in 1966, and retired in 1993 after 27 years of service. During the time Dale was with the Patrol, he rode motor for over 17 years.

In 1970, Dale married his wife, Mary. They had met as the result of a major accident she was in, caused by a drunken driver. Prior to their marriage, she had been a nurse at Deaconess Hospital. Together they have three children, all successful in their careers.

During Dale's early years with the patrol, Trooper John Mittmann, for whom he held great respect, was his mentor. Trooper Fred Swan and Dale often rode together.

Trooper Dale Olsen, shaking hands with Vice-President Walter Mondale, and Trooper Rick Jensen, circa 1981. *(Courtesy Dale Olsen)*

Fred P. Swan – hired by the Washington State Patrol in 1969

Fred Swan, 1980. *(Courtesy Fred Swan)*

Fred Swan was hired by the Washington State Patrol in March of 1969, commissioned November 7, 1970. He was assigned to Lincoln County, and stationed at Wilbur. He was transferred to Spokane in December, of 1973. The following narrative was written by Fred Swan:

In March of 1973, knowing he was a motorcycle rider, his sergeant, Ed Crawford, asked if I'd be interested in riding cycles. At the time there was a large number of fatalities at railroad crossings (15 one year) in the Spokane valley. After working with the county, stop signs were put up at the crossing. The 1966 Harleys that had been used for parades only were brought out of storage and assigned to Troopers Dale N. Olsen, Dan Davis, and Swan. Prior to this Troopers John Mittmann and Dave York had ridden them in parades. W.S.P. troopers attended a training session put on by Mel Griffiths from the Spokane Police Department, who later became a close friend of Swan. The railroad crossing assignment soon got the fatals down to zero.

In 1978 Troopers Swan, Olsen and Dan Davis attended the Seattle PD motorcycle training program. They all got new

1978 Kawasaki's and worked the valley together. They enjoyed a good working relationship with Spokane Sheriff's and Spokane City Police's motorcycles units. Swan will always remember the burnouts (or cooldowns) up Monroe Street after the Lilac Parade.

Later, the W.S.P. increased to 60 motor units throughout the state. Ten of them worked a roving unit throughout eastern Washington.

After visiting other agencies' two-week motorcycle training programs, Trooper Mike O'Brien from Everett and Swan developed the W.S.P. agency's program and became the head instructors. Swan taught the program for 10 years and was a motor officer for 23 years, at that time being the longest rider in the state. Joe Pass now holds that record.

Other officers that have ridden and worked the Spokane area during his career are: Troopers Jim Lamunyon, Rod Mittmann, Lee Boling, and Joe Pass.

Swan retired in November of 1995. However, he still rides motorcycles. He currently has two Harley Davidsons and one Honda.

The W.S.P. motor school was later patterned after the Arizona Highway Patrol school, which is nationally recognized as one of the best. Mike O'Brien and Fred Swan attended AHP instructor school and returned to Washington to set up the W.S.P. program. They both said they didn't think they would get through the program because of its difficulty and the demands for perfection required by the instructors. This is from two guys with a lot of previous motorcycle experience. Fortunately for the patrol, they both graduated and subsequently set up the program currently in use.

Trooper Dave Peretti, of Olympia made the following statement regarding his training and experience riding W.S.P. motor, which represented many typical circumstances and events the majority of W.S.P. motor officers encounter. Peretti was invited to submit his own bio, but chose instead to provide the following to Fred Swan:

Sometimes the value of this training isn't readily apparent until you have a few miles on patrol and are exposed to situations where these exercises are really needed. Of course the one variable is that some of us leave the academy thinking we're "experts." One of the things continually emphasized was the importance of "riding within your limits," which I apparently forgot within a few weeks of basic motor graduation. Now that I think about it, the driving instructors told us the same thing. Two of the many exercises we were taught were "counter steering" and "high speed braking." These two exercises have been critical in keeping riders out of trouble.

Unfortunately I had to learn their value by a close call. A nice sunny day and I'm riding in shirtsleeves thinking, "I can't believe I'm actually getting paid to do this." I liked working the 101 area west of Olympia because it is rural and beautiful. There was nothing like cruising around smelling fir trees and salt water. I was riding my new, highly polished, Kawasaki KZ1000, just off the Mud Bay interchange of Highway 101. I'm sitting on the adjacent frontage road, called Madrona Beach Road, watching the westbound traffic, when I spotted a bright yellow Corvette greatly exceeding the speed limit going westbound. I knew this guy was going to continue west and then north on 101 towards Shelton. All I had to do was go west on Madrona Beach, parallel 101 until I got to Holly Lane, (about a mile up the road), then entered 101 and I should have been able to slip right behind him.

My first mistake! Madrona Beach Road is actually the old state highway SR410 from Olympia to Shelton. It is narrow, like all the old state roads, and built with concrete panels separated by expansion joints. Time and weather caused these panels to erode and develop humps, which is ok if you are at the posted 35 mph, but not if you are well over it.

If you ever had a chance to ride a Kawasaki KZ1000 you would be impressed. These bikes were rockets. We could take off down the average freeway on ramp and be nearing 100 mph before entering the freeway. When working with the W.S.P. aircraft we often times had high speed cars stopped within a half mile. When accelerating they would press you right back against the radio box and were so smooth you could easily underestimate your speed.

My second mistake. As I pulled out onto Madrona Beach, I hit the throttle, smiling to myself as it accelerated. Nothing like the sound of a KZ1000 wound up tight. I am familiar with the road as I've worked the beat in a car for years. I navigated several small curves and humps easily. Now I'm approaching an uphill grade that I know goes straight to a hill crest, then straight downgrade before curving right. I roll on more throttle and top the hill. I'm thinking my timing is perfect on the Corvette. As I top the hill I glance at the speedometer and can't believe it, I'm nearly at 100 mph. Suddenly, the thought came to me, this isn't good. I look ahead and see the right curve at the bottom of the hill. Now I'm seriously calculating my closing speed and don't like my conclusion. This is going to take some serious braking.

One of the most difficult maneuvers in academy training was emergency braking. We were taught "threshold brak-

Fred Swan, 1979. *(Courtesy Fred Swan)*

Troopers Fred Swan and Rod Mittmann at Fairchild air show, during the 1980s. *(Courtesy Fred Swan)*

ing" which is braking just under the point of wheel skid. We would accelerate down the course at a set speed until reaching a set of cones where we applied the brakes and if done properly, stopped short of a simulated barrier. Effective motorcycle braking requires the largest effort on the front wheel. Too much front brake and the wheel skids resulting in a loss of control called a "high side." We saw several of these events in training and have seen riders launched over the handlebars in this maneuver.

I'm on the brakes hard now and watching the right curve approach. There are trees on both sides of the road making this a blind curve. Fortunately traffic is light on Madrona Beach with no oncoming traffic at this time. As I start into the right curve I'm still way too fast. I start "counter steering." Counter steering is another maneuver we were taught at the academy.

A motorcycle is basically a gyroscope that tends to stay upright and inherently wants to go straight. (I think it's something Issaac Newton figured out). To turn, you shift weight and turn the handlebars somewhat like you would on a bicycle which is effective up to a point. To accelerate or exaggerate the turn we were taught to push on the opposite handlebar inducing a lean. The instructors would stand on the drive course while we approached them on our bikes. At the last moment they would signal a left or right at which time you initiated a "counter steer" (Scary at

times as an instructor). The harder you push the more the lean. I now needed some serious lean here.

Now I've got my hands full just braking and counter steering into the curve. I am leaning all the way over on the right side and the floorboard is grinding and bouncing on the pavement. I'm at maximum lean and pulling as hard on the front brake as I dare, but it's not enough. I'm drifting to the left towards the center line thinking "this might get ugly." I keep drifting to the left and now I'm over the center line as I look ahead anticipating an oncoming car. The bike is hopping up and down on the uneven panels because of the heavy leaning and braking. I'm now completely in the oncoming lane and in the middle of the curve and still way too fast. The curve is clear, but now I'm headed for the oncoming shoulder which is gravel and all of two foot wide bordered by a drainage ditch. I go off the pavement onto the oncoming shoulder throwing gravel. I ease off the brakes and start to realize "Hey, this may only be an incident if all I do is go in the ditch!" I finally come to a stop upright. I'm facing northbound on the southbound shoulder and I'm shaking like a leaf.

In all the years I rode motors, that was the closest I ever came to an accident. Excellent training and a good dose of luck saved me. Thanks, Mike and Fred! Two of us dodged a bullet that day... me and the guy in the Corvette.

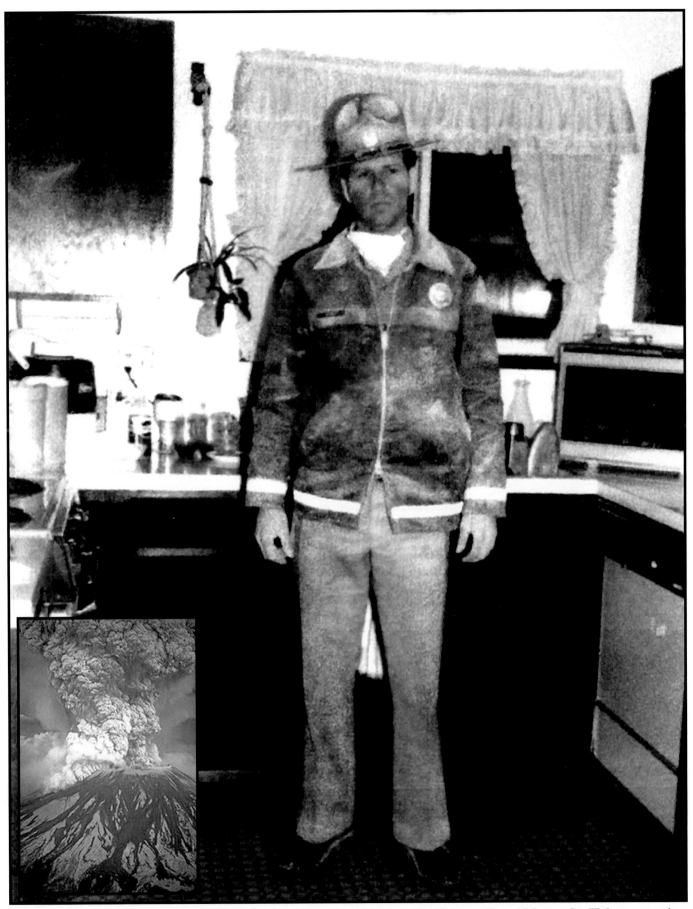

Trooper Swan on May 18, 1980, following the eruption of Mount St. Helens. (Inset)Mount St. Helens erupting on May 18, 1980. *(Courtesy Fred Swan)*

Trooper Swan at police motorcycle school in Phoenix, Arizona. *(Courtesy Fred Swan)*

Washington State Patrol, first drill team in 1991. *(Courtesy Fred Swan)*

Troopers Swan and nephew, Ben Heard, summer 1990. *(Courtesy Fred Swan)*

Motorcycle safety tips for new riders.

1. Always be aware of your surroundings; stay away from semi-trucks, pickups and trailers hauling loose materials.

2. Don't follow anything you can't see past. Always be looking far ahead.

3. Don't override your ability, know your limitations.

Don't let a group get you over your ability.

4. To avoid hitting an object or vehicle, always look ahead at your escape route NOT the object your going to hit. If you look at the object you're going to hit, YOU'LL HIT IT.

5. If you find yourself in trouble in a curve or corner, look way ahead around the corner and lean into it.

6. In case of a wobble, SLOWLY let off the throttle and FEATHER the rear brake.

7. Always check your vehicle equipment, tire pressure, etc.

8. Always be prepared for the unexpected. When approaching an intersection, driveways, and where someone can make a left turn in front of you.

9. The problem I see most lately are vehicles coming into your lane, especially at on-ramps. Always watch the cars beside you.

10. Keep your mind on your defensive driving. Don't be thinking about other things when riding.

James (Jim) W. LaMunyon – hired by the Washington State Patrol in 1973

Jim LaMunyon on his first bike in 1982, a 1980 Harley-Davidson. *(Courtesy Jim LaMunyon)*

James W. "Jim" LaMunyon's career was exceptionally noteworthy, as it was filled with accomplishment at a high level and diverse adventure within his chosen vocation.

Jim was born in Salem, Oregon, on July 13, 1951. He lived in Salem; Port Angeles, Washington; and Berkeley, California, up to the age of six. The family then moved to Boise, Idaho, and lived there from 1957 to 1961. From there they moved to Eugene, Oregon, where they lived from 1961 to 1967. The family's next move was to Spokane, Washington, where Jim lived from 1967 to 1973.

Jim has one younger brother still living and a younger sister who died in 1997, at the age of 39. He also has two younger stepsisters from his mother's second marriage.

His father, Weston W. LaMunyon, was born in Rising City, Nebraska, in 1926. He was a graduate of Midland College in Fremont, Nebraska, and later became a teacher and superintendent of schools in Nebraska. He later worked for Montgomery Ward in Oregon and Washington, and after that eventually attended Pacific Lutheran Theological Seminary in Berkeley, California. Following theological seminary, his father was ordained and was called to Redeemer Lutheran Church in Boise, Idaho. From there he went to United Lutheran Church in Eugene, Oregon, followed by Salem Lutheran Church in Spokane in 1967. He died in 1982 as a result of polycystic kidney disease.

Jim's mother was Shirley G. LaMunyon (Liudahl). She was born in Valhalla Township, North Dakota, in 1928, and moved to Salem, Oregon, with her family in 1936. She later became a Spokane public school teacher. After Wes died, she stayed in Spokane for ten years and in 1992, married her former high school sweetheart, Donald E. Clark. They lived together on a farm just outside of Silverton, Oregon, for the next 20 years. In 2012, they moved to Willamette Lutheran Retirement Community in 2012. Don died in July 2014, and Shirley died in November 2015.

Jim's education

Jim's early education began at Monroe Elementary School in Boise, Idaho. After moving to Eugene, Oregon, he attended Willard Elementary, Wilson Junior High, and South Eugene High School. In Spokane, he attended Shadle Park High School for his junior and senior years, graduating in 1969.

Following his graduation from high school, he attended Spokane Falls Community College, graduating with an associate of arts degree in 1972. In 1989, he attended one semester at the University of Louisville in Louisville, Kentucky (administrative officer's course). He received the Dean's Scholarship Award. For his junior and senior college years, he attended Whitworth College in Spokane. He did this while working full-time as a captain. In 1996, he graduated magna cum laude with a bachelor's degree in program administration.

During the time Jim attended Whitworth, he was the Northeastern Washington district commander for the Washington State Patrol. The courses he took were directly applicable to his management responsibilities.

Jim meets his wife

Jim met his wife, Beth (Elizabeth A. Ripple), in 1968 at a WSU-Stanford football game. The game was being played at Joe Albi Stadium in Spokane. During the game, he dropped something under the bleachers, which she saw and returned to him. Jim later found out who she was and called her for a date. Unfortunately, they didn't hit it off too well on their first date. Several months later Jim ran into her at a pizza restaurant on Monroe Street in Spokane and asked her out again. They have been together since then. They were married in 1972 and just celebrated their 44th Anniversary.

Beth's parents are Edmund J. Ripple Jr., who died in 2005, and Carmen Ripple, who is still living at the age of 91. Ed was the owner of Acme Printing in Spokane. Beth's grandfather, Edmund J. Ripple Sr. is recognized as the "Father of Spokane Softball," and is in the Softball Hall of Fame at the Spokane Arena.

Jim and Beth have two daughters, Sara and Julie. They are both married and each has a child. Jim and Beth have one grandson and one granddaughter.

Jim and Beth (Elizabeth) LaMunyon, circa 1975. *(Courtesy Jim LaMunyon)*

Jim's first jobs
on the way to becoming a trooper

Jim's first job was delivering newspapers. Following that, he was a life guard at a summer camp, worked as a busboy at the Shack Restaurant in Spokane, and worked at McDonald's and Taco Time before going to work at the Easter Seal Society in Spokane. He then worked for the Spokane County Sheriff's Office as a security officer in the jail.

A synopsis of Jim's
law enforcement resumé

• Original hire date was April 16, 1973, as a patrol cadet assigned to Walla Walla. Worked communications and performed administrative duties in the office. Was transferred to the Academy as a trooper cadet in September 1974, and commissioned as a Trooper on December 16, 1974.

Trooper Jim LaMunyon. Photo taken in 1980. *(Courtesy Jim LaMunion)*

• Assigned to Sunnyside working the Lower Yakima Valley until September 1975. Then assigned to the district office in Union Gap and worked the Upper Lower Valley until July 1977, when he was transferred to Spokane. Worked the Spokane West detachment until transferring to the Valley in 1979.

• Assigned to Motor in 1982. Promotion to sergeant in October 1983, assigned to Walla Walla. Transferred to Bellevue in February 1984, as motor detachment supervisor. Transferred to Olympia Headquarters in Personnel Section in December 1986. Supervised the cadet hiring unit and worked with all aspects of patrol employment. Promoted to lieutenant in April 1988 and transferred to Mount Vernon. Promoted to Captain and assigned to Spokane as District Commander in March 1992. Promoted to commander and assigned to Headquarters as Field Operations Bureau Commander in July 1997. Retired in July 2000.

• Went to work for the Washington Association of Sheriffs and Police Chiefs (WASPC) in September 2000. Over the next year, he completed a study on the feasibility of regional jails as an alternative to existing practices.

• In June 2001, was appointed acting chief of the State Patrol by then-Governor Gary Locke. Served in that position pending the appointment of Chief Ronald Serpas and then returned to WASPC.

• Directed other projects, including the jail booking information and reporting system, the Washington sex offender website, DNA Analysis Program, among others for WASPC, and was appointed deputy director. In 2007, was appointed as Executive Director of the Washington Auto Theft Prevention Authority. Retired in 2009.

• Worked with the National Highway Traffic Safety Administration (NHTSA) performing DUI program audits for several states from 1999 through 2008. Also involved in providing civil disturbance training through a federally funded program for local police agencies outside Washington State.

Reflecions on his career

Lieutenant Jim LaMunyon, ninth from left, with a group of Royal Canadian Mounted Police and fellow Washington State troopers during the "Peace Arch" celebration in 1990, on the US Canadian border. *(Courtesy Jim LaMunyon)*

During his career, Jim's favorite job was as a motorcycle trooper and sergeant. On the other hand, the worst job he ever had was not with the State Patrol. It was a contracted job cleaning out a house where a person had died and was not discovered for several days. That was his first introduction to the odor of a decomposing body.

Within the patrol there were jobs he liked better than others, but he felt he learned from each one and valued them all. He felt it was an endless learning experience that gave him something to be proud of. It taught him lessons that would be difficult to duplicate in other career tracks. He was able to see and experience events that many people only read about or watch on the news. Being a member of the State Patrol taught him about communication and how relationships are the key to getting through most situations. He learned that teamwork is essential in life, and you have to have people around you upon whom you can depend. It showed him the value of family and how important it is to have someone to greet you when you get home; how important it is to have someone to share your experiences with and be able to rely on for support.

As a trooper, the Patrol gave him educational opportunities and broadened his world. To Jim, the value of a career in the patrol is difficult to put in a few words, but it had so much to do with who he has become, his views of life, and his love of family. It tied him to an organization that is of great value to the citizens of Washington and made him part of its history. It also gave him many life-long relationships with many good people.

Greatest influences on his career

Most of the people with or for whom Jim worked for have touched his career in some way. He had so many good examples and so many talented people to draw from. He said if he had to identify just one person who had the greatest influence on his career it would be Trooper John Mittmann (see Mittmann section). Mittmann was the catalyst for Jim's seeking a career with the State Patrol. Jim's father had a lot

Jim LaMunyon transporting his motor, as his daughter Sara supervised. *(Courtesy Jim LaMunyon)*

Jim LaMunyon, sixth from left, prepping for DUI emphasis patrol with King County law enforcement agencies, circa mid 1980s. *(Courtesy Jim LaMunyon)*

to do with shaping him as a person and creating the foundation that allowed him to become a trooper in the first place. However, the person who has had the greatest influence on his "life" is his partner of 48 years, Beth. She has been there through a lot, has always been a good sounding board and counselor, and has never been afraid to challenge his thinking.

Jim's years on motor

Jim attended motor basic training in 1982. Following that, he rode motors for five years (1982 through the end of 1986). He rode motor as a trooper in Spokane until October 1983, at which time he was promoted to sergeant and assigned to Walla Walla as a detachment supervisor.

The patrol had expanded its motor program a few years earlier. As a result, there were motorcycle detachments in Everett, Seattle, and Olympia on the westside. In Eastern Washington they had put four motors in Spokane, two in the Tri-Cities, two in Yakima, and two in Wenatchee. Shortly after Jim

was promoted to sergeant, the patrol decided to put a second detachment in Seattle. They transferred him to the Bellevue office in February 1984 to supervise the newest detachment of motor troopers. He held that position until December 1986, when he transferred to the Personnel Section in Olympia.

As a motor trooper in Spokane, there were no assigned partners. He either worked alone or rode with whoever was assigned to work the same shift in the Spokane Valley. He often rode with Trooper Harry Minton. Harry was former military, very mature, and a good rider. Jim felt safe riding with him, as he was steady and had excellent judgement. Harry came up from the Tri-Cities when W.S.P. brought the extra motors to Spokane and eventually transferred back. Harry died as the result of a brain tumor several years ago. As a sergeant, Jim rode with all of the troopers assigned to the detachment at one time or another.

Being an escort for the Olympic Torch Run in 1984, for the Los Angeles Summer Games, was one of the

Troopers washing their motors preparing for working the "Water Follies," The Tri-Cities hydroplane boat races. *(Courtesy Jim LaMunyon)*

The Los Angeles games, Olympic Torch Run in 1984. *(Courtesy Jim LaMunyon)*

most positive experiences of Jim's career. The day started at 8:00 a.m. at Lake City Way in North Seattle. The patrol was with the torch until the escort was passed off to the Tacoma Detachment at the King-Pierce county line at about 3:30 p.m. that afternoon. The streets were lined with cheering spectators the entire day. In places, four lane streets were down to one lane because of all the people who had come out to see the torch.

The motor detachments also worked several major events throughout the state. These included the annual drag races in Spokane, Water Follies (hydroplane races) in the Tri-Cities, Seafair in Seattle, and Apple Blossom Festival in Wenatchee. The patrol escorted presidents, vice-presidents, foreign world leaders, and even Olympic champions.

In 1985-86, the Motorcycle Drill Team was formed at the suggestion of then Chief George Tellevik. The team, after several months of training and practice, performed at several festival parades in the Puget Sound region. It went on to perform in numerous events over the next decade until it was disbanded in

1996. The team served as an ambassador for the patrol and was a crowd pleaser wherever it performed. Jim served as its first drill master, and ten years later was the command officer tasked with reviewing the drill team status that led to the recommendation that it be disbanded for economic reasons. It had become a very costly enterprise and there were fewer motorcycle officers to draw from at the time. It was having a detrimental impact on the daily staffing needs of the detachments and districts where the motor officers were assigned.

Sergeant Jim LaMunyon at the Olympic Torch Run in 1984. *(Courtesy Jim LaMunyon)*

Jim's memorable experiences

• In 1985, in the line of duty death of Trooper Glenda Thomas on I-5 in North Seattle, Jim was one of the sergeants at the scene where Trooper Thomas was struck and pinned between two vehicles. He was also the ranking officer at the hospital when she passed from her injuries.

• The line-of-duty shooting death of Trooper James Saunders, in 1999, when he was Field Operations Commander. These were the two troopers with whose deaths Jim was directly involved.

• Seven State Patrol troopers and one commercial vehicle enforcement officer lost their lives in the line of duty during Jim's career. Each one of them had an impact. Most of them he knew, some better than others, but each loss was tragic, and they are all still remembered.

• Jim was no longer in the motorcycle program when Trooper Steven Frink died as a result of injuries sustained in a collision while pursuing a vehicle on Mercer Island. Trooper Frink was a member of the detachment Jim had formerly supervised when assigned to Bellevue. He was the only motor trooper killed while riding during Jim's tenure with W.S.P..

• As Field Operations Commander he was involved with the World Trade Organization civil disturbance in 1999 in Seattle; the Labor Day Rod Runs Long Beach Peninsula each year (included stabbing victims, street disturbances, street racing); the shooting death of Trooper Jim Saunders, in 1999 in Pasco; and student riots at Washington State University.

• As Captain (District Commander) freeway shooter incident in Spokane in 1996; Hells Angels in Spokane 1990s; bomb at city hall; raid on their clubhouse; North Idaho constitutionalist group's bank robberies and subsequent apprehensions in Spokane, mid-'90s; fire storms, ice storms, snow storms; eighty-six vehicle pileup on I-90 near Thor-Freya; and Applecup security in Pullman..

• As a lieutenant in Mount Vernon, floods, annual Peace Arch celebrations, oil line ruptures and spills, white supremacists honoring their fallen comrades with visits to what they viewed as a shrine, narcotics smuggling intervention efforts at the Canadian Border.

• As a trooper, along with Trooper Dick Pierce and some citizens, saving a drowning victim that was trapped in an upside-down car in a canal in the Yakima Valley.

The original Washington State Patrol Motorcycle Drill Team in 1986. Jim is sixth from the left. *(Courtesy Jim LaMunyon)*

Vice-President George H. W. Bush at Paine Field in Everett, Washington, with motors from the Seattle and Everett districts. On the far left is Lieutenant Trunkey and to his left is Lieutenant Jim LaMunyon. Bush was president from January 20, 1989 to January 20, 1993. *(Courtesy Jim LaMunyon)*

The 1986 Tri-cities Water Follies. Left to right: Dick Pierce, Gary Leach, Willy Hernandez, Tom Kline, Emmet Stormo, and Wayne Callecod. *(Courtesy Jim LaMunyon)*

Yakima Herald-Republic   Thursday, January 13, 1977

The above photo appeared in the *Yakima Herald–Republic* on Thursday, January 13, 1977. It stated the following: "For life-saving efforts, W.S.P. troopers honored. Not many awards are made to its own people by the Washington State Patrol, but two were given to a pair of Yakima W.S.P. district troopers Wednesday. Troopers Dick Pierce and Jim LaMunyon were presented awards of commendation by Capt. L. W. Woodmansee, Yakima District Commander, for their action in rescuing a man from a vehicle submerged in an irrigation canal.

"The incidents which led to the commendation occurred last September 20, near Laterals A and 1. On arriving at the scene, LaMunyon found Raymond Arrellio, 32, White Swan, on his stomach and an unidentified person pressing on him. LaMunyon checked Arrellio, found he wasn't breathing, and applied mouth-to-mouth resuscitation until breathing was restored, officers said. Meanwhile, bystanders yelled there was something still in the vehicle, which was on its top in the canal, submerged up to its rear axle. Pierce, followed by LaMunyon, went into the canal and discovered Juan Martinez, 22, Brownstown, inside the station wagon, ... With the help of four or five bystanders the troopers got the vehicle righted and extracted Martinez. The Sgt. said they believe that if it wasn't for troopers LaMunyon and Pierce, Martinez and Arrelio both would have become fatalities. . . ."

• The eruption of Mt. St. Helens and working the road-blocks and roads in Spokane following the eruption.

• The prison riots in Walla Walla in 1979, and being assigned to the prison yard walls after the prisoners destroyed their cell block and had to be housed outside in the yard.

• Duty in Kitsap County for the arrival of the first nuclear submarine at Bangor. Downtown Spokane civil disturbance after the drag races had been canceled in the early '80s.

• Along with Trooper Don Wigen, the apprehension of two armed bank robbers shortly after they had fled the bank and traveled south on Highway 27 from the Spokane Valley.

• There were fatal collisions that were memorable for one reason or another.

• Pursuits, building searches, felony stops, etc., that were part of being a trooper.

Oregon escapee arrested

Skagit Valley Herald

June 22, 1989
Two Sections

The following article was taken from the *Skagit Valley Herald* on June 22, 1989. It stated the following: Police arrest Larry D. Wamsley, 39, of Anacortes, Wednesday afternoon at Interstate 5 and College Way in Mount Vernon after discovering that he fled an Oregon State Penitentiary work party three years ago. Wamsley had been serving a 16 to 24-month prison term. The original charge against him was not immediately known. Oregon officials said today they will not extradite Wamsley, who was booked in the Skagit County jail for driving without a valid license. With Wamsley are state patrol Lt. Jim LaMunyon (left), trooper Jim Morse, and Mount Vernon officer Mike McLaughry." *(Photo public domain)*

The **Washington State Patrol troopers during the explosion of Mount St. Helens in 1980, at the Spokane Valley Office. From left: Bob McCluskey, Gordon Murashige, Gordon Sly, Jim LaMunyon, and Bob Aucutt.** *(Courtesy Jim LaMunyon)*

Some of the events that had the best feeling attached were the promotion and success of agency members that Jim supervised, managed, or directly worked with over the years.

Jim's happiest memories and biggest accomplishments

Personally, the marriage to his wife Beth, and the birth of his two daughters stand as the happiest times of his life. Professionally, his graduation from the academy, and being commissioned as a trooper followed by completion of motorcycle basic training, and being assigned to motorcycle duty was his second best memory.

The accomplishment he is most proud of is completing five years on motors without getting hurt. Developing relationships with wonderful people over the course of his career (both within W.S.P. and from other agencies and entities), expansion of the K-9 program, improvements to motorcycle equipment and uniforms, improvements to the W.S.P. Honor Guard, improvements to the W.S.P. Bomb Squad, development of the W.S.P. Aggressive Driving Team, work as member of a coalition of interested parties on the rules and regulations for bicycle events within the State, serving on the Washington Motorcycle Safety Advisory Committee in 1986-87, drunk driving apprehensions during his career, being a member

along with other W.S.P. personnel of an eight man rowing team, development of an advanced W.S.P. media relations program in Spokane, and helping others advance during their careers.

How he will be remembered

Jim LaMunyon will be remembered as someone who cared, who could be trusted, and relied on, who was thoughtful and sought the advice of others, and believed others were worthwhile and brought something of value to the table. According to his peers, he is someone who worked hard and never forgot what it was like to be in the field.

Retirement occupations

Jim has had boats since he was 16, spending much of his time on the water. Jim and Beth like to travel and also take care of their grandson two days a week. Due to Jim's parent's medical conditions, they spent the past several years traveling back and forth to Oregon and subsequently working on family matters following their deaths. Jim swims and exercises daily and works around the yard. He restores vintage furniture and likes building fences. He has polycystic kidney and liver disease and received a

Beth and Jim LaMunyon, 1974. *(Courtesy Jim LaMunyon)*

kidney transplant in 2007. As a result, he has done some volunteer work for Life Center Northwest by giving awareness presentations to drivers education classes in regard to the organ donation registry and his experience with transplantation. He also does presentations for kidney patients, at Group Health Cooperative, regarding his experience with kidney dialysis and transplantation.

The main lessons Jim has learned in life

Love and family come first. People and relationships are what it is about, not the things we tend to accumulate. You can't do this thing called life alone. You need an advocate at times, and you need to be an advocate for others at times.

Honesty, loyalty, trustworthiness, and dedication are not just cliché. They are tremendously powerful traits throughout your personal and professional life. Everyone is different. They have different backgrounds, experiences, education, thoughts, opinions, and aspirations. However, they are all human and have some things in common. They all bring something with them that you can learn from. You are only here for a short time. Influence the things you can while you are in a position to do so, and when your time is up know that others will follow you and bring something new with them.

We can all be replaced. You have an obligation to prepare others to take your place. Never give up. You can do so much more than you may have thought. Failure is not life-ending. It can be a catalyst for the greatest achievment if you pay attention and learn from the experience. Goals are difficult to achieve if you don't set them in the first place. Courage is not being fearless, it is the result of being able to cope with and overcome fear.

Doing the right thing is not always easy, nor is it the most popular action, but it needs to be done. Consider the consequences. If it doesn't feel right, there is a good chance that it isn't right. Amazing things can be achieved when you don't care who gets the credit. Rely on others. Surround yourself with people who are diverse in opinions and backgrounds. It enriches your experience and improves your decision-making.

Never forget where you came from and who helped you get where you are.

Learn from your mistakes and avoid making them again. Never say, "That's not my job." Take responsibility. Don't procrastinate. It will only get harder to complete the job as time passes.

Set an example. Don't expect people to carry a burden that you would not carry yourself. Follow-up. Trust others to do what is asked but check the progress. Be willing to step outside your comfort zone. It keeps you moving forward and learning new things. Take risks. You have to be able to adapt, and that sometimes means stepping outside the norm or policy, dependent upon the situation you are faced with. Life isn't always going to go as planned. You have to be flexible and adapt to the world around you.

Motorcycle Safety Tips:

1. Maintain awareness of your surroundings and circumstances.

2. Ride within the limits or your own skill and your equipment.

3. Constantly be on guard for other drivers around you.

4. Never assume that other motorists see you.

5. Be prepared to steer out of a situation instead of braking into it.

6. Always wear a helmet and appropriate safety gear.

7. Be cautious near overpasses, bridges, and shaded areas when temperatures are near freezing.

8. Maintain your equipment, especially tires and brakes.

9. Avoid braking into curves.

10. Steer around obstacles in the roadway and don't look at them as you approach. Looking at them draws you to them.

11. Always ride with your lights on so you are more visible to others.

12. If riding in pairs or groups avoid riding too close to one another. Leave yourself an escape route.

Julie (left) and Sara LaMunyon in 1986. They were in the process of testing new helmets for their father.
(Courtesy Jim LaMunyon)

Beth and Jim LaMunyon in 2016, following a full and rewarding career with the Washington State Patrol.
(Courtesy Jim LaMunyon)

Jim LaMunyon on motor, dressed for wet weather, circa 1983. *(Courtesy Jim LaMunyon)*

John R. Batiste – hired by the Washington State Patrol in 1976

Chief John Batiste, center of photo. *(Courtesy Jim LaMunyon)*

John Batiste was born to Jack and Pauline Batiste on November 25, 1954 in Louisiana, where he also grew up. He is the second oldest of eight siblings.

When Batiste moved to Washington, he attended Washington State University, where he played basketball for coach George Raveling.

Batiste became chief of the Washington State Patrol on February 14, 2005

Batiste took over as chief of the Washington State Patrol at a time when trooper morale was low, and wages were among the lowest of any law enforcement agency in the state. Also, a focus by the agency

Batiste participates in motorcycle drill practice. *(Courtesy Karen Miller, executive secretary to Chief Batiste)*

One of his most memorable experiences while on motors was being a member of the Washington State Patrol drill team. Also, among his best memories was getting to ride a motorcycle every day.

Concerning his many accomplishments, he feels fortunate that he has, in his position, been able to mentor others and help them achieve their goals. This fact shows by the way he is thought of by many of those who know him.

A good example of his reputation is a statement by his executive assistant, Karen J. Miller , who, when asked about the chief and what it was like to work for him, made the following statement:

> I've worked for the Washington State Patrol for nearly 18 years, and I have worked in the Office of the Deputy Chief since October 2006. I've worked indirectly with the chief's office during that time period. Chief John R. Batiste is one of the nicest men I have every worked with. He is genuine, caring, considerate, and passionate about the Washington State Patrol – and more than anything else – the people. He is a very humble man. The phrase I often hear him repeat is, "It is not about me." He is the epitome of "Service with Humility."
>
> In April 2016, he promoted me to the position of Executive Assistant, working directly for him. I could not be happier to be of service to him and to this agency. It is a very rewarding agency to work for, and I personally couldn't have asked to have worked with a better chief."

on certain traffic crimes, which some say reduced the flexibility troopers have to patrol their areas, were a few of the many obstacles.

"It's an organization that is suffering from some morale problems, and I think I can, indeed, help with that," Batiste said. "We can do a better job working with our people in helping them feel good about themselves and the organization."

His appointment brought praise from Sergant Bob Thurston, president of the Washington State Patrol Troopers Association. Thurston stated, "The governor made an outstanding selection. Batiste is easy to talk to, and he puts people first. That is a very strong quality that many of us would like to see in our leaders."

Batiste began with the Washington State Patrol in March 1976, as a cadet in the Everett and Bellevue areas. After trooper basic training, he worked as a trooper where he rode motorcycles from 1987 to 1989.

Batiste was promoted through the ranks of sergeant, lieutenant, captain, and deputy chief before becoming chief. He obtained his Bachelor's Degree in Law Enforcement Administration from City University and is a graduate of Northwestern University's Center for Public Safety School of Police Staff and Command, as well as a graduate of the Federal Bureau of Investigation's National Executive Institute.

Chief John R. Batiste is the 21st chief of the Washington State Patrol, originally appointed by Governor Christine Gregoire on February 14, 2005. He was again appointed as chief on January 16, 2013, by Governor Jay Insell, who stated Batiste had demonstrated the kind of results-oriented leadership that every agency needs.

The Washington State Patrol is the largest public safety, law enforcement agency in the state. They have statewide authority to always be available to lend assistance to county sheriffs and city police departments. However, their emphasis is on traffic enforcement and safety.

The State Patrol employs over 2,146 employees (1,067 sworn and 1,079 professional support staff). They have a yearly budget of $253,450,000. Chief Batiste oversees the day-to-day operations and manages the agency's six bureaus, which include Commercial Vehicle Enforcement Bureau, Field Operations Bureau, Fire Protection Bureau (State Fire Marshal), Forensic Laboratory Services Bureau (statewide crime laboratories), Investigative Services Bureau, and Technical Services Bureau.

Chief Batiste has been involved in a variety of activities and organizations, including his work with the Kenya National Police Force to create a National Police Chaplain Program and the South African National Police Force, to assist with training and procedures on ethical policing.

Chief Batiste is an executive board member of the Washington Association of Sheriffs and Police Chiefs; executive board member for the Western States Information Network; Washington Criminal Justice Training Commissioner; Washington Traffic Safety Commissioner; member of the International Association of Chiefs of Police (IACP), and past general chair of the IACP State and Provincial Police Division; American Association of Motor Vehicles Region IV board member; member of the National Organization of Black Law Enforcement Executives; and serves on the Washington State Forensic Investigation Council, and Governor's Emergency Management Council.

Batiste provides motorist assistance near the Tacoma Dome. (*Courtesy Karen Miller, executive secretary to Chief Batiste*)

Batiste conducts 1986 vehicle stop. *(Courtesy Karen Miller, executive secretary to Chief Batiste)*

Batiste and his partner on patrol on I-5. *(Courtesy Karen Miller, executive secretary to Chief Batiste)*

Sergeant Batiste conducts detachment meeting in 1988. *(Courtesy Karen Miller, executive secretary to Chief Batiste)*

In May 2013, Chief Batiste eulogizes Trooper Sean O'Connell, who was killed in the line of duty. *(Courtesy Karen Miller, executive secretary to Chief Batiste)*

A lineup of West Side W.S.P. motor officers.

West Side W.S.P. escort motor officers. At the far left is Sergeant Chet Pennington. *(Both photos courtesy Karen Miller, executive assistant to Chief Batiste)*

Joe Pass – hired by the Washington State Patrol in 1980.

Joe Pass at the Lilac Parade in 2014. *(Courtesy Joe Pass)*

Joe Pass was born and raised in Washington, D.C. The first job he had was with the Washington, D.C., Police Department.

On July 7, 1980, Joe was hired by the Washington State Patrol. His first assignment was as a radio cadet in Ephrata. He was then transferred to Moses Lake doing vehicle inspections. From there, he went to Kennewick as a regular cadet prior to being sent to the W.S.P. Academy. Following graduation, he was assigned as a motor trooper. In 1987, he attended the basic State Patrol motor school and began riding motor that same year. His motor partner at the time was Rod Mittmann. They both rode motor in Spokane, where he is presently working.

In 1990, Joe was promoted to narcotics detective. During that time, he worked the Federal Task Force

W
A
S
H
I
N
G
T
O
N

S
T
A
T
E

P
A
T
R
O
L

in the Tri-Cities until he was transferred back to Spokane. At that time, he choose to go on motor again, riding a BMW. He is currently riding a Honda 1300 ST.

On February 28, 2016, Joe was involved in a pursuit at which time the suspect drove his pickup into him, sending him to the hospital and his new motorcycle to the shop.

In 2014, Joe Pass received the Trooper of the Year award for his district. As a result, he was able to order the color of his new motor, which is metallic brown. *(Courtesy Joe Pass)*

From left: Craig Chamberlin, Will Thompson, Wayne Turner, Joe Pass, Jeff Sevigney, and Mike Brooks in front of a Blue Angels jet in 2014. *(Courtesy Joe Pass)*

The new motor Joe was awarded as the Spokane district Trooper of the Year in 2014. *(Courtesy Joe Pass)*

In 2015, Trooper Joe Pass was selected Trooper of the Year for his district. As such, he was awarded a new 2015 Honda motorcycle and was then allowed to pick whatever color he wanted to have it painted, he chose metallic brown.

Unfortunately, his new motor was destined for a bad experience before his odometer reached 500 miles. In February 2016, Joe was at the end of his shift, riding home on the two-lane highway near Valley Chapel and Hangman Valley roads. Suddenly, he noticed a Ford F-150 headed directly toward him in his lane of traffic. Joe narrowly avoided a head-on

crash, turned his motor around, and began a pursuit of the driver, all while radioing for assistance.

The chase was on and lasted for about 10 miles at speeds between 70 to 80 mph. As they continued, they were met by Spokane Deputy Sheriff Mike McNees, who took over the chase by patrol car, with Pass falling back to a safer distance.

The chase continued for about five or six miles with the deputy behind the pickup and Pass following both. Within a short time, Deputy McNees found an opportunity to perform a "pit maneuver" on the Ford pickup. Although McKees's maneuver was successful in stopping the suspect, it caused the vehicle to go into a 360-degree rotation, flipping it upside down. At the same time, Trooper Pass, not expecting this pit maneuver, ran into the pickup. Both Trooper Pass and the suspect were knocked unconscious and transported to the hospital, where they were both treated. Following that, the driver of the truck was booked into the county jail.

It was later learned that the suspect had an arrest warrant for driving with a suspended license and drunk driving. He also had a lengthy criminal record. Two years after this incident, the suspect died of cancer, which he had at the time of his arrest.

Spokane County Fairgrounds, 1989. *(Courtesy Joe Pass)*

Trying a new BMW, 2015. *(Courtesy Joe Pass)*

Olympia Peace Officer Memorial. Trooper Sean O'Connell, a fallen officer, being honored in 2014. *(Courtesy Joe Pass)*

Joe Pass as part of a presidential escort in Seattle, 2014. *(Courtesy Joe Pass)*

Pedestrian emphasis in 2016 on Monroe Street in Spokane, with Spokane Police Officer Ken Applewhaite.
(Courtesy Joe Pass)

Motorcycle show at the fairgrounds, sponsored by the Washington State Patrol, which included the Seattle Cossacks in 2014. The trooper on the left is Joe Pass. Wayne Turner in on the right. *(Courtesy Joe Pass)*

Working the escort of the president of China in Seattle. *(Courtesy Joe Pass)*

Donald Trump, the Republican candidate for president of the United States, and Joe Pass (both top and bottom), in 2016. The State Patrol is often called on to provide protection and escort for politicians. In many instances, they are asked to pose with the person they escort. *(Courtesy Joe Pass)*

Wayne Turner – hired by the Washington State Patrol in 1985.

Wayne Turner, circa 2011. *(Courtesy Wayne truner)*

Wayne Turner was born in Bremerton, Washington, to William and Darlene Turner. His father was a produce manager for Safeway, and his mother was a school teacher. He has three siblings, an older brother, older sister, and a younger sister. The first job Wayne had was working at a butcher shop from 1975 to 1978

Wayne joined the Washington State Patrol in 1985, and, while he was a W.S.P. cadet working in Vancouver, Washington, he met his future wife, who was a dispatcher for the patrol. They were married in Edmonds, Washington, in 1985. They have two children, a son and a daughter. The most positive influence in Wayne's life is his wife, encouraging and keeping him focused. In 1990, Wayne was af-

flicted with cancer, which he overcame and soon went back on the road. Wayne began on motor in 2003 and is still riding.

Some of the most memorable experiences in Wayne's life were getting married, having children, completing motor school, and buying an 11-acre farm. The accomplishment he is most proud of is raising great children. The thing he will be most remembered for by his friends and peers is why it took him so long to retire. The answer to that is simple – he loves his job and the opportunity to do good for people.

When he does finally retire, he looks forward to life and the chores connected to his small farm. He also enjoys working with horses on his farm, and when he finds time, water-skiing. He strongly feels his life has been guided by the Lord in all ways and has allowed him to be at the right place when he has been needed.

Wayne Turner working radar. *(Courtesy Wayne truner)*

William "Will" Thompson – hired by the Washington State Patrol in 1997.

Washington State Patrol escort for the cast of *American Chopper* from Northern Quest to the Spokane County Fairgrounds in 2006. From left: Joe Pass, Captain Otis, Paul Teutul Jr., Jeff Sevigney, Paul Teutul Sr., William Thompson, Wayne Turner, and Michael "Mikey" Teutul.

***American Chopper* was a reality television series that aired on the Discovery Channel. The father and his sons play the tough-guy team from their hit reality show *American Choppers*. The series centers on Paul Teutul Sr., and his son Paul Teutul Jr. They manufacture custom chopper-style motorcycles.** *(Courtesy Joe Pass)*

Will Thompson was born in 1970, and was raised in Sprague, Washington. His father and mother are John and Myra Thompson. He attended and graduated from the schools at Sprague. Following his graduation, he attended Spokane Community College and received an Associaes of Arts degree in criminal justice.

Will is the nephew of retired deputy motor officer, Marvin Patrick, of the Spokane County Sheriff's Office. Will worked for Spokane County from January 22,

1990, to September 1992. From there, he was the chief of police of the Sprague Police Department from September 1992 to March 1995, as the chief of police. In March of 1995, Will became a deputy for the Lincoln County Sheriff's Department. In 1997, he was hired by the Washington State Patrol. Following his academy training, he was assigned to Kelso, Washington, where he worked until June 2000, when he was assigned to motor in Vancouver. He worked in Vancouver until April 2005, when he transferred to Spokane and was assigned to motor, which is his current job.

Some of his most memorable duties were the various escorts of VIPs. To Will, he best part of serving on the State Patrol is the camaraderie with his peers.

Will became a motorcycle instructor in 2010. In 2013, he was assigned as the lead instructor for the Washington State Patrol motor school. This was among the top of his accomplishments, as it is one of the best in the nation.

During his off-duty time, Will enjoys most outside activities. One of the main lessons he has learned during his lifetime is that a person's future is often only a minute away.

From left: Will Thompson, Wayne Turner, Captain Jeff Otis, Joe Pass, and Jeff Sevigney. *(Both photos courtesy Joe Pass)*

From left: Ethan Wyncoop, Robert Spencer, Will Thompson, Jordan Rippee, and Lennie Walker.

Lee C. Boling – hired by the Washington State Patrol in 1977

Lee Boling at the start of the Spokane Lilac Parade in 1985. *(Courtesy Lee Boling)*

Lee Boling was born in 1953, in Sunnyside, Washington, to Clarence and Diana Boling. He has two sisters, one younger and one older. The family lived in Sunnyside and Othello for the first seven years of his life and then moved to Spokane. Lee's father was also on the Washington State Patrol and worked in Othello. His father quit the State Patrol when they moved to Spokane and went to law school at Gonzaga. He practiced law in Spokane until his death in an airplane crash in 1977.

Lee attended Roosevelt Elementary, Sacajawea Junior High, and graduated from Lewis and Clark High School in 1972. Following that, Lee enrolled at Eastern Washington State College and earned a Bachelor of Arts Degree in Psychology, as part of his preparation for becoming an attorney.

The first job Lee had was working for Avis Rent-A-Car in downtown Spokane. He also worked at Kentucky Fried Chicken as an assistant manager after he graduated from college.

Lee met his future wife, Barb Albers, by accident at the Park Inn at 107 West 9th Avenue in Spokane. They fell in love and were married in the summer of 1979. Finding and marrying Barb is the happiest part of Lee's life, along with raising his son and daughter, Stephen and Kristen.

On January 3, 1977, Lee joined the Washington State Patrol. He rode motor for three seasons, from 1984 to 1986. One of his most memorable experiences occurred at the Tri-Cities hydroplane boat races when his clutch cable broke at the hand lever. He looked at every bike shop in the Tri-Cities to no avail. He was told he would have to park his motor and ride with a car trooper. He was able to use a vice grip to engage the clutch for starting off, and once in motion, was able to shift without a clutch. This quick-thinking action kept him on the motor and able to continue arresting DUIs for the duration of the races.

Among his good memories on motor was, without a doubt, riding the perimeters of the Spokane Lilac Parade. It was the appreciation of the people attending the parade, and seeing their happiness as they applauded the motor officers as they rode by. Typically, the motor officers from the city, county, and Washington State Patrol would start out the parade by riding the full length of the course. Once completed, they would ride along the sidelines of the parade route to keep it clear and be there if any trouble arose. The Lilac Parade seemed to be the culmination of the public's appreciation for the police departments and their "thank you" for protecting the public in a professional manner.

The biggest influence in Lee's life was his father, who was always struggling to do better for his family but was always there to help others. Lee strove to be like his father by being hardworking and dedicated to the Washington State Patrol and his fellow officers. During his time with the patrol, he never asked anyone to do anything he would not do himself. He always tried to be side-by-side with his fellow troopers at every turn or obstacle.

The main lessons he has learned from his father and fellow troopers is try not to be quick to pass judgment, to wait for the whole story and the real facts. Lee believes that just when we think we know all and that we are smarter than the rest, God reminds us that he is in charge and only through Jesus can we gain patience and understanding. Without his faith, Lee doesn't believe he would have survived his 25 years of service with the patrol and still have the positive attitude he has today.

Lee retired from the state patrol in 2002, at the rank of sergeant. Since that time, he has kept busy restoring cars and boats, enjoying and setting a good example for his kids and grandkids. He also works with Spokane Fire District #8 as a commissioner.

Lee's father, Clare Boling, circa 1957

Stephen Boling 4, and Kristen Boling, 2, polishing Dad's motorcycle for Lilac Parade, 1984. *(Courtesy Lee Boling)*

Lee Boling and son Stephen, 1984. *(Courtesy Lee Boling)*

Rod Mittmann – hired by the Washington State Patrol in 1980

Rod Mittmann and Joe Pass. *(Courtesy Rod Mittmann)*

Rod Mittmann was born in Spokane in 1957, to John and Lillian Mittmann, and was raised there along with one older and two younger brothers. His father, John, was also a Washington State Trooper. Joining the patrol in 1950, his dad rode motor for 25 years. He was a greatly respected W.S.P. motor trooper.

Rod graduated from Central Valley High School and from there went to Whitworth College in 1977, taking up general studies. Rod is married and has four daughters.

The first job Rod ever had was loading lumber at a lumber yard. The best job he ever had was with the Washington State Patrol. The highlight and best part about his job with the patrol was the opportunity to help others. The biggest influence in his life has been his father.

Rod went on motor in 1987, and rode for 14 years. His most memorable experiences during his time with the patrol were escorting dignitaries, working the various fairs, and the camaraderie established with his teammates. The happiest memory he has during his time with the patrol was at his graduation from the W.S.P. Academy in June of 1983, when his dad pinned his W.S.P. badge on him. His most ma-

jor accomplishment was completing his career with the Washington State Patrol.

When asked how he thought people would remember him, he stated: "as the big, tall, ugly guy." To which he added "with a smile."

Rod's response to the question about the main lessons he has learned in life was: "Everything we do, everything that happens, all the joy in life comes from maintaining our faith in God and Jesus Christ."

Left to right: Tim Lenander, Tom Pillow, Rod Mittmann, and Joe Pass. This photo was taken in June 2002, in Ephrata, Washington, at the county courthouse. This program was designed by the W.S.P. to bring a rainbow into the lives of some Special Need Kids, which, by the smile, did just that. *(Courtesy Rod Mittmann)*

Rod Mittmann. *(Courtesy Rod Mittmann)*

Joe Pass and Rod Mittmann at an air show at Fairchild Air Force Base in 2002. *(Courtesy Rod Mittmann)*

Robert Spencer – hired by the Washington State Patrol in 1998

Robert Spencer, circa 2014. *(Courtesy Robert Spencer)*

Robert Spencer was born in May 1976, to Rick and Sharlyn Spencer in Cottonwood, Idaho. He has a sister who is two years older. His father managed a grain warehouse in Cottonwood. His mother's family had farmed the Palouse since the beginning of World War I. Robert's father met his Mother in Bremerton during the time his grandfather was in World War II.

The schools Robert attended were Nez Perce Elementary, Riverside Middle, and Riverside High School. Following that, he went to Spokane Community College, receiving an Associate of Arts in Administration of Justice. His goal was to become a law enforcement officer.

In 1985, his family relocated to Spokane, where both his parents raised. In Spokane, his dad worked for his grandfather's grain seed treatment business and later went on to own and operate a self-loading log truck. Robert's first job, while he was growing up, was working on his granddad's small farm in north Spokane County. The worst job he ever had was cleaning the stateline rest area for the Washington State Department of Transportation. The best job he ever had was being a Washington State Patrol motorcycle officer. He finds great satisfaction in helping victims of crime and putting those in custody who take advantage of others.

The greatest influence in Robert's career has been many of the people he has worked with in law enforcement. These include many of the officers, deputies, and troopers who know their job well and perform with high efficiency.

Robert has been on motor since 2015. He was certified on a BMW, which he rode for one summer and then transitioned to a Honda, to which he currently is assigned. His motor duty has been in Spokane where he often teams up with different W.S.P. motor partners. One of his memorable experiences was when about 20 W.S.P. bikes took the Washington State Department of Transportation ferry to Seattle.

Quite often the patrol is called on to assist city or county law enforcement. During one such time, Robert received a commendation from Spokane Polic Department when he assisted in an arrest of an armed carjacking suspect.

Robert Spencer personally owns a 2005 Harley-Davidson motorcycle. During his off-duty time, he has put over 82,000 miles on it. His advice for anyone who spends much time on a motor is to "do your best to keep the rubber side of your motor down."

Robert Spencer, circa 2014. *(Courtesy Robert Spencer)*

During a high speed course at Shelton, Washington. *(Both photos courtesy Robert Spencer)*

At Shelton, the Washington State Patrol Academy driving course's high-speed corner. *(Courtesy Robert Spencer)*

Rod Mittman and Fred Swan, early 1990s. *(Courtesy Robert Spencer)*

Joe Pass and Rod Mittmann at a Fairchild Air Force Base open house. *(Courtesy Robert Spencer)*